Sept 22/04

For Darryl Reed

Thank you for helping
me to gain some
understanding of the
social & political aspects
of the problem

In friendship

ECOVIOLENCE AND THE LAW

Supranational Normative Foundations of Ecocrime

By
Laura Westra

 Transnational Publishers

Published and distributed by Transnational Publishers, Inc.
Ardsley Park
Science and Technology Center
410 Saw Mill River Road
Ardsley, NY 10502

Phone: 914-693-5100
Fax: 914-693-4430
E-mail: info@transnationalpubs.com
Web: www.transnationalpubs.com

Library of Congress Cataloging-in-Publication Data

Westra, Laura.
    Ecoviolence and the law : supranational normative foundation of ecocrime
/ by Laura Westra.
      p. cm.
    Includes bibliographical references and index.
    ISBN 1-57105-316-6
      1. Offenses against the environment.   2. Environmental ethics.
    3. Social responsibility of business.   4. Human rights.   I. Title.

K5278.W47 2004
179'.1—dc22

                                        2004041238

Manufactured in the United States of America

For my grandfather Zoltan Dabasi Halász
Consigliere della Suprema Corte di Cassazione Roma
and the Family, his wife Margit,
my mother Kata, Sari, Mici and Zoli.
(in memoriam).

CONTENTS

PART I

PART II

PART III

ACKNOWLEDGMENTS

This book was written primarily to show the interdependence of human rights and environmental rights. After studying environmental ethics for many years, I have recognized that tying my position on biocentric wholism to human rights might strengthen the argument I have proposed: it is not only immoral to breach environmental regulations and to refuse to sign on to more demanding legal international instruments, but it should be illegal. In order to prove the harms inflicted on millions globally by economical means, I called upon the resources of epidemiologists and biologists as well as ecologists, and great thanks are due to William Rees, Colin Soskolne, Tony McMichael, James Karr, Orie Loucks and Robert Goodland as well as Roberto Bertollini at the Rome office of the WHO. I also relied on philosophers who have addressed some of these issues, especially Mark Sagoff, James Sterba and Louis Pojman. Finally, I could have never completed this work without the help and inspiration of Craig Scott, Shelley Gavigan, Judge Sharon Williams of Osgoode Hall Law School, as well as Jutta Brunnée, Nicholas Robinson, and Don Brown. Ron Engel, Brendan Mackie and Steven Rockefeller of the Earth Charter have also been a continuing source of inspiration, as well as Robert Bullard and Darryl Reed.

Special thanks are also due to the superb help of Librarians Marianne Rogers, Mary Aspioti, Sharona Brookman and Diane Rooke of Osgoode Hall and that of Lucy Brown from the University of Windsor.

I have tried to include all the changes and additions to laws and documents up to the end of 2003. I apologize for anything I might have missed and to the errors that, no doubt, remain, and I want to express my warmest thanks to John Berger of Transnational Publishers, who took a chance on a philosophy-turned-legal scholar.

Laura Westra
Osgoode Hall Law School
Toronto, Ontario
Canada

PREFACE

After working for about ten years on environmental ethics, particularly on the meaning and the implications of ecological and biological integrity, I became convinced that its converse, ecological disintegrity should be viewed as an attack on life, a form of violence to natural systems' structure and function, hence, to all living things at the macro level, and an assault on human life, and on the natural function of human organisms at the micro level. Ongoing interaction with scientists, ecologists, biologists and epidemiologists informed my conclusions, eventually confirmed by a document produced by the WHO/ECEH Rome Office (Soskolne and Bertollini, 1999). This document, entitled "Ecological Integrity and Sustainable Development: Cornerstones of Public Health," was the product of a workshop convened by the Rome Office of the WHO, involving the scientists of the "Global Ecological Integrity Project" (Social Sciences and Humanities Research Council of Canada (SSHRC)) (1991–1999). It brought into focus the work of several years of research and numerous publications, making explicit the connection between disintegrity including various forms of pollution, and its causes, such as hazardous industrial practices, and in general, the results of overconsumption and of the elimination of natural systems. It also emphasized the resulting fatalities, human morbidity, and the alteration, often irreversible, of natural human functions. In so doing, it was foundational for the argument I propose in this work: breaches of environmental regulations, whether domestic or international, are ultimately to be viewed as breaches of human rights law.

Humans are "rational animals," "social animals," but they are, first and foremost animals among others who, adaptable and capable though they are, still need some specific physical natural conditions to achieve optimum development. Hence, aside from needing security from deliberate attacks of violence from their fellow humans, they need first and foremost to dwell in a habitat appropriate to their nature: that is their first right, before political, civil and even, to some extent, economic rights. Henry Shue (1996) said it best, "basic rights" are rights to "security and subsistence." They are prior in time and in principle. Temporally, infants need "security and subsistence" if they are to grow to adulthood, hence, to a state to which the presence of civil and political rights become relevant. Social and economic conditions at this early stage must be such to ensure the presence of "security and subsistence," hence, to keep them safe and permit them to grow and develop.

We have seen recently vivid example of the possible conflict between the right to freedom and to a nonrepressive political and civil society, and stark basic rights. The recent war in Afghanistan reported as "liberated" people, whole families who had neither food nor shelter for their children. Indeed, women could remove the veil from their faces now, with all that this freedom may imply: nevertheless, that "freedom" could bring little comfort to a mother who only had a tiny amount of bread to share among many children, and who would fear that many of these would not survive the coming months.

The same is true of drought/famine stricken areas, even in free, democratic countries in Africa. These examples show that an environmental right to healthy habitats, that is, to land growing healthy uncontaminated food and to a climate that fosters this growth, is a human right (Weeramantry, 1997). In fact, these can be termed both basic and first human rights: without conditions of "security and subsistence," all else is insufficient.

If that is so, the traditional and still current thrust both in ethics and in the law, to a separation between human rights and environmental rights, is profoundly misguided: they are not separate fields of study or endeavor, they are closely interrelated. Thus, we can be the victims of this deprivation of rights, this form of violence, in both democracies and dictatorships, in poor countries or wealthy ones, although, as we shall see, the violence itself will take on different characteristics under different circumstances and in disparate locations. Children in Los Angeles can be under attack in a democratic country: their normal respiratory functions are gravely altered by the toxic particulates in the air they breathe, a circumstance over which neither they nor their parents have any control. African Americans in Chicago, Illinois, or Birmingham, Alabama, both in democratic affluent states, are under attack in certain areas because of the toxic-releasing industrial processes to which they are exposed, once again, with no choice, no way other than having the economic ability to leave the area, to control the circumstances that affect their health and normal function (Gaylord and Bell, 1995; Westra, 2001).

Similarly, Canadian citizens, especially infants, children, and the elderly in Walkerton, Ontario, suffered terrible diseases, died or continued their lives with compromised functions and diminished health, because of an e-coli epidemic of which they had no knowledge, and which arose because of industry-favoring regulations and privatization of necessary water facilities in the area (see Chapter 4). Note that these examples are taken from the normally accepted operations of economic enterprises, against a permissive regulatory background, in fully democratic countries in North America, and that, therefore, citizens under attack could not expect to be liberated, or to receive political asylum, or hope for better civil rights to redress the harms they had suffered. At best stricken families could hope for some amelioration of their circumstances or some monetary recompense. But under no circumstances could they harbor any hope that the activities that had produced the violence would be terminated and eliminated from the options available to a civilized society.

In addition, it is not only the presence of poisonous, toxic substances, whether as by-products of ongoing activities or as residual wastes, that cause physical harms, but also the lack of appropriately sized ecological reserves, areas of land (Noss, 1992; Noss and Cooperrider, 1994), and sea (Pauly, 2000), where natural system are respected as such and are not subject to the manipulation and exploitation by economic interests, so that they continue to supply those natural services for the commons outside the reserves (Daily,1997) upon which all life depends. The close connection between a safe, natural environment as a human habitat and human health coupled with normal function, is emphasized in the interrelation between macro and micro integrity, as the latter is not truly possible without the former.

Assaults upon humans, whether perpetrated with bare hands or with other instruments of violence, are crimes. If the deprivation of necessary ecological integrity, either by encroachment and manipulation of the wild, or inquination and pollution of inhabited areas is a present and constant threat to human health and function, ultimately to human life, then that *too* is an assault, therefore a crime that must be viewed, treated, and punished accordingly. The fact that in present day legal infrastructure it is not so treated represents an additional moral "crime" in itself.

The defense and protection of human rights must start like the defense and protection of all human life does: with the respect for basic rights. As a corollary, any policy or activity that ignores that necessity should be treated for what it is according to its effects even if a deliberate intent to harm may be lacking.

This is a radical proposal, and several objections may be advanced. The first objection is the point mentioned: what is lacking in this characterization of "ecoviolence" as "ecocrime" is deliberate intent. A counter objection may be offered in response: not all homicides are murders, and carelessness, criminal negligence, and willful blindness are all important and relevant legal categories, as we shall argue below.

Another objection is that even in democracies, there are often conflicts between local, immediate economic, or social advantages, and the presence of concomitant but distant harms, well beyond the reach of the free choice of local residents (Westra, 2000b). Here too it is possible to respond that international courts of law are intended to provide supranational justice in cases where local justice systems are insufficient to address issues that are too partisan or debated within a national setting. The International Court of Justice performs precisely this function in other human rights violations, such as genocide (see Chapter 1).

Finally, it could be objected that democracies depend upon national citizens' choices, hence, that appeals to the international legal instruments available to redress acts of aggression are inappropriate precisely because they lack this element of citizens' collective choice, something that cannot be appealed to at the global level. The answer to this objection can be found in the structure of international law, as it provides not only for interstate adjustments and settlements of disputes, comparable perhaps to noncriminal cases brought before national courts, but it also reaches beyond these to true universality at the cosmopolitan level, through the presence of obligations *erga omnes*, flowing from *jus cogens* norms, neither of which is dependent upon national or group choice, and should not be subject in principle to arbitration or settlement. The former are universal obligations, beyond those originating from covenants, the latter represent the highest principle-based, nonderogable norms. My focus on *jus cogens* norms generating *erga omnes* obligations should not be understood to mean that norms and *erga omnes* applications are limited to *jus cogens* norms. There may be basic rights that, however basic, do not rise to the level of being *jus cogens* but yet are sufficiently basic to be *erga omnes* norms: see the famous paragraph in *Barcelona Traction* (discussed below, Chapters 1, 3, and 7), which links *erga omnes* to basic rights, without necessarily qualifying these same norms as also being *erga omnes*. To date environmental cases have not reached this level either in national or international courts, and the meager list of international environmental cases include both arbitrations and settlements instead. Hence, the need for a new approach, as the current one has left the *status quo* of ongoing environmental harms largely unchecked.

It is this situation and this possibility available through international law that suggested my main theme and my approach, inspired by the important treatment of *jus cogens* norms in the work of Maurizio Ragazzi (1997; see also Barile, 1985; Hannikainen, 1988).

Given the presence of disintegrity almost worldwide today, unchecked by the presence of democratic governance at least in the most powerful Western countries, and the lack of concerned global action, despite the proliferation of environmental ethics analysis and argumentation (Westra, 1994; Westra, 1998), and of environmental legal instruments, I want to propose a different way of looking at the multiple environmental crises with which we live. The reader will judge whether this proposal has enough merit to make even a small difference in the protection and defense of all life, and of the "basic rights" of humanity.

In the first chapter, the reasons why ecoviolence can be seen as institutionalized are discussed. Three basic points emerge: first, other than capital punishment, which is aimed at specific individual wrong-doers, only war is both violent, inflicting bodily harm and often death, and is generally accepted worldwide when "just." Even in a just war there can be a deliberate intent to attack and to harm. Hence, only *jus in bello* considerations might be relevant to wartime ecoviolence. Second, the main focus of this strategy is to view the *effects* and the *consequences* of these environmental unprovoked and unjustified attacks as primary. A central question then is whether the international human rights instruments in existence may offer, through their language and intent, some avenue through which these crimes may be brought to justice. Third, and equally important for my arguments, with respect to war-related violence and to human rights connections to environmental justice, the principles governing just war theory from the time of antiquity, are based primarily on, or at least tied to, natural law, a doctrine that, from its origins in Aristotle, to its application to law in the work of Grotius, need not be tied to particular religious beliefs.

The second chapter continues the strategy here initiated of looking at results and consequences, in order to redefine ecocrimes, through the abundant literature available on health effects of various forms of disintegrity, not only the occasional catastrophic effects already termed "environmental crimes" (French and Mastney, 2001), but also to the equally catastrophic effects of day-to-day legal, industrial and agricultural operations, and the disposal of the waste they generate. The method used here is that of analogy, and I discuss this method in Chapter 2, starting with appeals to early scholarship on the topic, as well as examples available through recent treatments in both U.S. and Canadian law.

Chapter 3 considers why these crimes are allowed to continue routinely even in free and democratic countries, and why even "informed" citizens appear to have difficulties saying "no" to harmful, though legal practices. The question of civil disobedience and even that of resistance, from peaceful protests to the recent tactics of the "no-global" activists will be discussed as their worldwide opposition to the increasingly oppressive "ecological footprint" of the powerful corporate enterprise is one good sign in a sea of disinterest.

The first three chapters are intended to provide a theoretical framework within which to analyze our main concern, and on which to rest the defense of the first main argument of this work. Simply, environmental harms are assaultive in nature. Hence, they are not, as they are sometimes described, "quasi-crimes"; they are crimes, *simpliciter*.

The second part of this work, including Chapters 4, 5 and 6, turns to the real, practical concerns that lead to the second main argument: these crimes produce consequences that are global in nature, for the most part; minimally, they are never limited to the single effect, or the one area, where specific local citizens may vote appropriately, hence, make a difference. First, as noted in Chapter 3, there is great difference between Presently Threatened Populations (PTPs) and their possible reaction to immediate or visible threats; and Population under Delayed Threats (PDTs), who cannot—-for the most part—-appreciate the magnitude of the threats and their consequences, and are often unable to extend their concern to others, far removed from their immediate surroundings. Second, even in democratic countries, citizens are not able to have all the information they require to make a decision that is not colored by the political and economic interests of their governments.

A clear example of this recurring phenomenon would be the Fall 2002 campaigns by politicians complicit with their local oil companies, aimed at the residents of the Canadian Province of Alberta, and to Canadians in general, to prevent Prime Minister Jean Chrétien from signing on to the Kyoto Accord. Emphasizing possible job losses, the campaign omits all references to health or life effects, not only in Canada, where the motto is "we will adapt" but especially to those living in developing countries, where no "adaptation" is possible to people who have no air conditioning to cushion heat, no medical or social infrastructure to mitigate floods and disasters, and no government subsidies to cushion lost crops through drought, but can only face famine and death.

Chapter 4 examines these phenomena in detail through a recent Canadian case in Walkerton, Ontario. The seemingly routine acceptance of a pro-business government move to deregulation and the imposition of substantial budget cuts to both public health and environmental ministries, eventually led to a disaster. The pollution of one water well too close to hog farms facilities, coupled with exceptional rainfall due to present climate change, brought an e-coli epidemic bringing death and disease to a small Ontario community. If identifiable individual attackers or terrorists were to cause such death or other serious and lasting physical harms, the attackers would be jailed and indicted as criminals. But this institutional form of violence at Walkerton simply became the subject of a judicial inquiry, resulting in some regulatory changes, a new "Safe Drinking Water Act" and, at most, some financial offers to the stricken families.

Chapter 5 looks closely at criminal law, taking the Criminal Code (Canadian) as this work's example of national law governing assaults and homicides, emphasizing once again the analogous character of environmental crime, and comparing it with the vastly different treatment of the latter in courts of law, without any principled explanation of this phenomenon, other than the intuitive one: it is most often the poor, the misguided, often the oppressed who resort to assaults treated paradigmatically by criminal law as crimes, but it is the powerful corporations, with the support and complicity of democratic governments who, for the most part, engage in ecological assaults, that, my work argues, also merit being categorized within the law as crimes.

Despite the theoretical links and the analogies described thus far, the conclusion of Part II in Chapter 6 is that, even at best, national governments and their courts of law are necessary but not sufficient to restrain and mitigate, if not eliminate environmental violence. Hence Chapter 6 moves from one national-local exemplar (Canada), to another, by turning to one particular U.S. state government, that of Pennsylvania, where environmental rights are entrenched in the Constitution of that commonwealth. Yet, neither this move, nor the presence of other legal documents intended to serve a meta-regulatory function, e.g., binational agreements such as the Great Lakes Water Quality Agreement (GLWQA), and other negotiated covenants, appears to be strong enough to withstand the global power of big business, notably as embodied in the WTO and its rules. A way to respond to and check that power is what is necessary in order to stop the ongoing environmental violence and the result of the oppressive "ecological footprint" the WTO supports.

The strategy I propose in Part III, is to turn to the international level, specifically to another species of covenants, those that recognize and emphasize the gravest crimes against humanity. These give rise to *erga omnes* obligations, in defense of *jus cogens* norms, which are nonnegotiable, universal in character, and drawing normative force not only from positive international law, but also from the reasoning in the work of well-known publicists and from the general principles of law and justice, many of which can be traced, as is argued in Chapter 1, to principles of natural law. Analogous to and perhaps in some cases as instances of attacks on the human person, genocide, and crimes against humanity, ecocrimes should be proscribed globally, and a precautionary and holistic approach should be adopted in that regard, and this approach is defended in Chapter 7.

Chapter 8, describes the nature of the threats and harmful activities we have encountered in the other chapters, and considers the major obstacles that have emerged to the defense of basic human rights. When these threats are found and acknowledged, then it is imperative that we seek possible strategies that may succeed where present legal approaches have not. The strategies here suggested include a radical turn to a kind of Kantian Cosmopolitanism, seeking a form of global governance that is patterned upon the EU with its Court of Human Rights and its power over limited and partisan economic and political interests (while not requiring unitary world government as such) (Hurrell and Kingsbury, 1992).

As noted, the obstacles faced are—for the most part—founded on economic interests, and these center on globalization and multilateral economic treaties (e.g., NAFTA, FTAA), culminating in the rule of the WTO.

The latter is, appropriately, the focus of major protests, worldwide. These protests are organized by determined activists that represent a "bottom-up" strategy for change, a desirable development that would gain additional credibility for its mandate if the "top-down" strategy here proposed was found to be acceptable. This second approach would require, eventually, not only normative principles but also the presence of an institutional power equal to the WTO, to combat the effects of unprincipled economics in globalization. That was the main reason for proposing the EU as a template of a desirable goal, as that is the only body that has been able to defy the WTO in defense of the health of its people (Chapter 8), as legal-system government that is not subordinate to the economic logic of trade laws, even as it is also true that health enjoys no absolute priority over trade even in the EU order.

Aside from that strategy, I also propose the adoption of an International Environmental Court to remedy the present juridical deficit (Postiglione, 2001), and a serious consideration, or maybe even the official adoption of the Earth

Charter, as a globally generated universal ethic, and thus a reference point for interpreting current law and generating new law. After the 2002 Rio +10, in Johannesburg, the Supreme Court Justices of the World recognized the urgency and the necessity to reform environmental laws, and to fully inform the judges who must preside over these cases. The Earth Charter, I believe, would offer an ideal starting point for their deliberations (see Appendix 1).

*   *   *   *   *

In conclusion, many centuries ago, capitalism arose in agrarian England, as the economic motive and competitiveness replaced traditional values in the "enclosure movements." The "enclosures" provided "the most famous redefinition of property rights": they eliminated the commons, with no regard for human rights (Wood, 1999:83). Philosopher John Locke defended the right to property above all, although he predicated his defense on ensuring that enough would be left to be held in common. But he also espoused the defense of improvements as needed to impose value upon nature, an argument that supported the policies of his master, the Earl of Shaftsbury.

Through his friendship with Jefferson, the Lockean arguments filtered into the American Declaration of Independence. But these enclosure movements, brutal though they were in their effects against the people, only started what eventually became known as the "Tragedy of the Commons" (Hardin, 1968). What we encounter today, in the primacy of the economic motive over and above human rights including the right to a safe and healthy habitat, is the final "enclosure movement": it is once again mostly the poor and dispossessed of the world who are shut out of the natural global commons.

The benefits that would accrue to them are no longer available: whatever is left of the commons has become someone's property, and is used as such. Even the most simple natural goods are no longer available freely: clear air, pure water, safe sunlight, safe foods, all is unavailable to the poor. Drinking water must be bought; sunscreen is needed to protect us against the sun: both travel to the few locations that can boast of clean air, or at least housing removed from hazardous industrial operations; food in areas of famine and safely organically grown food where it is available, but it is laced with toxic substances: all are commercial goods.

The greatest tragedy is that, unless some radical and immediate action is undertaken, the existence of the "commons" will remain only a historic fact, not even a memory for future generations.

FOREWORD

As the title of this book avows, Laura Westra provokes thought and challenges us to re-examine the legal foundations for how society defines norms of
human behavior toward nature and toward each other in the realm of nature.
Human society has evolved within the biosphere of Earth, and humans (at least
to date) cannot exist apart from the Earth. Despite this reality, human society acts
with callous disregard for its impacts on the natural systems that sustain life.

Westra would have us rethink the limits of criminal responsibility. Living
safely within the biosphere is not merely a matter of amenities or entitlements. If
nations can promote global trade and communications and travel, she sees the
need for a concurrent promotion of supranational norms to define crimes against
the ecological foundations of life. The norms she would have us respect have been
ably restated in legal instruments, such as the World Charter for Nature adopted
by the United Nations General Assembly (UN Res. 37/7) or in the more compre-
hensively framed Earth Charter, endorsed by UNESCO in 2003 (see Appendices
1 and 3 to this book, and http://www.earthcharter.org).

Human society increasingly applies these norms through the now volumi-
nous body of environmental statutes that have been adopted in every nation, and
by the growing body of multinational environmental agreements and other
treaties that integrate and harmonize national conduct toward different aspects
of life on earth. These legal instruments are based on the findings of the environmental scientists around the world. All nations embraced the action plan to
prevent further deterioration of environmental conditions on Earth adopted by
the United Nations Conference on Environment and Development as Agenda
21. On many, if not all, issues of environmental stewardship, today there has
emerged a congruence of legal opinion and agreement about the measures that
constitute environmental protection, and on the acts that constitute environmental injury. When legislatures enact norms as positivist statutes, defining
crimes, enforcement follows.

It should surprise none, therefore, that there has emerged in many nations a
body of jurisprudence about criminal environmental law.[1] The consensus about

---

1. See, for instance, *Environmental Crimes*, prepared by the Criminal Litigation Committee
of the Environmental law Section of the New Yo4rk State bar Association (Albany, N.Y. 1995).

criminal behavior constituting environmental crimes is that if the actor, for instance, had knowledge that a chemical he used was hazardous, that was enough to establish his responsibility when his chemical causes harm to the environment. No greater *mens rea* is required (consider, for instance Section 3008(d) of the Resource Conservation and Recovery Act in the USA, 42 U.S.C. 6928(d)).

What appears not yet present in national patterns of environmental criminal law, however, is the widening of the scope of what constitutes criminal action from knowingly having the capacity to cause harm, to conduct that acts in disregard of a duty to prevent harm, or to affirmatively protect the environment. The predicate for such a broader scope is found in a number of national constitutions,[2] such as the *dirigiste* provisions of Federal Constitution of Brazil of 1988, in Chapter VI, Article 225 ("All have the right to an ecologically balanced environment, which is an assert of common use and essential to a healthy quality of life, and both the government and the community shall have the duty to defend and preserve it for present and future generations.").

When a person causes egregious, long-lasting and momentously destructive environmental harm, the magnitude of the breach of a duty to sustain life may well be considered to constitute a crime. We see this approach within national criminal law in the case of the act that causes death of a human being, and resulting prosecution for the crime of manslaughter.

Implicitly perhaps, Laura Westra's advocacy echoes the maxim of René Dubos, to "think globally and act locally." Laura Westra would have us recognize that there is—or must be—the global concept of an "ecocrime." Either nations through their national criminal legal systems, or the international community through appropriate international tribunals, would prosecute those who commit ecocrime. She surveys the issues of jurisprudence, and broader philosophical and sociological perspectives relevant to ecocrime, and that applies her survey to the case study of Walkerton, Ontario, Canada. She would have us generalize from the emergence of prosecutions for violations of human rights to universal standards to permit prosecutions for ecocrimes. There are, however, many impediments to recognition or enforcement of ecocrimes at both the national and international levels

Laura Westra's vision extends well beyond state practice today. If her work invites scholars to think further, and elaborate her ideas, it will be to critique whether her "normative strategies" to build the global approach to ecocrimes is realistic, or if competing or different approaches might be assayed. Much of her experience is described from Canadian law, and in this respect the work also provides useful insights for the comparative environmental lawyer. A book succeeds

2. See Appendix B, setting forth "Constitutional Rights and Duties" *in* Edith Brown Weiss, *In Fairness to Future Generations: International Law, Common Patrimony, and Intergenerational Equity* (Transnational Publishers, 1989).

when it both stimulates and educates. This volume will excite the reader to think unconventional thoughts, and enriches the tapestry of jurisprudence about the biosphere we call Earth.

Nicholas A. Robinson
Chair, Commission on Environmental Law
International Union for the
Conservation of Nature
and Natural Resources

Pace University School of Law
White Plains, New York

PART I

CHAPTER 1

A PARADIGMATIC CASE OF INSTITUTIONALIZED AND LEGALLY SANCTIONED VIOLENCE: THE JUST WAR

1. INTRODUCTION

In recent years we have become used to hearing news about violence: terrorism, wars, genocide, crime and assaults of various kinds appear to be a routine part of life today. We read about them, we see them on television and they have become such a part of day-to-day life that we have almost stopped being shocked each time another instance of violence is brought to our attention. What is often forgotten is that not all forms of violence are alike. Although all forms of violence should be impermissible, in the sense of being proscribed and punished, many forms of violence are not publicly viewed as such, rather they are tacitly accepted and institutionalized through the practices of present Western democratic institutions.

These are often insidious, covert kinds of violence, taken to be both legal and acceptable the world over, and viewed simply as unintended but acceptable side effects of the modern world we know. Some of these have been recognized and treated as separate problems. Some examples are hazardous technologies (McGinn, 1991), risky business operations (Draper, 1991), environmental violence (Westra, 1998), environmental racism (Bullard, 1994; Westra and Lawson, 2001), animal agricultural practices (Regan, 1983; De Grazia, 1996; Rifkin, 1992), agricultural practices including chemicals and biotechnologies, (Pimentel, 1991; Pimentel, 1993; Mellon and Fondriest, 2001; Rissler and Mellon, 1993), the use and trade of toxic substances (Cranor, 1993), and technology transfers to developing countries (Shrader-Frechette, 1991). Finally, low-dose chemicals that are also part of modern life, have been found to be endocrine disruptors and they represent violent intrusions into the normal functions of humans and nonhuman animals (Colborn et al., 1996). Useful as these ethical, scientific, or social issue discussions have been and still are as they continue to emerge, they all miss a unifying focus, as they are treated singly, not jointly as symptomatic of a major problem, a form of all-pervasive violent injustice.

This list of attacks in some sense shares the status of wars: they are, one and all, legal and institutionalized, that is, integrated within the life of modern democratic countries and global society. We may not find each form of violence everywhere in the world at any given time, but we may be sure that they do occur at different places, many of them concurrently. What all these forms of violence share is their apparent acceptability. Even those who may be aware of one or another of these attacks personally, or among their peers in their community, seldom march, organize protests, or petition politicians to stop the violence *now*. In fact, those who do protest and march may be viewed as extremists, crackpots whose cause(s) should not be taken seriously by serious citizens. At most, these forms of violence are viewed as unrelated aspects of modern life, disturbing perhaps, but essentially an unavoidable part of progress. I have discussed most of these forms of violence separately in other works, at one time or another. Through those discussions and the research upon which they were based, I was increasingly led to perceive a common thread: their legality and—in part, due to their legality—apparent social acceptability. In contrast to their apparent pervasiveness and general acceptance, no coherent, all-inclusive discussion of these issues appears in the literature to date. A recent (1999) collection of essays on institutional violence, for instance, devotes only two brief chapters to environmental violence. One addresses the issue from the viewpoint of ecofeminism, and proposes dismantling present power structures through the approach of "nondomination" thereby eliminating, "dualistic thinking" and the "hierarchies embodied in patriarchal thinking" (Fox, 1999:258). The other analyzes petrochemical agriculture and its approach to natural systems and to nonhuman animals (Boss, 1999:263–277). I will discuss some of the points raised in the latter in Chapter 4, below. The former tends to remain conceptual and theoretic; hence, it is somewhat peripheral to the ethical and legal—taken compendiously and with a conscious element of ambiguous crossover between ethics and the law, the normative—dimensions of public policy that form the main focus of the present work.

Of course there is another form of institutional violence, that has also been discussed and debated at length, the death penalty for certain violent crimes. But some modern countries today still accept the death penalty as a legal and just form of punishment. In the United States only certain states condone it (Baird and Rosenblau, 1995; Radelet, Bedau and Putnam, 1995). Hence, unlike war, it is not a global phenomenon. The death penalty does not share many of the characteristics of just war, because it is always aimed at a single individual; thus, it is not indiscriminate in its violent effects (although many single innocents, especially people of color, may die because of it). In addition, it is intended to punish somebody who might be a threat to other innocents, by eliminating future harms, although I am not arguing that capital punishment acts as a deterrent to violence, as this does not appear to have been conclusively proven (Nathanson, 1999:53–59).

In contrast, a strong Kantian argument may be advanced to support capital punishment as can be found, for instance, in the work of Louis Pojman. He puts his argument for the "classic retributivist position" as follows:

(1) Guilt is necessary condition for judicial punishment; that is, *only* the guilty may be punished.

(2) Guilt is a sufficient condition for judicial punishment; that is, all the guilty must be punished. If you have committed a crime, morality demands that you suffer evil for it.

(3) The correct amount of punishment imposed upon the morally (or legally) guilty offender is that amount which is *equal* to the moral seriousness of the offense (Pojman and Reiman, 1997:9).

Pojman acknowledges that there are severe problems with the way justice is administered in the countries where the death penalty remains, and that they require immediate attention and redress. He also acknowledges the contributing factors of poverty, urbanization, and drugs to criminality, but notes that the former, for instance, by itself, cannot be indicted as the main cause of murder: in India, one can walk among the poorest people in the world with near perfect safety, unlike the situation that exists in most large U.S. cities. The argument for deterrence is not conclusive, Pojman admits, but he views the elimination of capital punishment as a desirable goal, achievable only in truly civilized countries. Austria is a country that has abolished the death penalty, but the murder rate in the whole country per year may be compared to that of the city of Detroit alone, which is 732 (Pojman and Reiman, 1997:62).

For now, Pojman calls for an end to the discriminatory way in which the death penalty is applied in the United States, not the elimination of the law. In contrast, Jeffrey Reiman believes we may "do considerable good" by refraining from executing murderers, because:

> . . . though the death penalty is in *principle* a just penalty for murder, it is unjust *in practice* in America, because it is applied in arbitrary and discriminatory ways and this is likely to continue into the foreseeable future (Pojman and Reiman, 1997:68).

Hence, on balance, perhaps one may conclude that despite the cogency of Kantian arguments, abolitionists may be right because not only in the United States, but in many Islamic countries that retain the death penalty, it is not reserved only for the most heinous premeditated murders, but meted out for sexual transgressions as well, contrary to the proportionality that is basic to Kantian theory. Nevertheless, for Kant it is a question of justice, but also a question of treating each legally and morally competent adult as an *autonomous* person, who is responsible for his actions, although extenuating circumstances may be taken in consideration before sentencing.

The argument of this work finds support in Kantian theory, as we will see, at several stages; hence, it is important to recognize Kant's position on one form of institutionalized violence right at the outset. Of course, it is not necessary at this time to take a definitive position on capital punishment, as that topic is outside the main focus of this work. Nevertheless, capital punishment has been raised as relevant because an important point emerges from the above discussion: the question of seeking proportionality and juridical balance.

Causing the death of innocents, for Kant, is to commit the gravest crime, unless engaged in a war of self-defense, and this crime deserves the gravest penalty. We need to keep this point firmly in mind as we note the gravity of the effects of ecocrimes in Chapter 2, Chapter 4 and much of what follows, as we note how these effects are considered in the law and public policy.

In law, the question of the status of capital punishment is even more unsettled than it is in philosophy. In a section entitled "introduction to Human Rights Issues and Discourse," Steiner and Alston offer a "Global Snapshot" of "diverse human rights problems that plague the world" (Steiner and Alston, 2000:31). This survey is instructive for what it includes, for instance workers' rights, the rights of prisoners and the accused in the United States, women's rights, from systematic beatings to rapes, the harms of a globalized economy that emphasizes the gap between rich and poor, and the suppression of religious freedoms. It is even more noteworthy for what it fails to include: this "smorgasbord" of human rights violations excludes any and all references to environmentally induced famines, floods, epidemics, and other disasters aggravated as well as caused by climate change, as well as other, more obvious, disasters, from oil spills to e-coli and cholera epidemics.

After this overview, the status of capital punishment is discussed. The European Court of Human Rights proscribes capital punishment, as do 105 other states, whereas the United States and 89 other states, notably China, Iran and most Muslim states, Japan, India, and the Russian Federation remain retentionists (Steiner and Alston, 2000:32). As said in this work, we are not going to discuss capital punishment, although it is indeed a legal, institutionalized form of violence in much of the globe.

Beyond this issue of balancing, a discussion of the arguments for and against it will not help to clarify the central focus of this work, that is, the analysis of institutional environmental violence on the basis of existing discussions of a legal, globally accepted form of violence. But one legal form of violence has been openly discussed, and the conditions for its acceptability and legitimacy form a large body of philosophical and legal work today: war. For a war to be legitimate under international law, it must meet certain conditions that will permit its inception in principle. It must also follow certain guidelines and fall within certain specific limits in order to be a just war, not only because of the reasons for engaging in the war, but also through the details of its operation, in practice. Accordingly, it seems that war is the paradigm case of permissible institutionalized violence. The conditions under which it acquires its legal and moral legitimacy will shed light on when and under what circumstances any form of violence may meet the criteria that render it morally acceptable. In the sections that follow, I will start by examining various approaches to war morality, starting with the classical approaches to *jus ad bellum* and *jus in bello*, as here we will find the clearest possible answers about what might constitute an acceptable justification for violence, including the burden of proof that must be met by would-be attackers.

From this standpoint we should be able to bring to light common principles that will allow us to judge other forms of violence in the light of similar standards. Thus, instead of discussing technology, or the environment as separate topics and as discrete sources of violent harms, we will treat violence as unitary, simply as the basis for individual and collective harms. More specifically, indeed violence has many faces, many manifestations from the most brutal and physical, to the less obvious, nonphysical kinds, such as racism, colonialism, sexism, all of which are, according to Curtin and Litke,

> . . . systemic patterns of thinking and cultural organization that often result in the creation of institutionalized forms of justice. For example colonialism as a systemic form of violence, required the British to export a formal educational system designed to create a loyal elite among their subjects. Similarly, racism as a form of systemic violence may lead a legislature to create a racially biased legal system in the name of "justice." That is, systemic violence may create an atmosphere conducive to the creation of violent institutions (Curtin and Litke, 1999:xiv).

What remains foundational for the argument of this work is that, despite the many gradations and forms of violence, distinctions can be drawn between individual and institutional violence (the former the main focus of criminal domestic law), and between existing institutional violence and the basic, but vaguer, systemic violence and systemic oppression. For the most part, national criminal law acknowledges and proscribes individual violence, but it cannot address institutionalized violence because, in some sense, the legal system itself may be based on it in important respects, from the systemic point of view.

This work will not examine in detail all forms of institutional or even systemic violence. Its focus will remain the physical, biological violence against organisms and natural systems, and against organisms through natural systems. The goal will be to show how national legal institutions and instruments need to be critically examined from the perspective of respect for human rights. The proposed remedy will be found in public international law instruments, and in their approach to human rights, as well as in the supranational constitutional example of the European community. The starting point for the proposed critical examination will be a close examination of the legal treatment of one form of accepted violence against humans: war.

To this aim, the starting point of war and war morality makes good sense: war is the only legal, institutionalized form of violence that has been studied, discussed and analyzed through the centuries and that is still viewed globally as acceptable in certain specific circumstances, unlike the death penalty. The presence of this body of analysis and arguments about what might render violence morally permissible must be combined and brought together with the abundant scientific evidence presently available about all aspects of the common life of men and women in modern, technologically advanced affluent countries, as well as those in the developing world. The result of juxtaposing accepted rules for waging war to other aspects of violent attacks is intended as a first effort (to my best knowledge) to apply an extensive body of theoretical and moral knowledge to a new and emerging field of scientific and practical knowledge. The latter has been viewed as a negative aspect of many practices endemic and intrinsic to modern life in different areas, but its underlying preeminent characteristic, that of unconsented, unjustified violence perpetrated against innocents, has not been isolated and studied.

a. The Just War in Antiquity and Early Christianity

From the time of the Roman Empire and even earlier, the conditions of just war have been discussed and debated. Later theologians and philosophers of Christian times added their voices, and earlier Chinese, the Aztec empire, ancient Egyptian, Babylonian, and Greek philosophers all discussed the proper and improper ways of visiting violence upon one's enemies. The Roman Stoic thinker, Cicero, discusses the necessary conditions for *ius ad bellum* (or just war):

(1) War must be declared by proper authority.
(2) The antagonist must be notified of the declaration of war.
(3) The antagonist must be afforded the opportunity to make a peaceful settlement prior to the initiation of hostilities (Christopher, 1994:13; Cicero, 1928).

Clearly, even before Christian thinkers, violence among groups, cities, and nations was an accepted part of political life, but the conditions of its legitimacy was a cause for concern. Violence as such was not desirable.

Cicero also notes that war should be a last resort, turned to only when discussion is unsuccessful (Christopher, 1994:13)

It is fair to say that no other form of violence has enjoyed such a long history of concerned and concentrated study from so many and so varied sources. Hence, we can do no better than to attempt to understand under what conditions, in principle, violence might be morally justifiable.

In Roman times, there was a great deal of concern about the conduct of war or *jus in bello*. Despite their position of imperial power, the Roman Senate adopted "just" laws based on principles so obvious and reasonable that they must be universally recognized, and imposed them on herself and those nations with whom she interacted (Christopher, 1994:14).

Rome issued and proclaimed a *ius gentium* or world law, although there was no international cooperation leading to the formulation of such laws. To the Romans we owe the first detailed formulation of the duties owed to enemies, the *limits* of retribution, and the rights of noncombatants (those who lay down arms), as well as prisoners. Although no claim can be made that all violent conflict followed scrupulously the rules of war, the very existence of such rules creates a precedent for a clear dividing line between legitimate violence and violent crime. Although several aspects of the rules of war that were present in Roman times remain significant today, one well-accepted modern day position appears to be absent from the discussion, that is, the position of pacifism. In fact, although Roman emperors are known to have looked down upon Christians and their less than whole-hearted support of the war effort, this attitude might have been due to the Christians' refusal to worship the Emperor and to practice idolatry, rather than their pacifism.

Yet early Christians may have refused to offer violence even to their country's enemies, based on the passages from the Gospel that forbid violence even in retaliation. But aside from the clear prohibition against murder and the change from "an eye for an eye" to "love your neighbor" brought in by the Gospel, a certain ambiguity remains. On one hand, we read "All who take the sword die by the sword" (Matt.26:50–53); on the other, the lawful authorities are expected and even obliged to keep order in the community and to mete out retribution and justice, and this may be done by violent means, if required (Christopher, 1994:21).

According to this interpretation, two significant aspects of present war morality emerge clearly: the need for a duly recognized authority to administer violent retribution according to its lights, and the presence of the condition required to legitimize violent punishment, that is, the primary concern for the public good. Pacifism understood as the complete rejection of any form of violence, under any circumstances cannot be found in the Gospels or even in the convictions of early Christians. Considering the fact that early Christians were motivated by religious scripture rather than by the quest for solid argument, we might simply trace the history of just war theory showing the development of theories from their earliest roots in antiquity to today, and set aside, for now, the question of pacifism. We will return to it later in the chapter, through the recent work of James Sterba (1998).

Although Augustine worked on the question of what constitutes a just war, most of his doctrine was accepted and eventually incorporated in the work of Thomas Aquinas. Aquinas can be said to have summarized and systematized Augustine's thought to produce clear rules and principles (Christopher, 1994:52), in line with eternal law, and available to man through reason and codified in natural law. Natural law, thus, sets the boundaries of all human laws including the laws governing a just war. In the *Summa Theologica* (Q.94, A.2), Aquinas says: "Since however, good has the nature of the end, and evil the nature of the contrary, hence it is that all of those things to which man has a natural inclination that are naturally apprehended by reason as being good. . . . Therefore, the order of the precepts of the natural law is according to the order of natural inclinations" (Timmons, 1990:97).

These "natural inclinations" are:

(1) the "inclination to good in accordance with the nature which he has in common with all substances" that is the common inclination to self-preservation;

(2) the "inclination in accordance to the natural law which nature has taught to all animals, such as sexual intercourse, the education of offspring, and so forth";

(3) the "natural inclination to know the truth about God and to live in society."

War morality and—in general—rules pertaining to the use of violence are clearly derived from natural law, from both its first and third principles.

Self-preservation as a *duty* as well as a right is obvious, but the question of "living in society" and "pursuing truth" are no less important in that regard. Society must be constructed and organized in such a way that the conditions are not only appropriate for a peaceful communal life, but also for a life kept safe, and, thus, kept at the same time congenial to the pursuit of truth. For the latter, a form of governance must be sought that (1) respects the *natural* ends of man, and (2) administers justice by authority which may legitimately employ violence when required. The basis for legitimacy lies in two criteria; the foundation of natural law and—most of all—the common good.

But the "common good" of the state cannot flourish unless its citizens be virtuous, and "the proper effect of law is to lead its subjects to their proper virtue" (Thomas Aquinas, *Summa Theologica* (Q.92, A.1,.A.2), at 25–26; Christopher, 1994:53). The common good "requirement" in fact is so powerful that its presence or absence is sufficient to render a form of governance either legitimate or not. When laws are not enacted in support of the common good, understood in terms of the principles of natural law, then those very laws and the authorities promulgating them lose their legitimacy. They revert to being a form of violence instead, as Aquinas has it, "violentia cuiusdam." (*Summa Theologiae* I-II Bk. II, Pt.I, 93, 3, ad. 2).

Thus, the requirements of *jus ad bellum* rest upon four major premises: (1) that war be declared (as in Roman times); (2) that war be declared by the legitimate authority, that is, the duly sanctioned authority concerned with the common good; (3) that war be waged for a just reason and a good cause; and (4) that war be waged with good intention (e.g., with the intention of promoting the good, seeking peace, or punishing or avoiding evil). In addition, unlike Ambrose and Augustine, Thomas Aquinas responded to those who insisted on *caritas*, or love of our neighbor, rather than self-defense in case of attacks, by bringing another doctrine, that of "double effect." This position entails that when we intend a good effect or a good result to follow our action, then a concomitant bad effect might be permissible, provided that it is unintended either as a deliberate means to our end, or as the end itself.

For instance, when we are attacked, we have the right to self-defense, but our defense must remain proportional to the attack itself. Self-defense may even extend to lethal violence against our assailant, provided that our intention remains to preserve our own life, not simply to destroy his: in that case, his eventual demise remains "outside the intention, or accidental, instead" (Christopher, 1994:57; cp. *Summa Theologiae*, Q.64, A.7). This doctrine should be kept in mind, and so should the notion of proportionality, as one of the basic requirements of legitimacy, together with the pursuit of the common good, which remains primary. This presentation of just war doctrine is not intended as a complete argument in defense of a particular position, but as an overview of its historical doctrinal development. Particularly emphasized is the movement from an ancient nonreligious background to the religious aspects of the doctrine, and finally to the passage from a religiously based theory to a legal one, in *Grotius* (1625). This is an overview that ignores several modern problems, civil uprising, for instance, or the possibility of a "war of liberation" or even the existence of "ethical revolutions," initiated not by the so-called "legitimate authority," but by various peoples seeking independence or justice (Gilbert, 1994:84–92; see also Section 7.e). The question of civil disobedience will be discussed further below, in Chapter 3, Sections 6 and 8).

2. THE TRANSITION FROM MORALITY TO LAW: HUGO GROTIUS

Although the seeds were already present in antiquity, it is in Grotius' laws of war that we find clearly articulated the principles defining just what makes a war just, from two separate points of view: Christopher says: "Grotius' laws of war deserve examination from two distinct and independent perspective: *jus ad bellum* and *jus in bello*. His primary objective is to prevent war. Failing to prevent it, he seeks to minimize its brutality" (Christopher, 1994:86).

Nevertheless Grotius took for granted that war had to exist; his concern was with ensuring that when it did, it would be just, not with defending or upholding pacifism. The requirements of just war (as *jus ad bellum*), according to Grotius, include (1) a just cause, including self-defense, defense of one's property, violation of rights, or the punishment of an injury inflicted; (2) the criterion of proportionality, that is, the "good" to be achieved by war must proportionally offset the bad effects inherent in the war itself. Relative to the proportionality requirement, Grotius speaks in an almost modern voice, in a way that resonates well for those who seek a global perspective today, instead of a national one: "Kings who measure up to the rules of wisdom take account not only of the nation which has been committed to them, but of the whole human race" (Grotius, 1962, Prolegomena Ch. 24, at 18).

Proportionality is not only relevant to considerations of *jus ad bellum*, but also to the conduct of war, or *jus in bello*. Whether a war should be waged and how a war is waged, that is, what can happen within it, *both* must be governed by the principles of proportionality. The third condition for a just war is that it should have a reasonable chance of success (Christopher, 1994:91), as for Grotius life is primary, and war is necessarily an attack on life. The fourth and fifth conditions are that war must be publicly declared, and by a legitimate authority, as we saw earlier in Aquinas' doctrines. For a sixth condition, we need to consider war very seriously, and only undertake it in exceptional circumstances, when all else fails (Grotius, 1962, ch. 25, III, at. 579; Grotius, 1962, ch. 24, VII, at 575).

The other condition on which both Augustine and Aquinas insisted as the determinant one, or the one that might render even an otherwise just war immoral, that is, the presence of the "right intention," was not recognized as valid by Grotius. This omission is understandable if one considers that it is morality, not the law that usually deals with the role of intentions, as actions themselves may not be affected by the agent's motivations. On the other hand, Grotius adds details to the condition of *jus in bello* and insists on the importance of designing rules to limit the conduct of war. Grotius also believed that his criteria were relevant and valid among nations, just as they were within a state.

The national application of the criteria will be helpful in bringing the rules of war to bear on other forms of institutionalized violence. From the standpoint of *jus in bello*, our first consideration should be the distinction between innocents and noninnocents, based upon their role within the hostilities, not on their individual moral character (Nagel, 1974; Westra, 1986). Innocents are those who are not immediately threatening, according to Thomas Nagel (1974); hence, women, children, older men, prisoners of war, medical personnel, or those exercising their religious calling, are not to be harmed. Only in rare circumstances, when grave harm may befall many, it might be morally permissible to proceed in a way that unintended consequences of our actions may harm some innocents, provided the death of these innocents is neither intended nor foreseen.

Another important criterion is that of proportionality, not only in deciding whether the harms perpetrated by war are offset by the good expected as a result of war, but also within the operation of war. The questions to be asked are: Are civilian deaths minimized during the conflict? Are the targets sought absolutely necessary, and are the means employed to bring about military targets and objectives, specific enough and limited in the effects? A counter example to proportionality occurred during the Vietnam War through the use of Agent Orange (a defoliant), used to destroy natural landscapes and vegetation, thus exposing the enemy targets. Christopher says: "Defoliation resulted in extensive long-term contamination of large areas of the Vietnam countryside, contamination of water supplies, and destruction of indigenous wildlife" (Christopher, 1994:102).

Eventually the carcinogenic properties of agent orange were discovered, adding yet another immoral consequence to the ones listed above. Note that most of the consequences listed represent additional harms to noncombatants, both direct and indirect.

The property of inflicting harms to the innocent belongs to certain policy decisions and war activities, and it also belongs to certain weapons: indiscriminate weaponry of all kinds must be eliminated through the rules of war. By definition, indiscriminate weapons cannot discriminate between combatants and noncombatants, and nuclear weapons are a clear instantiation of this kind of weapon.

After this brief overview of classical war morality, in the next section we will turn to a recent treatment of war morality and pacifism.

a. A Question of Justice: War Morality or Pacifism?

In a recent work entitled *Justice Here and Now*, James Sterba (1998) argues for a reconciliation of just war theory and pacifism, and his argument is relevant to the present enterprise. Pacifism is a position according to which any and all forms of violence should be proscribed. But pacifism cannot be accepted by anyone who accepts that self-preservation is both a right and a duty, that one's children and family, minimally, have a right to be defended. This work will argue that while institutionalized violence is unacceptable, self-defense is appropriate. I have argued this position even as corollary to my position of biocentric holism (Westra, 1994) against those who objected that a generalized respect for environmental wholes and the parts within these wholes, entails equal respect for bacteria or viruses, for example. The answer is that within natural wholes, self-defense and even defense and protection of one's species are both natural and expected. It is also defensible on moral grounds from most theoretical standpoints, such as virtue ethics, deontology and in some cases, utilitarianism.

However aggression against noncombatants, that is, against anyone (or any nonhuman animal) without legal capacities and intentions against us, is not an acceptable and defensible activity. More needs to be said of this topic, that is, of the transition from sentient human to sentient nonhumans, and possible objections will be addressed in Chapter 4, although there is already ample support for animal rights or the consideration for animals and their inclusion in the moral community (Regan, 1983; Singer, 1993; Taylor, 1986; Sterba, 1998).

Returning now to war morality, Sterba summarizes the requirements of *ius adbellum* as just cause, as follows:

(1) There must be substantial aggression.
(2) Nonbelligerent correctives must be either hopeless or too costly.

(3) Belligerent correctives must be neither hopeless nor too costly (Sterba, 1998:151).

Points (2) and (3) may incorporate the concept of proportionality as intended by the Ancients, Medievals and by Grotius, but I suspect proportionality goes beyond questions of cost and probability of success; in fact one can think of instances where it might even be in conflict with points (2) and (3). One can imagine an internal uprising motivated by strongly defensible principles, or, in Paul Gilbert's terms, a "moral revolution" (Gilbert, 1994). In this case, a decision for swift and brutal reprisal may well be "neither hopeless nor too costly," in contrast with "hopeless and costly" protracted dialogue or other peaceful but less decisive choice. I question the sufficiency of the three points as they stand. When both proportionality (as in the case of a small portion of the citizenry engaging in a righteous uprising), and "right intention" are absent, justice may be absent as well.

In addition, Sterba argues that despite the difficulties present in the quest for "just cause," hence, for a just war, just war theory assumes that a just war is possible, at least in principle, and that it further incorporates the specifics that render just the *means* through which such a war is conducted. The requirements of (1) not harming innocents either directly as an end or as means to some far objective, and (2) ensuring that even the harm directed at combatants and aggressors (including "epistemological aggressors," that is, contributors to war effort), should remain proportional to their goal (Sterba, 1998:152), can be applied to other forms of violence, beyond the war situation, and we will do so in some detail in later chapters.

In contrast, pacifism, at least in its usual formulation, excludes the use of any violence, and it is often counterintuitive as we have seen in the example of self-defense, or the defense of one's child. We may well want to attempt to preserve as morally appropriate this sort of violence, while proscribing large-scale wars instead. Sterba suggests that a position he terms "antiwar pacifism," avoids the objections against all-encompassing pacifism; instead, he defines it as a position that holds that, "Any participation in the massive use of lethal force in warfare is morally prohibited" (Sterba, 1998:153).

This position avoids the counterintuitive difficulties present in pacifism, but excludes for the most part any form of mass-directed violence. Similarly, Thomas Nagel has emphasized the difficulties inherent in the conduct of war in modern times, and with modern weapons of mass-destruction (Nagel, 1974). However there are some important dimensions of conflict that may be left out of Sterba's account. These are all forms of principled guerilla warfare, "ethical revolutions," and so-called wars of liberation (Gilbert, 1994).

These forms of violence share the defense of self and kin on the ground of shared, defensible principles. They do not share, however, the large indiscriminate weaponry common to large-scale wars, or even the depersonalization and lack of respect for individuals and for their moral position that are equally widespread. Antiwar pacifism could be modified, perhaps adding further nuancing and more detailed conditions. In addition, Sterba's definition of combatants to include epistemological aggressors may also be problematic, as it moves from immediate retaliation and self-defense, to attacking planners and contributors, who might deserve punishment perhaps, but not necessarily death, any more than those who plan, but do not execute murders should be condemned to life imprisonment (Nagel, 1974; Westra, 1983; Sterba, 1998:170–171).

Another important aspect of institutionalized violence has been analyzed by John McDermott, in the context of morality and technology. McDermott has argued convincingly that the presence of large and complex modern information technologies militate against morality when applied to modern warfare (McDermott, 1997:92–97). When highly complex information technologies are combined with so-called "rational bombing programs," as they were in the Vietnam War, what follows adds to the immorality of indiscriminate, large-scale weaponry, as these technologies support a component of disrespect for human rights and democratic processes, beyond the already grim results of the violence that is being perpetrated.

In brief, the bombing program against South Vietnam was based on models which aimed for maximum effectiveness to provide opportunities to kill a calculable number of soldiers, as well "of course, as a calculable but not calculated number of non-soldiers." McDermott adds: "This is the most rational bombing system to follow if American lives are very expensive and American weapons and Vietnamese lives very cheap. Which, of course, is the case" (McDermott, 1997:93).

Another result of this technologically advanced program is that (1) it depersonalizes completely all human beings involved in the war, in direct conflict for instance, with Nagel's Kantian position requiring a direct personal justification of our violent self-defense (Nagel, 1974); (2) it requires centralization of the decision-making process that is therefore limited to highly trained personnel, a veritable elite of technocrats, who are neither elected nor charged with the responsibility for public welfare, but only with the execution of a specific program; and (3) it necessarily groups unconsenting or protesting citizens, defective or faulty equipment or programs together as "negative externalities." They are all characterized and treated as something that impedes the progress of the elite-chosen and implemented program, viewed exclusively from the standpoint of the objective to be achieved, as either positive (helpful) or negative (unhelpful).

Therefore, it can be argued that not only are technologically complex weapons unacceptable within the confines of legally acceptable violence (in a just war), but their design, use, and implementation is also immoral, over and above the physical harm they produce in combatants and noncombatants alike. The absence of democratic process and the lack of respect for individuals and groups beyond the "enemy" forces render modern weaponry and the information and intelligence processes needed for their deployment also harmful and immoral. This assessment of war-related technologies further supports Sterba's argument for antiwar pacifism (Sterba, 1998) provided the modifications proposed earlier are taken in consideration. The next step now is to attempt to extend and generalize the argument for just war.

3. WHEN IS VIOLENCE JUSTLY EMPLOYED?

If we reject complete pacifism and accept a modified version of antiwar pacifism in its stead, then we can accept that under certain conditions and in certain circumstances violence might be morally justified. But this work aims to extend and universalize the conclusions reached in war morality, in order to see whether and under what circumstances and conditions, the conclusions reached may be applicable to other forms of violence. In sum violence may be permissible when the recipients (or expected targets) of such violence have been notified well in advance, so that all other avenues may be sought for the resolution of the conflict. The notification and the decision to pursue a violent course of action must originate from the "proper authority." This is an interesting requirement, because proper authority itself involves a cluster of complex requirements. These include:

(1) It is only the representatives of the state (or the recognized community) that have the right to make the decision. Obedience to the leaders of such a community is part of the implicit pact under which citizens live.

(2) Both the obedience to the recognized authority and the hierarchical organization of the state are for the sake of order, hence, for the common benefit of the citizens themselves.

(3) The weighty decision to declare war must be taken by this authority because he (or they) alone have the capacity (due to their power) to see to the common good.

(4) The projected target of violence, or the antagonists in the expected conflict must have enough advance information to propose alternative settlements or other appropriate courses of action.

As we noted, these conditions were already clearly present in the war morality discussions of Roman times. In later times and with the advent of Christian morality and theories, primarily those of Augustine and Aquinas and eventually with the doctrines of Hugo Grotius, more conditions were added. For Grotius, the conditions governing *jus ad bellum* were just cause, proportionality, reasonable chance of success, as well as the previous requirements of declaration of war by a legitimate authority, and time to respond and reconsider the projected hostilities. However, Grotius rejected the condition of "right intention," because he argued that intentionality was a characteristic of agents, not of "relationships between states" (Christopher, 1994:95).

From the point of view of violence in general, all of these conditions are important and are relevant in various degrees when considering violence. The problem to be faced is simple and it bears repeating: current scientific research and philosophical analysis shows that the citizens of modern states, including those governed by liberal democracies, are exposed to violence engendered by complex modern technologies both as products and as processes, directly and indirectly, through global environmental threats. The producers and originators of these novel forms of violence have used several techniques to defend and bolster their position and their "right" to proceed freely. The means employed range from media manipulation and control, to engaging in campaigns lobbying for deregulations for some of their practices, to the maintenance of the status quo through legal maneuvers. They have often employed whole legal teams to find and use the right legislation to protect them and the knowledge they possess and fight not to share with the public (Korten, 1995; Draper, 1991; Westra, 1998). The latter is an approach used routinely to ensure that citizens will participate willingly in promoting their own harm, because the advantages of certain products and practices are widely disseminated, while the harms they produce are kept as a "trade secret" (Westra, 1998).

There are two separate but related questions that face us and need to be answered in detail. The first: What, precisely, exposes us to harm? We need to show just what physical harms arise from modern practices and life conditions, and this will be the topic of the next chapter. The second question: If some of these practices are not considered exceptional or illegal, but are legal and institutionalized, what does war morality say that can be extended to this area of violence, starting with the possibility of the common good to which the attackers might appeal to justify their continued activity? These two questions represent the bridge between the theoretical approach to institutionalized violence that might be potentially justifiable, that is, war, and the corporate/technological institutionalized violence, that has not been analyzed from that point of view.

4. ECOVIOLENCE AS HUMAN RIGHTS VIOLATION: A GLOBAL PERSPECTIVE

The environment is man's first right
We should not allow it to suffer blight
The air we breathe we must not poison
They who do should be sent to prison
Our streams must remain clean all season
Polluting them is clearly treason
The land is life for man and flora,
Fauna and all: should wear that aura,
Protected from the greed and folly
Of man and companies unholy.
(Ken Saro-Wiwa, "A Walk in the Prison Yard," 1994.)

The brief discussion of institutionalized violence in the context of war morality in Sections 2 and 3 of this chapter, traced some of the arguments employed to provide a justification for legal violence. We need to keep in mind the major points that will emerge in the rest of this work:

(1) The basis of my argument is that "ecocrimes" are a form of legal violence, in fact that they represent "crimes against humanity" (Bassiouni 1992);

(2) Not only are such crimes discussed in law primarily against the background of "war crimes," but the international law instruments—(Charter of the Nuremberg Tribunal (1945); International Military Tribunal for the East (1948) Conventions on the Law and Customs of War on Land (The Hague, 1899); Conventions on the Prevention and Suppression of the Crime of Genocide (1948); Convention Against Torture and Other Cruel Inhuman and Degrading Treatment or Punishment (1984); International Law Commission Report on the Draft Code of Crimes Against the Peace and Security of Mankind (1991))—all start their discussion against a background of the conditions prevailing in armed conflicts, and appropriately so;

(3) Hence, it *appears to be entirely correct to* show the similarities between environmental institutional violence, that is "ecocrime" (at least, in the moral sense), or the prevalence of environmental assaults that are not simply isolated, unexpected events, and other violent breaches of human rights regulations;

(4) From this point of view (as in (3)), another form of crime committed *outside a war situation*, that is, the violence perpetrated against women, often with the complicity of the state and its legal institutions, has been recently declared a form of torture, and elevated to the status of international crime (*The Globe and Mail*, March 2001); and finally,

(5) The question of responsibility for these crimes against humanity can be perceived and presented most clearly in the context of international law, although the U.N. and other international organs presently lack the ability to enforce and punish.

In some sense, ecoviolence appears to describe a form of attack that is somewhere between a breach of humanitarian laws, that is appropriate to the conduct of war, and human rights laws, pertaining to peacetime forms of violence. Although it appears to be more appropriate to think of ecoviolence as a breach of human rights law, the argument here advanced that it is a form of systemic violence makes it almost equally fitting to consider it under the category of humanitarian laws, that is, as a form of protection of human rights in a situation of violent conflict. Given the reality of North/South conflict, and the repeated conflicts between the "haves" and the "have-nots," exemplified by the violent demonstrations in Seattle, Geneva, Genova, Napoli, Québec, and elsewhere against the

WTO, on the part of coalitions that include prominent environmental and animal defense activists, this contention appears more than a facile exaggeration.

Accordingly, this section will start with a discussion of the Nuremberg principles and the question of responsibility for crimes in the categories covered by those documents. Section 5 will consider some of specifics of the violence proscribed under the Charter of Nuremberg. Section 6 will consider what rights, specifically, are protected by international human rights laws in relation to Shue's *Basic Rights*. . . . (1996). Section 7 will attempt to respond to various critiques, both conceptual and practical, advanced against the use of traditional human rights principles, based, at least in part, on natural law, and other essentialist principles that are foundational to the conception and the use of *jus cogens* norms.

The first thing to note about the protection of human rights, after the Nuremberg trials, is that many disputed the legality of those documents, based on the fact that the criminality of those actions had been established only *after* the crimes had occurred. Aside from the fact that the German Nazi government had a precedent in law, as they had altered their own promulgated law in order to introduce new provisions that substituted for *nullum crimen sine lege* (Section 2 of the German Penal Code of 1872), the principle of "legislative and judicial analogy" (Bassiouni, 1992:131), another condition was present that made the all-important difference. Bassiouni points out:

> The crimes committed during World War II which fall within the meaning of "crimes against humanity" were unprecedented in history. Not because the violations were unknown, but because the scale and the manner of their perpetration was until then unknown to mankind. The absence of positive law foreseeing such crimes was, therefore, inevitable, just as killing of Cain by Abel was inevitably a first (Bassiouni, 1992:139).

This is precisely the argument proposed here: "ecocrimes" can be so defined in international law, and they should be so entrenched, because they are a "first" as well, in their magnitude, their gravity, and the global reach of their effects. This is the first obvious similarity between crimes against humanity and ecocrimes, but further examination will disclose far more than a similarity between them.

Many of the points made by Bassiouni can be made about ecocrimes as well: they are unprecedented, and so is the "scale and manner of their perpetration"; so that not only their consequences, their *actus reus*, is similar, but so is their "scale and manner of their perpetration." Hence, we might rely on this Nuremberg precedent and arguments for its validity as law in the effort to criminalize environmental assaults.

There is also another aspect of international law that might provide a better avenue to curbing ecoviolence, that is the possibility of international prosecution through the ascription of individual criminal responsibility. Individuals can be ". . . charged on the basis of individual responsibility for having participated in the decisions or carrying out in whole or in part, these acts deemed violative of these rules" (Bassiouni, 1992:19). In addition, other traditional approaches to crime are also codified, as some of these war criminals were not only charged with crimes, but also with "having failed to prevent their occurrence, when, as commanders, they had a duty which they intentionally, knowingly or recklessly, disregarded" (Ibid.). The difference between the approach to these perpetrators and those in corporate boardrooms and institutional government bureaucracies is clear: the former cannot be protected by reasons of state, while the latter can appeal to trade secrets and even to some constitutional protections (for instance the Canadian Charter of Rights, Section (7)) to the extent they are considered legal persons (Chick, 1993; French, 1984).

In addition, public law demonstrates the ultimate responsibility of state officials to the common good, as that is what legitimizes their very authority (Hohfeldt, 1923; Simmons, 1979). From the work of Plato and Aristotle, through that of St. Augustine and Thomas Aquinas in earlier times, to recent work on the topic, including that of Bassiouni (1992:58), that is the accepted standard to legitimate authority. Hence, it is not sufficient to view human rights violations as violations of the law of one or another specific state: those in power may well be imposing laws that are in stark contrast with what is morally right, and whatever embodies the good of all within a state Aquinas contends that, in such cases, not only is a citizen not obliged to obey those "laws," but that he or she has a moral obligation to *disobey*, an early statement of "conscientious objector status," the first of its kind in medieval times.

Hence, individuals, at least in principle, always have the right and the duty to think for themselves and act morally, whether or not such action is commanded by their national laws. Aside from personal morality and obligation, even states have a similar obligation from an international point of view. Grotius said that, "kings have the right of demanding in punishment not only on account of injuries committed against themselves and their subjects, but also on account of injuries which do not directly affect them, but excessively violate the law of nature or of nations in regard to any person whatsoever" (Grotius, (1962:chs. XX,XL; Bassiouni, 1992:62–63).

5. OBLIGATIONS *ERGA OMNES* AND THE NUREMBERG CHARTER

This argument brings us to consider obligations *erga omnes*, as we will argue that it is through these obligations and the norms of *jus cogens* that we can best hope to control international ecocrime. These norms are not based on anachronistic principles, even though crimes committed through the environment are the products of a technologically advanced society, not present in Roman or Medieval times. What these obligations and norms emphasize is the universal morality that is, or should be, present in all articulations of substantive justice that can defend and support human rights. If we consider the nonderogable principles and norms embodied in the principles of Nuremberg, we can see other useful conceptual doctrinal tools for preventing environmental crime. For instance, the Nuremberg defendants were charged with "four counts":

(1) "common plan or conspiracy";
(2) "crimes against peace";
(3) "war crimes"; and
(4) "crimes against humanity" (Bassiouni, 1992:209).

Of these, three are appropriate and, in fact, applicable within our context: (1), (2), and (4). And both the Nuremberg Charter (1945), the Charter of the International Military Tribunal (82 U.N.T.S. 279), and other related documents like The General Assembly's Nuremberg Principles, represent the strongest articulations of the rules to govern legal forms of violence; hence, they are most useful for understanding and analyzing ecocrimes. Principle II of the General Assembly's Nuremberg Principles is a case in point: "The fact that internal law does not impose a penalty for an act which constitutes a crime under international law, does not relieve the person who committed the act from responsibility under international law" (Bassiouni, 1992:624). Another important point is emphasized in Principle IV: "The fact that a person has acted pursuant to an order of his government or of a superior does not relieve him of responsibility under international law, provided a moral choice was in fact possible to him" (Ibid. at 625). But the most important principle of all is Principle VI which holds that:

The crimes hereinafter set out are punishable as crimes under international law:

a. Crimes Against Peace:

(i) Planning, preparation, initiation or waging of a war of aggression, of a war in violation of international treaties, agreements or assurances;

(ii) Participation in a common plan or conspiracy for the accomplishment of any of the acts mentioned under (i).

b. War Crimes:

Violations of the laws and customs of war which include, but are not limited to murder, ill-treatment or deportation to slave labour or for any other purpose of civilian populations of or in occupied territory, murder or ill-treatment of prisoners of war, of persons on the seas, killing of hostages, plunder of public or private property, wanton destruction of cities, towns or villages, or devastations not justified by military necessity.

c. Crimes Against Humanity:

Murder, extermination, enslavement, deportation and other inhumane acts done against any civilian population, or persecutions on political, racial or religious grounds, when such acts are done or such persecutions are carried on in execution of or in connection with any crime against peace or any war crime.

From my point of view, the second principle establishes the first salient point: what is under consideration is not the positive law of this or that country; rather, what constitutes a gross violation of morality possesses universal validity. If an action can be characterized as this kind of crime, that is, one that infringes the tenets of natural law (Bassiouni, 1992:69), then the fact that a specific country has failed to criminalize it, or even that many countries have been guilty of the same carelessness, is irrelevant to the Charter's position. The fourth principle reinforces the difference between procedural and substantive justice: something that is entrenched as part of a state's positive law, still does not require obedience, if an individual's morality forbids it.

Bassiouni is correct when he describes the Nuremberg Charter as being, "between Law and Morality" (Ibid. at 69). In the 17th century, Grotius said, *"crimen grave non potest non essere punibile,"* a grave crime cannot be unpunished. How is a "grave" crime defined? Turning to Grotius again, we see that such a "crime" may not violate a state's "principles of legality," but it violates natural law, in turn defined as follows: "the dictates of right reason which points out that a given act, because of its opposition to or conformity with man's rational nature, is either morally wrong or morally necessary, and accordingly forbidden or commanded by God, the author of nature" (Grotius, 1962:ch. XX, n.811).

In essence, both Principle II and IV establish the primacy of universal morality over positivistic legalities of any country, and jointly require that those responsible will be indicted, whether or not the person charged has a position of power, or is expected to obey. Principle VI, on the other hand, outlines the factual elements that render certain acts criminal; in addition, it adds that even "planning," "preparing" (2(i)), and "participating" or being "complicit" (2(ii)) in the carrying out of "crimes against humanity," constitute crimes in themselves.

From the material standpoint then, the actions that can be considered "ecocrimes," are "murder," "ill-treatment," "devastations not justified by military necessity," and "wanton destruction of cities" (VI.b). There are also some elements of VI.c, especially the reference to "extermination" and to "racial" grounds that support the argument for criminalizing actions that infringe human rights from the standpoint of environmental justice. If we consider many of the acts indicted through Principle VI, we find great similarities between these acts and the *actus reus* of ecocrimes. Murder is surely no less such, when it takes place immediately, or slowly, even by increments, as through the administration of poisons or toxic substances. In the Canadian Criminal Code, for instance, Section 227 which required that a death follow an assault by no more than a year and a day, has been repealed (see Chapter 5).

There is also reference to ill-treatment, and it refers to the conditions to which civilians and noncombatants and prisoners may be exposed. But ill treatment may also refer to the conditions that result from ecocrimes: for instance, famine following droughts, or cholera and other diseases following floods when these are fostered and rendered acute by global climate change. When we willingly participate in activities that produce these effects, we are, at the very least, complicit in the violent conditions that form an inescapable part of the life of those most severely affected by those forms of ill treatment: the citizens of developing countries.

But we must note that the comparisons to military violence, noted at the beginning of this work, are disanalogous in one important respect: there is no just war in progress. Hence, all references to military necessity are out of place in this discussion: both devastations and wanton destruction of cities are the regular results of careless and reckless environmental practices, and they must be viewed as breaches of human rights, without countervailing benefits or any other common good being achieved. As Francis Biddle argued, "Crimes against humanity constitute a somewhat nebulous concept on, although the expression is not unknown to the language of international law" (Biddle, 1974).

Yet, nebulous though the concept might be, I think that an objective description of the consequences of ecocrimes, many of which are irreversible, others even produce terminal disease or are capable of affecting humanity in the real sense of inflicting DNA damage through toxic/chemical exposure, as well as through endocrine disruption (Colborn et al., 1996), provides a list of conditions and circumstances which fit that "nebulous" definition all too well.

Some argue that international law has always, to some extent, been concerned with whatever happens to individuals within states, although its primary focus has been the interaction between states. This historical concern can be expected, given that international law, like domestic laws, "had roots in an accepted morality and in natural law" (Henkin, 1989). Henkin, however, argues that beyond common traditions and common morality, "political-economic (rather than humanitarian or human rights)" concerns might have motivated International Law. Nevertheless, the main point at issue, from the standpoint of the tradition of morality and respect for human rights is the basic reason for the presence of international laws and international tribunals.

6. WHAT IS PROTECTED BY INTERNATIONAL HUMAN RIGHTS CHARTERS AND *JUS COGENS* NORMS? THE QUESTION OF SHUE'S BASIC RIGHTS

When we consider the language and intent of both international human rights and humanitarian laws, including the International Covenant of Civil and Political

Rights (ICCPR) (1966), as well as the International Covenant on Economic, Social and Cultural Rights (ICESCR) (1966), both of these instruments assert that their articles are based on "the inherent dignity of the human person," and that the "ideal of free human beings enjoying civil and political freedom and freedom from fear and want can only be achieved if *conditions* are created whereby everyone may enjoy his civil and political rights," as well as his "economic, social and cultural rights." (emphasis added) It is important to consider what these "conditions" might be. An Arab proverb says that, "The Palm Tree is beautiful, but only when a man's belly is full of dates." Hence, the conditions for physical survival are primary, before cultural or political considerations enter the picture. These conditions must include what Shue calls "subsistence rights." As Shue puts it, these: "Basic Rights are the morality of the depth, that is, they show us the limits below which they cannot sink in our treatment of all people." They are "basic," as the enjoyment of them is essential to the enjoyment of all other rights; they are "everyone's minimum reasonable demands upon the rest of humanity" (Shue, 1996:19).

These "demands," minimally, include "security rights" and "subsistence rights" (Shue, 1996:20). Ecoviolence represents an attack on both. The right not to be "threatened with murder, rape, beatings," ought to include the right not to be exposed to chemicals and toxics, radioactive materials, and every substance that produces morbidity, mortality, and may alter immune, reproductive, and other human functions at the present time, or even affect through DNA changes, future generations (Carson, 1962; Colborn et al., 1996; Westra, 1998; Gbadegesin, 2001). In addition, Alan Gewirth argues for the "necessary pre-conditions" of human rights (Gewirth, 1982:5), in a way similar to that of Shue. Similar arguments can be made for subsistence rights. But although there appears to be an unprecedented proliferation of human rights instruments (and we will examine some of the details of those documents below), some raise serious questions about the validity and even the universality of universal human rights (Baxi, 1999:125; De Sousa Santos, 1999:337).

Some of these questions take the form of attacks on the traditional concept and understanding of human rights. The aim of this work is to (1) show the closeness between ecoviolence and other forms of institutionalized violence; (2) demonstrate that the well-developed and well-established literature on war morality shows clearly the limits within which such violence may be legitimately used and imposed upon others, by showing the specific conditions and circumstances that may render a war legal and just; hence, by analogy, minimally that the need to find similar circumstances if ecoviolence is to be allowed to continue; (3) argue that not only direct causation of violence but also complicity, toleration, and even silence may entail responsibility for its effects, on the part of states, institutions, and individuals; and (4) that both humanitarian laws, intended to mitigate the horrors of armed conflict, and international human rights laws, intended to protect social, economic, cultural, civil, and political rights must rely and be based on respect for basic rights, lately defined by Shue as security and subsistence rights.

The passage in *Barcelona Traction* indicates that (see full discussion in Chapter 7, below) when we consider the language of international treaties and covenants, it is surprising that, amidst a proliferation of charters, covenants and declarations, there is very little that pertains directly to basic rights. Environmental violence attacks human beings in many different ways (Westra, 2000; and see Chapter 2). It might be useful to list some of these forms of assaults and their expected consequences here, as a frame of reference:

(1) increased exposure to UVA/UVB because of ozone layer thinning;
(2) exposure to direct impacts of global climate change, such as floods, extreme temperatures, and other weather changes;
(3) exposure to toxic wastes;
(4) exposure to toxic/hazardous by-products of industrial production, ranging from nuclear power to high-input agriculture;
(5) exposure to food additives and chemical residues in food production;
(6) long-term, low-level exposures to various chemicals and processes;
(7) exposure to climate-induced health threats from new or renewed infectious diseases;
(8) the loss of nature's services through loss of biodiversity, fragmentation of natural landscapes, and deforestation;
(9) increased presence of particulates and other pollutants in the air;
(10) the diminishing supply of safe water;
(11) direct contact with pathogens through encroachment on the wild (Soskolne, 1997, personal communication)
(12) increased hazards from the presence of bioengineered foods and transgenics, which may range from unexpected allergic reactions to unlabeled bioengineered food with unpredictable side effects (as in BSE), to the hidden antibiotics in transgenic fish;
(13) exposure to antibiotic-resistant strains of pathogens; and
(14) increase in communicable-disease risks through migration of persons based on immigration policies of governments and to accommodate refugees, to seek out qualified labor, and to travel (Westra, 2000:287).

A brief survey will disclose how little addresses directly the right to health and the right to noninterference of our physical biological systems, in any of these instruments.

We noted that two of the major covenants (ICCPR (1966); ICESCR (1966)) could be interpreted in a way that could address this concern to some extent. Slightly more explicit is the Convention on the Rights of the Child (1989), although its provisions remain weak and ambiguous. For instance, the Convention states: ". . . the child, by reason of his physical and mental immaturity, needs special safeguards and care, including appropriate legal protection, *before as well as after birth*." Although Article 1, defines a child as "every human being below the age of 18" and Article 3(1) states that "in all actions concerning children," whether public or private (including those undertaken by legislative bodies), "the best interests of the child shall be a primary consideration," both these laudable statements leave open the question of what protection might be accorded to a child *before* birth. Although present "political correctness" considerations force the avoidance of in-depth consideration of the morality and the justice of decisions that only consider the (adult) women's rights and choices, when these may come into conflict with the requirements of the unborn, we must remember that endocrine disruptors and other toxic and chemical substances attack the fetus in ways that are disproportionate in comparison with the dangers imposed on adults of either gender (Colborn et al., 1996). In addition, the rights to protection of the female fetus appear to be even less acceptable than those of their male counterparts, given that females are aborted with even more frequency than males, in some cases.

This is not the appropriate forum for advancing arguments for and against the right to life, and there is an abundant literature in bioethics that can be consulted (Warren, 1991; Thomson, 1990; Noonan, 1991; English, 1991; Beckwith, 1994). But it seems wrong not to mention that, in contrast to an ever-widening openness to rights of various kinds, something as basic as the protection of the rights of future generations should not be subjected to weak and imprecise regulations, especially when the stated goals include the protection of the child before and after birth.

The European Convention for the Protection of Human Rights and Fundamental Freedoms (1971), after the expected statement in Article 2 ("2.1—Rights and Freedoms), 1. Everyone's right to life shall be protected by law," has some interesting language in Article 10.2. Addressing the "right to freedom of speech," it acknowledges that, in its limitations clause, "the exercise of such freedoms, since it carries with it duties and responsibilities; may be subject to various conditions, prescribed by law, as these may be deemed necessary for 'public safety' or 'for the protection of health or morals'." Perhaps then the "freedom to advertise," market, and manufacture products that represent an attack on public safety and health, such as certain chemicals, or bioengineered foods, might be lawfully restricted under the provisions of this article.

The American Convention on Human Rights, is clear and decisive in the protection of life. Part I, Chapter II, Article 4, states:

1. Every person [previously defined as "human being"] has the right to have his life respected. This right shall be protected by law and, in gen-

eral, from the moment of conception. No one shall arbitrarily be deprived of his life.

Article 5.1 adds, "Every person has the right to have his physical, mental, and moral integrity respected." Another interesting point—one that has not been found in the other Charters and Covenants considered so far—is Chapter V, Article 32:

1. Every person has responsibilities to his family, his community, and *mankind.*

2. The rights of each person are limited by the rights of others, by the *security of all,* and by the *just demands of the general welfare,* in a democratic society (emphasis added).

If the provisions of Article 32 were fully implemented, the production, marketing, and waste disposal related to all toxic, chemical and nuclear substances, hazardous from "cradle to grave," that is, presently manufactured, traded, and disposed with a cavalier disregard for the life and rights of others, would be eliminated.

Finally, the African Charter on Human and Peoples' Rights (1986), adds some novel considerations, not formally explicit elsewhere, to its principles. For instance, the concern for "human and peoples' rights" (Preamble), and the explicit inclusion of the concept of "duties" on the part of everyone, as the complementary concept to "rights," are a welcome development in the right direction. Both of these innovative considerations re-appear and are reinforced in several articles beyond the Preamble. "Duties" are the subject of a whole chapter (Chapter II, Duties); Articles 27, 28, and 29 require that the exercise of one's rights take place, "with due regard to the rights of others, collective security, morality and common interest" (Article 27).

The consideration of "human peoples' rights," repeatedly joined in the text in this manner, is particularly interesting, and uniquely apt to protect whole populations from ecoviolent crimes, such as those who decimated the peoples of Ogoniland (Westra, 1998). However, neither duties nor the protection of peoples are specifically directed to the safeguard of the health, and the environmental protection of the habitat of either individuals or peoples. This duty would be particularly relevant for the bureaucracies and the leaders in a continent where toxic trade is rampant (Cranor, 1996; Gbadegesin, 2001).

In sum, even the language, let alone the practices of all these legal instruments, reflecting the concerns of their respective countries and institutions, are not truly conducive to a serious consideration of ecocrime or institutional violence imposed through the environment, nor yet to the legal restraints that are necessary to limit the vast damage inflicted upon all, but primarily on the vulnerable and the disempowered in developing countries by commercial and technological practices that are ruled, for the most part, by economic considerations.

It has been my argument that all these related points are and can be clearly supported in both law and morality, by a full understanding of the principles of natural law, and that these basic rights should be defended by *jus cogens* norms, and the duty to do so should be firmly enforced. This position is necessary because all forms of ecoviolence can be demonstrated to represent crimes against humanity, forms of genocide, and attacks on the human person, as defined and discussed in the work of Bassiouni (1992) and Schabas (1999). In the next section, we will consider both theoretical attacks against the traditional understanding of human rights here accepted as foundational, and some of the critiques and objections against that understanding, especially those voiced by non-Western scholars.

a. Humanitarian Law and Human Rights

Before turning to a philosophical consideration of the normative principles in support of both humanitarian and human rights law, it may be helpful to consider the connection between the two. The first connection can be found in the conditions of universality that apply in both cases (Provost, 2002:24–25; compare Provost, 2002:25, n.33). Provost adds that, in fact, "the human interests which humanitarian law seeks to protect are largely similar to those safeguarded by human rights law" (Ibid. at 26). A possible difference may be found, if humanitarian law is viewed primarily as imposing obligations on states and individuals, whereas human rights laws' primary focus is the protection of certain human rights from the state, especially in the case of first generation rights (Ibid. at 18–21). In addition, under the obligations imposed by humanitarian conventions, these rights cannot be waived either by the protected person or their states (Ibid. at 2002:33).

But the most basic human rights are similarly treated: for instance in jurisdictions prohibiting assisted suicide, the consent of suicide does not exculpate those who assist (Battin, 1996:393–400), so that the right to life itself is viewed as nonderogable, although there are countries, such as the Netherlands, where assisted suicide is legal. Similarly, the major separation between the protection of rights and the imposition of duties suggested by René Provost, is increasingly blurred as both the Covenants on Civil and Political Rights, and that of Social Economics and Cultural Rights, at least in their respective Preambles, say:

> *Realizing* that the individual, having duties to other individuals and to the Community to which he belongs, is under a responsibility to strive for the promotion and observance of the rights recognized in the present Covenant.

The closeness between the two types of law, however, are most clearly found in the *jus cogens* status of the strongest principles in both, and the *erga omnes* obligations imposed by most of their respective principles (Meron, 1989:10–23,

188–201). Both *jus cogens* norms and obligations *erga omens* will be discussed below, starting with the classical locus, *Barcelona Traction* (see Chapters 3 and 7).

At this point it is sufficient to show that the scholarly literature, while distinguishing one from the other, discusses both humanitarian law and human rights law in the context of universality, principled normativity, nonderogability, and, most significantly for the argument of this work, recognizing the insufficiency of both documents, and the lack of unifying instrument (Meron, 1983).

Humanitarian laws also provide cases analogous to those we will discuss below. When the interest of states conflicts "with the purpose of humanitarian treaties, which seek to subordinate the immediate military objectives of belligerents to higher, humanitarian interests" (Meron, 1989:217), then the interests of states cannot prevail. Analogously, we will argue that when the economic interests of states, regions or legal entities will seek to subordinate basic human rights, those interests should not prevail either. If appeals to state "necessity" cannot permit derogations from humanitarian law principles, when even the state's survival may be at issue, then all the more breaches of basic human rights cannot be permitted, when a state's interests are purely economic.

Addressing the "rationale underlying the concept of *jus cogens* and the public order of the international community," Meron cites Judge Mosler (H. Mosler, 1980, *"The International Society as a Legal Community,* at. 18–20), who defined the "public order of the international community" as follows:

> . . . consisting of principles and rules the enforcement of which is of such vital importance to the international community as a whole that any unilateral action or any agreement which contravenes these principles can have no legal force. The reason for this follows simply from logic: the law cannot recognize any act either of one member or several members in concert, as being legally valid if it is directed against the very foundation of law.

In the next section we will turn to the principles and norms, providing the foundation for both areas of law.

7. HUMAN RIGHTS AND NATURAL LAW: COMMONALITY AND DIVERGENCES

> I used to wonder why my parents' generation had been so blind to the wrongness of segregation; they were people of good conscience, so why had inertia ruled so long? Now I think I understand better. It took the emotional shock of seeing police dogs rip the flesh of protestors for white people to really understand the day-to-day corrosiveness of Jim Crowe. We need that same gut understanding of our environmental situation if we are to take the giant steps we must take soon (McKibben, 1999).

The basic argument we have been proposing is a simple one: natural law and the traditional understanding of human beings, based on Ancient Greek (hence, Western) philosophy and eventually translated into medieval terms by Aquinas then Grotius, is present in the rules of war and just war theory. One cannot understand just war theory without understanding natural law theory, and natural law theory originates with Aristotle and with a scientific, biological understanding of what it is to be, essentially, human in that sense. To put this in crude terms, the blood and the flesh of the protestors, and of the "good people" McKibben refers to, are the same. Aside from variations in skin color, the biological structure of human beings, hence, their capacity to suffer, is precisely the same. An obvious point perhaps, but a hard lesson to learn nevertheless, and one that must be learned if basic human rights are to flourish. This is the form of "essentialism" I wish to defend. This position is basic to any argument that can be made in defense of our biological integrity; thus, it is the most powerful tool humanity as a whole has against the assaults of corporate globalization, and its efforts to have us view humanity purely in economic terms.

One of the clearest expression of this assumption was reported in December 1991. Lawrence Summers, then vice-president and chief economist of the World Bank, issued some comments on a draft of the World Bank 1992 Global Economics Perspectives (GEP) Report, which was to be presented at the United Nations Conference in Rio de Janeiro, in June 1992. It started with the following words: "Just between you and me, shouldn't the World Bank be encouraging more immigration of the dirty industries to the LDC's I can think of three reasons." These were, in essence:

(1) "Measuring the costs of health-impairing pollution depends on the earnings lost due to increased morbidity and mortality," hence, "the economic logic behind dumping a load of toxic waste in the lowest-wage country is impeccable and we should face up to that";

(2) "I've always thought that under populated countries in Africa are vastly *under*-polluted, compared to Los Angeles or Mexico City"; and

(3) "The concern over an agent that causes a . . . change in the odds of prostate cancer is obviously going to be much higher in a country where people (live long enough) to get prostate cancer, than in a country where mortality is 200 per 1,000 under age five."

Harper's magazine produced this leaked memo under the heading "Let Them Eat Toxics," almost at the same time when a sober memo from the Washington Bureau of the World Bank appeared in the national paper of Canada, *The Globe and Mail* (Victoria Day Issue, Toronto, May 19, 1992), under the title, "World Bank Urges Green Consciousness; Environmental Practices Must Be Given Higher Priority, Development Report Says." One wonders whether, in the context of the previous "memo," this official document represents serious and sincere moral concern at all.

Human dignity and the human rights of citizens will never be respected as long as their life, morbidity and death are discussed and assessed purely in economic terms. In contrast, the work of the WHO supports public health *globally*, and appreciates the attacks human health is subjected to through environmental degradation fostered by globalization, as it did, for instance in "Ecological Integrity and Sustainable Development: Cornerstones of Public Health" (Soskolne and Bertollini, 1999).

It is important to understand that the assessment of human beings by Northwest powers, is far removed from essentialism, because it denies the reality of our common humanity, while it emphasizes superficial differences such as earning ability, technological development, or even skin color or racial background. The biological reality of each human needs to be accepted and defended from corporate assaults equally in domestic cases, where democracy and well-developed legal systems prevail, as was clearly shown in the cases against the tobacco industry, in Canada and the United States. Biological essentialism, or the acknowledgment that there are certain natural functions that our lungs perform, or certain reproductive functions and abilities that are specific to each gender in normal environmental conditions and without exposure to chemicals and toxicants, is the only basis from which we can advance claims to resist the unchecked proliferation of chemicals that affect those healthy functions (Pimentel et al., 1998; Carson, 1962; Colborn et al., 1996).

In addition, despite the presence of many legal instruments that support not only human rights in general, but, specifically, the rights of children, their normal functions and development are affected through the presence of pesticides, from both commercial/agricultural sources, and home and garden use. A recent study by Gillette on the Mexican population of the Yaqqui Valley (for the most part agricultural workers in large scale operations), compared to those living on the foothills with no agricultural exposure, showed the inabilities of one group of children (those who had been exposed to pesticides) to perform simple tasks that the other comparable group, without such exposure, could perform with ease at comparative ages. Even more ominous, because those pesticides function as hormone mimics, little girls who had been exposed to them, showed clear signs of puberty at age seven, and high cancer rates in their twenties (Suzuki, 2001).

Therefore, we must be prepared to say that *this* development, and *this* function are normal, and *those* that are influenced by toxic substances are not, rather than permit political correctness to deprive us of the strongest arguments to help us formulate a case against those who support and promote these hazardous practices and products. In other words, there must be a normal lung function for children, to enable us to say to those who sell tobacco or engage in practices that produce smog, that chronic bronchitis and asthma are *not* natural varieties of upper respiratory function. They are the results of the activities of corporate giants, operating with the complicity of democratic governments.

Similarly, if we concede that, say, infertility is simply a variation of normal function in all cases, or that reduced lung capacity might be no more than the challenge of a specific individual, we have lost; our position vis-à-vis powerful corporate giants, or complicit governments is weakened, as we play into their hands, and we give up our stand based on physical reality.

For these and similar reasons, I propose reconsidering natural law and essentialism in the biological sense. It is surprising to see the massive misunderstandings of the origins and scope of natural law in the human rights literature. Upendra Baxi addresses "the future of human rights" through "seven critical themes" (Baxi 1998:127). These themes include practical as well as conceptual critiques. Examples of the former might be Numbers 4, 6, and 7, which address issues such as market ideologies (6), globalization (7) and the use of "meta-narratives" for political ends (4). These critiques concern the misuse of human rights, rather than their conception, or the principles upon which they might be based. For now, only the conceptual attacks will be considered, and addressed in turn:

> First, the genealogies of human rights, both "modern" and "contemporary," their logics of inclusion and exclusion, and their "construction of ideas about "human";

> Third, the politics of difference and identity, which views human rights as having not just an emancipative potential but also a repressive one;

> Fifth, the resurfacing of arguments about ethical and cultural relativism interrogating the politics of universality of human rights, making possible, in good conscience, toleration of vast stretches of human suffering; (Baxi, 1998:127).

Human rights law appears to have evolved *at least in part*, from the framework of humanitarian law of war (Malanczuk, 1997:22; Brownlie, 1990:73; Schabas 2000:5). Malanczuk says: "The term 'international humanitarian law' . . . suggests that there is some synthesis between the laws of war and international human rights" (Malanczuk, 1997:342). Hence, the first point to note is, at least in that sense, human rights law is intended to protect primarily the physical, biological existence of human beings, as is the case with prisoners, the wounded, civilians in war, and the hospitals tending to them. It is important to keep in mind this original, basic concern, as it is much closer in spirit and reality to Shue's *Basic Rights* . . . (1996), than it is to political, social, or cultural rights that evolved in subsequent covenants, following the U.N. Declaration. These are all important, even vital rights; but if the principles upon which all human rights depend are in question, the first step must be to ensure that these principles are indeed the best possible to protect the basis of the enjoyment of all other rights.

The first "critical theme" proposed by Baxi suggests a similar approach. Yet Baxi attempts to pack too much into some concepts. Baxi says:

The very term "human rights," which I invoke constantly, is itself problematic. The abundance of its meanings may not be reduced to a false totality such as "basic human rights" inasmuch as all human rights are basic to those who are deprived disadvantaged, and dispossessed. Nor may we succumb to the to an anthropomorphic illusion that the range of human rights is limited to human beings; the new rights to a clean and healthy environment (or what somewhat inappropriately, even cruelly, called sustainable development) take us far beyond such a narrow notion (Baxi, 1998:128).

Baxi is correct in saying that "human rights" is normally intended as limited to "human beings," and I will readily concede that "sustainable development" is, to say the least, an oxymoron (unless spiritual or intellectual "development" is intended). In addition, it is equally correct that a healthy human's well-being and even "dignity" depend also on a healthy habitat (Shue, 1996); but that can be argued on the grounds of the intrinsic worth of all life, as whatever is hazardous to the bird, the fish, or the tree, or even that most valuable of all creatures, the earth worm, is ultimately hazardous to human beings as well (Daily, 1997; Westra, 1994; Loucks, 2000; Westra, 2000).

Baxi, however, is not correct in implying that, if all possible extensions and applications of a principle are not rendered explicit or spelled out within it, then the principle itself is flawed. The use that Baxi makes out of the standard of "human suffering" as that template of the best formulation of human rights, returns to the basic, biological understanding of what it is to be human, as I argued above. Baxi says: "I endeavor to relate the theory and practice of human rights to the endless variety of preventable human suffering" (Baxi, 1998:128). While not belittling the importance of political, social, and cultural rights, and the emotional and sometimes physical suffering that is caused by their absence, the most atrocious suffering is surely caused by the lack of physical security and subsistence rights, as Shue argues (1996). Natural law is basically concerned with the rights to protect our life and the development that we share with all animals. However, the major objections to the acceptance of natural law as foundational lie in misperceiving it as primarily based on religious principles. Reading its original formulations, this objection is easily confuted: natural law lies outside the range of limited, partisan tenets of any specific orthodoxy. The fact that there are many interpretations of natural law plays an important part in the lack of understanding usually accorded to it. It can be argued that today natural law is only available as mediated through the translations and interpretations of various scholars, most of which are proposed by specialists in law or other fields who appear to have no knowledge of its origin and meaning from antiquity on. That is why I proposed returning to the original formulation of natural law, as found in the work of the pagan Greek philosopher Aristotle, rather than mediated through Christian, Kantian, positivistic, or other traditional interpretations. When Aristotle's arguments for the existence of natural law are fully understood, then we shall be in a good position to evaluate all subsequent interpretations in the light of their

[margin handwritten notes: "OTHERS", "RETURNING / e ARIST / DON'T UPHOLD / NAT'L LAW", "PROB of slaves, etc.", "eg Taylor / MacIntyre"]

faithful rendering or interpretation of the original. Of course, coherence with Aristotle's own letter and intent does not make any interpretation "right" or "wrong" as such, but it will help to determine whether any interpretation or version can truly be classed a natural law at all.

In some sense, all texts are mediated by the reader: an Italian proverb says, "traduttore, traditore," indicating that anyone who translates, is a "traitor" in respect to the original text. Hence, our best bet is to read and understand, to the best of our ability, the originator of a doctrine in his original language, and also to consider as primary the interpretations and commentaries written closest to the time of Aristotle's life, such as those of Thomas Aquinas.

Hence, in order to fully understand natural law as one of the origins of human rights, and "their logics of inclusion and exclusion," and even the "construction" of ideas about "human," we need to examine without preconceptions the basis of natural law itself. We should start by remembering, *pace* Baxi, the role of nature in natural law, especially given its basic formulation in Aristotle. Of course, we will not find environmentalism in either Aristotle or Aquinas, but we will find the respect and the study of nature and its laws, viewed by both as basic. We will also discover that "individual good," for Aristotle, as for some of the tenets of the African Charter of Human Rights is the good of the community, because "man is a political animal" for him (meaning a social animal), as well as a rational one: the two are inseparable. The rationality here appealed to is not philosophical insight, or the specific convictions of ancient Greece: it is more akin to the instincts particular to the human animal.

a. The Laws of Nature and the Origins of Natural Law: Nature and Laws in Aristotle

Nature is central to Aristotle's argument in the *Politics*. This is routinely accepted by Aristotelian scholars:

> Aristotle conducted his study of things human in the fields of politics and ethics (and also of logic, poetry and oratory), side by side with a study of things natural (physics, medicine, and general biology). (Barker, 1973:xviii).

In addition, his "inclination towards the Ionic 'becoming'—the genetic doctrine of phusis" (Ibid. at xxix) ensures that nature will be and remain foundational for all his arguments, from the admiration he evinces for the beauty of perfected forms, to the presence of design in nature as such (*Parts of Animals*, 1., #3, 6 & 7). We noted that governance, citizenship, and the polis itself were discussed with reference to natural standards (of size, of completeness and the like). In the same sense, the constitution of the state will provide its "essence," the explanation of its identity as a "quasi-juridical person" (Barker, 1973:100–101). The constitution is analogous to the natural laws governing physical organisms (bk. III, ch.VI, 1278a40ff).

Like all natural entities, the state has two main ends (in this case, not just one end), for the association it represents. Aristotle starts with the basic "natural impulse" according to which "men desire to live a social life"; the other end is represented by the common interest: "The good life is the chief end, both for the community as a whole and for each of us individually. But men also come together, and form and maintain political associations merely for the sake of life." (*Politics* III, 6. 1278a40ff). Hence, the *essential* nature of a state, the laws that regulate it, exist for the sake of maintaining (1) life; (2) social association; and (3) the good life (Barker, 1973:iii). This simply reelaborates the theme clearly stated in Book I of the *Politics*, that "every polis exists by nature," and that the "nature of things consists in their ends or consummation," as "the end, the final cause is the best" (bk. I, ch.2, 1522b9ff, cited in Barker, 1973:5). The polis exists "by nature" and man is meant "by nature" to live in a social environment.

If we consider the modern, liberal democratic state, we find something that is in direct conflict with the Aristotelian view of *The State*. It does provide association, so it satisfies at least one condition Aristotle finds essential to the nature of the state. But note that the other two "ends" or reasons why men join together in political association are missing or under threat. In glaring contrast with the Aristotelian emphasis on the state's support of the common good, or the happiness that is based on the "natural end of man" as a moral ideal, in modern times even a token quest for that sort of good has been completely eliminated from present political institutions (Westra, 1998).

b. Thomas Aquinas: Nature and Natural Law

As we move to consider natural law in Thomas Aquinas, we necessarily pass from antiquity to the Middle Ages, a very different historical period. Yet it would be simplistic to assume that the difference is simply one of adding Christianity to Aristotle, or eliminating from his doctrine whatever is contrary to Christian thought. We need to understand how the concept of natural law evolved, as it did not leap a thousand years from the great philosopher, to a great philosopher/theologian, without maintaining some sort of continuity. We find the thread of this continuity quite early in a.d., in the definition attributed to a Roman jurist, Domitius Ulpianus (circa 170–228 a.d.).

Jus naturale est quod natura omnia animalia docuit (natural law is that which nature taught to all animals). This definition was also adopted by Justinian in the *Corpus Juris Civilis* (Crowe, 1974:261). Ulpian was known as a "great name" in Roman jurisprudence and, unlike other contemporaries, he distinguishes clearly between the "natural law" and the "jus gentium." Gaius (180 a.d.) instead "distinguishes only two kinds of law, the jus civile and the jus gentium, the latter being the work of natural reason" (Crowe, 1974:262).

What nature teaches animals, freely translated from Ulpian, is "to reproduce, (Ulpian adds, 'that is what we call marriage'), to educate one's offspring, and the like." *Jus gentium*, is the law used by humans, which is different "because it is held in common solely by human beings." Finally, there is civil law. This division, surprisingly, was the one preferred by St. Thomas, rather than Isidore's two-way division between *jus naturale*, incorporating whatever is natural to mankind, and is, thus, common to all nations and civil law. The former is natural because it is "independent of human conventions" (Crowe, 194:264).

Eventually Bonaventure, who does not write specifically on laws, adopts Ulpian's definition in his own *Commentary on the Sentences*. The tripartite definition can be roughly translated as follows: in the first sense, natural law represents what is found in both Gospel and laws: in the second sense, it is the law common to all nations, and it is mandated by right reason; finally, in a third sense, it encompasses what is most appropriately what nature teaches all animals (In IV Sent., d.33,a.1,q.1; Bonaventure, 1856:t.V.V.II, c.17).

There is no need to pursue further the history of natural law, interesting and varied though it is. The main point, at least according to Ulpian, Bonaventure, and St. Thomas, is the relation of nature, as nonhuman, that is a firm component of a true understanding of natural law. Nature remains the standard, the starting point, the basis to help us understand what natural law might mean, when we apply it to humankind. It is implicitly acknowledged: man and nonhuman animals (to insert the use of modern terminology) have several common characteristics: they are created and they are subject to identical or similar biological laws, so that a Cartesian split between nature and human reason becomes impossible. We are connatural with whatever is alive, though it might not be possessed of reason, at least insofar as we are considered as biological beings. The presence of biological nature is, thus, ensured in this conception of natural law.

We have traced briefly the role of the laws of nature, and of the concept of nature in natural law doctrines, from Ancient philosophy through the Middle Ages, looking at Aristotle and Thomas Aquinas. We were able to show the presence of several important principles linking morality and law through nature and to nature. If we are to understand the direction our laws should take today, in order to help correct the inability of modern governance to enact laws and regulations that are environmentally sound and that protect citizens, we should reconsider the doctrine of natural law.

We found a number of principles and arguments tying the historical, powerful natural law doctrine to nature, its processes and its laws. Particularly important, yet mostly absent from today's understanding of the proper role of governance and the law, are the following:

(1) The connaturality of human and nonhuman life, with the clear acknowledgment that the same laws and processes apply to both.

(2) Therefore, following the legal and regulative part of modern governance should equally reflect that reality in its mandates.

(3) Because of this reality, it is wrong, at least in principle, to act in ways that prevent the actualization of natural entities, according to their own natural unfolding. To prevent such entities from reaching their final form cannot be done routinely, as it is morally suspect (as well as prudentially suspect, according to environmental ethics and the precautionary principle.

(4) Objections aimed at discrediting the validity of natural law can be answered, and the common attacks on it from analytic philosophy can be refuted.

In the final analysis, whether implicitly or explicitly, much of the content of natural law, its core meaning including the value and importance of natural laws and functions, is present in today's civil and criminal laws. Of course, it is not fully understood, and the debt to past traditions is seldom acknowledged or accepted. It is, therefore, imperative to reexamine and clarify the full import and meaning of natural law doctrines, so that their implicit message can be rendered explicit.

No doubt this brief excursion into natural law helps to clarify its biological or "animal" aspects, hence, to show that it is not a question of "construction" of ideas about what it is to be human; rather it is a question of scientific observation, albeit only at the scientific level possible in 300 b.c. C.E. Harris lists the values, hence, the related rights, that natural law supports in Aquinas' formulation as,

> 1. "Biological Values," including life and procreation, both of which support the right of self-defense, in turn foundational for the rules of *jus ad bellum* and *jus in bello*, and the natural inclination "to engage in sexual intercourse and to rear offspring" (Harris, 1990:103).

These values do not attempt to make a statement about human choices, they simply observe what is true in the animal world and accept those basic tenets as typical of the animal part of rational animals, or humans. What can be learned from this simple exposition is that, whatever is inimical to the support of human life in its natural unfolding, is morally wrong and unjust, as Ken Saro-Wiwa recognized when he referred to "genocide" and "ecocide" in the same paragraph, as he noted the life-threatening conditions forced upon the Ogoni by the complicity of their own government and the actions of Royal Dutch Shell Oil (Westra, 1998).

According to Aquinas, that complicity would be sufficient to delegitimize the military government. Baker summarizes the legal implications of natural law as follows:

. . . the doctrine that law is the true sovereign and that governments are the servants of the law; the doctrine that there is a fundamental difference between the lawful monarch and the tyrant who governs by his arbitrary will: the doctrine that there is a right inherent in the people by virtue of their collective capacity of judgement to elect their rulers and to call them to account (Barker, 1973:ixi).

Under "2. Characteristically Human Values," "knowledge and sociability" are listed. The first clearly implies the right to education and to the pursuit of knowledge, including religious knowledge. The second implies the right to associate with others and form communities (Harris, 1990:104; Aquinas *Summa Theologiae*, bk.II, pt.I, Q.94, A.2). War is permitted as a just extension of self-defense, to the defense of one's community and rightful state. But when the state is radically injust, then the obligation is to disobey, not to be in any way complicit in its wrongful aims, because the state's legitimacy is lost when the "common good" is not served by its rulers. Speaking of man's obligation to obey a "prince," Aquinas says clearly, ". . . if he commands what is injust, his subjects are not bound to obey him" (Aquinas, *Summa Theologiae*, bk.II. pt.I, Q.104, A.6, reply obj.3).

c. Natural Law and Justice

A just law is a man-made code that squares with the moral law or the law of God. An unjust law is a code that is out of harmony with the moral law. To put it in terms of St. Thomas Aquinas: An unjust law is a human law that is not rooted in eternal law and natural law. Any law that uplifts human personality is just. Any law that degrades human personality is unjust (King, Jr., 1990:71).

Justice, in turn, is determined by the adherence of laws to the "common good." This understanding of natural law, based on the biological/scientific observations of Aristotle to a large extent, defends the theory from the objection of "constructivism," based on "Western" ideals. Aristotle was a Greek, and, if one would persist in viewing natural law as primarily a Christian theory, bear in mind that Jesus was clearly a birth citizen of the Middle East, not the West.

We can also respond to the "repressive" aspects of "human rights" based on "inclusion and exclusion" according to Baxi (1998:127). As we noted, animals and nature in general are only partially excluded. On the other hand, the natural environment can be reintroduced as natural habitat, on grounds of life-support and in defense of "subsistence." Incidentally, this approach is perfectly compatible with the respect for the intrinsic value of natural entities, in some forms of deep ecology, although it would not be appropriate to introduce those arguments here (Westra, 1994).

Inclusiveness and exclusion may also refer to humans judged incapable of full human dignity. On that issue, both Aristotle and Aquinas are "guilty as charged." For Aristotle, those who lived outside Athens were the "barbarians," and women did not have rational souls. Although for Christianity all humans are created equal, this was certainly not the case for the ancients, and the history of slavery and disregard for women's rights are clear in all historical descriptions of the development of human rights from the times of the *Magna Carta* (Nash, 1967). But it is precisely the presence of the biological/scientific arguments that Aristotle proposes that demonstrate the basic similarity of all human beings, and which are the best antidote to those deficiencies. They might help to redefine natural law in a more logical and comprehensive way, to elevate it to a doctrine of both foundational and contemporary value.

Finally, the repressive aspect of rights is hard to find and isolate in natural law, except if a specific form of knowledge is emphasized, that is, if "knowledge" is limited to the pursuit of Christianity. Clearly this emphasis will not be found in Aristotle or the Roman lawyers and Stoics who followed natural law, and this thrust can be deemphasized without losing the basis and the principles of natural law, as we saw, for instance, in Grotius (see Section 3, above). Can natural law accommodate peoples and individuals from a background that is different from the one of its origin? If we trace some of its history from the emergence of humanitarian law, to cases such as the *Nicaragua* case where the "International Court at the merits phase, applied general principles of humanitarian law, based upon Article 3 common to the four Geneva Conventions" (Brownlie, 1998:73), where the law had to be applied to an internal conflict, and the role played by the United States in that conflict was in question. In 1986, the International Court of Justice (Rep. No.14, 1986 I.C.J. 69) decided that "the United States had violated its customary law obligations (a) not to interfere in the affairs of Nicaragua and (b) not to use force against it" (Kindred et al., 2000:94). The fact that the rights were of a people quite different from that of the United States, did not prevent the Court from deciding against the aggressors on principle. The fact that, to my knowledge, nothing much was done to the United States by way of punishment, is a failure of the lack of punitive powers on the part of international courts, or perhaps of the respective powers, military and economic of the United States in contrast to those of Nicaragua. Both are deplorable circumstances, but they do not invalidate the principles upon which the decision was based (1949 Geneva Conventions—Common Article 3 (1950)).

The conceptual model we have considered is termed "modern" rather than "contemporary" by Baxi (Baxi, 1998:132). He contrasts the "modern" model with the "contemporary" one that is better in his view, at providing "the logics of inclusions." In the context of the present day "global village," inclusion of different peoples and perspectives appear preferable to the standpoint of a limited community such as that of Athens or of Medieval towns or states. We must not, however, lose sight of the fact that, whether or not the ancients were aware of the rights of others, be they "barbarians" outside the city walls or anyone living in far away lands, what we must be concerned with is the conceptual foundations of natural law, and its principles, not the interpretation of these principles as it existed over a thousand years ago. The problem is that if, in the interest of "inclusiveness" we attempt to eliminate "essentialism" as in "what it is to be a human being," we go too far in the wrong direction. One ought to remember that it is in virtue of our common biological makeup that we can say that *your* suffering and *my* suffering are the same, not because of some "metanarrative" or some particular political state configuration.

d. Natural Law Principles Versus Cultural and Ethical Relativism

> As it is you depart, if you depart, after being wronged not by us, the Laws, but by men; (from Socrates' response, in the *Crito* 53c 1–5)

It is not necessary to read modern authors to find clearly articulated beliefs about the difference between the basic principles of law and the sometimes wrongful or biased application of these principles by self-interested, or unthinking or even malicious men, as that contrast has emerged clearly from the time of Sophocles's *Antigone* to today. In contrast, ethical relativism goes even further than cultural relativism as not only it recognizes, as the latter does, the presence of different, culture-bound beliefs about right and wrong, but accepts any of these categories on the part of a "group," undefined (Stace, 1985:474; Pojman, 1989:24). The corrosiveness of this position, not to be confused with respect and tolerance of others' cultural practices that do not represent an attack on basic human rights, can be seen clearly in this presentation of the doctrine *of* ethical relativism:

[handwritten margin note: Look AT none PROMINENT DEBATES]

(1) *The Diversity Thesis*. What is considered morally right and wrong varies from society to society, so that there are no universal moral standards held by all societies.

(2) *The Dependency Thesis*. Whether or not it is right for an individual to act in a certain way depends on or is relative to the society to which he or she belongs.

(3) *Ethical Relativism*. Therefore, there are no absolute or objective moral standards that apply to all people everywhere and at all times. (Pojman, 1989:35).

To state the obvious, these three theses would justify Nazism, provided it was accepted in that society at that time, or apartheid, or the subjugation of women, under the same circumstances. But all these practices are considered morally distasteful and unacceptable, and other basic concepts, such as murder (as distinguished from killing in a war situation, or some executions perhaps), incest, and some conceptions of moral obligations between parents and children, appear in all cultures.

Moral principles are indeed "weakly dependent" on a community's beliefs. For instance, the Inuit believed that it is morally right to allow old people to starve, as a form of euthanasia; and "One tribe in East Africa throws its deformed children in the river because such infants *belong* to the hippopotamus, the god of the river" (Pojman, 1989:36). Possibly, some of the meta-principles that we embrace can apply: respect for property in the latter, and a form of respect for aged family members in the former, supporting a form of euthanasia as appropriate in their harsh environment. Hence, it could be argued, some universal moral principles apply but other, nonmoral cultural beliefs result in the wrong application of those principles in some cultures. Hence, it is better to embrace acceptance and toleration for all practices that do not represent a breach of the most serious moral principles in their cultural applications.

Ethical relativism, the thesis that moral principles derive their validity from dependence on society or individual choice, seems plausible at first glance, but when scrutinized closely is seen to have some serious difficulties. Subjectivism seems to boil down to anarchistic individualism, and conventionalism fails to deal adequately with the problem of the reformer, the question of defining a culture, and the whole enterprise of moral criticism (Pojman, 1989:37).

In times when the global presence of so many different peoples and cultures is obvious to all, it is almost viewed as reactionary to attempt to draw the (admittedly) fine line between tolerance and acceptance on one hand, and repression or even "imperialism" on the other. Yet, even in the times of the Roman Stoics, the thrust to cosmopolitanism was present, in the same sense that commonly accepted practices, including slavery, were at least viewed as necessarily limited and constrained by principles of justice (Lauterpacht, 1950:84). In those cases, long before the *Magna Carta*, the primacy of law and rationally recognized moral principles (not simply religious observances) were deemed to be superior even to the will of "kings." Lauterpacht notes these advances and says that, "By the end of the Middle Ages, the substance of what proved to be the doctrine of the natural rights of man was well established" (Lauterpacht, 1950:85).

But the question raised by Baxi is whether in today's multicultural world it is even possible to use absolute principles originating in one age, to another, where quite different cultural realities are present. For instance, because the present concern with ecoviolence and ecocrimes is the fruit of practices that rapidly multiplied became magnified and became incrementally more and more hazardous since that second world war (Carson, 1962; Colborn et al., 1996), we cannot expect to find anything in natural law to accommodate these phenomena. In a sense, ecoviolence (an evil), like multiculturalism (a good), are emergent phenomena that are not obviously or clearly covered by the provisions of international human rights legal instruments. As far as multiculturalism is concerned, there is an abundant literature on the topic, in relation to human rights. For instance, Jennings notes that, ". . . as more and more aspect of international law reach down through the states to corporations to other legal entities and to individuals, so international law has more and more to take into account and allow for differences of municipal law, differences of legal tradition, and differences of culture" (Jennings 1987:195). But to acknowledge these developing issues, and—in the case of ecoviolence—these "emergent risks" (Hiskes, 1998) do not necessarily require abandoning previous principles of natural law in their support of human rights. A "sociology of law" approach, such as the one used by Gutto (1993), helps to pinpoint and flesh out some of the problems; it does not help either to propose a solution to the perceived difficulties, or to find another, better common ground. Gutto admits this:

> Sociology of law is a hybrid developed from sociology (and to a less extent other social science disciplines) and legal science. It helps in *identifying social*, cultural historical, economic religious and political processes and conditions from which law, including human rights law, emerge from, rest upon, and in turn influence (Gutto, 1993:40) (emphasis added).

The problem with embarking upon this route to human rights is that it does not map out a better path, but rejecting a preexisting principle framework leaves a vacuum. Given the constant flux of political processes, including the wax and wane of ideologies, simply pointing to the latest development as legitimate might lead one to legitimize, for instance, Nazi laws, as evolving from "popularly accepted ideologies" *at that time*, or apartheid as right for South Africa, at the time when it reflected certain emergent social and political processes: in essence it would lead to total relativism, or the belief that something becomes right because a group, undefined in either size or scope, believes it to be.

In contrast, the distinguishing characteristic of moral universality is that rather than relying on authority or group choices, its conclusions are based on *arguments*, hence, on what is shared by all humans to help them to evaluate these arguments: the ability to reason, not traditions, or holy books. The recent work of the Earth Charter (see Appendix 1), has made a concerned effort in the last ten years since the last Earth Summit (1992), to bring together the wisdom and moral principles of all peoples, from North to South, and from East to West. The principles of the Charter combine respect for human beings and for all peoples' cultures, with an equal respect for nonhuman animals and for natural systems and functions (Rockefeller, 2002).

In law, universality is also defended in the lengthy and inspiring "separate opinion" by International Court of Justice's Vice-President Christopher G. Weeramantry (Gabcikovo-Nagymaros Project (1997), I.C.J. Rep., 37 I.L.M.168). Weeramantry says:

> The protection of the environment is likewise a vital part of contemporary human rights doctrine, for it is a *sine qua non* for numerous human

rights such as the right to health and the right to life itself. It is scarcely necessary to elaborate on this, as damage to the environment can impair and undermine all the human rights spoken of in the Universal Declaration and other human rights instruments (Weeramantry, 1997:3).

Weeramantry's opinion defends the right to treat the environmental reasons advanced by Hungary to justify its noncompliance with the original treaty with Slovakia to build a dam diverting the river Danube, as an obligation *erga omnes*. But he appeals to universality by presenting a scholarly dissertation on how all countries, from China to Africa, to Europe, from the time before Christ to modern times, considered environmental concerns to be the common rights of humanity, but also they were considered to be their international obligations.

The examples he offers range from the "royal edicts" dating from the third century b.c. in Ceylon,

> Mahinda, son of the Emperor Asoka of India, preached to him a sermon on Buddhism which converted the king. Here are excerpts from that sermon: "O great King, the birds of the air and the beasts have as equal a right to live and move about in any part of the land as thou. The land belongs to the people and all living beings; thou art only the guardian of it." [This sermon is recorded in the *Mahavamsa*, Ch.14]

"Do no harm" is the basis of all morality, from Ancient Greece on. In Buddhism, no harm can be caused to others, hence, *"sic utere tuo ut alienum non laedas"* is present in all laws and moral principles. Weeramantry adds:

> *"Alienum"* in this context would be extended by Buddhism to future generations as well, and to the other component elements of the natural order beyond man himself, for the Buddhist concept of duty had an enormously long reach (Weeramantry, 1997:10).

Other examples confirm the universality of these principles of respect and conservation, from sub-Saharan Africa, where two ancient cultures, the Sonjo and the Chagga (Tanzanian tribes), had created complex networks of "irrigation furrows," in order to convey water from mountain streams to the cultivated fields. The maintenance of these furrows was the sacred responsibility and duty of all citizens (Weeramantry, 1997:11).Weeramantry's historical survey ranges far afield in place and time, in order to demonstrate the *timelessness* and the universality of environmental concern and obligation, supporting laws and customs entailing sustainable development long before the concept became a modern by-word. In essence, the traditions of peoples everywhere show that; "Environmental rights are human rights" (Ibid. at 1).

Weeramantry's historical survey, however, does not show that different cultures chose these principles, and that, therefore, they represent legitimate sources of international law. It demonstrates, instead, that all peoples universally *recognized* the existence and the acceptability of these beliefs; hence, they are far more than the modern articulation of principles arising from a European country (Sweden), where Gro Bruntland led the present articulation of "sustainable development' principles.

Similarly, natural law, in its original formulation, embodies principles and beliefs that can be found in many civilizations; hence, it is well able to provide *not* the latest word on human rights, but the best *starting point* for a comprehensive and nonpartisan understanding of human rights, imperative in our complex and changing world.

Therefore, if we lose the template or standard provided by universal moral principles, we retain no ground from which to argue about the difference between different mores and unacceptable action. The right to wear a turban, or to refuse certain foods, or to wear a veil, must be respected as different cultural mores; but the right to segregate according to color or race, the right to eliminate minorities perceived as threatening, or the right to practice painful, nonconsensual mutilations on girl-children, all fly in the face of basic morality, whether funded in natural law, which proclaims the basic equality of all, regardless of color or ethnic origin, or Kantian belief in the respect due all humans (Westra, 1998). On what ground, or with what voice, are we to say to a cultural group or to any peoples that their accepted practices are in fact genocidal (Schabas, 2000) or represent attacks on the human person (Bassiouni, 1992) and are therefore unacceptable, although they are accepted in their community? If we cannot discriminate between acceptable and unacceptable practices on principle, we have little else to use to proscribe what some groups are prepared to do.

Maurizio Ragazzi, discussing human rights in relation to obligations *erga omnes* (through the examples provided in the *Barcelona Traction* case), lists (1) "acts of aggression," (2) "acts of genocide," (3) "protection from slavery," and (4) "protection from racial discrimination," stating:

> In giving the examples of the outlawing of genocide and the protection from slavery and racial discrimination, the International court wrote that obligations *erga omnes* may derive, in general, from the principles and rules concerning the basic rights of the human person (Ragazzi 1997:135–136; 1970 I.C.J. 32, para. 34).

Ragazzi adds that, relying on Fitzmaurice, ". . . a principle is something which underlies a rule, and explains or provides the reason for it" (Fitzmaurice, 1950:7; Aristotle, *Metaphysics*, 10112b34-1013 a23).

Hence, it is important that the principles be preserved and used as standards, even as the circumstances which provide the background for our activities, may be in constant flux. In sum, embracing ethical relativism would admit and permit far more negative decisions as legal and just, than it would eliminate. It seems clear that, if the Aristotelian background of natural law principles is fully understood, as is the development of natural law from ancient Greece to the Middle Ages, from Aquinas to Grotius, there are several points that may help rather than hinder the protection of human rights internationally. Some of these are:

(1) The basic rights to subsistence and physical security (Shue, 1996; see Section 6);
(2) The right to a safe habitat or environment that would not hinder the "natural" development and biological function of all humans (Ibid.);
(3) The right to social living, the right of all humans to live in a community that fosters their common good;
(4) The right to the acquisition and pursuit of knowledge, including religious knowledge;
(5) The right to a form of government that ensures (1), (2), and (3) above, so that the common good of all is protected;
(6) The right to rebel against any form of governance that does not respect and protect the rights listed in (1) to (5) above.

The sixth and final point, needs much more discussion because, like ecological degradation, the presence of diverse ethnocultural groups and their rights as "peoples" are anachronistic from the standpoint of natural law, although, I believe, they are compatible with it. Hence, peoples' rights will be the topic of the next section.

e. Natural Law and Moral Principles in Support of Peoples' Rights

I believe profoundly in the universality of the human spirit. Individuals everywhere want the same essential things: to have sufficient food and shelter; to be able to speak freely; to practice their own religion or to abstain from religious belief; to feel that their person is not threatened by the state; to know that they will not be tortured or detained without charges, and that, if charged, they will have a fair trial. I believe there is nothing in these aspirations that is dependent on culture or religion, or stage of development (Higgins, 1994:96).

This excerpt supports that argument of this chapter: the addition of environmental security or of safe habitats can be equally compatible with Higgins' position, as it is with that of Shue (1996). In contrast, anthropologists and social scientists tend to accept cultural relativism, and claims about the inappropriateness of universal human rights abound in their work as do such pronouncements as, "culture makes us, not biology"; or "we become what we are by growing up in a particular cultural setting; we are not born that way" (Kuper, 1999:2).

The aim of this line of argument is "that we can be made over into something *better*, perhaps learning from the tolerant people of Samoa, or the perfectly balanced Balinese" (Ibid.; emphasis added). But this argument is fallacious because (1) given the equal status of all cultural beliefs, there is nothing to prevent some of us, from learning from neo-Nazis, instead of Samoans; and (2) the very notion of "better" entails the existence of a universal standard of better and worse, the very notion that is absolutely denied by cultural and ethical relativists. These two objections are sufficient to show why ethical relativism, based on the obvious existence of cultural differences, not only takes an "is" for an "ought," but is both self-contradictory and incoherent (Stace, 1985).

The normative appeal to cultural relativism cannot be supported but we have to acknowledge that we will also not be able to find direct, explicit support for the rights of peoples in natural law, any more than we will find explicit support for a safe and healthy environment. Although we have indicated how a case could be made for the latter through the foundations of natural law, the former would be even harder to argue from that perspective. If cultural beliefs are insufficient to support the existence of peoples, then the first question is, what distinguishes people? Schabas discusses this question in his work on "genocide" (Schabas, 2000:105–111). The Universal Declaration of Human Rights (UDHR) (1948), alludes to "racial and religious groups" (UDHR Article 26(2)), while other scholars speak of "minorities," but believe that the reference to groups, be they "racial," "ethnic," "religious," "cultural," or "linguistic," is preferable to the former usage of minorities." Of course, there is another reason why "minorities" is incorrect: in some cases, the group suffering from discrimination may be a majority, as, for instance, Africans in South Africa.

But the basic question remains: who are the people, those who justly and rightfully deserve protection from the oppression of an unjust government? What are the grounds of "national identity" (Gilbert, 1994:106)? There are several models of national identity, and Paul Gilbert presents them in the context of the hardest possible test, that of terrorism: what makes a group not only one, but such that even violent terrorist action might be considered as the principled self-defense of freedom-fighters instead? He suggests two basic conceptions of peoples, (1) the "voluntarist model," and (2) the "ethnic model" (Ibid.). The voluntarist model is based on the liberal assumption that all people choose to associate with certain others because it is in their interest to do so. This assumption flies in the face of the reality of many instances of communities who persist in seeking independence despite suffering many harms because of their quest.

The ethnic model, in contrast, may be based on stereotypes about national character, or it may be based on an organic view of what makes a people, somewhat like natural kinds, viewed almost as zoological species (Gilbert, 1994:110). Ethnic conceptions often account for peoples on the basis of "cultural" rather than biological facts (Ibid. at 112). These cultural factors may include shared religion, language and shared aims and values. Sometimes a "national memory" of "folk memory" may be included to parallel, in some sense, "the nascent stage of personal identity," as peoples may not only share a present culture as a single nation, but they may also "share beliefs about a common past" (Ibid. at 115–116).

This brief presentation cannot do justice to a very complex contemporary question and one which, unfortunately, cannot be answered clearly in terms of customary law, as nations have very different regulations concerning nationality: for example, German nationality requires German ancestry, whereas French nationality is conferred by birth (Ibid. at 111). What makes the question so important is that once a community or group gains the status of one of the peoples, or nations, they acquire both rights, as emphasized for instance in the African Charter and other U.N. documents, but also obligations, not only to one another, but also to the world at large. The emergent existence of a community ought to be able to justify both self-defence on their part, but also fighting on their behalf, on the part of others, to protect their independent status.

Gilbert's main concern is the situation in Ireland. As he analyzes it from various points of view, he wants to compare it, at least in principle, to a just war, because (1) border disputes can never be solved by democratic means, as citizens of adjacent nation-states can only vote within their own borders, not to change the location of these borders; and (2) because once the crucial conclusion is reached that we are indeed dealing with separate peoples, rather than with a minority within a state, then various forms of violence, as I argued above, may be justifiable on their behalf.

Hence, we need to examine both negative and positive conditions to conclude there is indeed, a new community: it should be based both on voluntary association and on shared cultural characteristics and a shared traditional identity, not just one or the other. It should be seeking self-determination not only because "its members (have) a strong aversion to living together with others" in the existing national configuration, but because the emergent community would enhance the enjoyment of human rights in ways not possible in the status quo. Gilbert says it well:

> I suggest then, that the proper grounds for a group's claim to statehood are that it is living, or could live a decent communal life which could be protected or enhanced by statehood, so long as the life of similar groups is not thereby worsened in a way that they have a right to avoid (Gilbert, 1994:123).

Another, perhaps less popular and less obvious condition needs to be added: "It is not what people do desire, but what is desirable for them, that generates the right, though what is desirable for them is something that they are in a good position to judge" (Ibid.). We can note then, that the independence of peoples ought to be based on a "common good model" that includes both (liberal) "voluntarist" and "cultural" models, but also establishes principled conditions that ensure that no arbitrariness will suffice to support the emergence of a new association of peoples.

Will Kymlicka also finds the question of "illiberal cultures" (Kymlicka, 1997:94) a very difficult one, and he discusses its problems in a chapter on "Toleration and its Limits" (Ibid. at 152). He cites forms of religious toleration practiced by a state such that it permitted any form of religious organization on the part of minority communities: "In the 'millet system' of the Ottoman Empire for instance Muslims, Christians and Jews, were all recognized as self-governing units (or 'millets') and allowed to impose restrictive religious laws on their own members" (Kymlicka, 1997:156). But present day liberals strongly emphasize individual autonomy, sometimes to the detriment of communal interests. Their own ideology, however, would *prevent* the imposition of liberal values in a coercive way, whereas it would permit some appropriate but limited forms of persuasive pressure to support the emergence (or the presence) of other peoples even when these might act now in ways that run counter to human rights laws. In such cases, although Kymlicka does not propose the sort of tests to legitimacy that Gilbert does, it would seem that to accept the legitimate status of peoples would require that the common good be respected and given primacy. Their cultural and social common good may well be enhanced by belonging to these new communities, but the acid test remains whether those who belong to the new group, are not suffering from attacks on their basic rights as outlined above. If that were the case, once again, one could argue with natural law that the authority binding together the emergent community would lack the legitimacy required to support it.

8. CONCLUSION

This chapter proposed the argument that the present day use of chemicals, toxic substances and many other components of our technological age, are not well controlled by either national or international regulatory regimes at this time. The problems they cause are not just somebody's mistakes, or occasional accidents, they represent a systemic form of violence, legal, for the most part, and legitimized by the institutional acceptance of these harmful practices. Humanitarian laws forms the basis for human rights laws, and they originated and became codified at the same time as environmental violence; hence, ecocrimes were escalating because of the proliferation of untested and untried substances that were and are potentially harmful to life (see discussion in the next chapters). Thus, laws against violence of unprecedented gravity and magnitude are required, and they could well have their starting point in the laws that were designed to prevent the recurrence of equally unprecedented violence of great gravity and magnitude, such as those that took place in World War II. The Covenants against Genocide, Torture and other Crimes against Humanity, may well fit both sort of crimes.

Hence, starting with a presentation of the rules of war from antiquity to the time of Grotius, the similarity between crimes against humanity and ecoviolence was emphasized, through a consideration of the principles of Nuremberg. Then, various international human rights documents were discussed, in order to show how little in these documents supports explicitly the "basic rights" (Shue, 1996) that are foundational to the protection of human life and health. It is my argument that attacks on these basic rights, whether or not they are explicitly listed among those protected by the Conventions arising from humanitarian law, constitute serious international crimes, not only delicts (Pellet, 1998).

For this reason, they ought to be protected by obligation *erga omnes*, supported by *jus cogens* norms. Thus, we have turned to international law for the protection of human rights through principles such as those of natural law, precisely because customary laws alone appear to be incapable of dealing appropriately with the novel and global problems posed by these ecocrimes.

However, current literature on international human rights, especially from non-Western scholars, questions the ability of traditional principles, based on essentialism, to accommodate problems that are contemporary, multicultural, and global in scope. Hence, the second part of this chapter takes up each of these critiques and objections, ranging from the work of legal scholars, to that of anthropologists and sociologists. The reason for this detailed defense of natural law and traditional principles is that the argument proposed, is to defend threatened basic human rights, by appealing to Conventions, as nonderogable norms or principles. Hence, if the accepted principles are flawed and open to serious objections, they will not provide the absolute, universal basis that is needed to declare ecoviolence totally inadmissible.

I believe that through the last sections of this chapter, starting with a brief history and exposition of natural law, counterarguments were presented in response to the objections found in the literature. We were, therefore, able to demonstrate as well as possible when one is not dealing with an exact, physical science that current practices of Western technologically advanced liberal democracies must be limited and restrained through obligations based on principles that support the basic rights of all humanity.

INSTITUTIONALIZED ENVIRONMENTAL VIOLENCE AND HUMAN RIGHTS: INTERPRETATION AND ANALOGY IN THE JUDICIAL PROCESS

1. INTRODUCTION: RECOGNIZING "ECOCRIMES," ARGUMENTS FROM INTERPRETATION AND ARGUMENTS FROM ANALOGY

The previous chapter argued that environmental violence results in gross breaches of human rights, and the notion that such breaches deserve to be understood as crimes was also introduced. But to speak of crimes, whether international or crimes in general, is to assume that not only the physical elements of the offense (e.g., conduct and consequences) are present, but also that some form of the required mental or fault element should be identifiable. This chapter starts with evidence about the physical elements of environmental harms, supported by extensive epidemiological and medical research. But factual evidence of this sort has been seen, traditionally, as insufficient to treat actions that trigger the harmful events appropriate for criminal prosecution rather than civil litigation (Stuart, 1995; Canadian Bar Association, 1992). The emphasis on fault can also be traced back to the connection between morality and the law. In morality, the intent is often thought to be as important as the action itself, especially in virtue ethics or Kantian morality (Westra, 1998:ch. 7).

In addition, the importance of moral notions such as justice are inextricably interwoven with the law. Hart points out that notions of morality may enter the law either openly and explicitly, or slowly, and in a piecemeal fashion, through the juridical process; the principles of natural law are very much a part of these notions.

This impartiality is what the procedural standards known to English and American lawyers as principles of "Natural Justice" are designed to secure. Hence, though the most odious laws may be justly applied, we have, in the bare notion of applying a general rule of law, the germ at least of justice (Hart, 1961:202).

Yet it might be too sweeping to equate "natural justice" in law with natural law as such. John Finnis characterized, as follows, the connection between justice and natural law:

The distinctive claim of natural law is not that unjust laws are not law, but there are objective, valid normative principles to which law-the entire complex body of rules of positive law and their applications-ought to conform (Finnis, 1980:351).

Lloyd Weinreb, another natural law scholar, discusses the connection between justice and natural law, as he views it, as divided into "two branches," one pursuing "the problem of human freedom" and "political obligation"; the other, attempting "to discern a normative order in nature" (Weinreb, 1987:129).

The question of moral responsibility is always present in the judicial process; hence, Hart states that ". . . statutes may be a mere legal shell and demand by their express terms to be filled out with the aid of moral principles" (Hart, 1961:199).

Therefore, if principles of morality require intent, the expected and inevitable presence of these principles in the judicial process can lead through the careful interpretation and the use of analogy, to evolution of the law through attention to new circumstance, and to the need for new issues and problems to be fairly treated in the judgments, rather than the letter of the law being simply applied in ways that might be procedurally correct, but morally vacuous.

Criminal law may be defined as a set of nonderogable norms, the performance of which may not be necessarily desired. Hart describes the difference between two kinds of laws:

> We shall consider later the attempts made by jurists to assimilate those laws which provide facilities or powers and say, "If you wish to do this, this is the way to do it," to the criminal laws which, like orders backed by threats, say, "Do this whether you wish to or not" (Hart, 1961:28).

Hence, there is an asymmetry between the mental element required for compliance to criminal laws, and the clear intent expected to characterize a breach of these laws. If A wishes to assault or rape B, or he desires the anticipated result of the assault (although this is not necessary), yet he does not do the act, the crime did not take place. Hence, his mental state is not relevant until an act, with certain consequences appropriate to the offense has taken place, and this is right and appropriate, especially when we consider the gravity of the punishment to be inflicted. Yet it is less than obvious that this traditional approach is equally appropriate to aggregate harms of the sort that are committed in ecocrimes.

It is important to remember that Canadian criminal law does criminalize "attempts," "conspiracy," and "counseling" to commit crimes (under Section 24 of the Canadian Criminal Code; Roach, 2000:98–111), and therefore it does not contrast with the Nuremberg Principles (see Chapter 1).

In the last chapter we noted that crimes like genocide and crimes against humanity do not always require full purpose, and that, in certain cases, even actions such as joining a group may make one guilty and complicit in the crimes of aggression promoted by that group (see for instance the rules arising from the Nuremberg Trials, in Chapter 1, Section 5). Those harms are not the result of one person's aggression against another, for whom he feels a specific animosity. Instead, they refer to the practices or policies by several persons against many others belonging to a different ethnic, religious, or racial group—hence, my term, "aggregate harms" to describe the results of these crimes.

Perhaps then, viewing ecocrimes in a similar light, as analogical to these forms of crimes against humanity in light of the results that follows the commission of the crimes and the causative preparation or activity, may help us to reduce the high requirement for "knowledge," "purpose," and, in general, clear subjective fault element. Unlike homicide or assault, ecocrimes require no personal acquaintance—no hate or ill feelings between the actor and the recipient of the harm. Similarly, the crime of genocide and other crimes against humanity, do not require personal acquaintance with the targeted group members, although, minimally, a lack of consideration for their lives and well-being if not clear hate, may need to exist.

This difference might support a slightly different level of criminality for crimes of genocide on one hand (perhaps viewing these as analogous to the worst kind of premeditated murder), and ecocrimes, on the other. The latter might be viewed as forms of manslaughter or assaults instead. In essence, a central goal of this work is to argue that environmental violence should be placed within the realm of crimes, rather than torts. This does not exclude the possibility of gradual increases in gravity among kinds of environmental violence, and even for the most severe, it may not be necessary to view them in the same light as the most heinous crimes. The main point is that viewing ecocrimes as only civil or commercial regulatory breaches is insufficient and inappropriate to the harms they pose. Our method will lead us to examine the case law and its interpretations, as these are played out against the Canadian Charter of Rights and Freedoms, and in the United States, the Constitution and Bill of Rights and its Amendments, in both cases, within the limits of both evolutionary interpretation and analogical method. But before discussing these approaches, it is necessary to do more than claim the existence of serious harms including both morbidity and fatality, as well as the impairment, often irreversible, of our natural biological functions. This will be the topic of the next section.

a.   The Scope of Institutionalized Violence

There are certain other forms of violence that are all-pervasive and as prevalent in Western democracies as they are in the nondemocratic regimes of the developing world. They are *environmental* forms of violence, because they are perpetrated in and through the environment: they represent direct and indirect attacks on our health, our lives, and even on what we are and our species.

Sadly, they are hard to proscribe, regulate, and control, for many reasons. Their perpetrators are powerful, their influence is global but their activities may be said to lack malicious intent, and to be instead deeply entrenched in the very fabric of modern life. As scientific evidence mounts about specific attacks on human health in various parts of the globe, through various means, responsible parties, be they corporate, governmental, or other, attempt stalling techniques and use their considerable resources to mount an impressive self-defense. In general, they claim that the *means* of their attacks, either products, processes, or other activities, are "innocent until proven guilty," and that precise proof, in the legal sense, is not available. We had seen recently a detailed unfolding of that kind of strategy, as the tobacco industry defended its "innocence," albeit in the civil context (Cohen, 1996). In another case, a specific population was put at risk; after years of stalling amidst protestations of corporate innocence, Dow Chemical Corporation was recently found liable for the health effects of their silicon breast implants (Swanson, 1996; see also *The Globe and Mail*, "International News," A16, Aug. 19, 1997).

Speaking of the tobacco issue, Lester Brown views the payments the tobacco industry was forced to give state governments as a "retroactive tax" on cigarette sales as a positive precedent for environmental harms. He says:

> This is a massive precedent for the idea of a carbon tax on fossil fuels. As with the health care related costs of smoking, an analysis of the indirect effects on burning fossil fuels, including air pollution, acid rain, and climate disruptions, would be needed to determine the amount of carbon tax (Brown, 2000:11).

Brown hopes for a similar revolution in the environmental field, but his "precedent," while desirable and positive, remains only a step forward in the realm of torts. It is still inappropriate in the face of the terrible human rights violations produced: those who are in the final stages of lung cancer, or who have suffered heart attacks and strokes, will *not* get better because of the "retroactive tax." Similarly, the life-support function of natural systems, when depleted or eliminated by altered weather pattern, desertification, floods or water losses, will not get "better" overnight or even in the lifetime of those who are presently affected, or their children, especially since, like the sale of tobacco products, the harmful practices persist as *legal* activities.

The difficulties of demonstrating responsibility are compounded, because there also are cumulative effects of toxic substances, where each substance may be at the legal "safe" level, but the result of many such chemicals may be very harmful or even lethal. Then there are the health and other reproductive effects due to low-dose exposure to products and materials that are an accepted part of life in North America. In addition, there are the aggravating effects of global climate change, as well as the effects of environmental racism because too many are disproportionately affected, and bear burdens far in excess of possible benefits from practices resulting in environmental pollution.

In sum, the claim advanced that the imposition of environmental harms is a crime, raises many difficulties both in principle and in practice, where we see that liability even in civil law (tort) is both doctrinally and practically difficult to prove in law. We will consider the practical difficulties, and suggest possible strategies to overcome them, in the final chapter of this work. At this time, we will focus on some of the major theoretical difficulties. Even if we are convinced that the consequences of assaultive crimes produce results similar to those produced by environmental harms, at least four problems remain:

(1) The effect of assaults are always the result of "illegal wrongful acts" (which the law treats as wrongful in themselves), and this is true of only some environmental harms (French and Mastny, 2001:166–188); but many *legal* environmental activities also result in serious harms.

(2) No present criminal law views environmental harms as equal to other "regular" assaults, although they often impose comparable or even more severe harms. In a Canadian example of the conceptual gulf between crime and noncrime, a young man, in stolen medical garb, introduced himself as a "lactation specialist" to new mothers in a downtown Toronto hospital recently, and touched and fondled their breasts. When identified, the man was immediately taken to jail. In contrast in Walkerton, Ontario (see Chapter 4) many died and suffered severe and lasting illnesses because of an e-coli contamination of the drinking water, in the Spring of 2000. Despite a formal judicial inquiry and endless discussions in the media, to date no one has been considered for a jail sentence, despite the permanent irreversible harms caused.

(3) The question of the requirement of intent (see Chapters 1 and 5) remains an obstacle.

(4) The method of arguing by analogy to other areas of law from the *effects* produced, rather than solely from the *acts* committed, has a methodological pedigree in legal reasoning but has limited acceptance as a basis for inputting criminal responsibility because of the enduring acceptance of the requirement of intent.

In this chapter, our first consideration will be the results and consequences of ecocrimes (1) and (2), before turning to an examination of analogy as a method to view ecocrimes as criminal assaults (4), Chapter 5 will be devoted to an examination of intent (3), and the legal/illegal distinction (1) will be discussed in Chapter 7, in the context of international law

2. THE INJUSTICE OF CLIMATE CHANGE

> [A] nation's climate is an extraordinarily important ingredient in deter-
> mining a nation's quality of life and its economic possibilities. Because
> no theory of international relations justifies the right of any national act
> in such a way that it greatly harms another nation's quality of life, those
> nations that cause global warming violate the most basic international
> norms (Brown, 2002:86).

We will examine some of the many forms taken by ecoviolence starting with
the effects of global climate change. The problems we will discuss are interconnected and interrelated, so that most of them are aggravated by the presence of
another. Still it will be helpful to treat them separately, even if they are not really
separate, simply to appreciate the magnitude of the problems that we face. We are
familiar now with the effects of holes in the ozone layer and the corresponding
hazards of ultraviolet radiation. The consequences represent an institutionalized
attack on our immune system and on our health, and the effects are equally present on all exposed animals, and on crops and vegetation. It is institutionalized,
like all other hazards discussed in this chapter, because the activities that produced it were not illegal, or proscribed, but were part of a technologically
enhanced lifestyle that has been supported and even encouraged by corporations
and by political institutions intent on pleasing voters. Indeed, the public supports
these activities indirectly by their support of these products and the corporations
that manufacture them.

I have argued that a reduction in production is a necessary part of a first
"step-back" to encourage reduced consumption. But corporate interests have been
allowed to bring us to this point, where we are all at severe risk from various
exposures, including exposure to something that is so much a part of natural life,
that is, exposure to the sun's rays. It is even more disturbing that these corporate
giants intend to pursue growth and to discourage additional regulations, rather
than prepare themselves to acknowledge their guilt and attempt to make amends.

Scientific evidence mounts about the details of the hazards to which we are
exposed, in various measures, according to our geographical location (McMichael
et al., 1996:161–174). For instance, it has recently come to light that not only
"short wavelength UV radiation (UVB)" is carcinogenic, but "new data indicate
a carcinogenic role for long wavelength ultraviolet light (UVA) also." Squamous
cell carcinomas and melanomas can be induced in tests "by UVA alone or in combination with UVB" (Schmitz et al., 1994; see also DeLaat and deGrujil, 1995,
in support of the carcinogenicity of UVA). In addition, studies on the effects of
ultraviolet radiation have shown that UVB alters significantly the immunological
processes of human and nonhuman animals (Grantstein, 1990).

Climate change will have other significant health effects globally, with low
elevation, deltaic and—in general—less developed countries bearing the heaviest

burden of harm. The impacts, both present now, and envisioned through integrated models, consider both direct and indirect individual biophysical impacts, so that the *indirect* harm caused by changes in horticultural and arable crops, and *direct* harm caused through the increasing incidence of cyclones, floods, and droughts on humans, particularly those who are not buffered by the social infrastructures present in affluent countries, become evident (Warrick et al., 1996; Murray and Lopez, 1997). The close relationship between the preservation of the environment and the ecological services it provides to all life is more visible and better understood in less developed countries, where people live their lives in a state of pervasive poverty and are striving to survive. The depletion of forests, the loss of medicinal herbs, and other results of climate change, such as "flash floods, landslides, soil erosion," and the resulting degradation of agricultural lands, mean that the health of inhabitants is at grave risk, as it is in Nepal, for instance (Malla, 1996).

It is important to keep in mind that most less developed countries have not contributed significantly to the causes of global climate change, and that, therefore, their greater burden is even more unfair than it would be, were it the lot of affluent nations instead. In Africa, environmental disasters escalate and multiply the impact of "Africa's natural hazards," such as epidemics, endemic diseases, and the like. Other man-made disasters, armed conflicts, industrial hazards, and the forced movement of populations, food insecurities, and "cultural and political instability" also interact with climate changes and environmental degradation to make disease and other health emergencies a constant threat (Loretti and Tegegn, 1996).

Examples could be multiplied, but the authors of the *World Health Statistics Quarterly* express best the full impact of this deadly interface: "Disasters occur when hazards and vulnerability meet. Out of 100 disasters reported worldwide, only 20 occur in Africa, but Africa suffers 60% of all disaster-related deaths" (Loretti and Tegegn, 1996).

In fact, accident and disaster epidemiology has become an essential tool to study the health effects of disasters, and to emphasize the need for prevention and mitigation of human health effects. Healthcare preparedness should be made a prominent priority in disaster relief, and not be brought in only to aid after the fact (Lechat, et al., 1993–94).

This section started by citing a basic principle of international law: "Do No Harm" (to other states), through your activities, as stated for instance in the *Trail Smelter* arbitration (Chapter 7, Section 6). But according to the international panel convened precisely to examine and assess the impact of global climate change now and in the future, the international community was in danger already in 1995 according to the Intergovernmental Panel on Climate Control's (IPCC) *Second Assessment Report* (1995), which led to the adoption of the 1997

Kyoto *Protocol*. Swift action might have stemmed the raising tide of the disastrous effects, but—as we know—this did not happen, despite the IPCC estimates and recommendations.

Figure 2.1 Projected Changes in Global Temperature (Global Average 1856–1999 and Projected Estimates)

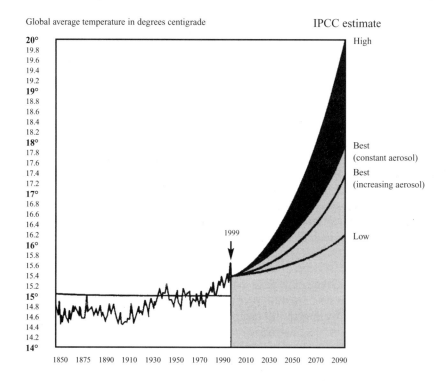

Source: U.N. Environment Program, Grid Ardenal, Climate Research Unit, University of East Anglia, Norwich, taken from IPCC Report 95.

The most recent *Summary for Policy Makers of the IPCC's Third Assessment Report* (February 2001), contains a number of specific predictions. It is too late at this time to prevent at least some global warming, under way in most areas of the world (see Fig. 2.1), and this temperature rise will produce impacts in sea and land alike, although not all areas will warm at the same rate (IPCC; *Second Assessment* Report, 1995, para. 2.10; Brown, 2002:89). The warming will cause both droughts and floods, intense storms and cyclones, while cities will suffer "life-threatening heat waves" and ecosystems, biodiversity and forests will all be modified in unpredictable ways. Food impacts due to changes in crop yields can be expected, especially in the tropics, and both glaciers and permafrost are already melting now, rendering already present water problems acute (Brown, 2002:89–91).

These impacts will affect the international community unevenly, and the most vulnerable, the poor in developing countries will suffer the worst effects of storm, floods, rises in sea-level, and in general, health effects and famines due to increasing desertification (Brown, 2002:93). This global injustice, perpetrated for the most part by the rich countries upon the poor, is one of the worst consequences of our "ecological footprint" (Wackernagel and Rees, 1996; see Chapter 7).

a. Other Forms of Environmental Violence

Another familiar area of health hazards is that of toxic waste exposure. A great deal has been done to analyze the impacts on human health of radioactive waste (Shrader-Frechette, 1982; Shrader-Frechette, 1993). The sheer persistence of radwaste, as well as its toxicity has shown the wastes of the nuclear industry to be one of the worst threat to mankind today. They represent a clear example of institutionalized ecoviolence: even such democratic countries as Canada or the United States do not offer voters a nonnuclear option as a source of power. But radwaste as well as other toxic agents must be eliminated from waste dumps (Rall, 1988).

In addition, novel criteria for testing and monitoring must be introduced. For instance, epidemiological studies disclose that the air around such sites is not classified as "representative for the possible health burden of exposed persons" (Eickmann, 1994). But gasses come out of toxic waste sites, and the air at these sites should be studied and compared to "normal" air, to detect possible hazardous variations. In contrast, chemical variations in the air may not be sufficient to make a solid case for the affected populations. Another difficulty that must also be addressed is that populations at risk may show only "nonspecific deterioration of health and well-being," rather than "overt clinical disease" (Von Schirnding and Ehrlich, 1992).

Toxic waste is also the locus of environmentally racist practices. That sort of waste is most often placed in areas populated by people of color in North America and also in less developed countries on the other continents (Bullard, 1994; Bullard, 2001; Gaylord and Bell, 1995). In all those cases, the health problems suffered by minorities is aggravated by the lack of healthcare availability in the areas where those populations live, and by the insensitive and inadequate legal and institutional infrastructure that does not offer either protection or redress (Westra, 1995).

Before ending in waste sites, many of these toxic substances are used routinely in industries, especially in agribusiness. Intensive agricultural practices impose risks well beyond carcinogenicity. A recent "Agricultural Health Study" based in North Carolina and Iowa lists many additional noncancer risks among all persons who enter into direct contact with pesticides and other agricultural chemicals (among these persons are agricultural workers, registered pesticide applicators, and their spouses). Some of the additional risks beyond cancer are "neurotoxicity, reproductive effects, immunological defects, nonmalignant respiratory disease, kidney disease," as well as abnormal growth and development in children (Pennybacker et al., 1996).

The products that have be shown to cause these health effects are also used in homes, lawns and gardens, and thus provide *direct* exposure. *Indirect* exposure may arise from "spray drift, laundering workclothes, or contaminated food and water." The effects of agricultural business practices and other *external* uses of these chemicals, parallel the *internal* exposure through ingested foods containing traces and even small quantities of these hazardous products. The general population is exposed to these hazards through accepted legal and regulated practices fully supported by present institutions. But when pesticide residues are ingested, they may be quickly metabolized and eliminated, or some have a highly acute toxicity and "show a strong tendency to accumulate in the body." In that case, the worse hazards may be connected "with long-term low-dose exposure" (Al-Saleh, 1995). In these cases, the institutional infrastructure may not recognize the health problems that arise at times far removed from the time of exposure. This means that not only are the institutions that support and permit these corporate practices and products morally wrong, but that the legal infrastructure of the institutions is equally at fault as it requires victims to carry the burden of proof (Brown, 1995). The problem is a twofold one: one is the issue of the *burden* of asserting a claim in civil litigation; the other is the question of the *quantum* (or standard) of proof (e.g., beyond a reasonable doubt in criminal law) (Roach 2000:42–44). To meet either of these two "burdens" represents a feat, for the most part, beyond the economic abilities of those who are victimized.

In another recent study, "ambient air was monitored" in an Australian town surrounded by banana plantations. Organochlorines and organophosphates were detected, but these were used mostly for nonagricultural purposes. Although the level of the agricultural pesticides used at the plantations did not appear to pose significant health risks (Beard et al., 1995), the *synergistic* effects of agricultural and nonagricultural chemicals have not been well researched.

Once again, as for toxic wastes, environmental racism also runs rampant in developing countries in the use of pesticides. Pesticides that are banned or restricted in developed countries are routinely used by large groups of agricultural workers in developing countries, and the full range of the health hazards generated by their exposure has not been fully monitored, although, fatalities are recorded (Shrader-Frechette, 1991). A recent article in the *Journal of Health Services* lists several effects on workers and the unsafe use of increasing amounts of these pesticides both in acute poisonings and in chronic health effects (e.g., neurotoxic and dermatological effects). The article argues that: "Policies that promote the use of pesticides should be critically evaluated. North-South and South-South research collaborators must be encouraged to address this global health problem" (Wesseling et al., 1997).

The problem is further aggravated by the fact that malnourished populations are much more vulnerable to the toxicity of pesticide residues. Together with the problem of product misuse, often originating from the lack of instructions in the language of the users, and the presence of restricted or banned pesticides, this should force global institutions and policymakers to rethink all strategies for pest control in the developing world (Dillon, 1995). Research indicates that radical rethinking should take place in regard to *all* agricultural practices and policies that involve chemicals, and there is no need at this time to review the abundant literature available on the topic (Tuormaa, 1995; Pimentel et al., 1993; Pimentel et al., 1991).

For the purposes of this work, all the evidence shows that the hazardous products and practices are, for the most part, legal and unrestricted activities (even if subject to regulation regarding levels of pollutants and so on), and part of an institutionalized and accepted lifestyle that is never brought into question as a whole. At best, studies that identify a specific problem may spur piecemeal legislation, or other standard-setting processes, enacted to respond to specific problems. But these sudden grave problems should be viewed as red flags, alerting us to the presence of an unsustainable and violent whole, a society that condones and encourages activities that constitute grave attacks on the physical integrity of individuals and their habitats. When air, water, sun, earth, and food are all contaminated and basically hazardous, then ecoviolence is being perpetrated on a regular basis, and the moral right to self-defense ought to be invoked to attack the legality of present institutions and eliminate these persistent attacks.

A study published by the *Japanese Journal of Hygiene* has recently proposed using a parallel method to the one used by the Denmark budget methods (Codex Alimentalius of the WHO/FAO Joint Committee), which establishes Recommended Dietary Allowances (RDAs) for each food intake. The proposed method could be called "Estimated Ecological Daily Intake" (EEDI), and it would calculate the daily intake of food additives and contaminants, based on volunteers' food consumption (Toyokawa and Nishikawa, 1994). This sort of research could be repeated at various locations and it might form the basis for an eventual series of class action suits by groups or even by government institutions on behalf of these groups, similar to the ones brought against the tobacco companies in 1997. If states in the United States can sue tobacco companies to recover the damages arising from health costs incurred because of these companies' practices, then legal actions against other hazardous industries might make a serious impact on the way these corporations conduct their respective businesses, and also on the general uncritical acceptance of those states' institutions.

A similar method might be designed to study the amount of exposure to low-level chemicals and toxics, such as hormone mimics and other endocrine disruptors that are not ingested (Colborn et al., 1996; Westra, 1998). These substances and their effects will be discussed in the next section in some detail.

Even more than the specific exposures of agricultural workers, or others involved in the manufacture or use of chemical products, low-level exposure is a threat to many in theNorthwest affluent countries, where the lifestyle is based on the uncritical acceptance of a myriad products and processes, all of which may affect us through low-dose exposures. Anyone who uses soft plastics and lives in an area where chemical endocrine disruptors exist (and that is pretty much everywhere) is at risk. As Colborn has it, "Living in a man-made landscape, we easily forget that our well-being is rooted in natural systems. Yet all human enterprise rests on the foundation of natural systems that provide a myriad of invisible life-support services" (Colborn et al., 1996:168). As seen in animals, endocrine disruptors attack all of us and our future through "widespread disruption in human embryonic development" producing frequent genital abnormalities in infants, as well as reduced sperm counts in males and infertility and reproductive difficulties in females (Colborn et al., 1996:171). Many of these harms are transgenerational; all are largely invisible and do not produce the clear, "smoking-gun" relations between causes and effects that may move present institutions to curtail or eliminate them (Westra, 1998).

We noted earlier some of the effects of global climate change. These changes are already having a significant impact on the spread of vector-borne infectious diseases, and on viral and parasitic infections. All changes in the ecology of a region entail changes in the vector populations. Large-scale movement of human populations contribute to this severe threat as well. The loss of tropical forests, global warming of air and oceans, and all other anthropogenic disturbances, all contribute to health threats.

Many believed that infectious diseases had been eliminated through the use of antibiotics, including smallpox, whooping cough, diphtheria, paralyzing poliomyelitis, tetanus, and many other diseases that are largely extinct. But the majority of "vector-transmitted diseases," such as cholera, and several forms of "severe respiratory tract infections" will continue to be "an important health problem" for the 21st century. Some of the causes include "lifestyles prone to infectious pathology, such as megacity urbanization," "industrialized foods . . . global commerce and tourism, . . . antibiotic-multiresistant microbial flora; environmental disturbances as a result of global warming, deforestation, the settling of virgin areas, dams, the large-scale use of pesticides, fertilizers and antimicrobials" (Kumate, 1997).

Some of the contributing causes cited by Kumate include drug addiction, "sexual liberation" and other nonenvironmental contributing factors. But, for the most part, the causes of the emergence and reemergence of life-threatening diseases are environmentally imposed and not subject to individual consent (like sexual orientation). Yet we might want to question this assumption as well. Although no research is available to my knowledge on this aspect of the problem, we might connect the sexual changes imposed by endocrine disruptors to the sexual "choices" that are thought to be freely intended, and cited as contributing factors to the presence of these diseases. If this connection is at least possible, then even sexually transmitted diseases arising from certain choices may not be "chosen," and may thus be listed under environmentally induced threats as well. There has been a general move to grant rights to those with sexual orientations beyond heterosexuality, in most Western democracies. Amended laws and regulations are based, for the most part, on the value of individual freedom and on egalitarian considerations. Yet, if the effect of these chemicals is to alter sexual orientation in humans as it often does in birds and marine mammals (Colborn et al., 1996), then granting rights after the fact does not change the impact of the violence that might have been done to these individuals and to their natural, original functions and sexuality.

The introduction of toxic materials and chemicals is not only a direct form of violence, but it contributes indirectly to the loss of "nature's services" (Daily, 1997). When systems are no longer capable of continuing their evolutionary paths, as they are not left unmanipulated or wild, the services they provide may be proportionately decreased as our interference with their structure and function eventually eliminates their ability to provide support for all life (Westra, 1998). A recent study, for instance, addresses our need for plant life: "Only green plants can convert the single carbon units of atmospheric carbon dioxide into the multi-carbon organic molecules on which all forms of life depend. Only green plants can provide the oxygen required by man and other aerobic organisms" (Bell, 1993). Further, the medicinal and nutritive services provided by a vast array of plants is eliminated when these are affected, depleted or rendered extinct, while so little is known about most of the diversity that still exists. E. Bell adds, "Nothing or virtually nothing is known about the composition of approximately 250,000 wild and little used species" (Bell, 1993; Harte et al., 1992; Wilson, 1993; Ehrenfeld, 1991). The elimination of biodiversity and of systemic function leads to repeated system collapse: this, in itself, is arguably the most severe threat to human health that we encounter (Jutro, 1991; McMichael, 1995). Additional impacts on human health arise from two other primary losses that face us: the loss of safe air and the loss of safe water (McMichael et al., 1996:43–68, 71–105).

Air pollution and the presence of particulates in the air lead to children's asthma in unprecedented numbers, and to the increasing presence of obstructive pulmonary disease in much of the Western world from Europe to North America (Anderson et al., 1997; Aunan, 1996; Hernandes-Garduno et al., 1997; Guidotti, 1996). Safe water, or at least somewhat uncontaminated water, is not available to 40 percent of the population of the world. This represents a factor clearly contributing to the reemergence of vector-borne diseases like cholera, as we saw earlier, and the role of unsafe water was evident in the cholera pandemic of January 1991 (Reiff et al., 1996; Colwell, 1996; McMichael, 1995). The cost of providing safe water worldwide, however, would be prohibitive; for instance, a public intervention to supply families with safe water in Latin America would cost between U.S. $1.50 and $4.00 per family (Reiff et al., 1996). Globally, although safe water has been taken for granted as "an essential public health need," it appears that the time when everyone will have to pay dearly for safe water is almost upon us (Middleton and Saunders, 1997).

These facts provide ammunition for the thesis of this chapter, and they offer an additional example of the injustice perpetrated by our "ecological footprint" (Rees and Wackernagel, 1996), as certain groups are disproportionally affected. For instance, most of the citizens in less developed countries cannot pay the required price for safe water (Rogers and Wofford, 1989); and infants have special needs, in comparison with the rest of the population: they "need three times more water than adults if the requirements are calculated according to body weight" (Dartois and Casemitjana, 1991).

We are also totally vulnerable to pathogens to which animals (such as apes) are routinely exposed, as we encroach on their wild habitats with our expanding populations. The sudden spread of the Ebola virus is a case in point: a disease that might be commonplace for one species, may be lethal for another. We are more familiar with another aspect of this phenomenon when we consider the encroachment on the habitat of one human group by another, as when the first North American colonists arrived in areas previously occupied by peoples native to those regions. In that case, the aboriginal people were the ones affected, because they were exposed to pathogens to which they had not developed an immunity. Yet it does not seem as though we have truly understood that lesson, clear as it was. Like that colonizing expansion, our encroachment into habitats of which we are not a part is uncritically accepted and part of "normal" modern life: it has become institutionalized.

The newest aliens within ecosystems and habitats, that is, bioengineered and transgenic organisms (both plants and animals) are also a regularly accepted and institutionalized form of ecoviolence perpetrated in various ways against human and nonhuman life (Westra, 1998). Altered animals are also forced to live in altered conditions, thus requiring food additives including antibiotics, in order to survive. This practice, in turn, gives rise to our own exposure to antibiotic-resistant strains of pathogens (Westra, 1998; Rissler and Mellon, 1991). Altered foods are also hazardous to the natural systems where they are introduced. Further, they are normally unlabelled, so that another threat to health arises from possible allergic reactions to the hidden components within previously acceptable and safe foods (Rissler and Mellon, 1991; Westra, 1993).

Finally, social conditions aggravated by conflicts (Homer-Dixon, 1991), as well as the environmental degradation we have briefly detailed here, engender the migration of entire groups and populations. Refugees, displaced persons, legal and illegal immigration all contribute to the spread of health threats to all areas of the globe. We may sum up some of these forms of ecoviolence as follows, although these headings are by no means a complete list of all possible harms of this kind:

(1)   increased exposure to UVA/UVB because of ozone layer thinning;

(2)   exposure to direct impacts of global climate change, such as floods, extreme temperatures and other weather changes;

(3)   exposure to toxic wastes;

(4)   exposure to toxic/hazardous by-products of industrial production, ranging from nuclear power to high input agriculture;

(5)   exposure to food additives and chemical residues in food production;

(6)   long-term, low-level exposures to various chemicals and processes;

(7)   exposure to climate-induced health threats from new or renewed infectious diseases;

(8)   the loss of "nature's services" (Daily, 1997) through loss of biodiversity, fragmentation of natural landscapes, deforestation;

(9)   increased presence of particulates and other pollutants in the air;

(10) the diminishing supply of safe water;

(11) direct contact with pathogens through encroachment on the wild (Soskolne, personal communication, 1997);

(12) increased hazards from the presence of bioengineered foods and transgenics, which range from
(a) unexpected allergic reactions from unlabelled bioengineered food, to
(b) exposure to food with unpredictable side effects (as in BSE), and
(c) to the hidden antibiotics in transgenic fish;

(13) exposure to antibiotic resistant strains of pathogens;

(14) increase in communicable disease risks through migration of persons to accommodate refugees, to seek out qualified labour, travel, and immigration policies of governments (Westra, 2000).

3.   INSTITUTIONALIZED ECOVIOLENCE AND ITS ETHICAL DIMENSIONS

Certain common features allow the grouping of all these disparate attacks on our existence. Most of these attacks are viewed as arising out of the "normal" functioning of Western industrialized societies. Another common feature is that, in all cases, there is *no* candid information available to the public about the "double effects" of products and activities we tend to take for granted. The role of the media (Korten, 1995) and of business practices such as trade secrets regulations

(Velasquez, 1991), conspire to keep us in the dark. Many of these products have become highly desirable, or even necessities through clever marketing; in some cases, even planned addiction has been part of the marketing process. Often immense corporate resources promote a product well beyond its intrinsic value, until it becomes a "must have" icon globally (think of Coca-Cola or MacDonald's in this respect).

In contrast, some other features of our list affect Northwest affluent populations in a way that is different from the effects on impoverished minorities in Southeast countries. For instance, low-dosage exposures arise directly from the industrial life-style of the Northwest. As Theo Colborn explains, it is the soft plastics, the petrochemical agricultural aids, and other taken-for-granted parts of our daily life that cause much of our hazardous exposure: in this regard alone, we are worse off than those who live at or below the poverty level in the developing world (Colborn et al., 1996). But Northwesterners are advantaged in some other ways: our affluence protects us from some of the effects of global climate change, including the resurgence of previous infectious diseases, and the emergence of new ones. The siting of hazardous waste facilities, on the other hand, is far more likely to put minority populations at risk, here or in the Southeast.

Although we are assured of protection, by our government institutions, such as "security of the person" (Canadian Charter of Rights, Section 7), or to "equal protection" (U.S. Constitutional Amendments 4 and 15), somehow the harms listed are viewed in a different light. They are not taken to be forms of crimes. They are either viewed as normal aspects of modern life, or as "acts of God," accidental events beyond our control. What is lacking is the acknowledgment of collective responsibility on the part of the risk imposers themselves, as well as on the part of whole institutions, including the governing bodies that aid and abet these activities. At most, our politicians and our judges accept unrealistic burden-of-proof expectations, as they neglect to factor in their decisions, the limits of scientific predictive capabilities, the impact of uncertainty and the importance of the precautionary principle, particularly in regard to environmental matters.

Aggressions and attacks are still thought of in the narrow sense of direct physical attacks on persons by other persons. I believe that a new approach is necessary, because these invisible harms are not acknowledged now: instead, they have become accepted taken for granted, that is, institutionalized. They are not viewed as unacceptable and abnormal, the way criminal acts are viewed. It is a crime even to carry knives and firearms (outside the United States), or bombs; it is not legal to have them or stockpile them, in most circumstances, regardless of actual use or even intent to use.

But toxic substances, hazardous chemicals, and even the practices that eliminate biodiversity, reduce and pollute wild habitats, and render clean water a rare resource, are also harmful to human life and health. They are even worse than guns, in some sense, as they require neither malice nor intent to be harmful; simple carelessness, negligence, lack of concern for nature's services (Daily, 1997), are sufficient to result in disasters, some of which are irreversible (such as the effects of nuclear waste). Of course, none of the effects I have mentioned are immediate, evident, or even directly causative of the harms they eventually produce. Like the small, cumulative doses of obscure poisons found in the urbane and elegant murder mysteries written by British authors, they do kill, slowly and inexorably. When they do not, they impose disease or they wreak havoc in various ways in the natural functioning of human beings (McMichael, 1995a; McMichael et al., 1995b; Colborn et al., 1996; Colwell, 1996; Forbes and Calow, 1996, Longstretch and DeGrujil, 1995).

My approach to environmental ethics is and has been biocentric and holistic: I have defended the intrinsic value of the integrity of systemic wholes (Westra, 1994; Westra, 1995; Westra, 1997). In my latest work I have also defended the rights of individual organisms (such as human beings) to retain their own microintegrity, as well as the integrity of their habitats. For now, leaving aside the needs of nonhuman animals and the protection of systems *for themselves*, I want to argue that my approach is necessary even if we limit ourselves purely to a consideration of the connection between environment and the right to human health, surely an easy goal to defend. What is the relation between ecological integrity and human health? Literature exists about the necessity to establish, respect, or restore wild areas (core areas) in order to reestablish within them the large fauna originally native to each habitat (to the best of our knowledge), and, at the same time, ensure that all the biota necessary to the functioning of each ecosystem are present on each site (Noss, 1992; Pimentel et al., 1992). In essence then, our first concern based on respect for others, ourselves, and all life should be the conservation of the resilience of the ecosystems on which human activity depends, and the ability of these systems to continue to provide valued ecological services to *all* biota. To achieve this, not only does the *quality* of ecosystems in the wild need protection, but also their *quantity* (in the sense of the size of the core areas required). A holistic approach is needed so that the separate channeling of legislation affecting pollution, agricultural practices, fisheries or forestry, can all be viewed through a perspective that *starts* from the necessary centrality of integrity, and only then moves on to particularities. Just as it is not possible to save animal species and communities without a primary concern for their habitat, so too, concern for individuals and communities of humans should start with respect for the habitat we share with the rest of the biota.

And the causal effect of inappropriate human activities does more than affect something "out there," external to the humans whose activities they are. As Aldo Leopold and others have shown, our human position as part of the ecosystem's biota, renders each imposition of inappropriate stress a reciprocal one: in an "upstream/ downstream" world (Leopold, 1949; Scherer and Attig, 1990), everything we do comes back to affect us in some way. The difficulty is that disrupting natural processes in large areas, not only disrupts the life and health of *their* biota, it also affects *ours:* cutting down forests, for instance, reduces the "services" their trees perform for all air, hence, for all forms of life that need to breathe. Introducing toxic and hazardous substances into waterways and oceans not only affects all the wildlife that depends on clean water for its life, it also affects all humans in various ways, as our own food supplies are affected, not only in the water, but also through evaporation that distributes the toxins on whatever is grown for food.

We are familiar by now with the almost automatic association between chemicals and their carcinogenic and mutagenic properties. Additional recent research shows no less ominous but different effects of "herbicides, fungicides, insecticides, nematocides" and most other industrial chemicals. Theo Colborn recently sketched a "Toxic Chemical Profile" of these substances and their effects: She shows that they:

(1) mimic natural hormones;
(2) antagonize hormone effects by blocking binding sites;
(3) react directly or indirectly with natural hormones;
(4) alter natural patterns of hormone synthesis, metabolism and excretion;
(5) alter hormone receptors' level (Colborn, et al., 1996).

These effects are supported by basic research involving wildlife, controlled laboratory toxicology tests and tests on human epidemiological exposure (Colborn et al., 1996). Although these substances affect gene expression, however, they are "organizational, activational, not mutational, as they do not affect the integrity of the DNA" (Colborn et al., 1996). What we do see is an almost endless series of sexual and reproductive effects, engendered by very low doses of most of these substances; the loss of structural integrity of male and female reproductive apparatus is followed by the loss of functional (reproductive) capacity, and often by the loss of natural gender orientation and parenting abilities (Colborn et al., 1996).

Many of these effects of low-dose exposure may be found in birds, fish, and mammals, including humans. The increasing frequency of these abnormalities is due to the worldwide exposure to chemicals we are experiencing. Colborn traces the first "wide-scale exposure to manmade chemicals" to the 1940s (after World War II), so that in the 1940s and 1950s a first generation was exposed. In the next 20 years (1950s to 1970s), for the first time, worldwide exposure in the womb occurred; hence, by the 1990s this generation itself reached reproductive age, thus continuing the pattern of exposure.

But not all the results of these low-dose exposures are clear, observable, sexually related, or represent examples of recognizable diseases. Some are far more subtle: they *are not* visible, for example hyperactivity, reduced head circumference, auditory/verbal deficits, poorer reflex functions, stress intolerance, and reduced average intelligence are just some of the problems increasingly found in populations in the Great Lakes area, for example. Colborn points out that even some economists are beginning to be concerned about the possibility of whole populations "whose intelligence, capacities and reactions are abnormal" (Colborn et al., 1996).

Therefore, we should become aware of the urgent and grave threats to our health, to the health and survival of our children, hence, to the survival of our species and that of all other species on earth. The effects of these chemicals ought to emphasize the "imperative of responsibility" to the very idea of humankind (Jonas, 1984) and, as the principle of integrity proposes, to all life on earth (Westra, 1994). Those who do not recognize their responsibility and continue to pursue their own agendas without considering the side-effects of their activities should be treated as guilty of "reckless endangerment," and of "assault causing bodily harm," and punished according to the laws governing these crimes. These harms are perpetrated directly by corporate and industrial enterprises for the most part, not by individuals, although they are aided and abetted by consumers everywhere, as they uncritically accept the goods these enterprises provide and market. Additionally, and beyond the direct harms discussed, there are various complex effects engendered by global warming and other changes, as these too affect health worldwide.

It is clear that we need to find some remedy for these and other such hazardous situations globally, because the list of environmental assaults on the physical integrity of ecosystems and, through them, on our own physical integrity and capacities occurs equally in Northwest affluent and in Southeast developing countries. The global distribution of the threats, from remote islands in the Pacific Ocean to pristine areas in the Arctic (Colborn, et al., 1996), demonstrate that geographical and political boundaries are not capable of containing and limiting environmental degradation and disintegrity. A careful study of the hot spots and locations where the worst hazards persist, shows that they are equally global in distribution. It seems that we cannot generally separate democracies from, say, military regimes and other nondemocratic states on the basis of the spread and severity of the environmental threats to which their citizens are exposed, although nondemocratic rule can produce exacerbated or at least different harms.

The "toxic doughnut" area in Chicago is a persistent threat to the life and health of residents (Gaylord and Bell, 1995), although it is located in a country that prides itself on its status as the "land of the free," and which routinely allows its leaders and politicians to praise its democratic institutions, in contrast with other undesirable forms of government the world over. Equally hazardous, Royal Dutch Shell Oil's operation in Ogoniland, Nigeria, uses the dictatorship of Gen. Sani Abbacha and its military clique, to enforce the acceptance of extreme health hazards on its citizens (Westra, 1998). Of course, those who oppose these hazardous corporate activities in Nigeria are brutally and violently repressed or murdered, while the Chicago residents are not.

The U.S. residents, primarily minorities in most large U.S. cities (Westra and Lawson, 2001; Bullard, 1994), are not imprisoned or executed, and the army is not sent in to restrain and eliminate their protests. In some sense, their plight is therefore better: they only suffer the physical harms imposed upon them by others, and their life and health are slowly, insidiously attacked and diminished. They only suffer from ecoviolence; they are not imprisoned and executed if they protest, as they might have been in Nigeria. But in some sense, their plight is even worse. Ostensibly possessing civil rights, basic education, access to information, and constitutional guarantees about freedom of choice, life and the pursuit of happiness, they are in fact manipulated to contribute willingly (but unknowingly) to their own plight. Aggressive advertising and marketing techniques cause the public to regard the products of modern technology as not only extremely desirable, but even as necessary, as things everyone should have. They regard these consumers choices as free, as corporate sponsors and originators employ trade secret and other hard-won rules and regulations to protect themselves, all the while keeping citizens in the dark about the effects and consequences of their choices.

At the same time, public relations departments work steadily so that questions about the risks and harms imposed, and whether they are and should be truly offset by the so-called benefits available, are raised as rarely as possible. Further, as David Korten shows, two other severe problems arise in connection with the pursuit of economic gain through techno-corporate activities. The first is a clear attack on democracy, as independent PR firms are hired at great cost to generate public movements and campaigns, with the double aim of selling their ideas and preparing the public to accept and actively pursue certain products and services. The second problem is that legislative modifications, regulations or deregulations favorable to business, are also sought. In some cases, corporations select and buy legislatures through campaign financing.

The result of these activities is that free democratic choices are neither truly free nor truly democratic. Korten cites Washington journalist William Greider:

> (the corporations') . . . tremendous financial resources, the diversity of their interests, the squads of talented professionals—all these assets and some others—are now relentlessly focused on the politics of governing. This new institutional reality is the centerpiece in the breakdown of contemporary democracy. Corporations exist to pursue their own profit maximization, not the collective aspirations of the Society (Korten, 1995).

The problem is embedded in liberal democracy in two senses:

(1) Corporations, as fictitious legal persons (French, 1984), are free to pursue their aims, unless it can be proven (in the legal sense), that some citizen or citizens are directly harmed by their chosen activi-

ties. Further, there is no overarching conception of the good for all, that can be contrasted with *their* pursuit of their own good, which is economic, rather than intellectual or spiritual.

(2) Because there is no good to guide public policy, aside from aggregate choices and preferences, and because the public can be, and in fact often is, routinely manipulated and under-informed, the myth of "one man/one vote" remains a vague ideal, not a reality (see also Chapter 3).

The arguments often proposed to justify these negative impacts, center on the alleged economic advantages provided by multinational corporate giants. But, as we indicated in the Chicago example, this economic advantage is not evenly distributed or fairly apportioned among rich and poor: Moreover, if we shift to the global scene, even economic advances depend on "relative" rather than on absolute income. The Bruntlandt Commission proposed a "3% global increase in per capita income." That would translate into a first-year per capita increase (in U.S. dollars) of $633 for the United States, and, among others, $3.60 for Ethiopia. After ten years, the respective figures would be $7,257.00 for the United States, and $41.00 for Ethiopia: a vast advantage for the "haves" over the "have nots." Korten adds: "This advantage becomes a life-and-death issue in a resource-scarce world in which the rich and the poor are locked in mortal competition for a depleting resource base" (Korten, 1995).

Objections may be raised about such polarized descriptions of corporate activities. For instance, David Crocker believes that demonizing corporations as such is philosophically fallacious and practically incorrect, as many corporations are good and seek to support and implement the common good in their activities (Crocker, personal communication, 1996). This objection, however, is open to a counterobjection. The main point at issue is not that this or that corporation is "bad" and needs to be stopped, but that Western democracies and their institutions appear to have no mechanism available, at this time, to protect the public from hazards and harms, many of which are—in part—self-inflicted under conditions of public misinformation and manipulation discussed earlier.

In this case, to say that there is no need to institute radical changes, and in particular to implement a system of criminal charges against the corporations is, I believe, like saying that, because many of us are generally decent people, who do not view physical assaults and murder as acceptable activities, there is no need for strong laws and sanctions regarding these crimes. Leaving to the corporate goodwill of individual firms the choice to either engage in harmful activities or not, within the ambit of the present loose regulative structures and unrealistic legal criteria (Brown, 1995), is to tacitly support the status quo and to condone the crimes perpetrated thereby. In the next section, we will discuss the strategy required, to treat these environmental assaults as crime.

4. THE ARGUMENT FROM ANALOGY: FROM INSTITUTIONALIZED ENVIRONMENTAL VIOLENCE TO ECOCRIMES

... analogical reasoning may be especially desirable in contexts in which we seek moral evolution over time. If the legal culture really did attain reflective equilibrium, it might become too rigid and calcified; we would know what we thought about everything, whether particular or general. By contrast, analogical reasoning has the important advantage of allowing a large degree of openness to new facts and perspectives (Sunstein, 1993:782).

What this work seeks to achieve is indeed "to seek moral evolution," through openness to "new facts and perspectives." Hence, analogy appears to be the appropriate method to employ, although it is by no means uncontroversial.

a. The Debate of the 1937 Dutch Congress on Analogy

Some early jurisprudence scholars took strong exception to the use of analogy, while others defended it. On November 13, 1937, a conference was convened in The Netherlands, to discuss "the problem of analogy" in penal law (Halász, 1938:358). The problems envisioned included the "debated question of *nulla poena sine lege*, so that the role of the judicial decision *arbitro del giudice*, is to proceed according to linguistic interpretation and "grammatical construction." But an examination of the ultimate will and thought process behind legislation leads to a considered interpretation, which may be extensive and far reaching. In that case, like in the case of analogy, one seeks the *ratio* of a specific disposition, in order to be able "to deduce another one."

In such cases, the difference between interpretation and analogy appears to be simply one of degree, in the sense that one may go somewhat farther than the other. In both cases the judicial aim is to "avoid the possibility of injustice and to safeguard the unity of penal law" (Halász, 1938:359). Apparently, the history of analogy as a legitimate method and tool oscillated between acceptance and rejection. The early debate here referred to argues that in the early 1800s through 1827, Dutch authors (for example, Kemper, 1809; Van Maanen, 1810) flatly rejected analogy. At the time of the conference, its use was "forbidden in penal law, but allowed at the level of the Supreme Courts." In France as well, the notion was strongly debated. For instance, Marc Ancel stated: "... le juge prend texte legale commme basé d'une construction juridique ... il lui fait produire toutes les consequences logique, naturelles qu'elle contient en germe" (Ancel, 1931). Examples are adduced to show that, while "to allow the country justice of the peace to reach decisions that depart from the letter of the law" is both undesirable and unjust. Others, like Taverne, respond that the hands of a magistrate must not be tied in the administration of justice: "the judge must be a faithful servant not a slave to the law" (Halàsz, 1938:366).

In that case, however, "interpretation " may be understood as "camouflaged analogy," whereas analogy itself is both "honest" and open. (Ibid.). The earlier debate hinges on whether interpretation and analogy are truly different in kind, whereas some believe that analogy does not benefit from the limits provided by the presence of the text in interpretation: the danger may be that of turning judges into legislators. The position of I.M. van Bemmelen is that analogy remains "a highly dangerous arm" in the hands of those with the power to restrict citizens' liberty. Roling and Langemeijer rely that "interpretation signifies the application of a norm that does emerge clearly in the legal expression," but "analogy signifies the application of the positive norm to facts that are not included [explicitly but that possess an intrinsic similitude to the acts the norm intends to punish" (Halász, 1938:368).

Finally, A.J. Marx (Germany) proposes the concept of "limited analogy" requiring (1) that the text be viewed as primary guide; (2) that the legislature should periodically review decisions of the Supreme Court, in view of becoming aware of possible *lacunae* needed to be filled, in order to render the use of analogy unnecessary in many cases; (3) that it be limited to serious crimes, not to regulatory breaches (Halász, 1938:368). Many of these categories will be important for our argument, as both problems and advantages of analogy already emerge in this early European discussion. We should now turn to some recent material on the topic.

b. The Role of Analogical Reasoning in Law: Some Recent Discussions

> . . . principles play an essential part in arguments supporting judgments about particular rights and obligations. After the case is decided we may say that the case stands for a particular rule. . . . But the rule does not exist before the case is decided the court cites principles as its justification for adopting and applying a new rule (Dworkin, 1978:2).

The question then is not only how do judges and courts make decisions, but how can they in effect make just decisions, or administer justice beyond the application of rules. This line of argument will help our case in two ways: first, and most important, it will support our contention that, given both the novelty and the gravity of the crimes we discuss, both principles and analogical ways of applying existing norms will be required; and second, the pivotal role of principles will also support our argument for moving from national to international law.

Speaking of rules, for instance, Dworkin cites Hart as he distinguishes between primary and secondary rules:

> The rules of the criminal law that forbid us to rob, murder or drive too fast, are good examples of primary rules. Secondary rules are those that stipulate how and by whom, such primary rules may be formed, recognized, modified or extinguished (Dworkin, 1978:19; Hart, 1961:89–96).

The authority of rules is based on their (U.S.) Constitutional foundation, and the limits posed by that constitution, and should not be exceeded therefore, by the rules that apply that Constitution. As we will see below (Chapter 7), it is precisely because of Constitutional limits, such as the extension of individual rights to corporations and institutions, especially when these are understood in conjunction with other factors, such as economic or political pressures, that our quest for environmentally constructive principles leads beyond state jurisdictions to international law.

The goal is to seek justice and respect for human rights and—*prima facie*— Ronald Dworkin is a defender of the latter as well the former, particularly in Rawls' understanding of the concept (Dworkin, 1978:150).

For Rawls, "reflective equilibrium" is a method of moral reasoning (Rawls, 1971:46–53). Dworkin says that Rawls' method is a procedure to achieve "the harmony of equilibrium" (Dworkin, 1978:165). It is an example of how a "reasoner seeking to resolve a problem casts about for examples that, either intuitively or by conventional association, promise to be fruitful sources for the problem at hand" (Sherwin, 1999:1181). Sherwin cites Brewer on this method, as he views this form of reasoning as one that produces a tentative "analogy-warranting rule," one that posits a logical relation, inductive or deductive, between the examples and the problem (Brewer, 1996:962). What is at stake, is a "reasoned elaboration," as opposed to allowing judges to exercise "discretionary fiat" (Hart and Sacks, 1994:147), a serious concern, as we saw with the use of analogy.

Despite this reasonable description of both process and result of analogical reasoning, doubts remain about the amount of discretion that should be allowed to judges, to exercise both their political and maybe their personal preferences (Rosner, 1990:86–98; Halász, 1938:358–368).

For environmental harms, it is imperative to transcend the narrow confines of present day environmental decision-making: in the context of state regulatory decisions, our examples from Canadian and U.S. domestic law will indicate, analogical reasoning should be employed (see Chapter 5 and 6). So far, however, it has not; hence, the effort to show that some forms of violence, resulting from environmental degradation, affect human beings in ways similar to the violence that is described and addressed in international humanitarian law (see Chapter 1). We will also argue that environmental harms affect victims in ways analoguous to the victims of assaultive crimes (see Chapters 5 and 6). This argument supports legislators and judges who might be willing to reach to the spirit and the implications of legal norms, beyond the simple letter of the rules.

Bassiouni argued that, at the time of the Nuremberg Trials, although neither the crimes for the harms were totally new in 1945, the scale and the magnitude of these crimes were indeed novel—hence, the many changes that were made in the laws and the way of considering certain issues. The same could be said of environmental harms. The example Bassiouni offered is of the first fratricide. Like that crime, environmental harms resulting from ecocrimes represent a violence that is radically new in reach, scope, and gravity today, although environmental disaster and pollution are part of the history of mankind.

Judge C.G. Weeramantry in his *Separate Opinion* of 1997 (*Gabcikovo/ Nagymaros Case*) attests to the long history of environmental concernsj from the time of the Assyrians, the Sumarians, in all times and in all areas of the world (see Chapter 1). However, the difference we note in present days disasters and harms, is not a difference of degrees in comparison with the past, but a difference *in kind*. Hence, the need to use analogy. Cass Sunstein says: "For analogical reasoning to work well, we have to say that the relevant, known similarities give us good reasont to believe that there are further similarities and thus help us to answer an open question" (Sunstein, 1993:744). Sunstein's argument starts with the example of "cross burning" as a form of "speech" that ought to be treated as a "threat of violence . . . outside the First Amendment" (Sunstein, 1993:765). He supports his analogy by arguing that "hate crimes" are also treated in a special way in U.S. law. In essence, analogies do help us discover inherent similarities between cases and between crimes; they may also help to discover legal and moral principles that are "ultimately freestanding" (Sunstein, 1993:775).

In this work, analogy has been and will be used in two ways. In one sense, it shows why one should argue that the factual components of environmental harms can and should be likened to individual assaults and to crimes against humanity, where whole populations might be affected. In another sense, the argument repeats the analogical argument with respect to the laws governing common assaults and crimes against humanity, on the diminished requirement for the presence of a mental element. The regulatory framework, especially the wider-reaching international instruments, should be applied to the factual consequences of ecocrimes.

5. INTERPRETATION AND ANALOGY: SOME CASES

For positive law is not always clear and undisputed. If it were, the function of judges would be purely automatic (Lauterpacht, 1968:103).

In the previous section Sunstein's important article on analogy was used to establish the general parameter of the application and use of analogy to cases. His main example is that of cross burning, in relation to the First Amendment of the U.S.Constitution (free speech). The Constitution provides the limit and decides the parameter of legal argument in any case, just as the Charter of Rights defines that parameter, and provides that limit for Canadian law. Sunstein' s starting point is his understanding of analogy: "In law, analogical reasoning has four different but overlapping features: principled consistency; a focus on particulars; incompletely theorized judgements; and principles operating at a low or intermediate level of abstraction" (Sunstein, 1993:746). Sunstein also argues that, because of its emphasis on particulars, analogy may be viewed as "a version of 'bottom up' thinking," a position also espoused by Richard Posner (Posner, 1992:446). Yet how can we simply compare facts, unless a standard of comparison, that is, a theory informs our thinking? If we consider Sunstein's own example, that of cross burning, it is an example of cases confronting the First Amendment (R.A.V. v. City of St. Paul 1, 112 S. Ct. 2538 (1992)). Cross burning, however, appears to be action not speech (Sunstein, 1993:759). A strong voice recently spoke out in favor of retaining a 50-year-old Virginia law banning cross burning, that of U.S. Supreme Court Justice Clarence Thomas. On December 11, 2002, Justice Thomas "condemned cross-burning as a symbol of oppression during 100 years of lynching in the south by the Ku Klux Klan" (Toronto Star, Dec. 12, 2002, A14). The justice added: "This was a reign of terror, and the cross was a symbol of that reign of terror. Isn't that significantly greater than intimidation or a threat?" (Ibid.). These arguments followed a case of cross burning by a white Virginia Beach, group, after a party in the yard of a black man, James Jubilee.

But more must be said in order to evaluate the connection between action and speech acts as they are sometimes called. There are more neutral ways of restricting cross burning, the use of "trespass law, or maybe just forbidding "acts . . . [that] produce anger or resentment," although this approach appears insufficient; finally, there might be a variant of the previous approach by the addition of qualifiers to "anger and resentment," such as expressions basing these on "race, color or creed." But perhaps what should be forbidden are acts of expression that are based on a specific viewpoint (Sunstein, 1993:760–762). The question is not only the content of the proscribed expressions, but the understanding of the meaning of "fighting words," on the basis of the reaction they will produce, rather than on the basis of the intention of the speaker (or, as in the case of cross burning, the actor). This is precisely the point made by John Stuart Mill in his famous work *On Liberty:* freedom of speech should not be curtailed except for the utterances made in public, that would inflame a crowd to riot or do violence (Mill, 1910). In that example, even one of the best known supporters of freedom, and of limits to the allowable restraints society may place on individuals and groups, clearly based his argument on the harm caused, rather than on the intention of the speakers. It is worthy to note that Mill's famous example does more than use freedom of speech in a way that illustrates the method of analogy; it also demonstrates that a constitutional right can be reunderstood (1) as a criminalizable act, and (2) largely on the basis of its effects on others (that is, on their rights and interests).

Within U.S. jurisprudence, the answer lies in part in the efforts of American courts to defuse Constitutional challenges by emphasizing their own neutrality, at least in principle. That neutrality, as Sunstein argues, can be set aside for reasons viewed as important, ranging from the permission of "bans on political advertising on buses" (Lehman v. City of Shaker Heights, 418 U.S. 298 (1974)), to banning "partisan speeches at army bases" (Freer v. Spock, 424 U.S. 828 (1976)). Yet clearly the most neutral of all positions from which to judge both speech and speech acts (or expressive acts), does not follow from the intent of the speaker or actor, or even from the reaction of those affected: it lies in the *objective* consequences, whether actual or clearly anticipated, such as the dire consequences that might follow from shouting "fire" in a crowded theater, even if the speaker merely intended this as a prank.

To flesh out this point in environmental terms, we can add to the objective consequences those consequences that precautionary thinking indicates will arise. If the basic rule in both domestic and international law is "Do No Harm," then, whether the harm is immediately evident as a physical result, or a delayed effect, the basic principle should remain intact, although the harm may be the consequence of an impermissible act or of a currently legal one. The role of harm in the recent development of jurisprudence, in both arguments and the disposition of cases, can also be traced in Canadian criminal law.

a. Interpretation, Analogy, and the Focus on Harm: Some Canadian Cases

The rule that you are to love your neighbour, becomes in law, you must not injure your neighbour (Lord Atkins, Donoghue v. Stevensons, (1932) A.C. 562, (1932) AII E.R. Rep.1,101 L.J.P.C.119 (H.L.) C580).

How the law interprets a norm is of primary importance, and the use of analogy appears to be a necessary tool to draw together seemingly disparate facts, under the aegis of the same principle. Interpretation serves a similar purpose. An example of this might be *Regina v. McLeod* (1993) 84 C.C.C.3d 336, 1993 CCC Lexis 3056),where the Yukon Court was presented with an appeal as follows:

Count #2. On or about the 23rd day of October, 1991 at or near Whitehorse, Yukon Territory, did unlawfully commit an offence in that: she did in committing an assault on Karen Mary Woodcock (née Mc Leod), use a weapon, to wit: a dog, contrary to Section 267(1)(a) of the Criminal Code.

The term "weapon" is used in the above section and it is defined in Section 2 as follows:

"weapon" means

(a) anything used or intended for use in causing death or injury to persons, whether designed for that purpose or not, or

(b) anything used or intended for use for the purpose of threatening or intimidating any person, . . .

In this case, all that is needed is to interpret, to understand, and lay out more fully the meaning of "anything," to show that something that is not an inanimate "thing" may have been meant. Given the presence of intent to do harm, the unusual sort of weapon should not have a bearing on whether the event constitutes an assault. The interpretation is therefore both logically and legally well-grounded without the aid of analogical reasoning.

The cases become more complicated when there is no clear intent, and the case then may be viewed as a challenge to the Canadian Charter especially Sections 7 and 11(d). This problem was faced squarely in the *De Sousa* case. "The Facts" are reported in part in the appeal:

> On Dec. 31, 1987 Teresa Santos attended a New Year's Eve Party in Toronto. Shortly after midnight, a fight broke out at the party. As she was attempting to gather her belongings, which were located at a table in the vicinity of the fight, Ms. Santos was struck on the arm by a piece of glass. The glass fragment produced a large gash on her left forearm which required seven stitches to mend the underlying pronator muscle in the arm, and a further seven stitches to mend her skin above the muscle (R. v. DeSousa, (1992) 95 D.L.R.4th 595).

Mr. De Sousa was involved in a fight, and as he threw a bottle against the wall, a glass fragment from that bottle struck a bystander, Teresa Santos. De Sousa's act must be considered in relation to the Criminal Code, and the relevant provision is Section 269:QT269. Unlawfully Causing Bodily Harm

> Everyone who unlawfully causes bodily harm to any person is guilty of

> (a) an indictable offence and liable to imprisonment for a term not exceeding ten years; or

> (b) an offence punishable on summary conviction and liable to imprisonment for a term not exceeding eighteen months.

It is important to note that it is sufficient that an act be unlawful. It is not necessary that the harm be subjectively intended before the act. Sopinka J. addresses this question:

> The mental element of s.269 has two separate aspects. The first aspect of the mental element is the requirement that an underlying offence with a constitutionally sufficient mental element has been committed. Additionally, s. 269 requires that the prosecution prove that the bodily harm caused by the underlying unlawful act was objectively foreseeable (Sopinka, J.; 2. Constitutional Sufficiency).

This case could be viewed then not as an example of interpretation of a norm, but of tracing the objective analogy between the consequences of certain unlawful acts, and the objectively foreseeable harm. The analogy appears to be between the harm from intentional crimes and the harm ensuing from an objectively dangerous, unlawful act. Sopinka J. adds: "I can see no reason why there should be a difference between the two categories of acts. There is no need to differentiate between criminal and noncriminal unlawful acts when one unifying concept is available." Perhaps one could say that it is not really one concept that is used and available, but that the unifying condition between somewhat different concepts, is that the resulting harm is analogous in the two cases. That will be the basis of the argument in Chapters 5 and 6: if the harmful consequences of certain acts are similar, if both entail consequences that produce adverse impacts on innocent persons, then the causal origins of the similar consequences ought to share some significantly analogous features. The consequences of certain actions produce significant harms, although the causative elements and the harms themselves may be quite different from one another. Note for instance the wording of Section 219 of the Criminal Code (Canada, 2001):

219.(1) Criminal negligence—Everyone is criminally negligent who

(a) in doing anything, or

(b) in omitting to do anything that is his duty to do, shows wanton disregard for the lives or safety of other persons.

The wording itself invites a consideration of what is shown by one's actions, not what was thought in the commission (or omission) of those actions. It seems that one can therefore do more than ensure that a certain mental element be present. One can interpret certain norms, when we cannot discover a clear fault element in the actor, that is, a clear intent to produce certain results, but the result is produced nonetheless.

It is important to acknowledge that this section occupies a contentious place in Canadian Criminal Law, often giving rise to split decisions by the Supreme Court of Canada in cases of criminal negligence (Tutton, (1989) 1 S.C.R. 1392, 48 C.C.C.3d 129; Waite v. the Queen (1989) 48 C.C.C.3d 1). In contrast, the Supreme Court restored the acquittal of a man charged with criminal negligence causing death (Anderson v. the Queen, (1990) 53 C.C.C.3d 481). Anderson had been drinking, but not excessively, as proven by a breathalizer test; but he went through a red light, hitting an oncoming vehicle broadside and causing the death of a passenger in that car. Sopinka J., after citing Sections 219 and 220 of the Criminal Code, adds:

The use of the word "negligence" suggests that the impugned conduct must depart from a standard objectively determined. On the other hand, the use of the words "wanton and reckless disregard" suggests that an ingredient of the offence includes a state of mind or some moral quality to the conduct which attracts the sanctions of the criminal law. The section makes it clear that the conclusion that there is a wanton or reckless disregard is to be drawn from the conduct which falls below the standard.

In this case the objective determination on the "impugned conduct" was not sufficient to overcome the lack of intent, as it was in the previous two cases instead.

Martin, J.A. (Ontario Court of Appeal) cites Lord Diplock in his disposition of the *Buzzanga* case (Regina v. Buzzanga and Durocher, 101 D.L.R.3d 488, 1979 DLR Lexis 4197):

> . . . Lord Diplock, however, defined intention in much wider terms. He said that where intention to produce a particular result is a necessary element of an offence, no distinction is to be drawn in law between the state of mind of one who, when he does the act, is aware that it is likely to produce the result but is prepared to take the risk, that it may do so in order to achieve some other purpose . . . (101 D.L.R.3d at 905).

This is a form of recklessness according to Martin, J.A. Now, according to McIntyre, J. of the Supreme Court of Canada, this approach can be extended to the crime of rape. Once again, he cites Dickson, J. "recklessness must also be proven in relation to all the elements of the offence, including absence of consent. This simply extends to rape the same general order of intention as other crimes" (Pappajohn v. The Queen, (1980) 2 S.C.R. 120, Dickson, J. at 146).

At a glance, the crimes here cited are quite different from one another *Buzzanga* deals with promoting hatred; whereas other cases such as *Pappajohn* for instance, are crimes of rape. What links these cases is the lack of a clear, indisputable intent on the part of accused. Another analogical link is the fact that in each case harm was caused. Analogically, the same argument can be extended to omissions:

> I see no rational grounds for excluding from conduct capable of giving rise to criminal liability, conduct which consist of failing to take the measures that lie within one's power to counteract a danger that one has oneself created, if at the time of such conduct one's state of mind is such as constitutes a necessary ingredient of the offence (Lord Diplock, R. v. Miller, House of Lords (1983) 2 A.C. 161, (1983) All E.R. 978, (1983) 2 W.L.R. 539, 77 Cr. App. Rep. 17, March 17, 1983).

What Lord Diplock is referring to once again is "being reckless," in yet another context, that of dropping a cigarette, and setting fire to one's mattress causing damages. These cases' consequences will be discussed in more detail in Chapter 5. The important point for now is to note that, despite the disparity of settings, factual elements, and even the specifics of ensuing results, the state of mind of the respective perpetrators, appears to be analogous and the harm is the result of the negligent, reckless or willfully blind act, in all cases.

b. The Fault Element and Analogy in Sexual Assaults

A Court relies on analogy whenever it draws on similarities or dissimilarities between the present case and previous cases which are not binding precedents applying to the present case (Raz, 1979:202).

We noted the use of analogy in comparing earlier court decisions with newer dispositions of criminal cases, for instance, in regard to assaults. Arguments from analogy attempt to reach further than simple interpretations of existing norms, yet they represent unique vehicles for incorporating different forms of fault and for replacing the former focus on the harms caused by the act, whether it is intended, or fully known in its consequences.

Argument by analogy shows that the new rule is a conservative one, that it does not introduce new discordant and conflicting purposes or value into the law, that its purpose and the values it promotes are already served by existing rules. This is the force of analogical argument but this is also its limitation (Raz, 1979:203).

What analogical reasoning does then, is to support "the continuity of applying and making law" (Raz, 1979:206–207), although the judicial law-making itself may not be conscious on the part of the judge in the case, who may prefer, or be socialized to think that s/he is simply applying the law. Yet, to interpret the "rationale of existing legal rules" and, even more important, "to show the harmony of purpose between existing laws and a new one" (Raz, 1979:208), is to be an active participant in moving law-making forward as may be required by new situations and conditions. The details of some of the new circumstances will be discussed together with the appropriate case law in Chapter 5. For now, we can note some areas where Charter challenges are avoided by reference to analogical circumstances in new situations or situations where there has been a change from the traditional ways of understanding social relation between interacting persons.

An example of changed circumstance might be seen in the *Cuerrier* case (see Chapter 5). What is new is the emergence of a highly contagious, incurable, and fatal disease, AIDS. Having unprotected sex while being fully aware of one's infected status, and without informing one's partners, constitutes a new form of risky, reckless behavior. The fatal harm caused may have no previous intent to infect any specific person chosen as a partner. In fact, neither the illness, nor the possible death of the partner may be desired. Nevertheless, the choice not to disclose one's health status is a case of "fraudulent misrepresentation." Cory, J. says: "The possible consequences of engaging in unprotected intercourse with an HIV positive partner is death. In these circumstances, there can be no basis for distinguishing between lies and a deliberate failure to disclose." The *Cuerrier* case introduces a novel circumstance in that an act that is not normally unlawful when consensual, becomes unlawful because of nondisclosure. Another sort of new case can increasingly be found not in new circumstances, but in a new understanding of those circumstances that have existed through history. Rapes and assaults against women have always existed, but they were limited, for the most part, to the most obvious and violent cases. With the increasing prominence of women's rights, not only the extent of the rape, and the intent of the accused, but the question of consent becomes prominent. Many examples may be found, such as the cases of *Ewanchuk, Pappajohn, Sansregret*, and others. The last two will be discussed in detail in Chapter 5. We can now turn to *Ewanchuk* (R. v. Ewanchuk, (1999) 1 S.C.R. 330, 1999 Can. S.C.R. Lexis 8) as a template of new developments and attitudes, confirmed and codified by a new judicial approach and emphasis, although the rejection of earlier attitudes is also present explicitly in the case.

The case involves a 17-year-old woman who met and conversed with a young man, then agreed she was interested in a possible job with his business and—at his request—willingly followed him to his trailer in the parking lot of a mall in Edmonton, Alberta. No full sexual encounter took place, but extended touching, rubbing, massaging and grinding did, interrupted at times when the woman said "No" at several points. She testified that he always stopped, but that she believed he had locked the trailer's door, and that she was afraid to prompt further assaults and possibly even rape, if she resisted too much.

This case is particularly important, because both the traditional approach to the assaults is cited, in the words of McClung, J. who had been the Appeals Trial Judge, and the new emphasis, as expressed by Mme. L'Heureux-Dubé. Mme. L'Heureux-Dubé (Gonthier, J. concurring) cites at some length statistics about the increasing presence of violence against women, which she views "as much a matter of equality as it is an offence against human dignity and a violation of human right." This is a case about "consent," and that makes the case especially noteworthy.

Consent has traditionally been viewed as based on the state of mind of the accused, and his perception and understanding of the willingness of his partner. McClung, J. saw the case as based on "advances that were far less criminal than hormonal," as he saw the accused as furthering his "romantic intentions." McClung adds that, rather than relying on the intervention of the court, this case was "better dealt with on site—a well-chosen expletive, a slap in the face or, if necessary, a well-directed knee." In addition, her moral character is brought into question, because she was an unwed mother and she was living with her boyfriend.

But the fundamental error, from the current perspective, is that her passivity was taken to imply compliance, hence to imply consent, L'Heureux-Dubé adds:

> This error does not derive from findings of fact but from mythical assumptions that when a woman says "no" she is really saying "yes," "try again" or "persuade me." To paraphrase Fraser C.J. at p.263, it denies women's

sexual autonomy and implies that women are "walking around this country in a state of constant consent to sexual activity."

The contrast between these two approaches, the traditional one based on the mental beliefs of the accused, and the recent interpretation of the law looking primarily to the harms, and not only *physical* harms, could not be more glaring. Susan Estrich also notes that, "rape is most assuredly not the only crime in which *consent* is a defense; but it is the only crime that has *required* the victim to resist physically in order to establish non-consent" (Estrich, 1986:1090) (emphasis added).

I believe that this clearly indicates another analogy between the "new," human rights based interpretation of the crimes of rape and assaults, and the approach to environmental crimes I propose. For the most part, unless massive protests are orchestrated, perhaps with the use of force and the destruction of private property, against harmful environmental practices, people are taken to be consenting to their own harms. Their aggregate and collective "No" is not loud enough to be heard. It is perhaps a stretch to seek an analogy between the assumed consent to sexual activity, and an assumption of consent on the part of general citizens to government sanctioned corporate activities (Westra, 1998). Nevertheless, in the case of women's "acquiescence," the courts now require a much clearer sign than "she did not protest" or "she did not fight." I am proposing that, analogously, assumed consent ought not to suffice when exposure to hazardous substances and processes (whether direct or indirect), is at issue.

c. Mme. Justice L'Heureux-Dubé: Applying Her Method Beyond Family Law

. . . [a] person's native language or mother tongue is understood and spoken without effort, in an intuitive and natural way. My hope is that for the generations that come after us, the language of equality will be spoken in this way, as their mother tongue (L'Heureux-Dubé, 1999:273)

Mme. L'Heureux-Dubé is clear: substantive justice requires equality based on the appropriate treatment of the vulnerable and of minority groups to eliminate the evil of discrimination. She also says:

I believe that if we are to be true to our commitment to enhance the quality of justice in the family law context among other, the focus of legal developments and reforms should be on the notion of equality. Our desire to for equality has its roots in our desire for justice. For inequality is injustice. From inequality and injustice flow oppression, and oppression has no place in the society which we are trying to mould for the future (L'Heureux-Dubé, 1997:105).

This passage opens the way to apply her principles beyond the realm of family law, as it can be applied in other contexts as she states. Basing our understanding on her own words here and in her other articles, judgments, and dissents, I believe that the essence of L'Heureux Dubé's work can be understood and characterized under four main headings:

(1) the quest for substantive justice;
(2) the elimination of discrimination;
(3) the focus on the "rule of reason" over precedent in judgments (a conceptual approach);
(4) the importance of going beyond case law in the judgments, by considering more than just the actions involved, that is, taking "judicial notice" of social facts and common knowledge (see *Moge* below) and looking to:
    (a) the context of the actions,
    (b) the effect of the actions,
    (c) the harms arising from the actions.

All of these categories, both conceptual and factual, can be used analogously beyond the human rights and family law setting which represents the main focus of L'Heureux Dubé's work (Egan v. Canada, (1993), 2 S.C.R.513; Moge v. Moge, (1992) 3 R.F.L.3d 345; Trinity Western, (1996) 27 O.R.3d, 132 D.L.R. 4th; A;G. Canada v. Mossop, (1993) 1 S.C.R. 554; Vriend v. Alberta Alta, (1994) 6 1 S.C.R. 493). This work seeks to pursue a similar approach albeit in a different context and through different avenues. But the methods she proposes add a further legal dimension, beyond showing why environmental harms are assaultive in nature, that is, beyond showing their physical/biological effects on humankind. These effects represent only part of the categories listed above in (4), under subheadings (b) and (c). But the imposition of physical harms and hardships also reveals itself, *ipso facto*, as an attack on those citizens' rights, and the right to equal treatment under the law being the most prominent of these.

She asks the cases to be approached in a different way, as "substantive justice" hinges on taking "judicial notice" of the context of the action to be judged and thereby freeing judicial reasoning from the overly legalistic constraints of proof, and considering primarily those involved in the activity and those affected by it. This approach is based on the language of Section 15.(1) of the Charter (in force since 1985).

15.(1) Equality before and under the law and equal protection and benefit of law—Every individual is equal . . . without discrimination and in particular, without discrimination based on race, national or ethnic origin, colour, religion, sex, age or mental disability.

These enumerated categories, and those that can be deemed "analogous" grounds of discrimination, are routinely appealed to in L'Heureux-Dubé's decisions and dissents. But these grounds are also judged by her to be insufficient to apply the "language of equality" to modern society, and to guarantee to everyone substantive equality (Liu, 2000:445). In order to achieve the latter, the effect imposed on individuals and minority groups must be considered as well.

Turning now to item (3) above, or "the focus on the rule of reason," the background of her position is uncovered. In a 1993 article entitled "By Reason of Authority or by Authority of Reason," Mme. L'Heureux-Dubé contrasts the civil law tradition in Québec, as it "favours the spirit and the content of civil litigation as well as doctrine over strict adherence to judicial precedent" (L'Heureux-Dubé, 1993:1), to common law tradition. After examining the approach of the two systems, she discusses how the Supreme Court of Canada "attempted to reconcile the seemingly contradictory principles of *stare decisis* in both systems" (Ibid. at 2). To clarify this point, she cites Smith and Kerby:

> In discovering the legislator's implied intention the civilian judge does not stop at adopting *by analogy* the rule laid down for some similar matter. He may formulate a rule by deduction from a principle legislatively stated: this is what de does every time he adapts the law to new circumstances (Smith and Kerby, 1975:293)

She continues:

> Consistent with the basic premise that the law is complete the civilian judge is obliged to decide every dispute. The fundamental obligation is expressed Art. 11 of the *Civil Code*, which reads: 11. A judge cannot refuse to adjudicate under pretext of the silence, obscurity or insufficiency of the law (L'Heureux-Dubé, 1993:8).

According to civil law, the judge has a somewhat different role than the common law judge. L'Heureux-Dubé explains that the civil tradition, "places a role of paramount importance on the doctrinal writings of legal scholars," as they are not only writing "about the law, but what they write is "fundamentally constitutive of the law" (Ibid. at 9). To return to tradition and principles, while insisting on the importance, in fact the primacy of reasoned argument, is required to apply her method to our problem. L'Heureux-Dubé says: "To look to the future is to turn to the past. It is from that vintage point that one can best measure both the importance and the direction of the changes that occurred as well as the trends they carry" (L'Heureux-Dubé, 1993:301).

It is necessary, as noted earlier in this work (see Chapter 1), to do more than look to the present context of judgment, to achieve substantive justice, the past traditions inform our understanding of both issues and situations and the general "principles of law" are explicitly part of international law (see Chapter 7).

These principles provide a framework within which to judge (morally) whether the proposed trend simply reflects modern societal values, or whether it is truly valuable in itself, as a step towards substantive justice.

Discrimination is always at issue in cases of environmental justice. For the most part, like the proverbial canaries in the mine, the first to be harmed by inappropriate environmental practices, and those who are harmed most severely, are the most vulnerable, that is, infants, children, fetuses, the aged, and women. This was the case in Walkerton, Ontario (see Chapter 4): those who died were mostly babies, children, and the aged. This is also a general trend for the effects of all kinds of pollution. Climate change affects the whole world with destructive floods, droughts and—in general—weather extremes. The poor in developing countries are most severely affected, as I have argued, because they lack medical and social support infrastructures or the financial ability to find alternative ways of surviving.

Hence, both nationally and internationally, unequal effects follow current practices. Current legal social practices, therefore, are a clear example of social values that indeed exist, but are not worthy to represent the goal or even the effect of present judicial trends: it is sufficient to consider unrestrained consumerism, or, in general, the primacy of economic motives, in that respect. Both perpetuate inequality, locally, nationally, and internationally. The most vulnerable are so because of enumerated or analogous grounds: age, race, ethnicity, and because of their residence in developing countries. In North America, the effects of environmental racism (Bullard, 1994; Westra and Lawson, 2001) again affect the vulnerable as described, especially people of colour (see R. v. Andrews, McIntyre J., (1989) 1 S.C.R. 143, at para. 18). This is the main reason for appealing to reasoned principles, beyond observing society's present beliefs and practices, before judging which rights do not conflict with basic human rights and fundamental freedoms. This equality-informed "judicial notice," perhaps not precisely as Mme. L'Heureux-Dubé intended it, would support a radically changed approach to environmental crimes. The approach to these crimes would gain by viewing some societal trends, such as consumerism, or privatization of government services coupled with the elimination of controls as "rights" that come in direct conflict not only with Section 1 of the Charter, but also with Section 7 and the "right to life and security of a persons." The right to life and security of persons should encompass the right of freedom from the imposition of morbidity or altered functioning of our body, and it would support the rights of the most vulnerable both nationally and globally.

Both situations are part and parcel of modern society: hence, the necessity to go beyond observing what obtains in society, call it "trend" and support it as a new "right." The rights of the poor, the vulnerable, and people of color internationally to be free from environmentally engendered assaults is defensible by reasons (as well as in international law), and does not pose a challenge (even principle) to Section 1 or Section 7 of the Charter. But the rights of the risk-imposers, that is of the corporate/industrial enterprise, and of the complicit governments and politicians instead, could not claim the same defense: profit making is not one of the fundamental freedoms, nor is it a "right: at any cost (be it of health or even life)"; hence, it should not be protected under Section 15(1) (L'Heureux-Dubé, in Egan v. Canada, (1993) 2 S.C.R., at 37 in dissent).

When we consider environmental crimes, Mme. L'Heureux-Dubé's method including all four categories outlined above, is fully appropriate to evaluate and judge the effects of environmental discrimination. Provided that the factual "context" is not taken to be fully determinant of the correct, just judgment, but remains to be examined in the light of reasoned principles, her approach can indeed lead to a better understanding and defense of human rights in the law.

6. FROM "INTERPRETING LAW" TO "MAKING LAW"

We have shown why our method was chosen. First, unprecedented new circumstances exist that render the former approaches to environmental harms both limited and insufficient. The traditional limits viewed all environmental harms as circumscribed to a specific geographical area, or commercial activity, without any understanding of the nature of the intra- and intergenerational impacts of those harms. Second, the ever-expanding considerations of human rights, both nationally and internationally, demand that we integrate environmental health harms within the laws that govern the global obligations we traced. Some of the causes of these harms, are backed by extensive epidemiological research and we studied them with the support of the World Health Organization (Soskolne and Bertollini, 1999).

The section that follows relates the harms described to moral considerations which, as we saw in Raz's, Hart's and Sunstein's discussions of the use of analogy, form an integral part of the judicial process. This is the easiest argument to make, and it has been made by Henry Shue (1996) and for the specific aspects of these harms by the many authors cited above in Section 2. It is a lot harder to go from "this is wrong," to "this is a crime," especially when intent is entrenched in our understanding of "crime." Historically, even such mass disasters as the *Bhopal* case, have been relegated to the realm of torts (Baxi and Paul, 1986). The *Bhopal* case is commonly discussed in most business ethics literature, and is too well known to require repetition at this time. Suffice it to say that it was alleged to try the case in India, would provide a *forum non conveniens*. Even more problematic, was Union Carbide's "Motion to Dismiss." The case was only one of the many dismissed when "brought by foreign citizens and residents, involving foreign accidents, because they are far more appropriately and conveniently tried in the foreign forum" (Baxi and Paul, 1986:29).

Yet, aside from attempts to ignore the carnage caused by Union Carbide, and the insurmountable difficulties involved in flying witnesses to the United States instead, or interviewing persons who are not familiar with either the language or the law in Western countries, Union Carbide's "Motion to Dismiss" also stated:

The complaints allege claims of negligence, strict liability, nuisance, and ultra-hazardous activity on behalf of Indian citizens living in India which must be decided in accordance with Indian principles of law, policy and socio-economic standards (Baxi and Paul, 1986:31).

From our point of view, aside from the obvious critique that can be brought against this disingenuous pronouncement, aimed at escaping the grave responsibility for the disaster, the main point is that even "negligence, strict liability, nuisance, and ultra-hazardous activity," still sounds like something that can be redressed as compensable, at least in elevated monetary terms.

The argument I propose instead, is to view Union Carbide as accused of "Crimes Against Humanity," for the gross breaches of human rights that their operation implied under normal circumstances, and for the disaster this operation created. In that case, The International Court of Justice at The Hague or eventually, The International Criminal Court at Rome, would provide appropriate *fora* for what amount minimally, to mass manslaughter or, perhaps, an entirely new judicial body (Postiglione, 2001). One would hope that such a change of venue may help to eliminate the continuing carelessness and recklessness, especially when it is directed to those in developing countries or—in North America—to people of color. This "juridical deficit" will be discussed in Chapter 8 (Postiglione, 2001).

Corporate crime or institutional crime of this sort must be treated as such because—for the most part—the victims suffer incompensable harms. The question of intent becomes moot: neither in Walkerton, Ontario (see Chapter 4) nor in Bhopal, those who lost a child or a parent can be compensated. Hence, it is basically false to consider and try these crimes under a heading that by itself—even in the best of circumstances—will not possibly elicit a just disposition in a court of law. Financial recompense is not sufficient to redress the injustice perpetrated in environmental crimes any more than the $100.00 payment Ewanchuck offered as recompense for the massage was sufficient to get his charges dismissed.

With disasters of this magnitude (such as Bhopal or Walkerton), it becomes obvious that both the quantitative and the qualitative parameters of environmental harms have changed dramatically in recent times, because of the exponential growth of technological power, and the corresponding scientific knowledge that demonstrate the multiple implications of each case. The burden imposed upon minorities in North America is discussed by Robert Bullard's seminal article "Decision Making" (Bullard, 2001:3–28). In this example, among other suggestions to redress the inequities that people of color suffer in the United States, Bullard proposes several changes in approach, notably, the "Prevention of Harm" (rather than relying on after-the-fact litigation); shifting the "Burden of Proof," that now forces the victim that has been harmed, discriminated against, or "disproportionately affected" to prove their misfortune, while, "Few poor or minority communities have the resources to hire the lawyers, expert witnesses and doctors

needed to sustain such a challenge" (Bullard, 2001:16). Finally, he asks to implement the next step: to "Obviate the Proof of Intent": "Laws must allow disparate
impact and statistical weight as opposed to 'intent'—to infer discrimination
because proving intentional or purposeful discrimination in a court of law is next
to impossible" (Bullard, 2001:18).

The question of differentiated impact is also brought into play in the arguments surrounding the use of affirmative action measures in employment.
Discrimination has both intentional and institutional aspects that disproportionately affect both women and visible minorities (Velasquez, 1998). But, one may
argue, some visible minorities in North America, such as Orientals, are not
demonstrably disadvantaged in any way that may require redress or compensation. In such cases, neither race nor ethnicity are good indicators of when possible quotas or other affirmative action practices should be put in place. Hence, the
use of "impacts" of past practices and attitudes on certain populations but not on
others, can be used to decide who needs to be justly compensated for past wrongs
and for future social goal achievement, and who does not, and Mme. L'Heureux-
Dubé's approach is best suited to achieve justice.

In conclusion, the use of analogy was proposed as it can be used to help
develop morally adaptive laws that can do justice to both changed circumstances,
and the developing sensitivity to human rights issues.

a. "Past Impacts" and "Future Social Goals": The December 13, 2002, Decision of the Supreme Court of Canada

As noted in the Section 5.c, devoted to Mme. L'Heureux-Dubé's judgments,
both her own work and other recent work on analogy admit the importance of (1)
desirable social goals; (2) past harmful impacts; and (3) the role of judges in
assisting to shape the law for the protection of the public interest. These principled and desirable goals are all present in a recent decision of the Supreme Court
of Canada in Québec. Following the introduction of the Tobacco Act of 1995, and
the Tobacco Product Information Regulations (enacted pursuant to Sections 17
and 33 of the Act on June 8, 2000), and the enforcement of large and explicit
package warnings, several tobacco companies (J.T.I. MacDonald Corporation,
Rothman, Benson and Hedges, Inc., and Imperial Tobacco Canada Limited), chal-
lenged the Tobacco Act (S.C. 1997, Chapter 13) in three separate actions. They
asked the court to declare the Act unconstitutional under the Canadian Charter of
Rights and Freedoms (Part I of the Constitution Act, 1982, being Schedule B to
the Canada Act, 1982 (U.K.), 1982, Chapter 11). The plaintiffs argued that the Act
violated their freedom of expression under Section 2(b) of the Charter, and other
rights under Sections 7, 8, and 11.

The difficulty in adjudicating this case is that these are basic and, in fact, fundamental rights that are in question, as freedom of expression is pitted against the

protection of public health and the public interest in general. This conflict also underlies the analogy that links this case to environmental cases, but, in the latter, the conflict is often with corporate freedom and free trade, not only with the freedom to advertise and promote products, as the freedom to produce and to encourage consumption must be restrained as well.

In essence, as we shall see below, public health is viewed as primary, and its protection trumps both the freedom to promote and free expression. As in Mme. L'Heureux-Dubé's judgments (see Section 5.c), we will find the major emphasis on harms and the harmed groups, and on the consequences of such harms. The foundation for both kinds of cases is solid science supporting the harm claims. The December 13, 2002, judgment used the extensive scientific evidence available on the effects of tobacco, and the Canadian Cancer Society intervened as did several doctors many of whom reported on the work of the World Health Organization and their findings on the effects of tobacco on individual health (these included Dr. Nancy-Michelle Robitaille; Dr. Leonard Ritter; Dr. Adrian Wilkinson, Dr. Richard Pollay, Dr. Ronald M. Davis and others). However, their evidence emphasizes some of the main differences between tobacco and environmental harms, although I argue that the analogy remains strong enough to support our claim that ecocrimes should be treated and regulated minimally, in a similar manner. Some of these differences are:

(1) Tobacco is physically addictive, whereas environmental disintegrity, a product of the technologically "advanced" lifestyle of affluent countries, is not addictive in itself. Yet the "lifestyle" is vigorously promoted as the desirable indication of modernity; hence, the corporate activities that produce the physical harms are only addictive in a figurative or emotional sense, not in the biological one;

(2) Tobacco produces a long and well-documented list of various forms of morbidity, whereas the discovery of ecological harms is more recent and less specific: in many cases there are cumulative and synergistic effects that produce the harm; in some cases, the capacity of the immune system is generally lowered, hence, it becomes far less easy to produce a specific list of directly caused diseases, unless the individuals at risk live or work close to the ecologically compromised site (e.g., a tannery, uranium ponds, heavy industrial or carbon monoxide emissions, or water infected with e-coli);

(3) Although the infringement of Section 7 of the Charter's "right to life, liberty and security of persons" is present in both cases in a physical sense that has not so far been clearly allowed, despite the efforts of the Canadian Environmental Law Association (CELA), the use of tobacco is—at least initially—a personal choice intended to produce pleasure. In contrast, there is no pleasure in breathing air containing particulates, or drinking unsafe water, although on the whole the modern lifestyle does provide some individuals with plea-

sures and satisfaction only indirectly linked to harmful industrial practices and products. Another substantial difference is the fact that there is little or no element of choice in environmental exposure: most North American states and provinces do not offer a voting choice that might eliminate these practices. For instance, in North America there is no no-nuclear political choice possible.

Thus, both similarities and differences in the factual aspects of tobacco use on one side, and of environmental violence on the other, manifest and support some aspect of the argument by analogy here proposed. Similarities (and some differences) can also be found in the law. But the facts had to be established first as the tobacco case could not be made without the scientific evidence of the effects of its use. So too the presence of credible scientific evidence linking pollution and disintegrity to human health effects is the necessary starting point of the analogy.

Before turning to the laws relating to the risk imposers through the manufacture and sale of tobacco products, and the risk/harm imposers through environmental hazards, we need to consider the basis for both arguments: the Constitutional questions that can be raised in both cases. The first Constitutional question hinges on the application of the "peace, order and good government of Canada" (pursuant to Section 91 of the Constitution Act, 1867, as being enacted pursuant to the criminal law power in Section 91 (27) thereof). The second Constitutional question is based on the freedom of expression as set out in Section 2(b) of the Canadian Charter of Rights and Freedoms, and whether this "does constitute a reasonable limit on that right as can be demonstrably justified pursuant to Section 1 thereof" (RJR-MacDonald Inc. v. Canada (A.G.), (1995) 3 S.C.R. 199, at 239–240).

These are the Constitutional question that frames the moral conflict between two fundamental rights, in legal terms. To be able to answer these questions, the next step is to identify the *purpose* of the law: what is the "evil or injurious or undesirable effect that the law is supposed to combat" (Ibid. at 238). First, it is desirable to introduce "extrinsic evidence," although clear rules on its admissibility are not available. But there are some very strong reasons for the introduction of such evidence:

[62] a) extrinsic evidence is not only permissible, but often essential; . . .

b) when examining legislative facts, the court must take into account the context in which the legislation is enacted; . . .

g) the court must have the best evidence available at the time;

The importance of extrinsic evidence is obvious in both the tobacco case and—in principle—in environmental cases: the quest for substantive justice is based on the understanding of both "context" of present harms and on the evidence of consequences. Only by facing squarely this evidence, will it be possible to see that we cannot simply "strike a balance between the claims of legitimate but competing social values" (McKiney v. University of Guelph, (1990) 3 S.C.R. 229, at 285–286, La Forest J.). La Forest's approach may be good and desirable when gains and losses envisioned are similar both in their nature and magnitude; then such a procedural justice ideal may suffice.

But the right to free expression is not equal to the right to life, which is primary, temporally, conceptually, and morally. The result of curtailing the freedom of expression of tobacco companies, is to restrict their promotional efforts, hence, at most, their sales and ultimately their profits. But, as Mme. Mme. L'Heureux-Dubé stated, there is no constitutional right to profit (L'Heureux-Dubé in dissent, Egan v. Canada, (1993) 2 S.C.R., at 37). There is, however, a fundamental "right to life and security of persons" (Charter, Section 7). The Supreme Court's judgment in, *RJR-MacDonald Inc. v. Canada (A.G.)* ((1995) 3 S.C.R. 199) in the section on Freedom of Expression (Section 2(b), in "Contextual Analysis," states:

> [217] We must ask ourselves what values are at stake in the case at bar. On the one hand, we have the constitutionally guaranteed freedom of expression; on the other, we have the right to life guaranteed under section 7 of the Charter. By extension, the Parliament is obligated to promote the health of all Canadians.

This paragraph is—to my knowledge—unprecedented in Canadian Supreme Court judgments, and it echoes, to some extent, the approach of the EU Court of Human Rights, in some of its groundbreaking judgments (see *Guerra v. Italy*, or *Lopez-Ostra v. Spain*, Chapter 8), where the right to life is extended to the right to "biological" or "physical integrity," precisely in environmental disputes. The passage therefore strongly supports the argument of this work as a whole. If Parliament is "obligated to promote the health of all Canadians," then anything that can be proven to represent an assault on the health of Canadians is to be clearly proscribed.

Ample scientific evidence is available, documenting the many harmful health effects not only of "environmental crimes" or disasters (French and Mastny, 2001), but also of the day-to-day business operations of corporate modernity, as recorded by the WHO and listed in this chapter (see Guidotti and Gosselin, 1999; Sampat, 2001). Climate change also produces desertification and floods that result in famines in the developing world (Brown, 2002; Pogge, 2001). All of these impacts and consequences are global in character, although the impacts vary from one area to another, and the geographical location of Canada, for instance, provides some advantage, as does the social infrastructure available to provide some mitigation to affected regions.

Nevertheless, if Parliament is obligated to protect the life/health of all Canadians, then it cannot limit its regulatory powers to the establishment of environmental regulations and of limits to industrial operations. These regulations and limits are negotiated with the risk/harm imposers themselves; that is, they are defined in cooperation with the polluting industries. Parliament should have the responsibility to ensure that its regulatory framework is capable of guaranteeing life and health: if that is Parliament's responsibility in regard to an activity that citizens, (1) find pleasurable, and (2) choose with some degree of freedom, then it seems clear that that responsibility is much greater when citizens have neither choice nor pleasure in regard to the harms they incur. Even the presence of a due diligence defense (see Chapter 5) ought not to apply, as the diligence, even when conscientiously practiced, still stops practices only at the prescribed "safe" level, something that bears repeating, is negotiated, not impartially researched and decided by noninterested parties (see Chapter 4).

Taking these factual difficulties into consideration, we can now turn to a reexamination of the proposed analogy between harm due to the use of tobacco, and environmental harm, from the legal standpoint of the risk/harm imposers. When considering the legal rights of the tobacco corporations, the law must start by considering the *Oakes test* (R. v. Oakes, (1986) 1 S.C.R. 103, at 137, Dickson J.), which sets out the framework for applying Section 1 of the Charter. The first requirement is to apply the civil standard of proof, "proof by a preponderance of probability," as the criminal standard of "proof beyond a reasonable doubt" would be too onerous. To justify limiting a fundamental right, a "pressing and substantial objective" is required (R. v. Sharpe, (2001) 1 S.C.R. 45, at 82). This is indeed the chief consideration underlying the *Oakes test*, and in either case, that is, in the case of tobacco use, and in that of exposure to environmental disintegrity, the harms imposed are amply documented, and in both cases do provide a "pressing and substantial objective" to the court.

The presence of this objective underlies the test itself, and its three components:

(1) The means must be rationally connected to the objective;
(2) The means must impair the right to freedom as little as possible;
(3) The deleterious effects of the means must be proportional to their salutary ones (R. v. Oakes, (1986) 1 S.C.R. 103, at 138–139).

But this test, like the Charter itself, must also be placed in its proper linguistic, philosophic and historical contexts (R. v. Big M Drug Mart Ltd., (1985) 1 S.C.R. 295, at 344, Dickson J.). On the same topic, Bastarache J. said:

The analysis under s.1 of the Charter must be understood with a close attention to context. This is inevitable, as the test devised in *R .v. Oakes* [1986] 1 S.C.R. 103, requires a court to establish the objective of the impugned provision, which can only be accomplished by canvassing the nature of social problems which it addresses (Thomson Newspaper Co. v. Canada (A.G.), (1998) 1 S.C.R. 877, at para. 87, Bastarache J.).

Mme. L'Heureux-Dubé wrote as follows in *R. v. Sharpe* ((2001) 1 S.C.R. 45, at 138–139.): "In keeping with the underlying purpose of s.l and the democratic values which it seeks to encourage, this Court has eschewed a formalistic and rigid application of the framework set out in *Oakes* in favour of a *principled* and *contextual* approach" (emphasis added).

Here she opens the door to allow attributing different values to particular rights and freedoms, thus supporting, in principle at least, the claim advanced above about the primacy of the right to life and health, with respect to any other fundamental value. Thus, the third component of the *Oakes* test, that is, the proportionality requirement can be met easily, because saving life and health surely weighs far more strongly on the side of "salutary effects" than on the side of the "deleterious effects" of limiting freedom of speech.

When we turn to environmental violence, the salutary effects must be sufficient to offset something far more serious than even the right to free speech (understood as the freedom to advertise in the most enticing manner possible, including lifestyle ads): they must be strong enough to offset the needed radical change of our present economic and bureaucratic institutions. Those affected, should the required regulations be adopted, would be the legal entities, the corporations whose power has increased exponentially from the time of their inception, but whose responsibility has been, legally, limited for a long time.

However, there are several problems we need to consider. First, when environmental polluters are viewed as "risk/harm imposers," like tobacco manufacturers, they bear no particular malice to any specific individual or population. Cory J. says:

> The common law has long acknowledged a distinction between truly criminal conduct and conduct otherwise lawful, which is prohibited in the public interest. Earlier, the designation *mala in se* and *mala prohibita* were initiated; today prohibited acts are generally either classified as either crimes or regulatory offences (R. v. Wholesale Travel Group Inc., (1991) 3 S.C.R. 216).

Environmental offenses presently fit under the category of regulatory offenses. But, as I have argued here, given the consequences and impacts, both present and past of these offenses, the appellation of "true crimes" is a better fit. Nevertheless, Cory J. adds:

> The objective of regulatory legislation is to protect the public or broad segments of the public (such as employees, consumers and motorists, to

name but a few) from the potentially adverse effects of otherwise lawful activity. Regulatory legislation involves a shift of emphasis from the protection of individual interests and the deterrence and punishment of acts involving moral fault to the protection of public and societal interests. While criminal offences are usually designed to condemn and punish past, inherently wrongful conduct, regulatory measures are generally directed to the prevention of future harm through the enforcement of minimum standards of conduct and care (Ibid. at 218–219).

The point is a valid one in principle: as with tobacco regulation, the prevention of future harm is an important consideration. Yet, when this emphasis prevents the recognition and the punishment of "past, inherently wrongful conduct," then it is important to find a way in the law to preserve both emphases through legislation, not just one.

The introduction of the due diligence defense is insufficient: the "absolute liability offence which did not permit of any explanation by the accused," as "the performance of the act alone was sufficient to establish culpability." *R. v. Pontes*, (1995) 3 S.C.R. 44, at 57, Cory J.), indicates that some offenses like those regulated by the Tobacco Act should belong to this category. One might counter that leaving environmental crimes to be controlled by regulations as they are now, may help with the prevention of harm, whereas the law tends to deal with grave crimes only after the fact.

Even the case that provides the starting point for this analogical extension is itself a case where prevention would have been highly desirable. But the very fact that the tobacco industry is and has been regulated, did not really suffice to prevent their crimes and the harms they produced. On the contrary, the regulatory framework, when breached, can be dealt with, at most, as a tort, giving rise to monetary compensation (see Chapter 4, the *Walkerton* case), whereas the threat of a real jail term for the rich and powerful corporate CEOs might have given them pause.

Thus, even when dealing with regulatory matters, and following the tobacco companies in their claim that the present situation represents an illegal search and seizure of their products, infringing the rights protected under Section 8 of the Constitution, still we cannot accept their argument . In *Hunter* (*Hunter v. Southam, Inc.*, (1984) 2.S.C.R. 145, at 159–160), Dickson J. addresses the question of "reasonable expectations":

> The guarantee of security from *unreasonable* search and seizure only protects a *reasonable* expectation. The limitation on the right guaranteed by s.8, whether it is expressed negatively as freedom from "unreasonable" search and seizure, or positively as an entitlement to a "reasonable" expectation of privacy, indicates that an assessment must be made whether in a particular situation the public interest in being left alone by

government must give way to the government's interest in intruding on the individual's privacy in order to advance its goals, notably those of law enforcement.

The main focus of how these matters ought to be handled in order to achieve substantive justice remains clearly in the public interest. That is also the main argument in environmental cases. As factual and contextual evidence is readily available for both types of harms, the government, unfortunately, still benefits in both cases, from a continuation of the status quo, through taxes on cigarettes, as well as taxes and job creation from successful but hazardous industrial or other commercial operations. But the quest for substantive rather than purely procedural justice should be emphasized, so that these companies would face the punishment consonant with the gravity of their crimes.

The burden of proof should also shift: industry ought to prove the safety of their products and operations, before they are allowed to operate, rather than allowing the public to become, in effect, guinea pigs to demonstrate the possible safety of their operations. Similarly, and to achieve the same purpose of public protection, "allowable limits" of noxious substances must be ruthlessly readjusted according to the precautionary principle, and with the input of impartial scientists and ethicists only, with no decisive industry participation. If any of these desirable developments will take place, then this cardinally important decision may help to restrain risk/harm imposers in all fields.

CHAPTER 3

INSTITUTIONALIZED VIOLENCE, CIVIL DISOBEDIENCE IN THE NATIONAL AND INTERNATIONAL STATE SYSTEM

1. CITIZENS, THE ENVIRONMENT AND THE LAW

The unexamined life is not worth living (Socrates).

Earth Day 1970 is often cited as the beginning of the modern environmental movement. Direct action has been a tactic often employed to bring the cause of the environment to the attention of the world. I have argued that the defense of individual (micro) integrity and of macro, or system integrity, cannot be separated; that the defense of human rights, particularly the right to one's biological integrity and unimpaired normal function, goes hand in hand with the defense of life's habitat (Westra, 1998).

This point was reinforced and emphasized in the recent violent protests at the World Trade Organization meetings in Seattle (1999). Rather than being limited to such well-known "action" groups as "Earth First" or "Greenpeace," demonstrators in Seattle included workers and labor unions, animal rights activists and defenders of endangered areas and species. Environmentalists, for the most part, have focused on arguments and legal actions, as they hoped to win their "battle" through new regulations and through the courts, in the application of existing laws (Swanson, 1999).

With the exception of the deliberate and courageous ecosabotage practiced by Earth First (their motto: "No compromise in defense of Mother Earth"), Greenpeace, and various tree-spikers in Canadian and U.S. forests in the Northwest, the norm for environmentalists has been limited to polite and legal protests. Yet, dating back to the civil disobedience of Henry David Thoreau, and to the "Quaker doctrine of placing oneself in harm's way in defense of principles" (Swanson, 1999), to the more recent protests against the Vietnam War, there is at least a continuing thread that sustains North American protests.

Still, such a strong reaction as the one that took place in Seattle has not been seen in a long time. A Canadian journalist, Madeleine Drohan, says, "strange but true: trade stirs fiery anger" (Drohan, 1999). But it is not trade as such that sparks and sustains the anger so clearly in evidence in Seattle. Some of the placards waved by the crowds better capture the main points of protesters: "Canadian

Water Not For Sale" or "The WTO—The End of Democracy," and perhaps best of all, "Life is Not a Commodity—Shut Down the WTO." Hence, not trade as such, but trade of *what*, and trade *how* were the main issues. Naomi Klein calls the converging movements of disparate groups and activists who come together in protest all over the world, "coalitions of coalitions." She further describes the phenomenon: "Thousands of groups today are all working together against forces whose common thread is what might broadly be described as the privatization of every aspect of life, and the transformation of every activity and value into a commodity" (Klein, 2001:81–82).

As biologist and ecologist James Karr (University of Washington) remarked, such furor and dedication among students had not been seen since the times of the Vietnam War. This supports our thesis: in both cases violence was and is the issue: violence against humankind, violence against nature, violence against animals, and against human rights. Thus, what happened in Seattle was not, as U.S. President Bill Clinton commented, "a really interesting hoopla" that simply showed "people's interest in trade" (Drohan, 1999). Instead, it was a strong revolt against the legal but violent intrusions into our lives, our health, and the normal function of humans, other creatures, and natural systems in the name of prosperity, technological advancement, and even progress.

The World Trade Organization purports to be the body of negotiation and international rules that best suit the 135 member countries, and the primary enforcer of them through their considerable power (global trade has grown from U.S. $58 billion in 1948, to $5.3 trillion in 1998). But regulation of agriculture, genetically engineered foods, and respect for workers' rights are all issues that should have been on the table at the Seattle WTO summit, and are not issues that can be decided without public input on one hand, or clearly outlined in defensible principles on the other.

Some advance the argument that insofar as the WTO is composed of national trade ministers from countries with democratically elected leaders, their procedures remain essentially democratic. But this argument is not sound as given—in fact, it emphasizes the failure of present democratic national governments to truly engage in a multinational discourse, and to be able to propose and support choices that represent the common good. No environmental hazard is truly limited in scope and sufficiently localized so it enables even local citizenry to produce a majority decision that is informed, fair, nonracist, and nonspeciesist (Westra, 2000a). In fact, often even local environmentalists (such as those in bioregional groups) intent upon defending some specific area within their turf, may not be willing to arrive at decisions that are truly sound from an ecological point of view. In a recent chapter entitled "At What Scale Should we Manage Biodiversity?," Reed Noss relates his problem in communicating with bioregionalists whose position was against incorporating global concerns in their local policies. Noss cites the representatives of a "biodiversity workshop" for the U.S. Bureau of Land Management in Redding, CA:

> We don't care about what's going on in Florida, the Rocky Mountains, or Southern California . . . We have serious problems we need to deal with right here in our own watershed . . . Why do we need to hear about mass extinction in the geological past, human overpopulation, or global warming? We have to put on a consensus response to the draft forest plan (Noss, 1998:96–116).

This attitude is one I have discussed with reference to the Canadian fish wars experience (Westra, 1998). "Think globally, act locally" sounds good, but unfortunately, it is not normally accepted even by ecologists and environmentalists, the main groups that ought to be receptive to such a message. Noss proposes a better alternative: "think at multiple scales, act at multiple scales" (Noss, 1998:97).

To better understand this problem, one might start by noting the difference between various categories of environmental hazards. Would-be-victims, or those who are most likely to be affected by the siting of a hazardous facility such as a dump site or a nuclear power station, belong to a category I will term "Presently Threatened Populations" (PTPs). Those who are facing a loss of natural habitat, replaced by a less threatening facility, such as a parking lot or the opening of new roads, whose presence does not pose an immediate or direct health threat, can be viewed as "Populations Under Delayed Threats" (PDTs). The former (PTPs) can indeed provide a balance to those who would impose a threat upon them, by offering a strong resistance and insisting on their rights to equal protection. PDTs cannot do the same, because of their usual and well-documented lack of interest in the widespread and long-term effects of a hazardous activity when an immediate advantage might be given to their limited group if they comply (Westra, 2000a). But is it sufficient to recognize the influence of parochial self-interest in the local citizenry, parallel to that found in corporate and world-trade attitudes? There might be some other issues at play. It is quite different to push exclusively for corporate profit without consideration for the possible harms suffered by affected parties outside one's group, whether these harms are immediate or delayed. It is quite another for a country's citizens, many of whom are informed on environmental hazards, to continue to make ecologically harmful choices. It is worth asking whether some other element might play a part in the basic passivity and complacency manifested in these wrong choices.

In keeping with the analysis of violence in war, there is another aspect that could be a contributing factor in this area, as it is in much of the gratuitous violence that is commonplace in war despite principles established at Nuremberg (Wasserstrom, 1974). In war, the problem is that of (unthinking) obedience to orders (Kelman and Hamilton, 1989), a problem already studied and discussed also in psychological research. The question is how (and whether) that problem also might be present in environmental violence. In practice, why do many who derive no specific or direct personal advantage from the status quo support it wholeheartedly, despite the future harms to which they might expose not only to others but even to themselves?

It is not, as it is in the context of war, a question of unquestioning obedience to superior orders. Rather, some aspects of the problem appear to foster the adherence to hazardous practices as well. Kelman and Hamilton outline three contributing factors that tend to weaken moral inhibitions against violence: "authorizations," "routinization," and "dehumanization" (Kelman and Hamilton, 1989). Some elucidation may be in order. The first characteristic of these crimes of obedience is the fact that the violence is authorized, hence being beyond individual consideration, and beyond the control of one's conscience. Of course individual citizens and consumers are not under the control of a superior army or of any other specific authority, whose function it is to direct their activities. The authority is much more subtle than that: it is the expectation of an unconcerned, overly optimistic and overconsuming society that somehow forces, or at least directs, compliance with the "ideal" of a modern state of the art citizenry. The preoccupation with fitting in, or being part of the crowd, and the desire to be perceived as a winner rather than a loser (note the language parallels with war and battles) is what tends to dull one's sensitivity toward others and set aside any sense of responsibility toward their plight, and even our own.

If we overconsume, it is because everyone does it, or at least, everyone would like to. If we insist on pursuing "technical maximality" (McGinn, 1997) in our life, despite the fact that the rights we insist on are totally unattainable to the citizens of developing countries, it is because we do not want to see the connection between what we believe we have a right to have, and the simpler basic rights of those who also have a right to *be*. The authority then is different, multifaceted, and such that we cannot really pinpoint those in charge and responsible for the apparent authorization to harm. We see others doing the same on television, we hear these practices described as part of our modern, technically advanced lifestyle, and we no longer feel the need to question the legitimacy of these activities or consider their consequences.

Thus, the authority is neither clearly spelled out, nor direct. It amounts to a diffuse, all-pervasive justification based on the institutionalized normalcy of practices so common in their everyday unfolding that no question needs to be raised. In this somewhat novel sense, authorization almost blends in with the next factor contributing to weaken our innate moral revulsion in the face of violence, that is, routinization. When an action or activity becomes routine, the need to question it is eliminated. It becomes what we always do, or what everyone does, and the assumption is that whatever questioning might have been necessary happened long ago, before the activity was adopted and institutionalized. In this way, all possible negative moral implications are relegated to someone else's analysis, in a distant past when—we believe—consequences and implications were confronted, analyzed and probably discarded.

Thus, routinization in relation to morality becomes what precedent is in relation to law. Actions acquire legitimacy simply because they have been presumably debated, then found acceptable or even right, at an earlier time. Precedent in law can be used to establish desirable goals upon which future moral decisions can be based (Westra, 1995; Westra et al., 2000). But because we are discussing precedent now, the unquestioning acceptance of the status quo simply supports a mechanized response. This is not acceptable as it represents the very antithesis of human moral responsibility. According to Kant, for example, our very dignity as human beings is based on our autonomy, or our ability to use reason to prescribe universally applicable moral laws to ourselves.

As Socrates said, "the unexamined life is not worth living," and that maxim applies to everyone in the present, not to a one-time examination upon which a decision was reached on the morality of an action in the distant past, once and for all. At best, we once might have had good arguments in support of a particular activity. At worst, no one ever examined it from the moral standpoint, and the activity was judged on its efficiency, or its desirability and acceptability or other such consequential perspectives. Hence, it would be morally irresponsible to accept unquestioningly any activity on the basis that it has been institutionalized in the past, and that it is routine. Further, as Aquinas argued in his presentation of the natural law principles, even original principles must be reexamined in the light of later factual conditions. No doubt, even the most well-intentioned individual in the earlier decades of the 20th century could not be held responsible for decision about actions with environmental consequences that have only become apparent in the last 30 years. Therefore, neither routine nor precedent ought to govern what we view as acceptable.

The final factor, dehumanization, follows from the two previous ones. What are the consequences of our activities on others? The first step in order to permit us to even open up this question, is to accept the moral considerability of others. Even those who find it hard to accept a biocentric or ecocentric ethic of environmental concern (Sterba, 2000; Westra, 1994; Westra, 1998) tend to accept that at least all humans must be morally considered, and that their basic rights should not be in question. In order to respect human rights, these must be attached to present, identifiable humans. However, most have difficulties with those who are geographically or temporarily removed, and even anthropocentrists are not exactly clear in their support of all humans, but at best defend the rights of those who are present here and now (Westra, 1998).

The well-known example of our vague reaction of distress when confronted with a far away disaster where thousands perish in Asia, but our very profound terror upon being informed that we are to lose even one finger is a case in point. Our reaction in this case not only manifests egoism, but it also emphasizes the dehumanization of the other, especially when this other is indeed different ethnically, racially, or otherwise. The violence routinely inflicted without hesitation or remorse by environmental means on faceless millions only becomes quite real when one of us is affected. Even then, the effort to find a culprit, or to blame this or that corporate manufacturer, is of paramount concern rather than acknowledging our cooperation in supporting the institutionalized violence of which this specific hazard is a part.

2. THE CLIMATE AND BACKGROUND OF THE "CRIMES OF OBEDIENCE"

Rebellion to tyrants is obedience to God (Thomas Jefferson).

In trying to understand why citizens of reasonably enlightened countries, governed by democracies, are so willingly led to rubberstamp activities, lifestyles, and regulations that ultimately harm them, we need to move beyond the obvious answer, the primacy of economic comfort. In a previous chapter we examined institutionalized ecoviolence through another lens connected with war: that of the psychological aspects of soldiers' training and motivation (see Chapter 1). Yet to speak of individual psychology may be slightly misleading as the general climate within which the crimes are perpetrated, often unnoticed and unrecognized as such, is one of political institutions and collective practices, not just of individual psychological inclinations. Several aspects of this political orientation have bearing on these forms of violence: (1) the question of language and common expressions; (2) the orientation of groups to question or not to question governance and authority; and (3) the commonly held beliefs about personal responsibility in violent situations, following upon the decisions of the Charter of the International Military Tribunal of Nuremberg (Wasserstrom, 1974).

The role of language emerges as an obvious tool of national power structures to achieve compliance with practices that might be deemed unacceptable were they presented to the public with a name that is truly descriptive. In Nazi Germany, as Hannah Arendt points out, there were 'language rules," a code name for the "normalization of atrocities": murder and liquidation were translated into "final solution," or "evacuation" and "special treatment" (Arendt, 1964). In the environmental context, such examples abound as well. At the time when the Newfoundland hunt of seal pups was a growing concern, the pro-hunt group referred to the massacre of defenseless baby seals as "culling the herds" or "fulfilling their fishery quotas," and "harvesting" their allotment. All of these expressions are also used today in other contexts. For instance, Japanese supporters of increased whaling quotas use them in attacking the arguments of animal ethicists, environmentalists, and all others who protest treating the whale, one of the most intelligent mammals on Earth, as a fishery catch.

These uses of language effectively achieve closure of all arguments against these practices before they can be heard and considered. Debates about the moral considerability of large mammals are not relevant if what is at stake is simply a fishery issue. In addition, arguments about the right of any special interest group to deplete an ecosystem upon which we all depend become moot if the issue is deliberately kept confined to local, immediate socio-economic concerns. The fact that even the local anthropocentric concerns are not well served for the long term by such practices and policies is never even brought to the table. Yet those who will be affected just as much as the species under consideration have a clear right to know. This was indeed the case in the Canadian fish wars, a war with no winners (Westra, 1998).

Obscuring language is an important part of the role of authorities as they mediate between their own interests and that of their allies, and the common good of the general public. But the language of "good" and "evil" or "right' and "wrong" is not ever used or considered, or it may be used, as it has been used by the Bush administration, as a public relation tool. As Mark Sagoff demonstrated, questions of rational values are ignored, as the focus is on consumers' preferences and market choices. This limits the consideration to psychological and emotional choices, individually aggregated, and leaving the community moral values untouched (Sagoff, 1988). For example, at the time of the awareness and panic about the chemical Alar in apples, the efforts of industry were directed toward altering public perceptions and alleviating public fear. This was the industry objective, rather than the obvious quest for immediate, impartial studies to determine the toxicity of the product in question while withdrawing both the product and fruit contaminated with it from the market. Note the lack of emphasis on the reality of the problem, coupled with a strong thrust to psychological manipulation of the public. This is routine with industry, as they call concerned people "hysterical," "ignorant" or worse (Shrader-Frechette, 1991; Shrader-Frechette, 1993).

In the environmental field, many should be able to understand the implications of goals considered to be normal and desirable, such as growth, development, progress, or even trade-off, when these concepts are presented as unmitigated goods. Environmentalists should know that the other side of growth is unsustainability and of development, overconsumption; and they should also know that progress may mask unsafe technology transfers or risky business sitings. "Trade-off" may well be another word for any of these evils, or even for environmental racism (Shrader-Frechette, 1991; Rees, 1998; McGinn, 1997; Rees and Westra, 2003; Westra, 1998; Westra and Lawson, 2001).

Another aspect of the problem emerges when people's general orientation toward those in authority is clarified. Kelman and Hamilton provide an interesting analysis of general types of possible responses to government authority that is somewhat more detailed than Kohlberg's analysis of moral development

(Kohlberg, 1984). Kelman and Hamilton propose three major categories of personal responses, based on "three orientations":

> (These) refer to the three components of the political system through which citizens may be bound and integrated in it. They represent three processes through which the legitimacy of the state is generated, assessed and maintained in the eyes of individuals (Kelman and Hamilton, 1996:268).

These political orientations are: "Rule orientation," "role orientation," and "value orientation."

The meaning of these orientations is such as one would expect from the terms that characterize them. The rule orientation describes those who follow rules and uphold them, as they are socialized to comply rather than to question. These persons see moral principles as largely irrelevant to the actions of both citizens and state: their level of moral reasoning can be described as "preconventional." They view their responsibility as limited to avoiding "sanctions for nonperformance" (Kelman and Hamilton, 1996:269).

Before continuing with the characteristics of the other two groups, two points are worthy of note with respect to rule orientation. The first is the connection between violence and group characteristics on one hand, and political process on the other. The second is that, as the authors themselves indicate, these characteristics also correspond to general economic and especially educational levels. As we shall see, only the value orientation group is prepared, willing, and able to question policies from the standpoint of principles.

The role orientation is somewhat different, although the absence of both questioning and the consideration of principles is still in evidence. This group consists of individuals who identify with the political powers and who feel that their obligation to the government overrides personal morality (Kelman and Hamilton, 1989:269). At this level of moral reasoning, only a threat directed to the government's status would prompt anyone to protest. Under normal conditions, they are reliable supporters of the government, and prepared to fulfill their role obligations, although this description might be better thought of as authority-oriented.

It is only those with a value orientation who act from internalized standards for evaluating consequences of actions, whose moral reasoning is at the "postconventional level," and who question and take an active part in formulating policies in the light of moral principles (Kelman and Hamilton, 1989:269). Without entering into the details of the origins of these orientations, what is terrifying is the fact that only those with high education and the professional and economic status to direct and control events may act on a value orientation. Kelman and

Hamilton say "the essence of value orientation is independent judgement in the face of authority's orders" (Kelman and Hamilton, 1989:332).

The recent evidence of the passionate involvement of people of all educational levels and positions in the protests against the G-7 gives one some hope. Perhaps when the anger and the passionate opposition to authority become truly overwhelming, even those who might—under other circumstances—be willing to acquiesce, might be prepared to act out their outrage, trusting their own "independent judgment."

Another impediment to activism lies in fragmenting activities and ensuring that tasks are apportioned to many, in order to produce a certain result, diffuses the sense of agency on the part of each actor, and with it the sense of responsibility owed to those who will be affected by the act itself. It is much easier to continue to play a part and to view one's contribution as a simple collaboration, rather than an act for which one might bear responsibility, if one feels like a powerless part of a large impersonal process, preordained by some authority. In contrast, "People who feel empowered and efficacious, who have learned to judge authority from independent alternative perspectives, and who participate in public decision-making from a pluralistic base, are inclined to see themselves as responsible agents" (Kelman and Hamilton, 1989:334).

The same contrast between passive acceptance and the rare questioning rebellion is played out, surprisingly, in the way we respond to the cancer epidemic that is sweeping the affluent Northwest. In the previous chapter, we surveyed the various forms of institutionalized violence fostered and magnified by climate change. Now we can ask how such passivity persists in the face of unquestioned and largely accepted violence to our health. The U.S. government's policies on cancer, like those in the rest of North America, are "piecemeal, fragmented and couched in language so vague as to render the ensuing regulations open to a variety of interpretations." Samuel Epstein adds: "Congress has often abdicated its authority and relegated it to regulatory agencies using vague, value laden terms, such as 'unreasonable risks' or 'feasibility." Epstein goes on: "Congress has thus allowed decision-making to evolve into an uneasy triangular relationship, involving besides itself the executive and the courts" (Epstein, 1978:317).

The question is how can we continue living and dying in such unquestioning passivity, when there is so much information on environmentally induced cancers all around us? Of course, if we question and raise our voices in public on these issues, we must be prepared to be called "hysterical"; if scientists, we will be called "unscientific." Epstein reports on the events following the arrival of Rachel Carson's *Silent Spring*, and the response of the scientific establishment dominated and supported by industry (Epstein, 1978:242). Responding to the barrage of misleading and libelous criticism levied against her, Carson responded as follows:

I do contend that we have put poisonous and biologically potent chemicals into the hands of persons largely or wholly ignorant of their potential for harm. I contend, furthermore, that we have allowed these chemicals to be used with little or no advance investigation of their effects on soil, water, wildlife, and man himself. Future generations are unlikely to condone our lack of prudent concern for the *integrity* of the natural world that supports all life (Carson, 1962:12; emphasis added).

Industry has worked hard to dismiss all scientific findings in support of Carson's position, despite the fact that the nonpartisan World Health Organization International Agency for Research on Cancer concluded that "there are no valid human data which can possibly justify the conclusions of safety claimed by industry" (Epstein, 1978:246; Pimentel et al., 1998). Of course, the authority is fostered by the powerful groups who would lose if pesticides and various other agricultural chemicals were to be indicted as hazardous. Epstein lists the major group in this infamous consortium:

In addition to the major agrichemical industries this consortium includes pest control operators, aircraft applicators; agribusiness concerns such as banks, utility companies, and farm equipment manufacturers; food processors; key politicians, especially from the corn and cotton belts; elements in federal agencies, especially the USDA; elements in state agencies, particularly state departments of agriculture; segments of the media, such as the chemical journals, rural newspapers, and chemical companies; house organs; professional societies such as those represented in the Council for Agricultural Science and Technology; elements in land grant universities; and consultants in other universities (Epstein, 1978:247).

One could also include the powerful petroleum interests who are an integral part of the agribusiness consortium, and perhaps the most powerful elements within it. The mantle of authority is clearly present in all these elements. Can one really question the legitimate authority of so many powerful, rich, politically experienced people, all apparently espousing the "safety" of chemicals and pesticides? Who could venture to speak out on the arcane world of chemicals, without the knowledge, the science, and the "hands-on" preparation of those thousands of experts?

In fact, the mantle of expertise and the unquestionable authority extends, at least in the minds of the many who use those products (with the support of government subsidies), even to those least qualified: the pesticide salesmen. Robert Van Den Bosch explains:

The greatest absurdity in contemporary pest control, is the dominant role of the pesticide salesman who simultaneously acts as diagnostician, therapist, nostrum prescriber, and pill peddler. It is difficult to imagine any situation where society entrusts so great a responsibility to such poorly qualified persons. . . . Pesticides rank with the most dangerous and ecologically disruptive materials known to science, yet under the prevailing system these biocides are scattered like dust in the environment by person often utterly unqualified to prescribe and supervise their use (Van Den Bosch, 1978).

The success of the efforts of the consortium, to ensure that the practice through which they thrive is institutionalized and fully accepted, depends significantly on the acceptance of those that Kelman and Hamilton termed rule- or role-oriented. It does not depend on the highly educated, outspoken and passionate critics of the status quo, whether on the issue of pesticides or biotechnology. One can also understand why these critics are easily dismissed as too far removed from the practicalities of the problem.

If principles of respect for life through ecology and the protection of integrity and biodiversity are viewed as irrelevant to the realities of the agricultural, forestry, and fishery practices, then no dialogue or exchange of information can even occur, and the unknowledgeable, uninterested, and even uncaring majority will continue to ally itself with those who regularly inflict damages on their health and that of their children. If the authorities who produce, control, and regulate these chemicals are all unanimous in their support, then the role of the applicator or the farmer or forester is simply to follow the rules designed by those who "know best."

Plato's "Cave Allegory" in *The Republic* comes to mind. Even if a philosopher were able to break away from the rest of his fellow citizens who are tied down in the dark and only acquainted with shadows of reality, and painstakingly ascend to the light of the sun to see reality for what it is, he would not be welcome when he returned to the cave. In Book VII of *The Republic*, Socrates describes what would happen when the philosopher who has now seen the light attempts to also enlighten his fellow citizens and share his knowledge:

> Now imagine what would happen if he went down again to take his former seat in the cave. Coming suddenly out of the Sun light, his eyes would be filled with darkness. . . . He might be required once more to deliver his opinion on those shadows, in competition with the prisoners who had never been released. . . . They would laugh at him and say that he had gone up only to come back with his sight ruined; it was worth no one's while to even attempt the ascent. If they could lay hands on the man who was trying to set them free and lead them up, they would kill him (Plato, *The Republic*).

Perhaps death is not the fate of those who speak against the status quo. But, even in academic settings, it is hard to swim against the current of public opinion, especially when the public has no desire to face hard truths or to revolutionize lives that are comfortable and even profitable as they are. For most people, the insidious violence is viewed as separate rather than recognized as directly causative and integrated within the activities they take for granted.

3. INSTITUTIONALIZED VIOLENCE AND RESPONSIBILITY: CAUSATION AND CONSPIRACY

When efficiency is the criterion of public safety and health one tends to conceive of social relations on the model of a market ignoring completely visions of what we as a society should be like (Sagoff, 2001:503).

The subject of psychological orientation in various groups, and of their views of government and public policy is not intended to exonerate citizens from responsibility, be they corporate or not. The analysis of responsibility for crimes committed jointly or through collective body, can also be found in war morality, particularly in the "principles of Nuremberg," where the question of moral and legal complicity in regard to violence is discussed in detail (Wasserstrom, 1974). A recent paper by Judith Lee Kissell (1999) analyzes complicity as a multifaceted concept. "Complicity" includes "encouraging," "enticing," "enabling," "ordering," and "failing to intervene," and one can cite examples from antiquity to the present that all fit loosely under the general heading of complicity.

Kissell says:

For example, we count as accomplices Aeschylus/ Aegisthus, who *encourages* Clytemnestra to kill her husband, Agamemnon; Shakespeare's Jago, who *entices* Othello to kill his beloved Desdemona; the mother who *enables* her child to become an alcoholic; the gangleader who *orders* a beating of a victim; the Western powers who, according to Margaret Thatcher, were complicit for *failing to intervene* in the former Yugoslavia (Kissell, 1999:1).

These examples demonstrate the wide latitude we accord to the concept of complicity in a variety of settings. Wasserstrom limits himself to the discussion of complicity in war in his discussion of the Charter of the International Military Tribunal (1947) at Nuremberg. Articles 6, 7, 8, and 10 address two main questions: the substantive description of crimes, or offenses, and the "conditions of individual responsibility" (Wasserstrom, 1974:136).

What forms of violence constitute war crimes? Article 6 describes them:

The following acts, or any of these, are crimes coming within the jurisdiction of the Tribunal for which there shall be individual responsibility.

a) Crimes against Peace: namely, planning, preparation, initiation or waging of a war of aggression, or a war in violation of international treaties, agreements or assurances, or participation in a common plan or conspiracy for the accomplishment of any of the foregoing.

b) War Crimes: namely violations of the laws or customs of war. Such violations shall include, but not be limited to, murder, ill-treatment or deportation to slave labor or for any other purpose of civilian population of or in an occupied territory, murder or ill-treatment of prisoners of war or persons on the seas, killing of hostages, plunder of public property, wanton destruction of cities, towns or villages, or devastation not justified by military necessity.

c) Crimes against Humanity: namely murder, extermination, enslavement, deportation, and other inhuman acts committed against any civilian population, before or during the war or persecutions on political, racial or religious grounds in execution of or in connection with any crime within the jurisdiction of the Tribunal, whether or not in violation of the domestic law of the country where perpetrated. (The Nuremberg Charter, 1945; International Military Tribunal; II Jurisdiction and General Principles, Article 6).

Many of the crimes described are easily translated into similar crimes of ecoviolence. Under (b) "murder" is not necessarily described as immediate, or evident at first sight. From the perspective of moral philosophy, murder is equally a crime if it is slow or delayed, as it invariably is when it is environmentally induced through cumulative small doses of chemicals or toxins. The wanton destruction of cities, towns, or villages can also be interpreted in an environmental sense. Consider for instance, "devastation not justified by military necessity." One could say then that ecological devastation to which we are exposed has nothing to do, for the most part, with war. Yet this is precisely why "devastation" as such (that is, as unconnected with war objectives) is termed a crime. (c) "Crimes against humanity" cover a lot of ground when it is defined (*inter alia*) as "other inhuman acts committed against any civilian population"; it offers especially fruitful grounds for our environmental perspective as these crimes remain such "whether or not in violation of the domestic law of the country where perpetrated."

We can now turn to our main focus in this section: what constitutes a conspiracy where individual responsibility is present, even in collective actions? The first thing to note is that participation in a common plan or conspiracy is sufficient to ensure one's responsibility as an individual. As Wasserstrom puts it: "Conspiring to do certain things is itself a crime." But, even more than this, responsibility is derived from membership in a group (Wasserstrom, 1974:137). The language of culpable conspiracy, such as "encouraging," "enticing," or "enabling" fits well within being part of a group membership.

Kissell defines conspiracy as: "an offense in which one agent, the accomplice, becomes responsible for the acts of, and the harm caused by another agent, the perpetrator" (Kissell 1999:2). Following this definition she adds: "complicity is an *offense* and not simply a collaborative action. Nevertheless, it is clear that even "planning," "encouraging," or even "enabling" are not in and of themselves harming anyone, when just two are involved, the accomplice and the perpetrator. It seems as though the situation is totally different when a group is involved. The one who delivers a hate speech to a group cannot claim innocence, when the inflamed group acts violently in consequence of hearing the encouragement to hate. The speaker cannot just claim he did not participate in the violence, and stood aside from it.

Speaking of the relationship between accomplice and perpetrator, Kissell emphasizes their "asymmetric relationship to the harm"; but when group complicity is at stake, the case is not so clear. It is not obvious that one can always distinguish between "cause" and "contributions" when a group conspiracy is at issue. Hitler at first "encouraged," then "planned," and finally "ordered" and "enabled" the killing of millions of Jews. He can certainly be seen as a perpetrator anyway, although he probably never personally, actively perpetrated a single violent crime, or killed a single Jew.

For all that, we can (and must) say that Hitler was indeed blameworthy and personally responsible for causing the atrocities he did not personally perpetrate. Nevertheless his causal agency is far more than a contributing factor. Because of the authority he represented, his beliefs and his expressions, aside from the laws he enacted, were directly causative of the harms that ensued. In that case, it seems that Kissell is mistaken when she claims that causation and complicit conduct cannot be equated. She says: "I can think of contribution as *causal* in the broad sense of being the object of inquiry that justifies censure. However, because it is not the same thing as a physical cause, it need not satisfy the necessity requirement, which in any case complicit conduct cannot do" (Kissell, 1999:5).

Wasserstrom provides a clearer understanding of group dynamics in violent situations, so that the mere joining of certain groups when these are known to promote a specific, explicit agenda, is sufficient to ensure the personal responsibility of all who join, for the ensuing violence. An example might be joining the Ku Klux Klan in the U.S. South, hence participating in its hate propaganda and its crimes.

For cases of institutionalized ecoviolence, we have no centralized "evil" authority we can point to, although, for instance, the demonstrators at the 1999 WTO protests had crystallized their movement against an organization, including corporations at least, if not against a specific person. On the whole, groups and organizations are much harder to characterize as "Evil, Inc.": they usually have at least some favorable sides, or some tentative good intentions, or even a few decent people in their organization, and all that might be to their credit. It is much easier in those cases, to be accused of belonging to a marginal group, or to be hysterical or irrational, if one dares to protest against groups and organizations. That is a danger that all protestors incur. Yet, the principles of Nuremberg help to understand how those who belong to certain groups can be viewed as conspirators, in regard to environmental violence, at least in the moral sense.

4. CITIZENS' RESPONSIBILITY AND THEIR CAUSAL RELATION TO HARM

An argument, which is often offered by public relations officers politicians and supporters of the status quo, is that no activity is risk-free and that, in accepting and actively seeking modern, technologically advanced lifestyles we thereby *must* also accept whatever risks such comforts might entail. I have responded to this line of argument as biased and unsound (Westra, 1998), and Shrader-Frechette has also examined this line of argument in relation to technology transfers to developing countries and found all arguments offered in defense of transferring hazardous or banned technologies as invalid and based on immoral premises (Shrader-Frechette, 1991).

We may raise that question once again from the perspective of the principles of Nuremberg. Is mere participation in a technologically hazardous society enough to brand the participants as guilty of complicit responsibility in the moral sense for any and all acts of ecoviolence their society's authorities perpetrate? Since we have used the example of Nuremberg, where complicity is clearly criminalized in the legal sense as well as viewed as immoral, we should perhaps turn to a military analogy between crimes against humanitarian laws and ecocrimes. Being in a war is, by itself, placing oneself in circumstances that may facilitate or even require criminal behavior. Induction places soldiers in an unavoidable position, analogical to the position in which those who live in technologically advanced, affluent countries find themselves: that is, both groups are forced in a sense, to participate in the world as we find it at the time. It can be argued that induction often puts soldiers in a position similar to the "moral blind alley" to which Nagel refers, in order to describe the position of a man faced with choices, none of which can be viewed as the morally right choice (Nagel, 1974). Yet, in the United States and in some other countries, induction is legally binding and, "all other things being equal, it is wrong to disobey the law" (Wasserstrom, 1974:137).

We do have moral choices in regard to the way we live our lives at least in principle. But do we? If one wants to achieve some measure of security for oneself and one's children, at least some hazardous practices might be unavoidable. The use of automobiles and airplanes to transport us to and from our work may be necessary, and we, as citizens, have little or no control over how those technologies are crafted. Does this mean that we ought to "drop out" of all that is part of technological society in order not to be accomplices to the devastation most of these practices entail? If we raise the classical question, of whether the harm could have occurred without the accomplice's contribution, the answer for most technologies commonly used in the Northwest countries is yes.

This might be, at least in part, the reason for the demonstrations against the policies of the G-7 and their meetings. Even practices like the "dropping out" of the 1960s such as the decision—say—not to eat food containing GMOs, or factory-farmed meat or fish, or to avoid driving to work, can only be practiced by those with larger than average incomes, and with the dedication, as well as the comparative economic luxury, to go the extra mile to attempt to live by one's conscience. But despite the growing numbers of people able and willing to live in this manner, they remain a minority and unable to peacefully influence the present world order. NAFTA and other such agreements remain the law, although large numbers of peaceful citizens in Canada have joined Maude Barlow's crusade against commodifying all that we have and even what we are, in some sense (Barlow and Clarke, 2002).

But the questions raised about causation may be more nuanced to help us understand the situation. Hart and Honoré, in their *Causation in the Law*, say: "The notion that a cause is essentially something that interferes with or intervenes in the course of events which should normally take place is central to the common sense concept of a cause" (Hart and Honoré, 1985). If this definition is accepted, then one individual's actions may not influence events in a society, but the aggregate activities or the social action of many may indeed make a difference. A case in point may be the European Community's ban of U.S. beef and other meats, coupled with the adamant rejection of biotechnology in agricultural products. My rejection of beef, or yours, while still being a contributing cause to the difficulties Monsanto has encountered in the European market, did not really make a difference in the reduction of the arrogant assumptions of compliance normally taken by Monsanto in their violent activities against all life-forms, natural systems, and ultimately all human beings affected by their products.

But the joint social action of the states of the European community certainly was able to produce just that effect, and make that difference. While the causality of common action cannot be denied, the term itself, social action that seems totally appropriate in this context, is a highly debated one. For instance, Colin Campbell says: "To date no theoretically significant criterion for distinguishing social action from action has been identified. Consequently the adjective 'social' is typically redundant" (Campbell, 1998:143). We may recognize with Campbell that, in general, "By transferring (meaning creating) . . . processes from intra-subjective to inter-subjective or social settings, the individual human being is effectively deprived of the ability to engage in willed, responsible action" (Campbell, 1998:148). But we have already discussed the difficulties encountered by actors attempting to reach independent decisions, in the face of media/corporate manipulation of public opinion. Perhaps social action should be termed public or collective action instead, as we must recognize the difference between the results and effects of the one (individual action) as opposed to the other (collective action). As Wasserstron shows, there is something distinctive about the collective but individual responsibility of those whose commanality of purpose renders them joint coconspirators when they willingly join certain violent groups and institutions.

Can we say the same about citizens who do not oppose the ecoviolent practices they have learned to take for granted? In other words, to what extent are "crimes of obedience" or—to be more precise in our context,—"crimes of acquiescence," crimes simply in virtue of participating in a common lifestyle? How much guilt should belong to each individual? Kissell emphasizes that it is fundamental to the idea of a self that I can choose and that: "Our practices regarding world-altering make us responsible for the world molds and shapes, limits or augments, our notion of self" (Kissell, 1999:6). If I may be blamed for my intentional conduct, and if such conduct results in a "particular violation of someone else's interest," then I will be held morally responsible for the "resulting fact."

But if these activities are so clearly causally conducive to harms, and somehow also indicative of my intent, although I intend no harm, then another dimension of the problem needs to be considered. In addition to the violence against physical life, there is also violence perpetrated against our free selves beyond the physical harms that disrupt our integrity and our functioning. This violence represents a fundamental attack on our personal selves, subtly subverting our intent and bringing about unwanted results, altering the world, and through it, harming those we did not intend to harm.

It seems that Wasserstrom's case for complicit responsibility on the part of those inducted in the army does not fully apply to citizens caught up in an overconsuming society, despite their contributions to the common harm through ecoviolence. The difference lies in the explicit commitment of the group joined to violence through a "common plan" or "conspiracy," commitments that are openly present in armies and those planning or preparing to wage wars or to initiate aggression. These open commitments are absent in modern society as a whole; hence, they are also absent in those acquiescing to a lifestyle that produces violent results.

In sum, citizens cannot totally escape their "complicity" or their responsibility for ensuing harms, but the presence of the circumstances outlined earlier in this chapter, tend to indicate that whatever culpability may be ascribed to their activities and their choices, by far the gravest burden of guilt rests on the shoulders of the corporate bodies and the institutions that both enable these activities, and ensure that they are viewed as "normal" practices.

5. INSTITUTIONALIZED ENABLERS AND THEIR COMPLICIT RESPONSIBILITY

In contrast to the ordinary citizen, when we turn to the question of "complicity" and responsibility on the part of those in authority, the latter understood as a combination of expertise, and economic and political power, the analogical appeal to Nuremberg gains credibility. The access to knowledge about specific products and processes is what the industry has (or can have, if it chooses to do so); it is also what the various government institutions can and should have, if equal protection of all citizens is more than an empty commitment. The scientists, who are supported by either, are the "experts" from whom the knowledge originates, and there is a lot of material already in the literature on their reluctance to commit the type of errors that would reflect poorly on their expertise and status. Scientists are far less reluctant to commit the type of error that might put the public at risk (Shrader-Frechette, 1991; Lemons et al., 1995). So, in the case of these three powerful groups, neither ignorance of the results of the practices they support, nor impotence in the face of powerful interests may be used as extenuating circumstances to limit or mitigate their responsibility. The only missing aspect for the criminality of these forms of ecoviolence is that of intentionality, although the concept of culpable negligence can be introduced in its stead (Westra, 1998; see also Chapter 5).

This aspect of their causal connection to harm can be viewed in a different way, and it can be assimilated to Nuremberg's principle. Even "planning, preparation, or initiating or waging a war or aggression" is not necessarily done with the intent to harm civilians or to commit murder or extermination. On the contrary, often war plans initiate with the quest for economic gain or economic protectionism, precisely the reasons prompting experts, institutions, and industry to pursue their joint hazardous activities.

Now the expression "responsibility is derived from membership in a group" (Article 10 of the Principles of Nuremberg) makes perfect sense. Conspiracy to commit crimes against humanity is never—to my knowledge—understood primarily as the desire to exterminate humans. It is a conspiracy that tolerates, maybe even expects, harmful side effects and takes them in stride to reach an ulterior purpose. The question of induction or deliberately accepting to be coopted into these enterprises, also makes more sense from this perspective. Some initial ignorance of the full extent of the effects of these activities can be expected at the outset, but continued disinterest in the scientific and political aspects of the activities and of their consequences, cannot be excused on the part of those who, unlike common citizens, would have access to the information that is often inaccessible to the rest of us.

The question of citizen and institutional responsibility for immoral practices is not played out in a vacuum: it is also exercised and practiced in the context of the laws of each land. Therefore, the next question that should be discussed is the interface between citizens, especially those living in liberal democratic countries in North America, and the laws they are expected to obey. *Prima facie* it would appear that laws are to be obeyed. The problem arises when there are conflicts between principles and individual conscience, and the law. Is it always possible to work to amend the laws that we might find unacceptable on moral grounds? Are we, in some sense assenting, even tacitly, to these laws, and perhaps acting inconsistently, even unacceptably, if we do not oppose, protest, and ultimately disobey them? These are some of the problems we will discuss in the following sections of this chapter.

6. APPLYING THE LAW OR BREAKING THE LAW?

> The position of the Catholic Church, now one of the most dominant moral communities in the United States, is not merely that some disobedient acts can sometimes be justified, but that some disobedient acts are sometimes obligatory (Perry, 1998:114).

This argument is almost a *verbatim* quote from Thomas Aquinas (see Chapter 1), and is also supported by many without any ties either to the Catholic faith or to secular natural law doctrines. Perry cites Ronald Dworkin: "A man must honour his duties to his God and to his conscience, and if these conflict with his duty to the State, then he is entitled, in the end, to do what he judges to be right" (Dworkin, 1978:186; Perry, 1998:114). From the times of Antigone, the conflict between divine and human law has been enshrined in the literature of many nations and in philosophy. But when a modern, consumerist society with strong laic convictions, is faced with choices, one wonders what role individual consciences may play against the background of the factual and psychological manipulation discussed in the first three sections of this chapter. In addition, at least in North America, the traditional response to conflict or disagreement is to seek peaceful, legal solutions, rather than seeking radical change. The effort is to "build precedents, case-by-case, to surmount racial segregation," as Martha Minow argues, for instance. She adds: "Some might idealistically, others more cynically, describe this process as the alternative to violent revolution. John F. Kennedy wrote, 'those who make peaceful revolution impossible, make violent revolution inevitable'" (Minow, 1991:728). We are becoming increasingly familiar with the forceful tactics employed by dissenters: the arguments advanced in defense of these tactics are many, but the effort to be *heard* and to have one's cause reported in the media, thus to achieve instant global reach, are among them (Westra, 1990).

a. A Question of Consent

The question then is: does dissent, even forceful dissent, have a place in democratic countries where—presumably—governments are elected and they enact and impose laws and regulations with the (implicit) consent of the governed? But, upon reflection, the presence of "consent" becomes far less obvious and defensible: "There is, of course, an immediate difficulty with these kinds of appeals to tacit, implied implicit or indirect consent. It is not immediately evident what citizens are consenting to" (Simmons, 1984:797). Consent, Simmons argues, may be construed as being based on voting or on residence. But, "going along with something" is not the same as consenting to it (Simmons, 1984:799). In addition, not everyone votes, and not everyone has a choice that is consonant with their will or even their conscience:

> Individuals in democratic societies do not possess the right to change laws, constitutional provisions, or public officials. Only majorities possess this right. There is then no sense in which my failure to exercise my right to do these things constitutes consent to the *status quo*. I have no such right. Nor is there any sense in which I have granted the majority to act for me in these matters (Simmons, 1984:799).

But, if even in democratic societies, existing laws cannot be said to be based on consent, then the question that arises is: what is the ground of our obligation to them? The same question may be raised about simply residing in a country, or the belief crudely expressed for instance, in "America: love it or leave it!"

The argument of Chapter 1 shows that, according to natural law, obedience to authority is limited by whether the authority is established and implemented for the common good. Finnis argues that, "The ultimate basis for a ruler's authority is the fact that he has the opportunity, thus the responsibility, of furthering the common good by stipulating solutions to a community's co-ordination problems" (Finnis, 1980:351). In a similar vein, Weinreb discusses the meaning of justice in relation to natural law and to our freedom (a prerequisite of morality). He states that justice, from this perspective is far more than justice from the perspective of positive law: ". . . justice is not confined to principles of social order deliberately enacted for a community's organization and governance. It expresses without restriction the idea of what a person is due, what he ought to be and to have" (Weinreb, 1987:234). In addition, "Justice depends on the exercise of freedom; but unless justice is reduced to mere chance, it appears to follow that the exercise of freedom must be in accordance to justice" (Weinreb, 1987:235). This close connection between freedom and normativity can be found in the Ancient Greek tradition, in Stoicism, and in Hellenistic thought, especially in Plotinus, long before Aquinas' articulation of natural law theory. Plotinus' conception of freedom is adherence to reason and morality, and he contrasts it with the actions of animals and small children who may choose what to do, but are, by definition, unfree, as are those who are mad (Westra, 1990).

For natural law, Weinreb confirms a similar understanding: "Freedom, it turns out, does not mean an absence of any order at all; it means a determinate order determined normatively" (Weinreb, 1987:235). This approach opens the door to civil disobedience and to the position of the conscientious objector, although in neither case is the authority of the law in general brought into question. We saw that, for Aquinas, a law that is not for the common good, is not law; it is "somebody's violence" (see Chapter 1). Clearly then, the question of consent has not been solved simply by living in a liberal democracy with periodic elections.

If I cannot logically transfer choice to a majority, it is also true that "silence virtually never gives consent" (Simmons, 1984: 800). Neither by "expressing a preference" through a vote, nor by residing in a country, can it be said that we give implicit consent to either laws or policies. Simmons adds: "Consent must, first, be given knowingly and intentionally. Second, binding consent must be given voluntarily" (Simmons, 1984:802). The question of informed consent will also be raised in regard to a well-known environmental case, the Gabcikovo/Nagymaros Dams case (see Chapter 7). The main point in the context of the present discussion is that neither democratic voting nor residence in a country support the argument that laws must be obeyed because the state, in some way, has obtained implicit or tacit consent from all its citizens. For Instance, Noam Chomsky indicts mass media as a significant and influential component of this problem. He describes their role in detail, and concludes that "the result is a powerful system of indeed conformity to the needs of privilege and power" (Chomsky and Herman, 2002:306). Speaking of the United States, the authors add: "In, sum, the mass media of the United States are effective and powerful ideological institutions that carry out a system-supportive propaganda function by reliance on market forces, internalized assumptions, and self-censorship, and without significant overt coercion" (Ibid.).

It is worthy to note that, in this sense too, international laws, with their multiple bases and origins, including moral principles, appear to have a more solid claim to allegiance and obedience from all: neither voting nor residence play a significant part in the obligation to abide by International Law (see Chapter 7).

b. Risk, Harm, and Consent

Some grave additional difficulties arise from certain forms of implied or tacit consent. In the previous chapter, we have described in some detail the harms and hazards to public health arising from environmental threats. I have argued against the common assumptions that consent to certain institutionally approved practices and corporate activities entails the consent to all possible side effects, including consent to be put at risk of harm. Even though we might derive some individual and collective benefits from those activities, it can be argued on moral grounds that consent to be harmed cannot be given.

From a moral (Kantian) point of view, we can argue against consent to harm, as long as harm is understood in the physical sense, not simply in the sense of being wronged, or not getting one's due (Simmons, 1979). But the claim that embracing the lifestyle of affluent Northwestern countries somehow entails giving tacit consent to the bad consequences that accompany that way of life needs to be examined from the standpoint of political theory as well. Tacit consent, in the context of one's political obligation to government institutions, may not be assumed simply because we are silent, or because we do not protest, particularly because tacit consent is almost never informed consent, as neither effort nor expense is spared to ensure that the public is not informed, when this is in the interest of corporate power (one example is the addictive nature of tobacco).

John Simmons argues that although "consent is called tacit when it is given by remaining silent and inactive," it must be expressed "by the failure to do certain things," when a certain response is required to signify disagreement. Unless characterized by the sequence described by Simmons, the tacit consent may simply represent (1) a failure to grasp the nature of the situation, (2) a lack of understanding of proper procedures, or (3) a misunderstanding about how long one has to decide whether to dissent (Ibid. at 80–81). Another possibility may be that a simple failure of communication has occurred. Thus, the conditions needed to establish the presence of tacit consent eliminate the possibility of simple, nonspecific voting in favor of some political institutions, without the particularity required for explicit consent to hazardous practices in question. After citing the problems inherent in John Locke's position on this question, Simmons adds that "calling consent 'tacit' on my account, specifies its mode of expression, not its lack of expression (Ibid. at 80).

Locke, Simmons argues, was confused about "acts of enjoyment" in one's country, such as enjoying public highways, police protection, and the like on the one hand, and "signs of consent," on the other. Because of this confusion, Locke believed that one gave tacit consent to one's government simply because one used and enjoyed a country's amenities. Similarly, some argue that if the enjoyment of some features of a system implies tacit consent for the system in all its activities, including hazardous ones, then by enjoying certain features of our modern, Western, technological lifestyle we thereby give consent to any and all side effects that ensue. Unfortunately this position is as confused as that of Locke, Simmons argues (Ibid. at 83–95).

Moreover, there are certain things to which we cannot consent in our social and political lives. Enslavement is a clear example. Humans are created free and only acquire the obligations of a nation's citizen through (explicit) consent. But, although consent is a powerful tool in general, its power does not extend to relinquishing one's inalienable rights, such as the right to life or to freedom itself; the right to self-defense cannot be abdicated. Thomas Hobbes says, "A man cannot lay down the right of resisting them that assault him by force to take away his life" (Hobbes, 1958).

Simmons says that Immanuel Kant argues for a similar position as well: "Kant holds that 'no contract could put a man into the class of domestic animals which we use at will for any kind of service;' that is because 'every man has inalienable rights which he cannot give up even if he would'" (Simmons, 1979:67; Kant, 1964). Kant holds human life to have infinite value, and he believes that humans cannot affect (or permit others to affect) their physical integrity for any advantage or any other consideration. Hence, it may be argued that the human rights that represent and support these inalienable human goods, such as life, freedom, and physical integrity, cannot be transferred or set aside, even if explicit consent were present. In this case there is a solid historical and theoretical basis for the somewhat novel position I am advancing in support of criminalizing those activities that represent an attack on our physical being. The difficulty of this position is compounded when one considers that the argument of this chapter raises the question of consent in two senses: (1) consent to risk and harm to oneself; and (2) consent by citizens to practices that produce diffuse, wide-ranging, and long-term harms, despite some awareness of the effect of our activities on others, indicating a degree of complicity, therefore some responsibility for the results, including, significantly, harms not just to other citizens (in the literal nationality sense), but to citizens of other countries.

To be sure, it is permissible and not immoral to trade off some of our freedom, in exchange for wages, provided we consent and that respect for our humanity is present in the transaction, or for a great common ideal (say, the defense of our common freedom from enslavement), or to engage in warfare in our own country's defense. Not all cases are so clear-cut that they evidently fall in either one camp (of permissible activities) or the other (of activities that represent an immoral trade-off); indeed, some, or perhaps even all, workplace activities normally entail at least some risk of harm. Even a philosophy professor who must drive her car or walk to her teaching institution exposes herself to some risk of traffic mishaps. If she were to remain at home and teach from her house, those risks would be avoided. But inactivity and a sedentary lifestyle are at least as hazardous to one's health.

In contrast, the public health threats considered here, whether directly posed by environmental conditions or indirectly caused by circumstances due to environmental disintegrity and degradation, are the sort of severe threats epidemiologists document (McMichael, 1995); they are not the occasional or possible chance happenings one may encounter in the circumstances outlined in the previous paragraph. The health threats I have in mind are of three kinds:

(1) health threats that seriously impair our natural capabilities (e.g., changes in our normal reproductive, intellectual, emotional, or immune systems);
(2) health threats that pose an imminent danger of death of individuals or groups;
(3) health threats including long-term, delayed, and mutagenic effects; like the reproductive effects in (1), there are threats to our *species*, as well as to the affected individuals.

These three types of effects have an undeniably negative impact on our rights, both human and legal, and we will consider these further, in order to understand why the risk thesis should be rejected.

c. Human Rights, Conscience, and Obligations

> *Creon:* . . . To transgress or twist the law to one's own pleasure, presume to order where one should obey, is sinful, and I will have none of it. He whom the State appoints must be obeyed to the smallest matter, be it right or wrong . . .

> *Antigone:* . . . That order did not come from God. Justice, that dwells with the gods below, knows no such law. I did not think your edits were strong enough to overrule the unwritten unalterable laws of God and heaven, you being only a man . . . (Sophocles, 1947:144,138).

In the previous section we discussed a specific case of consent, that is, the possibility of consent to our own harms: in these cases the basis of obligation to disobey or to resist may be self-defense, or the right to follow one's own conscience. The question of self-defense was taken up in the first chapter, through the use of humanitarian law and the application of several human rights instruments. At this time the argument will turn to the obligation to follow one's conscience.

Although there might be a strong obligation to obey the law, at least *prima facie*, the right to follow one's conscience appears to supersede it. In that sense, the argument of this work, as a whole, is aimed at showing the injustice present in many local/regional and state laws, supports civil disobedience and the allegiance to the stronger, clearer, universal principles that form one of the bases of international law. David Thoreau defends the importance of conscience and of principles clearly:

> Can there not be a government in which majorities do not virtually decide right and wrong, but conscience? Must the citizen even for a moment, or in the least degree, resign his conscience to the legislator? Why has every man a conscience then? I think we should be men first and subjects afterward (Thoreau, 1950:20).

In this sense, it is arguable that the presence of nonpartisans instruments and universal principles in international law elevates the latter to the high status to which Antigone appealed when she spoke of the "divine law," the "unwritten unalterable laws of God and heaven" that truly represent justice. This is probably an overstatement given that international law is certainly not exclusively based on principles, but is often influenced by the interests of the powerful. It is undeniable, however, that it is expected to uphold principles in a way that state regulations often do not:

> There is in fact, an intimate connection between the idea of the law of nature as the true source of legal justice and the notion of all humanity as a community of citizens equal in the eyes of nature. It is only within the structure of a wider system, in which the State has ceased to be an

absolute law and purpose unto itself, that the inviolate character of inherent human rights can receive adequate legal expression and that the sanctity of the individual human being as the ultimate subject of all law asserts itself in full vigour (Lauterpacht, 1968:94).

It may appear paradoxical to claim that one might have to disobey the law (national) in order to obey a higher (both in the normative and the positive sense) form of law and justice (internationally). Yet this is not pure philosophical theory; even less is it based on religious orthodoxy. This is the dilemma each soldier, for instance, must face, as he is ordered to kill, to attack, or to take prisoners from a certain ethnic group; it is also the question each leader must pose when even the majority of citizens appears to favor an action or a position that is either against the leader's conscience, or against the basic principles of international law.

Christian Bay suggests that "respect for the rule of Law . . . clearly must be contingent on, or limited by standards" that enable us to form a judgment about the purposes a specific rule promotes through politics. He adds: "The fundamental purpose of politics, as I see it, is not to perpetrate a given political order but to protect human life and basic human rights" (Bay, 1971:75). This is the crux of the dilemma: should soldier, leader, or citizen give allegiance to rules that contradict these basic rights? Often political systems disregard these basic tenets, for reasons that may include economics, efficiency, or political advantage (see Chapter 4 for the example of the Walkerton disaster).

When law and order supports injurious practices, hostile to both life and basic rights, and these are not obeyed or actively opposed, we have a situation quite different from that of the "conscientious objector" who lives in a country that disallows dissent. The latter's sole action is to refuse to act. In contrast, civil disobedience may range from peaceful demonstration to active, even forceful, opposition. The necessity for strong, explicit opposition may arise, and clearly does, increasingly, arise in democratic countries that fully support liberalism.

To return once again to Bay, we must part company with the letter of his position, although in preglobalization times, the spirit of his theory may remain defensible. He says: "The primary purpose of politics and government, I hold, is to protect human life, and *to expand the sphere of freedoms securely enjoyed by the individual*—all individuals mind you, on an equal basis" (emphasis added; Bay, 1971:79). In recent times, the individuals whose freedoms have expanded exponentially with corresponding exponential growth of the hazards to which the most vulnerable are exposed, include powerful corporate citizens, with largely unrestricted global power (Korten, 1995). Hence, it is only when the individual rights to be expanded are those uncritically advocated by "liberal political programs that increase their freedoms, equality, pluralism and distributive justice" (Kekes, 1997:44), with no restraint based on principle, that there will be no real protection from harm. In this case, one ought to restrict and curb national laws that may come into conflict with the principles and the instruments of international law. The opposition and the conflict appealed to are basic: to what extent should one allow free rein to regulators whose positions are only supported by procedural rather than by substantive justice?

In essence not all rights are created equal: the right to impose physical harms on innocent people globally for various goals such as technological advancement or profit, represents a criminal or quasi-criminal activity (to be discussed in Chapter 7), and should not be viewed as the practice and embodiment of defensible rights and freedoms. In this case, the resistance and opposition, even the use of force, may be more just and more justifiable than acquiescence and obedience.

d. The Law and Corporate Responsibility: *Doe v. Unocal Corp.*

A recent example of "holding multinational corporations accountable for egregious human rights violations" is the *Doe v. Unocal Corp.* (2002 W.L. 31063976 (9th Cir. 2002)) case, where the rights of persons not to be forced to work were found to be primary, before the corporate rights to collaborate with a government's military to ensure that the required workers would be forced to perform their tasks.

The case dates back to 1992, when Unocal Corporation "acquired a 28% interest in a gas pipeline project (Project) in Myanmar, formerly known as Burma" (Harrington, 2002:247). One of the main questions in the case is whether the Project actually hired the Myanmar Military (Military) to facilitate their operations, as some of Unocal's own employees suggested. The plaintiffs, villagers from the area where the Project was taking place, alleged that they had been forced "to serve as laborers on the Project," with threats of violence, and that, in order to protect the Project"s security, the Military, ". . . subjected them to acts of murder, rape and torture. One plaintiff testified that, after her husband was shot for attempting to escape the forced labor program, she and her baby were thrown into a fire resulting injuries to the woman and death of her baby" (Harrington, 2002:248). When two groups of villagers brought action for human rights violations against Unocal and the Project (under the Alien Torts Claims Act (ACTA) (28 U.S.C. § 1350 (2002)), the Ninth Circuit reversed the original verdict (Doe/Roe v. Unocal Corp., 110 F. Supp. 2d 1294,1306 (C.D. Cal. 2000)).

The treatment to which the villagers had been subjected was termed by the Ninth Circuit, the "modern variant of slavery," and Unocal's role, a form of aiding and abetting, to say the least. Unocal's earlier response that "the plaintiffs were barred from bringing this action by the "act of state doctrine," was not accepted by the Ninth Circuit (Harrington, 2002:249).

Although this case is not directly related to environmental harms, it is—in many ways—similar to the *Saro Wiwa* case (Westra, 1998:ch.5), in that the nefarious alliance between corporate crime and egregious human rights violations are clearly present, and so is the corporate support for the role of the military to ensure citizens' compliance through rape, murder, torture and terror. Scholarly writings on this case are divided on whether the concept of slavery should have been introduced by the Ninth Circuit, as forced labor is also proscribed in both national and international law. Tawny Aine Bridgeford argues that the Ninth Circuit was practicing judicial activism in this case (Bridgeford, 2003:1009). Andrew Ridenour instead argues that the use of slavery is entirely apt in this case (Ridenour, 2001).

Ridenour's concern is that municipal law should not be considered to determine when acts are brought before the courts under ATCA," as section 1350 of the Judiciary Act of 1789 (the Alien Torts Claims Act) . . . Permits Federal district courts to hear claims by aliens for torts committed 'in violation of the law nations'" (Ridenour, 2001:587). When we consider the import of ATCA's history, it is evident that an act intended to deal with matters of liability must deal exclusively with criminal matters instead: "Crimes such as genocide, slavery, summary executions, and torture [which] have been universally held by courts as violations of contemporary *jus cogens* and thus subject to liability under ATCA . . ." (Ridenour, 2001:588). The meaning of *jus cogens* was addressed in passing in Chapter 1 and will be discussed in detail in Chapter 7. In essence, violations so defined, according to *Barcelona Traction* see Section 7.b), must be of norms that are "universal, specific and obligatory" (Ridenour, 2001:587; Filartiga v. Pena-Irala, 630 F.2d 876, 881 (2d Cir.1980); see also Ragazzi, 1997); hence, they must be of a character *beyond* even the general concerns of customary international law. For the most part, international treaties are enacted for the interests of their signatories (Bridgeford, 2003:1022), and derogation from their mandates does not entail penalties other than economic or procedural (see Chapters 6 and 7), although customary law evolves over time "to include offenses that the international community universally prohibits" (Ibid.).

Ridenour remarks on the odd coupling of criminal and tort law in ATCA. He says: "While these violations are criminal in nature, international law allow states to fashion remedies under universal jurisdiction, which the United States has done in a civil form through ATCA" (Ridenour, 2001:589). Ridenour's important article was written in 2001, and in 2002 the International Criminal Court of Rome came into force. Eventually, perhaps ruling under ATCA will form the basis for additional criminal prosecutions best suited to these crimes of universal jurisdiction, that, like genocide, piracy, the slave trade, and war crimes, extend beyond the scope of state action.

The main point for our argument is that, although "no court ha(d) found a corporation liable for a violation of *jus cogens* under ATCA" (Ridenour, 2001: 590), until this case, a test for conspiracy is that "both public and private actors share a common, unconstitutional goal," hence, fit the Principles of Nuremberg as well (see Chapter 1). This is the incalculable importance of this case, not only to show a clear example of corporate liability, but also to establish the foundations for a possible eventual criminal prosecution, based on *jus cogens*, for the violations of which corporations were found liable.

Harrington notes that not only were human rights directly violated in Myanmar, but that, in addition, "Myanmar's rich pool of diverse natural resource is currently being exploited for the benefit of the military" (Harrington, 2002:240). He adds that 'heightened standards could translate into a victory for the environment'," at least if U.S. corporations could be forced "to adhere to U.S. standards," even when operating abroad (Ibid.). Given that U.S. standards on the environment, while better than those of most military regimes, whether in Nigeria or Myanmar, are hardly a guarantee of a "victory for the environment," it seems to me that the threat of criminality (albeit a remote one, as the United States is not a signatory of the International Criminal Court), might better serve to indicate to corporations, of all countries, the full extent of their responsibility.

7. THE FAILURES OF LIBERALISM AND THE ARGUMENT OF JOHN KEKES

> It is a remarkable feature of liberal thought that it pays almost no attention to the prevalence of evil (Kekes, 1997:23).

John Kekes lists the basic values of liberalism as "pluralism," "freedom," "rights," "equality," and "distributive justice" (Kekes, 1997:6–12). Liberalism implies the presence of pluralistic conceptions of the "good life," about which rational, self-interested agents can reach decisions, without any governmental interference to judge or prioritize possible forms or alternative conceptions of this good. But the political implications of this position are that the obligation of the government is to be completely neutral in this regard, although a liberal government's own support of this position clearly renders it self-contradictory.

In addition, we noted in Chapter 1 that the sole emphasis on individual freedoms and rights are clearly insufficient, for two main reasons. The first is outlined by Kekes:

> If individuals are ruled by compulsion, addiction, irrational prejudices, or uncontrolled and misdirected passion, and if the genuine choices they make are informed by ignorance, stupidity, manipulation and propaganda, then they lack freedom as much as if they had been subjected to external coercion (Kekes, 1997:7).

The second reason is that the emphasis on liberalism also tends to preclude communitarianism, a view supported by non-Western human rights instruments, such as the African Charter on Human and Peoples Rights (1986), but also in morality by "religious, tribal, ethnic, agrarian, hierarchical . . . conceptions of the good life" (Kekes, 1997:15; compare MacIntyre, 1988). Still worse, all the values listed as forming the platform or the core of liberalism do not take in consideration the real presence of evil in the world: the sort of evil that was discussed with full scientific evidence in the previous chapter, for instance.

The message of liberalism is that these values, and not others that may be found to be more important, desirable or defensible, (that they) alone are required to foster individual "autonomy." But, *pace* Kekes, autonomy's primary meaning in philosophy is associated with the moral theory of Kant or of virtue ethicists. As the roots of the word entail (e.g., *autos, nomos*), it is the ability to prescribe universal, rational laws to oneself (Korsgaard, 1996:25). It does not mean simply untrammeled freedom of choice, or offer support for arbitrary, individual preferences, whatever these might be. Hence, if it is used in the liberal sense, the term is used incorrectly. Kekes says:

> A moment of reflection of the morality and the politics of our age brings to mind mass murder, unjust wars, vicious dictatorships, concentration camps, *large scale preventable starvation and disease, oppression*, rampant crime, systematic torture, and an easily expandable list of further evils (Kekes, 1997:25; emphasis added).

The underlined issues are closely connected to the threats to life, health, and normal function described above (see Chapter 2). Therefore, if the autonomy fostered by the liberal platform of values is not defended by universal, rational moral principles, but is simply used to indicate the near-absolute freedom liberalism offers, to be a "preference consumer," then autonomy may be good or bad, depending on the individual disposition, character, and the context of the action.

This means that, in order to avoid misuse of autonomy, the latter must be curtailed: this, in turn, means "strengthening law and order, enforcing morality, and insisting on the moral education of citizens . . ." (Kekes, 1997:25). All these measures also mean "curtailing pluralism, freedom, rights, equality, and the supposedly just distribution of goods that protect actual and potential evildoers" (Ibid.). In addition to the choices viewed as "autonomous" in liberal terms, one needs also to take into consideration the possibility of nonautonomous choices.

Many individual character aspects enhance the neo-liberal "right" to do harm, while believing that one is motivated by high principles instead. These are, (1) dogmatism, (2) insensitivity, (3) ruthlessness: all possible forms of "non-autonomous wickedness" (Kekes, 1997:36). Yet the "liberal faith" in the perfectibility of human nature, when allowed free choice without oppressive regulations or restrictions, is misplaced, if we simply observe the present situation in liberal democratic states. It is also self-contradictory, because it assumes what liberalism is at pains to deny: (1) essentialism, or the existence of a specific human nature; and (2) the existence of better or worse standards or conditions for humans.

The existence of such standards are also implicitly denied when all choices and preferences, all conceptions of the good, are deemed to be equal (Kekes, 1997:39). Because of these practical and logical problems, liberalism cannot successfully curb evil in the countries where it is fully accepted and implemented, and the results affect disproportionately the weak and the vulnerable in developing countries, but also people of color wherever they are, and whatever their political presumption or form of government. In general one can therefore say that the liberal policy involves weakening existing curbs on people's conduct: how could this not lead to allowing more scope for evil actions? (Kekes, 1997:41).

Therefore, if Kekes's argument is accepted, the systematic violence, which provides the basis for the argument of this work as a whole, is itself based on an institutional problem: it originates from the failure of neo-liberal agendas to address and redress the injustices that result from it. Basic liberal values are undeniably important, both morally and practically, to any reasonable conception of the good life. But they ought not to be taken as "the only and most basic values": "Why are prosperity, order, civility, peace, a healthy environment, security, happiness and law-abidingness, not as important as those thought by liberals as basic?" (Kekes, 1997:43). The rhetorical questions raised by Kekes are the ones the liberals cannot answer: "Why could the preservation of peace not be worth curtailing some rights? Why could maintaining a healthy environment not be more important than some restriction of freedom?" (Ibid.). More and more common people of various interests, beliefs, and persuasions join not only in aggressively raising these questions and demanding answers, but they are willing to use more than just protests and civil disobedience to be heard. In the next section we will consider the question of civil disobedience and the use of force.

a.   From Liberalism to Justice?

Politically enacted law, if it is to be legitimate, must be at least in harmony with moral principles that claim a general validity that extends beyond the limits of any concrete legal community (Habermas, 1998:245).

The problem that leads to protests of all kinds is the rising awareness of the powerlessness of all citizens to control, guide, or restrain their own institutions even in democracies. Hence, this indictment of liberalism, as a major power in the societies of Northwestern democracies is far more than a theoretical exercise: it shows not only its inadequacies in relation to the presence of evil, as we saw in the previous section, but also in regard to justice itself. For instance, Sandel argues that both Dworkin and Rawls fix their attention primarily on individuals, understood aside from their communities, and that, therefore, no theory of the good may be based on those premises (Habermas, 1998:245).

Yet Norman Daniels argues that ". . . there was a congruence between acting in accordance with justice and the good for people" (Daniels, 2000:130). But,

Daniels himself argues, we are forced "to accept a reasonable pluralism about many matters of importance" (Ibid.). But can such a reasonable approach ever be reached when the primacy is given to individual autonomy and freedom, as it is in liberalism? Rawls's view of the prominent role of autonomy should be leading to a comprehensive moral view. It is unclear, however, where morality stands in this scenario. Daniels adds: "What is the deepest form of stability that can be achieved given reasonable pluralism? This is the central question raised by *Liberalism*. Rawls's answer to this problem is to recast justice as fairness as a free-standing political conception of justice" (Ibid. at 131). But what can it mean to have a "freestanding" and "political" concept of justice? Such a notion permits no appeal to principles or tradition; in essence, it does not appear to be compatible with either the legal or the moral sense of justice. Daniels adds:

> Within the public domain, when we debate matters of justice, we need not—indeed we should not—appeal to those deeper justifications at all. We simply build on people's agreement with the basic ideas, and restrict their reasoning about matters of justice to the kinds of considerations internal to the political conception of justice (Ibid.).

An ideal of autonomy that is not originating from or supporting of universal principles is not autonomy in the Kantian sense, or in the sense present in any version of virtue ethics (O'Neill, 1996; Westra, 1998). Hence, to make autonomy the primary principle, the primary goal worth pursuing in a society committed to pluralism and to a procedural (political) rather than substantive form of justice, is to ensure that no deeper meaning can be ascribed to it, and no specific good will be sought in that society.

Another possible approach to democracy and justice and autonomy, without some of the extremes of liberalism indicted by Kekes, may be found in the thought of Jurgen Habermas. He proposes "discourse theory," as this approach, ". . . invests the democratic process with normative connotations stronger than those of the liberal model but weaker than those of the republican model" (Habermas, 1998:245). This approach to both democracy and law formation appears attractive especially from a philosophical standpoint: it is based on dialogue, hence, on reasoned argument. It is reminiscent of both Athenian and Rousseau's democratic ideals. Yet, we no longer live in a small, homogenous village or township, and it is almost impossible to find a citizenry who shares the required characteristics of commitment to the polity, full information about the issues, and at least a basic goodwill toward one's fellows.

In contrast, in today's world we are faced with a great deal of apathy about all common issues of manipulation, secrecy, and unequal and unjust power structure, all of which militates against the possibility of considering others as fellows, let alone brothers and sisters. The great disparity present between North and South, and indeed, between the haves and the have-nots in modern liberal democracies works against the worthy goal Habermas describes as the expected result of the dialogue he advocates:

> However, the fairness of consequences is measured by the presupposi-
> tions and procedures, which, for their part are in need of rational, indeed
> normative justifications from the standpoint of justice. In contrast with
> ethical questions, questions of justice are not by their very nature tied to
> a particular collectivity. (Habermas, 1998:245).

The difficulty alluded to about justice in the moral sense, thus becomes acute when we consider justice in the legal sense. Rawls speaks of the first principle of justice as follows: "Each person is to have an equal right to the most extensive total system of equal basic liberties compatible with a similar system of liberty for all" (Rawls, 1971:302). Individuals are viewed as balancing "one liberty against another" (Ibid.). The basic liberties to be balanced in this way include equal participation in the political process, and equality under The Rule of Law. The Rule of Law includes the expected principles, such as "ought implies can," "similar cases ought to be treated similarly," "there is no offence without a law," "the judge must be fair and impartial," finally, Rawls sees "justice as regularity" (Rawls, 1971:235–238). Regularity, however, is a procedural, not a substantive category.

Hence, under liberalism, the sphere of individual rights to freedom has substantially shifted. Barry uses the Wolfenden Report as an example (Report of the Committee on Homosexual Offences and Prostitution, 1957) Barry remarks that, ". . . the sphere of personal liberty" was then extended "from matters of conscience . . . by the yoking together of religious and sexual practices" (Barry, 1973:37). This shift lends credence to the comments of Lucas on the Wolfenden Report:

> The absolute privilege which the early Protestants claimed for a man's
> spiritual relation with God, the modern liberals claim for a man's sexual
> relationship with his fellow men and women. A man's soul was once his
> impregnable fortress and now, at least, an Englishman's bed is his castle
> (Lucas, 1966:342).

This strong position on the supreme value of individual liberty, or liberal autonomy, must then be based on a remarkably thin theory of the good, if one is present at all. For Barry, Rawls is attempting to follow J.S. Mill or Aristotle, on differentiating between qualities of wants or pleasures. But Rawls's theory is not fully consistent on this point: "Without the 'Aristotelian principle,' the 'thin theory of the good' amounts to little more . . . than the definition of a man's good as getting as much as possible of what he wants" (Barry, 1973:30). But such a thin theory cannot possibly support the basic understanding of justice in law, as that understanding must be principled enough to oppose various thin versions of what both individuals and even groups (internationally or transnationally) may want. Social norms are not simply translated into legal norms, that it is not a matter of simple correspondence between the two. In fact, even when there appears to be a correspondence, it is only perceived or expected, but it remains "contingent" only, as legal norms are not necessarily oriented to vindicating social norms.

Hence, once we admit that there be more to the law than a simple mirror-like reflection of social norms and choices, Rawls's thin theory of the good cannot provide the additional normative content required by justice, beyond simple procedural fairness. In the environmental arena, this need is most evident in the conflict between ecological and health protection on one hand, and the primacy of trade protectionism on the other, and this will be the topic of the next section.

b. The WTO and the Conflict Between Trade, Health, and Human Rights

Article XX

General Exceptions

Subject to the requirements that such measures are not applied in a manner which would constitute a means of arbitrary or unjustifiable discrimination between countries where the same conditions prevail, or a disguised restriction on international trade, nothing in this Agreement shall be construed to prevent the adoption or enforcement of any contracting parties of measures. . . .

(b) necessary to protect human, animal, or plant life or health; . . .

(g) relating to the conservation of exhaustible natural resources if such measures are made effective in conjunction with restrictions on domestic production or consumption ("Chapeau," and (b) and (g), (Agreement Establishing the World Trade Organization (1994)).

This document, like the Agreement on the Application of Sanitary and Phytosanitary Measures (1994), is entirely oriented to trade, not to the protection of health and the environment (see, for instance, *Appellate Body Hormones Decision*, EC Measures Concerning Meat and Meat Products (Hormones), AB-1997-4, WT/DS 26/AB/R,WT/DS48/AB/R). In the *Hormones* case, as in the other cases (*Australia/Salmon* case and the *Japan/Agricultural Products* case), the government appealing the use of substances or products judged to be harmful to human health, lost their cases.

These decisions may represent violations of human rights, but they are defended purely on economic grounds, although clearly, there are other values at stake, including democratic values, such as the right to due process. For instance, Robert Howse raises the obvious question: because of their role as transnational organizations with power over individual states, what of democracy in this context? Howse claims that democracy is not implemented by responding "to widespread fears of citizens about risks"; instead, the WTO decisions ". . . can and should be understood not as usurping legitimate democratic choices for

stricter regulations, but as enhancing the quality of rational democratic deliberations about risk and its control" (Howse, 2000:2330). Howse adds that "popular
choices should be respected," but only "if the choices have been made in awareness of the facts" (Ibid.). But that is precisely the point raised here: the facts provided by the corporate interests who wish to avoid regulation and their hired
experts may be far removed from the true facts of the case. Right decisions are
only taken after all scientific sides of a debate are heard, with those affected by
the decision casting the deciding vote and the Precautionary Principle is brought
into the decision (Shrader-Frechette, 1991:46–50; Tickner, 1999:162–186;
Ashford, 1999:198–206).

Perhaps the basic error lies in expecting these documents, specifically and
openly oriented to deal with *trade*, to also provide health and environmental protection that we all require, and that humanity should have a "basic" right to have
(see Chapter 1). However, given the lack of other instruments of equal or superior enforcement and implementation power designed for our protection, it is hard
to see why we should reduce our expectations of fairness and justice, principles
that govern all laws, including civil laws pertaining to trade. We need to be aware
of this cardinal problem: "free trade" has been described as a "Corporate Charter
of Rights and Freedoms" for Canada (Barlow and Clarke, 2002), and the notion
of an "economic Constitution for North America" was proposed by then President
Ronald Reagan (Laxer, 1991:209). For a country less rich and powerful than the
United States, such as Canada, the effect of WTO judgments may include "trading away one's national sovereignty" (McBride and Shields, 1993:162–164), and
may include a number of consequences far beyond "trade" issues (Wallach and
Sforza, 1999:chs.2 and 3). In some sense, what is at stake is the existence of sovereignty itself.

In the 17th century, Jean Bodin set out clearly a view of the limits of sovereignty: ". . . all princes and people of the world . . . [are] subject to the laws of
God and Nature" (Bodin, 1962:92). This understanding of the limits of human
planning and decision-making, even in commercial relations, is still held by many
today, although God/Nature are combined in one concept. For a popular understanding, the limits of liability in insurance claims routinely exclude the effects
of such disasters as earthquakes, by terming these "acts of God." Nevertheless,
humanity as a whole has lost most of the understanding of its own limitations
(Rees, 2000). Dupuy says:

> Humankind is engulfed by the planetary environment, even though
> whole people tend to behave as though they were outside of nature. In
> antiquity all was sacred, except humankind. Mountains, spring, the
> winds, and the sea were deified; people did not enjoy any particular
> rights. With the advent of Judeo-Christian reversed, and Man alone is
> scared. Nature having become secularized, has been treated as if it were
> at man's disposal, indeed as if it were a reservoir of riches subject to

unlimited exploitation. Today, we have begun to understand that we cannot retain this dualistic vision (Dupuy, 1991:201).

But we ignore and depreciate nature and its complex processes and interactions only at our own risk and peril, as we saw in the last chapter. In fact, we are placing the very continuity of life at risk, as we increasingly impose disproportionate burdens on people of color and people in developing countries, as well as future generations and the whole environment (Westra, 1998; Westra and Lawson, 2001).

Part of what is at issue is the increasing dissonance between the proliferation of explicit "green" "soft law" instruments that give primacy to our habitat and to humanity, and the even greater proliferation of "trade-as-sovereign" documents. These, for the most part, express a few green sentiments in their nonbinding Preambles perhaps, but continue to view cases and issues as "business first." In the first group, we can include such documents as the U.N. Convention on the Moon (1979); The Convention on the Law of the Sea (1982); The Rio Declaration (1992); The Vienna Convention of the Protection of the Ozone Layer (1985); The Montreal Protocol on Substances that Deplete the Ozone Layer (1987), as adjusted and amended in 1990, 1992, and 1995, and others pertaining to forests and to the Common Heritage of Mankind (1982, UNCLOS and the 1979 Moon Treaty).

All these documents make explicit the principles invoked in the International Court of Justice decision (Barcelona Traction, Light, Power Co. Ltd. ((Belgium v. Spain), 1970 I.C.J. 50, 54 (Feb. 5)), that is, the principle that states do not only have obligations to one another, but they have obligations to humanity as a whole, obligations *erga omnes*, and these are particularly directed to "respect for the rights of man and the environment" (Dupuy, 1991:202; see Chapter 7).

Dupuy's position parallels my own but, to be fair, "the rights of man and the environment" are by no means explicitly coupled in *Barcelona Traction* (Barcelona Traction, Light and Power Company, Ltd. (Belgium v. Spain), 1970 I.C.J. 3 (Feb. 5). Although this pivotal case will be discussed below, it is important to understand both what the judgment does say and what it does not; hence, what might be required to bridge the gap between its explicit language and the point made by Dupuy:

33. When a State admits into its territory foreign investments or foreign nationals, whether natural or juristic persons, it is bound to extend to them the protection of the law and assumes obligations concerning the treatment to be afforded them. These obligations, however, are neither absolute nor unqualified. In particular, an essential distinction should be drawn between the obligations of a State towards the international community as a whole, and those arising vis-à-vis another State in the field of diplomatic protection: they are obligations *erga omnes*.

34. Such obligations derive, for example in contemporary international law, from the outlawing of acts of aggression, and of genocide, as also from the principles and rules concerning the basic right of the human persons, including protection from slavery and racial discrimination. Some of the corresponding rights of protection have entered into the body of general international law . . . others are conferred by international instruments of a universal or quasi-universal character.

The first step to establish the linkage to the environment that Dupuy wants to establish, and that I and others have argued for in the previous chapter (see Chapter 2, see also P. Taylor, 1998), is the meaning of "basic right of the human person" and their connection to "fundamental rights" (Meron, 1986;184–185). What is at issue here is the presence of nonderogable rights, giving rise to obligations *erga omens*, thus, not all human rights, many of which are state-specific, like the right to a nationality, a passport, or a country's free education or health care.

However, increasingly, human rights are considered to be protected by universal obligations. Theodor Meron says: "But the most interesting feature of this development is that the growing acceptance of the *erga omnes* character of human rights has not been limited to the basic rights of the human person only" (Meron, 1986:187).

Meron adds that, in fact, ". . . one of the accomplishments of the United Nations has been to consolidate the principle that human rights are a matter of concern that the international community is entitled to discuss (U.N. Press Release (Geneva) HR/1/1733, Aug. 6, 1985, at 2; see also U.N. Doc. A/40/348, 6–7 (1985)).

The next step is the need to connect, explicate, and interpret the language of *Barcelona Traction*, to render explicit the intimate relationship between human rights and environment.

I believe that there are no less than two explicit concepts one can refer to in this regard: "acts of aggression," and "the basic rights of the human person." In the previous chapters I have first argued that ecoviolence is very close to other forms of violence such as the one present in armed conflicts (Chapter 1); then I reported on the ample evidence that has emerged in recent times about the dependence of the survival and normal function of the human person, on their habitat, the environment (see Chapter 2).

If my argument in Chapter 1 is found to be plausible and the evidence provided in Chapter 2 is accepted, then the connection between the right to life, implying the right to "living" (Cancado-Trindade, 1992; see Chapter 8B), hence to basic health and normal function, is clear. In this case the relation between *erga omnes* obligations proscribing acts of aggression, and outlawing breaches of the "rights of the human person" is rendered explicit. Moreover, when the acts arise out of the corporate activities of the North, and these have significant impacts on whole regions and population in the South, then even the concept of genocide may be appropriate (see Chapter 7).

Thus, this is far more than the expression of nice sentiments about the environment or about human rights: the justification for these obligations follows logically from the very arguments that corporations use to support their rights to negotiate on a level of parity with states. If there is a difference between a crowd or a mob, and a corporate body, because of their unity of purpose, represented by the Corporate Intentional Decision-Making Structure (CID Structure), as French argues (French, 1984), and if that difference allows a corporation to become a separate legal entity, beyond the individual existence of those who compose it, then, if we also accept Dupuy's argument that "humankind forms a biological community," we must also accept his conclusion: "The result is that it must constitute a legal entity" (Dupuy, 1991). It is inappropriate and logically inconsistent to say that legal entities will have standing in the law, even standing and power beyond those of legitimate states, if, and only if, they represent specific economic interests, but not if they represent the basic, biological interests of that community of life. Neither appeals to economic interests, nor even to democracy, should supersede such basic concerns, as Shue, for instance, argues (Shue, 1996; see Chapter 1).

In addition, present liberal democracies do not offer the conditions and circumstances in which citizens' protection and that of their habitats can be ensured through the enactment of fully protective laws, embracing the Precautionary Principle. Reed argues: "First, no actual democracies entirely satisfy the conditions for the generation of legitimate law. Second, not all ethical concerns can be adequately addressed through the process of law (viz., they may require more immediate action, etc.)" (Reed, 1999:33). I have argued that neither present corporate approaches, nor liberal/democratic national states' laws appear to be able to defend even the most basic rights of their citizens, especially in North America (Westra, 1998:chs.3 and 8). Hence, the argument that emerges is not that going beyond sovereignty is, in all cases, an unmitigated evil, but that the reasons for so doing cannot and should not be purely economic.

In general a "Common Resource," includes commercial and economic rights, but it ought to go beyond these to the primacy of the public interest. The same should be said of decisions pitting economic interests against the common interests of mankind in the preservation and defense of its life-support systems (Karr, 1995; Karr, 2000; Westra, 1998; Westra et al., 2000:ch.1). When viewed in this light, our common human moral right to the protection of nature, clearly supersedes the commercial rights of any economic group or corporation: their rights exist, but they should not trump the right to life and life-support conditions for all humanity. In the next section we will move from theory to practice, to look briefly at some of the cases decided by the WTO, before turning to an examination of how the world's people can and should behave in the face of such attacks to their basic security, in the light of the recent forceful demonstrations at all WTO meetings (see Chapters 6 and 7, for discussion of the legal aspects of these questions).

c. A WTO Case: The *Shrimp/Turtle Decision* and Its Implications

1. We must preserve and where possible restore the integrity of natural systems—soils, water, air, and biological diversity—which sustain both economic prosperity and life itself (Daly, 1996:13).

In the same chapter of his seminal work, *Beyond Growth*, speaking of the GATT and the WTO as "highly suspect" and "requiring considerable changes," economist Herman Daly says: "13. Decisions affecting development should be open and permit informed participation by affected and interested parties, that require a knowledgeable public, a freeflow of information and fair and equitable opportunity for review and redress" (Daly, 1996:17). The second point lists the conditions under which GATT and the WTO should operate, in order to support sustainability. It indicates just how far the reality of WTO regulations are from both No. 1 and No. 13.

A brief discussion of how a WTO case actually plays out will help to determine whether any of these conditions are even possible within the present regulations. From the 1999 WTO Ministerial Conference in Seattle, increasing forceful and widespread protests, in all countries where the meetings were held, indicated that not only environmental groups, but citizens of most countries and many persuasions were involved. These groups were not only dissatisfied, but appeared to be outraged with the lack of transparency in the WTO deliberations and decisions, and the lack of considerations for all the issues necessary for just sustainability (See Daly's principles).

The last meeting of the WTO in Doha, Qatar, ended November 14, 2001, and it described the issues to be discussed in the trade negotiations of 2005 (at paragraph 45), as well as referring to their attempt to promote "reform and liberalization of trade policies" (at paragraph 1). But further "liberalization" seems to imply more of the same policies that have been found wanting already. Environmentalists, however, expect not more of the same, but a completely different orientation for their policies. They want international trade rules that support environmental protection; they also want countries to be free to set stricter environmental regulations and—when disputes arise—they want environmental concern to be given precedence (Esty, 1994:1260). But none of the cases heard and adjudicated by the WTO demonstrate an interest in responding to these concerns in a concrete manner.

Two of these cases are the *Shrimp/Turtle* and the *Tuna/Dolphin* cases (United States Prohibition of Shrimps and Certain Shrimp Products, WTO Doc. WT/ DS58/AB/R (98-0001) October 1998; United States Import Prohibition of Certain Shrimp and Shrimp Products, WTO Doc. WT/DS58/R (May 15, 1998); The Dispute Settlement Body adopted the Appellate Body Report and the Panel Report, as modified by the Appellate Body Report, on Nov. 6, 1998; also United States Restrictions on Imports of Tuna, 39 GATT BISD 155 (1993), reprinted in 30 I.L.M. 1594 (1991); United States Restriction on Import of Tuna, DS29/R (1994), reprinted in 33 I.L.M. 839 (1994). The first *Tuna/Dolphin* case was brought by Mexico against the United States). Both cases exhibit clear evidence of North/South conflict: the *Shrimp/Turtle* case could also have been named the *India-Malaysia-Pakistani-Thailand v. United States*, whereas the *Tuna/Dolphin* case was brought by Mexico against the United States (Atik, 1998:6).

Our example will be the *Shrimp/Turtle* case, a case ostensibly protecting the South against the intrusion of the North in its domestic policies. The Southern states listed had lucrative shrimp exporting operations. However, their fishing practices were lethal to many sea turtles, an endangered marine species. The United States proposed the use of Turtle Exclusion Devices (TEDs) as mandatory to ensure the acceptability of shrimp in their markets. The states mentioned above resisted the U.S. position on how shrimping was to be done. Although sea turtles are a protected species, the Southern states argued that "goods must be permitted to flow across borders without regard to the processes used to produce them" (Atik, 1998:7). The Uruguay Round of WTO meetings confirmed the viability of this position. But in this case, the United States, whatever the economic aspects of their position, *did*, in fact, propose an import ban to avoid supporting through trade "goods produced in an ecologically irresponsible manner" (Ibid.). The extermination of an endangered species is an irreversible harm to the global commons: it has no measurable economic dimensions, in the sense that it is, like many others, an incompensable harm. Hence, Atik's proposal that the case should be viewed as a "taking" is wrong: although that approach suggests a desirable outcome, it does so for the wrong reasons, if the intent is "compensation" (Atik, 1998:8).

In contrast the idea of financial redress has merit on both moral and legal grounds. Morally, if TEDs were beyond the means of the Southern states initiating the action, then the right response would have been to provide those, who depended on shrimp for their economic survival, with the economic and technical help required. From the legal point of view, a precedent of sort can be found in The Vienna Convention for the Protection of the Ozone Layer (1988). Article 4, "Co-operation in the Legal, Scientific and Technical Fields," especially 2.(a) and 2.(b):

> 2. the Parties shall cooperate, consistent with their national laws, regulations and practices and taking into account in particular the needs of

the developing countries, in promoting, directly or through competent international bodies, the development and transfer of technology and knowledge. Such co-operation shall be carried out particularly through:

(a) facilitation litation of the acquisition of alternative technologies by other Parties;

(b) the supply of necessary equipment and facilities for research and systematic observations;

Also, the Montreal Protocol on Substances that Deplete the Ozone Layer (1987), in Article 5, "Special situation of developing countries," offers special conditions for the latter's compliance with the provisions of the protocol. It also recognizes that the developing countries' implementation "will depend upon the effective implementation of the financial cooperation as provided by *Article 10*, and the transfer of technology as provided by *Article 10A*." Article 10 provides a "Financial Mechanism" and, under Article 10.3, establishes a "Multilateral Fund" for this purpose.

This "precedent" in law would therefore suggest that instead of speaking of compensation to the developing countries for trade losses, or, even worse from the environmental point of view, permitting them to continue their unsustainable practices in the name of free trade—a fair and just answer can be found. Perhaps another environmental "multilateral fund" can be established to serve a purpose similar to that of the one designed for the Montreal Protocol. The proposed "fund" would help alleviate the trade difficulties and the obvious injustice in pre-scribing measures that the "appellants" in *Shrimp/Turtle* could not meet, while enforcing the ecologically sound measures that must be acknowledged as neces-sary when a common concern of mankind is at issue. This concern is not, how-ever, what the Appellate Body Report refers to as a "shared global resource," when referring to sea turtles (Panel Report, at para. 7.52).

The difference between the two ways of understanding sea turtles as the Report itself recognizes, is that "shared global resource" implies "a common interest in the resource concerned" (Ibid.), but it does not recognize the basic point at issue: the point of so viewing sea turtles, or the ozone layer, or forests, is not to "share" them in the sense of exploiting them in a "fair" manner. Rather, it is a question of preserving them as direct or indirect components of the life-sup-port systems on which we depend (Westra et al., 2000:ch.1).

It is the fact that the basic dimension of the problem is not recognized and accepted that is one of the major issues motivating the intense and forceful protests of the WTO that, it seems clear, will not abate until this fundamental attack on all life is eliminated.

Vandana Shiva addresses this question clearly, as she discusses the "violence of reductionism," although from a somewhat different point of view. She says it is:

(a) Violence against women . . .
(b) Violence against nature . . .
(c) Violence against the beneficiaries of knowledge . . .
(d) Violence against knowledge . . . (Shiva, 1989:26).

This violence is based on the "suppression and falsification of facts" (Ibid.), because, *pace* Howse, there are no incontrovertible facts on which alone you can base economic or environmental decisions and from which you can derive ecologically sound policies, especially in the age of chaos and of complex systems theory in science. Shiva cites an earlier work, by Feyerband: "There is no 'scientific method,' there is no single procedure or set of rules that underlies each piece of research and guarantees that it is scientific and therefore trustworthy" (Feyerband, 1978:10; Shiva, 1989:27).

Yet, despite her strong beliefs about the violence perpetrated on nature (and knowledge and women), Shiva, in the tradition of her great compatriot, Gandhi, does not counsel the use of force in return. She proposes the *Chipko* movement as an example of nonviolent struggle on the part of women who, by embracing trees, protected their native forests in India, and inspired countless women all over the world (Shiva, 1989: 207–210).

Her approach was successful, as was that of a more recent case of peaceful resistance, the effort of a single woman, Julia Butterfly Hill, to save the Redwood trees in Humboldt County, California. Julia intended to save a thousand-year-old tree, "Luna" by stopping Pacific Lumber/Maxxam in their operation. Julia lived on a small platform 18 stories above ground in the tree, from December 10, 1997 to December 19, 1999. When she finally touched the ground, "a preservation agreement and deed of covenant to protect Luna and create a 20-foot buffer zone into perpetuity was documented and recorded" (Hill, 2000:243).

It is unfortunate that such stellar examples and sound beliefs appear to be insufficient to counter the relentless advance of all-pervasive, global power of an organization like the WTO. This chapter considered the responsibility of citizens and other legal entities in national states and beyond. We would have been remiss had we not included the possibility of peaceful, legal protest, before turning to consider civil disobedience, and even the use of force as possible responses to the violence to which we are exposed.

8. CIVIL DISOBEDIENCE: FORCEFUL OR NOT?

Few changes on this planet have taken place solely because of non-violent action. To remain non-violent totally is to allow the perpetuation of violence against people, animals and the environment (Watson, 1982: 26).

Thus speaks the radical activist of the Sea Shepherd Society, Paul Watson. His thought is echoed by that of Dave Forman (representative of Earth First!):

... Wilderness for its own sake, without any need to justify it for human benefit. Wilderness is for wilderness. For grizzlies, and whales and titmice, and rattlesnakes and stinkbugs. And . . . wilderness for human beings. Because it is the laboratory of three million years of human evolution and because it is home (Forman, 1993:188).

This radical line of argument supports, in some sense, the approach of Chapter 1: ecoviolence *is* violence indeed, it is unwarranted, unprovoked, totally disproportionate aggression. Hence, the question at issue now is a twofold one. (1), Is it morally and legally permissible to respond to violence with some degree of force, at least when all other approaches appear to fail (appeal to self-defense)? (2) Is it morally and legally permissible to respond with some degree of force in defense of principle or in protest against immoral laws and activities?

It is to the second of these questions that we will turn at this time, as the first question was discussed in Chapter 1, through an analysis of humanitarian and international human rights law. Although resistance to tyranny in defense of human rights has a long history, many representatives of this defense are and have been, traditionally, nonviolent. Among these are Gandhi, Martin Luther King and David Thoreau stand out.

Yet civil disobedience may be defined as "the deliberate violation of law for a vital social purpose" (Zinn, 1971:103). But this definition does not address the "means of disobedience": must they be entirely nonviolent to retain their justification? Thoreau in "A plea for Captain John Brown" argued that: "It was Brown's peculiar doctrine that a man has a perfect right to interfere by force with the slaveholder, in order to rescue the slave. I agree with him." (cited by Zinn, 1971:105). In addition, Gandhi himself in *Young India* said: "I do believe that where there is only a choice between cowardice and violence, I would advise violence" (Ibid.). Camus, in *The Rebel*, like many others, reluctantly faces the dilemma of those who stand against unjust laws and principles. The first point to consider, even for nonconsequentialists, is what is at stake. If human rights are at issues, especially the basic rights of the most vulnerable, then, when the force is directed against property rather than life, we might need to reconsider absolute prohibitions against force. We noted that self-defense is morally and legally acceptable provided it is both focused and proportionate. Might it not be the case that a similar argument might be made in support of the defense not only of the human life in general, but even of all life-support systems and all life within them, beyond humankind? Zinn argues that: "Planned acts of violence in an enormously important cause, (the resistance against Hitler may be an example), could be justifiable" (Zinn, 1971:111).

The principles to be protected are such that, even if national laws do not explicitly embody them, they are clearly present in international law instruments, as was noted in Chapter 1 (see also Chapter 8 for details). Christian Bay expresses this point well, in regard to the right and the duty of civil disobedience:

A strong case for exalting the law (and indirectly the lawyer) can be made from my own political ground of commitment to no system but to the sanctity of life, and the freedoms necessary for living, in so far as laws (and lawyers) were to operate to protect all human lives, in the priority for those most badly in need of protection (Bay 1971:74).

He does not encourage or even sanction force even in the support of such an obviously desirable project. But we also need to consider what we mean by violence as an integral part of civil disobedience. As we have used the term ecoviolence to characterize unjust and too permissive laws and practices that constitute attacks perpetrated (legally) in and through the environment, it might be best to refer to force instead for our possible response. In this manner, we need not confuse attack (ecoviolence) with self- or principled defense (I have referred in a different context to self-defense 1 and self-defense 2, respectively, for the self-defense of physical self and of one's principles (Westra, 1990). Hence I will continue to use the diction force to refer to the alternative to peaceful demonstrations.

Nevertheless, even the most radical strategists among the proponents of Earth first! describe "monkey wrenching" as "nonviolent self-defense of the wild." Forman says:

"Monkeywrenching is non-violent resistance to the destruction of natural diversity and wilderness. It is not directed toward harming human beings or other forms of life. It is aimed at man-made machines and tools" (Forman, 1993:193). In fact, although these tactics are illegal in most nations, they are not necessarily immoral: these activists are well-aware of the seriousness of their mission and the necessary limits to their activities (unlike those who direct and command the corporate and institutional activities these environmentalists are committed to halt): "They remember that they are engaged in the most moral of all actions protecting life, defending the Earth" (Forman, 1993:194). Therefore, the question of proportionality will have to be foremost in the mind of activists: no one should put lives at risk for a right that is not as grave, or to prevent an action that is not irreversible.

a. Some Final Considerations

This chapter discusses the mixed responses of citizens to the environmental harms to which they are exposed. On one hand, after the 1999 Seattle demonstrations, we have seen the emergence of forceful protests joining disparate groups and interests with a common target: the economic hegemony of the WTO and the G-7, the lack of transparency, of concern for human rights, and for our common habitat exhibited by those bodies. On the other hand, majorities, under liberal democratic governance, have not exhibited the same concerns beyond, at best, their own immediate worries, and even then only for the most visible and immediate threats.

We noted that: (1) the protesting groups are increasing both in quantity and in the level of those protests; but also (2) the forms of governance based on economic control, are also increasing both in number and power. There are psychological and social reasons why the second escalation is permitted, tolerated and—in some cases—enthusiastically embraced. The reasons we have analyzed are based on individual responses and also on institutional and corporate goals; hence, questions were raised about both individual and institutional responsibility.

In Chapter 1 we noted the rise of legal instruments for the protection of human rights, following the emphasis on humanitarian law after the Second World War and the Tribunal of Nuremberg. The principles of Nuremberg lend support to the understanding of harms arising from unsound ecological practices as ecocrimes. Criminal offenses present specific forms of *actus reus* starting with either an act or omission, that is, with the conduct of some individual or legal entity; they include the circumstances of the act(s) or omission(s) and the consequences caused, that is, the harm(s) produced. Not every crime contains all forms of *actus reus* (for instance assault does not require "harm," but "assault causing bodily harm" clearly does).

In this chapter we have considered primarily the conduct of all agents involved, and the causality leading from the acts (and omissions), to the consequences, hence, the harms that ensue. Chapter 2 described those consequences in some detail, and argued that using analogy as a method, it was possible to take humanitarian and human rights law and the actions (and omissions) they indict, and apply those standards and principles to environmental assaults. Chapter 1 established the basic, principled orientation of this work, starting from humanitarian law as based on natural law (and through it, to just war theory), as well as positive law, but judging the latter from the standards of justice provided by the former (Weinreb, 1987).

But the acceptance of these standards not only implicitly permits, but actually requires civil disobedience when principles of justice are not embodied in the law citizens are asked to obey. Hence, if the basic rights of all, globally, not only are not respected, but are under attack, as indicted by the scientific and epidemiological research of Chapter 2, the acquiescence itself may be an injustice. When we considered the institutional, causative aspect of these harms, categories like "complicity," "conspiracy" as well as "causation" were discussed, still relying on analogy between economies and genocide and other crimes against humanity according to the principles of Nuremberg. Corporations and other powerful institutions are viewed, minimally, as enablers, but also as conspiring to commit criminal activities.

Given the violence perpetrated through these harms, the next problem is the possible conflict between freedom of conscience, and abiding by the law, in the light of the forceful protests that, increasingly represent the counterpart and the response to the immense, economically based power that is the ultimate source of ecoviolence.

The power of the G-7 and its organs can be judged more clearly from the normative framework we have adopted, based on natural law, as represented traditionally by Aristotle and Thomas Aquinas, and through the recent scholarship of such thinkers as Finnis and Weinreb. The measure of the rightness of the law is whether it supports the common good of all, universally: if it does not, it does not meet the standards to which a just law must conform.

We have not argued that, in principle, laws are not to be obeyed, that there is no such obligation. Instead, laws should be obeyed, provided they conform to the standards of substantive, not only procedural justice. When these standards are not met, then the presence of liberal democratic procedures and of civil/political rights in the countries under consideration are insufficient to justify acquiescence. In that case, protesting, objecting, and noncompliance indicate that one of us is not willing to participate in unjust activities, and that one does not consent to these activities even if an elected government is supporting them.

It would be best if the rejection of unjust practices could be indicated peacefully, rather than forcefully. Great revolutionary thinkers like Gandhi, Martin Luther King, and others showed that it can and should be done in that manner. But today it seems as though it is not as easy to do that. This is not a sociological study, and it cannot yield a clear answer to the question of why it seems to be necessary to compensate for the victimization of many, and the acquiescence of most, with noisy, even forceful responses. It might be the anger at the failure of decades of polite, academic condemnation to achieve any substantial amelioration of the situation; or perhaps the role of the mass media which thrives on reporting forceful outbreaks but no polite academic findings and arguments.

What appears to be clear is that the domestic legal system of single states form power alliances when these are in their interests, subscribe to minimal standards of justice both internally and internationally, and even abide by international treaties only when it is convenient for them to do so, as in the case of G.W. Bush's rejection of various international treaties. Yet, at least in principle, and because of the multiple sources of international law (see Chapters 7 and 8), moral principles and justice are present internationally and could provide better human rights protection than domestic laws.

At any rate, the next chapter will examine the failure of a liberal democratic government to protect its own citizens from grave harms. We will see that this example provides more than anecdotal evidence because it typifies what can and does happen in an advanced, developed Western democracy, when procedural legal protection and the primacy of the economic motive supersede human rights and ecological necessity.

PART II

CHAPTER 4

RESPONSIBILITY AND ACCOUNTABILITY FOR ECOVIOLENCE: THE EXAMPLE OF WALKERTON

1. INTRODUCTION—WALKERTON, ONTARIO

Negligent motoring and negligent manufacturing significantly threaten the public interest; yet Western judges seem more comfortable punishing counterfeiters and prostitutes than imposing sanctions against those who inadvertently take unreasonable risks (Fletcher 1971:401).

In May 2000, an outbreak of the deadly e-coli virus struck Walkerton, Ontario, a small rural town, killing as many as 18 people at the latest count although, according to later official sources, the total deaths acknowledged by Provincial authorities was only seven. The initial public outrage started with a question: how could this happen in an affluent democracy like Canada's Ontario Province? In early June, the banner headlines multiplied, as the circumstances, background and implications of the case became clear: "Ontario ignored water alert" (S. Bourette, *The Globe and Mail*, June 7, 2000, A1) is a typical report of the crisis: "Ontario's Environmental Ministry warned as early as 1997 that shutting down its water testing labs could lead to the kind of water disaster that has hit Walkerton, Ont. and killed at least seven people, internal documents show." Ontario's Premier, Mike Harris, had pursued a policy of (1) privatizing water testing services without ensuring that medical officers of health were informed if harmful bacteria were detected; (2) revising "Ontario Drinking Water Objectives," shifting the treatment costs to municipalities, without guaranteeing that smaller municipalities would continue to keep tabs on water quality; (3) disbanding "teams charged with inspecting municipal water treatment plants" (John Ibbitson, "Harris's Denials are Floundering," *The Globe and Mail*, June 8, 2000, A7); (4) giving priority to "infrastructure projects to aid economic development" (R. Machine, "Water Sewage Not a Priority for SuperBuild," *The Globe and Mail*, June 8, 2000, A7); and as a general policy Mike Harris had clearly stated that provincial debt reduction would be his main objective, *not* the protection of environmental and public health, repeatedly, as part of his election platform.

Despite the opposition of the Liberal Party and the many environmental and human rights groups who protested, Mike Harris was reelected for a second term in 1999 precisely on his "pro business/lower taxes" platform. But the general public would assume that basic safety would be ensured for all citizens, that public health would not be or become an issue. Yet it would be difficult for Harris to claim ignorance of the present trends in Canadian water issues.

This example is of a case unexpected in a country like Canada, especially in one of its richest and most populous provinces. It is important to keep in mind, however, that the Walkerton case study cannot be fully written yet, as its history is still unfolding at this time. Even more important, at this time, (1) Walkerton is only described as an example of an ecodisaster that can happen anywhere, even in a democratic country, and close to home, not only in some developing country under some military regime; and (2) Walkerton is also different in that the ecocrimes committed are systemic, institutional, and the result of practices some of which are legal, taken for granted, not the result of some specific activity by a specific actor or actors, as is often the case in other case studies, such as those written in Bhopal (Baxi, 1997), or the *Saro-Wiwa* case in Ogoniland (Westra, 1998).

Normally case studies include a clear chronology and perhaps details not only about the facts at issue, but also about the individuals or companies involved. Hence, although we will describe, broadly speaking, some of the political and regulative background, against which the Walkerton events unfolded, no effort will be made to provide a specific chronology of events, or to indict a specific individual, company, or group, as is normally done in case studies. What we hope to do, is to show the nature of the sort of "ecocrimes" that are systemic, diffuse, and institutional; Walkerton is a clear example of this sort of disaster.

Hence, I will argue that (1) breaches of environmental regulations are ecocrimes and ought to be treated as such, not only as quasi criminal; (2) the "emergent risks" (Hiskes, 1998) posed by ecocrimes are not easily dealt with either by tradition, regional/national means, let alone by a weakening system supporting deregulations as we will argue below; ecocrimes are not sporadic, occasional offenses, they are instead institutional forms of violence often practiced through nonpoint pollution, that is, pollution that does not come from one, identifiable source, in the careless and often negligent pursuit of other goals, mostly economic ones. Section 4 of this Chapter will turn to the question of moral and legal responsibility, and the way these regulatory breaches are viewed in common law. It is important to understand these breaches as real crimes: unlike other ecodisasters, primarily in developing countries (Gbadegesin, 2001; Westra, 1998; Baxi, 1997), or in North American minority neighborhoods (Gaylord and Bell, 1995; Westra, 2001; Bullard, 1994), Walkerton is an example of the results of legal, institutionalized practices, without illegal acts being committed or the taint or racism.

After considering the governance aspect, and the regulatory framework, Section 5 of this Chapter will turn to the question of corporate responsibility for ecoviolence. Although we have argued that only the good of all people justifies governmental power and authority (see Chapter 3), this responsibility does not rest equally on corporations and on business in general as they do not have the good of the people as its primary concern. Whether or not the area megafarms or a single farm operation was the major trigger for the disaster at Walkerton, the relationship between democratic governments, their regulatory systems, and public safety must be reexamined, for their failure to meet their protective obligations (Westra, 1998:ch. 3; Pogge, 2001). Section 6 shows that the regulatory framework as presently in place already raised concerns for the Canadian government as early as 1985, as a Law Reform Commission studied some of the problems outlined in the previous page. The conclusions of the Working Paper of the Law Commission will help to conclude that serious efforts must be made to view environmental regulatory breaches as real crimes, with all the consequences that this "turn" implies.

As we noted in Chapter 3 (Section 6.d), the economic interests of institutions, corporations and individuals, appear to pose the gravest threats to the possibility of achieving environmental security. Some argue that the root of the problem is the form of governance of the country affected by environmental disasters. But, as we shall see, even in a country with no dictator or other repressive form of governance, citizens may be at serious risk. (Westra, 2000a).

We will consider the example of Walkerton, together with the ostensible reasons for permitting, in fact encouraging, practices that have documented harmful effects. The desired results intended in this case, are the ability of industry to provide abundant meat at low prices, thus enabling everyone to buy and eat as much as they desire. But, although catering to public preferences is often viewed as one of the goals of liberal democratic governance, in this case, the "preference" is in direct conflict with the public good (see Chapter 3). In brief, a diet based on animal meat and fat, laced with various chemicals, as required by factory farming conditions, and by the economic interests of industrial producers, is not "good": it is as harmful to humankind as are illegal drugs. Not only is it harmful to public health, it carries serious implications for public health services, strained to the limit by the recurrence and growth of "Western man diseases" (Burkitt, 1991), such as cancers and heart disease.

The true beneficiaries of factory farming are the corporate owners of these operations and, perhaps, the bureaucracies that may get rewarded for their support of these operations (see Section 2.a). The relation between these operations and farming in general will be discussed with the thrust to deregulation and the support for markets rather than citizen's safety in Section 2.a, and the legal regulatory frame work in Ontario and Canada, in Section 3.

After much prevarication and name calling among politicians, the problem came to a head on the front page of Canada's most conservative and pro business newspaper (a victory in itself). Citing *The Globe and Mail* once again, on June 7, 2000, Andrew Nikiforuk's special report entitled "National Water Crisis Forecast—

Study Blames Declines Supply on Lax Attitudes, Climate Change," placed the finger right on the problem. Canada's foremost water ecologist, David Schindler (University of Alberta) predicts that:

> . . . the combined effects of climate change, acid rain, human and live-stock wastes, increased ultraviolet radiation, airborne toxins and biological invaders will result in the degradation of Canadian freshwater on a scale hitherto unimaginable (D. Schindler, *The Globe and Mail*, June 7, 2000, A5).

Once again, as it had happened for many years (see Chapter 2), the underlying ecoviolence was not isolated as a major issue, and the list of problems Schindler outlines have been, at best, viewed as *separate* problems, each requiring an individualized response. Schindler, correctly, views all separate effects as arising from a combined, unified cause. I have called the "cause" disintegrity, or that condition of climate, air and land that engenders and sustains multiple water disasters. The lax attitudes cited by Schindler are also the basis of much of the stress that fosters climate change, so that a lack of moral imperatives, demanding responsibility, not only rights, and supporting appropriate laws and regulations is fundamentally at fault.

We need at least a certain percentage (Westra, 1998; Pimentel, Westra and Noss, 2000) of the Earth to be left as wild or undeveloped, in order to provide all life with nature's services (Daily, 1997; Westra, 1998; Noss, 1992). We also need to keep the rest, both land and water, in a state of health (Rapport, 1995; Callicott, 1999). Most of all, we need to accept as Schindler does, the ecosystem approach (see Chapter 6) as a holistic means to understand the problems and to design and implement a solution.

Walkerton is an example of the acceptance of practices and policies chosen under the same problematic conditions as those outlined in our discussion of contingent valuations (Westra, 2000a). We can address the choices that have resulted in the litany of disasters Schindler describes. In most cases, including that of Walkerton, reductionist, rather than holistic, end of pipe solutions were (and are) sought and the institutional response is limited to an effort to isolate the failures of government, bureaucrats, or others to monitor the grave conditions of the natural systems involved, including air, water, and land. But no effort or even mention is made of isolating the underlying causes, the practices and choices that North Americans (in this case, Canadians) have made over the years, that have brought these environmental matters to a head. Schindler says: "People don't appreciate the impact of multiple stressors on our water supply and we have a history of underestimating problems. And when you put all these things together, nasty things tend to happen" (D. Schindler, *The Globe and Mail*, June 7, 2000, A5). Only the holistic approach truly captures the reality of what is happening. Hence, so long as we continue to view each problem as arising from a separate stressor, we will accept individualized, fragmented responses as adequate. I am arguing that only when we understand the role of multiple stressors on a system, that is on a whole, can we start to move to appropriate public policies.

The Walkerton disaster shows precisely the role of multiple stressors on ecosystems, as well as the multiple instances of violence arising from these stresses. The violent attacks combine to affect human health at most obvious levels. An outbreak of disease (engendered by e-coli) in the water supply and the resulting infection, morbidity, and fatality for men, women, and children, is undeniably a violent attack, fostered by disintegrity including the lack of appropriately sized natural, wild areas, and environmental degradation.

2. DIET CHOICES, PREFERENCES, AND MEGAFARMS

This section will not address the indefensible violence against nonhuman animals in factory farms: these have been documented all too well in many books, and evaluated and discussed by many ethicists. Descriptive works like *Slaughterhouse* (Eisnitz, 1997) or *Prisoned Chickens, Poisoned Eggs* (Davis, 1996), or *Milk The Deadly Poison* (Cohen, 1998) tell a shocking story of violence and inhumanity. Philosophical works like *The Case for Animal Rights* (Regan, 1983), *Animal Liberation* (Singer, 1976), discuss and analyze the practices that support our preferred affluent Western diets. Jeremy Rifkin's *Beyond Beef: The Rise and Fall of Cattle Culture* (1992), ties in the unethical diet choices to the global injustices engendered by overuse and overconsumption that are as hazardous to our environment as it is to our health and to the survival of those in impoverished countries in the Southeast. Aside from questions relating to the responsibility and accountability of bureaucrats, businesses, and institutions of Walkerton, there is a question that was not raised in the newspapers, why that sort of hazardous business was encouraged to locate in the area, without imposing limits or other regulatory restraints to where and how it should operate. The underlying motive can be primarily economic, when we consider the single and the corporate business operations involved. When we consider the motivation of the Ontario government, the economic motive, even if present through business support, is normatively insufficient and legally suspect. Governments should not licence or permit to operate, operations that do not function for the public good, or—at least—that do not impose public harms.

Examples of environmentally hazardous operations, may be the opening up of highways with multiple lanes, or even the presence of large hospitals, sources of copious toxic wastes. Both examples indicate that the side effects, intrusion into the wild for the former, hazardous waste for the latter, should be mitigated; but in both cases the public good is served by both operations. Clearly, both should take steps to function in a more environmentally safe manner, in order not to give rise to "double effect" harms to the public. But the basic usefulness of both cannot be denied.

In the same way, we need to consider the question of diet preferences leading the desirability not only of farms producing meat in traditional ways, that is,
keeping animals in natural conditions of life, but also factory farms, intended to
produce large quantities of meat at prices low enough to enable most citizens of
affluent Western democracies to eat abundant meat at all meals. But factory farming raised animals, must be fed large amounts of antibiotics and other chemicals
to keep them alive in unnatural conditions of confinement, and they are also fed
growth hormones and other medicines to bring them as soon as possible to full
size and the market. The question then is whether this progress is indeed in the
public interest, or whether the harms imposed are significant enough to justify
legal countermeasures to control these practices.

In relation to both human rights to be free from harm, and the justice dimensions of environmental effects of the "cattle culture," Rifkin outlines the effects,
such as famine, in developing countries. When cattle are fed grains that would
feed hundreds of thousands of people in the South, and instead produce meat for
the taste preferences of those who can afford it, this is not only an environmental
wrong, but also a breach of justice. Of course, even turning everyone in developed countries to vegetarianism, in the interest of global justice, would not be
enough, unless the monumental distribution and political problems were settled
first (Pogge, 2001).

The science supporting this position is readily available (Pimentel and
Goodland, 2000; Pimentel et al., 1997; Daly, 1996; Brown, 1995), and so are the
normative analysis of these practices.

For most of the philosophers, it is the unspeakable violence against the individual animals that is the target of their arguments. I will accept these arguments
as given and will not attempt to compare or evaluate them, as there is an abundant literature that has already done much of that work. I will use their joint
(though nuanced) agreement that the violence perpetrated upon animals in the
quest of consumer preferences is immoral, and use that as a starting point for the
arguments of this chapter and this section.

The result of accepting that argument is to accept that what takes place in
factory farming is institutionalized, legal violence. What we must add is that the
violence eventually returns to us, magnified and unexpected, when we exercise
our right to enjoy what we prefer to consume. The ecoviolence that boomerangs
back to us follows through these considerations: (1) ecoviolence through animal,
agricultural practices; this leads to (2) ecoviolence through ecosystem disruption,
representing both violence to the system, and (3) to us through resulting health
effects; the consequence is ecoviolence against (4) both individual and public
health. The latter in turn includes several interrelated but separate attacks. It is
both sad and puzzling that we accept these attacks fostered by a global economic
enterprise that supports a hazardous diet for all who want it and can afford it,

without regard for the resulting "Western man's diseases" or for the violence upon which the diet itself is based.

Thus, beyond the violence against so called "farm" animals, the question about the common good raised in the previous chapter demands answers: it is not enough to say, look at what happened at Walkerton, and what the government of Ontario or of Canada did or did not do.

A question raised in Chapter 3 resurfaces: why did we empower politicians, freely and democratically chosen, to support such hazardous choices? These choices are, at the same time, a threat to our health, to other living creatures, and to our joint habitat. Of course, another question comes first: can we truly claim that our preferences are truly ours and freely chosen? The questions raised in Chapter 3 become more relevant again: does our knowledge of the consequence of our preferences, spotty and incomplete though it is, render us complicit in the violent results of those preferences? And, most puzzling of all, what leads even the citizens of democratic countries, where at least some information is available to them in principle, to participate in practices that are ultimately going to harm them? These questions were considered in theory in Chapter 3, but the major issues of global justice are not even relevant or primary in this context, when we consider our own diet choices, as most of the harms occur to the individuals whose choices they are. In that case, questions of distance in time and space need not occupy us now, although the question of the distance between rural practice and most consumers, even within the same region, remains relevant, as most meat-eaters only encounter it packaged, in supermarkets.

Diet choices are manipulated by those who gain from selling food that is harmful when it is grown, processed and even consumed (Epstein, 1989). This touches each one of us as closely as we can be touched: our immediate survival depends both on our nourishment and on our habitat. Both are under attack, as we are, from current diet choices. We are bombarded with advertisements about fatty, unhealthy food choices we know are harmful to our health and to that of our children. In addition, at least in Northwest democracies, we also know that our government's bureaucracies have other priorities than the protection of human health. In the introductory section of this chapter, we saw that Canadian Mike Harris (Ontario's Premier), candidly admitted that his priority was reducing the debt and supporting business. This frank confession was uttered while a television interviewer raised question about the unprecedented spread of disease, the mounting number of deaths, and while yet another agricultural community, St. Thomas, discovered e-coli in the water of a local nursing home.

The connection between diet choices and the e-coli outbreak starts with the existence of megafarms that produce what we believe we need and we are entitled to have, together with the morally culpable negligence of those whose responsibility is to ensure protections for our life and physical integrity. This example (Walkerton) shows the factual sequence leading to the disaster that occurred.

The first step lies in a political system that only pays lip service to the common interest in ecological/health protection, as legally established by national environmental acts, such as Canadian Environmental Protection Act (CEPA) (1999) and by the binational (Canada/U.S.) regulatory mandates of the Great Lakes Water Quality Agreement (GLWQA (1978), ratified 1987), but does not really incorporate the binding requirement "to protect and restore the integrity" of the Great Lake Waters and of that basin, with all that it would imply for the conduct of business in the area.

The second step may be considered the election of a government that implements disastrous ecological and health deregulation, under the heading of bringing about a "common sense revolution," that places openly economic interests above environmental protection and the basic rights of Ontario's Canadians. Note that each step can be deemed to be "normal" "routine," a legal aspect of institutionalized practices. But the "megafarms" raise public and individual health problems that do not arise from small family farm operations such as the ones that were present in that Ontario region for years. Consider for instance hog farming. In a feature titled "Fear of Farming," Alana Mitchell, John Gray and Real Seguin cite some "Porcine Statistics":

12 million: Canada's current (record) hog population
36, 000: number of hog farms in 1986
13,000: number of hog farms today
280: pigs per farm in 1986
917: pigs per farm today
(Mitchell et al., *The Globe and Mail*, June 3, 2000, A11).

Similar percentages are present in Ontario and in Quebec and bovine statistics report equally large numbers and rapid growth. The phenomenal growth of the megafarms reflects public and individual health problems that do not arise from the operation and the products of the small family farms operations of the past. The epidemic proportions of "Western man's diseases," all fostered by cheap, available fat and meat products is related to our diet. The World Health Organization (WHO) has publicized the "Mediterranean diet," in stark contrast with the practices of affluent Western countries (with the exception of Italy, a country that boasts the most longevity in the world today). We are taught, enticed and convinced to prefer unsafe diets, whereas what is healthy and safe is the opposite: red meat never, or no more than once a month at best, chicken (normally raised or free range) once a week, at most, for the rest, fruits, vegetables, olive oil, grains and natural starches, and fish.

We reap the result of ignoring the reality of our needs and our best interests at our own cost, and at the cost of those who are disproportionately affected by our practices. These injustices range from the use of grain protein (thus limiting protein intake to those who can afford it in its form as meat). This practice, as many have shown, deprives those who are starving of possible available grains, to satisfy our taste preferences (Rifkin, 1992; Singer, 2000). We also reap the results at many other levels, as agribusiness and factory farms have grown enormously. Farmers themselves suffer, minimally, noxious odors and other discomforts:

> The Hern family has watched the factory farm evolution up close. For the better part of 140 years, they happily farmed 20 acres near Kirkton, 50 kilometers north of London, Ont. Then some newcomers moved into the neighbourhood. "I now have 10,000 hogs one mile from my bedroom," David Hern says. The result is waste equal to that produced by 40,000 people.

But, of course, there is more involved than a bad smell: the threat to the near neighbors and to the rest of us is just as real: hog waste, like cattle manure is not treated. Cattle and hogs can transmit e-coli through their feces, or from cattle hides after butchering. Some U.S. research shows that cattle raised in overcrowded feedlots in Nebraska and in general fattened at Midwest feedlots are breeding grounds for e-coli, that is actually found in 72 percent of the lots investigated (*The Globe and Mail*, July 3, 2000, A11).

The factory farm is therefore the source of severe individual and public health threats, but it is also at the same time the source of serious environmental damage, and the epitome of gross disregard for the life, health, and integrity of individual animals. There is more than a casual connection between these forms of violence, and the harm that eventually rebounds upon us reaches beyond the savage treatment of so called "farm animals." It is worth noting that J. Baird Callicott in his classic treatment of the topic, "Animal Liberation: A Triangular Affair" (Callicott, 2000), although he does not argue on the side of animal ethics, strongly indicts agribusiness practices. He says, of the consumption of meat:

> Meat, however, purchased at the supermarket, externally packaged and internally laced with petrochemicals, fattened in feed lots, slaughtered impersonally and, in general, mechanically processed from artificial insemination to microwave roaster, is an affront not only to physical metabolism and bodily health, but to conscience as well (Callicott, 2000:60).

We distance ourselves from the violent treatment meted out to animals that we only encounter, eventually, as slabs in a supermarket cooler. Similarly we tend to think of agribusiness as just business, that is, as something unrelated to suffering or violence, just a normal, legal part of everyday life. In fact we admire and even treat as celebrities those whose business thrives and becomes increasingly larger and more profitable year after year. Even environmental damage is often thought to be something else, something other than and unrelated to the concern with violence, or with our health.

When we see (1) animal violence; (2) environmental violence; and (3) violent attacks on our health, for what they really are, the connection becomes clear, as does the cause and effect sequence, and the eventual deadening of our ability to be morally awake and emotionally sensitive to violence in all its forms. Eventually the violence has a boomerang effect as it rebounds on us. Difficult questions remain unanswered: for instance, why do we continue to accept as inevitable this (meat based) diet, these practices with their tripartite violence: to nonhuman animals, to natural systems to human organisms? Underlying all three, there is also a global injustice in the pursuit of institutional practices that decimate biodiversity, despoil nature, and reduce those in developing countries to famine-stricken masses (Rifkin, 1992; Singer, 2000; Rachels, 2000).

It might be possible to at least understand, if not condone such a cluster of immoral choices and preferences, if the results produced unadulterated good for the choosers. However, the opposite is true. Given what goes into the meat and the milk we consume, the hormones, antibiotics, and other chemicals, together with the dirt and contamination to which all these products are exposed through the slaughtering and butchering processes (Eisnitz, 1997; Cohen, 1998; Davis, 1996), it is clear that they present grave threats to health, even beyond diet considerations.

For the latter, Jeremy Rifkin reports on an accidental experiment as it happened to Danish nationals. Due to the naval blockade of 1917,

> . . . the Danes were cut off from incoming shipments of food. The government was subsequently forced to begin to ration out food, and encourage the country to give up its meat, and eat mainly a potato based diet. In time, some three million people became vegetarians and the death rate from disease fell some 35% (Parsons, 2000; Rifkin, 1992).

The reverse is shown by the increase in cancer and heart disease in Japan, as that country moves away from its traditional low meat diet. Of 2.1 million deaths in the United States, 1.5 million are due to dietary factors, primarily high consumption of cholesterol and fat in meat. The hormones, synthetics, and other substances including bioengineered and transgenic substances that are present in the feed, hence, in the animals we eat, add to the now well-documented health risks. Perhaps the most publicized of these recent times has been the presence of Bovine Growth Hormone (BGh) followed by the infamous outbreak of "mad cow" disease (McCalman et al., 1998).

In conclusion, the violence practiced on animals to support our choices and preferences for certain foods, is tied to the violence we receive from these choices and preferences in our diet.

a. The Impact of Deregulations and Other Effects of the Common Sense Revolution

One of the key elements in the Walkerton tragedy may well be the present legislative and regulatory framework in Ontario. Even before the tragedy happened, Canadian Environmental Law Association's (CELA) *Intervenor* described the situation in Ontario's farming communities as "Rural Ontario" Industrial Hog Barns, Industrial Waste" (25(1) *Intervenor* 5 (Jan.–Mar. 2000)). In the previous section, we described some of the effects of having industrial hazardous facilities in farming areas. We did not enumerate in detail all the human health problems arising from this form of violence against animals. Antibiotics are fed to pigs, as "thousands of animals are kept together in huge barns, sows producing more piglets, and piglets fattened by the shortest possible time before slaughter" (Ibid.) Animals under these violent, inhumane and unnatural conditions require antibiotics to survive to market.

A recent issue of *Nucleus*, the magazine of the Union of Concerned Scientists (23(1), *Nucleus* 1 (Spring 2001)), makes the same point in "Pearls Before Pigs" (Mellon and Fondriest, 2001). Too many antibiotics that can be considered "key" to human medicine, are "routinely fed to livestock"; some of these are tetracycline, penicillin, and erythromycin, all of which are used for healthy livestock. While the European Union has banned growth hormones, promoting uses of antibiotics that are used for humans, in the United States, for instance, their use has increased by 50 percent (Ibid. at 2):

Figure 1 Amount of Antibuitics Fed to Healthy Livestock Each Year During the 1990s

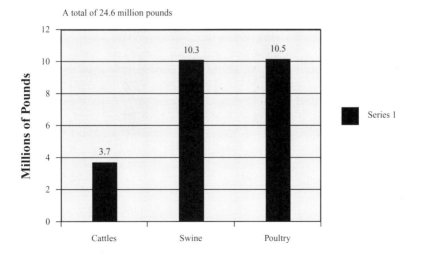

A total of 24.6 million pounds

Antibiotics Fed to Healthy Livestock Compared with Antibiotics Used to Treat People

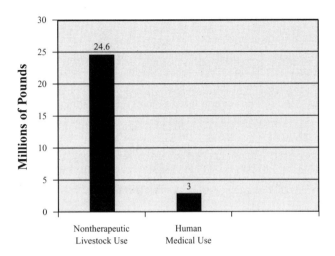

Increase in Nontherapeutic Antibiotic Use in Livestock Since 1985 Millions of Pounds

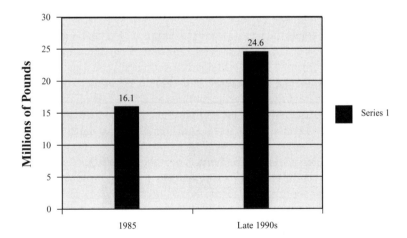

It is almost obscene to think of using medication in this way, for the profit of some, when children in developing countries are dying from the lack of some of the same medications. Nevertheless these statistics further support the point made in the *Intervenor.* Even more immediately hazardous are the other threats arising from "intensive livestock facilities":

Intensive livestock facilities produce enormous quantities of highly toxic manure. A single hog will produce two tons of manure per year. Ontario's 4 million hogs produce as much raw sewage as the entire human population of the province, without the benefit of a single sewage treatment plant (25(1) *Intervenor* 5 (Jan.–Mar. 2000).

This represents the most hazardous aspect of these industrial farming operations, later confirmed by the general conditions and background to the events in Walkerton. In addition, "the odour associated with a hog barn is dramatically worse than the odour which comes with a normal farming environment' (Ibid.), and this odor of manure itself, can have "severe health impacts." Bruckmann adds:

Manure contains over 150 gaseous compounds, including hydrogen sulfide, ammonia, carbon dioxide and methane. Residents living near intensive livestock facilities report headaches, nausea, and the exacerbation of asthma and respiratory problems (Bruckmann, 2000:5).

Even before the Walkerton tragedy, it was clear that the existing regulations were totally inadequate: as long as what amounts to a hazardous industrial operation continues to be improperly defined as farming, the nature of the actual operation is not properly understood and cannot be controlled realistically, as I argued in the previous section. In fact, the regulatory infrastructure intended to support "small scale farms and other rural residents," in effect harms them by supporting and protecting large corporate operations and industrial interests instead. The latter are in conflict with the economic interests of small Ontario farmers, and with the right to life, security, and health of all Ontario citizens.

The problem is and has been a two-pronged one: on one hand, the regulatory framework itself is deeply flawed as we will argue below, as it is unclear, imprecise, and couched in language that cannot provide clear and tight guidelines. On the other, the deregulations imposed during the last five years by the government of Mike Harris, have removed whatever measure of security was provided by monitoring and controls provided by previously existing laws. Ontario's Environmental Protection Act (OEPA) (1990) lags behind the 1999 CEPA, as we will see in the next section; many of the concepts present in the latter are still absent from the former, for example a reference to the Precautionary Principle. But deregulation, instead of keeping pace with science's recent discoveries, including scientific recognition of its own inability to be fully predictive (Kay and Schneider, 1995), virtually eliminates the monitoring and controls that protected the public before its inception.

The problems generated by specific industrial practices masquerading as "farming," represent the most evident and obvious cause of the contamination resulting in the Walkerton tragedy. The CELA "Five Year Report" (Clark and Yacoumidis, 2001) clearly shows no less than ten areas where the so-called

'Common Sense Revolution" has aggravated, multiplied or fostered environmental problems in the province. The authors list the "Top 10 Things Wrong with Environmental" protection:

(1) Ministries and agencies who protect the environment have too few staff and too few funds to do their job.

(2) The government loads environmental responsibilities on small municipalities on one hand and limits their ability to protect the environment (e.g., in 1998 the provincial government enacted protection to large scale, industrial livestock facilities with the *Farming and Food Production Act* but after Walkerton, the province has temporarily relented and permitted municipalities to pass interim control by laws to limit further factory farm development).

(3) "The Common Sense Revolution" thinks environmental protection is red tape: In fact in 2000, the "Red Tape Commission" became a permanent legislative body.

(4) "New laws and regulations do not adequately protect the environment" (as an example, although under the Living Legacy Strategy (July 1999) almost 400 new "protected areas" will be created, mining and sport hunting may be permitted there).

(5) "The government beefs up enforcement, but will not commit to prevention and planning."

(6) "Under the Common Sense Revolution, protected areas are not protected."

(7) "The provincial government refuses to act when it should to protect the environment" (With reference to Walkerton and the protection of "large scale industrial facilities," "the province was reluctant to even consider a regulation to protect the environment and human health from the farm emissions").

(8) "Industry self regulation and self monitoring increase the risk of environmental damage."

(9) "Common Sense protects game animals and commercial fisheries, not wildlife . . . (The Ministry of Natural Resources (MNR) issued *Beyond 2000 . . .*) "a strategic directions document" of its management activities. Its tone and emphasis is on "management and consumption of natural resources, and insufficient emphasis on the protection and conservation of natural systems.")

(10) "The Revolution fumbles national and international environmental protection initiatives" (This point emphasizes noncompliance with GLWQA and the expiration of the Canada Ontario Agreement regarding the Great Lakes Ecosystem (March 2000); Ontario as "the major obstacle on a Federal/Provincial agreement on Climate Change" (Ibid. at 7–14).

After this initial introductory chapter, the second chapter of the document, on "water," indicates many of the failures that eventually led to Walkerton. Ostensibly, the "Ontario Drinking Water's Objectives (1994)" state: ". . . if the water contains any indicators of unsafe water quality, . . . the laboratory will immediately notify the MOE District Officer, who will immediately notify the Medical Officer of Health . . ."

Unfortunately, however, "Not following these guidelines is not against the law. The guideline itself is not enforceable" (Ibid. p. 17). But Ontario's water problems, although most evident in water quality issues, are equally real in relation to water quantity: "Throughout the summer of 1999, Great Lakes levels and levels in watersheds throughout the province reached historic lows" (Ibid. at 20).

Yet permits are routinely given to bottling companies to remove water from Ontario's aquifers. When this reduction in availability is coupled with continued and largely uncontrolled pollution, the future for Ontario's water is as grim as that for Canada as a whole (Barlow, 1999).

The desperate need for regulatory action to control "nutrient runoff from agricultural operations," was noted as early as 1995, when Walkerton was identified by Health Canada as a 'high-risk area for infection from e-coli because of the large local density of cattle operations (Clark and Yacoumidis, 2001:24). But the agency charged with the regulation of farming operations, OMAFRA, has, a "primary client group . . . the Ontario farm industry." The Special Report of the Environmental Commissioner of Ontario (July 27, 2000) adds: "It is open to question whether the ministry can overcome this conflict of interest and effectively regulate this same industry" (Ibid. at 24, 101, n.61).

Even aside from bias, lack of resources, and of determination to truly eliminate the grave water problems besetting Ontario, any new initiatives are kept reactive, aimed at fixing problems rather than preventing them, thus little hope can be had that Ontario will lose its place as "North America's third worst polluter" (Ibid. at 26).

Although all ten points noted are highly relevant, some aspects of this list are particularly important, not only for understanding Walkerton, but also for the overall argument of this chapter: they are (3), (5), (8), (9), and (10), above (and the last two are closely related to (6)).

The first, (3), above deals with "decision making" discussed in Chapter 3 of the Five Year Report. In line with the basic understanding of that chapter, most of problems discussed in this section, are indicative of a basic underlying approach: the primacy of economic and business interests not only over environmental protection, but over health and safety of Ontarians and people in general. The *Intervenor* describes the government's approach in the five years of the "common sense revolution" as "deregulation, defunding and devolution," and the emphasis on facilitating business enterprise, regardless of its impact on natural systems and, through them, on human life as well. The consistent elimination of red tape, giving rise to an act for its implementation, is a clear commitment to declaring a democratic government that owes its political legitimacy, in principle, to the promotion of the citizens' common good (Gilbert, 1994), to business and corporate interests instead.

Efficiency, at the cost of stakeholders' participation (Ibid. at 34) and at the cost of expert information, is a serious flaw, not a desirable government goal. Public accountability, according to Carl Dombeck, Chair of Appeal and assessment Boards," means that "the boards must account to politicians for cost reduction and expediting hearings," for the ultimate aim of "reducing the cost of doing business in Ontario" (Ibid. at 32). In addition, even the Environmental Commissioner, originally with first incumbent Eva Ligeti, a position intended as a watchdog and control on government's activities, is now filled by a personal friend of the Premier, a man who is involved in that political party (Ibid. at 36). The negative impact of Gordon Miller's personal bias on his role, was obvious after Walkerton, as he repeated and emphasized the human error statement Mike Harris endorsed as "explanation" and as attempt of exculpation of the government's pivotal role in the tragedy.

Beyond eliminating careful and serious study of all issues, as evidenced by their redefinition of red tape, there are at least two other grave problems in the decision-making structure of Harris' government, the promotion of industry's self-regulation (see also (8), above), and the corresponding quest for a "balance of industry and non industry representation" on Boards and technical advisory committees (such as the Technical Standards Safety Act (1999)) (Ibid. at 40).

There is no possibility of a "partnership of trust and a balance between voluntary and regulatory actions" (REVA, August 1999), between parties who share little other than unequal power, where one party is most often the attacker (environmentally speaking), and the other, the victim. If we acknowledge the existence of ecoviolence, from local to global threats and health effects on all populations (Westra, 2000), then it is not possible to pair as partners actors with such disparate interests, goals and powers. As one would not expect abusers to help to define, enforce, and punish assaults on women and children, so too it is naive to expect such partnerships to yield desirable results in the protection of all life. It may be naive to hope that business would be excluded completely from either the domestic or the international law regime formation. But the international approach to exclude corporate interests at least from NGO status, hence from open participation in treaties and the discussions that give rise to them, at least shows that the influence of these economic interests may be unavoidable in practice, but it is, and should not be openly welcome, in principle.

The present state of the global commons (Brown, 2000; Pimentel, Westra and Noss, 2000), attest to the unreality of such a partnership as a goal (see also (8) above). The final remarks of this section will address the problematic relationship between Ontario's revolution and the commitment of Ontario and Canada, to the vital global goals of protection of natural systems. "Protected areas are not protected," and "lands for life and Ontario's Living Legacy Strategy" are both misleading and public relation slogans, far from the reality of the situation. The language employed appears to refer to the necessity to protect systemic integrity, in a specific percentage of any region, as science has convincingly proven the importance of preserving unmanipulated and unexploited lands in order to ensure the presence of nature's services as Gretchen Daily explains (Daily, 1997). Reed Noss has also shown the necessity of keeping large percentages of lands wild, in order to conserve the natural diversity that best supports megafauna, and through it, all life and nature's services on land; James Karr has made the same point with strong scientific evidence in regard to inland waters and rivers (Karr, 1995; Karr and Chu, 1999; Karr, 2000) and Daniel Pauly has done the same for marine reserves (Pauly, 2000).

The necessity for areas of ecological integrity in order to support all life within and without their boundaries, is also present in the regulations, vision, and mission statements and constitutions of most nations, including the Liberal Policy Book (where, following Monte Hummel's suggestion, only 12 percent is listed as the required percentage) (Hummel, 1990). After the first appearance of the language of integrity in the Clean Water Act (U.S., 1972) integrity has appeared in any number of preambles, regulatory documents, and legal or programmatic statements, from the Constitution of Brazil (Chapter 6, "Meio Ambiente") to the statement of the "Union of Concerned Scientists," to the final draft of the Earth Charter (Westra, 1994; Westra, 1998).

The "Global Ecological Integrity Project" (SSHRC, 1992–1999; NATO, 1999), has united a number of scientists to study and define the concept, while detailing the consequence that follow upon that understanding. The work of that group and their arguments cannot be repeated at this time and it is available in print (Pimentel, Westra and Noss 2000). Nevertheless, it is clear at (1) there are compelling scientific reasons for understanding, protecting, and restoring, as much as possible, ecological integrity in appropriately sized areas in all regions including Ontario; (2) simply referring to "healthy systems is insufficient, because ecosystem health is compatible with careful use and manipulation, whereas integrity supports total lack of human activity in the protected areas, and correspondingly safe practices everywhere else, in order not to have a deleterious impact on protected areas through hazardous activities elsewhere; and therefore (3) integrity (and health) related language should be carefully defined because of the pivotal role they play in various acts, including the GLWQA where integrity is also left undefined (Westra, 1994). It is not possible to follow a mandate the goal of which is left unclear and undefined. Taking the integrity mandate seriously would entail "living in integrity" (Westra, 1998), that is, ensuring that (1) appropriately sized wild areas be established or reestablished everywhere; and (2) commercial and urban activities be judged acceptable only if they have no seriously adverse effect on both wild (core) areas, and in the buffer zones established, like half-way houses, around the core, permitting healthy use of natural systems (Noss, 1992; Noss and Cooperrider, 1994).

Although the CELA document does not refer to integrity specifically, it appears to support the measures that are conducive to its implementation: true conservation, respect for protected areas, and concern for national and international obligations, all require ecological integrity as a basic goal. For instance the GLWQA states:

> The purpose of the parties is to restore and maintain the chemical, physical and biological integrity of the waters of the Great Lakes Basin Ecosystem where the latter is defined as: The interacting components of air, land, water and living organisms including humans within the drainage basin of the St. Lawrence River (GLWQA (1978), ratified 1987; Westra, 1994:21).

However the CELA document refers without comment to the *Beyond 2000* list of "desired outcomes" that include, 'the long term health of ecosystems" (Ibid. at 79). But health is a component of integrity and necessary though not sufficient to achieve the goals that the CELA document itself argues ought to be achieved. For instance, no recreational activities in protected areas, no hunting or fishing in natural reserves, goes beyond the goal of health: an organic farm is based on a healthy system, so is an area devoted to sustainable and organic forestry practices. But integrity requires no utilization whatever, in order to preserve the natural services referred to earlier (Noss, 1992; Noss and Cooperrider, 1994; Ulanowicz, 1995; Karr and Chu, 1999).

3. REGULATORY AND LEGISLATIVE FRAMEWORK OF WALKERTON

> Each offence must be sentenced in accord with its specific facts but pollution offences must be approached as crimes, not as morally blameless technical breaches of a regulatory standard (R. v. United Keno Mines, (1980) 10 C.E.L.R. 43 (Terr. Ct. of Y.T.). Chief Judge Stewart, at 47; cited in R. v. Village of 100 Mile House, (1993) B.C.J. No. 2848 DRS 94 07390), 22 W.C.B. (2d) 131.

In this section we will consider the actual acts and regulations the Ontario/ Canadian framework within which the crimes committed in Walkerton can be assessed, in order to determine what, specifically, needs to be revised and changed to prevent further disasters. The relevant acts for Walkerton, were the Environmental

Protection Act (1990:ch.E.19), and the Ontario Water Resources Act (1990: ch.O.40). It is also instructive to study the instruments used to apply for a license to operate a water works, the education requirements for those in charge, and the Canadian Environmental Protection Act (1999). The language of these acts is highly problematic, because of its vagueness and imprecisions. This problem is often present in international covenants (see Chapters 6 and 8): however, the explicit presence of normative principles as an important, necessary component of international law (Kindred et al., 2000), could at least potentially, lead to better law, and better environmental implementation.

In contrast, the language of these provincial legal instruments is not ecologically helpful. "Adverse effect" is defined in some detail, but the explanations, ranging from (a) to (h) are entirely slanted toward human use of the environment, not to any intrinsic value for the natural environment, even less to the natural services (Daily, 1997) that all natural areas perform for the benefit (and the survival) of all life within and without their confines. Some examples will suffice: (a) "impairment of the quality of the natural environment for any use that can be made of it"; or (f) "rendering any property or plant or animal life unfit for human use," clearly demonstrate the bias in conceptualizing and understanding the "natural environment." Even (b) "injury or damage to property or to plant or animal life," starts with a reference to "property," so that the implication is still on of human use. Therefore this definition does not take seriously the need for "wild lands" in quantities sufficient to perform the services Gretchen Daily describes in detail:

- purification of air and water;
- mitigation of floods and droughts;
- detoxification and decomposition of wastes;
- generation and renewal of soil and soil fertility;
- pollination of crops and natural vegetation;
- control of the vast majority of potential agricultural pests;
- dispersal of seeds and translocation of nutrients;
- maintenance of biodiversity, from which humanity has key elements of its agricultural, medicinal, and industrial enterprise;
- protection from the sun's harmful ultraviolet rays;
- partial stabilization of climate;
- moderation of temperature extremes and the force of winds and waves;
- support of diverse human cultures;
- providing of aesthetic beauty and intellectual stimulation for the life of the human spirit (Daily, 1997).

If this aspect of the protection of natural systems is ignored as the CELA document discussed in the previous section indicates, then Ontario's present regulations do not take into consideration stated national and international goals, where the protection and restoration of integrity are required.

Part II of the Ontario Environmental Protection Act (OEPA), under "General Provisions" carries a strong prohibition in the document:

> s.6. (1) *Prohibition:* No person shall discharge into the natural environment any contaminant and no person responsible for a source of contaminant shall permit the discharge into the natural environment of any contaminant, from the source of the contaminant, in any amount, concentration or level in excess of that prescribed by the regulations.

However, even this prohibition is followed by an "Exception": Subsection (1) does not apply to animal wastes disposed in accordance with normal farming practices (R.S.O. 1990, Chapter E.19, Section 6).

The same pattern is followed in Section 13.(1).

> *13.(1) "Ministry to be notified when contamination exceeds permitted levels."*

Every person,

> (a) who discharges into the natural environment; or

> (b) who is the person responsible for a source of contaminant that discharges into the natural environment, any contaminant in any amount, concentration or level in excess of that prescribed by the regulations shall *forthwith* notify the Ministry of the discharge

> (2) *Exception.* Subsection (1) does not apply to animal wastes disposed in accordance with *normal farming* practices (R.S.O. 1990, 1999 Chapter E.19, Section 13).

And, finally, the next section:

> 14.(1) *Prohibition.* Despite any other provisions of this Act or the regulations, no person shall discharge a contaminant or cause or permit the discharge of a contaminant into the natural environment that cause or is likely to cause an adverse effect.

This last, strong prohibition is also marred by the Exception (2) that follows: Like Section 6 and Section 13, "animal wastes" are routinely exempted not only from the "prohibition," but also explicitly from reporting "forthwith" to the Ministry, the occurrence. The underlined words (Section 13.(2)), "normal farming practices" are never discussed or defined although, as we quoted Bruckmann in the *Intervenor*, there is no comparison between "normal farming" and the industrial practices that are present throughout Canada, and specifically in the Walkerton area.

Normal farming practices are neither detailed nor defined, nor is the distinction between farming in general and factory farming as an industrial, not a family enterprise, even discussed.

It is worth noting that this is not only a problem with OEPA, but also one that needs to be addressed, specifically, under the Nutrient Management Act (2001) (Bill 81), and the Canadian Environmental Law Association has made a submission to that effect to the Ontario Ministry of Agriculture, Food and Rural Affairs (R.D. Lindgren, Counsel, August 13, 2001; Report No. 407).

This grave omission was also noted repeatedly in the previous section in the discussion of CELA's "Five Year Report," and it was addressed specifically by Elizabeth Bruckmann in "Rural Ontario: Industrial Hog Barns, Industrial Waste" (25(1) *The Intervenor* 5 (Jan.–Mar. 2000). Aside from the details about this sort of operation, in general, the thrust to industry self-regulation and self-monitoring, "increases the risk of environmental damage" (Clark, 2000:12). Clark adds: "The province was, therefore, prepared to pass a new statute to protect factory farms from municipal by laws, but is reluctant to even consider a regulation to protect the environment and human health from farm emissions" (Ibid.).

Other sections of the Ontario Environmental Protection Act (OEPA) detail the procedures surrounding the granting of a "certificate of approval," and the powers of the Director in that regard, without, however, any attempt to prescribe scientific competence on the part of a Director, or make that a requirement of their position, given the Director's responsibility for environmental and human health.

The same lack of precision with a corresponding apparent lack of concern for public safety is present throughout the document. At Section 176.(1) *Registration*, or the mandate to "monitor, record and report to the Ministry," any number of contaminants and wastes "that will or are likely to be generated," also prescribes no time frame for the required reports, and it does not prescribe a specific response on the part of the minister. This is not a minor point. If the Children's Aid Society, for instance, were to require no clear time frame for doctors to report child abuse, or for the society to intervene, such abuse could continue unabated and uncontrolled, and the child's at-risk rights would be violated under the Charter (Section 7), just as I believe our rights are violated, by the total absence of serious, timely mandates to protect public health and safety (Muldoon, "Editorial," 24(2) *Intervenor* (Apr.–June 1999)).

The only point that might give rise to some hope in future developments, is the consistent division between the penalties assigned (or assignable) to individuals, and those assignable to corporate bodies (see, for instance, Section 187, (1) and (2), or (4), (5) and again (7) and (18), all subsections of the same section 187).

The Ontario Water Resources Act (1990:ch.O.40), in Section 15. Section 15 allows inspection of water facilities by provincial officers "without warrant or court order," "at any reasonable time and with any reasonable assistance." It also promulgates the following directives under Section 16.(2).(4) 3, ". . . to sample, analyze and report to the quality or quantity of any waters, 1998.c. 35, s. 49." The same act also says that "Discharge of polluting material prohibited in Section 30.(1), and specifies "sewage" under Section 31. However, it still allows the Director to have the power to amend, vary, or revoke as "the Director considers desirable" any order that had been issued. Nevertheless, Section 32 "Measures to alleviate effects of impairment of quality of water" remains delightfully vague with respect to both details, timelines, and procedures. See for instance Section 32.(5) of this document: "to monitor and record the quality and quantity of any water specified in the order and to report thereon to the Director," equally lacks specificity or any details; although details may be specified elsewhere.

In contrast, the Water Works and Sewage Works (0. Reg. 435/93), is far more specific in its "Operating Standards," as it prescribes specific training standards and educational levels for the operators of water facilities, for example, a grade 12 education (Sections 2.1, 3.2, 4.(1), 2.5(1)2.i), applicable to all levels of operators, and, in addition, a requirement for "at least forty hours of training each year:" (Section17.(1)). The act does not refer to the way these requirements could be circumvented by "grandfather clauses" that, in reality, resulted in the continued, unquestioned reappointment of totally unqualified, or grossly under qualified, employees in Walkerton (Christensen, 2002:98–99). Examples could be multiplied: it is undeniable that the 1999 CEPA is far more comprehensive and detailed than the documents examined, for instance, in the work of Diane Saxe, prior to the Conservative government's election, and the implementation of the so-called "common sense revolution." However, it is too easy to blame all environmental problems on Harris' Common Sense Revolution, although, as we saw, many arise clearly from that general approach. Nevertheless, Saxe's influential work indicates a number of serious problems embedded in the earlier legislative framework, and these undoubtedly paved the way for the disastrous "Deregulations" listed by CELA's "Five Year Report." In sum, Saxe noted the following problems:

(1) Regulatory offenses often set "clear numerical limits" to define both amount and concentration allowable for the emission of contaminants; but only a few are ever tested and standards developed;

(2) For the most part, regulations rely on "guidelines," "objectives" and the like, all of which lack legal status (in that they are not binding);

(3) Even when the specific allowable numbers are incorporated in a binding document, these numbers are based on limited research;

(4) "[T]here are far more contaminants than there are standards," and the limits themselves are "systematically set too high";

(5) "Even when standards do exist and can be discovered for a particular contaminant," public demands for (a) "complete removal of the contaminant," and (b) a totally risk-free result cannot be met, for the most part, "without shutting down economic activity";

(6) Companies "object to cleaning up anything which cannot be scientifically proven to be dangerous." This is very much a lower standard.

(7) At best standards are negotiated, not based on "solid science"; and

(8) Even the objectivity and measurability standards of standards remain in question, as very few laboratories can perform these highly expensive tests, and they are, at best, open to a large margin of error (greater than 100 percent) (Saxe, 1991:20–27).

Saxe's work gives evidence in support of all her claims, and it is not necessary to reproduce that evidence here. But it is clear that most of the difficulties she mentions have not been mitigated, in the years following her presentation of these problems; in fact, some have been exacerbated, as noted in the "Five Year Report."

Science, and corresponding international environmental regulations, have moved forward since 1991, for instance, through the presence of complex systems theory as applied to environmental issues in North America and Europe, especially in the Scandinavian Countries (Ulanowicz, 1995; Kay and Schneider, 1995; see Chapter 6), and through the formulation of international standards and goals with global participation, such as Agenda 21, and other treaties following upon the Earth Summit (1992) (Brown, 2000). Therefore, several additional points must list beyond those present in Saxe's analysis.

The first point (1) to be noted is the total absence in the CEPA, to my knowledge, of Principle XV of Agenda 21, of the documents of the 1992 Earth Summit: the Precautionary Principle. Raffensperger and Tickner say that the Precautionary Principle, "like sustainability, is neither a well defined nor a stable principle" (Raffensperger and Tickner, 1999:16); They add:

Neither concept has much coherence other than it is captured by the spirit that is challenging the authority of science, the hegemony of the cost benefit analysis, the powerlessness of victims of environmental abuse, and the unimplemented ethics of intrinsic natural rights and intergenerational equity (Raffensperger and Tickner, 1999:16; compare Jordan and O'Riordon, 1999:19–23).

The principle however, is accepted by the United Nations and the European Union; the United States has appointed a special representative to ensure that the guidelines of U.S. EPA comply with Agenda 21 (Brown, 1995; Brown, 2000).

Hence, the Precautionary Principle ought to play a much larger role in the provincial and federal regulatory systems than it appears to do at this time. The Principle poses a serious challenge to the basis of environmental regulation:

> Precaution reflects the mood of distrust over the introduction of risky technologies, processes and products that are assumed to be forced on the unknowing and susceptible public by commercial interests, allied to governments, and exerting manipulative, self interested power over consumers (Raffensperger and Tickner, 1999:17).

This is not the appropriate locus for an in-depth discussion of the Precautionary Principle, but it is important to note its absence, despite the existence of a strong presence of the Principle in much of the current environmental literature, from risk assessment, to environmental ethics, to policy making and global regulative instruments, and although the Precautionary Principle is present in the 1999 CEPA, it is not present in the Ontario Environmental Protection Act.

The second major point (2) hinges on the much-debated question of scientific objectivity. Saxe points out that the standards are not based on "solid science." Much more needs to be said on that topic:

(1) "Solid," purely "objective" science is a myth. Even if bias values can be eliminated, at least in principle, methodological values are intrinsic to science, and noneliminatable (Shrader-Frechette, 1991).

(2) The presence of complexity now acknowledged in science eliminates even the possibility of full predictivity (Kay and Schneider, 1995; Ulanowicz, 1995; Ulanowicz, 2000).

(3) "Science" as a basis for public policy has been discussed from various ethical and political points of view, such as feminist (Longino, 1990); moral (Shrader-Frechette, 1991); racial (Bullard, 1995) once again eroding any argument for scientific "objectivity."

(4) The presence of complexity has been recognized in many areas, such as its role in endocrine disruptors and hormone mimics in individuals and in natural systems, as well as the cumulative and synergistic effects of all chemical substances (Colborn et al., 1996).

(5) The regulation of toxic substances is increasingly becoming a global concern (Cranor, 1991; Soskolne, 2000).

(6) The recognition of the meaning and the far-reaching impact of ecological disintegrity, not only for natural ecological systems, but also, increasingly, on human health (McMichael, 1995; Westra, 1998; Soskolne and Bertollini, 1999; Pimentel, Westra et al., 2000).

(7) The recognition of the hazardous "other face" of overcomsumption and business as usual in Northwest affluent countries (Westra and Werhane, 1998) and the impact of our "ecological footprint" (Rees and Wackernagel, 1995), on a global scale, and especially on populations of developing countries.

(8) Following upon (7), the recognition of the need for environmental justice as a substantive and determining consideration, when all environmental laws and regulations are passed at any level, and in any locale (Rockefeller, 2000; see Chapter 1; Appendix 1).

Both Saxe's list and my addenda, from the standpoint of complex systems theory, ecological footprint analysis, ecological integrity, environmental justice, epidemiology and the Precautionary Principle, show the flaws of the regulation we have considered. If sound science is a red herring because it cannot be relied upon to predict the precise limits of just how and where, specifically, our activities become harmful, then seeking the unattainable standard of certainty only allows for the continuation of ecoviolence and environmental injustice.

The legislative framework was flawed, and therefore impotent in its mandate to protect both the public and the natural environment in 1990. It would have been insufficient even in the context of the science and knowledge available at the time of *Silent Spring* (Carson, 1962). Nothing in the last 30 or more years since that time has improved the situation Carson deplored. In addition, the last ten or 15 years have seen the acceptance and codification of scientific complexity and uncertainty leading to the absolute necessity for caution and restraints (Ulanowicz, 1997; Goerner, 1994; Karr and Chu, 1999; Colborn et al., 1996; see Chapter 7).

The 1993 Environmental Bill of Rights is intended to increase public participation in decision-making. This is a laudable goal, but, when viewed against the facts we have noted, in regard to public information and general concern (Westra, 2000) in relation to the very instruments intended to protect the public we have examined cursorily, I am not convinced we can expect any significant gains. The whole participatory process, as it is designed, appears to be more like a public pacifier (Shrader-Frechette 1982), than like a significant move toward the protection of human and systemic health. It is not encouraging to notice that similar moves toward codes of ethics or other public declarations intended to include and encourage public participation have been also organized by a number of organizations and industries: the tobacco industry, the chemical industry, the breast implant industry (Westra, 1998), the nuclear industry (Shrader-Frechette, 1982), and even scientific associations such as American Plant Pathologist Association, have employed and supported public relations campaigns to improve their public image and quiet public fears. Intended to demonstrate these bodies' goodwill and interest in public health and concerns, they have been, for the most part, nothing but cosmetic cover-ups of the same operations aspiring to profits, not the protection of public health.

Ultimately, public acquiescence renders citizens complicit in the causation of the very harms that place everyone at risk (see Chapter 3; Westra, 1998). This scenario is particularly disturbing, given the presence of clear references to the Precautionary Principle and to many other of the concerns listed above, in the Canadian Environmental Protection Act (1999:ch.33). Much of the content of the

"Preamble," if fully enforced, would respond adequately to many of the critiques to the Ontario Environmental Protection Act critiqued above. Some samples of that document's language will suffice:

> Whereas the government of Canada is committed to implementing the precautionary principle that, where there are threats of serious or irreversible damages, lack of full scientific certainty shall not be used as a reason for postponing cost effective measures to prevent environmental degradation.
>
> The government of Canada recognizes that the risk of toxic substances, in the environment is a matter of national concern and that toxic substances once introduced into the environment, cannot always be contained within geographic boundaries.

Still within the Preamble, there are some strong references to "the protection of the environment and human health," and somewhat more vague references to "the control and management of the risks of any adverse affects of the use and release of toxic substances, pollutants and wastes."

The sections on "Administrative Duties" cement the "duty" of the government to "exercise its powers," according to Section 2.(1)(a), "In a manner that protects the environment and human health, applies the precautionary principle."

But in Section 2.(1)(b), once again the language of the act becomes so vague that the "duty" previously announced becomes no more than one among many considerations required for making a decision. The administrative duty in Section 2.(1)(b) is to "take the necessity for protecting the environment into account in making social and economic decisions," a position hardly sufficient to accomplish the duty named in Section 2.(1)(c): that is to "implement an ecosystem approach that *considers* (emphasis added) the unique and fundamental characteristics of ecosystems."

If the Canadian government is serious about these duties, then more than considerations appear to be required: to consider protecting and regulating, is not the same as doing so, and this appears to be in direct conflict with the Preamble. If the government recognizes the need for the protection of human health, to use the Precautionary Principle in regard to a host of substances, including biotechnologies and other toxic and polluting wastes, then this should also be recognized as a duty, not a consideration, among other "economic" factors.

Finally, as the CELA "Five Year Report" indicates in points 9 and 10, there is an apparent contradiction between some of the most recently articulated goals of the Harris government and the mandates of the Ministry of Natural Resources

(MNR) and even the CEPA (1999). Point 9 as we noted, addresses the question of the protection of wildlife and endangered species. But, for instance, "Fish" does not refer to wild fish stocks, it "means fisheries," and the MNR's Beyond 2000, in general, "places too great and emphasis on management and consumption of natural resources, and insufficient emphasis on the protection and conservation of natural systems" (Northwatch, 2000).

But part of CEPA 1999, *Administrative Duties* (Section 2.(1)), uses strong language in favor of environmental protection, such as the protection of "(j) the environment, including its biological diversity and human health, from the risk of any adverse effects of the use and release of toxic substances, pollutants or wastes." The 'Duties of the Government of Canada" are outlined as follows:

2.(1)(a) exercise its powers in a manner that protects the environment and human health, applies the precautionary principle that, where there are threats or serious or irreversible damage, lack of full scientific certainty shall not be used as a reason for postponing cost effective measures to prevent environmental degradation, and promotes and enforces enforceable pollution prevention approaches;

(a.1) take preventive and remedial measures to protect, enhance and restore the environment;

(b) take the necessity of protecting the environment into account in making social and economic decisions;

- implement an ecosystem approach that considers the unique and fundamental characteristics of eco systems;
- endeavour to act in cooperation with governments to protect the environment;

In contrast CELA, point 10, for instance, notes that, in March 2000, "Ontario emerged as the major obstacle to a federal provincial agreement on climate change at a meeting in Vancouver." Similarly, the joint responsibility of Ontario and Canada for the Great Lakes ecosystem is not well served, if the articulated aims of the GLWQA are not explicitly respected and supported. Cooperations with governments, whether provincial or otherwise, is necessary because, as I have argued, no environmental harm is ever, ultimately, a purely local occurrence, as, sooner or later, close by or far in time or location, the results are always global and extended (Westra, 2000a).

The gravity and reality of these threats makes it important that we consider once again the status of environmental offenses, and the question of responsibility in regard to their consequences.

4. CAUSATION AND RESPONSIBILITY IN THE LAW: ECOVIOLENCE AS "REAL CRIME"

In the realm of regulatory crimes, where offences have been designed to control the behavior of enterprises created by enabling legislation for the primary purpose of pursuing profits; where entire structure of corporate law insulates the individuals involved from personal responsibility for their actions; and where the consequences of failing to meet regulatory standards may mean the loss of human life, community, or irrepairable damage to the environment, what does it mean to say that an accused charged with an absolute liability offence who has failed to meet the standard of compliance in the legislation, may be "morally blameless"? (Sheehy, 1992:118).

Elizabeth Sheehy captures in this passage much that has been said here in order to defend the label of ecoviolence for these crimes. The responsibility for these violent acts, performed through the environment is therefore systemic and diffuse, and the reality of these circumstances renders the causal connections hard to trace.

First, what was the proximate cause of the e-coli epidemic in Walkerton? We can point to the deregulation and the cuts to environmental protection in general, which virtually eliminated the government's obligation to monitor the safety of the Walkerton water supply; or we could consider the lack of qualifications, and the dishonesty of the government bureaucrats entrusted with public health; or we could go even further back in time and question the presence of multiple farming operations including factory farms, all producing legally untreated waste much too close to drinking water facilities. Or perhaps we should view all of these as contributing causes. We can point to Mr. Stan Koebel in the role of cause, a man who was neither trained nor prepared for the grave responsibility that was his to handle. He claimed he did not understand the gravity of the situation, and was not sure what to do, or even whether doing anything specific was required. But testimony heard at the inquiry appears to support a different story: Koebel knowingly falsified reports for years, therefore he had to know the public health dangers to which he exposed Walkerton citizens, or there would have been no reason for falsifying documents. It will be useful to turn to the Law Reform Commission of Canada, Our Criminal Law (1976;19, 22, 33, 36, 38, 40) to pinpoint more clearly the causal relations between ecoviolence and those responsible, and to establish the criminality of the actions involved. The work of the Commission discusses the need for reforms within the criminal law, a position also supported by the argument of this work. In Chapter VII, "1" Scope of Criminal Law," attempts to define "true crime" in relation to regulatory offenses. Criminal acts are "morally wrong"; they must also be such that they seriously threaten and infringe "fundamental social values": primary among these, not surprisingly, are "crimes of violence."

If we speak of criminalizing those responsible for the legislative infrastructure of Canada or of Ontario (or both), and to similarly indict corporate persons, then we must start by being clear about the characteristics of both types of offenses: "true crimes" and regulatory offenses. What characterizes acts of real crime within the criminal code? The Commission suggests that we should be able to answer the following questions in the affirmative:

- Does the act seriously harm other people?
- Does it in some other way seriously contravene our fundamental values as to be harmful to society?
- Are we confident that the enforcement measures necessary for using criminal law against the act will not themselves seriously contravene our fundamental values?
- Given that we can answer "yes" to the above three questions, are we satisfied that criminal law can make a significant contribution to dealing with the problem?

In the light of the evidence (Westra, 2000; McMichael, 1995; McMichael, 2000), on the links between environmental violence and global morbidity and fatality, as well as the evidence of our own local disaster, I think there is no doubt that the first question can be answered in the affirmative.

What about the second questions? Again, respect for the life and the basic subsistence rights of all human beings, regardless of race, creed, gender, and location, are indeed fundamental human values internationally (Shue, 1996). As we shall see in the next chapters, these rights are codified in all manners of International Charters, Commissions, rules and regulations. If our democratically elected governments do not have the duty to protect us and our subsistence rights, including the right to a healthy, livable habitat, then our most basic and fundamental values are at stake. Hence, we can easily answer both the second question in the affirmative as well (see also Chapter 5).

The third question, however, is where the problem lies. In Canada today, after the Charter came into force, but also traditionally in the Anglo Saxon world, civil liberties are placed very high on the hierarchy of fundamental values. I have argued that life and subsistence conditions, in any society, ought to be prior and primary, and therefore that both stigma and even imprisonment in varying degrees, ought to be appropriate punishment in principle for those who commit assaults, but also for those who fail in their duty of care for others, whether or not death was foreseen or foreseeable (Westra, 2000). For the latter, their assaults or negligence are not focused in time, place, or even on one victim, but they affect whole communities through their actions. The causative link may not be a single one, let alone "the" cause, but that does not stop the prosecution of more diffuse crimes, such as the selling or importing of a prohibited substance.

An even clearer example of what I would term responsibility for diffuse harm, can be found in the aggravated assault case of *R. v. Cuerrier* ((1998) 2 S.C.R. 371). The case concerned a man, advised by a public health nurse in 1992 that, because he was HIV positive, he was to use condoms when engaging in sexual intercourse, and that he was to inform all prospective sexual partners of his condition. Cory J., in his factual background exposition, adds, "the respondent angrily rejected this advice. He complained he would never be able to have a sex life if he told anyone he was HIV positive."

Eventually Cuerrier formed a relationship with KM, who, in February 1993, was informed by another public health nurse that, while her tests were negative, Cuerrier was indeed HIV positive. After their breakup, Cuerrier formed another sexual relationship with BH, again not disclosing his condition. Subsequently, when the second woman also found out, Cuerrier was charged with two counts of aggravated assault. In addition, a question was raised about whether uninformed consent was still truly consent, given the dishonesty of the accused, who Cory J. added, engaged in "fraudulent misrepresentation." Cory J. said:

> The possible consequences of engaging in unprotected intercourse with an HIV positive partner is death. In these circumstances there can be no basis for distinguishing between lies and a deliberate failure to disclose. Without disclosure of his HIV status, there cannot be true consent.

When Cuerrier was advised of his duties with respect to all future sexual partners, there was no specific person named or intended, nor was any question raised about his intent to do harm, or to cause death. But the possible death of any partner in his case, could be viewed reasonably as a "consequence within the risk" (Hart and Honoré, 1985:94). Like the environmental harms we have described, the lack of openness and transparency on the part of the risk imposers, was termed "fraudulent misrepresentation," and his actions described as "aggravated assaults," although it would have been hard to prove *mens rea* in his case (see Chapter 5 for a discussion of *mens rea* in assault cases).

Lack of transparency on the part of risk imposers, misrepresentations about the possible gravity of the risks, and unconcern about the negligence with respect to the duty of care, are all typical in environmental crimes. When one engages in intercourse, especially with a stranger, there is also, even in the best of cases, some element of risk, but so is an element of choice or preference gratification. No such element can be found in those who are exposed to ecoviolence in general, or even specifically, to contaminated water as in Walkerton. Even the element of risk we noted would always be present with new sexual partners ought not to exist when citizens are dealing with a necessary service provided by these citizens' government.

To return briefly to the "four questions" raised in the 1976 Working Paper on "Criminal Law," the first three are questions of principle, but the other is a practical question, hence, the list is not entirely consistent. It is one thing to ask "is this right," quite another to ask "is it efficient" or "will it work." Normally, questions of principle, of right and wrong, are not debated from the standpoint of efficiency. Nor are laws concerning serious issues cancelled or repealed when they do not prove to be totally successful. For example, in Sicily and most other areas of Italy, Mafia associations and activities are criminalized. It would be absurd to say that, because these laws have not been efficient enough to eliminate Mafia activities, these activities should be decriminalized instead. In contrast, most people will argue that other measures should be taken, in addition to criminal prosecution, and that approach is desirable for the reduction of ecocrimes as well.

We have shown that there are strong similarities between the physical harms caused by ecoviolence and those arising from assaults (see Chapter 2). Therefore, it can be argued that all harms to our physical integrity, function, and life ought to be treated in similar fashion, if justice is to be served. Neither the immediacy nor the proximity of the causes(s) is readily visible in environmental crimes, but this difficulty ought to be noted, but not used to reduce or even avoid the responsibility for the final consequences and effects of these crimes. However, just as the harm is "diffuse" and nonspecific for the most part, so is the responsibility.

Reflecting on the antecedents of the case, we note additional causes: had untreated waste not been present near the water wells in question, Mr. Koebel would not have been faced with a situation he could not handle. Glanville Williams says:

> It may also happen in a particular case that the consequence is produced by the simultaneous operation of two conditions), i.e. but two independent causes such that either of them would have been adequate to produce (the consequence) (Williams in Hart and Honoré, 1985:235).

Hence, we can argue that perhaps *neither* Keobel's nonactions or omissions, *nor* the farms' untreated waste as such represent *the* cause of what eventually happened. But we might want to look at these and other circumstances as "concurrent causes" and "contributory negligence," rather than hope to find "the" cause, hence, more easily discover a perpetrator. Hart and Honoré provide a suggestion: "When joint or several tortfeasors have contributed to the same harm, the obvious rule is that each should be liable for the whole harm" (Hart and Honoré, 1985:235).

This appears to be a better principle for both torts and crimes, because we can immediately start tracing back decisions, and the application of regulations for months, maybe even years, and still find additional causes in a long series of contributory causes. In this case, as in most environmental cases, it would be almost impossible to isolate the *conditio since qua non*, the closest or most proximate cause:

What we do mean by the word "proximate" is that because of convenience of public, or a rough sense of justice, the law arbitrarily declines to trace a series of events beyond a certain point. This is not logic. It is practical policy (Pasgraf v. Long Island R.R. Co., 248 N.Y. 339, 162 N.E. 99 (1928), per Andrews J. in Hart and Honoré, 1985:90).

The question we must keep in mind is not about logic or practical considerations, however, it is about *justice*, beyond the rough approximation cited above. A better way of approaching causation in the case of "emergent risks" can be found in the case of *Snell v. Farrell* ((1990) 72 D.L.R.4th 289). The question addressed in this case of medical malpractice was the cause of Mrs. Snell's eventual eye nerve atrophy (and loss of sight) following an apparently botched eye operation. The loss of sight resulted "from a loss of the optic nerve's blood supply." Neither the plaintiff's expert nor that of the defendant "was able to express with certainty an opinion as to what caused the atrophy in this case, or when it occurred." Sopinka J. continues citing Turnbull J. (Court of Queen's Bench), who remarked that, "the trial judge was satisfied that the facts of the case at bar" brought it "within an emergent branch of the law of causation, whereby the onus to disprove causation shifts to the defendant in certain circumstances" (citing House of Lords in McGhee v. National Coal Board, (1973) 1 W.L.R. 1).

From our point of view, the most relevant statement by Sopinka J. appears in his discussion of "Causation Principles":

> The traditional approach to causation has come under attack in a number of cases in which there is concern that due to the complexity of proof, the probable victim of tortious conduct will be deprived of relief. This concern is strongest in circumstances in which, on the basis of some percentage of statistical probability, the plaintiff is the likely victim of the combined tortious conduct of a number of defendants, but cannot prove causation against a specific defendant or defendants on the basis of particularized evidence in accordance with traditional principles. The challenge to the traditional approaches manifested itself in cases dealing with non traumatic injuries such as man made diseases resulting from the widespread diffusion of chemical products, including product liability cases in which a product which can cause injury is widely marketed and manufactured by a large number of corporations (at 294).

If we consider all the events that contributed in various ways to the final (and ongoing) event or disaster, we must add each single element that played a part, no matter how negligible. This is particularly apt, when studying the result of the introduction of various substances into a biotic system to which they are not native, or at least not native in the present quantities (Karr and Chu, 1995). Unless each contributing cause is isolated and these are then brought together as a whole, there is no hope that a solution will be found to avoid such disasters in the future.

In the previous section, we noted the flaws and lacunae present in the legislative framework that defines environmental (regulatory) offenses. Those who approved those regulations certainly bear a strong responsibility for the consequences of their reckless and negligent work. Imagine a city planner who failed to have stop signs or traffic lights installed at a very busy intersection. No doubt, the drivers of any car involved in a collision would bear a responsibility for the accidents that ensued. But it is the responsibility of city planners, the municipality, and other bureaucrats to ensure that lights would be placed where needed, and they would be working; also it is their responsibility to ensure that those not abiding by those signals would be punished.

In comparison, a legislative framework that is so imprecise that, even if some people were intent on following the letter of the law, that "letter" would be very hard to detect, is to fail totally to provide a regulatory system that can establish clear guidelines, and therefore protect public health adequately (Muldoon, 1999). Hence, like those who would neglect to put up signals to control and direct traffic in a way that protects the public, the absence of clear stop signs to prevent continued hazardous activities appears to be a contributory cause to the eventual e-coli epidemic in this case. Nor can we term this contribution too small to be significant. Remote though it might have been, the imprecise and incomplete formulation of rules and terms is *not de minimis* (Hart and Honoré, 1985:226).

In general, there is no question about governments and ministries having a "duty" of care to the public with whom they are entrusted: the good of the citizens, hence, the protection of their life and health, minimally, is the condition that legitimizes their authority over citizens (Simmons, 1979; Hobbes, 1958; Hohfeld, 1923; Gilbert, 1994). With reference to the Canadian government, in the previous section we noted that the Canadian Environmental Protection Act (1999), in a section entitled "Administrative Duties," refers to such duties as "Duties of the Government of Canada." This section of the act concludes with: "(2) Nothing in this section shall be construed so as to prevent the taking of any action to protect the environment or human health for the purposes of this Act."

The same section at (2).(1)(g), adds the duty to "establish nationally consistent standards of environmental quality." Hence, if the government of Canada acknowledges these duties to both "environment" and "human health," and clarifies that nothing is "to prevent" appropriate preventive action, combined with the duty to provide "nationally consistent standards of environmental quality," then the series of events culminating in the Walkerton disaster are in clear conflict with the Canadian government's own, acknowledged duties. The Ontario Ministry ought to admit to both actions and omissions as part of the links to the chain of causation leading to the epidemic.

On the question of causation, Hart and Honoré argue that the three questions one needs to ask, in order to recognize what caused the harm, hence, who is responsible, in relation to the duty of care, are the following:

whether the defendant was under the duty of care, whether he was in a legal sense guilty of negligence to the plaintiff, and whether his action was the proximate cause of the plaintiff's injury, are really one and the same (Hart and Honoré, 1985:04).

The "one question" the authors suggest, citing Denning, L.J., who says that "simple is better," is: "is the consequence within the risk?" (Denning L.J. in Roe v. Minister of Health, (1954) 2 Q.B. 66, 86). The many, repeated references in the Canadian Environmental Protection Act (1999), to "duties to avoid harm to the environment and human health" confirms the Canadian government's awareness of multiple environmental risks, as does the reference in that act to the precautionary principle. Being fully aware of the threat of risks, further questions can be asked about the role of "interpersonal transactions":

> They are relevant whenever causing, inducing, helping, encouraging or permitting others to act, is a sufficient ground for criminal responsibility, even though the statutory of common law rule under which the liability arises is not expressly formulated in these terms (Hart and Honoré, 1985:363).

The role of a ministry, whether provincial or federal, is one of "causing," "encouraging," and "permitting" in regard to the corporate bodies whose operations provide the sources of the risks. This complicit relationship holds true in most environmental crimes, as it does in disasters where specific workers, employees of one or another corporation are exposed to disease or fatality (Glasbeek and Tucker, 1993).

Unfortunately, we do not have a Mr. Cuerrier, or any other single clear wrong doer who is easily identifiable in ecocrime. But some of those who bear responsibility for ecocrimes are beginning to emerge in the instructive case at Walkerton. We noted the role of the legislative framework within which the crimes have occurred, as well as the duties and responsibilities of the ministry and, more generally, of all government bodies toward their citizens. In the next section we will discuss the other persons whose obligations must be examined, that is the corporate and business persons, whose activities through their products, processes, trade practices, and wastes, may well be the primary risk-imposers among us.

5. CORPORATE RESPONSIBILITY AND ACCOUNTABILITY FOR ECOVIOLENCE

> Pollution, population growth and environmental crusading are expected to put enormous pressure on the world's supply of fresh water over the next ten years. Some of Canada's largest engineering companies are gearing up for the day when water is moved around the world like oil, or wheat, or wood. . . . What will be important is who has the right to sell it to the highest bidder (*Report on Business*, in Barlow, 1999:21).

In the previous section we focused primarily on governmental institutional responsibility. Political theory, moral principles, and the national legislative framework ensure that ministries and other government bodies have a duty of care, a responsibility for the citizens in the regions they govern. This, however, is not true of corporate bodies, especially the powerful multinational corporations who operate at many levels and in many countries, under diverse jurisdictions. As we noted, it is extremely difficult even to characterize their hazardous activities as crimes although, when these crimes are perpetrated, multinationals operating in various countries cannot claim state immunity, unless they are true representatives of their countries in their foreign operations. (I.L.C. Draft Articles on Jurisdictional Immunities of States as adopted at 43rd Session, 1991, and recommended to U.N. General Assembly, Article 10, 30 I.L.M. 1554 (1991)).

Many view these harmful activities as providing "countervailing benefits" (Shrader-Frechette, 1991), to the impoverished populations where they operate, without considering the fact that, for the most part, the benefits accrue to the corporate shareholders and officials, the harms to the unconsenting and uninformed recipient of the harmful technologies they produce and distribute (Shrader-Frechette, 1991). Moreover, if the legislative and regulatory framework of Northwest democratic countries is insufficient to provide full protection to their citizens, one can assume that in regions where much less public information, literacy, and participation prevail, it would be unrealistic to expect better, tougher protective measures to be present.

The legal and moral status of the corporation should be discussed in the context of *mens rea* requirements for assaults convictions in corporate crimes. To sum up, briefly, corporations are indeed legal persons, and there are several theories that address the meaning of that terminology (Chick, 1993; French, 1992:134–145).

There are many theories formulated to address this question. For our purpose, it will be sufficient to mention three major positions: the "Fiction Theory," the "Legal Aggregate Theory," and the position that is taken to be most appropriate, the "Corporation's Internal Decision Structure," clearest approach to predicate corporate intentionality (French, 1979:102–105). The "Fiction Theory" has its roots in Roman jurisprudence, but its main flaw is that, in relying on the description of "legal fictitious persons," it ignores the biological existence of real persons, as well as, by implication, of any others. The "Legal Aggregate Theory," recognizes the biological reality of persons and grants priority to these legal subjects, while treating corporate persons as purely derivative, and identifying them only with "directors, executives and stockholders" (French, 1979:102). In so doing, however, Aggregate Theory supporters are choosing arbitrarily where to ascribe responsibility, and make it impossible to distinguish between a group (or mob) and corporate reality.

A case in English law demonstrates the difficulties embedded in the first two theories. In *Continental Tyre and Rubber Co., Ltd. v. Daimler Co. Ltd.* (1915), K.B. 893), a company whose directors and shareholders were German subjects and residents, was incorporated in England and carried on its business there. The question was whether Continental Tyre should be treated as an English subject, and could bring suit in an English Court (while Britain was at war with Germany). The Court of Appeals' majority opinion (five to one) was that, "the corporation was an entity created by statute," hence that it was "a different person altogether from the subscribers to the memorandum, the shareholders on the register" (French, 1979:102). Hence, the corporation's biological composition may not be identical to its true "personhood" or its intentional structure.

It is also worthy of note that not all who are subjects of rights can in fact be the administrators of rights, and infants, fetuses, animals, future generations and ecosystems are relevant examples of entities that have been declared at one time or another to have some rights, although it has never been argued that any of these could administrate their own rights (Stone, 1974). If we accept a nonspecific description of a person, such as the subject of a right, we can at least make the following claims:

(1) Biological existence is not always necessary to personhood;
(2) The subject of a right is "the noneliminatable subject of a responsibility ascription" (French, 1979:103).

Responsibility is the necessary correlative of a right. In this sense, it goes beyond simply being the one (or the corporate person) who performed an action. We must address the question of intent. For corporations and institutions, the Corporate Internal Decision Making (CID) structure is the locus of the intentionality we intend to establish. Through the CID structure corporate power is deployed, setting in motion a series of actions flowing from a central, hierarchically made decision, but involving the "acts of biological persons who . . . occupy various stations on the organizational chart of the corporation " (French, 1979:106).

An advantage of this approach is to be able to maintain corporate responsibility while also, at the same time, retaining the ability to consider varying degrees of intent or of desire to bring about a certain result, the product of corporate ordered activities. French's argument strongly supports corporate responsibility and, because of its inclusivity, could easily be extended to other institutional bodies, as long as these, too, are possessed of "internal decision making structures." In fact, his argument can be used to apportion responsibility (perhaps even liability) to various players in the *Walkerton* case, as it involves both corporate and institutional "persons." Can French's argument help to redefine the *mens rea* question? French assumes the presence of intentionality; would that impose a heavier burden upon the Crown in regulatory offenses cases? Perhaps we can argue that the CID structure approach *implies* intentionality as corporate activities are performed by subjects of rights in all cases where an action has been performed or omitted. But neither institutions nor corporations may be free to be the subjects of rights without accepting the corresponding full responsibility toward all other right holders, be they individual or corporate.

In other words, once a corporate body has been distinguished from a mob or an aggregate, and is, in fact, *defined* by its CID structure, then it is clear that its very nature is to be capable to intentional agency: that is the root of its "person-hood." In addition, because it is not a biological entity, it can also be argued that such persons are not capable of the emotions that characterize individual biolog-ical entities. Corporate persons then, can only intend, rationally, whatever activ-ity they choose; such actions cannot be the result of sudden impulses or passions (provocation), fear for its own life (self-defense), or addiction (intoxication). Neither mental disorders nor automatism or any other syndrome will be possible. Hence, in a sense, by claiming to be persons, yet admitting they are not individ-ual, biological ones, corporations may represent the clearest examples of pure purposefulness, or desire to bring about certain results, including the activities whose results are the physical elements of an *actus reus*.

If this line of argument is accepted, the Crown's burden of proof in regard to the mental element of a corporate fault, will be substantially reduced and sim-plified. Once the physical elements of the fault are present, and after they can be causally connected to the corporate person, the mental states that connote its agency are limited to variants of intent, and may range from the purposeful desire to bring about a certain result, to the certain knowledge that the result will occur, the probability or possibility (recklessness) that a result might follow.

But corporations do have aims, goals, and purposes, as do institutions (and many of these are even codified in their statements of intent or codes of practice). Thus, the only conclusions one can draw is that, for the most part, and barring sabotage or people acting outside the corporate perimeter on their own, whatever corporations actually do is something they decided, planned out, and fully intended to accomplish (for the possibility of a due diligence defense, see Chapter 5). That guarantees the responsibility of the perpetrators. Chick argues that the United States has had a long time to define and regulate corporate rights in rela-tion to Constitutional law. However, he adds: ". . . it was only through the accep-tance of one particular corporate personality, the "aggregate theory," that American courts even decided that corporations were entitled to claim constitu-tional rights" (Chick, 1993:15). But the aggregate theory is not correct, and that is why it is not generally accepted as the best way to understand corporate per-sonality and function. The reasoning employed in order to link corporations and Constitutional protection, is that individuals, those who compose the corporation, should not lose Constitutional guarantees because they join together in a lawful association. I find this argument to be incoherent: if the lawful association is to provide the associate with a new entity, with legal personality and corresponding rights, then it is not logical to argue that the new body is nothing but an aggregate of persons, and nothing more. If the newly formed association is *one*, rather than as French argued, a mob or a heap with no unitary defining characteristics, then there appears to be no grounds for requiring special status for it, any more than it would be to require and demand such status for any crowd.

French is correct in saying that, to enjoy some rights (and legal status), something more is required than a mass of individuals. There has to be something that makes many into one, at least in one respect. He found this unifying element in the CID structure (French, 1979) of the corporate/institutional body. It is not sufficient to say that each component part of the association has rights and duties, true though it is. There are simply no grounds for additional legal status and personality, unless we can identify something that serves to unify the corporation. The CID structure provides unity through purpose, and therefore provides that ground. However, the additional entity, as it acquires the right to be and to act, like single individuals, single citizens, has duties and obligations.

It is possible to argue that corporate personality theories have been manipulated and are still discussed from the standpoint of political ideals (Romano, 1984:923). But what remains clear, is that in order to be one person, there must be something to permit such terminology as an undirected crowd or mob has no status as such, beyond that of the individuals that comprise it. On that basis, therefore, the CID structure theory of corporate personality can be accepted as the most accurate, and several points will follow; to sum up:

(1) We cannot accept diminished responsibility of any sort for it, because as a separate unit, different from its human components, I can never claim defenses or mitigating circumstances based on human frailties and emotions (see Chapter 6);

(2) Based on similar reasons, the lack of human features, we need not claim for it the status of "vulnerable accused" in courts of law, and seek for it corresponding Charter protection (Sheehy, 1993);

(3) Having been accorded independent status and rights in the law will entail corresponding duties and responsibilities: individual purposes cannot be persued without considering the rights of others as imposing on individual freedom. So too the corporation must assume full responsibility for all their activities and their results.

In *R. v. Wholesale Travel Groups Ltd.* ((1991) 3 S.C.R. 154), Cory J. argues that the Charter was primarily intended to protect "vulnerable members" of society, hence, as in (2) above, no corporate institution, especially one provided already (legally) with "limited liability," should be able to appeal to the Charter for protection.

In essence, the Charter's primary focus is the protection of individual rights, an intensely and particularly "liberal" focus, according to Chick and the sources he cites (Chick, 1993:56–57; Hutchinson and Peter, 1998; Sopinka, 1989):

> Those who take the view that individual rights must always come first, and . . . must take precedence over collective goals are often speaking out of a view of a liberal society which has become more and more widespread in the Anglo American world (Taylor, 1992:440–441).

I have argued that liberal democracy, as presently implemented in Northwest affluent countries, has failed to protect even the citizens in the nations where it prevails, let alone those who, though geographically or temporally removed from decision-making institutions, are bearing the gravest risks (Rees, 2000; Rees and Wackernagel, 1994; Westra, 1998). This is true because collective and community rights are not respected, nor are the natural systems and processes on which we depend for life and health, and the case study of Walkerton, discussed in this work, is a clear example of this general trend.

The protection of the common good is neither an institutional not a corporate priority in the environmental context. The same is true in the area of employee's rights, for workers employed in risky businesses, and it is constructive to compare the two (Draper, 1991).

A well-known Canadian mining disaster can be analyzed in a similar way as the legislative framework for the protection of the workers is as lacking as that intended for the protection of citizens from environmental harms. In their discussion of the *Westray Mine* disaster, Harry Glasbeek and Eric Tucker point out the repeated, unpunished disasters brought about by unconstrained corporate activities. Among several points worthy of note, some could be equally repeated for the ecoviolence in Walkerton' for instance:

(1) Invariably, the inquiries reveal that the deaths and injuries are attributable, at least in part, to violations of existing mine regulations;

(2) This finding inexorably leads to statements of firm resolve that their will be no recurrences, no more violations, no more disasters. But, as the records show, these oft-asserted goals are never realized (Glasbeek and Tucker, 1993:14).

The assumptions underlying these glaring breaches of human rights are that somehow the employing corporations, the law dispensing institutions, and the affected workers are all working towards similar or at least compatible goals (Glasbeek and Tucker, 1993:15–16). This is both untrue and indefensible on the basis of evidence. There is no deep and substantive consensus between corporate owners and their employees, although the latter, especially in male dominated industries, tend to frown on manifesting any concern about workplace safety and risk, as not "manly" enough. Similar viewpoints were also expressed, by the male population in Lewiston, N.Y. (see Section 6), while the women, the wives and mothers who had to watch their children and families sicken and die, had the courage to join together and speak up. This is a recurrent theme, not only in corporate/employment hazards, but equally in the case of environmental hazards.

A risky business (Draper, 1991), such as a corporation disposing capacitors laden with PCBs (Westra, 1994) or the nuclear industry attempting to site a waste disposal facility against the citizen's will in Nevada (Schrader-Frechette, 1993), are viewed by the men in community as a possible source of employment and the risk involved is considered an acceptable part of doing their job, even viewed as a "heroic exercise of manly confrontation," itself understood as a test of toughness, rather than an unwarranted and unconsented risk to be avoided (Glasbeek and Tucker, 1993:28). In all these cases, workplace/health concerns and ecoviolence/health concerns, are treated in a similar manner, both in the public mind, and by the boardrooms and the institutions that could control such risks.

We should question our acquiescence in the context of our liberal democratic political system, as we reconsider the corporate/institutional "facilitator" who enables and supports the risks and condones the harms. One of the major causes of our unthinking support of "business as usual" is the tranquilizing effect of marketing and advertising campaigns, within the context of what I have termed "the failure of liberal democracy" (Westra, 1998:53). Thomas Homer-Dixon shows democracy's lacks in his work. He says:

> If you only have procedural democracy in a society that's exhibiting environmental stress and already has cleavages, say ethnic cleavages, then procedural democracy will tend to aggravate these problems and produce societal discord, rather than social concord (Homer-Dixon, 1994).

The same point can be made about economic cleavages, rampant in a capitalist system, whose openly avowed goal is increased production, increased profits, not global justice, conservation, and respect for the natural systems on which their very activities depend.

6. CONCLUSIONS

The question of responsibility and accountability is hard to answer, not only for Walkerton, specifically, but also for ecocrime in general. Positive support in common law for the argument of this chapter can be found in the Law Reform Commission of Canada.

The Law Reform Commission of Canada (Working Paper No. 44, (1985)), is entitled "Crimes against the environment"; it contains a section where "Mental Element" is described as follows:

1. That the mental element for a crime against the environment should be intention, recklessness or negligence.
2. That the degree of negligence required for criminal liability should be that which falls well below the standard of reasonable care required for ordinary or civil negligence.
3. Whereas intentional or reckless pollution could by exception incur criminal liability under this new code offence even in the absence of harm or damage to human health, negligently harming or endangering the environment should only incur such liability if the pollution causes or risks death or bodily injury (Ibid. at 68–69).

The responsibility for these crimes appears to belong to regulatory legislative and institutional bodies as well as to corporate ones. To some extent all of us who accept the cosumerist, technologically advanced lifestyle prevalent in affluent Northwest countries as well as in nondemocratic states in developing countries, are, in a sense, both victims and complicit in the harms, as we live in an upstream/downstream world (Scherer and Attig, 1990).

Humans are, by their very nature, "patch disturbers" (Rees, 2000:142), but, for the most part, their goals and plans have neither consideration nor understanding for the role of their habitat and their total dependence upon it.

Reed Noss says:

Biology—the science of life—and planning (for example regional planning or land use planning) have been considered totally separate disciplines, pursued by different training and different interests. But, at a time when the ecological integrity of the Earth is declining rapidly and human land use is the major cause of this decline (Ehrlich and Ehrlich, 1981; Wilson, 1992; Noss and Cooperrider, 1994) effective conservation requires that we bring biology and planning together (Noss, 2000:193).

And here, of course, lies the problem: the focus remains economic, whether on the obscene growth of capitalist consumption, or on the unconcerned emphasis on who owns and controls the means of production, rather than on the injustice of ecofootprints due to both overproduction *and* overconsumption. Ecofootprint analysis discloses the hard truth:

The human enterprise now grows in part, by drawing on cumulative stocks of natural capital. Regrettably, unlike our ancestors, modern humans can no longer simply move on to greener pastures, when our planetary patch wears out. This means that, contrary to prevailing international development models, so called First World material lifestyles are simply not sustainably extendible to the entire world population (Rees, 2000:150).

Neither space, nor yet our chosen topic, will permit an in-depth analysis of capitalist vs. socialist systems, and some believe that some environmental advances could be made under the latter (Faber, 1998). The point at issue remains that the goal of increasing incomes and economic capabilities everywhere is a naive pipe dream, no more. Equalization requires substantive and radical stepping back on the part of everyone in democratic affluent Western societies, far removed from what Vandana Shiva termed "absolute poverty" (Shiva, 1989).

I have argued elsewhere that this is a moral imperative for all those, workers or owners who are overconsuming now (Westra, 1998; Brenkert, 1997; Daly, 1997; Brown, 1997).

Even the International Business Council for Sustainable Development (BCSD),

. . . has recognized that "industrialized world reductions in material through put, energy use, and environmental degradation of over 90 percent will be required by 2040 to meet the needs of a growing world population fairly, within the planet's ecological means (BCSD, 1993:10; Rees, 2000:154).

We must, therefore, accept that the basic, crucial question at this point in time, is not how to fairly divide the industrialized pie between corporations and workers. Rather, both groups must moderate their demands in proportion to their present economic means, in the interest of a livable habitat for all, and in defense of global justice.

In conclusion, to return to our example and to the question of responsibility and accountability in regard to Walkerton (but also for ecoviolence in general) it is clear that the emphasis on economics is wrongheaded and misguided from the standpoint of morality and from that of substantive justice as well.

Mark Sagoff said it best in *The Economy of the Earth* (1988). In his discussion of another ecodisaster, the nuclear and toxic wastes buried (but not forgotten by the residents) at Lewiston, N.Y., and the morbidity and fatalities that followed, he attacks cost benefit methodology and all decisions based on preferences (and willingness to pay), rather than on what is right (Westra, 2000). Sagoff says that the theory on which this approach is based, is indeed "neutral" among our values, having first imposed a theory of what value is. Sagoff adds:

"No matter how much people are willing to pay three will never be the square root of six. Similarly, segregation is a national curse and the fact that we are willing to pay for it does not make it better but only makes us worse" (Sagoff, 2000:472).

What we need instead, is a moral theory that supports respect for persons and therefore prescribes protection for their environment. In Lewiston, people "demanded to know the truth about the dangers that confronted them . . ." Sagoff says: ". . . the residents of Lewiston asked for an explanation, justice and truth, and they were told that their wants would be taken care of" (Sagoff, 2000:473).

History repeats itself today, and it is equally morally repugnant when it happens in Canada, and when the waste is organic rather than nuclear. I cringed and waited for a public outcry (one that did not happen) when Walkerton residents were offered economic redress, and were asked to sign away their rights to sue, to indict those who were guilty of numerous crimes, in exchange for money. In contrast, I have argued that indeed crimes, assaults, and negligent homicides and infanticides were committed at Walkerton, that human health and life were respectively compromised and taken away. The conclusion then is that all those responsible ought to be stigmatized, charged with all the offenses whose results were disclosed at the inquiry, and eventually convicted and jailed; they should not be allowed to compound the tragedy of their crimes toward Ontario citizens with a monetary payoff.

In the next chapter we will look beyond domestic environmental law and consider how criminal law deals with assaults and homicides, because, as we have already argued, these are in many respects analogical to the effects of ecoviolence (see Chapter 2).

7. POSTSCRIPT: THE TRAGEDY OF WALKERTON TWO YEARS LATER

Two years have passed since the events following what journalists and the Canadian Environmental Law Association (CELA) termed "Tragedy on Tap" (Lindgren et al., 2001). The Walkerton inquiry under Commissioner Judge Dennis O'Connor carefully established the lines of causality, the presence of numerous unchecked errors, the negligent actions of untrained, unqualified and careless personnel, who were neither supervised nor reviewed by appropriate bureaucracies.

CELA's lawyers who supported and represented the Walkerton residents, wanted to defend their interests and to ensure that their rights were respected, at least within the parameters of existing regulative infrastructures. They also wanted to redress the regulatory deficits and the policy gaps that instituted a significant part of the events leading to the tragedy. The main focus of their efforts was to establish a "safe drinking water act," its purpose, "the protection of human health through the control and regulation of drinking water systems and drinking water testing" (Ministry of the Environment, Ontario, Oct. 29, 2002), but Commissioner O'Connor issued 28 recommendations in the *Report of the Walkerton Inquiry* (Part One). Four of the 22 recommendations that gave the Ministry of the Environment "lead responsibility," were implemented in advance of the release of Part One of the Report (Ministry of the Environment, Oct. 29, 2002):

- conducting annual inspections of municipal drinking water systems;
- inspecting municipal drinking water systems for certification and training standards;
- developing criteria for "groundwater under the influence of surface water";
- implementation of time—limited certificates of approval.

Since the release of Part One, four more recommendations were also implemented:

- requiring continuous monitoring of chlorine and turbidity;
- ensuring resources are provided for inspections;
- the development of communal drinking water systems training courses for operators; and
- implementing regular meetings between Ministry of the Environment Offices and local health units.

Other recommendations offer specific protocols and procedures and include the possibility of unannounced facility inspections by the ministry.

Most important of all is the recommendation to design and implement an Ontario Safe Drinking Water Act Proclaimed on October 29, 2002. Part Two of the *Report of the Walkerton Inquiry* focuses on five areas including "Watershed—based source protection," and a new Nutrient Management Act, posted for comment on the Environmental Bill of rights Registry on August 20, 2002, (comments period ended October 19, 2002). The two parts of the first regulation are (Ministry of the Environment, Oct. 29, 2002):

- content requirement for nutrient management plans (NMPs), which set out the best way to use nutrients in manure, commercial fertilizers and other nutrient—rich materials, in order to maximize economic benefits while minimizing environmental effects.
- the categories of livestock operations which will require the NMPs, and when they will require them.

The second point is particularly important, as the events of Walkerton indicate: whether the "culprit(s)" in that instance was a family farm who attempted to take "due care" within the murky and incomplete infrastructure present at the time or not, the principles involved are the same.

The Ontario government announced a "bold plan to develop a watershed-based source protection framework in Ontario" (Ibid. at 5). But the Great Lakes Water Quality Agreement (GLWQA) has had an even "bolder" plan in existence, as it demands the "protection and restoration of the biological and chemical integrity" for the whole area already, and has done so since 1978 (see Chapter 6).

In addition, the Nutrient Management Act is still dependent upon the Farm Practices Tribunal, an institution that is expected to pass judgment *first* on what does or does not constitute a "normal farming practice," hence on what is still, today, categorized as exempt from polluting prohibitions.

Both the Safe Drinking Water Act, and the Nutrient Management Act, provide ways of mitigating some of the harms arising from farming and industrial "farms" and their operations. Note that the NMAs lacks a Purpose Statement, or a Preamble, like all other environmental laws have: Richard Lindgren (2001) recommends that:

> The NMA should be amended to include a public interest purpose statement that provides that the purpose of the Act is to protect the natural environment and public health in Ontario from adverse effects caused by nutrient management and other agricultural activities.

Noting that the "normal farming practices "exemptions persist, Lindgren notes:

> . . . section 61 of the NMA amends section 6(2) of the Environmental Protection Act so as to provide that the section 6 prohibition does not apply to animal wastes disposed of in accordance with both normal farming practices and regulations made under the NMA. While this kind of clarification is welcome, it begs the question of why the other agricultural exceptions under the Environmental Protection Act have not been similarly amended by the NMA. More fundamentally, it begs the question of why these agricultural exceptions still remain within Ontario's environmental laws (Ibid. at 13).

Some Canadian and American areas' legislation require Cumulative Effects Assessments (CEAs) for environmental impact assessments, that is, these assessments must take into consideration much more than the bare facts of a proposed project. William Ross says: "Cumulative effects are effects of the project under review in combination with the effects of other past, present and future human activities" (Ross, 1998:267). Those who propose a project, at least in the Province of Alberta, where these CEAs are required, must identify the "valued ecosystem components" (VECs) of a proposed project, then proceed to show that cumulative effects would not adversely affect VECs, before the project can be deemed acceptable by environmental authorities. This approach is essential for any regulative framework that intends to take both environment and public health seriously, although they are clearly highly demanding.

Unfortunately, this seriousness is not much in evidence even in post-Walkerton Ontario. For instance, one of the recommendations of the Walkerton Inquiry, requiring "regular meetings" between local Ministry of Environment (MOE) office and health unit personnel, says: "Any affected operator of laboratory *should be invited* to attend the meeting" (Recommendation 5, Implemented May 2002) (emphasis added). This is hardly the approach of a determined administration to redress the grave wrongs done to its citizens, let alone to prevent or to punish criminal negligence. Lindgren et al., "Overview," *Tragedy on Tap* (May 15, 2001), points out that (1) there is still no public right to safe drinking water; (2) there are few mechanisms for holding drinking water suppliers or governmental officials accountable, whereas the EU, several U.S. States, England, Wales and Australia, all have much better, earlier, and clearer directives to protect their citizens (Wordsworth, 2001:16–24). Speaking of the inadequacy of Canadian water laws, David Boyd says:

> Many Canadians believe, incorrectly that they have a right to clean, safe water. While this right may exist at the philosophical level, it does not exist under Canadian law. There is no such thing provided in Canada's Constitution, the *Charter of Rights and Freedoms*, or in the common law. As a judge in the BC Supreme Court recently ruled in a lawsuit where citizens sought unsuccessfully to halt logging activities in their watershed, "There is not before me an established case for the concept of a right to clean water" (Boyd, 2003:25; Red Mountain Residents and Property Owner's Association v. B.C. (Ministry of Forests), (2000) 35 C.E.L.R. (N.S.) 127 (B.C.S.C.))

Hence, we can conclude, some of the major questions raised in this chapter have not been fully answered, even by the introduction of two new acts, and there appears to be little hope of finding ecologically sound and public health oriented answers in the near future. In contrast to the mandate to find "solutions that maximize economic benefit while minimizing environmental effects," as cited, we will see in our concluding chapter (Chapter 8) that the European Court of Human Rights of the Council of Europe clearly demonstrates that the right to life includes implicitly the right to biological integrity and normal human function, hence that it is incommensurable with questions of economic benefit (*Guerra v. Italy* and *Lopez-Ostra v. Spain*). These cases clearly imply and take as fundamental to their position that environmental rights are human rights, as Judge Weeramantry stated and will be discussed below (see Chapter 7), and that the latter cannot be respected and defended without equal respect for the former.

CHAPTER 5

THE CASE FOR CRIMINALIZING ECOVIOLENCE: CAN IT BE DONE THROUGH CANADIAN NATIONAL LAWS?

1. INTRODUCTION: IS VIOLENCE "QUASI-CRIMINAL"?

The previous chapter argued that ecoviolence, whether local, regional, or global, should be treated as a crime. Because it is not, for the most part, a crime committed by one person against another, ecoviolence does not truly fit within our definitions specified by the Criminal Code. All activities related to the environment are considered as regulated by several acts, and breaches of those acts are treated outside the Code under the rubric of "regulatory offenses." Viewed as quasi criminal these offenses are not subject to the high requirement of proving *mens rea* in order to recognize the culpability of the offender.

Elizabeth Sheehy explains the history of this division:

"True crimes" are said to require proof of *mens rea* which is subjectively tested from the point of view of the accused's actual state of mind. In contrast, public welfare offences those regulatory offences created to serve the public interests, used the legal concept of absolute liability (Sheehy, 1992:111).

This passage represents the background against which the important *Sault Ste. Marie* case was played out ((1978), R. v. City of Sault Ste. Marie, 85 D.L.R.3d 161). The facts of the case are simple. On November 18, 1970, the city of Sault Ste. Marie agreed that Cherokee Disposal and Construction Co. Ltd. would dispose of all city waste. Cherokee was to supply both site and labor, as well as all material and equipment. The company selected a site near Cannon Creek (close to Root River). They decided to follow the area or continuous slope method: the garbage would be compacted in layers and each day natural sand or gravel would be used to cover each layer.

The Cannon Creek area was the location of several fresh water springs at that time, but Cherokee dumped material to cover them, before proceeding as planned with the layered garbage. Because of the resulting pollution, Cherokee was convicted under Section 32(1) of the Ontario Water Resources Act (1990). The question was whether the city itself was also guilty. The original trial judge found that, because Cherokee was not a city employee, their responsibility ended with the hiring. At trial Judge Vannini found the city to be guilty (under strict liability). The Divisional Court set aside that judgment, but found that the charge required *mens rea*. The case eventually reached the Court of Appeal, where the majority agreed that proof of *mens rea* was required. Mr. Justice Dickson dissenting said:

> the inescapable inference to be drawn from the finding of fact of Judge Vannini was that the city had known of the potential impairment of waters of Cannon Creek and Root River and had failed to exercise its clear powers of control (Dickson, J. In R. v. Sault Ste. Marie, 85 D.L.R.3d 161, at 162).

The point at issue here is the question of *mens rea*. Dickson J. adds:

> The distinction between the true criminal offence and the public welfare offence is one of prime importance. Where the offence is criminal, the Crown must establish a mental element, namely, that the accused who committed the prohibited act, did so intentionally or recklessly, with knowledge of the facts constituting the offence, or with wilful blindness toward them. Mere negligence is excluded from the concept of the mental element required for conviction (Ibid.).

Dickson J. also emphasizes the "generally held revulsion against punishment of the morally innocent." These points will be addressed below, in this chapter and the next. But, even more disconcerting, is the fact that many of the difficulties we encounter in regard to environmental offenses is their characterization as regulatory offenses in the law, and the resulting implication that they are less serious harmful than real criminal offenses.

The first hurdle is that very label, regulatory offenses, as this title places the ecoviolence offense within a context that is entirely inappropriate to it; grouping it together with false advertising, or importing of controlled goods, under the Export and Imports Permit Act (1985), is wrong in itself. Environmental offenses, in contrast to many of these other offenses, have life and death impacts on the population or have grave, and possible irreversible consequences for their habitats (Sheehy, 1992). Considering the facts of the Walkerton example (see Chapter 4), we quickly discover that the series of regulatory offenses that took place were not only perpetrated by the expected actors in such cases, industry, or corporations, but also by the institutional regulators themselves.

Accordingly, looking for remedies for the present situation might start with a serious reexamination of the categorization of offenses in general. This cannot be accomplished by case law decisions, or even by judicial *fiat* or interpretation. But what I have attempted to prove so far, as I presented both evidence and arguments, is that because of technological advances, and because of over half a century of uninformed, unconsidered choices by nearly all states and institutional systems, the hazards to which we are all exposed through these regulatory offenses have grown exponentially in dangerousness and unpredictable consequences. The role of governments and regulators needs serious consideration. While it is true that so called "stigma" attached to the prosecution of corporate bodies is not a serious concern (Sheehy, 1992), a parallel prosecution of governments or other regulatory institutions may have much more deleterious consequences. We do not expect our businesses necessarily to protect us, but we vote for a government and a system of laws, both of which, we believe, are intended to do just that.

Perhaps a commission or a working group ought to be convened to separate regulations governing business practices from the sort of public welfare offenses where life is at stake. Regulatory offenses may include acts that mislead the public, defraud the public, or put the public at risk to have their own activities rendered illegal, as when a realtor performs certain services for a client without a valid licence. The public has a right not to be misled or defrauded, but there is a difference in kind, not only a difference of a degree, between an injury that threatens or thwarts our plans or our property, and one that puts at risk our physical integrity or our life. The law recognizes this difference in the way it deals with thefts, on one hand, and assaults and homicides, on the other, particularly in sentencing. This difference is a precedent of sorts.

Another example and perhaps another sort of precedent can be found in the way the tobacco industry has recently been dealt with, without complete criminalization, yet in a matter that is different from the ways other commercial activities are treated (for instance, in respect to their freedom of advertising). (RJR-MacDonald Inc. v. Canada (Attorney General), (1995) 3 S.C.R. 199). The heavy toll that industry has taken over the years and continues to take every day in lives, disease, and addiction, should be instructive for law-makers, especially when one considers that although some people derive pleasure from smoking, and demand the freedom to continue in that practice, self-destructive though it is, no one, to my knowledge, claims pleasure in the diseases caused by environmental contamination. The e-coli epidemic in Walkerton is an example.

In conclusion, with the example of tobacco companies, we ought to be able to learn from its history of lies and deceptions, not to trust either corporate assurances, or the way we presently regulate corporate activities (see Chapter 2). The trail of death that is disclosed by that industry's history might encourage law makers to at least reconsider the way they categorize other life threatening commercial activities.

The second major hurdle is the question of institutional responsibility in general, as well as through its complicity in corporate crime. Sheehy relates parts of the Supreme Court's majority opinion in *Wholesale Travel*, a case where the Court of Appeal had characterized the offense one of "absolute liability." Sheehy relates in part Cory J.,'s writing the majority opinion:

. . . he began with the proposition that legislation may be "regulatory" rather than "truly criminal" if it deals with conduct which is not "inherently wrongful," but is instead designed to protect those unable to protect themselves from the adverse effects of "otherwise lawful activity" (Sheehy, 1992:116).

Cory J. even ventures that a "lesser degree of moral fault" suffices for the prosecution of "social welfare offenses" when these are "designed to secure social ends such as the presentation of a competitive market" (Ibid.).

This analysis may well apply to *Wholesale Travel*, a case where misleading and defrauding the public were at issue, but an attack on the physical integrity of the person is inherently wrongful, as is causing a death, whether it occurs within hours, weeks, or years from the time of the offense.

Similarly, there is a vast difference between market objectives and life threats; hence, the important issue is which activity is the law prepared to treat as "otherwise lawful," despite overwhelming ecological, epidemiological, and toxicological evidence to the contrary.

Regulations, as Sheehy points out, are designed "to control the behaviours of enterprises created by enabling legislation for the primary purpose of pursuing profits" (Sheehy, 1992:118) Her point emphasizes the second major hurdle we encounter when trying to apply substantive justice to those cases. Enabling, as we noted in Chapter 3, when we considered the principles of Nuremberg, is a form of causing, and it renders the enabler complicit in the commission of crimes. In general, the law deals with causation and responsibility in similar ways. Hart and Honoré assert: ". . . to say that someone is responsible for some harm is to assert (*inter alia*) that he *did* the harm or caused it" (Hart and Honoré, 1985:65). The concept of causation also includes cases "where harm is the consequence of one person providing another with reasons or opportunities for doing harm, as cases of "inducing" or "occasioning" harmful acts" (Ibid. at 71). Causation was discussed in detail in Chapter 3. For now it is simply clear that, although it is important to ensure that corporate crime is acknowledged and punished, this is necessary but not sufficient for substantive justice. The role of institutional responsibility must be flagged and detailed, no matter how difficult that might be. We will be in the paradoxical position of having to employ the law and use legal arguments to critique not only those who break the law, but also the very institutions whose function it is to administer and perhaps even to design the laws in question.

The third and final hurdle we must consider, is less basic than the other two: it is simply necessary to examine what is problematic about the way the law is applied in regard to regulatory offenses, with special emphasis on the use of *mens rea* or its absence in regulatory offenses. This will be the main topic of the present chapter. The main object of this chapter is to consider ecocrimes in comparison with other (recognized) assaults, in order to support the thesis that environmental regulatory offenses are:

(1) different in kind from most others in the same category;
(2) instead, much closer, materially, to assaults; and that
(3) there appears to be a trend in case law, toward giving more weight to the public welfare recently.

This trend, if present, would perhaps help to diminish, correspondingly, the concern with the challenges this approach may pose to the Charter (Section 7).

There has been, historically, a sharp division between criminal offenses and regulatory offenses, as the latter are considered to be "not truly criminal" (Stuart, 1995:160). How are we to seek to identify the fault element of "subjective *mens rea*," so necessary to support responsibility for these offenses? "Public Welfare Offences" (Stuart, 1995:149) are different from other assaults and violent crimes. This "difference" introduces many difficulties, for instance, in cases of environmental racism. Robert Bullard, one of the foremost scholars in that field, lists the "Principles of Environmental Justice" as follows in a seminal article:

- the right to protection
- prevention of harm
- shift the burden of proof
- *obviate proof of intent*
- redress inequities (Bullard, 1995:9–22; emphasis added)

Both the shifting of the burden of proof and "obviate proof of intent" are particularly relevant to the argument in this chapter and the previous one. In regard to the latter, Bullard says: "Laws must allow disparate impact and statistical weight—as opposed to 'intent'—to infer discrimination in a court of law is next to impossible" (Bullard, 1995:18).

It seems clear that racist discrimination is not the only area where we might need to heed Bullard's advice. But note that intent normally comes into play only when some crime has been committed. In environmental justice, as in the case of other public welfare issues, what we must accomplish is to stop the imposition of hazards before the harm occurs, rather than wait until there are bodies to count. That is why it is vital to be able to infer discrimination from companies' precedents in citing risky facilities and other potentially hazardous practices. Consider that in the last chapter's example, it is probably true that no one who was ultimately responsible for the deaths that occurred, performed their contributory part with anything like purpose or even knowledge. If such a high test should remain the norm, it would become almost impossible to bring racist and other ecoviolent assaults to justice.

The difficulty lies primarily in the form of fault to be found in ecoviolent crimes, In Canadian criminal law, the first cases to address the question of the mental element in the context of regulatory offenses are the *Sault Ste. Marie* case, and the *Motor Vehicle Reference* case. A recent article by James Stribopoulos (1999) traces the history of *mens rea* considerations, before and after these two cases, and addresses the normative component of these issues with reference to the Canadian Charter of Rights and Freedoms (Part I of the Constitution Act, 1982, being Schedule B of the Canada Act 1982 (U.K.) Chapter 11, proclaimed in force April 17, 1982). The importance of *mens rea* considerations cannot be overstated. Speaking of the cases mentioned, Stribopoulos says:

> In these initial decisions the court elevated the need for *mens rea* into a constitutional requirement for all criminal offences. At the same 'time these decisions evidenced a clear preference for a subjective (or descriptive) view of *mens rea*. This narrow approach to *mens rea* limits its meaning to a question of whether the accused intended or was reckless in bringing about, the prohibited act, consequences or result (*actus reus*) (Stribopoulos, 1999:228).

The implications for environmental justice were discussed above. It is admittedly impossible to prove a person's intent to discriminate except by observing the person's actions, and thus applying an objective, rather than a subjective standard (Bullard, 1995).

This chapter will examine the relationship between environmental regulatory offenses and true crimes, or assaults. In the next section negligence and risks will be discussed (Section 2); in Section 3, we will continue our examination of negligence and the causation of environmental harms and the regulation of public safety; in Section 4, constructive liability, recklessness and willful blindness will be discussed; Section 5 will return to regulatory offenses and their relation to *mens rea*; Section 6 will consider Walkerton as an example and compare it to *Sault Ste. Marie*; Section 7 will return to the question of *mens rea* in assault cases; Section 8 will address the defense of due diligence for environmental regulatory offenses; and conclusions, based on the *Hydro-Québec* case, and the trends it manifest, will be the topic of Section 9.

2. NEGLIGENCE AND RISK IN ENVIRONMENTAL CRIME

From a common-sense point of view, criminal negligence appears a good category to use in our effort to characterize ecoviolence or environmental crimes without a clear, specific focus. By specific focus, I mean something like the latest oil spill next to the Galapagos Islands: one disabled vessel with an environmentally hazardous cargo; no specific intent to kill wildlife and despoil wild ecosystems: yet clearly a shipping operation and negligent or careless monitoring of traffic, much too close to a unique, ecologically sensitive area.

It is relatively easy to trace responsibility in such a case, and even to ascribe liability. But what are we to say in the numerous cases where we discover multiple causes, numerous players with varying degrees of power and responsibility and no simple, one-to-one relationship to one another, but the crimes engendered by a series of cumulative and synergistic effects instead? It is clear that, distasteful as this might be to those who are committed to subjective awareness of consequences and clear intentionality for a crime, the only thing that can be done to trace the sequence of events back to its many causes, and to understand its history, is to start by observing the consequences, the facts, or the *material* elements of the crime. We must also keep in mind the symmetry is an established principle in law (McLachlin J. in R. v. Creighton, (1993) 83 C.C.C.3d 67).

This pragmatic approach corresponds to the objective understanding of negligence that is found in common law, in contrast with that subjective standard of responsibility, that represents the perception of negligence found in European countries, such as Germany or Russia (Fletcher, 1971:407). For Canadian as for British law, "because negligence is 'objective' or 'external,' it is not a form of *mens rea*" (Ibid.). Yet the continental understanding may import "an element of will" into the negligent act, in a way akin to our willful blindness (Ibid. at 409, n.25), as the knowledge of risk is key to seeing the willful element.

In British law, the category of "homicide by excessive risk-taking" (Fletcher, 1978:259) comes very close to a description of what happened in Walkerton, and what happens in general, in all (or too many) cases of ecoviolence, although some demonstrate clearly the resulting harm within a reasonable length of time, while other cases do not. Note that in Canadian law criminal negligence is defined as action that manifests "wanton or reckless disregard for the lives of safety of others." The *Bhopal* case, or *Walkerton* itself, provides an almost instant and clearly visible causal connection between the perpetrator of ecoviolence and the homicides and other harms that follow. Floods, famines, and cholera pandemics (Colwell, 1996), fostered, and to some extent engendered by global climate change through anthropogenic stress, do not provide a similar causal link sufficient to establish specific culpability. Recently, Nicola Lacey and Celia Wells have argued that:

> Not only are there more man-made events as technology grows, but technology also affects the previously "natural" flooding is the best example here. What looks like a natural disaster is often attributable to some human industrial or agricultural activity, further upstream (Lacey and Wells, 1998:574).

However, although there are many early cases where corporations were charged and prosecuted, for instance *Cory Bros.* (R. v. Cory Bros. and Co. Ltd. and Others, (1927) All E.R. Rep. 438), rulings were handed down confirming that a "corporation could not be indicted for an offence against the person" (Lacey and Wells 1998:575). We will return to this problem below.

Fletcher argues that there are "three important factors" (points) to be considered before assessing the culpability for the risk incurred: first, "the likelihood of causing death under these circumstances;" second, the dimension termed "the gravity of the risk"; third, "the benefits of the risk," or the presence of "countervailing benefits" (Fletcher 1978:260). Fletcher also points out: ". . . the profound difference between being mistaken about whether there is risk at all and being mistaken about whether the benefits of the risks outweigh its costs" (Ibid. at 261). These points should be considered in order. First, we have noted that ecoviolence consists of various harms and even death inflicted through environmental means. For the most part, negligence is understood according to an objective standard (interpreted according to the "conduct of a reasonable person"). Yet some U.S. decisions (for instance Commonwealth v. Welansky, 316 Mass. 383, 55 N.E.2d 902 (1944)), hold "that the actor must at least know of the facts that constitute the "risk," and, "inadvertence, merely being inattentive to a grave and unjustified risk, cannot properly be regarded as culpable" (Fletcher, 1978:263).

Perhaps a common citizen could claim inadvertence, or "being inattentive to the possibility of grave risks," but this excuse could not be adduced convincingly by those elected to be responsible to the general public, or by those whose business it was to run the various operations, as it is their specific area of expertise. This pattern is not unique to Walkerton, as it is repeated with variations in most Northwest affluent countries wherever economic interests of any group supersede the health of citizens and of their habitat. Both those who lobby for deregulation and free markets, and those who push for workers' interests, when either of these conflict with environmental protection or a precautionary approach (Brown, 1995; Raffersperger and Tickner, 1999) in regard to public health, must be aware of the risks and the potential harm they are promoting (see second point).

The third point raises another important question, that of the possibility of countervailing benefits. What are the examples Fletcher uses to elucidate this point? He speaks of a doctor performing a very hazardous operation in order to attempt to save a life, or a police officer being forced to shoot at an armed and dangerous felon in a crowd (Fletcher, 1978:261). For both cases, two conditions obtain:

(1) The risk-taking is related to a life-saving activity;
(2) The life that is at risk is one of those the risk imposer is trying to save/protect.

In other words, this is the best possible reason, in both cases, for undertaking a risky activity. In both cases, one could actually (in the case of the operation) or potentially (in the case of a citizen in the crowd harboring the escaping criminal) either receive or reasonably expect consent. For the first case, in most democratic countries, a surgeon needs the patient's consent for any operation, let alone a particularly risky one, and that consent must be informed and uncoerced. For the crowd situation, one could visualize a parallel response: it would be reasonable to expect that anyone in a crowd, upon discovering that an armed and dangerous felon was present, would not only permit, but request armed police presence for protection.

What of Walkerton or any other location at risk of ecoviolence? These cases are in sharp contrast with the previous examples. First, no such lifesaving conditions are present in most if not all cases of ecoviolence: in Chapter 4 we argued that a cheap and easily available meat diet is deleterious to health, not lifesaving, and that—at best—there are some economic benefits to be gained by the collaboration between bureaucratic and industrial institutions, but no such obvious benefit as saving lives. On the question of countervailing benefits, Fletcher's examples do not include economic benefits as possibly counterbalancing the risk of death, and we can extend his analysis to include morbidity as well as mortality (Soskolne and Bertollini, 1999). And in many cases, even genetic mutations affect, negatively, the human race (Colborn et al., 1996).

A possible exception to the "economics first" argument may be found in the presence of real public benefits arising from corporate activities such as (1) the research for life-saving drugs; and (2) the much touted "green revolution" for enhanced (nonmeat) farm productivity. Yet, the former is a benefit that is unevenly spread and distributed, as the main targets of research are—for the most part—to cure affluent men's diseases, and eventual breakthroughs such as new AIDS/HIV drugs, are not made available according to need, but only according to the ability to pay. For the latter, the eventual results of the "green revolution" proved to be ecologically unsound and unsustainable in the long term.

From the moral point of view, the most damning argument against speaking of benefits to be weighed in the balance, is the question of justice and fairness, particularly appropriate in our context. In Fletcher's examples, the risks are imposed to those who are *already* at risk, and the benefits sought, are to remove the risk of death. Not only is it disingenuous to compare economic advantage with lifesaving, but the comparison is fallacious in another important sense: the benefits that may accrue are not intended solely for those at risk through ecoviolence, and, in fact, harms and benefits may be apportioned to totally different groups. The elderly people and babies most at risk from e-coli in the *Walkerton* case were not the same group who reaped benefits either from the tax cuts and the corresponding cut-backs in monitoring and controls (government/bureaucracies), or from the operation of the farms (mostly industry), or the Ontario citizens whose preferences were satisfied.

This pattern is repeated in all areas of environmental risk of violent outcomes, and even the instruments often used to ask the public for their consent for risky activities, are grossly insufficient in the present reality of lack of transparency and information in which those potentially at risk give their consent (Westra, 2000a).

Parallel cases have also been made for the immorality of hazardous technology transfers. In her seminal work *Risk and Rationality* (1991), Kristin Shrader-Frechette speaks of the "countervailing benefits," together with the "social progress argument," as two of the arguments representative of what she terms the "isolationist strategy," practiced by transnational corporations in regard to "Third World risks, as developing countries' populations, are 'isolated' from the regulatory régimes enforced in the corporations' home countries." (Shrader-Frechette, 1991:146–156).

I have pointed out elsewhere that the concept of isolation is very close to that of segregation. It is particularly fitting to the interaction with developing countries, as even the standards required by the North American home base regulations of multinational corporations and their governments, remain isolated from a wider, global context, and distant stakeholder's protection is minimal or nonexistent. One of the clearest examples of this approach is the sale of banned pesticides in developing countries: the profits are reaped by transnational corporations, the morbidity and mortality that ensue represent the benefits left to those distant populations, as they are the ultimate recipients of those reckless practices.

In fact, Fletcher's insightful analysis of negligence supports the argument that criminal negligence is a good way to approach ecoviolence, which is primarily corporate/institutional crime, resulting in assaults to the person on a grand scale. For instance, Fletcher says: "Analyzing negligent and intentional acts in terms of objectivity, subjectivity, justification and excuse demonstrates the underlying structural unity of both forms of criminal responsibility" (Fletcher, 1971:430).

3. NEGLIGENCE, CAUSATION, AND THE CRIMINAL REGULATION OF PUBLIC SAFETY

So, whereas the police generally adopt a "them and us" approach to criminal law-breaking, the dominant mode for many regulatory agencies is negotiation and compliance (Lacey and Wells 1998:496).

The sort of offenses that are termed regulatory and presented as quasi-criminal, are not materially different in their results from other forms of assaults and homicides, except in the ways they are viewed and treated in the courts. Some suggest an analysis in terms of corporate/capitalist crime and that committed by poor individuals. This analysis is important but insufficient as two other aspects of the problem are not emphasized within it: (1) the parallel presence of institutional crimes, whether these institutions are socialist, totalitarian or capitalist, democratically elected or not (Westra, 1998:2); (2) the insufficiency of local-regional power in environmental decision-making, in the face of the global reach of all hazards, including local ones (Westra, 2000a).

If we accept Lacey and Wells' argument about the technological-global reach of these offenses (see Chapter 4; see also Westra, 1998; Bertollini and Soskolne,

1999; Pimentel, Westra and Noss, 2000), the consequences of environmental crimes are closer to "genocide," even in the sense of "omnicide" as Ken Saro-Wiwa had it (Westra, 1998) than they are to breaches of local regulations; international laws treat the former as a grave crime warranting indictment by the International Court of Justice, while the latter is treated through negotiations and compliance. This represents a grave injustice. The very characteristic of regulatory offenses fosters this inappropriate and immoral model, as Lacey and Wells indicate:

> The three main characteristics of the regulatory model are, first that the form in which these offences are defined often omits any mention of the consequential harms; secondly, that liability is technically 'strict,' and thirdly, that the model of enforcement is based on a consultative, us-and-us, rather than them-and-us, conception of the regulated employer or company (Lacey and Wells, 1998:507).

We have emphasized the question of consequential harms of regulatory offenses. Leslie Sebba argues that, "the seriousness of the harm inflicted" does, increasingly reflect the new "penal philosophy," incorporating public attitudes toward *lex talionis*, that is, based on the gravity of the act as determinant of the appropriate treatment and punishment of the offenders, and what can be considered to be their "just deserts" (Sebba, 1980:71; J. Crim. L. & Criminology 124:127–135). Yet some argue that even strict liability may provide an improper basis for the imposition of criminal sanctions, since it can lead to the punishment of the "faultless" (Richardson, 1987).

But how is this "faultlessness" understood and defined? Keeping in mind that ecoviolence (that is violence that follows breaches of environmental regulation) does not always produce immediate and visible harms, but that the eventual harms may well prove to be such on a grand scale; we must acknowledge that the results are different in kind from most cases of common assaults and homicides, aside from war situations. It is even more vitally important to keep in mind that the goal of a regulatory framework is not primarily to punish a wrong-doer after a crime has been committed, but that, "The primary role of the regulation is preventive rather than retributive and the criminal law is employed in order to deter noncompliance" (Ibid.). In addition, although both the Canadian Charter of Rights and most other constitutional instruments support the right of the accused until proven guilty through strict procedures, it is increasingly clear that, for the most part, the "strict liability regulatory offender is not a 'blameless innocent'" (Ibid.). Once again we must consider the necessity to weigh "the problem of unequal treatment" through the imposition of strict liability as a standard, against the harms and disasters engendered by noncompliance. Richardson believes that

> ". . . complete equality for regulatory offences is beyond the scope of any criminal justice system and that the need to prevent serious harms, Thalidomide and Bhopal, for example, should take priority over strict equality of treatment"

(Ibid.). Keeping in mind that compliance and compromise are far from the usual ways criminal law operates, one must wonder at their use in the environmental regulatory framework, when even the notion of corporate manslaughter has now entered the public consciousness, and corporate and institutional responsibility has been well documented (French, 1984).

Another question is whether negligence might represent a better way of classifying regulatory offenses, hence, perhaps a better way of preventing the harms that ensue, by making it more difficult to slide into compromises. Negligence as such is controversial: is it a "state of mind"? Or is it, following Henry Terry, ". . . conduct, not a state of mind"? (Edgerton, 1926:849).

If one opts for the mental theory, a further question arises: does negligence require a certain (indifferent) state of mind, or should it be defined by the capacities of the normal or standard person? In other words, do subjective or objective standards define it? Edgerton cites Sir John Salmond:

> Negligence consists in a certain mental attitude of the defendant towards the consequences of his act. . . . He is guilty of negligence . . . when he does not desire the consequences, and does not act in order to produce the consequences, but is nevertheless indifferent or careless whether they happen or not, and therefore does not refrain from the act notwithstanding the risk that they may happen (Edgerton, 1926:850; Salmond, 1965:21).

But if negligence is the "mental attitude of undue indifference with respect to one's conduct and its consequences" (Edgerton, 1926:850), then it appears to be a form of *mens rea*. It is also culpable inadvertence or lack of due care, hence, it is linked to the strict liability offences that permit a due diligence defense.

But note that "due diligence" is a defense that suggests that certain actions were performed, and certain measures had actually been taken, not only thought about. It would appear that, if due diligence and due care can be demonstrated as acts a corporation or other institution performed to offset the charge that they had not practiced due diligence, then, I believe, a description of their "state of mind" would not suffice as a proof that the accused were not guilty.

There is no question that inadvertence, undue indifference, inattention, and other mental states and attitudes are the prelude to the damage or the injury on which a suit can be based or expected. But it is the damage, the injury that is the result of the inappropriate mental attitudes that we must prevent, not simply the states themselves. Edgerton says:

> Negligence neither is nor involves ("presupposes") either indifference or inadvertence, or any other mental characteristic, quality, state or process.

Negligence is unreasonably dangerous conduct—i.e. conduct abnormally likely to cause harm (Edgerton, 1926:852).

Edgerton also emphasizes the importance of due care in this respect:

Freedom from negligence (commonly called "due care" does not require care, or any other mental phenomenon, but requires only that one's conduct be reasonably safe—as little likely to cause harm as the conduct of a normal person would be (Ibid.).

Following Edgerton, the conclusion that can be reached is that negligence ought to be judged on objective grounds, and that the mental state of those accused of negligence in this sense should have less relevance than either their conduct or the actual results both immediate and far-reaching, of their acts.

4. CONSTRUCTIVE LIABILITY, RECKLESSNESS, WILLFUL BLINDNESS, AND OBJECTIVE DANGEROUSNESS

"Constructive Liability" exists where responsibility is attributable to an actor for a result without requiring proof that it was foreseen or foreseeable" (Healy, 1993:265).

The previous section concluded by arguing for an objective standard for negligence, rather than a mental one. To continue the argument in support of attributing criminal liability for regulatory offenses regarding the environment, we need to also examine recklessness, omissions and other related forms of fault. It is useful to start by considering *Leblanc v. the Queen* (1975) 68 D.L.R.3d 243). The accused, a bush pilot, "was charged with criminal negligence causing death contrary to s.203 of the Criminal Code." What is important from our point of view is not the sort of episode that gave rise to specific charges in this case, but what was said in several places, as the courts rejected Leblanc's appeal. The wording is quite instructive. At one point, for instance, the headnote to the actual appeal stated: "The requisite *mens rea* for criminal negligence is 'advertent negligence' and although the act itself will, in most cases, prove the *mens rea*, it is open to the Crown to prove it by affirmative evidence." Although this editorial has no legal weight, it indicates the general thrust of the judgment in the case. More to the point, Dickson J. (Laskin C. J.C., and Beetz J. Concurring) said: "On a charge of criminal negligence the requisite *mens rea* is determined by an objective standard, so that similar fact evidence cannot be admissible to prove any subjective intent (at 244). "In a discussion of *Creighton* and other cases purporting to pose a constitutional challenge, Patrick Healy says:

Parliament can impose criminal liability and punishment as it sees fit, provided that it acts within legislative jurisdiction and observes the fundamental principle of proportionality between elements of liability and the proposed punishment. This principle excludes imprisonment as punishment for offences of absolute liability. In rare circumstances the gravity of the offence and the punishment will require proof of an element of recklessness in the proscribed act. Otherwise the principle of proportionality does not exclude liability for some form of negligence or for constructive liability (Healy, 1993:265).

This passage affirms the traditional standards, while clearly indicating the recent shift to objective standards for faults of negligence. Healy views the last 20 years of "Canadian jurisprudence" as moving away from strict *mens rea* requirements in many cases. He adds: "There is abundant evidence in recent decisions and legislation of a growing shift toward the sanction and punishment of what people do and the effects of their conduct" (Healy, 1993:267). This conclusion is particularly encouraging from our point of view, as the cases he cites in support of this claim are certainly not all regulatory offenses, in fact they are *both* assaults and regulatory offenses, thus providing additional support for the claims advanced here and in the previous chapter about the similarity between assaultive and environmental regulatory offenses crimes (e.g., R. v. Wholesale Travel Group, Inc., (1991) 3 S.C.R. 216; DeSouza and Others, in Healy, 1993:267, n.7).

It is this progression from Charter-mandated emphasis on intentional mental states for criminal liability, to a combination of objective, reasonable person standards, and the material elements of fault (the act more than the actor), that supports my argument and may allow it to move forward, from a philosophical, normative argument about what ought to be (critical morality) to what might eventually be a final goal of substantive justice.

Healy also addresses the question of what constitutes constructive liability; he says: ". . . constructive liability exists where responsibility is attributed to an actor for a result without requiring proof that it was foreseen or foreseeable" (Healy, 1993:269).

The constructive aspect here described exceeds the reality of the *Walkerton* case, chosen as an example of ecoviolence for our discussion. Both industry and government institutions had enough knowledge and expertise, or at least access to those with such expertise, that the harms that ensued were at least foreseeable, minimally, as contradicting EPA (R.S.O., 1990:Ch.E.19; Pt. II, 6.(1) and 5.14(1)), notwithstanding. There is an exception envisioned in Section 13(2), in regard to farm wastes, and that "exception" recurs in all acts. Given present technologies, used in all farming, and also given the magnitude of the waste produced by factory farming, much "exceptions" appear to be inappropriate.

In *R. v. Creighton* ((1993) 83 C.C.C.3d 67), McLachlin J. emphasizes several points that are applicable to our present problem. First, she cites Lord Ellenborough C.J.:

He who deals in a perilous article must be wary how he deals, otherwise, if he observes not proper caution . . . he will be responsible. . . . (It is) a universal principle that when a man is charged with doing an act of which the probable consequences may be highly injurious, the intention is an inference of law resulting from doing the act . . .

and also,

. . . when a person began doing wicked acts for his own base purposes, he risked his own life as well as that of others. That kind of crime does not differ in any significant degree from one committed by using a deadly weapon, such as a bludgeon, a pistol or a knife. If a man once begins attacking the human body in such a way, he must take the consequences if he goes further than he intended when he began" (Ibid.).

Hence, both the "thin skull" rule and an objective standard are sufficient to ensure that what started as a dangerous negligence in regard to emissions, or negligent omissions in regard to monitoring and controls, represents, minimally, the foreseeable risk of bodily harm. When infants and the aged are disproportionately affected, equity and fairness needs to be considered very seriously. McLachlin J. adds:

I turn first to the distinction between appreciation of the risk of bodily harm and the risk of death in the context of manslaughter. In my view, when the risk of bodily harm is combined with the established rule that a wrongdoer must take his victim as he finds him and the fact that death did in fact occur, the distinction disappears (Ibid.).

If certain groups (children and the aged) were disproportionately affected, one must also consider the equality rights (Charter Section 15(1)) of those harmed, and a constitutional challenge ought to be instituted on the part of the citizens. What is happening now instead, is that the citizens are asked to acquiesce to a government "payoff." To paraphrase Mark Sagoff, "they ask for justice, for answers about why this terrible thing happened to them," and they are offered economic redress instead (Sagoff, 1988).

It is true that the facts as they presently stand in Walkerton do not appear to manifest the desire to do bodily harm or to kill on anyone's part. More uncertain is the question of recklessness, whereas willful blindness appears far more plausible. McIntyre defines recklessness in R. v. Sansregret ((1985) 17 D.L.R.4th 577):

Recklessness involves knowledge of a danger or a risk and persistence in a course of conduct which creates a risk that the prohibited results will occur (Ibid).

Colvin proposes returning to Caldwell (1981) for some illuminating passages that set the stage for subsequent debates between those favoring a "subjectivist" vs. those preferring an "objectivist" understanding of recklessness (Colvin, 1991:140ff.). Caldwell had apparently been engaged to do some work by the proprietor of a hotel, with whom he eventually had a disagreement. One evening, when drunk, he set fire to the hotel. Although no serious damage was done, he was tried on two counts of arson, under the Criminal Damage Act, 1971 (U.K.) Chapter 48. He pleaded not guilty to a serious count under Section (2), which reads:

A person who without lawful excuse destroys or damages any property whether belonging to himself or another—

(a) intending to destroy or damage any property or being reckless as to whether any property would be destroyed or damaged; and

(b) intending by the destruction or damage to endanger the life of another or being reckless as to whether the life of another would thereby be endangered; shall be guilty of an offense (Colvin, 1991:141).

In this case, Lord Diplock's analysis of recklessness appears to reject the requirement for a subjective awareness of the risk, and—in addition—concludes that the defense of intoxication is irrelevant when recklessness is alleged. He says:

"Reckless" is used in the new statutory definition of the *mens rea* of these offences is an ordinary English word. It had not by 1971 become a term of legal art with some more limited esoteric meaning than that which it bore in ordinary speech, a meaning which surely includes not only deciding to ignore a risk of harmful consequences resulting from one's acts that one has recognized as existing, but also failing to give any thought to whether or not there is any such risk in circumstances where if any thought were given to the matter it would be obvious that there was (Colvin, 1991:142; Commissioner of Police of Metropolis v. Caldwell, (1982) A.C. 3341, (1981) 2 W.L.R. 509, 73 Cr. App. R. 13, (1981) 1 All E.R. 961, at 966).

The last sentence of this judgment imports the objective element of *mens rea* to which Canadian courts have often objected within the context of recklessness (R. v. Tutton and Tutton, (1989) 48 C.C.C.3d 129; 189 CCC Lexis 2608). The objective interpretation of recklessness is, clearly, the preferable one for environmental offenses where, paradigmatically there is no connection or even acquaintance, between many perpetrators working together to bring about hazardous circumstances, through the institutional or corporate CID Structure (French, 1984), and the public at risk. In *Sansregret* McIntyre J. says:

Negligence, the failure to take reasonable care, is a creature of the civil law and not generally a concept having a place in determining criminal liability. Nevertheless it is frequently confused with recklessness in the criminal sense and care should be taken to separate the two concepts. Negligence is tested by the objective standard of the reasonable man. . . . In accordance with well-established principles for the determination of criminal liability, recklessness, to form a part of the criminal *mens rea* must have an element of the subjective.

Lord Diplock concludes: "It is, in other words, the conduct of one who sees the risk and who takes the chance. It is in this sense that the term recklessness is used in the criminal law and it is clearly distinct from the concept of civil negligence (ibid.)."

This may well be the case, and it ought to be questioned from a moral point of view, as Stribopoulos has argued (Stribopoulos, 1999). Recklessness then is a category in criminal law, and it includes the awareness of risk and the reckless willingness to take the chance. The link to Sansregret emerges when we consider that willful blindness also includes a certain recklessness in not following through in one's reasoning, to the consequences that would surely follow one's act. In neither case is clear knowledge, let alone intent, directed at a specific party, present. An example relating to both classes of acts might be that of war crimes where a subjective element, that is, a form of intent directed at a specific person or group is often absent, and those who actually commit the crimes (not order, command, or direct them) are often less than fully aware of what the result of their actions might be.

Hence, it is not sufficient to say that negligence, with its objective standard is not appropriate for criminal cases, only for civil ones that do not require a *mens rea* element. R. A. Duff also discusses negligence and recklessness in detail. He says:

> Though most (and especially the most serious) offences require intention or recklessness, some need involve only negligence (S and H, pp. 352–5); one who drives without due care and attention commits an offence of negligence (Road Traffic Act 1988, s.3), as do employers who fail to ensure, as far as it is reasonably practicable, the health, safety and welfare at work of their employees (Health and Safety at Work etc., Act 1974, 5.2(l)) (Duff, 1990:9).

Duff also raises the question we have been grappling with all along: "Why . . . should intention or recklessness be so crucial to criminal liability?" (Ibid. at 11), and this is true whether we consider individual actors or institutional ones.

For now, it seems that the level of violence and harms imposed in Walkerton and potentially (or actually) present in all environmental harm cases should suffice to reduce or even eliminate the constitutional question normally raised in regulatory offenses. This appears to be especially true when the (potentially) innocent accused is not a vulnerable individual, but a powerful institution who, because of its very nature, can impose grave physical harms, but can only suffer economic ones, as it cannot become ill, suffer pain, whether physical or mental, or die, except figuratively, or to be imprisoned.

5. REGULATORY OFFENSES: BETWEEN *MENS REA* AND ABSOLUTE LIABILITY

In the previous section we considered the status of regulatory offenses from a perspective that included "negligence," constructive liability," "recklessness," in relation to "willful blindness" (Sansregret), in order to show that environmental regulatory offenses are truly "crimes," and that they should be viewed as a category apart, because of their grave effects on human health. The traditional starting point is not helpful: regulatory offenses are not "true crimes." Don Stuart cites *Dherras v. De Rutzen* ((1895) 1 Q.B. 918), outlining a "threefold classification of absolute responsibility offences":

(1) acts "not criminal in any real sense" but which "in the public interest are prohibited under a penalty;
(2) public nuisances"; and
(3) Proceedings not "criminal in form," but "really only a summary mode of enforcing a civil right' (Ibid. at 922); Stuart, 1995:150).

It is necessary to keep in mind, as stated at the outset, that the understanding of what may be contrary to the public interest has changed dramatically (or should have changed in that manner) in the last hundred years, as highly sophisticated, all-pervasive forms of harm have emerged. Many of these are not only lethal, but they also result in genetic modifications, hence, posing a threat to the human race as such, as well as to specific individuals and populations (Westra, 2000).

Moving ahead from Sherras about 50 years, we find the *Beaver v. the Queen* ((1957) 166 C.C.C. 129) case, where two brothers sold a package they represented as heroin to an undercover agent, while evidence showed they had believed it to be sugar of milk." They could be not only convicted for misrepresentation but also for possession, as the *mens rea* element was not required. That is, they were not required to intend to sell heroin; possession of the forbidden substance was sufficient to convict (Stuart, 1995:150). Thus, perhaps "possession" and the use of hazardous substances destined to be placed in the environment might be sufficient as well.

Closer to our environmental concern is the *Pierce Fisheries Case* (Pierce Fisheries Ltd., (1969) 4 C.C.C. 163). In an eight to one majority decision, the Supreme Court of Canada "upheld the conviction despite no *mens rea* requirement" for the possession of 26 undersized lobsters (as part of a purchase between 50,000 to 60,000 lbs. of lobsters). Ritchie J. made at least two relevant points as he said—*inter alia*—". . . this legislation was not criminal, but rather a conservation measure in the public interest"; and "To require proof of *mens rea* would make it virtually impossible to obtain a conviction for this offence."

Stuart does not think much of the *Pierce Fisheries* decision, as he argues that "there was no integrated approach providing clear criteria for subsequent cases" (Stuart, 1995:153). It is worth noting that the single dissenting voice in *Pierce Fisheries*, Mr. Justice Cartwright, had cited in Beaver, Chief Justice Lord Goddard in *Harding v. Price* ((1948) K.B. 695, at 700):

> The general rule applicable to criminal cases is *actus non facit reus nisi mens sit rea*, and I venture to repeat what I said in *Brend v. Wood* (1946) 62 T.L.R. 462,43. It is of the utmost importance for the protection of the liberty of the subject that a court should always bear in mind that unless a statute either clearly or by implication rules out *mens rea* as the constituent part of a crime, the Court should not find a man guilty of an offence against the criminal law unless he has a guilty mind.

To some extent cases involving possession of narcotics or other more general regulatory offenses are helpful to set the stage for the pivotal *Sault Ste. Marie* decision.

A lot has been written on the *Sault Ste. Marie* case, and the case is cited in most criminal law books. For our purpose the progressive change in *mens rea* requirements in assault cases, appears to be more relevant than studies that are limited to merely regulatory offense cases. Of course, before embarking on such a course, the case ought to be made that the physical elements of the *crime* are similar to those occurring in assaults. This point was argued in the previous sections, and—factually—in Chapter 2, where I showed that ecoviolence is indeed a form of violent assault against citizens.

It is hard to deny that the material fault element is substantially different in assault against a single individual on one hand, and assaults against a group or population on the other, because of the differences in scale and the presence of unspecific victims. But physical harm to over 2000 people (as in *Walkerton*) surely cannot be, in itself, necessarily the lesser crime. In Chapter 3 I have argued that according to just war theory and to the principles of Nuremberg, when large numbers are targeted, only a previous hostile action on their part—in some cases—justifies retaliatory violence (*jus ad bellum*). Harm caused by acts of omission or commission through regulatory offenses affecting civilian populations cannot ever claim justice in responding to violence with violence, as no violence has been offered to institutions and corporations in such cases. No Walkerton victim, to my knowledge had performed terrorist or seditious acts.

In contrast, the institutional conspiracy that was clearly present for prolonged periods prior to the crisis, is clearly proscribed, and even termed a criminal act in itself, by the Nuremberg Principles (see Chapter 3). Hence, if we cannot find any reason by which to justify violent acts on the part of an institution or corporation, and if neither excuses nor justifications apply to these legal persons, then violence against a large group ought to be viewed through the lens of the criminal laws pertaining to assaults and the imposition of physical harms.

We need to keep in mind that, important though the *Sault Ste. Marie* case is in law, it and other cases like *Wholesale Travel, Pierce Fisheries* and even *Beaver*, are not cases where there was an assault perpetrated on the public, that produced actual and present harms (including death) to anyone, at the time the courts made their respective decisions. This is a common situation in environmental harms, as some of the diseases induced, or the early death caused by these forms of ecoviolence are not immediately visible. In fact, the main point of the pertinent regulations is precisely to prevent such wholesale harms and multiple deaths, not simply to condemn and punish them after the fact.

6. THE WALKERTON EXAMPLE: DISSIMILARITIES AND SIMILARITIES BETWEEN *SAULT STE. MARIE* AND *WALKERTON*

The Walkerton example can be addressed from a number of standpoints, all indicating lack of concern for the public interest and carelessness and negligence in protecting the common good. The megafarms allowed to operate in the area, in addition to the traditional farms already present, combined to bring the toxic load present in the environment to the point of exposing all citizens to an extremely dangerous and even fatal disease, although the specific contaminant appeared to come from an earlier farming operation, combined with an unusual level of rainfall. The megafarms are not to be deemed innocent, even if the work of the O'Connor Commission may exonerate them in this instance. These operations would still retain the status of unexploded bombs, in a sense, as they are placed among an unknowing public, unaware of their potential hazardous effects. Hence, they would still represent a form of reckless endangerment of the public, once the effect of one farm's untreated manure is multiplied many times, to match the large difference in porcine numbers between the present culprit and the large existing, ongoing and untreated operations. It is noteworthy that no common good, no general gains accrued to all in the region, as the benefits were distributed to the area's businesses, while the burdens were imposed primarily on the most vulnerable.

It is somewhat premature to be writing on Walkerton at this time, as eventually more problems, and possibly some helpful moves might emerge in the future. But, so far, among the plethora of issues discussed by the Walkerton inquiry, the question of unequal protection was not addressed. In this case, the youngest and the oldest were disproportionately affected, contrary to Charter Section 15.(1), which prohibits, *inter alia*, discrimination due to age. In contrast, most of the public's attention and that of the media, were devoted to the weakest link in the institutional chain of command, the uneducated, untrained employee who neither knew nor cared about the effect of e-coli in the town's drinking water, and also some attention was focused on the lack of responsiveness and effectiveness on the part of those charged with monitoring the institution.

Serious as those regulatory offenses were, they were not as grave as the lack of principles and serious regulations governing the protection of public health and safety through the environment at both the provincial and the federal levels. Many scientists pointed out these failures after Walkerton (see Chapter 4), and the recent reoccurrence of a similar problem (tainted water) emerging in Battleford, Saskatchewan in the Spring of 2001. For instance, Michael M'Gonigle writes "Safety isn't the only issue" (*The Globe and Mail*, May 2, 2001, A17). He argues against quick, "crisis-response" approaches, in favor of serious responses, reflecting "three lessons"; we need to understand that "Fresh water is a scarce resource"; we must "focus on managing our excessive demands," before looking for additional supplies"; we also must learn to consider water as a resource in its full cycle, not only when it is supplied to us from nature, fresh and free of charge. In fact a "superficial bill" adding "a new layer of bureaucracy" is not the answer, if we do not also, at the same time, take seriously the systemic issues involved, beyond the occasional "disasters," termed by M'Gonigle, "the tip of the iceberg."

From our viewpoint, the effects we note are indeed institutional, systemic, and require a radical change of approach and perspective. The effects on both environment and populations, even the little we know today, are sufficient to advance the need for a major revision of the way regulatory offenses are viewed, handled, and punished at this time.

Therefore, aside from the fact that the *Walkerton* case is only an inquiry at this time, I would like to consider some of the major similarities and dissimilarities between *Walkerton* and *Sault Ste. Marie*.

Dissimilarities

   (a) *Sault Ste. Marie:* Breach of regulations with possible and even probable deleterious environmental consequences, against the public interest (per Dickson J.) The City of Sault Ste. Marie was charged that it did discharge, or cause to be discharged, or deposited materials into Cannon Creek and Root River, or on the shore or bank thereof, or in such place along the side that might impair the quality of the water in Cannon Creek and Root River, between March 13, 1972, and Sept. 11, 1972. The charge was laid under Section 5.32(1) of the Ontario Water Resources Act, R.S.O. 1970, Chapter 332 (formerly Ontario Water Resources Commission Act).

   (b) *Walkerton:* Breach of several regulations with consequences including (a) environmental degradation; (b) physical harm to many individuals; and (c) multiple homicides and infanticides.

(a) *Sault Ste. Marie:* Based on a single wrongful decision by the city's officials to award the waste disposal contract to Cherokee Disposal and Construction Co. Ltd. (agreement, Nov. 18, 1970). "Under the terms of the agreement, Cherokee became obligated to furnish adequate labour, material and equipment" (per Dickson J.). Hence the City awarded the contract without retaining proper control of the manner in which such work would be carried out.

(b) *Walkerton:* a series of institutional wrongful decisions including the following:

   (a) commission granting permission(s) for the operation of mega-farms, without appropriate controls or thorough studies of probable consequences.

   (b) commission cutting funding for the institutional checking and monitoring of the conditions of the ecosystems where the wells and the farms were located.

   (c) commission not providing appropriate regulatory infrastructures to control farming activities in the region.

   (d) commission not providing well-trained and well-qualified personnel to supervise and test the wells.

Similarities

(a) *Sault Ste. Marie's* main focus: The institutional/governmental responsibility is primary, or at least coprimary and coextensive with the responsibility of the contractor performing the activity resulting in the fault (compare earlier discussion of CID structure in Chapter 4, Section 5).

(b) *Walkerton's* main focus: The institutional /governmental responsibility is primary, or at least coextensive with the responsibility of the owners/operators of *all* farms in the area, as well as the responsibility of the water facility employees.

(a) *Sault Ste. Marie's* main legal focus: The court reaffirmed the legitimacy of strict liability offenses wherein the accused (for instance a corporation), may avoid the imposition of criminal liability only be establishing a defense of due diligence on the balance of probabilities.

(a) *Walkerton's* main legal focus *(NB: proposed, not established):* Whether the events of Walkerton support the imposition of at least liability for a regulatory offense, if not a criminal form of culpable homicide (still allowing the possibilities of a due diligence defense).

Because of the dissimilarities noted as (a) and (b) above, "strict liability" appears grossly insufficient. It could at most provide a starting point for additional findings of fault.

Let us return to the major, glaring difference, that is, the *visible, proven* presence of physical harms and multiple homicides and infanticides. Recall Dickson's belief that "his judgment does nothing to 'dilute or erode' the basic principle that, when an offence is truly criminal, there is a mental element to be determined subjectively" (Stuart 1995:157; R. v. Sault Ste. Marie, (1978) 40 C.C.C.2d 353). Dickson's well-known tripartite division is as follows:

(1) Offenses in which *mens rea* consisting in some positive state of mind such as intent, knowledge, or recklessness, must be proved by the prosecution either as in inference from the nature of the act committed, or by additional evidence.

(2) Offenses in which there is no necessity for the prosecution to prove the existence of *mens rea*; the doing of the prohibited act *prima facie* imports the offense, leaving it open to the accused to avoid liability of proving (on a balance of probabilities) that he took all reasonable care. This involves considerations of what a reasonable man would have done in the circumstances. The defense will be available if the accused reasonably believed in a mistaken set of facts which, if true, would render the act or omission innocent, or if he took all reasonable steps to avoid the particular event. These offences may properly be called strict liability.

(3) Offenses of absolute liability where it is not open to the accused to exculpate himself by showing that he was free of fault (Stuart, 1995:159; Sault Ste. Marie ibid. at 373–374).

It is worthy of note that Dickson has "no difficulty in characterizing the pollution offence as one of public welfare since it was "enacted in the interest of public health" (Stuart, 1995:159). One wonders whether Dickson would view the *reality* of the violation of public health standards, resulting in homicide and other harms as "not criminal in the true sense."

Once the connection to public health is made (Soskolne and Bertollini, 1999), the presence of widespread disease and death must lead even what was originally characterized as a regulatory offense, in another direction: either in the direction of evidencing some form of *mens rea*, or in that of absolute liability. It is the first of these two avenues that I believe might be the most promising one, the one most likely to support the sort of conviction and punishment that would fit a crime of this magnitude, and serve as a possible future deterrent. Stuart remarks that even deciding that pollution (like other regulatory offenses) is not truly a crime, is a "faulty criterion for substantive classification" (Stuart, 1995:161) and he adds that "the distinction between truly criminal and public welfare offences has not been substantially drawn (Ibid.). Regarding *Sault Ste. Marie*, Stuart even raises the question whether "a negligence inquiry would have been preferable" to the one which produced the decision reached (Ibid. at 171).

Even though the justices of the Supreme Court in 1978 (at the time of the *Sault Ste. Marie* case) were not aware of the full implications of pollution offenses, after 20 years of increasingly harrowing ecodisasters, ignorance can no longer be claimed. We have seen the full impact of one global disaster after another, from the results of global climate change, produced by many (and ongoing) corporate practices supported by equally ongoing public choices, to specific ecodisasters from Bhopal to the Exxon Valdez spill, to the Royal Dutch Shell Oil ecocide in Ogoniland, Nigeria (Westra, 1998).

Here at home, we can no longer ignore the implications of the e-coli disaster, nor the many voices raised in warning that Walkerton may be repeated again and again in Ontario and in Canada as a whole, unless drastic changes are made. We must also keep in mind that even when the results of the violent assaults are not immediately evident, as they were in Walkerton or in Ogoniland, pollution's insidious consequences not only attack individual humans and populations, but also future generations, by inflicting genetic damages. Ken Saro-Wiwa appropriately called these attacks, "omnicide" (Westra, 1998). Hence, it must be acknowledged that calling pollution "not really a crime" manifests a deplorable lack of information and even—following the Criminal Code—a form of willful blindness (*Sansregret*). McIntyre J. describes the facts of this case as follows. The 20-year-old lover of a bright, articulate and well-employed 31-year-old woman is told of her wish to terminate the relationship, after almost a year of abuse on his part. The young man returns twice to her house, breaking in, in the early hours of the morning, "raging, furious and threatening," the first time with a file, the second, with a knife. Both times the woman attempted to ward off the explicit threats to her life by talking of a possible reconciliation and consenting to intercourse. The second time she was told to stand naked in the kitchen, her hands tied behind her back, while he struck her repeatedly "with sufficient force to draw blood," and while he struck the wall close to her, several times, with his knife. Once again she consented to intercourse, in fear of her life. After she was allowed to leave for work and had driven the young man where he wanted to go, she called the police to accuse him of rape in addition to breaking-and-entering and forcible confinement. The trial judge agreed to all charges except rape, as he believed that the appellant did not enter the house with the intent of making a sexual assault on the complainant, rather that Sansregret "honestly believed the complainant was giving him a free and genuine consent to intercourse," hence that it was a case of "an honest mistake of fact."

When the case came to the Supreme Court of Canada, this defense leading to Sansregret's exoneration on the charge of rape, was not allowed. MacIntyre J. said:

> Wilful blindness is distinct from recklessness because, while recklessness involved the knowledge of a danger or risk and persistence in a course of conduct which creates a risk that the prohibited result will occur, wilful blindness arises when a person has become aware of the

need for some inquiry declines to make this inquiry because he does not wish to know the truth.

That is indeed the position of corporate risk-imposers and institutional bureaucracies, who through the abundant information flowing through the mass media, as well as their own specific research and expertise, must be willfully blind if they do not follow through to acquire and accept full knowledge of the circumstances wherein they act.

After the tobacco trials, we have had in front of our eyes a clear example of criminal activities on the part of large multinational corporations, who proceeded, with full knowledge of the expected result of their activities, to addict countless millions of children and adults, condemning them to incurable disease and untimely death.

Stribopoulos sees clearly the conflict between the decision in Sault Ste. Marie (and other such related cases), when "the Supreme Court took the Canadian Criminal law to the brink of making an exclusively descriptive view of *mens rea* into a constitutional requirement" (Stribopoulos, 1999:283). If such a subjective (descriptive approach) is "the exclusive gauge of defining 'moral innocence' in Canada" (Ibid.), the normative content of *mens rea* will be lost. Stuart claims that, ". . . the subjective awareness principle has now proved to be the fairest test of fault and an ideal vehicle of restraint" (Stuart, 1995:250). The subjective understanding of the fault element denotes the intent to perform a certain act, and thus achieves a certain result. In *R. v. Buzzanga and Durocher* ((1979) 101 D.L.R.3d 488, 1979 D.L.R. Lexis 4197), Martin J.A. acknowledgeable that there are cases

> . . . where an intention to produce a particular consequence is essential to constitute the offence, an act is not done with the intent to produce the prohibited consequences unless it is in the actor's conscious purpose to bring it about, and that actor's foresight of the certainty of the consequences is not synonimous with an intention to produce it.

The intent is the subjective element of fault. But Martin, J.A. adds that even if "recklessness satisfies the mental element denoted by the word 'willfully,' when used to denote . . . ordinary *mens rea* . . . for some purposes recklessness may denote only a marked departure from objective standards."

Stribopoulous is clearly concerned that too much could be eliminated from *mens rea* if only subjective intent, rather than objectively observable circumstances and consequences, could be used to determine fault. One wonders who will be restrained by Stuart's approach, and Stribopoulos, in contrast, responds that what Stuart takes to be correct, "fails to account for the unprincipled and counterintuitive results that this approach forces us to adopt" (Stribopoulos, 1999:285).

Perhaps the major part of the problem is the grouping of environmental regulatory offenses with cases like *Wholesale Travel* where business practices and economic concerns were at issue. These attacks, though clearly wrong, are not in the same category as physical assaults. It is my contention that, given our present degree of knowledge, and even the common awareness of the consequences of the other (environmental) regulatory offenses, listing the latter together with the former is a grave mistake, one with far-reaching consequences, as it permits the courts to characterize the results of some of the worst disasters known to men as not truly criminal, despite the fact that they are not "acts of God" but the direct results of negligent or careless institutional human behavior.

7. *MENS REA* STANDARDS IN ASSAULT CASES: THEIR RELEVANCE TO ECOVIOLENCE

The previous section argued that often constitutional challenges are not challenges to justice in its substantive, true sense. We also noted that while some legal scholars find procedural components to be sufficient for the fundamental principles of justice, many do not. We concur with the latter. Cases of environmental regulatory offenses may be treated in a procedurally fair way, but it is becoming increasingly clear that considerations of true justice are systematically excluded because of the way such issues are classified, and also because of the way they are treated in the courts. I have argued that environmental violence should not be considered simply a regulatory offense, because in recent times it has acquired the characteristics of assaults, through the imposition of unconsented "force" and bodily harm (Soskolne and Bertollini, 1999; Pimentel, 2000; Westra, 1998; Westra, 2000; McMichael, 1995).

This point can be argued, evidence can be adduced to support it, but the desired change cannot be accomplished by any single individual. For now, we can begin to consider whether the charge of ecoviolence for regulatory offenses, changing them to assaults, might render the *mens rea* requirement easier or more difficult to handle, and whether under a changed status, a former "regulatory offense" might weigh in better on the side of public welfare rather than on that of the Charter rights of the perpetrators, whoever they might be. Our present aim is to trace the way the courts have balanced the conflict between the public interest and welfare on one side, and the constitutional rights of the accused in cases of assault on the other.

The argument of the previous chapter shows that environmental regulatory offenses should indeed be classed as "true crimes" (*pace* Dickson J.), because of the characteristics they exhibit. The Criminal Code is illuminating in this regard, as it shows what is actually *present* in the law, when we do not start by misrepresenting ecoviolence as "regulatory offenses," thus excluding other classifications as *a priori*.

The starting point may be Section 217 (Part VIII—Offences Against Person):

217.*Duty of persons undertaking acts*—Everyone who undertakes to do an act is under a legal duty to do it if an omission to do the act is or may be dangerous to life.

219.(1) *Criminal Negligence*—Everyone is criminally negligent who

(a) in doing anything, or

(b) in omitting to do anything that it is his duty to do, shows wanton or reckless disregard for the lives or safety of other persons.

Following up on Section 219, Sections 220 and 221 discuss the substantial penalties to be imposed for causing death or bodily harm by criminal negligence. Assault is defined in the Criminal Code at Section 265.(1), as follows:

A person commits an assault when

(a) without the consent of another person, he applies force intentionally to that other person, directly or indirectly;

(b) he attempts or threatens, by an act or gesture, to apply force to another person if he has, causes that other person to believe, on reasonable grounds that he has present ability to effect his purpose; or

(c) while openly wearing or carrying a weapon or an imitation thereof, he accosts or impedes another person or begs.

For our purpose, (a) is the telling part of this definition, as the harmful force may be applied directly or indirectly, thus fitting the model of harmful environmental practices. Still on the topic of assaults, Sections 268 and 269 are the most interesting for our purpose:

268.(1) *Aggravated* assault—Everyone commits an aggravated assault who wounds, maims, disfigures or endangers the life of the complainant.

269. *Unlawfully causing bodily harm*—Everyone who unlawfully causes bodily harm to any person is guilty of

(a) an indictable offence and liable to imprisonment for a time not exceeding ten years; or

(b) an offence punishable on summary conviction and liable to imprisonment for a term not exceeding eighteen months.

The physical elements of crime can easily be identified not only in *Walkerton* (where the bodily harm had already occurred), but also in all environmental hazards, especially now that Section 227, restricting responsibility for death to "one year and one day" after the occurrence of the attack, has been repealed (Repealed 1999, Chapter 5, Section 9(1)).

We are in a difficult position now as we attempt to single out the possible mental elements in crimes for which we have, at this time, no accused. We will have to limit our analysis to deal with theoretical accused persons only: this necessity ought to help to preserve the fairness of our assessment as we will indicate what could have been the mental element, from the physical elements of the crime alone, although this approach would seem to limit us to an objective standard. The best starting point may be a consideration of *Walkerton*, followed by other possible instances of ecoviolence and environmental crimes in general. What is obvious is that these are not the sort of crimes where one person, or even a conspiracy (see Chapter 3) *intended* the consequences with full knowledge, had the disease and deaths as their purpose, or even meant to cause death and bodily harm. Yet Dickson J. believes that in *Sault Ste. Marie*, "the accused who committed the prohibited act did so intentionally . . . with knowledge of the facts constituting the offence." The reason for importing at least this element of *mens rea* is found in the concepts of causing and permitting, as both imply some knowledge. Dickson J. adds, speaking of cause and permit:

> These two words are troublesome because neither denotes either full *mens rea* nor absolute liability. It is said that a person could not be said to be permitting something unless he knew what he was permitting (*R. v. Sault Ste. Marie*, (1978) 85 D.L.R.3d 161, 1978 D.L.R. Lexis 3456).

Note that Dickson J. refers to a person. In the light of our earlier analysis of the personhood of institutions and corporations, it is clear that in those cases, their CID structure entails *necessarily* that both institution (the city in *Sault Ste. Marie*) and the corporation (Cherokee Contracting), not being prey to human weaknesses and passions, indeed "knew what (they) were permitting": that they intended the prohibited act although they did not intend the possible (and probable) public health hazards or harms, despite the fact that such results and consequences are commonly known.

Lowering the standards for this sort of knowledge from full intent, to "knowledge of the facts constituting the offence," Dickson J. inserts a wedge of sorts between the prohibited act (pollution), and the prohibited result (public health harms), thus allowing the defense of "due diligence."

8. AN ASIDE ON DUE DILIGENCE

It is unclear how any person (let alone a knowledgeable institutional or corporate one) could have "knowledge of the facts constituting the offence" and yet had taken the due care required to move the offense beyond the realm of absolute liability. We can concede that the intent that could be described as "subjective foresight of consequence of death" (*R. v. Martineau*, (1990) 58 C.C.C.3d 353) was absent in *Sault Ste. Marie* as it would be in Walkerton. Yet if one knows that—say—to push a knife in a person's chest is a prohibited act, one must, presumably know why that is the case. And the consequence of inflicting (minimally) a serious wound cannot really be separated realistically from the wielding of the knife. Nor can one say that such a prohibited act was committed with due diligence as the act implies at least some culpable consequences.

Specifically, the due diligence requirement has been examined in detail in the work of Dianne Saxe (Saxe, 1991). Saxe argues that:

> the judicially created defense of reasonable care usually referred to as "due diligence" can play an essential role in protecting the environment, if defendants are obliged to show a sufficiently high degree of environmental care in order to benefit from the defense (Saxe, 1991:216).

Saxe also believes that the standards required (over ten years ago), were both demanding and expected to rise in the years to come (Ibid.). Her point is that, if the standards are both high and clearly expressed, then the corporation would have a strong interest in investing in environmental compliance " to protect them from liability" (Ibid.).

This hopeful scenario did not appear to come to pass in the later nineties, and it is not really present now. Although the economic motive of ensuring protection remains a strong one, the controls, monitoring, and enforcement structures are not. The institutional aspect of the problem needs to be taken seriously into consideration. Many factors militate against the success of the due diligence standard, and these emerge clearly in the Walkerton inquiry. I propose the following, not as an exhaustive list, simply as a tentative, initial list of difficulties that complicate the issue of how corporations prepare to comply:

(1) The presence on the Canadian labor scene of unions and other instruments that protect and reward workers for seniority rather than ability or improved, current qualifications, especially in the environmental field where science is constantly showing causal connections that promote new hazards (see the contrast between the "paper requirements" of education and testing, and the actuality of allowing Stan Koebel's seniority to supersede even those minimal requirements, Chapter 4);

(2) The institutional/governmental bodies' power to cut funding to environmental monitoring and enforcing programs;

(3) In general, as in (2) the power of institutions to establish priorities on a purely (or primarily) economic basis;

(4) The lack of scientific/laypersons' checks necessary even for demo-cratically chosen, local activities that might benefit certain groups, while gravely harming others (see Chapter 4);

(5) The lack of transparency and open information about the true effects of products and practices;

(6) The economic ability of corporations to mount advertising and mar-keting campaigns that reinforce the problems as in (5) (Korten, 1995);

(7) The lack of accountability of institutional/corporate partnerships, especially multinational ones, to the global, general public and per-haps to an international tribunal;

(8) The "other side" of economic consequences of noncompliance: monetary penalties are easily internalized as allowable, tax deductible expenses and passed on to consumers, hence, my emphasis on criminalization and different penalties, despite Charter protection (Westra, 1998);

(9) The presence of multinational treaties and international trade agree-ments, all of which offer "out-of-the-country" options for both pro-duction and marketing, and an easy way to escape "standards" set in Canada. Without an international criminal process, Royal Dutch Shell Oil can perpetrate in Nigeria crimes that the standards set and enforced in the Netherlands would never permit (Westra, 1998:ch.5; ibid. ch.9).

My argument is that if we discriminate between causing a monetary loss both in classifying crimes and in sentencing, when the defendant is a private citizen, then we need to carry this distinction through to when it is institutions and cor-porations who are at fault. We do not view, sentence, or punish the pickpocket or the thief, as we do those who commit assaults and homicides. Consistency requires that these distinctions be followed throughout the legal system, if it is to merit the appellation of a system of justice.

The courts and legislature appear to attempt periodically to take new steps to protect the public and to apply a precautionary principle to certain activities, while assuming full knowledge and awareness for corporations whose research departments are far superior even to governments' departments of research (Westra, 1998). On October 13, 2000, a Canadian Court reached a decision that appears to accept this conclusion, as the B.C. Court of Appeals convicted "Imperial Oil for discharging MMT into a harbour":

The court insisted that Imperial, a big company with many experts, must know the toxicity of every chemical in its plants. Having a good general safety system that allocated precautions based on known risks was not enough (R. v. Imperial Oil, (2000) B.C.C.A. 553; (2000) B.C. No. 2031).

One can therefore argue that cases like this one, involving not only a very large, very powerful corporation, but also one that had *already* found out many times what it meant to be criminally responsible for environmental damages (compare Exxon Valdez disaster, Velasquez, 1993), unfortunately indicates that even high "due diligence" standards are necessary, but not sufficient to improve corporate behavior and thus also environmental conditions.

What most often happens when a corporation discovers some possible riskiness in an otherwise profitable product or operation, as it happened in the DBCP case (Velasquez, 1993:421–424): Having been alerted by its own research scientists that the pesticide DBCP was shown to shrink testes size and cause tumors in rats, Amvac Corporation discontinued testing and did not alert the workers who handled the manufacture and production of the risks involved. It is only when, much later, the high rate of infertility in its Mexican workers was discovered that the true facts came to light.

In addition, as I have claimed above, further international ramifications were also present in the end. The U.S. EPA found that if DBCP were completely banned, "farmers would suffer a $400 million loss for crop damage in the first three years of the ban" (Ibid. at 424). Dow and Shell declined to resume production after the EPA intervened, and this produced a "window of opportunity" for Amvac, who now recouped its losses by shipping the pesticide to less developed nations, where often illiterate farm workers with no protective gear, would not be expected to read the warnings and take the precautions that might prevent the infertility and cancers, as proven before the U.S. EPA ban.

Once again, in this case, the indications were present, but the corporation was willfully blind to them. McIntyre J. explains (in *Sansregret*):

There are two senses in which a man is said not to know something because he does not want to know it. A thing may be troublesome to learn, and the knowledge of it, when acquired, may be uninteresting or distasteful. To refuse to know any more about the subject or anything at all is then a wilful but real ignorance.

Glanville Williams adds *(inter alia)*, that, in the case of willful blindness, "He suspected the facts, he realized its probability; but he refrained from obtaining the final confirmation because he wanted in the event to be able to deny knowledge" (Williams, 1955).

There is a well-known case where even the documented presence of "due diligence" is insufficient to dispel liability, that is, *Rylands v. Fletcher*, the topic of the next section.

a. "Nonnatural Use" in *Rylands v. Fletcher* and Strict Liability

> There have been . . . common law developments moving ort law away from fault and closer to a regime of strict liability. For example, the objective theory of the reasonable person, the use of statutes in negligence litigation, the doctrine of *res ipsa loquitur*, contributory negligence legislation, and other developments have indirectly edged negligence law toward a stricter form of liability (Linden, 1997:499).

Although the argument of this work has been that it is best to understand differently the nature of environmental offenses by viewing them primarily through their consequences and the harm they cause, avoiding the "due diligence" defense might be a good start to an approach that manifests more concern for our human rights. To this aim, it is worth considering strict liability offenses starting with *Rylands v. Fletcher*, a domestic case from the U.K. which is both environmental in its application, and foundational in spelling out clearly, especially in the appeal phase, the very principles that national as well as international legal systems too often attempt to avoid.

The case is taken to be basic to strict liability jurisprudence, and even the description of the case is illuminating "Liability of surface areas—without negligence or willfulness." (*Rylands v. Fletcher*, (1868) 3 L.R.-H.L. 330, 37 L.J. Ex. 161; 19 L.T. 220; 33 JP 70, HL as the final appeal after the Fletcher v. Rylands, (1866) LR 1 Exch 265, Exch, revg (1865) 3 H&C 774). The case is a simple one:

> A was the lessee of mines. B was the owner of a mill standing on land adjoining that under which the mines were worked. B desired to construct a reservoir, and employed competent persons, an engineer and a contractor, to construct it. A had worked his mines up to a spot where there were certain old passages of disused mines; these passages were connected-with vertical shafts which communicated with the land above, and which had also been out of use for years, and were apparently filled with marl and the earth of the surrounding land. No care was taken to block up these shafts, and shortly after water had been introduced into the reservoir it broke through some of the shafts, flowed through the old passages and flooded A's mine: Held A was entitled to recover damages from B in respect of this injury (Fletcher v. Rylands (1866)).

Although the court at first instance found that B did not owe damages to A because he did employ competent contractors to do his work on the reservoir, and because he was not aware of the presence of mines and passages beneath his operation, the Appeals Court reversed the judgment. The well-known passage from *Fletcher v. Rylands* is the judgment for the plaintiff on the following grounds; Manisty, J.:

2. The principle of law which governs the case is that he who does upon his own land acts which, though lawful in themselves, may become the source of mischief to his neighbours, is bound to prevent the mischief from occurring, or in the alternative to make compensation to the persons injured. This will be peculiarly the case when the act done consists in the construction and use of artificial works, for the purpose of collecting and impounding in vast quantities an element which will certainly cause mischief if it escapes (at 269).

It is very enlightening to see that it is not simply what happened that renders a person guilty, even though there was neither knowledge nor intent to cause the damage on his side, but the fact that the technologically altered condition of the property, and the risks inherent in this alteration, not its natural functioning was that through which the damage occurred, made all the difference. On the same topic, Blackburn J. (at 270) adds: ". . . but the difficulty here is in saying that what was rightful in the first doing, became wrongful in the continuation. The other side will contend that their duty was to take care, but not successful care." Almost all pollution-related environmental offenses are well-covered in these passages (although conservation issues are not). Whoever alters a natural system ought to take full responsibility for the eventual consequences, foreseen or unforeseen, that may follow upon that alteration, and this question will be addressed in detail in the next chapter.

To say that it is unrealistic to expect such responsibility to attach to whoever owns, alters, and controls the property and the operation upon it, does not begin to address the question of equity in such cases. Blackburn, J. was equally astute in noting that, in this case (and we can add in most cases of transboundary pollution resulting in ecocrimes), it was a lawful, not an illicit act that caused the harm. Blackburn J. (at 271): "When a party alters things from their normal condition so as to render them dangerous to already acquired rights, the law casts on him the obligation of fencing the danger, in order that it shall not be injurious to those rights." It is worth noting that only economic harms and damages are present or envisioned in this case; hence, this absolute liability position would be even easier to support when the harms and damages concern human health instead, or even human life.

It is encouraging to note that the present reliance on due diligence as a defense is not even proposed for this case. Chief Baron and Martin B. (Fletcher v. Rylands, (1866) LR 1 Exch 265, at 279), proclaim a principle of law that, were it enforced, would eliminate many of the problems we have discussed, and serve well to protect the environment:

We think that the true rule of law is, that the person who for his own purposes brings on his lands and collects and keeps there anything likely to do mischief if it escapes, must keep it in at his peril, and, if he does not do so, is *prima facie* answerable for all the damage which is the natural consequence of its escape. He can excuse himself by showing that the escape was owing to the plaintiff's default; or perhaps that the escape was the consequence of *vis major*, or the act of God; but as nothing of this sort exists here, it is unnecessary to inquire what excuse would be sufficient. The general rule, as above stated, seems on principle, just (at 280).

Simple, reasonable, and clear, this instance of domestic law inspires or should inspire equally clear and reasonable peremptory norms, even though the details of the environmental hazards are not set out in detail. The question details is covered nicely below, by Chief Baron and Martin B.: "And, upon authority, this we think is established to be the law, whether the things so brought be beasts, or water, or filth, or stenches (at 280)."

Linden summarizes the "Scope of Strict Liability" in relation to the case: "Under the traditional view of *Rylands v. Fletcher* a strict liability will be imposed if two elements are present: (a) non-natural use of land, and (b) escape" (Linden, 1997:503). The importance of "non-natural use" cannot be overstated, despite the fact that the concept has been used as an escape valve in environmental cases. For instance, many argue that "an overflow from a domestic water heater, or other home plumbing systems" would not be covered by *Rylands v. Fletcher*, and neither are "authorized sewers and storm drains" as they are viewed as "ordinary and proper for the general benefit of mankind" (Linden, 1997:504). Nonnatural use, therefore, became a use that exceeds accepted technologies and usual practices, rather than retaining the original meaning of the alteration to a natural system, a meaning that appears preferable when you consider the original case itself. But the meaning the courts ascribed to the expression is that of unusual activities or activities that were not ordinarily expected in that area or location.

The case law following upon *Rylands v. Fletcher* and using its principle, appears to be, for the most part, departing from the simple meaning I have proposed for nonnatural, that is, not the product of natural evolutionary processes. If one accepts as natural any number of activities that are based on man-made equipment or technologically enhanced processes and machinery, one has departed radically from the words and—I would add—from the spirit of the *Rylands v. Fletcher* principle. Linden discusses a great number of such cases (Linden, 1997:503–508). He says: ". . . non-natural came to mean special, exceptional, unusual, out of the ordinary. In the same way, the word "natural" took on the meaning of normal, common, everyday, or ordinary, rather than primitive or in the state of nature" (Linden, 1997:504).

The same view is expressed by Newark (1961:557–558), as he argues that "natural" means primarily that which exists by nature and is not artificial. In the secondary sense, however, it can mean that which is ordinary and usual even though it may be artificial. Newark supports his contention through U.K. case law, as Linden does, adding North American cases.

But it is important to retain the original sense of nonnatural as something that would not have come about in a natural way, or without direct human intervention, especially because of the many instances of such nonnatural uses of land, through which grave harm is inflicted, such as biotechnology in agricultural practices, or the chemical-induced global climate change (Brown, 2002). *Rylands v. Fletcher* imposes absolute liability and, in general, all cases involving environmental risks ought to be considered, minimally, under this category. Tony Honoré discusses "responsibility and fault" in tort law, and he explains this point through his discussion of the case of a ship officer "who was competent and experienced but who did not possess the certificate required by law" (Honoré, 1999:101). The officer negligently involved his ship in a collision, but he denied that the lack of a certificate was "causally relevant" (Ibid.). As "the basis of liability was fault," it is "rightly held that the lack of a certificate was irrelevant, since the officer would have navigated no better had he possessed one" (Ibid.). Honoré adds: "Since strict liability is liability not for wrongful conduct, but for engaging in risk-creating activity, there would have been no need in this case to show that the lack of a certificate was causally relevant" (Honoré, 1999:101).

All activities that arise nonnaturally in the sense I proposed as basic to *Rylands v. Fletcher* impose a certain amount of possible risk. In addition, all technological innovations, by definition, have no history upon which one may rely to ensure their safety, especially since, for the most part, only the manufacturer or originator of the equipment or process is ultimately competent to provide government agencies with the required test results.

Hence, one could propose that liability "based on causing harm," be replaced by "liability based on risk allocation" (Honoré, 1999:115). Far-fetched, perhaps, but also useful to put risk-imposers on notice that even their potential for causing harm is duly noted, before harm appears. I have proposed the example of a person having explosives taped under their jackets, while walking into a crowded square (Westra, 1998). Even if there is no intention of detonating the explosives, and, in fact, if by chance they do not go off, the magnitude of the risk, even in its uncertainty, ought to suffice to find the risk-imposer criminally liable in the law, although many disagree, and some would term the person "just lucky" (Ripstein, 1998). In the next sections we will see some other possible ways of taking environmental harms seriously.

9. ECOVIOLENCE AND THE "PEACE, ORDER AND GOOD GOVERNMENT" CLAUSE OF THE CANADIAN CONSTITUTION ACT (1867)

The argument of this chapter has been an attempt to show that, whether regulators or bureaucrats or even the public are fully aware of it or not, environmental regulatory offenses are different in kind from other regulatory offenses, because the results they produce, sooner or later result in effects similar to those produced by assaults or murders. In that case, the natural environment, when so altered and laced with toxic substances, simply holds a different, slower-acting sort of weapon. A major problem is that assaults and the infliction of harms upon others, appear to demand a perpetrator who is not only aware of his actions, but also of the results that will, or may occur. The force required to perpetrate an assault, can be direct or indirect (Section 265.(1)(a)) of the criminal code, and the "weapon," under Section 2 of the Criminal Code ("Interpretations") means anything used, designed to be used, or intended for use

(a) in causing death or injury to any person, or
(b) for the purpose of threatening or intimidating any person, and, without restricting the generality of the foregoing, includes a firearm.

Hence, there is no necessity to use a conventional weapon in order to commit an offense against a person. Even more encouraging, the time limits between the assault and a person's death, are no longer subject to the "year and a day" rule, since Section 227 was repealed ((1999) (Chapter 5.5.9.(1)). Finally, even the most serious difficulty addressed in this chapter, the *mens rea* requirement for serious crimes against the person, appear to be optional, as Section 2 talks about "any thing used," not only "intended," or "designed" to be used, in a manner to cause injury or death.

Throughout this chapter we have grappled with the knowledge and intent requirements of true crimes, while repeating the words of legal scholars who continue to view environmental regulatory offenses as "quasi crimes," or not true crimes without, unfortunately clear scientific evidence to permit the alleged distinction between crimes and offenses that do not, *prima facie*, appear to fit that appellation.

Aside from the specifics of the arguments proposed, the major points at issue, both in the chapter and this work as a whole are: (1) the status of regulatory offenses; it appears to be inappropriately characterized at this time, as their import and effects render them "true crimes,' therefore they should be treated as such; (2) local and even regional and national regulatory regimes are insufficient to deal with the damages and harms that are transboundary in nature and global in their reach; for these reasons, therefore, (3) both perpetrators and complicit enablers of ecocrimes should be tried, convicted and punished, without making intent or even an unattainable full knowledge of the consequences of their activities, the *conditio sine qua non* of their culpability.

R. v. Hydro-Québec ((1997) 3 S. C. R. 213), provides support for all three points, through language that is both clear and thorough on the first two points, and therefore permits the conclusion drawn on the third. The judgment in *Hydro-*

Québec, in a split five to four decision (La Forest, L'Heureux-Dubé, Gonthier, Cory and McLachlin J. J.; Lamer C. J., Sopinka, Iacobucci, and Major J. J. dissenting) stated that there were solid grounds to affirm federal powers over such a diffuse and grave threat as PCB contamination. Hence, both criminal law powers and peace, order and good government powers, were appropriate, in addition to the already existing provincial powers to regulate toxic substances. It is not necessary to spend time on the details of the appeals of the case and the parties involved. From our point of view we must consider what the strong language of the case can do in support of the major points listed above.

While it is indeed true that regulatory offenses are covered under criminal law, they are not presently treated as true crimes. This chapter has argued against that position, citing the similarities between the consequences of environmental regulatory offenses and those of assaults and other crimes against the person. La Forest J. states that, "Under s.91(27) of the Constitution act, 1867, Parliament had been accorded plenary powers to make Criminal Law in the widest sense" (Ibid. at 2). In addition, Parliament also has the right to decide what threatening evil they wish to suppress. The protection of the environment is a "wholly legitimate public objective in the exercise of criminal law power." Recognizing the significant threat imposed by highly toxic but long-lasting PCBs, and the grave risks of serious harms to both animals and humans, these clearly fall within criminal law power, even without seeking to add "Parliament's jurisdiction to make laws for the peace, order and good government of Canada."

There was a dissenting argument, to the effect that the goal of environmental regulations is to regulate, not to prohibit environmental pollution. This argument did not prevail, as the "federal-provincial consultative process" is only that; therefore, having consulted the provinces, Parliament "is free to pass whatever regulations it sees fit in order to address the threat posed by substances qualifying as toxic" (Ibid. at 32). The reason for this supervening power is cited at 35 (by Laforest J.):

> A crime is an act which the law, with appropriate penal sanctions, forbids; but as prohibitions are not enacted in a vacuum, we can properly look for some evil or injurious or undesirable effect upon the public against which they law is directed.

> Is the prohibition then enacted with a view to a public purpose which can support it as being in relation to criminal law? Public peace, order, security, health, morality: these are the ordinary, though not exclusive ends served by that law

This passage clearly indicates the presence of a "legitimate public purpose," because a toxic substance is defined under Section 11 of CEPA, as,

(1) having or that may have immediate or long-term harmful effects on the environment;

(2) constituting or that may constitute a danger to the environment on which human life depends; or

(3) constituting or that may constitute a danger in Canada to human life or health (Ibid. at 40).

And these are "not cumulative requirements": a substance therefore may be brought under federal control even is it is not presently known to have a harmful effect on life or health (Ibid. at 41).

Hence, it appears that the "true crime" argument that was advanced in this chapter, leading to full prohibitions and serious sanctions, rather than fines, is supported by this judgment.

The next question is a jurisdictional one. Why invoke Parliamentary powers, when the existence of provincial regulations is intended to deal with these problems?

La Forest J. in his judgment, citing the "leading case" on this topic, *Friends of the Oldman River Society v. Canada*, says:

The protection of the environment has become one of the major challenges of our time. To respond to this challenge, governments and international organizations have been engaged in the creation of a wide variety of legislative schemes and administrative structures (Ibid. at 85).

Recognition of the scope and gravity of the threat entails that there are many possible avenues open to Parliament to deal with this emergent public problem, without "offending the division of Powers" between the provincial and federal government. The powers of the Constitution permit "the creation of environmental crimes," provided they "actually see *to outlaw* the behaviour, not merely regulate it" (Ibid. at 61).

The same gravity, when recognized, should prevent the consensus and compliance approach to regulation that is used in provincial regulation and instruments, but is totally inappropriate to all forms of assaults. The judgment proposes that, rather than persist with models of legislation better suited to earlier times, when less technological complexity prevails, the Constitution "must be interpreted in a manner that is fully responsive to emerging realities" hence to the nature of the subject matter to be regulated (Ibid. at 86).

An additional, obvious reason is that the environment must be viewed as a national concern, is and that no toxic substance can remain at a single location, in a single province. Hence, the "Peace, Order and Good Government" clause of

Section 91 is as relevant to the question of releasing PCBs in the environment, as is the criminal law power (Section 91(27)) of the Constitution Act (1867) (Ibid. at 90). However, the "issues" portion of the judgement states that, if the "criminal law power" is sufficient to the purpose, then it becomes unnecessary to involve the national concern doctrine (Ibid. at 110).

The main point is that, as the pollution seriously affects both the natural environment and Canada's citizens, its prevention is "a public purpose of superordinate importance," and "it constitutes one of the major challenges of our time." Peter Hogg also sees the *Hydro-Québec* decision as "taking criminal law power well beyond the conventional limits of criminal law" (Hogg, 2000:3). The judgment affirms that the highest powers and the most stringent legal structures must be invoked and utilized (R. v. Hydro-Quebec, (1997) 3 S.C.R., 213, at para. 123). Gonthier J. is cited for his pronouncement in *Ontario v. Canadian Pacific Ltd, (1995) 2 S.C.R. 1031:*

> Everyone is aware that individually and collectively, we are responsible for preserving that natural environment. I would agree with the Law Reform Commission of Canada, *Crimes Against the Environment supra*, which concluded at p. 8 that: . . . a fundamental and widely shared value is indeed seriously contravened by some environmental pollution, a value which we will refer to as the right to a safe environment (at 124).

It seems clear that the seriousness of the language in much of this judgment, supports *both* the full criminality of environmental "assaults," and the need *to add* national (and—as I will argue below—even international) dimensions to the legal instruments used to combat this evil.

The final point is more debated, and less clear in this judgment. La Forest J. acknowledges that even the higher power invoked is "of course subject to the fundamental justice requirements of s.7 of the *Canadian Charter of Rights and Freedoms*, which may dictate a higher level of *mens rea* for serious or true crimes" (Ibid. at para. 2). There is a tension between the need for sweeping reforms in the public interest, and the intention to cling to a Charter requirement that is hard to fit into the environmental situation and the multiple actors responsible and complicit in the commission of these ecocrimes.

In this chapter I have also argued that it is precisely the issue of fundamental justice, understood as substantive, not only as procedural justice that makes the difference in this case. When the criminal law power is used to eliminate a crime that is diffuse, multisource, and systematic, it is nearly impossible to pin one specific individual down to intent, just as Robert Bullard argues for cases of environmental racism (Bullard, 1995). Without repeating previous arguments, it seems that the recognized gravity of the multiple threats involved and their pervasive and persistent character are sufficient to support the position that the rights of the accused, in this case, usually of institutional/corporate/bureaucratic persons, by definition neither vulnerable nor disadvantaged, and not subject to imprisonment *qua* entities, and thus not having the same consequences of limiting *mens rea* as would be the case for humans, whose negligence, willful blindness, and recklessness may still need to find a place. In that case, those consequences cannot be weighted more heavily than the health, safety, and security of all Canadians.

In conclusion this judgment supports the emergence of the need to employ criminal law power at the federal level to prohibit activities that present grave threats to the environment and all Canadians, not only to regulate in a collaborative manner with industry and all polluters some negotiated emission or release standard and then hope for compliance. This sounds like a very general assessment of the circumstances. But much of the language of this judgment is equally general and universal in tone. Gonthier J. says it well in the rest of the passage cited above from *Ontario v. Canadian Pacific*; after referring to the right to a safe environment, he adds:

> To some extent, this right and value appears to be new and emerging, but in part because it is an extension of existing and very traditional rights and values already protected in criminal law, its presence and shape even now are largely discernible. Among the new strands of this fundamental value are, it may be argued, those such as *quality of life*, and *stewardship* of the natural environment. At the same time, traditional values as well have simply expanded and evolved to include the environment now as an area of interest of direct and primary concern. Among these values fundamental to the purposes and protections of the criminal law are the *sanctity of life*, the *inviolability and integrity of persons*, and the *protection of human life and health*. It is increasingly understood that certain forms and degrees of environmental pollution can directly or indirectly, sooner or later, seriously harm or endanger human life and human health. (cited at para. 124).

It is the presence of these basic values (and basic rights) that fuels the quest for more demanding and more exhaustive environmental laws. In fact, after a number of global environmental disasters like Chernobyl, Bhopal and Exxon Valez focused public awareness on the consequences of environmental negligence, the U.S. enacted the criminal enforcement of environmental protection, adding criminal convictions and jail time to the long-standing existing regime of tort liability. It is worth looking at these changes and place them in the context of recent past and present trends in U.S. environmental law in a brief summary, in the next section. U.S. present laws, as we shall see, would add an interesting dimension to the pursuit of justice so absent in the Walkerton case (see Chapter 4).

a. Criminal Enforcement of Environmental Laws in the United States: Knowledge Requirement and the Elimination of *Mens Rea*

The U.S. Congress made environmental pollution a federal crime in the Refuse Act of 1899; hence, a violation of the Refuse Act is a public welfare offense, for which violators are held strictly liable (Cooney et al., 1999:5) These offenses are considered "real crimes," and jail terms are routinely assigned:

> From the crucial events of October 1982 until April 7, 1995, Justice obtained indictments against 443 corporations and 1,068 individuals. During that time, 334 organizations and 740 individuals were convicted by plea or verdict. Justice recovered $297 million in criminal penalties, $125 million of which was obtained from the *Exxon Valdez* oil spills alone. Sentences totaling 561 years of imprisonment (not counting actual time served) were imposed against those convicted (Ibid. at 8).

In addition, the Water Quality Act of 1987 (Pub. L. No.100-4, § 312, 101 Stat. 7, 42–44 (codified at 33 U.S.C. § 1319(c)), eliminated the requirement of a "negligent or willful mental element," and replaced it with a hierarchy of offenses, whereby knowing acts could be punished as felonies (Cooney et al., 1999:8) The differences between misdemeanors and felonies remained somewhat problematic although the EPA in 1982 identified several factors, to distinguish between the two; these criteria assist in defining the need for criminal prosecution in specific environmental cases (Perry Memorandum, Regions I-X, Criminal Enforcement Priorities for the Environmental Protection Agency, Oct. 12, 1982):

- *The scienter requirement*—criminal prosecution is normally limited to cases in which the prospective defendant has "guilty knowledge" or intent to violate the law;
- *The nature and seriousness of the offense*—this factor focuses on the "extent of environmental contamination or human health hazard" resulting from the prohibited conduct;
- *The need for deterrence*—this factor primarily targets particularly deliberate offenses or those that result in serious environmental contamination or human health hazard;
- *Compliance history*—repeated environmental violations may trigger criminal enforcement to achieve effective individual deterrence; and
- *The need for simultaneous civil or administrative enforcement action* (Cooney et al., 1999:13).

The first of the five criteria relates to the Canadian *mens rea* requirement, and, with the question of deterrence, it is perhaps the most important from our point of view.

The difference between "misdemeanors" and "felonies" remained somewhat problematic although the EPA in 1982 identified the factors listed above.

On the question of the *mens rea* requirement, although the Department of Justice (henceforth, Justice) was concerned with retaining *mens rea* in the traditional understanding of criminal prosecution, recent judicial decisions have effectively eliminated this requirement (Cooney et al., 1999:8). Richard Lazarus remarks that the government's success in securing convictions has been based on "its ability in most criminal law contexts to persuade the judiciary that environmental offenses require only a diminished *mens rea*" (Lazarus, 1995:9).

Many of the cases in question involve "midnight dumpers," but often they also involve "conspiracy, aiding and abetting; submission of false statements; mail fraud, perjury and obstruction of justice" (Cooney et al., 1999:6, n.11), thus making it easy to invoke the "public welfare offense." Technically, any violation of an environmental statute may be prosecuted criminally, but enforcement officers cannot locate and prosecute all infractions; hence, they must rely, to some extent, on corporate self-regulation. As well, the whole program of criminal prosecution encounters difficulties as struggles arise between Washington and local prosecutors. Even when the local EPA office can provide all necessary evidence, the Department of Justice may be reluctant to prosecute unless it can be certain to secure a conviction (Cooney et al., 1999:9). Justice must exercise its own judgment on this question, and it must be convinced of its ability to provide concrete explanations that will be found satisfactory by all, as it is not easy to resolve policy disputes by appealing to neutral principles: "The problem is especially acute when the mental component, ordinarily the principal determinant of criminal cases, is no longer an element of the offense" (Ibid.).

In some sense, Justice's approach is desirable: they are concerned with establishing viable precedents, thinking of future prosecutions that might need to rely on these successes. Yet treating environmental crimes primarily as administrative problems, that is, in keeping with the focus with the regulatory aspect of these violations, is problematic in itself. The criminal thrust was fueled by public outrage at a series of disasters such as Love Canal, Chernobyl, Bhopal and Exxon Valdez. But it is wrong to expect that only obvious disasters based on immediately visible consequences are worthy of serious prosecution because, increasingly, the science and public health components of environmental crimes are readily available in the literature (see Chapter 2).

In 1990 Washington attempted to regain authority by granting the Attorney General the right to veto prosecution. But 1994 Attorney General Janet Reno issued another policy directive, dividing all cases into national interest cases and lower priority cases (Office of the Attorney General, Bluesheet Revision to the U.S. Attorney s Manual on Environmental Crimes, Aug. 23, 1994). Although this approach is better than allowing centralized political decision-making to affect prosecution, this division does not acknowledge the fact that all environmental cases have both local and national (and even global) relevance. There is no such thing as a fully contained, local environmental adverse effect, although there are degrees of containment.

Richard Lazarus notes the emphasis on administrative law, as less complex, less open to scientific debates of interpretation (Lazarus, 2000:703). Speaking of the decisions of the Supreme Court's Justices, he says:

> For most of the Court, most of the time, environmental law has become no more than a subspecies of administrative law, raising no special issues or concerns worthy of distinct treatment as a substantive area of law. Environmental protection is merely an incidental context for the resolution of a legal question (Lazarus, 2000:632).

In addition, although U.S. laws appear to be better fitted to prosecute environmental crimes than—say—Canadian laws, they only apply where a statute is present. Lacking statutes to preserve wild lands, or corridors or to support nonnegotiable scientific standards that might include cumulative and synergistic effects of effluents and pollution, some of the worse problems may not be solved even by these enhanced prosecutorial rules.

We noted that (1) *mens rea* and (2) deterrence were the most important questions for the purpose of this work. Starting briefly with the latter, it is worth noting that some regional EPA offices, such as California and Ohio, have created specific task forces that target such area as the "mishandling of pesticides, failure to report leaking under ground storage tanks, falsification of environmental documents" as well as whole "critical geographical areas" such as the U.S./Mexican border (Cooney et al., 1999:20). The Ohio EPA has also shifted from prosecuting "midnight dumpers," to established businesses intent on improving their profits and competitive advantages: "Such companies may simply regard civil penalties as a cost of doing business, and can be brought into compliance only through the individual deterrent of criminal prosecution" (Ibid.). We alluded briefly to deterrence in Chapter 1, on the topic of the death penalty. Although that question remains undecided, as it is overshadowed by issues of fairness and equal treatment, in this case the evidence appears to be clearer, and the reason to hope for deterrence appear based on common sense.

Corporate interests find it too easy to reduce all values to economic ones, so that the difference between (1) harms to human life and health, and even human rights, and (2) possible harms to corporate economic goals, are perceived as different in degree, rather than in kind. The shock of a criminal prosecution, as argued by Cooney et al., may possibly bring home the vast gulf present between harm (1) and harm (2), thus to emphasize the grave responsibility borne by corporate offenders for harm (1), and the latter's incommensurability with harm (2).

Turning now to the knowledge element in U.S. law, regarding environmental crimes, we need to consider several aspects of that question. First, environmental crimes are viewed as general intent offenses; where knowing violations are not truly defined, allowing instead the courts to give meaning to the term "on a case-by-case basis" (Cooney et al., 1999:23). The concept is often understood to mean that the defendant had "mere consciousness" of an act or omission (Ocean Dumping Act (1971), 33 U.S.C. § 1411(a)), which amounts to a "violation of law, regulation or permit," without demanding proof "that the defendant had knowledge of the relevant statutory provision" (Cooney et al., 1999:23, n.155).

Second, the "Public Welfare Offense Doctrine" applies "when the substance involved is so inherently dangerous that the defendant's knowledge of the legal issues can be presumed" (Cooney et al., 1999:23). Third, the "Crime of Knowing Endangerment," created by Congress "to deal with particularly offensive conduct that directly threatens human life" with graver penalties, is an important tool to approach these crimes. All that is required other than the presence of graver consequences, is general intent, which is shown when evidence demonstrates that the "discharger knew it was dealing with a material that could harm humans or the environment" (Cooney et al., 1999:18). Examples include discharge of "dioxin from paper mills, arsenic from metal operations, vinyl chloride from other industrial operations" and the like. Cases that involve less lethal materials or compounds are misdemeanors and, for those cases, "negligently violating a permit" represents sufficient knowledge.

In contrast, aggravated felonies require a knowing violation and proof that the defendant "knows at the time that he thereby places another person in imminent danger" (Cooney et al., 1999:27).

Individuals may be charged with environmental crimes on the basis of "(1) direct evidence, (2) wilful blindness/conscious avoidance, (3) circumstantial evidence, and (4) the responsible corporate officer doctrine" (Cooney et al., 1999:29). The last of these requirements is particularly relevant in cases where it is hard to show knowledge through other means. Under this doctrine, criminal liability can be imposed on:

(1) a corporate officer,
(2) who is directly responsible within management for the conduct in question,
(3) who knew that they type of improper activity allegedly committed by his or her subordinates was occurring (Cooney et al., 1999:30).

The doctrine permits imposing liability on officers at corporate headquarters, who have no direct responsibility for the operation of the offending facility (Ibid.), when this facility is not located nearby. Liability is imposed solely by virtue of the position of responsibility of the corporate officer in question. The strongest support for this doctrine can be found in Britain (United States v. Britain, 731 F.2d 1413, 21 E.L.R. 21092 (10th Cir. 1991)), where a city's public utilities' director was charged with allowing the discharge of pollutants into a local creek, in a case reminiscent of Walkerton (see Chapter 4). If U.S. laws had been applied In Walkerton, as environmental crimes are subject to a *de minimis* knowledge requirement, it would have been easy to argue that, whatever his educational failings (see Chapter 4), a public utilities employee such as Koebel, who knew enough to falsify reports to the ministry, would be aware of the dangerousness of the presence of e-coli bacteria in the water supply, and would certainly meet the *de minimis* requirement, as above.

Similarly, the Ontario Premier who initiated the deregulation, and monitoring cuts spiral, eventually leading to the documented deaths, could not avoid criminal prosecution, but would be charged under the corporate officer doctrine. One wonders why some of these approaches to environmental crime have not long since been introduced in Canada and internationally, and whether perhaps there might still be time for an interpretive appeal to U.S. approach for the Canadian case, as no criminal prosecutions have been initiated to date. In contrast, Lazarus argues that even in the United States, present Supreme Court decisions are viewing the precedents upon which many environmental felony prosecutions have relied, as becoming increasingly unstable (Lazarus, 1995:9), thus possibly leading to a regression away from environmental protection.

In sum, although, both strict liability and the U.S. approach to environmental crimes appear to be preferable to what Canadian laws did in Walkerton (see Chapter 4), I believe that the analogy between environmental harms and assaultive crimes serves best to bring out the gross human rights breaches that follow the occurrence of these crimes. In the next chapter we will consider the possibility of entrenching what Bosselman terms "ecological human rights" (Taylor, 1998) directly into a national constitution (the Constitution of the Commonwealth of Pennsylvania), before turning to the regimes of international law covenants.

CHAPTER 6

FROM NATIONAL TO INTERNATIONAL ENVIRONMENTAL LAW

1. BEYOND NATIONAL ENVIRONMENTAL REGULATIONS

The Walkerton example discussed in Chapter 4 indicated several difficulties endemic to the functioning of environmental regulations and controls in a Western democracy. A brief summary will help to review some of the difficulties that emerged. First, the regulatory climate itself is one of compromise and collaborative interaction between regulators and bureaucrats on one side, and corporate actors, on the other. Second, the strongest language in the environmental regulatory instruments can be found in the Preambles or in other nonenforceable sections of those documents. The result of these practices is that, whenever a prohibition might affect negatively the business interests of some corporate player, an exception is tacked on, after the stern-sounding prohibition.

Often, the language of the document itself is unclear, and major concepts are left undefined. A clear example might be the use of the language of ecological or biological integrity (from the time of the U.S. Clean Water Act of 1972), present in any number of documents, but always left undefined (Westra, 1994). In the Walkerton example, for instance "farming" in all environmental regulations is allowed to mean both family farming and factory farming, despite the vast differences in the respective environmental impacts that result from each of these practices (Chapter 4).

Third, whether explicitly or implicitly, economic considerations consistently "trump" environmental and health concerns, in several ways: (a) "deregulation," "self-regulation," and "cutting red tape," are all blatant forms of courting and supporting the corporate enterprise, whether or not these practices result in immediate or long-term public harms (see Chapter 4); (b) privatizing monitoring and control protocols, once again suggests that the rights of citizens to protection may be left to the decisions of the market, and to the untutored, uninformed, or economically motivated choices of private enterprise, rather than being the first obligation of any government in power; (c) budget cuts to both environmental and health care, even when coupled with tax refunds, once again demonstrate that essential environmental and health services are viewed a s secondary, despite the government's responsibility to maintain and support public health a basic human right (Shue, 1996). It seems obvious: all the problems we have described, the attitude of compromise/collaboration between would-be-regulators and those who resist regulations, the imprecise and vague language of legal instruments, the primacy of economic considerations, and the influence of power politics, are equally present, and probably even magnified at the international level. But international law includes explicit principles, the work of publicists and *opinio juris*, as well as customary, positive law. At the national level, at best, judges may choose to apply some principle or cite a jurist at the Appellate or Supreme Court level. In addition, *erga omnes* obligations and *jus cogens* norms my be appealed to (albeit sparingly) in international law; these may also be appealed to in both arbitration and judgments of the International Court of Justice, and incorporated in covenants, as we will see in Chapter 7.

In addition, not only are human rights are not fully respected because of omissions of care and respect in national environmental laws, but the argument of Chapter 5 showed the similarity between assaults, even manslaughter as defined by the Canadian Criminal Code (2000), and environmental attacks or ecoviolence against human individuals, groups, and populations. Case law shows that, at least in Canada, both the factual and the fault elements present in manslaughter may be shown to be equally present in environmental assaults, that is, in ecocrime (see Chapter 5). The case is not so clear for assaults that do not result in death, although I have tried to make that argument as well. Part of the difficulty is that Canadians do not have a constitutional right to a healthy environment, although critics have made a strong case for including such rights in Section 7 of the Canadian Charter of Rights and Freedoms (Muldoon, 1999). Nevertheless, the reference to the "health" of Canadians as an imperative, when environmentally risky activities are considered, is clearly stated in the 1999 CEPA (see Chapter 4).

In this chapter, we will start by considering this strategy: would it help to entrench the right to a healthy environment in the Constitution as a human right of all citizens? The Commonwealth of Pennsylvania is the only one of the United States where this Constitutional right is explicitly present, and the consequences of this unique constitutional amendment will be considered in Section 2.

Our analysis will show that, despite the obvious desirability of entrenching environmental rights in state Constitutions, this step is not often taken. If it were, not only would constitutional amendments serve to erect protective walls for the defense of citizens' lives and health, but the practice would add to the list of customary principles of international law, so that the legal effects of such additions would be doubled.

The first part of this work has painstakingly described ecoviolence in its nature as gratuitous, unprovoked attack, and in its effects that represent, for the most part, clear human rights violations.

Hence, treating environmental protection as a Constitutional right appears to be a necessary first step in the right direction. Breaches of human rights in international law, or constitutional rights in national law, provide the first parameters of criminality, before attempting to establish the regulatory regimes that will exhibit the requisite "equity, justice, transparency and fairness," in response (Brunnée and Toope, 1997:29).

However, the same internal pressures and economic and political interests at play in the example of Walkerton, Ontario, are equally in evidence here, at the national level: noncompliance with both the spirit and the letter of the law, economic interests and public apathy (the latter a clear presence in most liberal political organizations) are contributing factors (see Chapter 3).

In the next section we will consider the role and function of binational agreements, as we move from domestic towards international and transnational governance (Scott, 2001). The classic case from which principles of international environmental law are derived is the *Trail Smelter Arbitration*, which was decided by an arbitral tribunal, after the International Joint Commission offered its own fact-finding and recommendations (see Chapter 7). The International Joint Commission is particularly important for having established this "precedent," but also because, through its role in the Great Lakes Water Quality Agreement (GLWQA), it helps to support and institutionalize the ecosystem approach in international and in customary law.

We will then also consider the role of regime formation and the history of "new law" through the emergence of progressive principles for the protection of human rights and the proliferation of multilateral treaties for the protection of the environment and, through it, our health and basic rights.

From a consideration of treaties and customary law, we will turn to some cases that show clearly the progressive importance and acceptance of legitimate universal, common concern, such as the Nuclear Tests case, and the Gabcikovo/Nagymaros case.

This chapter is intended as a "bridge" of sorts to the discussion of ecocrime in international law in Chapter 7, and the question of state responsibility for these breaches of human rights.

2. THE ENVIRONMENTAL AMENDMENT TO THE CONSTITUTION OF PENNSYLVANIA

The people have a right to clean air, pure water, and to the preservation of the natural, scenic, historical and aesthetic values of the environment. Pennsylvania's public natural resources are the common property of all the people, including generations yet to come. As trustees of these resources, the commonwealth shall conserve and maintain them for the benefit of all the people (PA Constitution, Article 1, Section 27; approved May 18, 1971).

This text, as we shall see, is open to several interpretations, and is less than precise. Nevertheless, it makes a strong statement in defense of peoples' rights to the protection of the "commons," especially if the text of this article is understood and explicated in ecological terms. "Clean air," "pure water" and, in general, the preservation (rather than the "conservation") of the natural environment require the full protection and, where necessary, the restoration of ecological integrity (Karr and Chu, 1995; Karr, 2000; Westra, 1994; Westra, 1998; Noss, 1992; Noss and Cooperrider, 1994).

But a strong preservationist policy, such as the one advocated by the ethics of integrity (Westra, 1998; Brown et al., 2000) and by the principles of the Earth Charter (Rockefeller et al., 2000; Miller and Westra, 2002), is clearly inimical to the primacy of trade and economic development, unless strong restraints are mandated by an ecologically motivated policy. Hence, the question that arises is whether even such a clearly worded Constitutional amendment can, in practice, carry out its protective role. John C. Dernbach has recently attempted to answer this question in a great deal of detail, first, through an examination of the Article's "Interpretive Framework" (1999), then through a follow-up article on "Environmental Rights and Public Trust" (1999). His findings support the thesis that,

> As its early supporters feared, the Amendment seems to have more symbolic than substantive value, inscribed on plaques and quoted in speeches, but rarely used in decision-making (Dernbach, 1999:696).

If it could be proven that at least there has been a clear indirect impact from that Amendment, providing a better interpretive framework in a general way, that might be a modest, but desirable outcome. But Dernbach's conclusion appears to be supported by the evidence of case law. In the best known case, *Commonwealth v. National Gettysburg Battlefield Tower* (311 A.2d 588 (Pa. Commw. Ct. 1973)) "the courts held that the Amendment created a self-executing public right" (Ibid. at 696), but ruled that a commercial venture on that property did not violate that right. The Amendment could have a very powerful role through the substantive rules it proclaims, but it needs to be fully understood and positively applied: ". . . Article 1, Section 27 needs to be understood primarily on the basis of government responsibilities. While citizens' rights are an essential part of the Amendment, such rights should be directed primarily at enforcement of government duties (Dernbach 1999:699).

Of course, if environmental and other regulatory instruments were already capable of providing the required protection, there would be no need for judicial enforcement of the Amendment. Dernbach adds: "Where legal gaps exist however, courts shall enforce the substantive rules contained in the Amendment" (Dernbach, 1999:699). Dernbach analyzes the Article into two component parts: the first part "creates a right in the public to clean air, pure water, and the preservation of certain values"; the second part establishes the Commonwealth as the trustee of all these resources, with the duty to conserve them and protect them for future generations (Dernbach, 1999:402). It seems undisputable that a trustee has an absolute duty not to allow the capital of her trusteeship to be attacked, although there might exist special provisions attached to the trusteeship that would enable her to allocate the interest derived from the capital in ways that are consonant with the intention of the trust.

In principle, one could do no better than to entrench such an amendment in all constitutions, including the Canadian Charter of Rights and Freedoms. It is essential to trusts that the distribution and the use of the interest is separate from the preservation of the capital: for the latter, no "wise use" is permitted. In environmental terms this principle applies to the difference between what is sustainable and what is not. Unfortunately, although it is a matter of simple observation to decide what was the original investment (or capital) in monetary terms, and what is the subsequent earned interest that can be allotted for various purposes without affecting the continued existence of the capital, this is not true in the case of natural systems.

In natural systems, we are dealing with complex biological wholes (Goerner, 1997), not economic units, and any such clear divisions and limits are totally artificial (see next section for a discussion of complex system theory vs. Newtonian mechanism in all ecological considerations). In order to err on the side of safety, if err we must, not on the side of irreparable overconfidence, we must rely on the Precautionary Principle.

Although Article 27, Section 1 does not explicitly invoke the Precautionary Principle, the substance of its mandate and its language clearly implies it: a trustee must protect and "maintain" the capital, and—in order to do so—must be able to identify it.

a.   *Commonwealth v. National Gettysburg Battlefield Tower, Inc.*

In *Commonwealth v. National Gettysburg Battlefield Tower, Inc.* (302 A.2d 886 (Pa. Commw. Ct. 1973), *aff'd*, 311 A.2d 588 (Pa. 1973)) a company was attempting to build a 307-foot tower and the State argued that, ". . . the tower's visibility throughout the Gettysburg battlefield would interfere with the public right to preservation of the natural scenic, historic and aesthetic values of that environment" (Dernbach, 1999:705). It is noteworthy that the reason why the court could rule in this case, in favor of the protection of "historic" and perhaps "aesthetic" values, was because of the "environmental rights" portion of the Amendment, not on the basis of the trusteeship mandate. The trusteeship of the Commonwealth's natural resources and their preservation was not relevant, because the tower was to be built on privately owned lands. But one may wonder whether taking both parts of the Amendment seriously would therefore require the Commonwealth to restructure the amount of land, air, water, in sum the quantity of natural resources that could, in fact, be privately owned.

If an insufficient amount of land is left to remain as the public property of the Commonwealth, the trust cannot be executed. In other words, the Commonwealth must ensure that it retains sufficient capital to ensure its use in perpetuity, by present and future generations. This point is emphasized morally by the Principle of Integrity and the Second Order Principles that follow upon it (Westra 1994; Westra, 1998). The need to retain a certain amount of land as a public, common good, in order to ensure the presence of nature's services (Daily, 1997), has been also emphasized by scientists from Aldo Leopold (1949); see also Westra, 2001), through the Wildlands Project (Noss, 1992; Noss and Cooperrider, 1994), and it is a principle of conservation biology, as well as sound ecology (Karr and Chu, 1995; Karr and Chu, 1999; Pimentel et al., 1991). Therefore, should the Commonwealth feel impelled to permit the sale of most state-owned lands, without ensuring that at least 20–25 percent of these lands were kept back in their natural state, that is wild, and unmanipulated (Westra et al., 2000), it would be impossible for Pennsylvania *ever* to carry out the obligations of its trusteeship. "In the Gettysburg case, on appeal, the Court found that, ". . . the tower, while conspicuous, would not transform the scene of present day Gettysburg" (Dernbach, 1999:707). In addition, the court concluded that "the historical Gettysburg area was already 'raped' by development" (Dernbach, 1999:707; Gettysburg Tower, 13 Adams County L.J. at 85). It is hard to believe that a site that represents both an important historic value, and the locus of a natural resource should be recognized as a brownfield and accepted as such. Dernbach (1999:707, n.57) lists present commercial activities as including among others, "a junkyard, motels, fast food restaurants, souvenir stands, an amusement park and a gasoline service station."

b. *Payne v. Kassab*

We can contrast the treatment of Article 27, Section 1 in the *Gettysburg* case, with the use of the notion of trust in the Amendment in *Payne v. Kassab* (312 A.2d 86 (Pa. Commw. Ct. 1973)). In *Payne* the facts are quite different from the previous case discussed, as the dispute in *Payne* was the land that was part of the "River Common," and the project envisioned would eliminate large trees and, in general, use part of "the state's public natural resources" to widen a street in an area presently located in a commons (Dernbach, 1999:709). But the court's decision took into consideration all reasonable efforts that had been made to mitigate some of the project's adverse impact, and ordered that some safeguards be employed.

The effect of this decision, viewed in law as "an all-purpose test for the Amendment" was to make it clear that courts would and could do little better for public-owned lands, than they did for private property. Dernbach concludes that in *Payne*, "the public trust part of the Amendment is deprived of any substantive content": ". . . the state's responsibility for publicly owned resources—the resources over which it has the greatest control—is not to conserve them or preserve their values, *but rather to manage their degradation* under the Payne test" (Dernbach, 1999:713, emphasis added). The final decision was not made on moral or substantive legal grounds, but on the basis of a market analysis instead (Sagoff, 2000). But courts are intended to pursue substantive values, such as justice, not to give primacy to economic goals. Therefore, even though the cost/benefit analysis in *Payne* favored the economic results of increased traffic through the area, over the less visible effects of preventing environmental degradation, this does not appear to be an acceptable reason for the decision reached, especially in the light of Article 27, Section 5:1. Mark Sagoff says:

> Environmental economics fails as a normative science because it cannot tell us why or in what sense an efficient allocation is better than a less efficient one. Lacking all normative content, terms like "utility," "well-being," or "welfare" fail to move environmental economics from the "is" of WTP (willingness-to-pay) to the "ought" of value or valuation (Sagoff, 2000:455).

c. Preserve or Conserve?

This apparent misunderstanding and misuse of Article 27, Section 1 shows that by altering its language from the obligation to "preserve and maintain" public trust resources, to "conserve and maintain" (although "preservation" was retained in the first sentence of the Article), the courts were, at best, prepared to support "sustainable development" (Dernbach, 1999:704; 717; compare Dernbach, 1998:1). But, as I have argued with significant scientific support, "sustainable development" is an oxymoron, as it falls far from the ideal of sustainability, given today's environmental conditions (Pimentel, Westra, and Noss, 2000). In essence, preservation in areas large enough to ensure the presence of natural services, is vital to guarantee conservation for present peoples and future generations, and only the use of the Precautionary Principle coupled with strong normative principles, might support the letter and the intent of Article 27, Section 1, cost-benefit analysis.

In conclusion, despite its high-sounding language, the Article does not appear to have been used successfully by the citizens of Pennsylvania to protect the very rights the Article was introduced to ensure. The Article's history of failures as a defender of the common good, include a list of hazardous activities. Speaking of Pennsylvania's citizens, Dernbach states:

> They have not been able to use the [Payne] test, for example to prevent a stream relocation project to remedy existing hazardous conditions, to prevent the construction of pumping stations and other facilities to direct water from a stream to supply water for cooling a nuclear generating station, or to overturn permits approved by the State Department of Environmental Resources (Dernbach, 1999:723).

In a state "dominated by iron, steel, coal and railroad interests" (Dernbach, 1999:727), even a strongly worded Constitutional Amendment has been insufficient to protect the public from harms and environmental degradation.

Given the present institutional setting of most states, but also of Canada's provinces, I have no reason to believe that even the introduction of a "Right to a Healthy Environment," in the Canadian Charter of Rights, would do any better for the protection of life. Dernbach recognizes that the value of life protection is implicit in "natural values" and he cites, as we have done, Gretchen Daily's work on nature's services (Daily, 1997:369; Westra, 1998). He also acknowledges that these natural services are, for the most part, irreplaceable (Dernbach, 1999:143). It is disheartening that neither the Canadian nor the U.S. governments, and not even the government of the Commonwealth of Pennsylvania, are capable or willing to incorporate this factual and scientific reality in their regulatory infrastructure.

The ultimate impotence of Article 27.1, is supported by the analysis of how and why constitutional amendments come into being (Ruhl, 1999:245). After discussing the history and substance of most U.S. Constitutional Amendments, Ruhl affirms that an environmental quality amendment (EQA) "does not belong in the constitution." He says:

> The problem for the champions of biodiversity is that, without exception, every EQA proposal made in the past and being put on the table today is an absolute failure in the sense of approaching what makes a sound amendment to the constitution. Indeed, no commentator or legislator who has proposed an EQA would be constitutionally sound, as opposed to being good for the environment (Ruhl, 1999:250).

It is surprising, to say the least, that in 1999 an informed scholar can oppose "constitutionally sound" and "good for the environment." The reason for this opposition, according to Ruhl, is that, of the four goods and categories under which he places constitutional amendments, there seems to be no precedent for an EQA. He groups these goods as follows: "(1) altering the operational rules of the government; (2) prohibiting specified government action; (3) creating or affirming rights; or (4) expressing inspirational goals" (Ruhl, 1999:253). Note that the hypothesis being advanced here is not, that such amendments cannot work in practice (and I would regretfully concur with this conclusion, at least in a limited sense), but that in principle any such amendment is constitutionally unfit.

I believe that this thesis can be refuted using Ruhl's own categories. For instance (1): the present operational rules of the U.S. government strongly support corporate interests over public health and other noneconomic and nonpolitical public rights. The presence of ombudsmen, of "congressional fellows" taken from industry to work within the government, and the currently accepted media slant on most corporate activities, are all in need of a thorough overhaul (Korten, 1995).

The second category (2) might house an amendment that would place common good limits to some of the supporting, enabling functions the government uses in order to pursue its business first activities. These functions range from protectionism, to trade secrets regulations, to many legislative regimes whose only goal is to foster the economic growth of business and to protect its operations. Examples of the latter are instruments regulating toxic substances (Cranor, 1993) and the national and international transport of hazardous waste (Soskolne, 2001). In general, when economics take precedence over other values, including moral values and the common good, just solutions cannot follow (Borman and Kellert, 1991; Sagoff, 1988; Sagoff, 2001).

As was noted in Chapter 4, that approach was clearly the underlying cause of the Ontario (Walkerton) tragedy (see Chapter 4). Turning to the issue of (3), an opposition between the citizens' right to life and an EQA can only be imagined. For instance, the Canadian Charter of Rights, ensures the security right of all citizens. And security may be understood as a right in the environmental sense (Shue, 1996; Brunnée and Toope, 1997). Richard Ullman, for instance, defined a "threat to security" as follows:

> [any action] or sequence of events that (1) threatens drastically and over a relatively brief span of time to degrade the quality of life for the inhabitants of a state, or (2) threatens significantly to narrow policy choices available to the governments of a state or to private, nongovernmental entities (persons, groups, corporations) within the state (Ullman, 1983:133; Brunnée and Toope, 1997:96).

In addition, most should by now be aware of the evidence linking environmental degradation, including the loss of wildness, to a variety of human diseases and to grave functional impairments including reproductive impairments and even DNA mutations (Colborn et al., 1996; McMichael, 1995; Westra, 2000; Soskolne and Bertollini, 1999; see also Chapter 2 for details). In that case, Ruhl's focus on the good of the environment being in opposition to the Constitution, is simply wrong: surely the Constitution of the United States, like all democratic constitutions, must start with the right to life and to the freedom from physical harm for all citizens.

From this perspective the easiest category to defend is (4): "aspirational goals." The defense and preservation of our home, the Earth, a vitally needed habitat for all humankind, should need no defense as a goal superseding almost all others. In essence, the short-term, immediate goal of fostering a strong economy, tends to be the goal few seem to question. Yet all economic activity needs, minimally, resources, energy, and well-people to man the activity and utilize the products.

Unfortunately, all regulatory regimes that do not manifest an understanding of this basic fact, if they ignore or neglect ecological reality for more palatable present human preferences, are doomed to a short-lived success at best (Rees and Wackernagel, 1996; Rees, 2000; Goerner, 1994). Therefore, it is sad that Ruhl is probably correct when he concludes that "An EQA is unlikely to find its way into the Constitution in the foreseeable future" (Ruhl, 1999:281).

But if, as Ruhl has argued, there is little hope, for both social and legal reasons, that an EQA might appear in other state constitutions, or in the U.S. Constitution itself; and further, if it appears that even the presence of such an amendment does not make a significant difference in environmental decision making when it is present, then we may need to transcend national regulations and laws to achieve fair and just results. Perhaps agreements between nations may better serve the cause of human safety and security.

3. STATE COOPERATION AND TREATIES: A BETTER ROAD TO ENVIRONMENTAL PROTECTION?

> Piracy being excluded, the Court has to look for some new and peculiar ground: but in the first place a new and very extensive ground is offered to it by the suggestion, which has been strongly pressed, that this trade, if not the crime of piracy, is nevertheless crime, and that every nation and indeed every in individual has not only a right, but a duty to prevent in every place the commission of crime. It is a sphere of duty sufficiently large that is thus opened out to communities and their members. But to establish the consequence required it is first necessary to establish that the right to interpose by force to prevent the commission of crime commences, not upon the commencement of the overt act, not upon the evident approach towards it, but on the bare surmise grounded on the mere possibility. (Le Louis, 2 Dodson Rep. 238, Judgment—Sir William Scott, at 248).

Sir William Scott is addressing the issue of slave trading, in terms that tend to place the action in the realm of emergent, if not present, *jus cogens* norms (Ragazzi, 1997:215). He ends his judgment by admitting that, as it is not as yet, the established practice of all states, and even less, international law to view the slave trade as a crime, it cannot be so considered, despite the fact that most would agree with his moral position against slavery and the slave trade.

But the point made in this passage is precisely the main point of this work: we need to appreciate the activity to be proscribed first and foremost in its true nature (in our case, viewing environmental degradation as a crime), before we can even start to place it in the appropriate legal context.

The second important point emerging from *Le Louis*, is the need for a clear international norm, one that has accepted the corresponding *erga omnes* implications. *Le Louis* shows without a doubt the problems that arise when a universal moral norm conflicts with a treaty or state practice, or is not at a certain time, fully operative in either context. The strong beliefs of most people, their revulsion in the face of an activity (such as the slave trade) that ought to be proscribed everywhere, is insufficient, unless either a treaty exists with signatories from all countries globally, or the delict is raised to the status of crime, or the activity is viewed as impermissible in customary law (see Chapter 7).

It seems that the possibility of cooperative regimes ought to be considered first, in order to ascertain whether state cooperation might be easier to achieve than it would be to accept the onerous task of proving conclusively and convincingly the criminal status of an immoral activity, like violence in any form, including environmental violence.

Yet, aside from the status of the activities that result in environmental harms, there is another aspect of the problem that militates against the possibility of relying on all states to ratify a treaty that is ecologically sound, but not necessarily conducive to the short-term economic interests of some states. This other aspect is the way a specific environment is viewed.

The problems we noted so far, however, may persist because the rules for international responsibility of states themselves may well prove an obstacle to the achievement of environmental protection: "like the national norms on delictual responsibility, the law of state responsibility, struggles with both the limitations of the legal systems it is to enforce and the shortcomings inherent in its purpose" (Brunnée, 1993:832). The next question that arises then, is what can the role of the state be in the environmental context, and whether transcending the state and domestic law would truly provide a significant difference in results. We saw that, even at best, domestic law, when it establishes the presence of a quasi-crime, and if responsibility has been ascribed to an individual or a corporate agent, the result is limited to fines and monetary compensation to those affected (see Chapter 4).

But, even aside from moral principles that are explicitly constitutive of international law (in contrast with municipal law), state responsibility in the international context demands more than fines. First, what is the meaning of "state responsibility"?

> "State responsibility" simply put is the name public international law gives to the normative state of affairs which occurs following a breach by a state of one of its international legal obligations (whether that obligation derives from treaty law, customary law or other recognized sources such as 'general principles' of law) (Scott, 2001:47).

This description sounds essentially similar to a breach of domestic regulatory obligations in some ways. For both domestic and international law, for the most part, damage must be demonstrated before it can be decided that a violation has occurred. But further obligations, beyond compensation, are present when we move from domestic to international law:

> The breach of a (primary) rule of international law triggers certain secondary obligations. These are commonly considered to include duties to: 1) discontinue the act; 2) apply national legal remedies; 3) re-establish the situation existing before the act in question or to the extent that this impossible, pay corresponding compensation; 4) provide guarantees against repetition (Brunnée, 1993:833).

In essence then, there are three further obligations beyond No. (2), "apply national legal remedies," that accrue to the state, when viewed from an international, transboundary perspective.

a. International Law-Making and the Rise of International Environmental Law

Since the Stockholm Conference of 1972, there has been an increasing proliferation of multinational treaties dealing with the environment. They deal with issues ranging from long-range transboundary pollution, and the protection of the ozone layer, to the control of the transboundary movement of hazardous waste, the conservation of wild fauna and flora and national habitats (Birnie and Boyle, 2002:3–9). The importance of these conventions cannot be overstated. They represent one of the major sources of international environmental law, although as such, limited as they are by customary law and often negotiated by interests inimical to environmental protection, they are insufficient to their task of environmental protection.

Birnie and Boyle cite the Preamble to the Convention on Biological Diversity (1992) (Birnie and Boyle, 2002:5–6), to emphasize on of the major problems with those instruments: the lack of biocentric perspective:

> *Conscious* of the intrinsic value of biological diversity and of the ecological, social, economic, scientific, educational, cultural, recreational and aesthetic value of biological diversity and its components,

> *Conscious also* of the importance of biological diversity for evolution and for maintaining life-sustaining systems of the biosphere,

Although these passages reflect both the presence of the intrinsic value (Callicott, 1989:63–74, 129–156; Westra, 1994), and are both holistic and biocentric in tone (Westra, 1998; Sterba, 1998), it took a long time beyond 1982 to see the emergence of legal instruments, approaches and principles that are not entirely anthropocentric instead (Birnie and Boyle, 2002:6).

For this reason, international environmental law, even as it formulated and applied today, is often unable or unwilling to protect the environment, thus to fulfill its required role. The goal of international environmental protection includes at least four objectives (Birnie and Boyle, 2002:7):

(1) It "provides mechanisms and procedures for negotiating necessary rules and standards" as it "constitutes the process of international environmental governance";

(2) It is intended to prevent and mitigate harm. This is the primary role of treaties, but increasingly, institutions considers "soft law" guidelines and the recommendations of important NGOs such as the IUCN (Birnie and Boyle, 2002:25–26);

(3) It assesses compensation for environmental damage, although it is weakened by the fact that many sources of both damage and harm are presently legal (see Chapter 7), and that the most serious forms of environmental damage are incompensable, as not all ecosystem functions can be reinstated within one or two lifespans, once destroyed;

(4) It may be used to establish the presence of environmental rights and to establish the parameters of environmental crimes, as we argue in this work (see also Birnie and Boyle, 2002:ch.5).

The final point is of great importance for the argument of this work: the increasing emphasis on human rights (see for instance the African Convention on the Conservation of Nature and Natural Resources (1968)) tends to advance the argument for categorizing breaches of these regulations as giving rise to obligations *erga omnes* (Peel, 2001:85–87).

Aside from the vital considerations of monitoring, control and compliance, the thrust is toward humanity's and—I would add—all life's legitimate interest in the protection of the Earth's habitats. The presence of these international instruments means that, ". . . the management by a state of its own environment," is no longer purely an internal matter (Birnie and Boyle, 2002:ch.5). In order to speak of "global climate change," or the protection of "tropical forests," the concept of "common concern" had to be introduced into international dialogue (see Section 4.b).

This argument supports and in some sense duplicates the argument advanced earlier after the lengthy paragraph from *Le Louis*. The starting point appears to be the emergence of a concept, an understanding, even a definition, as all of these then permit the development and eventually the application of certain regulations as appropriate to the nature of a specific delict or crime, based on the understanding. It might be a "chicken or egg" question to ask whether it is the perception and the conceptual understanding that is primary, or the regime formation within which the problem is confronted, analyzed, discussed, categorized, and eventually placed within certain parameters.

Some of the advantages of regime formation, giving rise to binational or international meetings, conferences and conventions, and treaties, must be acknowledged. Thomas Gehring speaks of international conferences and the development of regimes:

> Frequently these conferences develop into permanent for a for the negotiation and adoptions of new instruments of international law, or as the case may for major revisions of existing ones. Due to their political character, conferences of parties are often held at a high political level—occasionally even at the ministerial level.

> Regulations developed in these fora, and governing a defined area of international environmental relations, shall be labelled international environmental regimes (Gehring, 1990:35).

It is clear that with the presence of diverse individuals, many of whom are possessed of roughly similar intellectual powers, ability, and education, but who come from different backgrounds and represent divergent beliefs and interests, that there will be a tremendous potential for knowledge sharing and exchange. These fora may eventually be able to establish a knowledge base for future decisions. Yet the reason for the creation of regimes carries an inherent problematic, as List and Rittberger view it: "regimes are created for *specific issue areas*, which are in turn part of a larger, *theoretically determined policy area*" (List and Rittberger, 1992:89). The quest for a common knowledge base would be particularly important to establish a starting point for future law-making, given the uncertainties and complexities of today's science, on which much of eventual regulatory norms must depend (Goerner, 1997). Gehring adds: "The cognitive and normative aspects of the process are mutually reinforcing: changing knowledge demands an adoption of normative prescriptions, whereas agreed upon norms induce the generation of technical knowledge" (Gehring, 1990:35). It would be naive to believe that credible knowledge alone would be sufficient to generate agreement among states, and prompt them to implement necessary measures. The undeniable political dimensions of the eventual international law instruments that emerge from these regimes show that agreement, if not real consensus, is reached with great difficulty and, unfortunately, through many compromises, in order to retain a critical mass of states sufficient to ratify and perhaps become signatories to the treaty in question.

These political dimensions are not entirely benign, however. Some of the powerful states may exert pressure on the others, in order to achieve less stringent regulations, or weaker criteria for their own benefit, at the detriment of the environment. In contrast, some regime may work "to close gaps" left by previously negotiated treaties (Gehring, 1990:43–44). Further, the political difficulties that arise in multilateral regimes, hence in treaty formation, are also present in the "normative expectations" (Gehring, 1990:41), that are intended to shape the emerging treaty or convention. These difficulties, at least in principle, ought to be minimal, when we consider a binational regime that gives rise to binding obligations to only two countries, who share similar aspirations and outlooks: Canada and the United States.

b. A Freshwater Binational Regime: The Great Lakes Water Quality Agreement and the International Joint Commission

Canada and the United States have a responsibility, not just to one another as subjects of international law, but to Canadians, Americans and other members of the human race to protect the environment and to reduce to a minimum adverse effects of the utilization of a common indivisible resource (Williams, 1986:201)

When we turn to a binational agreement from a universal (political) principle such as the Common Heritage of Mankind (CHM), we start with two apparent advantages: (1) as a binational agreement following upon the Boundary Water Treaty (1909), this regime may boast solid roots in international law; and (2) the agreement is based on the ecosystem approach, which "requires consideration of the whole system, rather than individual components," and a management that "respects the need for maintaining ecosystem integrity" (Brunnée and Toope, 1994:55). The second point is reinforced by the Great Lakes Water Quality Agreement (GLWQA) (Nov. 22, 1978, TIAS No.11, 551; Nov. 18, 1987, Can TS No. 32).

Article II of the 1987 Protocol (Nov. 18, 1987) says in part:

The purpose of the Parties is to restore and maintain the chemical, physical and biological integrity of the Great Lakes Water Basin Ecosystem.

In addition, Article II(a) defines the Great Lakes Water Basin ecosystem as "the interacting components of air, land, water and living organisms, including humans within the drainage basin." This detailed definition is particularly significant because (a) it clearly introduces biocentrism in a binational regulation, hence in international law; and (b) it reinforces the holistic perspective of the document by using the language of integrity, arising from the work of Aldo Leopold (Leopold, 1949; Westra, 1994).

This emphasis presents an important development in international environmental law, important because it emphasizes what Jutta Brunnée terms "environmental security." She says:

The broader conception of environmental security is crucial because, at least in the long term, security, even in the traditional sense, can be ensured only if the environmental sense is emphasized. Only when ecological balance is maintained, resources are protected, and supplies ensured, will the potential for conflict be significantly reduced (Brunnée, 1995:1742).

In addition, both biocentrism and environmental holism are necessary to the goal of supporting global ecological interests. It is only in the second half of the 20th century that these interests have gained prominence. Yet, public international law as it existed then and still exists today, is not particularly welcoming to these new developments and to the emerging environmental concern. Brunnée adds:

> The first challenge is rooted in the very foundations of public international law. As a legal order built upon the sovereignty of states, international law does not readily accommodate the development of rules and regimes premised upon ecological unity (Brunnée, 1995:1744).

Hence, at least as far as its principles are concerned, that is, the principles of the GLWQA Protocol are concerned, it would appear that the International Joint Commission (IJC) is in an ideal position to promote ecological goals. The next question that arises is whether the ostensible legal mandate of the IJC to support, maintain, and implement the explicit goals of the GLWQA, can be effected within the present regime. Toope and Brunnée argue: ". . . that régime formation should be conceived along a continuum from mere dialogue and information sharing, to the creation of more formal cooperative frameworks, to the hardening of substantive, sometimes binding norms" (Toope and Brunnée, 1998:273). The authors also counsel patience in waiting for the unfolding of this desirable sequence of events.

It is unfortunate that, at least in the case of the IJC and the GLWQA, there has been no "hardening" to any norms that may be termed substantive, let alone "binding." For instance, the initial thrust to "zero discharge" (Muldoon and Jackson, 1994:14), a goal consonant with that of restoring and protecting integrity, has simply petered out, at best, to a series of emission reductions that produce minimal results, and that do not take in consideration the precautionary approach. In contrast, the 1978 Amendment to the GLWQA at least implicitly, adopts the Precautionary Principle, by including "lists of toxic or potentially toxic substances" in that protocol (Toope and Brunnée, 1997:52).

The idea that eventually a convergence of goals in a regional context is not only desirable but possible, is supported by the goal of "transboundary ecosystem management" and the "six thematic amendments" it includes, which provide for:

> (1) specific reporting deadlines and clear roles for the governments involved, as well as the International Joint Commission; (2) three priority lists of toxic or potentially toxic substances; (3) commitment to biannual consultation to consider the need for new objectives; (4) geographic

"areas of concern" for which so-called Remedial Action Plans can then be developed; (5) "Lakewide Management Plans for Critical Pollutants"; and (6) increased public involvement (Toope and Brunnée, 1997:53).

Despite this ecologically sound mandate, the results are, for the most part, poor. Meetings glorify minimal industry emission reduction and tentative, highly limited and localized public involvement, and this is clear to anyone attending these meetings including this author. Anecdotal evidence, perhaps, but the results of years of biennial meetings which have not improved the quality (or quantity for that matter) of the Great Lakes bear witness to the results of years of lax policies (Barlow, 1999; Kay and Regier, 2000:121).

Yet the importance of the ecosystem approach is explained and supported by Lynton Caldwell:

A holistic approach means identifying and taking account of all factors of significant relevance to any situation. In a pluralistic political economy unaccustomed to holistic thinking, this comprehensiveness of outlook and analysis would be a salutory corrective to the tendencies of society to attack problems in a linear, or single-purpose basis (Caldwell, 1993:196).

The holistic thrust of the ecosystem approach has a background in complex systems theory and chaos theory, and it is a clear result of "ecological thinking" and of the emerging "ecological world hypothesis," as explained by Sally Goerner (Goerner, 1994:4). In essence, as Lovejoy has it, "There are no separable problems anymore" (as cited in Goerner, 1994:3). Any policy or political regime that contends otherwise, is not based upon the global reality in which we live. Goerner adds:

Basic ecologism creates a root metaphor for evolving ecological universe. The deep ecological vision creates a literal one, i.e. a physically based understanding of an evolving, order producing universe that consists of and is governed by ecological dynamics (Goerner, 1994:10).

But the contrasting, analytic, Newtonian beliefs, are not only inaccurate, in the sense that they do not provide us with an accurate picture of the real world, but "they are also dangerous" (Goerner, 1994:15). The danger lies in their belief in "technique" and "control," as they foster a "dominator" mentality (Eisler, 1988; Goerner, 1994:15) and as they provide "an excuse for an ethics of power" (Ibid.).

Nonlinear, non-Newtonian beliefs provide the basis for the ecological approach: however, not everyone understands and embraces such a novel concept. In fact, although the approach recommends practices that are radically different from "policies traditionally dominant in the United States" (Caldwell, 1993:195), at least these practices would be based on ecological realities, instead of shortsighted economic interests.

This is the reason for Toope and Brunnée's defense of the ecosystem approach for binational and even for international law: this approach emphasizes a necessary step for both sustainability and justice. It also becomes clear why, although the IJC's mandate includes the responsibility to "oversee the implementation of the agreements" and although "its decisions may possibly provide a model for ecological management," unfortunately, as Caldwell himself anticipated, "countervailing political considerations have intruded to truncate the effectiveness of the IJC itself" (Caldwell, 1993:195).

If the nonholistic, mechanistic perspective justifies an "ethic of power," as we saw, then clearly the economic and political ambitions of both states (Canada and the United States), will impede the desirable progression of "binding norms," as these would imply a corresponding loss of power and control: "Application of ecological concepts would find a major obstacle in the indiscriminate treatment of land as a commodity" (Caldwell, 1993:195). The same argument would apply, *mutatis mutandis*, to water. Complex systems theory and the ecosystem approach imply and demand "a new way of organizing human relations with the natural world": ". . . an ecological approach to land policy implies fundamental changes in the rights and responsibility of individuals, corporations and government agencies" (Ibid.).

But simply establishing the principles implicit in the ecosystem approach, as Toope and Brunnée show, is insufficient to ensure that the full potential of the IJC will come to full fruition, in the context of today's regimes. I am less optimistic than these authors in the future potential for such a radical change, because I do not believe any state today is willing to entertain the possibility of relinquishing control, or admitting that their present control and domination are unrealistic and ephemeral.

In many ways, the IJC would be ideally placed to effect sound ecological policies; Canada and the United States have a history of peaceful interaction and many shared beliefs and interests. In reality, their core assumptions about property rights and control, and also about what constitutes sound science, form a formidable barrier to the achievement of any long-term positive goal, based on ecological reality. We will need to search further afield to seek more positive answers.

4. THE NEED FOR AN INTERNATIONAL REGIME BASED ON THE ECOSYSTEM APPROACH AND THE PRINCIPLES OF INTERNATIONAL HUMANITARIAN LAW

Over the last decade environmental degradation and resource scarcity have come to be perceived as threats not only to human well-being and prosperity but also to international security (Brunnée, 1995:1742).

The argument of this work supports Brunnée's new understanding of security in the environmental sense. In fact I would like to propose a third dimension of security beyond the two she lists. Brunnée says:

> The term should be understood to have two dimensions. On the one hand, in placing emphasis upon the environmental dimensions, security means maintaining an ecological balance, at least to the extent necessary to sustain resource supplies and life-support systems. On the other hand, in emphasizing the dimensions of security in the traditional sense, the term refers to the prevention and management of conflicts precipitated by environmental decline (Brunnée, 1995:1742).

Not only these two senses are proposed, but the connection between the two aspects is recognized. In the Canadian Charter of Rights and Freedoms, we find a guarantee to all citizens of "the security of persons." That, properly understood, is the third sense of environmental security advocated and defended in this work. Chapter 2 documents the impacts of environmental degradation and disintegrity on human health. Chapter 4 presents the example of a Canadian public health disaster. Chapter 5 traces the assaultive aspects of the consequences of environmental harms. In addition, in Chapter 1, Shue's conception of basic rights (Shue, 1996), defines these and, in fact, lists security even before subsistence. Thus, it is not only a potential for conflict that is engendered by environmental degradation, but also an immediate or delayed harm to individuals and populations above and beyond a conflict situation.

The previous section discussed the holistic perspective required, and Chapter 4 argued for the necessity of global perspective, given the global reach of the health effects of any environmental hazards. The development of both ecological thinking and other related legal concepts is a symptom of a new and ongoing movement not only in normative theory, but also in law. Brunnée says:

> Environmental harm was legally relevant only when it coincided with a significant interference with the territorially based interests of another state. Therefore, much ecologically significant harm triggered no international rights or obligations (Brunnée, 1995:1745).

This change is one of pivotal importance in the interests of justice, but also in support of survival: hence, the relevance of international law in this respect cannot be overemphasized. International law should no longer be viewed as, "a 'fringe' specialty, well-meaning even noble, but naive and largely irrelevant to the real world" (Trimble, 1990:811; Shields and Gamble, 1989:40). This move represents more than the desirable inclusion of a specific sort of concern (environment or public health). It also brings into prominence the move from a fully accepted formalism, and a legal position where "the judicial [and other decision maker's] task, is said to be to discover and enforce, in particular cases, extant correct rules" (Chen, 1989:11).

Yet, according to Trimble, Chen's approach to ensure that international law advances the "basic values of human dignity or of a free society" (Ibid. at 19), tends to support "Western cultural imperialism" (Trimble, 1990:815), and—ultimately—the "property rights of multinational corporate interests" (Ibid. at 816). In contrast, many other values prevalent in African and Asian societies, are not present in this approach (Mazrui, 1986:11–21; Baxi, 1998:125). In fact, rather than assuming the existence of one, broadly construed world order, it is preferable and more realistic to view the present situation as one that places humanity at the crossroads, or what Richard Falk calls a "Grotian moment," calling for radical change:

> We have two or three decades, at the most, to bring a new system of world order into being. . . . We are living along the precipice of dire calamity. The danger is no longer alone a matter of fear for nuclear war, but the cumulative and interrelated dangers that stem from steeply rising curves of violence, population and pollution in a world of sinking space and dwindling resources (Falk, 1970:xiii).

Trimble criticizes Falk's work because he does not seem to understand the message it embodies. The state's role is indeed "fundamentally inconsistent" with the alleviation of the conditions that Falk describes and that this work has analyzed with the support not only of ecology, but of epidemiology, conservation biology, agriculture, fisheries, forestry, and ecological footprint analysis in general. We have argued that "acting locally" is most often far removed in both concept and effect from "thinking globally." Falk's argument, for example, for the use of international law to prevent the use of nuclear weapons as "functional equivalent" of chemical and biological weapons, is correct, although Trimble says instead that, "The use of international law for this argument is neither normative nor persuasive" (Trimble, 1990:821). Trimble contradicts his own position in the footnote to the above passage, as he argues that "signatory nations never intended that the earlier treaties on chemical and biological weapons be structured to cover *all* new forms of warfare and weaponry" (Ibid. at n.55). But Trimble himself had argued for the incompleteness of the "same old positivist rules" (Ibid. at n.820). Hence, it is not consistent to say that at a certain point in time, signatory states had not intended a certain result, when the failures of the positivist approach that would enshrine treaties and state practices exclusively, is the very point at issue.

According to Falk, we are in a "normative abyss": what is lacking is the presence of both principles and of contact with (ecological) reality. Neither can be found by appeals to the signatories of treaties designed to provide specific, limited obligations, not obligations *erga omnes*. Nuclear weapons and the relative U.N. Advisory Opinion of July 1996 will be discussed in Section 4.a, below. For now, although Falk pronounces himself somewhat "more positivist" than Weeramantry, nevertheless he cites Weeramantry at length, as moving "dramatically" away from positivism and manifesting instead "a strong set of naturalistic tendencies" (Falk, 1998:191), which is not diminished by Weeramantry's belief that these "natural," "humanistic," and "normative" aspects are already embedded in domestic and international law.

Weeramantry, therefore, supports the humanitarian, universal principles stated in Chapter 1. Like Weeramantry's, that argument is guided by universalism, a position that Falk hesitates to call by its name of natural law, understood in the original, Aristotelian sense, that is fundamental to any defense of basic human rights.

Although that is not his explicit argument, implicitly Falk's position not only supports the role of international law in the development of a new global order, but also the need for norms and universal principles based on natural law. This position is the only one that is consistent with seeking a new order, beyond formalism and positivism, both of which are insufficient to respond to the grave difficulties Falk outlines.

a. The Evolution of International Protection of Human Rights

In our search for an Ariadne's thread to lead us through the intricacies of international relatives we stumble upon a new concept creeping in and out of the intricacies of international reality: the "common heritage of mankind" (Cassese, 1989:376).

As we attempt to weave our way from domestic law and undisputed state sovereignty, to the goal of ensuring the primacy of international human rights beyond sovereignty with regard to humanity's habitat, we need to take stock, by repeating some of the earlier points made in this work, in the interest of a better understanding of the historical and political aspects of our quest.

When we consider the historical development of international law, we note that the powerful Western countries have tended, as much as possible to support the status quo in law, through the respect for the "freewill of states" and the prevalence of custom and of positive law. In contrast, the developing countries and those in Eastern Europe, albeit for separate motives, supported the formation of principles and rules beyond those based on the agreement and cooperation of states. Cassese's insightful analysis shows that, while in earlier years a "hobbesian or realist tradition" prevailed, which saw each country's position as essentially self-defensive in regard to other states, a later Groatian or internationalist conception of state interaction emerged, emphasizing "cooperation and regulated intercourse among sovereign States" (Cassese, 1989:31). Finally, the universalist, "Kantian outlook" emerged: "which sees at work in international politics a potential community of mankind, and lays stress on the element of 'transnational solidarity'" (Ibid.). The latter approach, together with a strong thrust toward the emergence of *jus cogens* norms and of obligations *erga omnes*, represent the preferred agents of change of developing countries, as they press "for quick, far-reaching and radical modifications" (Ibid. at 123).

In contrast, Eastern European countries, "prefer to proceed gingerly, believing as they do, that legal change should be brought about gradually, as much as possible through mutual agreement" (Ibid.).

Nevertheless, both Eastern European and developing countries joined in supporting Article 53 of the Vienna Convention on the Law of Treaties (1969). Cassese remarks:

> To developing countries, the proclamation of *jus cogens* represented a further means of fighting against colonial or former colonial countries—as was made clear in 1968 at the Vienna Conference by the representative of Sierra Leone, who pointed out that the upholding of *jus cogens*, provided a golden opportunity to condemn imperialism, slavery, forced labour and all the practices that violated the principle of equality of all human beings and of the sovereign equality of all states (Ibid. at 176).

For Eastern European states (such as Romania and Ukraine), *jus cogens* was viewed as "means of crystallizing once and for all, peaceful coexistence between East and West" (Ibid.).

Despite the support of both of these "blocks," Western countries were initially "on the defensive" before bowing to the inevitable will of the majority, and the need to espouse norms consistent with their own legal traditions (Ibid. at 177). It is instructive to consider that it is the weakest countries, those who felt most disempowered by Western alliances and treaties, who enthusiastically supported an approach that characterized the "new" law (although the "old" *Le Louis* case here cited demonstrates a similar position). E. Jimenez de Arechaga (Uruguay) termed these developments "a flagrant challenge to international conscience" (Ibid. at 178; Vienna Conference, Official Records, para. 48). I have argued that we are all disempowered in the face of mounting environmental threats to our health and survival, and the monolithic powers that support global trade and current economic policies instead of life. Perhaps that is why we see protesting groups joining forces from developing countries, but also from Western environmental and animal defense groups. At any rate, Cassese summarizes the "three principles that emerge and become codified" in the 1969 Vienna Convention:

> First, it introduces restrictions of the previously unfettered freedom of States;

> Second, there is a democratization of international legal relations;

> Third, the Convention enhances international values as opposed to national claims (Ibid. at 189).

Both *jus cogens* norms and obligations *erga omnes* will be discussed in Chapter 7. For now, let us turn to a controversial principle arising within the "new law" paradigm, one that did not quite live up to its true potential, at least so far: the Principle of the Common Heritage of Mankind. The concept appears *prima facie* to step forward, but this does not represent the whole picture. Birnie and Boyle say:

> An important factor contributing to the classification of living resources as common property is that they have generally been so plentiful that the cost of asserting and defending exclusive rights exceeds the advantages to be gained. A regime of open access in these circumstances has generally been to everyone's advantage. However, as Hardin has observed, the inherent logic of the commons, remorselessly generates tragedy, as the availability of a free resource leads to overexploitation and minimizes the interest of any individual state in conservation and restraint (Birnie and Boyle, 1992:118; see also Birnie and Boyle, 2002:97–100).

b. The Principle of the Common Heritage of Mankind

Law does not spring anew, old concepts evolve and new ones emerge to fit new fields of human enterprise. In this manner, the unique historical developments manifesting themselves in the emergence of a North-South cleavage have been responsible for the introduction of a new international legal concept, the Common Heritage of Mankind (CHM) Principle (Larschan and Brennan, 1983:305).

The new legal concept, CHM, can be defined as follows:

(1) the area under consideration cannot be subject to appropriation; (2) all countries must share in the management of the region; (3) there must be an active sharing of the benefits reaped from the exploitation of the area's resources; and (4) the area must be dedicated to exclusively peaceful purpose (Goedhuis, 1981:218–219).

This appears, at least *prima facie* to be a wonderful addition to the small arsenal of ecologically constructive concepts. Nevertheless the language employed in that definition shows clearly its incompleteness and deficiencies. If an area is ecologically sensitive and—in that sense—important enough to fit the CHM concept, then both managing it and exploiting it, may be contrary to the continued preservation of the area, a goal implicit in the CHM designation. All future generations comprising mankind would be deprived of any benefit whatever if the area were to be both managed and exploited.

That goal would be far better served if both present and future humankind were managed instead, so that their exploitive activities could be controlled and even excluded from the area to be designated as a common heritage: the area's existence and the natural services it may provide for all life both within and without its immediate confines, is what is primarily at stake (Daily, 1997; Westra et al., 2000:ch.1; see Chapter 2).

In essence, future generations or mankind can only benefit from nonexploitation which, in turn, is based on regulated restraint, or management of present human enterprise. Although the CHM principle is not yet established as either a treaty obligation or as an obligation *erga omnes*, and it remains a "political principle" at this time (Larschan and Brennan, 1983:306), it has emerged in international discourse because developing countries have been seeking a New International Economic Order (NIEO).

The developing nations, largely disempowered by free trade and the economically and politically powerful G-7, are attempting in this way to influence public policy opinion, at least in regard to areas "outside the traditional jurisdiction of states: the deep seabed, outer space and, to a lesser degree, the Antarctic" (Larschan and Brennan, 1983:310).

Our concern is with the national systems of Earth, so that only the deep seabed and Antarctica are relevant to the argument of this work. The first point worthy of note in this regard, is that this political principle is too accepting of the *status quo*, hence, it is not capable of protecting our common heritage as stated, because this natural patrimony of mankind does not only lie in areas that do not interest the Northwest affluent states. Oceans, old forests, lakes, rivers, and all other areas where biodiversity still abounds are surely part of the global commons and should be protected urgently, before their tragic loss may deprive all life of the support they provide (Noss, 1992; Westra, 1994; Ulanowicz, 1995; Daily, 1997).

Hence, the reference to the "benefits" of exploitation is clearly an oxymoron, unless one interprets benefit in a purely economic and short-term sense, that appears to be contrary to the letter and spirit of a principle aimed at benefiting mankind as a whole not only a rich and present minority.

Are we, for instance, to consider the global commons as *res nullius*, despite the tragic consequences that may follow the free and unrestricted appropriation of these areas by technologically advanced countries and other legal persons, bent on immediate economic exploitation? Or are we to consider it *res communis*, together with air and sunlight (*Black's Law Dictionary*, 1979:1173)? The 1974 separate opinion of Judge De Castro in regard to the *Fisheries Jurisdiction* (U.K. v. Iceland, 1973 I.C.J. Rep. 3), shows clearly the fallacy of this approach, as he states that "fish stocks in the sea are inexhaustible" (Ibid. at 97). But neither clean air nor safe sunlight (see Chapter 2) are presently available to most people on Earth, and fish stocks themselves are often sadly depleted or have crashed into extinction (Westra, 1998).

The argument of this work implies that the Common Heritage of Mankind Principle should be applied as *territorium extra commercium* as Bin Cheng proposes, except that instead of "management, exploitation and distribution," our concern should be with preservation, nonmanipulation, and respectful treatment, as these concepts, not the former, would ensure that mankind as such may enjoy the benefits of an unspoiled nature.

Here is Cheng's important passages discussing some of these concepts:

> While *territorium extra commercium* and *Territorium commune humanitatis* (for CHM) shared the same characteristics that they cannot be territorially appropriated by any State, they differ, in that the former is essentially a negative concept, whereas the latter is a positive one. In the former, in time of peace, as long as a State respects the exclusive quasi-territorial jurisdiction of other states over their own ships, aircraft and spacecraft, general international law allows it to use the area or even abuse it more or less as it wishes, including the appropriation of its natural resources, closing large ports of such ports of such space for weapon testing and military exercises and even using such areas as a cesspool for its municipal and industrial sewage. The emergent concept of the common heritage of mankind, on the other hand, while it still lacks precise definition, wishes basically to convey the idea that the management, exploitation and distribution of the natural resources of the area in question are matters to be decided by the international community (or simply the contracting parties, as in the Moon Treaty?) and are not to be left to the initiative and discretion of individual States and their nationals (Cheng, 1980:337).

Larschan and Brennan, in contrast, are primarily concerned with distributive issues: they argue convincingly that even defining certain areas as protected under the CHM Principle, in practice only appears to protect the "Group of 77," given that the "one nation-one vote procedure of the Assembly is cosmetic" (Larschan and Brennan, 1983:323). The Council empowered to make executive decisions is dominated by states "on the basis of investments, social system, consumption, production, special interests and equitable geographical distribution" (Ibid. at 322).

Our concern, instead, is with long-term preservation, not with the present distribution of the economic benefits of the global commons. The distributive approach, as Cheng points out, permits the use of the patrimony of mankind as a "cesspool," hardly appropriate to the Common Heritage of Mankind (Cheng, 1980:337). Even with its weaknesses, it would have been highly desirable to retain the use of the principle, beyond open space, the moon, and the deep seabed (Birnie and Boyle, 2002:97–100). The Antarctic Treaty System (1991), protects the area and the related ecosystems "in the interest of mankind as a whole" (1991 Protocol to the Antarctic Treaty on Environmental Protection, Preamble); and most obvious common heritage, the air we breathe, has not been so designated; rather the "global climate" has been referred to as a "common concern." In other environmentally related Preambles, the expression used is "world heritage of mankind" (Convention for the Protection of World Cultural and Natural Heritage, 1972) (Ibid.). In the next section the question of nuclear weapons will be discussed as an example of the development of international customary law in the protection of the environment, beyond the protection of immediate, economic harms to a specific state, as was the case, for instance, in the *Trail Smelter Arbitration* (see Chapter 7).

c.   Nuclear Weapons and the Opinion of the World Court

The International Court of Justice has issued an advisory opinion of great weight on the legality of nuclear weaponry. It is the first time ever that an: international tribunal has directly addressed this gravest universal threat to the future of humanity (Falk, 1998:147).

Before considering the International Court's opinion on the question of nuclear weapons, it is best to consider the context against which these weapons are developed, and the international pleadings of Australia and New Zealand as part of that context. Nuclear power, in all its applications represents one of the most hazardous products and process on Earth (Shrader-Frechette, 1982). As such, it is one of the clearest cases demanding immediate concern and legal action on several fronts: it is hazardous in the mining of its required materials, or throughout the "fuel cycle" (Shrader-Frechette, 1982:15; Draper, 1991); it is hazardous in all its uses, not only as a weapon (Shrader-Frechette, 1982:25–44); and it is especially hazardous in it disposal phase (Shrader-Frechette, 1993). Nuclear power is indeed "risky business" from cradle to grave (Draper, 1991), and the results of its impact exhibit all the characteristic harms this work confronts: immediate harm to human health, delayed threats to health, life, and normal function, and long-term harm to the "diversity of life" (Wilson, 1992) and to its very survival, through direct and indirect (genetic) impacts (Colborn et al., 1996). Finally it is extremely and unpredictably hazardous through its disposal (Shrader-Frechette, 1995; Shrader-Frechette, 1993; Goodwin, 1980:417–49).

It is not hard to find extensive and clear philosophical support not only for the immorality of the use of nuclear weapons, but also for threats intended as nuclear deterrence (Wasserstrom, 1985:15; McMahan, 1985:141; Ullman, 1985:191; Bok, 1985:339). In law one finds direct reference only to two aspects of nuclear power use: (1) testing; and (2) the threat and use of nuclear armaments. This is somewhat surprising: the occurrence of a terrible accident such as Chernobyl, as well as the routine production of low-level ionizing radiation through the normal, peacetime operation of nuclear power stations, has not been officially pursued in international law, to the best of my knowledge, although both have been discussed in the literature (Handl, 1988:203). For instance, despite the presence of an old, often malfunctioning power station like Fermi, right over the Canadian border in Windsor, although it is located between Michigan and Ohio, no legal cases have arisen from these hazardous circumstances.

On the other hand, Nevada has been battling federal orders to accept substantial quantities of radwaste, but—so far—the Yucca Mountain site has been successful in refusing to accept the facility, as officials agreed that they should and could not "impose something voters do not want," and because "leaving a potential catastrophe for the future is not an ethically defensible option" (Shrader-Frechette, 1993:250–251).

On the question of the legality of atmospheric nuclear testing, Australia and New Zealand instituted separate proceedings against France before the International Court" (Ragazzi, 1997:173). Atmospheric Nuclear Tests clearly spread unwarranted radioactive material indiscriminately to any and all countries adjacent to the tests. Even France, who wanted to test, did not attempt to conduct such tests over its own soil. France must have recognized that the atmospheric tests were neither desirable nor risk free, as they defended their strategy: France claimed it needed to perform these "last tests" in order to end atmospheric testing altogether. This declaration ensured that "the International Court did not pronounce either jurisdiction or the merits of the cases, relying on the obligation undertaken explicitly by the French government" (*Nuclear Test Cases*; *Australia v. France*, 1974 I.C.J. Rep. 253; *New Zealand v. France*, 1974 I.C.J. Rep. 457, at 467–70).

But the importance of the case does not lie with the majority view expressed above. Rather, the four judges who wrote a forceful dissent (Judges Onyeama, Dillard, Jiménez de Arechago, Sir Humphrey Waldock) asserted that the "object of the applicant States was to obtain a declaratory judgment" instead (1974 I.C.J. Rep. at 312 and 494; Ragazzi, 1997:175). The pleadings in these cases show that the intentions of the states were not simply to stop France on this single occasion, but to make a universal point of principle. France, according to these pleadings, had violated important rights: the protection of New Zealand's sovereign rights to be free of radionuclear fallout and contamination. This was described as a right that belonged to "all members of the international community" (Ragazzi, 1997:175).

Hence, especially for New Zealand, the obligation was *erga omnes*, and all states possessed correlative rights of protection. The fact that France (with China) had not been a signatory to the Treaty Banning Nuclear Weapons Tests in the Atmosphere, in Outer Space and Under Water (Moscow Treaty, 1963) was not relevant. Nevertheless, the additional fact that 104 states did become parties to the Moscow Treaty over the next ten years, enabled Australia and New Zealand to argue that, "customary rule had gradually emerged" in the International community, and New Zealand to assert, at the same time, the *erga omnes* character of France's obligation (Ragazzi, 1997:177). Ragazzi "infers" that the obligation is indeed *erga omnes*, from the following arguments found in the pleadings:

the obligation

(a) is stated in "absolute" terms (the dictum refers to "absolute" and "unqualified" obligations);

(b) reflects a "community interest" (the dictum refers to the "concern of all States");

(c) protects fundamental goods, namely "the security, life and health of all peoples" and the "global environment" (security, life and health are also some of the basic goods protected by the four examples of obligations *erga omnes* given in the dictum);

(d) has a prohibitory content (like the four examples given in the dictum);

(e) is not owed to particular States, but to the "international community" (the dictum refers to the 'international community as a whole'); and

(f) its correlative rights of protection 'are held in common' (the dictum provides that' all States can be held to have a legal interest' in the protection of obligations *erga omnes*) (Ragazzi, 1997:179)

The "dictum" here referred to is the one found in the *Barcelona Traction* case (see Chapter 7). This argument is of foundational importance, because it introduces the principled approach sought later by the WHO in opposing the use of nuclear weapons.

The WHO submitted a question requesting an advisory opinion on "the legality of the use by a state of Nuclear Weapons in an armed conflict," to the International Court of Justice, as follows: "In view of the health and environmental effects would the use of nuclear weapons by a state in war or other armed conflict be a breach of its obligations under international law including the WHO constitution?" (Adv.Op., 1996 I.C.J. .66)

Several states argued that the question went beyond "the WHO's proper activities." The Court added (at para. 10) that:

". . . three conditions must be satisfied in order to found the jurisdiction of the Court when a request for an advisory opinion is submitted to it by a specialized agency: the agency requesting the opinion must be duly authorized, under the Charter, to request opinions from the Court; the opinion requested must be one arising within the scope of the activities of the requesting agency (Kindred et al., 2000:363).

Despite the interest and the competence of the WHO to assess and evaluate the health effects of the use of nuclear weapons, at first the Court judged that the final condition had not been met, as the WHO was not a state able to wage a war, or enter into a conflict, and it did not use these weapons. Hence, the U.N. General Assembly had to bring the question to the Court once again. The Court held that neither "customary" nor "conventional" international law authorizes specifically the use of nuclear weapons (by 11 votes to three); and that the threat or use of nuclear weapons is also not specifically permitted, and that,

> . . . it follows from the above-mentioned requirements that the threat or use of nuclear weapons would generally be contrary to the rules of international law applicable in armed conflict, and in particular the principles and rules of humanitarian law; however, in view of the current state of international law, and of the elements of facts at its disposal, the Court cannot conclude definitively whether the threat or use of nuclear weapons would be lawful or unlawful in an extreme circumstance of self-defence, in which the very survival of a State would be at stake. . . . (the President casting his vote to break the 7 to 7 tie).

This opinion, despite its ambiguous tone, was viewed as an important decision, and it shows the transition from state treaties as sole arbiters of the status of nuclear armaments, to an opinion whose history and background served to bring a normative issue to the forefront of public opinion (Falk, 1998:172).

Falk traces the history of the movement that culminated in that request, from several groups in civil society, as ". . . the push to achieve elimination [of nuclear weapons] often merges with the view that weapons of mass destruction cannot be reconciled with international humanitarian law" (Ibid.).

Falk shows how world opinion as well as the work of many committed nongovernmental organizations prepared the groundwork for the very possibility of asking for an opinion, from the time of the London Nuclear Warfare Tribunal (1985), where those weapons were defined as "unconditionally illegal," hence, that even a threat of their use would amount to a "crime against humanity" (Falk, 1998:173).

The main point that emerges is that neither politics nor economic factors, nor even the advantage of groups of nuclear states, could be allowed to decide on the use of these weapon. Hence, at first the U.N. General Assembly and the WHO referred a difficult question to the World Court, and although the question could be evaded as "health," narrowly construed not the use of weapons, was the WHO concern; later, an opinion was given. Implicit in both the original request by the WHO and the eventual opinion is the fact that, "Nuclear Weaponry, with its global implications, raises question of legality that affect not just the citizenry of the nuclear weapons states, but the entire world" (Falk, 1998:174). This position supports, once again, the-*erga omnes* status of the question at least in principle, given the careful phrasing of the Court's statements. Falk does not use this language in regard to either the question or the Opinion itself, but he adds:

> Although not so formulated the radical element in this request was to transfer the question of nuclear weapons policy from the domain of geopolitics, where it had remained since the first attacks on Hiroshima and Nagasaki, to the domain of international law (Falk, 1998:175).

And if it has not transferred the question to treaty law, clearly both incomplete and insufficient to deal with this global threat, then Ragazzi's argument for placing its normative aspect among the few *jus cogens* norms generating an *erga omnes* obligation appears to be correct.

Another element appears to be present in all the legal approaches to the status of nuclear power, whether its tests or the weapons it provides is the implicit presence of the Precautionary Principle. In the next section the Principle's role will be discussed through an older case to which the Principle is indeed foundational.

5. THE *GABCIKOVO/NAGYMAROS CASE*: NORMATIVITY AND THE PRECAUTIONARY PRINCIPLE IN INTERNATIONAL LAW

> The protection of the environment is likewise a vital part of contemporary human rights doctrine, for it is a *sine qua non* for numerous human rights, such as the right to health, and the right to life itself. It is scarcely necessary to elaborate on this, as damage to the environment can impair and undermine all the human rights spoken of in the Universal Declaration of Human Rights and other human rights instruments (I.C.J. Separate Opinion of Vice-President Weeramantry:3).

These important words were written as a separate opinion to the well-known case. One's first impression is that a case that started with a treaty concluded in 1977 between Hungary and Czechoslovakia, intended to build twin dams in both countries "for the production of electricity, flood control and improvement of navigation on the River Danube" (Kindred et al., 2000:631), was based on many scientific assumptions that must be discarded today. In earlier times, it was common to consider exclusively or primarily the economic, and perhaps the social dimensions of a project. It took several decades for some understanding of the real impact of some of these "local," "economic" decisions to be fully appreciated; and even today it is often hard to ensure the incorporation of environmental considerations in all projects (Goerner, 1994; Caldwell, 1993).

The twin dams were extremely significant, in different ways, to their respective countries. By the late 1980s, Hungarian Prime Minister Miklos Nemeth, who was facing strong opposition to the project from his country's environmentalists, suspended all work on Nagymaros; while on the Czech side, despite some minor environmental protest, the dam was near completion by that time (Deets, 1998:1). Because bilateral talks could not reach a decision, the EU convinced the parties to bring the case to the I.C.J. Article 2 sets out the Court's responsibility:

Article 2

(1) The court is requested to decide on the basis of the Treaty and the rules and principles of general international law, as well as such other treaties as the Court may find applicable,

    (a) Whether the Republic of Hungary was entitled to suspend and subsequently abandon, in 1989, the works on the Nagymaros Project and on the part of the Gabcikovo Project for which the Treaty attributed responsibility to the Republic of Hungary;

    (b) whether the Czech and Slovak Federal Republic was entitled to proceed in November 1991, to the "provisional solution" and to put into operation from October 1992 this system, described in the Report of the Working Group of Independent Experts of the Commission of the European Communities, the Republic of Hungary and the Czech and Slovak Federal Republic dated 23 November 1992 (damming up of the Danube at river kilometer 1857.7 on Czechoslovak territory and resulting consequences on water and navigation course);

    (c) what are the legal effects of the notification, on 19 May 1992, of the termination of the Treaty by the Republic of Hungary.

(2) The Court is also requested to determine the legal consequences, including the rights and obligations for the Parties, arising from its Judgment on the question in paragraph 1 of this Article.

The most important point arising from this case, is the impact of an emergent ecological world view in the last two or three decades, giving rise to what Jacqueline Peel terms "an almost meteoric rise in profile within the body of international law" (Peel, 2001:82). During this period, multilateral treaties have proliferated, and one can find any number of conventions for the protection of nonhuman animals, from polar bears to whales, of biodiversity and of natural systems. Yet, although "soft law" in the protection of the environment, has entered everyone's consciousness from 1972 to 1992, for the most part, the global environmental situation has continued to deteriorate, as has the compliance of state and nonstate actors.

Another important point emerges as well: as long as states believe that international law is mainly a question of obeying *pacta sunt servanda*, and are correspondingly cagey about entering into bilateral or even multilateral agreements that may eventually inconvenience them, any truly international dimension of the protection of the global commons will be lost. Peel argues that "the crucial test for the new rules developed by the ILC will be their ability to promote better compliance by states" (Ibid).

In the next chapter, we will discuss both the 1996 International Law Commission (ILC) Draft Articles, and the new 2000 Draft Articles on State Responsibility, and the work of the Special Rapporteur Professor James Crawford (see Chapter 7). We will argue that the 1996 iteration of the ILC, Article 19(3)(d), for instance, came closest to expressing the main point of this work, considering what constituted "international crime," defined as follows: "a serious breach of an international obligation of essential importance for the safeguarding and preservation of the human environment such as those prohibiting massive pollution of the atmosphere or the seas." The question of "international crime" will be discussed below. For now, the main points are to consider the preservation of the human environment an issue of "essential importance," and a serious "breach of an international obligation," is in direct conflict with any legal instrument that limits responsibility to the fulfillment of agreement obligations. When the global commons are at issue, as noted in the previous section, and in Ragazzi's analysis of what constitutes an obligation *erga omnes* according to the dictum in the *Barcelona Traction* case, the obligation of state and nonstate actors cannot be exhausted by agreements that predate recent science by several decades, and that do not recognize the global implications of all environmentally hazardous activities.

This is precisely the case with *Gabcikovo/Nagymaros*. It may well be true that the Hungarians came to view the construction of the twin dams as an undesirable legacy of the Russian regime that oppressed them, while the Slovaks viewed the project as an "important achievement of the Slovak nation in the modern world" (Deets, 1998:17). But, whether or not either of the two states fully understood this or not, the main issue—as Weeramantry justly points out—is one of sustainability:

> When a major scheme such as the one under consideration in the present case, is planned and implemented, there is always the need to weigh considerations of development against environmental considerations, as their underlying justice bases—the right to environmental protection and the right to development—are important principles of current international law (Weeramantry, 1997).

The fact that the right to both environmental protection and to development have a strong presence in international law (for instance, in Article 1 of the Declaration of the Right to Development (1986), makes the latter an inalienable human right), does not help to solve the problems arising from conflicts between the two rights, despite the Stockholm Declaration (Principle II), which considers both "essential."

The proliferation of multilateral environmental treaties (Weeramantry, 1997), is undeniable, and the "concept of sustainable development is . . . a principle accepted not merely by the developing countries, but one which rests on the basis of worldwide acceptance" (Ibid). This becomes a major consideration, when one remembers that the science that helped to draft some of these conventions, and that supports them and gives them their rationale is—for the most part—science that was not recognized as such 20 to 30 years ago. This fact is foundational for two major points: on one hand, the scientific information that eventually changed the picture, was not available to either Hungary or to Slovakia, when the treaty was signed originally. On the other hand, if one acknowledges this fact, any treaty signed at a time prior to the availability of full scientific information about the circumstances of the case, ought to be null and void.

A similar argument is routinely made for contracts in domestic law from the standpoint of business ethics (Velasquez, 1998). Anyone who signs a contract to purchase a property, is expected to know, and to be made aware of the circumstances and conditions under which she signed the contract. If she was not informed about all the circumstances regarding the transaction, then her signature on the contract was not given under conditions of free and informed choice. In order for such choice to be both "free" and "informed," contracts must be undertaken without either coercion or ignorance.

If the environmental reality of the Danube ecosystem and the possible consequences of disrupting that system were not available at the time the treaty was signed, then, like any other contract where information was not fully disclosed at the time the contract was executed, the treaty itself ought not to be binding on either party. It seems clear that no one was attempting to commit a fraud, by deliberately withholding information. Nevertheless the fact remains: Hungary signed in good faith as did Slovakia, although neither party was fully aware of the implications of what they were signing.

The later fact that one country, Slovakia, did not deem the emerging ecological information important enough to supersede its need for cheap electric power, or its need for a national project that might enhance its status in the international community, ought not to render their misguided reasons for abiding by the Treaty, binding on Hungary as well. Speaking of commercial agreements, Manuel Velasquez says: "An agreement cannot bind unless both parties to the agreement know what they are doing and freely choose to do it" (Velasquez, 1998:330). In addition, one of the four conditions that have traditionally been considered as significant for the understanding of contractual rights and duties, is the fourth one, "4. The Contract must not bind the parties to an immoral act" (Velasquez, 1998: 330). Arguably, disrupting and, to some extent, destroying a vitally important ecosystem like that of the Danube delta, is morally wrong, because of the present and future consequences. Whatever the consequences may turn out to be, they will affect not only the present inhabitants of the area, including all the species in that natural system, but also future generations to whom obligations are due (Brown-Weiss, 1990).

Finally, the importance of disclosure and consent is also emphasized in bio-medical ethics, where the assumption is that whatever the procedure for which consent is sought, it is specifically intended to benefit the person who is asked to consent, a presumption that is lacking from environmentally significant disrup-tions, if the benefit is intended to be a biological one. The separate opinion of Judge Spotswood W. Robinson III in *Canterbury v. Spence*, is a clear example of the significance of consent in this context:

> The root premise is the concept fundamental in American Jurisprudence, that "[e]very human being of adult years and sound mind, has a right to determine what shall be done with his own body. . ." True consent to what happens to one's self is *the informed exercise of a choice that entails an opportunity to evaluate the options available* and the risk attendant upon each (emphasis added, 464 F.2d.772 D.C. Cir. 1972).

In international law, both the Nuremberg Code of Ethics in Medical Research (1948) and the Declaration of Helsinki (rev. October 2000, Edimburgh), address the issue of consent, although in a different context, that of medical experimen-tation, but still for the subjects' own good: for both voluntary, fully informed con-sent is central to the legality and to the moral acceptability of an activity. Despite the vast difference in context, the basic lesson is clear: whether we are dealing with an economically valuable business transaction, or a medically beneficial pro-cedure, neither one can and should take place without full, informed consent, although in international law the stability of treaties is strongly emphasized.

In the case under discussion, neither country appeared to be fully informed of the scientific and moral implications of their actions, as these implications and consequences became clearer, and even gave rise to several legal instruments in later years. (As a parallel example, if a patient were to be informed of certain risks, yet be willing to consent to a procedure at the first time, but if he should subsequently become aware of emerging scientific knowledge later, adding to the risk factors to which he had consented, surely the first, consent could be revoked on these moral grounds.)

When one adds the presence of the Precautionary Principle, once again cod-ified as soft law in Agenda 21(XV), in 1992, the combination of these factors supports to some extent the final decision of the I.C.J.

> B. Finds, by thirteen votes to two, that Hungary and Slovakia must nego-tiate in good faith in-the light of the prevailing situations, and must take

all necessary measures to ensure the achievement of the objectives of the treaty of 16 September, 1977, in accordance with such modalities as they may agree upon (Case Concerning the *Gabcikovo-Nagymaros Project*, Hungary/Slovakia, I.C.J. 25 Sept.1977, G.L. 90.92;49).

But the same changed circumstances which mandate and support the new negotiations, would also support adding some clear limits to any good faith negotiation that remains purely bilateral, when the common good is at stake in the ecological sustainability of the region. Recognition of this basic factor ought to move the negotiations in a different direction, one that would include impartial scientific observers, perhaps provided by WHO and UNEP, in order to safeguard the global interests of the international community. This approach would entail that the obligations of state and nonstate actors would be identified as *erga omnes*, rather than remain simply bilateral commitments. In essence, because of the introduction of the Precautionary Principle into international law discourse, and because of its increasing presence at least after 1992, the argument about the possible (even probable) negative consequences of damming the Danube, ought to prevails on those grounds alone, even without appealing to the concept of informed consent. Hence, although Weeramnatry's is only a separate, dissenting opinion, its importance as contribution to international law and as a statement or moral principle cannot be overstated.

6. CONCLUSION: ENVIRONMENTAL RIGHTS AS BASIC HUMAN RIGHTS

The ingrained values of any civilization are the sources from which its legal concepts derive, and the ultimate yardstick and touchstone of their validity. This is so in international and domestic legal systems alike, save that international law would require a worldwide recognition of those values. It would not be wrong to state that the love of nature, the desire for its preservation, the need for human activity to respect the requisites for its maintenance and continuance are among those pristine and universal values which command international recognition (Weeramantry, 1997:14).

Although, as we noted, Falk does not recognize the obvious connection, Thomas Aquinas' principle of natural law clearly (1) places its basic locus universally in human reason; and (2) recognizes that lawmakers must *apply* (not simply repeat) these basic universal principles to their own evolving and changing societies, provided that the basic, inalterable message in not lost in the application. This is simply another way of appealing to "pristine and universal values," or to the "ingrained values of civilization," and Weeramantry does a masterful job of tracing these universal environmental values to all civilizations, thus neutralizing the oft-repeated critique of natural law as limited to a specific religion, or even as an element of Western imperialism (see Chapter 1).

Thus, the utter universality of the quest for sustainability predates colonialism, North/South conflicts, and the rise of positivism in international law. Weeramantry adds: "If the Treaty was to operate for decades into the future, it could not operate on the basis of environmental norms as though they were frozen in time when the Treaty was entered into" (Weeramantry, 1997:17).

The related question of state responsibility will be discussed in the next chapter. But the reliance on universal principles appears to be preferable to a positivistic "counting of (States') heads." Fernando Tesón argues that "excessive reliance on democracy" is a flaw; he adds: "Unrepresentative governments are unacceptable in International Law; the tyranny of the majority is also unacceptable, even when it appears disguised under the cloak of "substantive deliberative process"" (Tesón, 1998:130).

The same argument, *mutatis mutandis*, can be made about multilateral agreements: even when these are procedurally correct, and accepted by all the involved international "citizens," unless universal normativity is introduced to judge these decisions, moral correctness, justice and fairness cannot be guaranteed: "The positivist argument for making governmental behavior the touchstone for the validity of democracy is ultimately contingent and irrational, like most arguments from authority" (Tesón, 1998:128). Tesón relies on deontology, a well-accepted antidote to utilitarian/majoritarian answers to human rights problems, to provide the needed corrective. His approach therefore supports universalism and human rights, although his basis is Kantian, rather than naturalistic, like Weeramantry's. Still speaking of *Gabcikovo/Nagymaros*, Weeramantry says:

> Environmental rights are human rights. Treaties that affect human rights cannot be applied in such a manner to constitute a denial of human rights, as understood at the time of their application. A Court cannot endorse activities which area violation of human rights by the standards of their time, merely because they are taken under a Treaty which dates back to a period when such action was not a violation of human rights (Weeramantry, 1998:17).

Today we can cite yet another confirmation of the insights of those who understand the global reach of an informed ecological world view. On the 100th anniversary of the Nobel Prize, 100 Nobel laureates became signatories to a groundbreaking statement:

THE STATEMENT

> The most profound danger to world peace in the coming years will stem not from the irrational acts of states and individuals but from the legitimate demands of the worlds disposed. Of these poor and disenfranchised, the majority live a marginal existence in equatorial climates. Global warming, not of their making, but originating with the wealthy few, will affect their fragile ecologies most. Their situation will be desperate and manifestly unjust.

It cannot be expected, therefore, that in all cases they will be content to await the beneficence of the rich.

If then we permit the devastating power of modern weaponry to spread through this combustible human landscape, we invite a conflagration that can engulf both rich and poor. The only hope for the future lies in co-operative international action, legitimized by democracy.

It is time to turn our backs on the unilateral search for security, in which we seek to shelter behind walls. Instead, we must persist in the quest for united action to counter both global warming and a weaponized world.

These twin goals will constitute vital components of stability as we move toward the wider degree of social justice that alone gives hope of peace.

Some of the needed legal instruments are already at hand, such as the Anti-Ballistic Missile Treaty, the Convention on Climate Change, the

Strategic Arms Reduction Treaties and the Comprehensive Test Ban Treaty. As concerned citizens, we urge all governments to commit to these goals that constitute steps on the way to replacement of war by law.

To survive in the world we have transformed, we must learn to think in a new way. As never before, the future of each depends on the good of all. (Our Best Point the Way, *Globe and Mail*, Dec. 7, 2001, A19).

In the next chapter we will explore possible ways of following this mandate through *jus cogens* norms in international law.

For now we will discuss a document that, like the Statement of the Nobel Prize Scientists, couples respect for the intrinsic value of natural systems and processes, with respect for human life and for peace, the Earth Charter. Recently that document has inspired the second draft (2000) of the International Covenant on Environment and Development (Commission on Environmental Law of IUCN—The World Conservation Union, in cooperation with the International Council of Environmental Law). Such a document, if able to incorporate the most significant aspects of the Earth Charter, would represent an important innovation and an important step towards more ecologically responsible legal regimes. (See Chapter 8, Part B, for a discussion of ecological rights; Taylor, 1998).

a. The Possible Role of the Earth Charter and the Draft Covenant on Environment and Development

II—Ecological Integrity

5. Protect and restore the integrity of the Earth's ecological systems, with special concern for biological diversity and the natural processes that sustain life (The Earth Charter, see Appendix I).

In 1972 the nations gathered at Stockholm agreed that environmental protection should be added to the core agenda of the United Nations, together with peace, human rights, and equitable social and economic development (Rockefeller, 2002:xi).This belief was emphasized and supported by many at the 1992 Earth Summit at Rio de Janeiro. In 1994, the Earth Charter Initiative worked to develop a document that would start by accepting the complete interdependence of humanity with the global natural systems, and that would involve all countries and nationalities from both the North and the South. As Rockefeller explains it,

> The product of a decade long, world-wide cross-cultural dialogue on shared values, the *Earth Charter* reflects an effort to build on and further develop the ethical visions in the *Stockholm Declaration* (1972), the *World Charter for Nature* (1982), the *Rio-Declaration* (1992), and a variety of non-governmental covenants and declarations (Rockefeller, 2002:xii).

The Earth Charter is an "ethical vision," but it is also a compendium and reworking of soft law. In addition, the International Draft Covenant of Environment and Development (2000 Revision), is presently under consideration and its wording is being reviewed by an IUCN-CEL Committee, to ensure that the main principles of the Earth Charter, are preserved within it. After the Committee's work is completed and the Covenant manifests as much as possible the spirit, if not the letter of the Earth Charter, in its articles, the IUCN will ensure that it is presented for ratification to all states, as it proposes to bridge "the sectors of environment and development" (Edith Brown-Weiss, Covenant, Foreword).

The Covenant is thus intended to regulate "relations between humankind and nature" (U.N. Secretary-General Report, at 18), and to create "an agreed single set of fundamental principles like a "code of conduct . . . which may guide states, intergovernmental organization and individuals" (Covenant, at 14). Turning now to specific provisions of the Covenant, both Objectives and Fundamental Principles repeat and support the main concerns of the Earth Charter, although the Covenant is much less detailed than the Charter, and less specific, thus manifesting, even in draft form, many of the same problems of vagueness and lack of prescriptive specificity of most international covenants, no matter what the topic.

This vagueness is not the result of chance: through negotiations most international agreements are negotiated "down" from their original intent, through blocs and alliances fostered by the most powerful countries and intended to ensure that business as usual will prevail in the interest of those countries, and that the regulatory regime under consideration does not cause too many impediments to affluent Western countries (Koskenniemi, 1992). Although it involved NGOs and citizens from countries all over the world, this has not been a problem for the Earth Charter; hence, the latter could speak with a strong voice indicting harmful practices and explicitly defending life and the intrinsic value of both natural systems and processes, as well as biodiversity.

Even in the Draft Covenant, there are at least two major omissions that would prove fatal to the real spirit of the Earth Charter in the document, if not corrected. The first is the important connection between human health and human rights. In the Earth Charter, Principle 2—*Care for the Community of Life with Understanding, Compassion and Love*, and 2(a), "Accepting that with the right to own, manage, and use natural resources comes the duty to prevent environmental harm and to protect the rights of people," the connection between environmental harm and human rights is rendered explicit. In addition, Principle 6(c), "Ensure that decision making addresses the cumulative, long-term, indirect, long distance and global consequences of human activities," ensures that the connection between environmental harms and human activities and practices is spelled out.

In contrast, the Covenant's Articles 4, 5, 6, and 7 only state the following:

Article 4—Interdependent Values—Peace, development, environmental protection and respect for human rights and fundamental freedoms are interdependent.

Article 5—Intergenerational Equity—The freedom of action of each generation in regard to the environment is qualified by the needs of future generations.

Article 6—Prevention—Protection of the environment is best achieved by preventing environmental harm, rather than by attempting to remedy or compensate such harm.

Article 7—Precaution—Lack of scientific certainty is no reason to postpone action to avoid potentially irreversible harm to the environment.

Some of the key concepts are preserved, but the question of long-term, long-distance and cumulative harms, resulting from human activities is not addressed, nor are duties as well as rights emphasized. Human health itself is not even mentioned.

Yet a number of high levels, U.N. sponsored WHO meetings on Environment and Health with Conferences in Frankfurt (1989) and Helsinki (1994),culminating in a "Declaration of the Third Ministerial Conference on Environment and Health" (signed in London on June 18, 1999), clearly connected environmental harms to human health and thereby to human rights.

It is both wrong and illogical to exclude the important scientific findings of the WHO in regard to human health in general, and in relation to environmental conditions, specifically in any document that is aimed at preventing environmental harm and promoting sustainability (Soskolne and Bertollini, 1999; McMichael et al., 1996). The spurious separation between "environment" and "humankind" militates against Articles 4 and 5 of the Draft Covenant, and against the main principles that animate the Earth Charter:

1. Respect Earth and Life in all its Diversity

a. Recognize that all beings are interdependent and every form of life has value regardless of its worth to human beings.

Hence the respect for human beings cannot be separated from respect for their habitat, one that they have in common with the rest of life. It is clear that if this connection were emphasized and made explicit, grave consequences would follow for present practices and institutions. For instance, when the activities of tobacco companies were fully disclosed and, eventually, the consequences of those practices scientifically documented, many business and institutional activities were severely curtailed as such rights as freedom of expression were pitted against public rights to health and life (see Chapter 2; see also ECJ examples in, Chapter 8).

When linkages are openly acknowledged between climate-induced disasters, temperature extremes, and soil erosion leading to desertification and famine, then state supported but unsafe business practices and—in general—a status quo that privileges trade over life, will be brought into question. The changes required will be drastic for both institutional practices and the law, as not one industrial enterprise (e.g., tobacco companies) but all of them, will have to admit their responsibility.

To their credit, the Covenant's drafters do not emphasize or give primacy to trade, the way the WTO tribunals and rules do. For instance their Article 30 under "Trade and environment," in subsection (c) lists "trade measures for environmental purposes do not constitute a means of arbitrary or unjustifiable discrimination or a disguised restriction on international trade," as one of a number of considerations, not the primary one (see Chapter 8). Nevertheless if the trade connection is imported into the Covenant and made explicit, as it is not in the Earth Charter, then surely the link to public health must be not only listed, but emphasized, as only in this way can the connection between human rights and environmental rights become evident. Hence, even the planned review conference, mandated by Article 63 of the Covenant, to take place every five years, should include the WHO, and not simply as observers.

This Draft Covenant represents a "bridge" of sorts between the failure to protect so clear in most other environmental international instruments, and the *erga omnes* obligations that best define environmental duties, as I will argue in the next chapter. Insofar as the Draft Covenant will add the connections and the emphases I propose, and will not allow signatories to further water down and erode the underlying normative message of the Earth Charter, it may well become one of the first international legal instruments committed to the joint protection of humankind and their habitat, and it is indeed encouraging to note its adoption by the UNESCO Resolution of October 16, 2003 (see Appendix 3).

PART III

CHAPTER 7

HUMAN RIGHTS VIOLATIONS AND ECOCRIMES: POSSIBLE EXAMPLES OF OBLIGATIONS *ERGA OMNES*, BASED *ON JUS COGENS* NORMS

1. INTRODUCTION

Men should speak with rational awareness and thereby hold strongly to that which is shared in common—as a city holds on to its laws, and even more strongly (Heraclitus, DK 114).

The people should fight for their law as for their city wall (Heraclitus, DK 44). (Owens, 1959:47)

In the previous chapter we saw the persistent problems caused by both the form and the application of regulatory instruments riddled with imprecisions, vagueness, and inconsistencies, in the face of mounting threats. Local human-made "dykes" are, even in the best of conditions, powerless to hold back raging (and raising) seas. If these "dykes" or "walls" are not well-built, if they present crevices and other imperfections right from the start, then we must turn to stronger, more solid bulwarks for our protection.

I argue that the weak "dykes" and "walls" represent the regional and state laws, that are apparently powerless to halt or even to mitigate the mounting threats to which all humankind is exposed through their environment. In contrast, this stronger, better fortified wall can be found in international laws. The need to shift the responsibility for environmental regulations and their enforcement to the international scene, has been felt for some time; some place the origin of this shift in the advances in science and technology, leading to new activities, and the "creation of wholly new branches of international law," and the "much greater awareness of the plight of millions of human beings who suffer." The authors trace our mounting awareness of all these issues to the efforts of nongovernmental organizations and of the "modern mass media" (Kindred et al., 2000:3).

Before turning to international law we need to raise questions about the function of the rule of law in the international community. In turn, questions related to its function require an understanding of its nature. Scholarly opinion appears to be divided between those who subscribe to a strongly positivist position on the nature of international law (Brownlie, 1998:2) or even a "policy-oriented position," as Brownlie terms the approach of Myres McDougal, W. Michael Reisman and others of the "Yale school" (Brownlie, 1998:8–10), and those who tend to emphasize the historical and theoretical background of international law, as most explanatory of its nature, dating from the concept *ius gentium* in Cicero (Malanczuk, 1997:1; see Chapter 1).

I would place H. Lauterpacht among the latter (Lauterpacht, 1968:73) because his focus, like mine, is on the full understanding of international human rights, starting from the historical background of the concept. Malanczuk emphasizes the importance of this approach: "International law has a number of special characteristics making it completely different from highly developed national legal systems which are connected with the existence of a modern state and its apparatus" (Malanczuk, 1997:3). Hence, without denying the presence and the importance of observable, positive national laws, the existence of wrongful acts that represent an injury to the whole international community appears to be basic and foundational in their importance for international law. When we add to the abstraction "whole international community," the specific reality of grave injuries to the human beings that constitute this "community," then it is clear why the presence of human rights violations must be used to show the role "naturalists" and their principles play against the reductionist role of "positivists."

Hence, when one considers Article 38(1) of the Statute of the International Court of Justice (as signed 1945), the importance of the ultimate moral principles, embedded in "natural law" (in its full historical sense as discussed in Chapter 1), must be kept in mind:

Article 38(1) of the Statute of the International Court of Justice

(1) The Court whose function is to decide in accordance with international law such disputes as are submitted to it, shall apply:
  (a) international conventions, whether general or particular, establishing rules expressly recognized by the contesting States;
  (b) international custom as evidence of a general practice accepted as law;
  (c) the general principles of law recognized by civilized nations;
  (d) judicial decisions and the teaching of the most highly qualified publicists of the various nations, as subsidiary means for determination of the rules of law.
(2) This provision shall not prejudice the power of the Court to decide a case *ex aequo et bono*, if the parties agree thereto.

Hence, the basic components of international law are treaties, customary law *opinio juris*, and the universality expressed primarily through the "general principles" (Malanczuk, 1997:36–56).

This work recognizes the presence of all the sources enumerated in Article 38(1), but it would place (c) squarely in the place of the present (a), although this is not necessarily the accepted position, and Melanczuk, for instance, sees the "hierarchy of rules" much as it is written. In fact he suggests that the rule of *jus cogens* can be derived from custom, and possibly even from treaties, but "probably not from other sources" (Melanczuk, 1997:58). This position ignores the very *raison d'être of jus cogens* norms, that is, the need to have some principles to appeal to in case treaties agree to legalize some practice that flies in the face of universal morality and justice. To reduce norms of *jus cogens* to the same level as other sources of international law, rather than giving such norms the status of "final arbiter" may effectively eliminate the presence of morality and justice, except in the case where consensus might be present. Of course the need for international laws, and the presence of an International Court of Justice and of an International Criminal Court owe their very existence to the reality of conflict and disagreement, not consensus, in the international arena.

In addition, conflict is complicated by the lack of a realistic "balance of power" among states, such that might lend some semblance of justice to the "consensus model" that appears to prevail in today's international community. As long as nations in the world are divided between the "haves" and the "have nots," there does not exist a level playing field in which all interests are the same, and cooperation is sufficient to ensure a just result. This same conflict was noted in Chapter 4 in relation to the interaction between government institutions and corporations on one side, and Canadian citizens, on the other. The presence of the e-coli disaster in Walkerton, Ontario, shows clearly why such a commonality of interests is simply not present. The disparity of goals and interests at the international level has been graphically shown by the protests at the WTO meetings, whether these took place in Seattle, Geneva, Napoli, or Quebec City. Michael Glennon raises some of these questions in his current work. He says:

> Can transnational balance of power principles adequately serve the needs of the modern world for stable and just peace? Can principles of peace and justice be vindicated by a modern, if metaphoric, "Concert of Europe"? Given the unique predominance of the United States, what role should it play in a system that is, in fact, all (American) power and little balance? Might the world community approach an unplanned order with at least some measure of optimism? (Glennon, 2000:3).

It is this imbalance, one that puts justice itself in a precarious position, that demands the presence of protective "walls," supported by underogable norms and principles. The presence of the latter, in fact, is also the main reason why international law appears to offer "some measure of optimism," compared to national (Canadian) laws where—in the environmental field—"consensus" and "cooperation" appear to be the twin goals of the regulatory framework. That approach, as evidenced by the spreading and escalating presence of environmental disasters and tragedies, is inappropriate, because a nonconfrontational stance ignores the reality of power and economic advantage of corporate powers and corporate supported institutions (see Chapter 4).

Previous chapters have shown that, for the most part, breaches of environmental regulations carry consequences more similar to criminal assaults than to regulatory offenses. In addition, the global reach of these ecocrimes is so wide that, even if internal laws were well designed and honestly and impartially applied, no one country alone could legislate against such hazards as transboundary pollution, toxic waste trade, climate change, and the loss of border straddling fish stocks. Hence, both the reach of the consequences, and the possible regulation of the activities giving rise to these harms have clear international dimensions.

2. "MANAGING THE WORLD"? THE GLOBAL DIMENSIONS OF GOVERNANCE

We have noted the problems of community-based decision-making and the lack of principled, universally driven action endemic to those decisions. The question now is what can and should take the place of that form of governance. The problem is that, on one hand localized, responsive government appears to be highly desirable, but on the other hand, many of the problems we must deal with are global in nature and, as we saw, they are not satisfactorily handled at the local, regional level. Maurice Strong says: "The challenge is to strike a balance so that the management of global affairs is responsive to the interests of all people in a secure and sustainable future. Such management must be guided by basic human values" (Strong, 2000:308). Of course, there lies the major difficulty: if by "basic human values" Strong intends principles of respect for life, racial justice, and rights for all humans, then there will be a potential conflict between these high ideals and the reality of decision-making not only at the regional level, but also at the national one. And that is the most important aspect of the primacy of principle and values: they are the only basis for an institutional structure that would have not only the principles, but also the power to stand up to those institutions who use their power to achieve their economic goals, without giving too much emphasis to ethical considerations, like the WTO, for instance. Speaking about his "few ideas . . . about the changes that need to be made," Strong calls for "The establishment, based on UNEP, of a much strengthened world environmental agency with a status equivalent in influence to that of such international agencies as the World Trade Organization" (Strong, 2000:297). Strong does not discuss in detail the reason why we need a "much strengthened *world* environmental agency," but from the context we can conclude that the overwhelming power of bodies such as the WTO demand the presence of a countervailing power on the side of the defense of life and of our common habitat.

In addition, he attempts to define the "boundary conditions that should prescribe global priorities" (Strong, 2000:314). Strong's aim is to differentiate the regulations that remain most appropriately the province of the "principle of subsidiarity" (Ibid. at 313), that is, the issues that benefit from governance closest to the people immediately affected by its decisions from those that cannot be so described. The United Nations, according to Strong, has an organization, a global membership and a mandate that alone can deal with issues of global reach (Ibid. at 313). These ideas are general enough that it would be hard to argue against them. The devil, of course, is in the details. What are the "boundary conditions," that is, the issues that should have primacy "at the international level," as they "can have a major effect on the security, survival and well-being of the entire human community or major portions of it"?

Strong suggests a starter list:

1) Strictly controlling the manufacture and use of nuclear, biological and chemical weapons of mass destruction. Much progress has already been made on this issue since the end of the Cold War, but there is still a long way to go before the world community can ensure itself against this form of self-destruction.
2) Limiting the amount of carbon dioxide and other greenhouse gases from human sources that can be allowed to build up in the atmosphere.
3) Limiting the destruction or compromise of the earth's biological resources.
4) Limiting the discharge or transport by any country of hazardous or noxious substances that can inflict damage beyond its borders.
5) Limiting a country's intrusion into or undermining of the security or economy of other countries.
6) Defining the extent to which a government can suppress human rights or commit violence against its own people without justifying repressive action on the part of the international community.
7) Protecting the global commons—the oceans, the atmosphere, Antarctica and outer space (Strong, 2000:314–315).

It is clear that no single country can possibly be responsible for any of the immense global risks listed on Strong's "starter list." Not one of these risks is such that any nation can unilaterally protect humanity from their "emergent" presence, to use Hiskes' term (Hiskes, 1998).

All the practices that result in the risks mentioned on the starter list, appear to have happened because of social preferences, international treaties, and cooperation between certain specific nations, fostered by greed, negligence, and disinterest in the fate of citizens in areas affected by our activities. The activities impose serious risks on all citizens, whether or not they are aware of their own precarious position. This is why we need the international perspective in both regulations and institutions: when popular voices arise from ignorance or from disinterest even in the citizens' own fate, then democratic institutions cannot properly direct the governance of their region.

We noted earlier that local and regional "free choices" give rise to many problems, despite the presence of high levels of education and information in affluent Western democracies (see Chapter 4). Note that it bears repeating, democracies suggest "a contemporary variant of an embedded and endemic inequality in their democracy;" and this fact is based on another unavoidable fact, "democracies almost always have market economics" (Midlarsky, 1997:319). As Jules Coleman observes: "Liberalism is committed to markets, not to efficiency as such" (Coleman, 1995:435). In addition to these indictments, neither liberalism nor modern democracy is committed to either justice or fairness as such, as the commitment to markets may be (and most often is) in direct conflict with other moral commitments.

These international dimensions not only permit, but in fact require that ecocrimes be regulated by international laws.

3. STATE RESPONSIBILITY

The aim of this work, as outlined in Chapter 1, has been a two-fold one: it is intended to demonstrate that environmental offenses are best viewed as crimes (see Chapters 4 and 5); and that they cannot be handled well in the sole context of national laws. Maurice Strong argues, as we saw in the last section, that the United Nations should be the best source of law to deal with what amounts to a series of global violent threats, well beyond the control of any single state (Strong, 2000:308). Strong, therefore, has a great deal of confidence in the United Nations, and in the UNEP. He also trusts the viability of such international global instruments as the Earth Charter, a document he helped draft with Steven Rockefeller, and helped support and ultimately present the charter to several states, including the Netherlands and Costa Rica and to many cities, for instance Urbino, Italy, that accepted the Charter (Ibid.; Rockefeller, 2002; Westra, 1998; Miller and Westra, 2002).

The thrust of the Earth Charter combines a strong biocentric defense of ecological integrity with a decisive declaration of its support of human rights while respecting the interconnectedness of all life. Unfortunately it is not a legal document at this time (see Appendix I). Strong recognizes that his starter list is so vital that acceptance by just a few states would be insufficient, as it must be enforced by all upon all. The question then is, even if one agrees with Strong in principle, how is this result to be achieved? In practice, what is the law of state responsibility? The first question may be why would environmental protection even be considered a state obligation?

I believe this last question has been answered sufficiently in the previous chapters, and it will be addressed and summarized in the following sections. It is a grave responsibility of all states, because, not to protect the environment is to be negligent in regard to human rights, not only those within each state, but also the rights of all other humans whose lives will be affected (see Chapter 2).

In this work I will use "responsibility" in two senses, each of which will be clarified by the context wherein it is used:

(1) The public international law term to indicate the legal state of affairs following a breach of state obligation;
(2) As a moral term, to indicate the general duty or obligation owed to those who are or might have been harmed by an activity, on the part of those who initiated that activity or sanctioned it.

Peter French ties the concept of responsibility to that of legal personhood. As we noted earlier, the CID structure is what renders corporations, like natural persons, capable of intent (see Chapter 4). French also traces the history of "legal personhood" from Roman times. He defines it as follows: "A legal person may be described as any entity recognized in law as supporting such capacities as instituting or defending judicial proceedings" (French, 1992:134). Roman law identified "legal personhood with legal status," and always conceived it "as a privilege and not a matter of right" (French, 1992:135). The implications for corporate and—I might add—for institutional responsibility, are obvious. A privilege tends to impose more responsibility than a "natural" right: it should be earned. In addition, both corporations and institutions are ideally suited to assume and bear responsibility for the future: given their life is not limited, hence institutions can best bear the responsibility for long-term harms, as they will also coexist with future persons, unlike humans, whose life span is limited.

There are many difficulties confronting the notion of state responsibility: to say that the state is accountable "for a violation of international law," appears to be the most general and abstract way of viewing state responsibility, although additional questions could be raised:

(1) Are states only liable for acts or also omissions;
(2) Is "intention or malice" necessary for a violation to occur;
(3) Are states alone responsible, or are specific individuals acting on the state's behalf responsible as well;
(4) Can some violation be defined as "criminal" (Higgins 1994: 148–150).

On the first question, the *Corfu Channel* case (Merits) (U.K. v. Albania, 1949 I.C.J., 4, 17–23), appears to be, first of all, a case of "omission": Albania omitted to inform the British Warships of the possible presence of mines in the Channel. The same case also applies to the second point. It does not appear that there was any malicious intent on the part of Albania. Although there was a failure on the part of Albania to take the appropriate steps to protect vessels in their Channel. Kindred et al. make the general point, that there might be, ". . . no need to establish the intention of the State in order to trigger responsibility leading to a regime of 'objective responsibility,' also called 'strict' or 'risk liability' (Kindred et al., 2000:608). Strict liability, in Canadian criminal law is the common standard for environmental regulations. As such, after Sault Ste. Marie (R. v. Sault Ste. Marie, (1978) 85 D.L.R.3d 161, 40 C.C.C.2d 353, (1978) S.C.R. 1299), a defense of "due diligence" may be advanced, in contrast with "absolute liability," that does not admit of this defense; states too have an obligation, "a duty of care to prevent injury" (Higgins, 1994:157; see Chapter 5).

In the environmental field, in addition, the responsibility of the state extends not only to the activities of the state and its organs and agents, but also to the "activities of private persons and firms" (Ibid.), what in international human rights discourse is now called the "duty to protect." So far we have considered state responsibility for illegal acts. But the classic *Trail Smelter Arbitration* (see below) is a clear example of a far more typical environmental hazard: one arising from legal commercial activities. Higgins analyzes state responsibility from the standpoint of the International Law Commission (ILC): She says, "the only requirement is causality," which entails that "responsibility is based on result, not fault" (Higgins, 1994:161), although not presently the case on international environmental law. Canadian Supreme Court Madam Justice Claire L'Heureux-Dubé supported a parallel position in her judgments and dissents in family law cases: she supports an interpretation of "equality rights" (Section 15(1) in the Canadian Charter of Rights and Freedoms, that considers first the result and consequences of, say, laws that are discriminatory towards women after a divorce, or on an affected minority group as a whole. I have argued that a similar approach can and should be used fruitfully for consequences that include environmental harms (see Chapter 5).

a. State Responsibility for Environmental Harms

> . . . an important function of the traditional approach, that of assigning responsibility and channeling compensation, does not meet the challenge posed by environmental degradation. It does not provide for the cooperation, coordination, planning, prevention and flexibility necessary to respond to ecological needs (Brunnée, 1993:330).

Ellen Hey also considers the deficiencies in international environmental law, and believes that the instruments presently available for the protection of the environment are "limited primarily" because of the "non-compulsory nature and the inner-state character of the procedures that are available" (Hey, 2000:1). Because of these failures, the Dutch Minister of the Environment J.P. Pronk, "expressed support for the establishment of an international environmental court" (Hey, 2000:3). Yet many of the environmental cases that could have been heard by an environmental court, also could have been (and, in fact, had been) decided by other courts, as they also intersected with other issues such as international water law, or human rights law, or "international law related to the use of force" and other related fields (Hey, 2000:6). Hey's argument supports the argument of Section 2 of this chapter, especially in relation to "human rights" and the "use of force" (the Legality of Threat of Nuclear Weapons, Advisory Opinion, ICJ).

Of course, the dangers perceived by Brunnée, such that of "leaving the larger ecological issue unaddressed" (Brunnée, 1993:830), will persist, if we continue to allow environmental assaults to be judged only in the context of other civil judiciary tribunals, and if we continue not to view them as crimes, rather than only delicts. One of the major problems is precisely the reality of states' responsibility, versus the paradox of states' interests. The *Trail Smelter Arbitration* demonstrates the paradoxical nature of interstate environmental disputes. On one hand, the states involved desire to keep their interaction at a reasonably friendly, cooperative level; on the other hand, they want to be compensated for damages but without insisting on meeting environmental standards that might be too high for them to meet in the future, or too low a burden of evidence to support the claims involved, because, although in the immediate case (*Trail Smelter*), it might have been to the U.S. advantage to ask for more, it would not have to their advantage to establish a precedent in law they might have to meet in the future:

> The element of reciprocity of risk on the other hand, seems to explain the initial unwillingness of the United States to pursue the matter, given the heavy industrialization of the US side of the border further east, and its accompanying concern that a dangerous precedent could be set (Mickelson, 1993:228).

It is this difficulty, that is the presence of common economic interests that may support "unholy alliances," from the environmental point of view, alliances that militate strongly in favor of turning instead to peremptory norms in support of the cause of ecology, as I have argued in this chapter. Another major difficulty is the global character of the problems, which "makes the pinpointing of responsible states and victims virtually impossible" (Brunnée, 1993:834). Finally, the complexity of the biotic systems affected, eliminates even the possibility of defining precise safe standards in technologically advanced societies. This renders impossible the full understanding of what might constitute serious damage, for instance. Brunnée argues that a combination of all these factors explains why even grave and "clear violations of international law such as the Sandoz spill in the Rhine, the Chernobyl reactor incident of the Gulf War, have not been followed by a pursuit of available state responsibility channels" (Brunnée, 1993:835).

And if even the gravest cases are not followed up, and the myriad smaller daily infractions of environmental safety are also not tried, then there is little hope that a strong *corpus* of case law will be created, and that the scarce precedents presently available will be augmented, so that they might assist with more than the restatement of some basic principles. In fact the existence of global disastrous consequences of acts not prohibited by either domestic or international laws, clearly indicates the presence of large lacunae in the structure and in the instruments of international environmental law, unless we reconsider our present approaches in some radical new way, such as the proposal to criminalize ecoviolence, for which I have argued in this work.

In the next chapter we will consider another aspect of our problem: whether corporate, institutional and other nonstate actors will be recognized to be responsible for the consequences of ecocrimes, by the Courts. The emergence of prosecutions of nonstate agents under Alien Torts Claims Act (ATCA) and the coming into force of the International Criminal Court of Justice (July 2002), can be counted as positive steps in this quandary.

b. International Liability of States for Injurious Consequences Arising Out of Acts Not Prohibited by International Law

In a shrinking world, where any activity that modifies fragile ecological patterns tends to have repercussions beyond national borderlines, it becomes even more necessary to establish standards suited to save those natural cycles and thereby to ensure the foundations of human survival (Tomuschat, 1991:58).

State responsibility arises both when an unlawful act has been committed and when there are harmful consequences from legal activities. In both cases *jus cogens* norms can be invoked to deal with environmental damage (Ago, 1989: 237; Tanzi, 1987:1). Two points must be clarified before proceeding. First, on the question of fault versus consequences, the hostages case in *United States v. Iran* (1980 I.C.J. 3, at 69, 70), shows that the duty of the Iranian government was to take "every appropriate step" to bring "the flagrant infringements" of international law to a speedy resolution, in fact, "No such step was taken," although states have the duty to regulate private actors in their territory. In this cause it appears that the fault element makes this an even stronger case that "Iran had violated . . . its obligation toward the United States" (Kindred et al., 2000:324). Another point of clarification is that of moral implications of *jus cogens* norms, beyond their legal status.

In *Wiwa v. Royal Shell Petroleum* (ATCA, March 2002), for instance, it is clear that because no state was involved, one could not bring a case against Shell for the breach of a treaty obligation; Shell had to be charged with the breach of *erga omnes* obligations supported by *jus cogens* norms, because of the moral and legal principles they violated, in flagrant conflict with international law, especially "crimes against humanity" as will be argued below. The second problem is the possibility that although the harm is visible and present, the act that generated the harmful consequences, was itself legal. The classic example is once again, the *Trail Smelter Arbitration*. As various forms of technology become more widespread and complex, the environmental harm that ensues, whether it is immediate or—as it is most often the case—delayed, it becomes precisely what this work suggests: a legal, institutionalized form of violence, producing harms that are often irreversible (see Chapter 2).

The problem of transboundary harm was first considered in a study by a subcommittee of the International Law Commission in 1963 to deal with the "conspicuous gap" left in international law by the exclusion of "liability that derives from . . . legal grounds" (Tomuschat, 1991:38). Several Rapporteurs and many iterations of that particular aspect of state responsibility uncovered several major points.

First, states are in a position to control specific activities. Hence, they should bear responsibility for the consequences arising from such activities. This appears unobjectionable. The second point, however, is more debatable, as it raises the question of transboundary liability for the "global commons," as introduced by Rapporteur Barboza (1989 ILC Rep. 242, para. 348). The third point follows upon the other two: often negative effects are produced that reach well beyond the intended effects, thus producing a "normative gap" that ought to be addressed by international law (Tomuschat, 1991:42). Fourth, modern scientific developments have indicated the immense scope of environmental problems such as climate change, global warming or biogenetic engineering, all of which are "dangerous activities" and "for whose consequences states must bear full responsibility" (Tomuschat, 1991:43).

Finally, whether the dangerous activities are undertaken by public or private sources, states must ensure that they assume full responsibility for all activities that place human rights in jeopardy. In addition, no private person or institution can ensure prevention, as a state can and must:

> Experience has taught that more often than not damage to the environment cannot be made good after it has occurred. When a species of animals has disappeared it cannot be revived again. Soil that has been contaminated may have to rest for decades before it can be recultivated. Radioactive particles that have escaped a nuclear installation pose a threat to their environment as long as their radiation continues. The ozone layer, once destroyed may never build up again. Thus the primary goal must be to prevent harm from occurring. Second pollution caused by a major disaster, but also pollution caused by accumulation, may easily take on such huge dimensions that both in financial and in technological terms, reparation is simply impossible (Tomuschat, 1991:46).

Against this background, we can consider now some specifics.

For instance, the 1996 ILC Report Chapter 4, defines the state obligation of "due diligence." Germany and Switzerland disagreed on absolute liability for the pollution of the Rhine by Sandoz, but "the Swiss government acknowledged responsibility for lack of 'due diligence' in preventing the accident through adequate regulation of its pharmaceutical industries" (Kiss and Shelton, 1997; 1987:719–727). The Convention on the Protection of the Rhine (1999), following the Rhine Action Programme adopted in 1987 (8th Ministerial Conference of the Rhine States, 1987), after the Sandoz accident (Birnie and Boyle, 2002:325), adopts the ecosystem approach and is aimed at the sustainable development of the Rhine area, thus controlling not only the actions of the riparian states, but those of all States involved in industrial activities having an impact in the area (in the case of Sandoz, including Switzerland).

The United Kingdom defined due diligence as "such care as government ordinarily employ in their domestic concerns" (at para. 9). A U.S. definition can be found in the *Alabama* case (U.S. of America v. United Kingdom, Great Britain and Northern Ireland):

[A] diligence proportional to the magnitude of the subject and the strength of the power which is to exercise it, a diligence which shall, by the use of active vigilance, and of all other means in the power of the neutral, through all stages of the transactions, prevents its soil from being violated; a diligence that shall, in like manner deter designing men from committing acts of war upon the soil of the neutral against its will.

Returning to international law, the elements of the ILC Convention's work on legal transboundary environmental harm were "prevention, co-operation, and strict liability for harm," but they were considered "too controversial" (Birnie and Boyle, 2002:105). The 2001 amended draft of this convention, divided the topic into two parts, "prevention and liability" and the main concern remained the former, not the latter (Birnie and Boyle, 2002:106). Although the latest draft prescribes "all appropriate measures that must be taken to prevent or minimize the risk," it does nothing to prohibit the activites that give rise to transboundary harm (Birnie and Boyle, 2002:107).

Risk itself "is defined to encompass both 'a low probability of causing disastrous harm' and 'a high probability of causing significant harm'," (Birnie and Boyle, 2002:115). However, neither "disastrous" or "significant" are defined, and neither international lawyers, nor judges or even scientists can hope to express with any certainty what might constitute the desired "clear and convincing" scientific proof of possible harm.

In addition, the standard of due care or due diligence must be proportional to "the degree of risk of transboundary harm in the particular instance," and can be expected to change with time and must take in consideration ". . . location; special climate conditions; materials used in the activity;" and so on. Higgins, who analyzes state responsibility, rather than liability, states that "the only requirement is causality," which entails that "responsibility is based on result, not fault" (Higgins, 1994:161). Special Rapporteur James Crawford explains:

> In particular article [1] stated that every internationally wrongful act of a State entails its responsibility, and article [3] identified two and two only elements of an internationally wrongful act, (a) conduct attributable to a State which (b) is inconsistent with its international obligations. There was no *distinct or separate requirement of fault or wrongful intent for an internationally wrongful act to be held* to exist (Crawford, 2002: 12; emphasis added).

Hence, even in the latest iteration of the ILC, international law does not require intent for the commission of a "crime" (although this language is no longer part of the ILC), and Higgins' point stands. Thus, the common argument of corporate or institutional wrongdoers, adducing lack of intent as exonerating or at least mitigating their responsibility, cannot be defended as even the due diligence defense is not allowed internationally.

In contrast, the problem of defining a state or institutional wrongdoing as crime, hence different in kind from other delicts, is no longer as clearly stated as when Article 19 of the ILC (1996) was in existence (see Appendix 2). Crawford admits that regimes appropriate to corporate crime could apply to state crime, but he views the absence of (1) precise definition; (2) "adequate investigative procedures"; (3) due process; (4) appropriate sanctions; and (5) "some method by which the State can, as it were, come clean, expunge the record," as providing definitive arguments against the use of the concept of crime in regard to the state (Ibid.), thus the necessity to focus on state liability for now, without losing sight of the desirability to appeal to more serious charges in the future.

One wonders whether the same five elements could not be raised in regard to the accepted crimes of genocide and crimes against humanity, all of which cannot truly be perpetrated without a state's acceptance or participation, and which cannot simply be described as "a pejorative way of describing serious breaches of certain norms," as he thinks other possible state crimes might more appropriately be termed (Ibid.) We note that if genocide and the like are still considered crimes, why are environmental offenses (previously an example of crimes in Article 19) left out, despite the immense damages to human life and habitat documented in Chapter 2 and elsewhere. Crawford's analysis states that Article 19 had been viewed as "divisive" and that states could not agree on the language most appropriate to express Article 19 in a better way.

It is wrong that these self-interested objections aiming not at better expression of commonly held values but at the protection of self-interest on the part of

powerful countries, were viewed as more significant than the solid arguments provided by a majority of publicists who wrote to defend the principles behind
Article 19, whatever the flaws of its presentation. It would seem that absent the
problem of intent, the consequences following environmentally hazardous activities should align these activities with other crimes against humanity, although the
consequences are not always clear and dramatic.

In the environmental field, especially in regard to public health consequences,
harms and losses are seldom, if ever, immediately visible or appreciable in their
full range of consequences. For instance, our earlier discussion of endocrine disruptors shows the example of a harm that consists in the alteration of normal sexual function (e.g., male sperm count reduction), caused by a combination of
factors in synergy. In addition, the harm is not immediately detectable (see
Chapter 2). Still, it is clearly wrong and immoral, as well as illegal, to interfere
with a person's normal function, without their explicit, informed consent.

The claim that there is no specific intent to produce that result in an identifiable person, as Crawford pointed out, cannot be sufficient to absolve the
causative agent(s) of any wrongdoing. Nor is it sufficient to claim that the activities giving rise to the described consequences were legal at the time they
occurred, and might even be legal today. In fact, Article 3 of the International Law
Commission (1988 ILC Rep. Ch. 4, at www.un.org/law/ilc/reports/1998/
chp4.html), is short and to the point on this issue: *"Prevention.* States shall take
all appropriate measures to prevent, or to minimize the risk of, significant transboundary harm." Special Rapporteur Srenivasa Rao (May 8, 1998), says:

> The objective of prevention of transboundary damages arising from haz-
> ardous activities had been emphasized in principle 2 of the Rio
> Declaration . . . and confirmed by ICJ in its advisory opinion on the
> *Legality of the Threat or Use of Nuclear Weapons*, as forming part of the
> corpus of international law (1 Y.B. I.L.C. 61 (1998).

Rao adds that the European Commission had drawn up various schemes to
prevent transboundary damages, and that its work emphasized that, because of
scientific developments, there was an "enhanced ability to trace the chains of causation, that is to say, the physical links between the cause (the activity) and the
effect (the harm);" hence, that prevention was indeed the key (Ibid. at para. 25).

Mr. Barboza, another special Rapporteur, also indicated that "the duty of prevention should continue to be treated as an obligation of conduct and not one of
result" (Ibid. at para. 29). On this topic, Alain Pellet added that "the statement that
only (*seulement*, in the French version) significant harm or damages was required
to be prevented by States was most inappropriate" (Ibid. at 63 para. 41).

Pellet's point especially supports the claim here advanced that visible, or otherwise detectable grave harms are only part of the kind of harms that ought to be

proscribed. Even an otherwise moderate hazard may become part of a cumulative or synergisitic scenario that eventually transforms it into a severe harm.

It is also useful to consider this document's efforts at defining due diligence. For instance at (6), in the Commentary following Article 3 (Prevention):

(6) The obligation of States to take preventive or minimization measures is one of due diligence, requiring States to take certain unilateral measures to prevent, or to minimize a risk of significant transboundary harm. The obligation imposed by this article is not an obligation of result. It is the conduct of a State that will determine whether the State has complied under the present articles.

Note that this commentary may conflate prevention with minimization, two quite disparate concepts. Are we to prevent harm or simply to accept that it will occur, and attempt to minimize it? Once again a comparison with assaults is in order: the criminal code does not make allowances for an attack attempting to minimize the harm inflicted, although the resulting harm, as well as the measure of awareness or intention will make a difference in how the case is considered, tried, and punished. This is a recurring problem we noted earlier in regard to national laws as well (see Chapter 5).

In fact, because the notions of responsibility and fault are closely related in international law, the whole regulatory infrastructure should be questioned. Gehring and Jactenfuchs (1990) say:

However, highly complex industrial activities create risks which can be minimized but not completely eliminated. The concept of state responsibility does not foresee any duty to compensate for damage due to activities which are not prohibited by international law. Furthermore, according to traditional international law, established legal wrongfulness of any activity having caused transboundary harm entails the obligation to cease its operation.

It appears logical that, if a similar factual harm is produced by a legal activity, a similar obligation to cease should prevail. But, at the present time no prohibition is codified in international law to stop "lawful" hazardous activities and, for the most part, states have a strong interest in continuing and even promoting many of these activities. In addition, even

. . . establishing too close a link between fault and the obligation to compensate for damage frequently does not result in an internationally accepted ban of a particular dangerous activity, but rather in a refusal by the source state to compensate, since any acceptance of the duty to compensate would imply acknowledgement of a violation of international law and thus endanger the future operation of the activity in question

(Gehrig and Jachtenfuchs, 1990, at www.ejil.org/journal/Vol4/No1/art9.html).

This is the main reason why in the next chapter we will propose initiating a reform of international law on environmental matters, and for establishing a new court to hear environmental cases (Postiglione, 2001; see Chapter 8).

The present "juridical deficit" (see Chapter 8) is even more obvious when the question of the "actors involved in an equitable balance of interests" (Article 12) of the International Law Commission is considered:

> *Article 12.* In order to achieve an equitable balance of interest as referred to in paragraph 2 of Article 11, the State concerned shall take into account all relevant factors and circumstances, including:
>
> (a) the degree of risk of significant boundary harm and of the availability of means of preventing such harm, or minimizing the risk thereof or repairing the harm;
>
> (b) the importance of the activity, taking into account its overall advantages of a social, economic and technical character for the State of origin in relation to the potential harm for the States likely to be affected;

Subsections (c) and (e) also emphasize the "availability of means" to prevent the harms, and the "possibility of carrying out the activity elsewhere or by other means or replacing with an alternative activity." The repeated reference to "economics" introduces a disanalogy into the discourse: economic losses or harms cannot be compared with losses of life or physical integrity (Guerra v. Italy, (1998), 26 EHRR 357). Although the precautionary principle is recognized, subsection (f) refers to "the standard of prevention," the number of factors to be taken into account demonstrates the problem of weighing factors that are neither equal in gravity nor comparable.

The right to life is basic in law and, for instance, the European Convention for the Protection of Human Rights and Fundamental Freedoms (1950), has that right in its Article 2, and throughout the article by juridical extension, the right is coupled with that of "physical integrity" (*Guerra v. Italy*). Hence an activity that has even the potential to expose us to grave risks to life and our "physical integrity" means that the state is allowing a corporate entity to use present and future generations as guinea pigs, effectively to test the result of their activities, and this practice should be eliminated. Further support can be found in Article 8(2) under "Right to respect for private and family life." Subsection (2) proscribes "interference by a public authority with the exercise of this right," except, inter alia, *"for the protection of health* or morals." (Council of Europe Publishing, 1999:13; emphasis added).

After the Johannesburg Earth Summit (2002), the UNEP organized a "Global Judges Symposium" intended to "Fortify Environmental Law Principles." Justice Arthur Chaskalson, Chief Justice of South Africa, said

> Our declaration and proposed program of work are I believe, a crucial development in the quest to deliver development that respects people and that respects the planet for current and future generations and for all living things (*Environment News Service*, Sept. 9, 2002, 1).

This is a significant development, and we will return to it below in Chapter 8.

c. Transboundary Harm and State Responsibility Revisited

It is wrong that the prevention of harm does not appear to be an "absolute duty" in international law, as indicated by the lack of Nuremberg style tribunals for Chernobyl, Bhopal, and the present Global Climate Change clearly demonstrates. Yet the International Law Commission Draft on State Responsibility (1996), states:

Article 3—Elements of an Internationally Wrongful Act of a State

> There is an internationally wrongful act of a State when: (a) conduct consisting of an action or omission is attributable to the State under international law; and (b) that conduct constitutes a breach of an international obligation of the State.

The important point is that neither in this article, nor in others is there a reference to damages or harm, as a condition of international responsibility (Kindred et al., 2000:604). Perhaps, as Graefrath suggests, following the recognition of norms and of values, "the implementation mechanisms" may still lag behind (Graefrath, 1989:255). The final question of state responsibility is that of ascribing criminal responsibility to states, and the viability of such a course of action. We will return to this problem below, in our discussion of the ILC's former Article 19, and the presence of some of the concepts of that article in the 2000 formulation of the ILC.

At any rate, for the purpose of this work, the civil responsibility of states is less important than the possibility of ascribing criminal responsibility to them. Civil responsibility and fines or economic incentives, are the normal way to deal with environmental offenses in national law (see Chapter 5). The regulatory attitude as demonstrated in Chapters 4 and 5, is one of seeking "consensus" and "cooperation," rather than engaging in decisive confrontations; these are indeed laudable goals, when those who participate in the "dialogue" enjoy a parity of power, both economic and institutional, and when the *actus reus* does not inflict physical damages on the victims(s). On the question of "power," as it was shown in Chapter 4, that is an unrealistic expectation even in a democratic country like Canada, where strong economic interests, supported by governmental infrastructures can pay lip-service to inclusiveness and respect for all, while blocking legally the ability of citizens to participate effectively. Trade secret regulations by and large do not permit citizens to know the results of the exposures they are asked to accept, and other mechanisms employed for the most part legally, do not permit enough information to allow free choice.

Because of the flaws in national environmental regimes, exemplified by the events at Walkerton Ontario (see Chapter 4), and because the consequences of environmental offenses are such that (1) they are not always immediately and locally visible; and (2) they are such that fines, reprimands or other economic incentives and disincentives are not truly appropriate, I advocate turning in addition to international law, where the consequences of these crimes and their true nature can be held up for condemnation by the whole international community. In Chapter 2, the full global consequences of ecoviolence were described, supported by epidemiological findings (Sieswerda and Soskolne, 2000; Soskolne and Bertollini, 1999), and some of these findings will be summed up in the next section, in relation to international crimes of aggression. A similar comparison was drawn in Chapter 5, by showing the similarity between ecoviolence and the consequences of assaultive crimes, involving the unconsented use of force, ranging from rapes to homicides. For these crimes, no due diligence defense is available (nor should it be), no monetary incentives or fines.

My argument is that a full understanding of the consequences of environmental offenses should remove them from the realm of quasi-crimes and place them squarely where they belong, among other violent crimes. In Chapter 5, the main difficulty, that is the ascription of some form of intent to perpetrators, if not full *mens rea*, then at least negligence or willful blindness, and the like, to the institutions and commercial enterprises that either perpetrate or are complicit in the commission of these crimes, was addressed in detail. It is worthy of note that it is just as hard to isolate the "perpetrator(s)" in a world of complex, synergistic, and cumulative interactions of hazardous substances, in the national context, as it is to do so internationally. The question of appropriate punishment is also equally difficult in both contexts.

In Chapter 4, the very possibility of reaching a unitary decision was shown to depend on the Corporate International Decision-Making Structure CID structure common to both corporations and governmental institutions (French, 1984). The CID structure approach applies to both domestic and international institutions. This is basic to the argument of this work: the true reach of environmental offenses can never be fully appreciated when only their local consequences are taken in consideration (see *Trail Smelter Arbitration*, below). Another example although no "case" or even "arbitration" took place, is the 1970s situation of the INCO (Sudbury, Ontario) copper smelter. It had reduced through its emission, the whole area in and around Sudbury, to a "moonscape," devoid of any vegetation. The effects of acid rain on human health were also well documented. In response to the complaints by both local citizens and unions, INCO erected the infamous "super-stacks" still present today. These were huge chimneys that simply redistributed the pollution beyond Northern Ontario. Sudbury is green again, but the effects on the flora and fauna even in protected areas as far as South Carolina and Ohio, are legion (Brunnée, 1988:13–14; compare Brunnée, 1988:141–142).

Even domestic problems, when solved in the manner dictated by democratic dialogue with local citizens, legally, can still produce international ecoviolence. Hence the two-fold argument of this work to show: (1) the criminal, violent consequences of all environmental offence and, as Higgins indicated, even of many legal practices; and (2) the international, global reach of both legal and illegal activities, hence the need to consider them both "serious" and "grave," and as attacks on the basic interests of all citizens, and all citizens, and all states—that is, as crimes.

In this chapter I am not concerned with identifying which individuals specifically may also be culpable, and the degree of their possible culpability, because the first step is to recognize the responsibility of states in this regard. Without their complicity, and support, corporations could not operate, and regulations, whether shortsighted, weak, ineffective, or even favoring the economic interests of some against the basic rights to life and health of others, could not exist. As well, in Chapter 3, the question of individual and even group responsibility was considered. The main issue now is whether a case can be made for state responsibility, and whether the appellation ecocrime can stand the test of international law.

Edward Wise discusses international crimes in the context of domestic (U.S.) law, in comparison with international crime, and proposes establishing an international criminal code (Wise, 1989:923). He is speaking against the background of international laws that included Article 19 (then draft only) of the ILC (see Appendix 2). It is instructive to study his discussion, in order to see how much can be preserved without the support provided by Article 19. The argument here proposed is that both states and individuals could be subjects of criminal responsibility under international law (Tunkin, 1974:396). Wise adds that, according to Oppenheim,

> The comprehensive notion of an international delinquency ranges from ordinary breaches of treaty obligations, involving no more than pecuniary compensation, to violations of International Law amounting to a criminal act in the generally accepted meaning of the word (Oppenheim, 1955:339).

Oppenheim also defines criminal acts in both material and formal terms:

The essence of a criminal act, as distinguished from a contractual or tortious wrong actionable at the instance of the injured party, is the fact that it injures, and is punishable by, the whole community at large. Nor are the seriousness, the destructive uses, and the heinousness of the act irrelevant to the question of the determination of its criminal character (Oppenheim, 1955:192; Wise, 1989:928).

Both of these definitions aptly characterize the sort of violent, widespread acts considered here. Neither of these attempts at definition appears to depend exclusively, if at all, on Article 19 of the ILC. But Wise correctly notes that the adoption of that article was not accepted universally:

The Commission's concept of an "international Crime" has been criticized. There are two basic objections. First in the more usual formal sense of the term, to call conduct "crime" implies that it is liable to be followed by criminal proceedings and punishment. But there are no international criminal proceedings, or international agencies empowered to inflict punishment on States.

Second, while the imposition of punishment on a collectivity may not be impossible, the problem of holding an entire population responsible for the acts of its government, since any sanction must ultimately fall on all members of the collectivity (Wise, 1989:929).

Yet, if Wise is correct in saying that for "normal delictual responsibility," state responsibility is "usually analogous to liability for a tort" (Ibid.), then it is clear that limiting all state responsibility to tortuous liability is simply insufficient to justly accommodate wide variations of wrongdoing. On his second point, that difficulty is not limited to criminal prosecution; one needs only to think of the grievous impact of economic sanctions to Iran on the population at large to see that the problem is endemic to state responsibility as such, not only to any novel form of state crime.

Wise might be closer to the mark in his analysis of what is a crime, a distinction he finds "embedded in accepted distinctions between criminal and civil proceedings, between punishment and delictual liability (Wise, 1989:925). The notion of punishment is surely an odd one in regard to a state, unless punishment consists of economic measures or sanctions, and it is hard to attempt to specify the appropriate punishment for state crimes (Cassese, 1986:49). But one needs only to consider that states, where persistent genocide or unwarranted attacks against humanity occur, are already eventually punished by the presence of NATO's peace-keeping forces, such as those who intervened in the recent attacks on Kosovo's Albanian population. According to Chapter VII of the U.N. Charter, Articles 41 and 42 describe the sanctions that may be imposed upon states "to maintain or restore international peace and security" (Article 39). These include the possible use of force by members of the United Nations, when economic sanctions do not succeed (Article 42).

The sequence is clear: first, a state disregards human rights on a continuing basis (vs. Article 34, Chapter VI, U.N. Charter). Later, punishment was meted out in an effort to terminate the human rights abuses through the use of force (Chapter VII, Articles 39–42). The latter indicates the progression of responses that may take place "With Respect to Threats to the Peace, Breaches of the Peace and Acts of Aggression." If it can be shown that ecocrimes are also Acts of Aggression, then an argument can be made in favor of intervention on behalf of the affected populations.

In any case, given that, for these recognized crimes, with or without the existence of Article 19 of the ILC, a sequence of actions on the part of the international community is already codified, starting with Article 33, Chapter VI, it is unnecessary to ask what a state punishment for crimes might be. We are speaking of state responsibility toward the whole international community, but not only *erga omnes* norms, also rather *jus cogens* norms that may support the invocation of the "countermeasures" part (Part III) of the 2000 version of the ILC. *Jus cogens* norms are at stake because these harms are both grave, serious and affecting the fundamental interests of the international community (Article 41 and 42). Only in this manner can we hope to improve the global situation today. Still, Wise is correct when he says that, "Indeed, one of the central problems confronting international criminal law is the problem of imposing restraints on the conduct of those whom the modern state has cloaked with official authority" (Wise, 1989:937; Williams, 1939:93).

4. *JUS COGENS* NORMS AS APPLIED TO ECOCRIME

Verdross, one of *jus cogens'* earliest advocates, explained that the concept of *jus cogens* was quite alien to legal positivists, but the situation was quite different in the natural law school of international law (Janis, 1988:361).

Over the last few years, we have seen increasing public unrest and even violence in defense of global human rights, understood as encompassing the right to a healthy, protected environment. The chosen target was and is currently the WTO and the high-powered economic representatives of today's richest nations. The main objections to these meetings and their agendas, I believe, address what is presently lacking in the substance of their deliberations: (1) the lack of explicit human rights concern; (2) the lack of environmental and public health concern; (3) the lack of openness and transparency in their eventual agreements.

The main emphasis on the part of the protesters, is on both "civil and political rights," as well as "social and economic rights," both of which, as we saw earlier, ought to imply the right to life and the healthy conditions required to support this right. Article 53 (see Chapter 1) of the Vienna Convention on the Law of Treaties ((1969), in force 1980), however, spells out explicitly the existence of norms that cannot be "forgotten" or simply ignored through other treaties or agreements arranged for the economic advantage of certain states:

A.53 Treaties conflicting with a peremptory norm of general international law (*jus cogens*). A treaty is void if, at the time of its conclusion, it conflicts with a peremptory norm of general international law. For the purposes of the present Convention, a peremptory norm of general international law is a norm accepted and recognized by the international community of states as a whole as a norm from which no derogation is permitted and which can be modified only by a subsequent norm of general international law having the same character (1969) 1155 U.N.T. S.331, in force 1980).

This article sets the stage: on the basis of Article 53, given the clarification of what is an international crime according to the description of examples of *ius cogens* norms in the former Article 19 of the International Law Commission (1996), although this article is strongly positivistic, thus not entirely helpful from our point of view.

If these articles and the corresponding obligations to which they give rise are taken seriously, then the so-called "hooligans" who riot and protest against the environmental abuses fostered and supported by certain WTO policies, might be seen in the light of freedom fighters, not only engaging in self-defense, but even in the defense of our common humanity and our common rights (Gilbert, 1994). The character of *jus cogens* norms is precisely that of providing the strongest possible citadel in defense of humanity; their role is to rise above the economic and power interests of various states, that could band together (and often do), for purposes that conflict with the respect due to all humans.

Hence, *jus cogens* norms are uniquely apt to provide and defend substantive global justice beyond the purely procedural emphasis present in many other legal instruments. Bassiouni says: "The term *jus cogens* means "the compelling law" and as such a *jus cogens* norm holds the highest hierarchical position among all other norms and principles" (Bassiouni, 1996:67).

I believe that the Article 19 of the 1996 ILC Draft here cited, despite its demise in the 2000 Draft of that document, remains an important, landmark document, at least through the discussions of that article by leading publicists, such as those cited in the collection of articles on *International Crimes of States*, edited by Weiler, Cassese, and Spinedi (1989). Hence, I believe that doing away with the language of Article 19, especially with the distinction it proposes between crimes and delicts, does not succeed in eliminating either the realities Article 19 intended to address, or the difficulties posed by them, and the learned debates on all these issues. In fact, Chapter III (ILC, 2000), "Serious breaches of essential obligations to the international community," reintroduces the difference in kind between certain sorts of breaches of international obligations and others (described in Article 19), by the "back door," so to speak, as we see in the language of Articles 41 and 42:

Article 41—Applications of this Chapter

1. This Chapter applies to the international responsibility arising from an internationally wrongful act that constitutes a serious breach by a State of an obligation owed to the international community as a whole and essential for the protection of its fundamental interests.

2. A breach of such an obligation is serious if it involves a gross or systematic failure by the responsible State to fulfill the obligation, risking substantial harm to the fundamental interests protected thereby.

Article 42 [51, 53]—Consequences of serious breaches of obligations to the international community as a whole

1. A serious breach within the meaning of Article 41 may involve, for the responsible State, damages reflecting the gravity of the breach.

2. It entails, for all other States, the following obligations:

    (a) Not to recognize as lawful the situation created by the breach;

    (b) Not to render aid or assistance to the responsible State in maintaining the situation so created;

    (c) To cooperate as far as possible to bring the breach to an end.

3. This article is without prejudice to the consequences referred to in Chapter II and to such further consequences that a breach to which this Chapter applies may entail under international law.

The language of either article can be interpreted to say, more vaguely and imprecisely perhaps, and in the context of consequences, rather than through the description of examples, what the former Article 19 said, more explicitly and clearly, although Rapporteur Crawford may disagree with this assessment. Chapter II, in turn, describes the "Forms of reparation," for "internationally wrongful acts," and names "restitution, compensation, and satisfaction" (Article 35) as constituting, singly or "in combination," "full reparation." But when we turn to the articles listed above, the language used is different in kind, not degree, between "breaches of an international obligation," and "serious breaches of essential obligations to the international community as a whole and essential for the protection of its fundamental interests" (Article 41). Article 42 adds that, the "damages" assessed should reflect "the gravity of the breach."

I find it hard to accept that the different language addresses simply differences of degree, on a continuum. It does not seem to be the case that one sort of language refers to—say—economic damages under $1 million, the other, economic damages over that limit. The international community as a whole can only be affected in a way that makes it reasonable and appropriate for them to react as a whole. It is unlikely that a scenario can be found that shows economic damages to support such an even-handed, global response. The difference we are trying to pinpoint, may be one between "subjectively injured," and "objectively injured" states (Dupuy, 1989:180).

An example may be that of massive pollution of the Mediterranean basin: Mediterranean states are directly injured, but the "objective interests" of countries as far away as Australia or New Zealand ensures that they, too, will feel and be "indirectly injured" (Spinedi, 1989:247, citing Sir Ian Sinclair).

This is a good example, because the converse was true about the *Nuclear Tests* case (Australia v. France, (1974) I.C.J. Rep. 253; and New Zealand v. France, (1974) I.C.J. Rep. 457). Both of these reflect the interests of a much wider constituency than that of the immediately and directly affected states.

Like aggression or genocide, both of which represent the most widely accepted, least controversial forms of these sorts of injuries affecting the international community, I argue that grave environmental pollution (in the quantitative or qualitative sense, as we will see below), should indeed be treated as a crime, whether or not the term "crime" is present in the language of any international law instrument.

The 2000 iteration of The International Law Commission has eliminated the language, but retained some of the approaches and the distinctions in Articles 41 and 42 (above). That is why placing all these internationally wrongful acts in the same category, the one that contravenes *jus cogens* norms, makes good sense: the effects of widespread environmental pollution, climate change, nuclear threats, food and water scarcity or contamination, share the characteristics of doing injury to the most basic human rights in all States, and evoking widespread global condemnation.

Alain Pellet notes that not only is there a difference of degree between what can be termed a delict and what must be termed a crime, but there may also be a difference in kind between some illicit acts and others: "Malgré une thèse souvant soutenue, il n'y a pas la une simple différence de degré entre ces deux categories de faits internationalement illicites, mais, bel et bien, une différence de nature" (Pellet, 1997:291). Pellet explains further that it is more than the society of states that is affected, it is a question of affecting humanity as such. And this is more than a theoretical argument, it is necessary to recognize the difference between an act of genocide and a "banale" violation of a commercial treaty's clause, a dispute between two states. It is the former, not the latter, that primarily has "humanity" as its target.

There are indeed differences between illicit acts that can be termed delicts, and crimes. Only the latter run counter to nonderogable norms; hence, only illicit acts of extreme gravity will fit this understanding. Yet, even Pellet recognizes the flaws in the list of examples provided in former Article 19.3. Most of them are questionable, Pellet argues, because the concepts used are "open and indeterminate":

> . . . les examples données font appel à des concepts eux-mêmes largement ouvert et indéterminés: violations "grave" (quantitativement ou qualitativement?); violations "à une large échelle"; obligations "d'une importance essentielle"; "aggression" (aggression armée ou également aggression economique?) (Pellet, 1997:298).

No doubt the specifics are insufficient and do not add the clarity required in such a foundational distinction. But we must consider the spirit as well as the letter of the relationship between the concept of crime and that of *jus cogens*, keeping in mind both Article 53 and Article 64 of the Vienna Convention of the Law of Treaties (1969, in force 1980).

When Pellet wholeheartedly approves of the distinction between crimes and delicts, he appears to have in mind the preeminent position of international crimes, as breaches of human rights in relation to other wrongful acts. Lauterpacht for instance, speaks of the Nuremberg Tribunal, as "the basis of codification of international law on the subject": "In an indirect but compelling manner the enactment of "crimes against humanity" constitutes the recognition of fundamental human rights, superior to the law of the Sovereign State (Lauterpacht, 1968:38). Lauterpacht also considers the role of the Security Council (Chapter VI and Chapter VII of the Charter), in order to understand the relationship between human rights and peace.

The correlation between peace and observance of fundamental human rights is not a generally recognized fact. The circumstances that the legal duty to respect fundamental human rights has become part and parcel or the new international system upon which peace depends, adds emphasis to that ultimate connection (Lauterpacht, 1968:186).

Speaking of the "General Principles of Humanitarian Law," Brownlie remarks upon the repeated appearance of this concept, for instance, in the *Nicaragua v.*

United States of America case (1986 I.C.J. 14) (six passages in the judgment) (Brownlie, 1998:14). It is worth citing the court's interpretation of the collective right to self-defense (Article 51 of the Charter);

> . . . [with] regard to the existence of the right of self-defense and in particular collective self-defense], the Court . . . notes that in the language of *Article* 51 of the United Nations Charter, the inherent right (or "droit naturel") which any State possesses in the event of an armed attack covers both collective and individual self-defense (at para. 102).

Particularly significant from the point of view of our argument, is the dubious translation of "droit naturel," easily understood as "natural right," as "inherent right" instead. The right to self-defense is one of the cornerstones of natural law (see Chapter 1), and perhaps the translation used is intended to disguise the presence of natural law in humanitarian law theory. This switch begs the question: if the right to defend myself inheres to me (or to a state), why is this the case, unless the argument of natural law supports self-defense, by providing the principle upon which it is based. Brownlie also notes that "there is an incremental progression toward an *actio popularis*," although even the presence or an obligation *erga omnes* may not be sufficient for the court to take action. In the *East Timor* case (1995 I.C.J. 90):

> . . . In the court's view, Portugal's assertion that the rights of peoples to self-determination as it evolved from the Charter, and from United Nations practice, has an *erga omnes* character, is irreproachable. However, the court considers that the *erga omnes* character or a norm and the rule of consent to jurisdiction are two different things (1995 I.C.J. 90, at 102, para. 29; Brownlie, 1998:77).

This point indicates just how problematic is the actual implementation of human rights protection, and we will consider this question in detail below. For now, we note the existence of another clear crime, accepted as such, and distinct from what Pellet terms "banale" disagreements between two states.

The existing literature on crimes under international law shows a difference in emphasis between those who see *jus cogens* norms as based on universal principles, such as those of natural law (Ragazzi, 1997), and others, such as Brownlie, who appear to emphasize the procedural aspects of these breaches of international law. Speaking of the laws of war, and of the Hague Convention of 1907 concerned with just war, and the 1949 Geneva Conventions IV (Civilians) and the punishment of those responsible Brownlie says:

> This is often expressed as an acceptance of the principle of universality, but this is not strictly correct since what is punished is the breach of international law . . . and the case is thus different from the punishment

under national law of acts in respect of which international law gives a liberty to all states to punish, but does not itself declare criminal (Brownlie, 1979:305).

I believe that Brownlie envisages "crimes against humanity" in the context of war or genocide, so that it might be difficulty for him to agree with the "extension" to "ecocrimes" for which I have argued under that same category, although these crimes can and do occur in peace time.

Although Alain Pellet's analysis does not refer specifically to environmental crimes, his position is closer to the intent of this work. Connecting delicts with civil considerations and crimes with penal ones, seems to be a step in the right direction (Pellet, 1998:303), although Pellet warns that one should not confuse domestic law categories with international ones (Pellet, 1998:306).

The legal consequences also help to understand the difference between delicts and crimes in public international law. Examples of consequences might be the presence of punitive damages for crimes but not for delicts (1996 ILC Article 42), or the requirement to restore the status *ex quo ante*, or *restitutio in integrum* (1996 ILC, Article 45), or even the general requirement to give full assurances or guarantees that the act will not be repeated (1996 ILC Article 46). Another consequence of real crime is that the state becomes transparent and the agents through whom the illicit act was committed (Pellet says, ". . . les agents par lequels il a agi (et/ou qui ont agi sous son couvert) voient leur résponsibilité individuelle engagée sans qu' ils puissent se prévaloir de leur qualité officielle" (Pellet, 1997:311).

Finally, even the discovery and indictment of the responsible agents, does not free the state itself from its own responsibility for the act (Ibid.) All these consequences, as well as the examples intended to clarify the nature of the acts themselves, distinguish delicts from crimes, as Pellet argues. Responsibility is at "the heart" of the international community.

Pellet advances a final argument in support of his position on the necessity for the concept of crimes, one that ties in with our position on corporate and government complicity in institutional violence, and with our hope to find some new remedy through international laws on crime. Pellet believes that the concept of crime at this level, might help to strengthen the present weak constraints imposed on the most powerful states (Ibid.); and—I would add—on the most powerful transnational institutions as well, and we will consider useful strategies to promote change, in the next chapter. Pellet says: "Ils sont le minimum sur lequel la communauté internationale ne peut transiger, sauf à perdre le peu de cohésion acquise au cours des siècles et qui demeure fragile et fragmentaire" (Pellet, 1997:315).

Once again, eliminating the language does not eliminate (1) the difference between categories of internationally wrongful acts any more than it does away with (2) the way these grave or serious acts are viewed and treated by the international community. It does even less to change the way this category of offenses ought to be treated. At the start of this chapter, the way international law is formed and applied was discussed, citing Article 38(1) of the Statute of the International Court of Justice: (1) international conventions; (2) international customary law; (3) general principles of law (4) judicial decisions and the work of highly qualified publicists (above) although (4) represents more a subsidiary means of determining the sources of law or of law-creating processes, rather than being a direct source, as such. It is clear that at least the last three sources maintain and support the difference between kinds of internationally wrongful acts, and, as we saw, the first source, while no longer obviously stating the existence of that difference, supports it in the way it treats the consequences of the sorts of acts which the whole community views as serious or grave. Spinedi says:

> There is not yet general agreement concerning the existent *lex lata* of other special legal consequences attaching to particularly serious wrongful acts, besides the right to take measures provided by the UN Charter. However, the opinion according to which international customary law already recognizes the existence of wrongful acts which affect all States and entitle them to react, is gaining wider and wider acceptance both in socialist, western and third world countries (Spinedi, 1989:246).

Spinedi adds (in the context of the previous presence of Article 19), that "most of the objection" to the possible existence of state crimes that injure all states, stems from the concern that the appropriate reaction to these crimes may be misunderstood. Their existence does not entitle all states to engage in reprisals: it simply affirms the right of all states, "whether directly injured or not," to claim, "before an international tribunal. . . the cessation of the wrongful act, the *restitutio in pristinum* (when possible) and the adoption of measures apt to prevent the repetition of the breach" (Spinedi, 1989:247).

No doubt there are those who disagree. For instance McCaffrey sees no need for a difference in kind between wrongful acts, supporting different forms of responsibility. He views these differences simply as differences of degree, "on a continuum" (McCaffrey, 1989:249). In contrast, De Fiumel says: "I believe that the notion of international crimes of State is so important that it should be set within the strictest framework possible" (De Fiumel, 1989:251). Roberto Ago, in turn, argues, in "The Concept of International Community as a Whole: a Guarantee to the Notion of State Crime?" that the main question is the related one of "who is to decide when a rule is one of *jus cogens*." He says that specificity is required on the question of these crimes: "First of all it must be clear that the *opinio juris* of all the essential parts of the world today agree that there is an international crime (for instance, that genocide, or acts of aggression, are international crimes, is something I feel we can be sure about)" (Ago, 1989:253). Finally, still on the debate in regard to the former Article 19, B. Graefrath acknowledges that "we are forced to think not only in bilateral terms, but very much in community terms, whether we want to or not" (Graefrath, 1989:254). Once again, this passage emphasizes the presence of *erga omnes* obligations, but also of the development of *jus cogens* norms. Graefrath addresses the question:

> Another important step is that we try to protect certain basic values, and that is, I think, the main idea behind singling out some grave violations that are now called crimes. They are called crimes in connection with terminology that has existed 40 years or more; the ILC merely relied on a language that was already *common* and *was used in international instruments* (emphasis added; Graefrath, 1989:254).

The depth, hence the importance of Graefrath's argument cannot be overstated. Legal instruments, clearly, are work-in-progress. They are intended, *inter alia*, to codify the protection of the basic values here referred to. But the existence of basic values and norms does not necessarily and immediately produce the regimes and instruments required for their implementation: "There is always a certain gap between rules and reality" (Graefrath, 1989:255).

Hence, I strongly believe that the latest iteration of the ILC Draft Articles (2000) and the exclusion of the explicit (though imprecise), language of Article 19, does not represent a positive step in the development of the "implementation process" to which Graefrath refers, but represents instead an unfortunate step back, that further confuses an admittedly difficult issue. The elimination of Article 19 does not advance the project to be more effective than it has in the past (Ibid.).

From the standpoint of the argument of this work, the next sections will attempt to show that ecoviolence "should be viewed in the same light as the unequivocal crimes of 'genocide,' 'attacks against the human person,' and all forms of unprovoked and unjustified 'aggression.'" The clear condemnation of all these internationally wrongful acts will then support my conclusions in regard to environmental offenses, if that case can be made.

In addition, one can consider as a very positive development, the emergence of an International Criminal Court (ICC), although the court is concerned primarily with acts of individuals, not states. Williams says:

> An independent, just and effective international criminal court (ICC) is an imperative for the twenty-first century. The ICC will have jurisdiction over most serious international crimes. Its value is not only in prosecuting and punishing perpetrators of crimes, such as genocide, war crimes, crimes against humanity and potentially aggression, but in its deterrence capability (Williams, 1998:23).

Neither in this work, nor in the Rome Statute of the International Criminal Court (1998), is there a clear reference to the environment (except in the context of "War Crimes").

The Preamble refers to a "shared heritage" and the concern "that this delicate mosaic may be shattered at any time." It also mention "the use of force against the territorial integrity . . . of any State," and even "the well-being of the world." Hence, the language of the Preamble can be viewed as potentially inclusive of ecocrime, if the "shared heritage" includes the natural systems on which we depend; if "integrity" is also understood in its qualitative as well as its quantitative sense, and if the "well-being of the world" also means, as it should, available safe water, air, and food. None of these "extensions" appear to stretch too far the meaning of the Preamble's major points.

Ellen Hey notes that:

[the] International legal system . . . has not been amended to accommodate to the societal changes that evolved during the second half of the 20th century. These changes are best characterized by the terms "globalization," "interdependence" and "transnational relations" (Hey, 2000:26).

Yet, despite the importance of the environmental issues that continue to emerge, Hey does not believe that "an international environmental court" would solve all the problems that face us; however, A. Postiglione, for instance disagrees (Postiglione, 2001). I believe that the answer is to be found first in the ratification of the ICC, which came into force in July 2002 as more than "60 States have ratified it" (as of March 2004, 93 states have ratified it) (Williams, 1998:29). The next chapter will examine international environmental law in detail. For now, although it is not in force at this time, the ICC appear to represent the best hope to deal with ecocrime in the future, although its present statute does not include environmental crimes.

The next question remains: is it right to advance the claim that ecocrimes ought to be elevated to this highest level? I believe that there are sound reasons for advancing this claim, and I will present my reasons below, under six headings:

4.a Ecocrimes as a Form of Unprovoked Aggression (see Chapter 1, Barash, 1998);

4.b Ecocrimes as Attacks on the Human Person (see Chapter 2; Soskolne and Bertollini, 1999; McMichael, 1995; McMichael, 2000);

4.c Ecocrimes as a Form of Genocide (Schabas, 2000; Westra, 1998);

4.d Ecocrimes as a Breach of Global Security (Homer-Dixon, 1996; Homer-Dixon, 1999);

4.e Ecocrimes as Attacks on the Human Environment (Noss and Cooperrider, 1994; Karr, 1999; Karr, 2000; Westra, 1998);

4.f Ecocrimes as Breaches of Global Justice (Rees, 2000; Brown, 2000; Brown, 2002; Westra and Lawson, 2001; D'Amato, 1990; Brown-Weiss, 1990).

a. Ecocrimes as a Form of Unprovoked Aggression

We noted in Chapter 1 that, just as human rights instruments start from a serious consideration of armed conflicts and the crimes that are perpetrated in the pursuit of some other goal (for instance "war necessity," and deal with the respective treatment of "combatants" and of "civilians") (Nagel, 1974; Hare, 1974), so too a parallel argument was proposed, characterizing environmental "regulatory offenses" as "ecocrimes," often committed in the pursuit of other goals and "necessities," such as economic advantage, or even "progress." What makes a war crime, according to *jus in bello*, is a practice that offends the dignity of all human beings, without consideration of race, religion or political affiliation. But often these war crimes manifest a component absent from ecocrime: that of deliberate intent, and this is true of genocide as well, as I will argue below, and the same could be said of crimes against humanity.

War crimes are aimed, for the most part, at the "enemy." But those who suffer from the consequences of ecocrime are not the enemy, they are fellow human beings, not violent aggressors. This fact separates sharply ecocrime from war-related acts of aggression. However, one could argue that ecocrimes, like breaches of *jus cogens* norms, can be crimes of commission or of omission (Bassiouni, 1996:9). In addition, the general context wherein the ecocrimes take place, that is, outside a possible armed conflict that might be judged to be a just war, means that there can be no possible mitigating circumstances. This fact leaves assaults that may well be committed without full *mens rea*, but they may involve negligence, willful blindness, or contributing causality.

It is important to note that the Charter of the United Nations, in its strong condemnation of the "Use of Force" in Article 2 addresses the question of "threat or use of force" in subsection 4. But in Chapter 1, Article 2(4) addresses the question from the standpoint of "territorial integrity or political independence of any state," and does not indicate concern for any possible violence against the citizens within these states, even if perpetrated or allowed by the states themselves.

In addition, there are some ambiguities in the language of Article 2. For instance, "threat or use of force" may be understood literally, as referring only to armed attacks. But according to Canadian criminal law, assaults may be perpetrated through the use of any weapon, or anything used as such. The argument of Chapter 5 is that environmental regulatory offenses have the character of assaultive crimes, and the argument should be extended to international law. To pursue activities that will deprive citizens of their health, life, or normal functions, is to assault them, hence to apply unwarranted and unconsented force to them.

International law acknowledges by its practices, that punishment may be imposed upon a nation, by economic sanctions, for instance; and the devastating health effects of Western economic sanctions upon civilians in Iraq are a matter of public record. Hence, it can be argued that aggression is a concept that may be understood and fleshed out in various ways.

Another ambiguous expression is "territorial integrity." Because of the obvious relations between territorial integrity and armed aggression, the concept is primarily understood in quantitative terms. From our point of view, the most important sense of the expression is qualitative instead. Attacks on the qualitative integrity of any nation are not obvious: they are insidious, hard to prove, and often manifest a very strange set of circumstances, whereby nonpoint violence is practiced and neither the substances involved, nor the harmful results that follow upon these diffuse activities are readily identifiable. Substance X or Y may well be safe at the level expressed, provided it is the only substance at that location, to which citizens are exposed. Because of cumulative and synergistic exposures (that is, incremental exposure, and exposure in conjunction with substances A, B and C), it is at times extremely hard to find the smoking gun responsible for the harm (McMichael, 1995).

Even harder to fit within the international law scenario, is the fact that, if one waits to see the harmful results of environmental exposure (rather than taking a precautionary approach), it is far too late to redress injuries that have occurred; as even the most generous influx of funds will not turn back the clock to fully restore either the individual bodily integrity of affected citizens, or the ecological integrity of the region or regions of the territory under consideration. This particular aspect of the problem can be approached considering the *Nuclear Tests* cases (see Section 4). In contrast Chapter 6 Article 34 of the U.N. Charter could be interpreted as referring, perhaps indirectly, to the defense of human rights within a state:

> Article 34. The Security Council may investigate any dispute, or any situation which might lead to internal friction or give rise to a dispute in order to determine whether the continuance of the dispute or situation is likely to endanger the maintenance of international peace and security.

In addition, Article 51 of Chapter 7 refers to the "inherent right of individual or collective self-defense," thus distinguishing between unacceptable and acceptable violence, the latter in self-defense, never as a form of unwarranted aggression.

The latter is defined in the Definition of Aggression (1974) along similar lines. It reads, *inter alia*, "the fundamental purposes of the United Nations is to maintain international peace and security and to take effective collective measures for the prevention and removal of threats to the peace, and for the *suppression of acts of aggression*, or other breaches of the peace " (emphasis added). On this question, Article 5 is even clearer. Its intent is not to characterize internal, unjust aggression within states, but it makes two important points. The first is "Aggression gives rise to international responsibility." The other is ". . . that no special advantage resulting from aggression . . . is or shall be recognized as lawful."

The only form of violence that may be considered just is self-defense. Self-defense is also permitted according to natural law theory, provided it remains proportionate to the attack one is repelling. But ecocrimes, exposing humans to unhealthy and hazardous environmental conditions, represent attacks on non-threatening individuals, not on attacking combatants. In such cases, neither rules of war, nor any principle of national or international law could possibly condone inflicting harms upon those who are not harming others. The proscription of aggression is part of the universal moral law, aside from specific treaties among states (Ragazzi, 1997:102). Some believe that "customary international law" underlies peremptory norms (Trumpel and Sands, 1988:364), whereas Bassiouni suggests that *jus cogens* norms are based on natural law (Bassiouni, 1997). Bassiouni appears to be correct, as the argument for universality and underogability supports the absolutes of natural law, beyond the desirability of widespread state approval. In other words, appeals to the moral or natural law, are objective, not subjective as Trumpel and Sands argue, according to their understanding of natural law (Trumpel and Sands, 1988:367).

As H. Lauterpacht argued as early as 1950, "there is nothing inevitably arbitrary about the law of nature. On the contrary, it has been a constant challenge to arbitrariness in the name of what is in the, long run universal, because generally accepted, and commendable to reason and to the nature of man, including his sense of justice" (Lauterpacht, 1968:100).

It is sheer nonsense to reject natural law because of its alleged "religious," hence partisan, point of view. Such a viewpoint ignores clear historical evidence: both Aristotle before Aquinas, and Grotius after him, were supporters of natural law, yet not committed to the Christian faith. Grotius clearly states that natural law "would have a degree of validity even if we should concede . . . that there is no God" (*Proleg.*11; Lauterpacht, 1968:100).

It is so far from being arbitrary, that Aquinas can be termed the first "conscientious objector," on grounds of conscience, not faith, as he firmly believed that the only possible justification for a government's or a sovereign's power, is the good of the governed: all the governed. Failing that, the government's power becomes tyranny; the laws themselves no longer merit that appellation: they become *violentia cuiusdam*, a "somebody's violence," which should not be obeyed. In fact, our obligation, in that case, is to resist such laws and follow our reason and our conscience instead (see Chapter 1).

Lauterpacht adds that, while natural law is not amenable to proofs as precise as those found in support of physics or mathematics, in later times it influenced thinkers as diverse as Hobbes, Locke, and Jefferson. He says:

> The authors of the Declaration of Independence referred to its principles as expressive of self-evident truths. There is, in that confident application of the Euclidean principle of self-evident truths to the notion of natural rights of man as assertion which is far from being arbitrary, of a direct relation between natural rights and scientific laws (Lauterpacht, 1968:101).

The point is that any basic presentation of natural law, aside from possible nuances about other issues, forbids aggression, but permits self-defense, and that is clear in the work of Grotius and Aquinas, and any other natural law scholar. Similarly, in the *Barcelona Traction* case, speaking of obligations *erga omnes*, the International Court of Justice stated:

> such obligations derive, for example in contemporary international law, from the outlawing of acts of aggression, and of genocide, as also from the principle and rules concerning the basic rights of the human person (*Barcelona Traction*, 1970 I.C.J. 34).

Article 34 of the Year 2000 ILC Report on State Responsibility states:

Article 34—Scope of International Obligations Covered by the Part.

1. The obligations of the responsible State set out in this Part may be owed to another State, to several States, or to the international community as a whole, depending on the character and context of the international obligation and on the circumstances of the breach, and irrespective of whether a State is the ultimate beneficiary of the obligation.

As well, in the Corfu Channel case (merits), speaking of the obligation of Albanian authorities to notify British vessels of the presence of mines at sea, the court said:

> Such obligations are based not on *The Hague Convention* of 1907, No.VIII, which is applicable in time of war, but on certain general and well-recognized principles: namely *elementary considerations of humanity* (emphasis added; Corfu Channel case, (1949) 4 I.C.J. Rep. 7).

The language and concepts in these two cases can be taken to be applicable not only to aggression in conflict situations, but also, as we argued in the previous chapters, to ecocrime. This point will be emphasized again in the next section.

b. Ecocrimes as Attacks on the Human Person

There are many ways in which ecoviolence attacks the human person, and we have discussed many of these in the previous chapters. The most pernicious and less visible of all these attacks (see Chapter 2 for a listing of several environmental attacks on the human person), are the ones that interfere with our normal functioning through endocrine disruptors (Colborn et al., 1996). We will return to this theme when we address the question of genocide, below.

At this time, a recent document produced by the WHO (Rome Office) will help situate this question in context (Soskolne and Bertollini, 1999 WHO). In 1995 A. J. McMichael published his seminal work, *Planetary Overload*, following upon the WHO publication, *Our Planet, Our Health* (Report of the WHO Commission on Health and Environment, 1992). In 1997, the WHO (Geneva) also published another document, *Health and Environment in Sustainable Development Five Years After the Earth Charter*. In December 1998, the WHO (Rome Office) convened a workshop based on research of the "Global Ecological Integrity Project" and in 1999 published a document entitled, "Global Ecological Integrity and 'Sustainable Development': Cornerstones of Public Health," in which the main points required to support the claims of this section emerge clearly.

The authors start by explaining both the long-term perspective they take, and the presence of concerns that are "more compelling" in this work, as they state:

> The combination of these circumstances means that the message contained in this document could actually trigger global actions, where previous efforts, whether in the form of conference reports, books, agency reports or movies, did not (WHO, 1999:x).

This "pilot" workshop served to bring together two sciences that had so far been viewed as separate: ecology and public health. In fact, the report admits that, up to that time, "scientists have not systematically linked life-support systems with human health concerns at the global level" (Soskolne and Bertollini, 1999:2). This new focus forced scientists, accustomed to consider public health risk assessment from the standpoint of a specific threat, to evaluate matters from the standpoint of a "scenario based risk assessment as the method conducive to identifying and establishing important ecological connections to human health." The harms described in Chapter 2, are similar to those listed by Karr and Chu (1995) and reported in this document:

Ecological and Biotic Impoverishment, or Loss of Life-Support Systems

1. *Alteration of Earth's Physical and Chemical Systems (Indirect depletion of living systems)*

    Soil depletion
    Degradation of water
    Chemical pollution
    Climate Change, globally
    Alteration of global bio-geo-chemical cycles
 2. *Direct Depletion of Non-human Living Systems*
    Renewable resource depletion
    Crop homogenization
    Habitat destruction and fragmentation
    Extinction
    Diseases, red tides, and pest outbreaks
    Alien taxa (growth of foreign organisms)
 3. *Direct Depletion of Human Living Systems*
    Epidemics
    Emerging and re-emerging diseases
    Reduced quality of life
    Reduced human cultural diversity
    Economic deprivation
    Environmental injustice (WHO, 1999:5).

The WHO document authors explain that this "kind of organization" has distinct advantages, as it permits the following:

(1) It illustrates the breadth of the challenge;
(2) It makes the human-environment connection explicit;
(3) It illustrates the common underpinning of ecological and human health challenges as well as social concerns (WHO, 1999:6).

There are several basic points that emerge from this innovative consideration of ecological systems and human health:

(1) First, both the former and the latter are dependent on the "integrity of ecosystems and the ecosphere";
(2) Most cities and other "urban regions" may support healthy populations, but their health is based on using more "productive," healthier ecosystems elsewhere, that is, these systems are used through the "ecological footprint" of those cities (Rees and Wackernagel, 1996);
(3) The use of far away natural systems described in (2), is not sustainable and many indices describing the state of the biosphere point to the reality of these hazardous circumstances (WHO, 1999:6).

As we acknowledge the connection between environmental disintegrity and health, we can once again briefly sum up some of the hazardous trends discovered and analyzed in this report. Chapter 2 was devoted to a careful listing and analysis of all the attacks on human life and health that occur through the environment. A brief review might be in order at this time. Global climate change aggravates and exacerbates all the hazards listed by Karr and Chu (1995). In essence, what used to be severe storms in the province of Québec, a normal occurrence in winter in an area where snowy weather is the norm, turned in 1999 into an unprecedented ice storm, a major disaster. Our example in Chapter 4, that of the Walkerton, Ontario, e-coli outbreak, was also initiated not only by negligence and multiple system failures, but also by unusually heavy rains that precipitated the problem's occurrence. Soil erosion and floods bring famines especially in the developing countries, where medical and social infrastructures are lacking or minimal, so that a flood in Germany or the Netherlands, cannot be compared in its consequences with the devastating results of a flood in Africa or India.

The risks from UVA/UVB exposure are not limited to rich sunbathers in affluent countries. Inuit people in the Arctic, for instance, suffer a loss of their immune system's ability to protect them because of that exposure. Exposure to radioactive and toxic wastes affect disproportionately the powerful, rich countries in the Northwest and the vulnerable minorities and the people of developing countries who suffer from toxic trade (Westra and Lawson, 2001) and exposure to pesticides and herbicides banned in the Northwest (Shrader-Frechette, 1991). The risks of cancers from these exposure are well-known and documented (Epstein, 1978). But the other risks to reproductive and parenting functions, intelligence and ability to concentrate and—in some cases—to DNA were also listed in Chapter 2.

The point of this litany of disasters and harmful, often irreversible, consequences of multiple exposures, is that they do not arise from mistakes, or occasional culpable errors, but they are accepted as the norm, the results of the normal, legal way of conducting business and regulating technologically advanced life in the 20th and 21st centuries. These assaults are not limited to a specific locale: they appear in various forms and with varying severity everywhere; hence, it appears appropriate to elevate these assaults to the level of international crimes, and to proceed to describe and stigmatize them as such, even if full prosecution of those responsible remains a difficult and debated issue at this time (Ragazzi, 1997:16–17).

c. Ecocrimes as Forms of Genocide

When we consider genocide, we encounter the problem debated in Chapter 5, that of the possible *mens rea* component of the crime. Article II and Article III of the Genocide Convention (1951), define the crime:

> Article II—In the Present Convention, genocide means any of the following acts committed with intent to destroy, in whole or in part, a national, ethnical or religious group, as such:

a) killing members of the group;
b) causing serious bodily or mental harm to members of the group;
c) deliberately inflicting on the group conditions of life calculated to bring about its physical destruction, in whole or in part;
d) imposing measures intended to prevent births within the group;
e) forcibly transferring children of the group to another group.

Article III—The following acts would be punishable:

a) Genocide;
b) Conspiracy to commit genocide;
c) Direct and public incitement to commit genocide;
d) Attempt to commit genocide;
e) Complicity in genocide. (Convention on the Prevention and Punishment of the Crime of Genocide (1951); Schabas, 2000:565).

But, note, crimes against humanity or even against the human person, do not appear to be defined by a specific intent to achieve a certain result. For instance Article II(d) talks about "intending," Article II(c) says, "deliberately inflicting" and the introductory, defining section speaks of the "intent to destroy."

It is therefore clear that genocide is one of the international crimes where intent appears to be required. William Schabas adds: "But in cases that cannot be described as purely accidental, the accused's mental state may be far from totally innocent" (Schabas, 2000:206).

In fact, degrees of culpability may be appropriate in this crime, and the degree of intent may affect the way punishment is meted out. But intent is not the only requirement for the crime of genocide. The Rome Statute of the International Criminal Court (1998), Article 30, declares "that the *mens rea* or mental element of genocide has two components," that is, "knowledge and intent" (Schabas, 2000:207). Perhaps full responsibility and the gravest punishment should be assigned to those with a "plan," a "project" involving a "conspiracy" to commit genocide. It may be best to Cite Article 30 in full:

Article 30—Mental Element

1. Unless otherwise provided a person shall be criminally responsible and liable for punishment for a crime within the jurisdiction of the Court only if the material elements are committed with intent and knowledge.

2. For the purposes of this Article, a person has intent, where:
   (a) In relation to conduct, that person means to engage in that conduct;

(b) In relation to consequence, that person means to cause that consequence *or is aware that it will occur in the ordinary course
of events* (emphasis added);

3. For the purposes of this article, "knowledge" means awareness that
a circumstance exists or that a consequence will occur in the ordinary course of events. "Know" and "Knowingly" shall be construed
accordingly.

An appeal to the crime of genocide appears more tenable when knowledge
of consequences to take place in the natural course of events, is concomitant with
the awareness that whatever consequences will ensue, these will affect a specific
group. Hence, ecocrimes consisting of dumping or otherwise polluting or eliminating natural systems, clean air or water supplies, will best fit the category of
genocide when it is known to the actors that (1) the consequences will affect primarily people in developing countries or people of color in developed Western
countries, and/or (2) the consequences will affect disproportionately, or more
gravely those in developing countries or people of color in the "home" country
from which the activities originate, wherever they are ultimately carried out.

An example of this sort of ecocrime, might be the presence of "toxic trade"
(Gbadegesin, 2001) and the disposal of hazardous material to countries like
Africa, or the results of the activities of Canadian mining companies in the devel-
oping world: "Accidents at Canada-owned mines in just the last five years have
resulted in massive toxic waste spills in Kyrgystan, the Philippines, Guyana and
Spain" (Seck, 1999:139).

If we understand "knowledge" in Article 30, in a sense similar to the knowledge present at least as willful blindness in domestic assault cases (see Chapter
5, especially *Pappajohn*), then we have both a group targeted deliberately, negligently, or through a refusal to accept that consequences will follow, "in the normal course of events." When they are perpetrated by either a state or a corporate
actor, these crimes deserve the gravest punishment applicable, short of death and
life sentences that, unfortunately, cannot be imposed. But, if knowledge and
awareness are at least necessary (if not sufficient) to indicate genocide, then perhaps we may be able to bridge the gap between *mens rea*, or clear intent, and a
simple consideration of the factual consequences of ecocrimes.

In Chapter 4, it was shown that although, for the most part, *mens rea* could
not be proven when regulatory offenses are committed, although these may have
serious environmental consequences and health effects, this lack was insufficient
to eliminate the causal connections between the act, or omission, and the harms
or deaths that ensued.

The need to prove *mens rea* was shown to be particularly relevant in the
Ontario case study discussed (Walkerton case study). The Canadian Charter of

Rights and Freedoms (1982) Section 7 requires protection of vulnerable accused persons, and the protection under this section of such powerful individuals and legal persons as corporations and institutions, we argued, did not fit the spirit of that law, or its intent. When we consider international crimes committed by powerful heads of states, officials or even whole bureaucracies, then it should be even easier to reject any claim of vulnerability, requiring special protection. It is the public at large, and the countries or global citizens that need to be protected, not the accused, whose abuse of power ought to be punished, whatever its motive (see Chapter 1).

Therefore, even if it is hard to pinpoint a motive, other than personal gain in power or other advantage, and a lack of care for the rights of others, we need to consider seriously whether a move to criminalize ecoviolence on a grand scale, as a form of genocide, may be the only way to attempt to protect especially the most vulnerable populations, regardless of the presence of a clear intent or at least motivation. Schabas reports on a number of countries who concurred with the position held by Gerald Fitzmaurice: "Motive was not an essential factor in the penal law of all countries. Motive did not enter into the establishment of the nature of the crime its only importance was in estimating punishment" (Fitzmaurice, UN. Doc. A/C.6/SR.75 (UK); Schabas, 2000:248).

Many other countries concurred that, insofar as genocide is concerned, "motive was of no importance" (Venezuela, U.N. Doc. A/C.6/SR.69); that ". . . to prevent the destruction of those groups, the motive was of no importance" (Norway, U.N. Doc. A/C.6/SR.69); Panama noted that the addition of motive was "unnecessary," "since no provision was made for it in any penal code" (Panama, U.N Doc. A/C.6/SR.75); and Brazil simply noted that "motive" was only relevant "in the penalty phase" (Brazil, U.N. Doc. A/C.6/SR.69); Schabas, 2000:248).

In the Ad Hoc Tribunal for Rwanda case *The Prosecutors v. Jean-Paul Akayesu* (ICTR-96-4-T, Summary of Judgment, Sept. 2, 1998) a clear position on intent is taken at No. 42, where *dolus specialis* is equated to "specific intent": "Genocide is distinct from other crimes inasmuch as it embodies a special intent, or *dolus specialis*. But at No. 44:

> On the issue of determining the offender's specific intent, the Chamber considers that intent is a mental factor which is difficult even impossible to determine. This is the reason why, in the absence of a confession from the accused, his intent can be inferred from a certain number of presumptions of fact.

On the other hand, in the work of the International Criminal Tribunal for the Former Yugoslavia (1995 *Tadic* case No. IT-94-1-AR72, Oct. 2, 1995), although the defense filed a motion "challenging the jurisdiction of the ICTY," "disputed the legality of the establishment of the ICTY by the Security Council" and objected on several other grounds, the Trial Chamber dismissed the motion (Steiner and Alston, 2000:1159). Eventually the Trial Chamber found Tadic guilty on several counts, but it described the law as "quite mixed" with respect to the need to prove "intent," and for the requirement that intent be "inherent in crimes against humanity" (Ibid. at 1171).

Nevertheless, in its judgment of July 15, 1999, the Appellate Chamber "affirmed the convictions of Tadic, while reversing several holdings of the Trial Chamber" (ibid.). From our point of view, the Appeals Chamber, ". . . concluded that Article 5 of the Statute did not require all crimes against humanity to have been committed with a discriminatory intent" (Tadic Appeal Judgment, at 285; Steiner and Alston, 2000:1172).

Another question that must be considered is the question of "command responsibility," discussed earlier in this work, from another perspective (see Chapter 3). For instance, the Annex of the Statute of the International Tribunal, established by the U.N. Security Council, under Chapter VII, for the "serious Violations of International Humanitarian Law (former Yugoslavia)," discusses these issues in Articles 3 and 4. For instance, Article 3(b) conspiracy to commit genocide; (c) direct and public incitement to commit genocide; and (d) complicity in genocide. In addition, "command responsibility" is not limited to humanitarian law:

> Most important, it is found that not only military commanders, but also civilians holding positions of authority, are encompassed by this doctrine. Furthermore, for the attribution of criminal responsibility, not only persons in *de jure* positions of superiority, but also those in such position *de facto*, may be held criminally responsible (Kindred at al., 2000:740).

Hence, both those who commanded and those who carried out the commands resulting in genocide against a whole group or part of one (Annex, Article 4.2.(c) can be viewed as criminal, albeit there might be some mitigating circumstances, especially for those following commands in some cases.

This debate replicates to some extent the questions raised in regard to mens rea in assaults in Canadian domestic laws (see Chapter 5), the presence of "strict liability" in Canadian laws after *Sault Ste. Marie* (see Chapter 5), for the criminal prosecution of environmental regulatory offenses (see Chapter 4), and it appears to support my position that proof of intent should not be required, where objective evidence in clear. In the United States, Pennsylvania for instance, is the only state to incorporate "the Right to a Healthy Environment" in its Constitution (PA. Const. Art.I, § 27; see Chapter 6). It is instructive to cite it in full once again:

Article I, Section 27:

1) The People have a right to clean air, pure water and to the preservation of the natural, scenic, historic and esthetic values of the environment.

2) Pennsylvania's public natural resources are the common property of all the people, including generations yet to come. As Trustee of these resources, the Commonwealth shall ensure and maintain them for the benefit of the people.

In the U.S., environmental crimes, such as felonies and misdemeanors give rise to jail sentences and produce a criminal record, without requiring proof of intent, or *mens rea* (Brown, private communication, Apr. 20, 2001) (see Chapter 6 for a discussion of the Pennsylvania Constitution).

Much more needs to be said on this conflicted topic. For now, there appears to be at least some significant support for the elimination of the "discriminatory intent" requirement in international law for genocide and crimes against humanity. One final point might be useful: although most "environmental justice" prosecutions are not criminal in the United States, one of the major representatives of the movement strongly advocates the elimination of the "intent to discriminate," requirement for all cases of "environmental racism" (Bullard, 1994; Bullard, 1995).

Based on these clarifications, there are two specific forms of ecocrime that can be clearly termed forms of genocide. One is the toxic and chemical waste trade and the other highly hazardous industrial practices that occur routinely in developing countries, many of which would never be permitted in the home states of the institutions whose practices they are. Consider toxic wastes sent to Africa (Gbadegesin, 2001:187) as an example, or the well-documented activities of Royal Dutch Shell Oil in Nigeria's Ogoniland (Westra, 1998:ch.5).

The other form of genocide, far less obvious or visible, was noted at the start of the section on crimes against the human person, the presence of hormone mimics and endocrine disruptors (Colborn et al., 1996). In Chapter 2 we noted the multiple effects these substances have on normal human functions. These effects include alterations to normal reproductive functions. Reproductive anomalies in animals, due to persistent chemicals in their habitat, or to abnormal temperatures, may lead to the predominance of one-gender births (Westra, 1998); in humans there may be reproductive failures and parenting inability. In either case, not only specific individuals and populations may be at risk, but—through DNA mutations—the human race may be at risk as well (Colborn et al., 1996).

d. Ecocrimes as a Breach of Global Security

David Barash writes on peace, but he says: "A central American peasant was quoted in the *New York Times* as saying, "'I am for peace, but not peace with hunger'" (Barash, 1998:130). He follows up this remark with a description of the components of "positive peace":

> The troubling relationship of human beings to their natural environment must also be reworked, perhaps in fundamental ways. A world at peace must be one in which environmental, human rights and economic issues all cohere to foster maximum well-being; ecological harmony cannot realistically be separated from questions of human rights or economic justice (Barash, 1998:130).

Environmental degradation coupled with, and fostered by global climate change engenders agricultural conditions that lead to famine. As Homer-Dixon has shown, environmental threats to security are additional to those discussed so far, and they include threats to "human physical, social and economic well-being" (Homer-Dixon, 1991:76). When certain populations find themselves without the resources desperately needed for their survival, they could engage in aggression to achieve that goal. Examining the causes of violent conflict, Homer-Dixon says: "Environmental change may contribute to conflicts as diverse as war, terrorism, or diplomatic and trade disputes" (Ibid). No state is self-sufficient, and transboundary problems arise because of changing environmental conditions, as an international version of the "problem of the commons" (Hardin, 1968:1243–1248) emerges worldwide. There is abundant scholarly literature on the question of hunger and the morality of imposing famine conditions, particularly to the vulnerable and the innocent, Hugh LaFollette and Larry May say:

> Children are the real victims of world hunger: at least 70 percent of the malnourished people of the world are children. By the best estimates, forty thousand children a day die of starvation (FAO, 1989:5) . . . Unless others provide adequate food water and care, children will suffer and die (WHO, 1974:677–679; LaFollette and May, 1996:70).

In essence, as we saw in Chapter 1, public international law started to define crime against human rights in the context of violent conflict or wars. War is still the locus of unspeakable violence. If environmental conditions are such that people are driven to violence for survival, or by environmental assaults on their life, then that is another way, aside from war itself, where global security may be put at risk. More recent statistics of the consequences of climate change and environmental degradation shows that, according to the United Nations Food and Agriculture Organization, Statistics (FAO), about 35,615 children died from conditions of starvation on September 11, 2001.

Relevant Statistics

- Victims: 35,615 children (source: FAO)
- Where: undeveloped (poor) countries
- Specialty programs: none
- Newspaper articles: none
- Messages from the president: none
- Solidarity actions: none
- Minutes of silence: none
- Rock Concerts: none
- Organized forums: none
- Pope messages: none
- Alert level: zero
- Military mobilization: none

Imagine a "United we stand" effort to eradicate hunger. This lack of commitment on the part of Northwest affluent countries is also emphasized in the work of Pogge on globalization (see Chapter 8; Pogge, 2001).

The connection between environmental degradation and conflict can also be supported by two additional considerations. For instance, colonialism and international post-colonialism, both emphasized the "wants" of European commercial interests, over the "needs" of African people. Omari Kokole pointed out the need to "increase food production in order to reduce the need for food imports, purchased at a high environmental price (export of timber, of incidental crops, of Mazrui's 'dessert and beverages' economies)" (Kokole, 1995:177). As long as foreign interests promote exports geared to their own preferences, there will not be an incentive to treat the African environment in a way that respects its sustainability and the basic requirements of its inhabitants. In addition, many African states bear political divisions and borders that do not respect the natural, clan-based divisions between pastoral and agricultural groups. This causes endless conflicts as it does not respect the traditional lifestyle of different groups and their habitats (Adams, 1995:181). Hence, violence is caused by clashes based on environmental degradation, inducing scarcity, but also by ecologically unsound policies by Northwest institutions (Westra, 1998).

A final consideration unites environmental and specifically war threats that is the presence of nuclear armaments in their whole life-cycle, from cradle to grave. Ragazzi addresses the question of nuclear armaments in connection with the disputes on nuclear testing, as an example of "the relationship between the concept of obligations *erga omnes* and the concept of *jus cogens*" (Ragazzi, 1997:206).

No doubt especially today there are many nonconflictual uses of nuclear power, but the test to which New Zealand and Australia objected involved weapons of war. France argued that because at that time the "community of states as a whole" as required by Article 53 of the Vienna Convention on the Law of Treaties "had not accepted formally the existence of jus cogens norms, therefore it could not accept an appeal based on that argument" (Ragazzi, 1997:208). Yet France had conducted atmospheric nuclear tests from 1966 to 1972, adducing as a justification, that these tests were necessary to bring France's ability to conduct tests exclusively underground to its conclusion (Ragazzi, 1997:173; see also Ragazzi, 1997:173, n.44.).

The main problem faced by Australia and New Zealand was that, while the Moscow Test Ban Treaty (1963); had been in place for a long time and had, by the time Australia and New Zealand brought their case to the International Court, no less than 104 states as signatories (excluding France and China), still it could not be claimed that all states had agreed. However, Australia made the case that its territorial sovereignty had been breached by exposure to nuclear fallout, and New Zealand also asked for "protection of its sovereign rights," including "the right to be free from nuclear tests . . . and to the preservation of the environment" (Ragazzi, 1997:175).

Both states appealed to *erga omnes* obligations, as the preservation of the environment as well as the right to be free from radioactive fallout were listed as rights belonging to "all members of the international community" ("Request for the Indication of Interim Measures of Protection" submitted by the Government of New Zealand," I.C.J. Pleadings, Nuclear Tests (1973 I.C.J. 99, at 135). Neither state believed that the obligations referred to depended on actual proofs of harm. From our standpoint, the indisputable harm arising from exposure to radioactive fallout (Shrader-Frechette, 1982) is sufficient, even before the introduction of the Precautionary Principle ((1992) Agenda 21, Principle XV), to give credence to the claim that this ban was indeed worthy of the status of a peremptory norm, hence that it was not opposable by any state, whether or not it was part to a treaty banning nuclear tests (see Chapter 6).

The *Nuclear Tests* pleadings and the disappointing judgment that ensued (Ragazzi, 1997:174), straddle the line between 4.d "ecocrimes as breaches of global security" and 4.e "ecocrimes as attacks on the human environment," as both New Zealand and Australia indicated indirectly, in the language of their pleadings. Not only tests, but all uses of nuclear power are highly hazardous, hence suspect from our point of view: human mortality and morbidity are expected consequences of any exposure, even aside the use of nuclear weapons in armed conflicts. They are indeed hazardous from "cradle to grave" (Draper, 1991), from the mining of uranium yellow-cake, to all forms of use and manufacture of its products, through the disposal of radwaste even the so-called "low level" radioactive sort, with a half-life of forever in normal human terms (Shrader-Frechette, 1993; Shrader-Frechette, 1997).

e. Ecocrimes as Attacks on the Human Environment

Why should attacks on the human environment, rather than just direct attacks on the human person, be termed crimes? I believe that the simplest answer is that, for humans, like all other animals, our habitat is an absolute requirement for our life and health; it is in fact inseparable from what we are as persons. The Genocide Convention had recognized one aspect of this truth by terming "crimes against peoples" the destruction of cultural icons and symbols of a civilization (in the Secretariat Draft Article 3(e), although this "cultural aspect" of Genocide Convention was rejected by the U.N. General Assembly (UNGA); see also the Rome Statute of the International Criminal Court (1998) Article 8(c)(ii) "War Crimes"). But this makes sense: many people identify with the religious and the cultural symbols of their civilization; to harm or destroy these symbols is to harm or to attempt to destroy them. But the Earth, the living natural systems are humanity's "icons" and "symbols": to destroy the human environment is a form of attack on human populations, even aside from health effects caused thereby. Although, as indicated, by "cultural icons" and symbols of civilization clause was not accepted by the UNGA, the Statute of the International Tribunal for the Former Yugoslavia (14 Hum. Rts. L.J. 211 (1993)), under Article 3, "Violations of the Laws and Customs of War" subsection (d), states: "(d) seizure of, destruction or willful damage done to institutions dedicated to religion, charity and education, the arts and sciences." Thus, the language of this article is quite similar to that of the rejected clause of the Geneva Convention (1949).

But the habitat wherein we dwell is also a basic life necessity: uncontaminated earth, air, and water are as necessary to us as they are to earthworms and insects (Loucks, 2000). We are often reminded that, unlike other creatures, humankind is extremely adaptable: we can survive in more than one habitat, we are not entirely dependent on one area or one region. But this is misleading on several counts. Rees terms humans "patch disturbers" (Rees, 2000). This means that, like certain other species, we tend to disrupt and consume an area, then move on to another region, one that might still provide for our needs. Unfortunately we have literally run out of places to use and destroy. Ecological footprint analysis (Rees and Wackernagel, 1996) indicates that the only way we can continue to maintain (let alone materially improve) our present consumerist lifestyle, is by using areas well outside our living spaces both as "sinks" and "sources" (Rees, 2000). The moral implications of these practices will be the topic of the next section (4.f). It is hard to find these scientific findings and moral indictments in laws that embody parallel principles. Once again, humanitarian law may provide the best starting point to make our case, especially when an instrument designed to indict criminal behavior in conflict situations, explicitly extends its reach. For instance, the "Report of the Secretary-General Under Security Council Resolution 808" (Dec. 5/2504, May 3, 1993, in 14 Hum. Rts. L.J. 1998 (1993)), notes the legal basis of an International Tribunal for the Former Yugoslavia. The language closest to our intent can be found under Chapter II, "Crimes Against Humanity":

47. Crimes against Humanity were first recognized in the Charter and Judgment of the Nuremberg Tribunal, as well as in Law No. 10 of the Control council for Germany. Crimes against humanity are aimed at any civilian population and are prohibited *regardless of whether they are committed in an armed conflict international or internal in character* (emphasis added).

This clause is somewhat ambiguous: is the "regardless" to be applied to the disjunct "international or internal," regarding armed conflicts, or can it be interpreted to apply to the presence (or absence) of an armed conflict as background to these crimes? The latter would be a more helpful interpretation from our point of view, and it seems at least possible to look at this report in this sense.

Aside from considerations about human justice and fairness, the work of conservation biologists has clearly shown that humanity, like all other life on Earth, needs the presence of large wilderness areas (Noss, 1992), in order to sustain all life through the presence of natural services (Daily, 1997). As the work of the WHO shows, all life depends on the presence of healthy natural systems, but also of a certain percentage, and the exact figures are still under debate, as they range from 20 to 50 percent of the Earth's surface, kept as wild and unmanipulated as possible, in order to retain these natural services through the ecological integrity of these areas (Karr and Chu, 1995; Karr and Chu, 1999; Noss and Cooperrider, 1994; Westra, 1998; Pimentel, Westra and Noss, 2000).

It is outside the scope of this work to elaborate on that theme which is well supported by science elsewhere. It is interesting to note that for instance, The Netherlands demonstrates its basic agreement with this position, as its environmental regulations term the "fragmentation of landscapes," a "form of pollution" (Bilthoven, 1996). Those documents state that, not unlike other forms of pollution, or noise, or the presence of chemicals, human health is affected by the fact that all, or most of the Netherlands is "developed" and it is hard to find any area of ecological integrity within it at this time. Hence, there are movements to close roads, in order to ensure that larger areas be left unused by humans, just as it is argued by the "Wildlands Project" in North America in order to restore the presence of megafauna and thus to normalize systemic functions (Noss, 1992).

The existence of these multiple threats, of cumulative and synergistic effects on human health and life, support the argument of this work as a whole: environmental regulatory offenses are not what they are purported to be. Whether directly harmful, as hazardous pollution, contaminated water, air or soils inflicting illness or death on individuals and populations, or indirectly harmful, affecting our habitat in the many ways that undermine life and health (see Chapter 2), the effects are widespread attacks. It is therefore important to elevate such offenses to the level of crimes, especially in public international law, where they can then impose non-derogable duties on all states, for the protection of humanity and life.

f. Ecocrimes as Breaches of Global Justice

Injustice is caused by ecocrimes in several different ways, and each one will be considered in turn: (1) by economic means through the "ecological footprint" of affluent countries; (2) by means of practice that affect disproportionately racial and ethnic groups; and (3) by practices that do not consider the rights of future generations.

(1)—Ecological footprint analysis indicates that, because no area of the world is entirely self-supporting and self-contained, those who are wealthy enough to overconsume, take a portion of the Earth's available resources, and available "sinks" for their wastes, from those who are not able to protect themselves. In essence, it is the "growth" itself, the consumption that is not in line with the total availability of planetary resources, that constitutes the glaring injustice, as those who can afford it, routinely exceed their fair share of the Earth's resources (Rees and Wackernagel, 1996).

Our present global situation can be defined as Rees does, as a "Historic Turning Point," as he points out that the research of Robert Goodland and Herman Daly clearly indicates that "the growth in the energy and national throughput of the world economy cannot be sustained," as we have now reached "an historical turning point in economic development" (Rees, 1998:113; Goodland, 1991; Daly, 1991). Ecological sustainability demands the availability of resources sufficient to "sustain" the growing population, although not necessarily to satisfy all the preferences of those who can afford choice.

Rees adds:

The "ecological footprint" is therefore defined as the area of productive land and water(ecosystems) required on a continuous basis to produce the resources consumed and to assimilate the wastes produced by a defined population, wherever on Earth that land is located(Rees, 1998:115).

Significant goods and services are imported even in productive areas with favorable climates, to sustain the local populations. This means that the actual area utilized is much larger than the one the specific town or city occupies. The difference between the two, that is, the area occupied and the area utilized, becomes more and more significant, the more unproductive the area under consideration. In his previous work, Rees compared Fraser Valley, B.C., an area that "only" requires about 20 times its size for its ecological footprint, and Riga, Latvia, where the requirement exceeded 120 times the city's size, because of its inclement weather and corresponding lack of productivity (Rees and Wackernagel, 1996).

Clearly the resources that are not local, as well as the waste disposal areas that are placed at a distance from the city itself entail that others, living in the additional used areas, will be deprived of their natural capital. The effects of such global "trade," even if compensation is present, are insufficient to retain just allocations, given the resource and space scarcity that afflicts the whole planet. To put this more bluntly, there are not enough available resources to sustain both the lifestyles of Northwest affluent countries, and even a modest "progress" in consumption and standards of living on the part of developing countries.

The crux of the matter is that, in order to serve justice and fairness in the allocation of all natural resources, those who live in the Northwest must resign themselves to accept serious limits to their choices, and even strict retrenchment of their present consumption and development patterns (Westra, 1998). The latter in today's circumstances, must be reinterpreted as intellectual and spiritual development only, as economic development, as argued above, is not sustainable, and it is not just to the overwhelming majority of people in the world who cannot even begin to approximate our use of resources, our consumption, or our unsustainable lifestyle.

If people's economic and social development opportunities is stunted because of our (Northwest) overconsumption and overuse, that is in clear conflict with the International Covenant on Economic, Social and Cultural Rights (1966).

For instance, Part I, Article 2 states:

2. All peoples may, for their own ends freely dispose of their natural wealth and resources without prejudice to any obligations arising out of international economic co-operation, based upon the principle of mutual benefit, and international law. In no case may a people be deprived of its own means of subsistence.

This Covenant entered in force in 1966, that is, many years before full information about what "freely" disposing of "their natural wealth" really meant. Its last sentence is a telling one: there is a clear conflict between the "freedom" to dispose of one's resources—perhaps based on the mistaken belief in their presence in perpetuity—and the reality expressed in the last sentence. You cannot deprive a people of their sustenance, but that is, for the most part, what global trade is doing right now (Rees, 1998; Goodland, 1998).

(2)—The next aspect of "ecocrimes as breaches of global justice," confronts the practices alluded to briefly under the heading of "genocide" and of "attacks against the human person": it is a question of environmental racism versus environmental justice (Bullard, 1995), a perspective not often found in the works of the advocates of "free trade or of "development." The question is who is the recipient of the hazardous conditions that represent the "other side" of the technological and advanced lifestyles of affluent societies: the wastes, the effluents, the risky facilities and operations are most often not in the "backyard" of those who enjoy the benefits. Those who enjoys the so-called benefits of advanced, consumerist lifestyles, are—for the most part—not the people who must live near the factories, the dumps and the recycleries (Gaylord and Bell, 1995).

Nor is the problem only affecting urban minorities in North America. The problem, in all its painful and unfair aspects, is one of global dimensions: toxic trade (Gbadegesin, 2001), hazardous dumping (Kwame-Appiah, 1998), or trade in banned chemicals (Shrader-Frechette, 1991) are present in most developing countries. These countries have become the "sinks," the cesspools and dumping grounds for the refuse of the developed world.

Environmental racism, I have argued, wears many masks and manifests many "faces" (Westra, 1995; Westra and Lawson, 2001). It may show itself as "progress," or as "trade," or even "opportunity for development": in each and every case, the waste, thus the hazard, originates in the Northwest, and is supported by Northwest money. The locations are those where the weak and the vulnerable are forced to coexist with the very substances that will affect their immune systems, ruin their health, and shorten or terminate their lives. This outrage is perpetrated under the guise of trade, while multinational corporations practice the "isolationist strategy" as they effectively "isolate" the moral and legal restraints that pose at least some limits to their activities in the home countries, from the required universal dimensions these limits ought to have in order to support real justice (Shrader-Frechette, 1991). Union Carbide could not and would not do in the United States what it did in Bhopal, India, where both regulatory framework and a strict monitoring system were absent.

Because of their excruciating poverty, and lacking any hope of improving their circumstances, people in developing countries tend to accept any work, no matter how hazardous. But in so doing, not only are unjust hazards imposed upon them (as a "choice" dictated by starvation is no choice), but their freedom is also absent, for the same reason (Shrader-Frechette, 1991). Should they attempt to resist, however, their fate is often immediate, brutal reprisals, and even death, as in the case of the Ogoni in Nigeria (Westra, 1998). Therefore the living conditions imposed upon those who must live near a hazardous operation or waste site are inhuman enough to fit under the conditions that define genocide. Hence, the practices that enforce such choices are criminal and the International Genocide Convention, Article II(c) defines the act: "deliberately inflicting on the group conditions of life calculated to bring about its physical destruction, in whole, or in part."

Unfortunately, the many "masks" behind which environmental racism (to use its most appropriate name) hides, often carry benign, even helpful connotations. But the results exchange the health, the life, and the normal physical functions of impoverished or otherwise weak people of color, for economic or other advantages for the powerful North Europeans and North American people of wealth.

These are the current geographical and ethnic aspects of environmental injustice. But the harms perpetrated do not cease here and now: they often manifest insidious transgenerational effects.

(3)—The final question under this heading is that of intergenerational justice, a question addressed by many in both ethics (Partridge, 1990; DeGeorge, 1981; Parfit, 1984; Westra, 1998), and the law (Brown-Weiss, 1990). Edith Brown-Weiss views duties to future generations as "an obligation *erga omnes*" (Brown-Weiss 1992; D'Amato, 1990). The concept of obligations to future generations is fully entrenched in both ethics discourse and in that of international human rights. Yet the notion is not without serious difficulties: the most notable one among these is the problem of ascribing rights where there is no clearly identifiable or specifiable person or group to which we can point as possessing the rights to which our obligations are correlative (Parfit, 1982; Westra, 1998). In addition, there is a problem not only with the identity and specificity of future persons, but also with their possible existence. "Potential persons" have not fared well in the literature (English, 1975; Warren, 1991; Thomson, 1990); and the rights of nonhuman persons have been found to be equally debatable (Stone, 2000; Regan, 1983). I have argued that, starting from the respect for global nature, ecological integrity helps to reconcile the diffuse respect and responsibility to the future, with the difficulty posed by requirements for specificity (Westra, 1998). Brown-Weiss states: "What is new is that we now have the power to change our global environment irreversibly, with profoundly damaging effects on the robustness and integrity of the planet and the heritage that we pass to future generations (Brown-Weiss, 1990:198). On the basis of this reality, we can revisit the difficulties alluded to by Derek Parfit (1984) and reemphasized by D'Amato (1990).

g. The Future Generations Argument and Parfit's Theory X

Derek Parfit deals at some length with future generations in *Reasons and Persons* (1984), and he encounters serious problems in the attempt, as many others have done. But he starts, it is important to note, with "persons," individuals; hence, he is heir to all the problems that arise through that approach. After proposing, discussing, and ultimately rejecting several theories, he says:

> I am searching for theory X, the new theory about beneficence that both solves the Non-Identity Problem and avoids the Repugnant Conclusion. More generally, theory X would be the best theory about beneficence. It would have acceptable implications when applied to all the choices that we even make those that affect both the identities and the number of future people (Parfit, 1984:405).

In contrast, the approach I propose requires no special consideration of either identities or numbers of future people. It proposes that future generations should be viewed not as an aggregate of individuals but as wholes. This seems appropriate because, particularly from the point of view of environmental considerations usually coupled with future generations issues, the future includes the natural systems, with all their biotic and abiotic components; that is, it must refer to wholes, not just to aggregates or communities of individuals considered singly and apart from their natural habitats.

Concern for the future hinges on the quantity and quality of safe air, water, and land that will be left for all. This clearly includes the continuation of the processes and functions appropriate to the specific landscapes and the changing climates of various futures. And if future generations can be viewed as wholes—that is, not as numbers of individuals or as separate though indeterminate communities of humans—then most of the problems arising from attempting to put faces and numbers on future generations are no longer as damaging to the argument in their support. Future generations must instead be considered as wholes, connected and interdependent with all other future forms of life and with natural processes at future stages of evolution which cannot be clearly defined but must continue to have the undiminished capacity to support life. From this perspective we no longer need to concern ourselves with improbable calculations about their probable "happiness" or "wretchedness," their future wants or preferences. From the integrity perspective, we are concerned with only one major aspect of the problem: the interface between future generations and the natural life-support systems that we leave them. Arguments about how much oil or other resources it would be appropriate for us to use in light of future generations' needs (DeGeorge, 1981), or about whether "future people are different, in morally relevant ways from present people" (Kavka, 1982), or about the importance of "the temporal location of future people or ignorance of them, and the contingence of their existence" (Ibid.) lose much of their significance.

Our primary moral responsibility is to the optimum capacity of natural life support systems. Our present respect and protection is intended precisely to preserve their future evolutionary paths and trajectories, including whatever changes in communities, populations, and interactions these might entail (Kay and Schneider, 1995). Not only is the lack of precision and predictability about the future not a particularly serious problem about "futurity," it is also necessarily accepted as part of "embracing complexity" and of the "ecosystem approach" (ibid). Its central focus remains the "causal necessity of integrity" (Ulanowicz, 1995).

The integrity perspective precludes attempting to predict whether the unmanipulated, evolutionary development of wild areas will lead in specific directions. We do know that these areas, and an attitude toward the Earth that does not conflict with the needs of such areas, are central to our present concerns about human and nonhuman life and health. It is the capacity of these systems to retain an optimum number of choices, based on their temporal and geographical locations, as well as on the information available through the biological diversity appropriate to each system, that is the primary good.

Moreover, we are not expected, in this scenario, to be ideal observers, and either arrange or calculate any future human chance at happiness: our obligation is to preserve our/their life-support systems in perpetuity. This appears to be a less stringent demand than those advocated through other arguments in support of future generations. In contrast, this position demands a much tougher stance now and is ultimately more respectful of all possible future developments and choices. By rigorously forbidding actions that would diminish natural systems' capacities, in essence it does preserve maximum human choice without paternalistic attempts at defining or limiting those choices. As the respect is aimed at all life, this position is neither speciesist nor racist or gender biased: its primary focus is the respect for life in the most general form; yet its mandates are far more restrictive than mandates attempting to "balance" present preferences alone.

We have considered briefly some of the ways in which institutional environmental violence fits within the ambit of internationally proscribed activities, and appears to merit the appellation of crime. The list provided above is not intended to be exhaustive: it simply indicates to some extent the direction required for a new perspective on environmental violence.

5.   A QUESTION OF BASIC RIGHTS

We have appealed to a variety of legal instruments, established for various purposes, but, one and all, in some way intended to protect human rights internationally, that is, reaching beyond the "wall" provided (procedurally) by state sovereignty, and substantively, by such notions as "reasons of state," or "progress," or "national purpose" or even "development." Historically, the first human rights to be protected have been negative rights, the right not to be coerced, or detained illegally, or harmed by their own rulers. Positive rights instead are "enabling" rights, intended to provide persons with ways of flourishing in their own ways (Shue, 1996:182; see Chapter 1).

There is no need to rehash that abundant literature at this time. We are not concerned, at this time, with "claim-rights" (Hohfeld, 1923), or even legal rights, but with the most basic of all human rights, irrespective of nationality, status, or ethnicity. Instead, the basis of this argument is the infinite value of human life in the Kantian sense, and the respect due to everyone. Fernando Tesón says: "The argument for human rights is universal since it is derived from the Kantian Categorical Imperative" (Tesón, 1992:55). Tesón adds that, because of this origin, international law is linked to human rights, "not to national interest, rights of governments, or other notions similarly rooted in the primacy of state sovereignty" (Ibid.). Our main concern then is with those rights that Henry Shue defines as "basic." These are primarily the right to "security," and the right to "subsistence" (Shue, 1996). Rights are correlative to duties, therefore, if it can be established that all are entitled to certain rights, then there are corresponding obligations to ensure they these rights are honored: "Basic rights then, are everyone's minimum reasonable demands upon the rest of humanity" (Shue, 1996:19). These go far beyond the negative rights to noninterference: "The infant and the aged do not need to be assaulted in order to be deprived of health, life or the capacity to enjoy active rights. The classic liberal main prescription for the good life—do not interfere with thy neighbor—is the only poison they need" (Shue, 1996:19). A parallel case can be made for all the vulnerable, disempowered people in developing countries, as well as the poor, and especially minorities, in affluent ones. But according to our evidence, the problem is not only that they are "left alone": it is that they are especially under siege, although we all are to some degree, from multiple sources, and by means of multiple threats. Basic rights are the right to security and the integrity of one's person, and the right, minimally, to subsistence, for Shue (see Chapter 1).

The list of ecocrimes we have described above, threatens the security of persons through attacks that rival deliberate murders, rapes, or beatings in severity. Their integrity (or what I have termed "micro-integrity," (Westra, 1998), refers to the full complement of normal capacities and functions of a human being and freedom from environmentally or industrially caused disease. Subsistence refers to the presence of enough food and water and other necessities of life, and these include: ". . . unpolluted air, unpolluted water, adequate food, adequate clothing, adequate shelter, and minimal preventive public health care" (Shue, 1996:23). These are the essentials of life, and those who have no access to them are in the worst possible position, as Shiva as it, they suffer "absolute poverty" (Shiva, 1989):

> People who lack protection against violations of their physical security can, if they are free, fight back against their attackers or flee, but people who lack essentials such as food, because of causes beyond their control, often can do nothing and are, on their own, utterly helpless (Shue, 1996:25).

Shue argues for "inherent necessities" or "simultaneous necessities," without which all other rights are not only insufficient, but also meaningless: "The enjoyment of the other rights requires a certain degree of physical integrity, which is temporarily undermined or eliminated, by deprivation of security or subsistence" (Shue, 1996:30). Hence, the argument is not that there are international human rights, and also other, separate, different rights, to a protected environment but that the latter is absolutely basic to any other human right of any kind. Therefore security and subsistence rights represent the necessary foundation of civil, political, social, and economic rights.

6. DEALING WITH ECOCRIMES: SOURCES OF INTERNATIONAL LAW

The aim of this chapter is to show why most breaches of environmental regulations should be considered criminal acts until and unless the overwhelming evidence points to the opposite. Article 38.2 surprisingly limits the power of the International Court by the parties' agreement, especially in the context of the Court's power to decide *ex equo et bono*, hence not through something that should be decided by agreement in the case of crimes.

The argument so far has indicated that international conventions, expressly recognized by most states are not enough, and that peremptory norms should guide and prescribe obligations *erga omnes*, as the best way to mitigate and eventually eliminate the tragic consequences of environmental inaction and carelessness. We also need to consider the role of international custom, and judicial decisions, in order to confirm the conclusions tentatively reached so far. It is not sufficient to show that the nature of illicit environmental acts, or even the consequence of lawful acts affecting the environment can, and most often do, produce consequences much closer to large scale attacks, or crimes against humanity, than to what might be expected from breaches of regulatory regimes (see Section 2). It is not even sufficient, although it appears to be necessary, to show the clear connection between environmental crimes and breaches of International instruments designed to defend human rights (see Section 3), and to examine in some detail the dual role of international law as such (see Section 4) finally, even to address state responsibility and the difference between delicts and crimes (see Section 5).

We need now to turn to an additional examination of what is already present in international law regarding the environment (see also Chapter 6), in order to show whether the conclusions reached at this stage are indeed correct, that a radically new way to address environmental issues is absolutely necessary.

a. International Custom Through Cases and Arbitrations

The Stockholm Conference consecrated the ideas among others, that (a) the environment is a global entity to be protected in its entirely (although this does not diminish the importance of particular rules applicable to different sources of pollution and to different components of the environment), and (b) environmental protection is a necessary condition of the promotion of peace, human rights and development (Ragazzi, 1997:154–155).

We should reconsider briefly the three "classic cases" that provide the best sources of international case law in regard to the environment, in addition to the *Nuclear Tests* case. The first of these, in chronological order, as well as in order of importance, is the *Trail Smelter Arbitration* (U.S. v. Canada (1931–1941), 3 R.I.A.A. 1905),where the Tribunal found that:

... no State has the right to use or permit the use of its territory in such a manner as to cause injury by fumes in or to the territory of another or the properties or persons therein, when the case is of serious consequences and the injury is established by clear and convincing evidence.

The language of the Tribunal's judgment is clearly dated, but one may want to apply the findings of this case, where the United States justly sought compensation from Canada, to the present situation where, for instance, "Global warming is a process that is no longer discounted in the international legal system, although the severity of its impact on the Earth is still debated" (Kindred et al., 2000:1017), yet the present U.S. government refuses to take responsibility for its own activities and ratify the Kyoto Protocol (to the United Nations Framework Convention on Climate Change (1997).

The United Nations Framework Convention on Climate Change clearly defines Climate Change, and in Article 1.4 defines "emissions": "'Emissions' means the release of greenhouse gasses and/or their precursors into the atmosphere and their interactions." In principle then, the U.S. refusal to curb its emissions runs counter to the principles and the letter of international law, completely ignoring the import (among other principles) of the Precautionary Principle (Article 15 of the Rio Declaration, (1992). Sharon Williams recognizes that the ". . . holding of the tribunal in *The Trail Smelter Case*, has today become an integral part of international environmental law and can be said to have widespread acceptance by states" (Williams, 1984:246). The language of the *Trail Smelter Arbitration*, however, is even more vague and imprecise than that of former Article 19 (International Law Commission) on "crimes," discussed in the previous section, nor does it take into consideration state responsibility for the "shared resources or the global commons" (Brunnée, 1993:831), as it considers *Trail Smelter* only as a civil case.

The second classic case is the Corfu Channel case (Merits) (U.K. v. Albania, (1949) I.C.J. Rep. 4, 17) Although the case concerns Albanian responsibility for failing (or omitting) to warn British Warships of the presence of mines in its waters, this is not—strictly speaking—an environmental case. But the language of the court can be integrated and extended to continue and support the point made in the *Trail Smelter Arbitration*, about state responsibility. The judgment found the state (Albania) to be responsible, in these words:

Such obligations are based not on the Hague Convention of 1907, No. VIII, which is applicable in time of war, but on certain general and well-recognized principles, namely: elementary considerations of humanity, even more exacting in peace than in war; . . . and every State's *obligation not to allow (knowingly) its territory to be used for acts contrary to the rights of other states* (emphasis added).

This passage establishes the following: (1) that humanitarian considerations are not limited to war circumstances; and (2) that the *Trail Smelter* rule "do no harm" held in this case as well.

The third case, the *Lake Lannoux Arbitration*, completes the trilogy as support for the existence of customary duties to avoid causing transboundary environmental damage and to make reparation for such damage, should it occur (Mickelson, 1993:220).

Together, this trilogy of cases and arbitrations present the main elements in international environmental law that are neither domestic laws nor principles, or rules, or articles taken from various instruments. Using primarily the latter, Mickelson argues that the use of those documents "perpetuates the notion that international environmental law has developed in a virtual vacuum," and that it is, for the most part, "a decontextualized invocation of abstract principles" (Mickelson, 1993:233). Nevertheless, she also claims that this judgment is incorrect, invoking "the rich body of material that does, in fact, exist." I find this statement not to be supported by facts: a survey of much of the major scholarly literature on the topic simply reveals different interpretations or analyses of the same basic cases. These interpretations are indeed "rich" in theoretical arguments, but it is important to note that none of these cases is even remotely applicable to the grave environmental problems we face today: the only one that is truly environmental, the *Trail Smelter Arbitration*, at best, involves economic damages to a specific agricultural community, in a specific area. In addition, the independent research of the International Joint Commission, as well as other factual research upon which the arbitration was based, also cited insect infestations and climate variations as additional contributive causes to the problem (Mickelson, 1993).

The patterns prevailing in current problems, are not present in *Trail Smelter:* that is, considerations of grave ecological disasters with global implications are absent from that Arbitration, so that, in the final analysis, we are only left with one major *principle, sic utere tuo,* as a standard and guide arising from this "case study." Some of the major differences between the situation in the *Trail Smelter* and today's global problems are:

(1) a full comprehension of the scope of the harms imposed (such as the effects of disruptions of ecosystem functions on human health), beyond simple economic consequences;

(2) a full comprehension of the scale of the harms imposed (such as the effects on the ozone layer), with consequences affecting populations far removed from the location of the environmental hazard;

(3) an understanding of the possible mutagenic effects of the harm such as changes in normal human functions and development, affecting even future generations;

(4) an appreciation of the substantive justice issues involved when environmental harms disproportionately affect certain populations more than others;

(5) an appreciation of the need for the Precautionary Principle, when evaluating an activity that might produce environmental harms.

Hence, we can conclude that not only is the case law meager in regard to international environmental law, but it is almost irrelevant with respect to the real issues we face today. One could argue that here are, in addition to the few environmental cases and arbitrations, several international human rights cases, some involving aboriginal peoples (Lubicon Lake Band v. Canada, Communication No. 167/1984; or the ICCPR case Ilmari Lansman et al. v. Finland, Communication No.511/1992: Finland. 08/11/94), where the ostensible primacy of human rights, both of the individuals and of peoples, are indivisible from environmental right. These cases view the environment as a fundamental human right of peoples, because it is basic to aboriginal cultures, not in the physical sense of a necessary basis of all human life, as argued for the most part in this work.

In contrast, other cases heard before the European Court of Human Rights (*Lopez Ostra v. Spain*; *Guerra v. Italy*), come closer to the spirit and the argument of this work and they will be discussed in the Chapter 8.

7. CONCLUSIONS

Obviously the rationale underlying the concepts of *jus cogens* and public order of the international community is the same: because of the decisive importance of certain norms and values to the international community, these norms merit absolute protection and may not be breached by states, whether jointly by derogation right claimed under a treaty, or severally by unilateral legislative or executive action (Meron, 1989:222).

I have argued elsewhere that it is immoral and unjust to speak of the hazardous effects of the modern, affluent lifestyles, as necessarily entailing the harm that is thereby engendered, as there is no necessary connection between consent to the lifestyle, and the passive acceptance of the latter (harmful consequences) (Westra, 1998; Westra, 1997). I will not repeat those arguments here: the basic one is the absence of consent on our part, because of the absence of full information and in many cases, the lack of alternatives (Westra, 1998). We are kept in the dark through corporate trade secrets, deliberate publicity campaigns and marketing that misinforms and other business practices (Korten, 1995). But even if we were to become aware in some manner of what we are exposed to, often in affluent countries, democratic ones even, there are no choices: neither in Canada nor in the United States can one vote against nuclear power, for instance, or factory farming. In developing countries, the hazardous conditions of environmental exposure may well be related to survival through work or even food laced with banned pesticides or other hazardous substance. Again, both of these possibilities, common today, negate consent and acceptance of the hazards.

In addition, for the grave threats present through the large-scale ecological damage which appears to be the norm, even the customary strict liability standard of dealing with environmental harms is grossly inadequate because it allows for a defense of due diligence in contrast with absolute liability that permits no defense (see Chapter 5). Many of the harms listed in Section 4 refer to either irreversible damages or to "incompensable harms," such as the imposition of cancer to infants and children (Shrader-Frechette, 1991). Hence, the present regimes ". . . based on the premise that the covered activities must continue, and the attendant risks can be adequately addressed by way of a compensatory scheme," (Brunnée, 1993:840) are totally insufficient and a radical change is necessary.

It is worth repeating that one of the accepted sources of international law is based on general principles of law accepted by states. Unfortunately as indicated in Chapters 4 and 5, national (Canadian) environmental law is equally prone to compromise, and to the acceptance of vague instruments and standards as we see clearly in their handling of the *Walkerton* case. The argument of this chapter has been that the present instruments of international law dealing with the environment are insufficient and incapable of performing the tasks humanity needs: they cannot protect us and the natural systems that are our necessary habitats. I have proposed that state obligations *erga omnes*, based on *jus cogens* norms, rather than agreements or covenants, should be used in order to attempt to reverse the present highly hazardous trends. The main claim advanced has been that the complexity of our natural systems and the complexity of our new (and untried) technologies combine to result in hugely injurious consequences, many of which are irreversible.

In this scenario, environmental offenses take on the coloration of assaultive crimes, and when they occur on a grand scale, of global crimes against humanity. We need at least to understand the true impact and reach of environmental harms, and then to view them in international law as crimes rather than just delicts, so that even those who are partially responsible, or complicit in some way, can be forced to give guarantees to avoid recurrences, but also to be publicly branded criminally responsible.

Another interesting question that was not fully addressed at this time is whether Ellen Hey's proposal for a special International Environmental Court might help correct the present difficulties. Hey, however recognizes that an environmental court would require a great deal of expertise in many scientific areas, as well as other areas of law (Hey, 2000:8). This possibility will be discussed below when we address the practical implications of the proposal to criminalize environmental offenses (Postiglione, 2001). For now, it is important to acknowledge the presence of other options, other possibilities that might serve to mitigate the problems many international law scholars acknowledge, and that have been discussed in this chapter.

The arguments for criminalizing environmental offenses are several, as we have seen, but the major difficulties relate on practical grounds, to the desire of states to limit economic exposure by not specifying clear enough standards, or expecting appropriate compensation, let alone assurances that the noxious activities (some of which are perfectly legal, as in *Rylands v. Fletcher*), will not be repeated. Yet, if these questions are left to be addressed by treaties, these might well be ignored by some of the most powerful players, as the Kyoto Protocol is not ratified or honored by the present U.S. administration. The Union of Concerned Scientists speculates on several possible scenarios that might develop in that regard. The United States might pretend to agree, but string out the time of negotiations; or they might propose "concessions they know the Europeans and other countries won't (and shouldn't) accept, with the intent not of reaching a deal, but of shifting the blame for the breakdown in the negotiations" (Meyer, 2001:8). In contrast, another possibility might be that if other countries including the European Union, should go ahead with the Tokyo agreement without the United States, big transnationals would then bring pressure to bear on the United States because of their preference for homogenized global trade conditions.

Hence, without denying the possibility of other options, this work simply suggests that to elevate environmental offenses to the status of international crimes under the headings explored in Section 4, might be a step in the right direction. Other possibilities will be discussed in the next chapter, as well as the possible role of the International Criminal Court, the example of the EU as well as other United Nations instruments including the Earth Charter (see Appendix 1).

All this chapter intended to achieve was to show why activities that are presently treated as regulatory offenses (1) have the character of violent crimes, but are not treated accordingly; (2) appear to have been left largely unregulated and uncontrolled thus far; and (3) do not appear to have any assured mitigation or—better yet—elimination, under the present "compromise and compliance" regimes. Aside from these practical reasons, environmental offenses are wrong on moral grounds. Hence, I have argued, it is appropriate that they should be proscribed by *jus cogens* norms, as these are based on principle, and as such they support *erga omnes* obligations, and they should not require multinational agreement to be justifiable. On grounds of principle and of equity, this shift of focus appears to yield better possibilities of success, as I attempted to show.

CHAPTER 8
FROM THEORY TO PRACTICE

PART A: SOME OBSTACLES TO SUPRANATIONAL AND INTERNATIONAL GOVERNANCE

1. A REVIEW OF SOME OBSTACLES

In order to protect the biosphere, we can make provisions for the power of sanctions to be exercised by a specific institution. This was provided for in the Declaration adopted by twenty-four States at the Hague on April 3, 1989. Having taken as their motto "My country is the planet," they studied the idea of an authority endowed with superstate powers capable of directing policies and responsible not only for controlling the conduct of States, but also for taking sanctions against those who violate the fundamental principles that are the basis of respect for the global environment. Such an approach is not possible without acknowledging that humankind has a right to integrity and, in the end, to survival (Dupuy, 1991:204).

This lengthy quote is exceptionally appropriate to introduce the last chapter of this work. So far we have shown why (1) ecological harms are equivalent to assaults resulting in harms to health and life; (2) why the nature of the harms indicates the need to view them as crimes, akin to other "attacks on the human person," "crimes against humanity" or even, in some cases, as "genocide"; (3) why the nature and the scope of domestic (common) law is insufficient to address the problems in (1) and (2); and (4) why we need an international law regime, giving rise to one or more supranational entities, capable of achieving at least a parity of power with such regulatory bodies as the WTO, NAFTA and all instruments whose primary goal is so-called "free trade" (Strong, 2000; see Chapter 7).

In this chapter we hope to discover a possible path to sounder environmental practices to protect life, globally. First, we must consider the obstacles to be overcome to achieve this overall goal. Then we must turn to the consideration of possible regimes for environmental agreements, and to the study of existing examples of supranational organizations such as the EU, as a template of legal institutions to come.

In the previous chapters, the focus of the discussion was a twofold one: (1) the criminal aspects of environmental harms, and (2) the difficulty of coping with this factor within the Canadian domestic (common) law. In Chapter 2, we proposed the use of analogy to move towards more progressive case law, and noted some interesting developments arising primarily from judicial decisions in the area of sexual assaults and in that of the protection of human health. Both broad categories have also been argued for on the grounds of individual and collective moral responsibility. Considering the difficulties encountered in attempting to indict the institutionalized, systemic violence that characterizes much of the harms caused by environmentally unsound practices, should help to isolate some of the major obstacles to overcome.

The first obstacle has not arisen in previous discussions: it is the question of jurisdiction. Although the problem has not been addressed before, it must be addressed before any conclusion can be reached. The other major obstacle in both domestic (common) law and international instruments, is the domination of the economic motive, culminating in the decisions of institutions like the WTO (see Chapter 6). The economic domination of certain countries and "blocks" of rich nations can be viewed as the major obstacle faced by environmentally sound regulations, and even more, by the hope for environmentally concerned compliance with existing instruments. This is also the most serious block to North/South cooperation, in itself a grave block to international comity.

The stark contrast between economic interests and ecological conscience is obvious and compelling. It dominates all aspects of state and nonstate interaction as noted by Dr. James Orbinski (1999 President of Médicins Sans Frontieres) when he said, "The law that privileges property over the right to exist is an outrage" (Orbinski, in lecture, Osgoode Hall Law School, April 2, 2002).

Domestic regulations are also influenced by political regimes and their constituents and supporters, especially in the affluent North American democracies. They are also complemented by a general attitude favorable to self-regulation, and the quest for managerial and procedural, rather than substantive environmental standards (Plus 1162, ISO 14001 and Compliance in Canada, 2002). This attitude is coupled with a determined emphasis on consensus building, rather than on responsibility ascription and prosecution (Downs et al., 1996; Koskenniemi, 1992; Handl, 1997; Chayes, et al., 1995, Falk, 1998).

The third obstacle follows upon the second and is equally political in tone: the very language and composition of regulations, both in the domestic and the international realm, reflect the concern to permit business to operate with minimal controls and restraints, although in international regimes these regulatory instruments are clearly debated and negotiated, unlike their domestic counterparts. Even when Preambles and other Statements (see CEPA, 1999, Chapter 4) sound a strong note in favor of ecological and health controls, the reality is a collection of low-key or nonenforceable articles most of which lack the teeth required to protect human and ecological health. We will need to consider all these obstacles before turning to possible ways of overcoming them through the law. A fourth obstacle is the difficulty of restraining, limiting, or even prohibiting legal activities that cause harm. From the legal point of view, our first concern is the question of jurisdiction, and that will be the topic of the next section.

a. A Question of Jurisdiction: Environmental Harms, Human Rights, and the "Juridical Deficit"

. . . On February 28, 2002. . . . Judge Wood's opinion found that plaintiffs' allegations met the requirements for claims under the *Alien Torts Claim Act*, in that the actions of Royal Dutch Shell and Anderson constituted participation in crimes against humanity, torture, summary execution, arbitrary detention, cruel, inhuman and degrading treatment and other violations of international law (Feb. 28, 2002, Wiwa v. Royal Dutch Petroleum Co.).

Environmental harms/human rights violations are hard to place and prosecute from the standpoint of jurisdiction: are we to consider the nationality of all those affected? Or are we to consider all those who contribute to the harms, including both complicit states and corporate bodies and including diversely incorporated companies, within a multinational corporate empire? And how is a diffuse harm, originating from multiple actors, to be analyzed in terms of the three aspects of jurisdiction: (1) jurisdiction to prescribe;(2) jurisdiction to adjudicate; and (3) jurisdiction to enforce (Bederman, 2001:176)?

The first raises the question of which court, hence which state may have the authority "to prescribe rules that impact the conduct and behavior of individuals" outside its own national borders. The second addresses the most obvious aspect of the problem: which state has the right to rule on a matter in a specific dispute that might have taken place outside its borders, and might not have caused harm to its own citizens. The third raises an even harder question (in practice): even winning a case and receiving a favorable judgment, leaves unanswered the question of how to enforce a court's decree (Ibid.). The problem is exacerbated because, following the changes in human rights, international humanitarian, and economic law, international organizations and even individuals (both biological and juridical) "have attained some measure of international legal personality" (Kindred et al., 2000:11). Bederman analyzes these aspects of "jurisdictional problems," from the starting point of the Lotus Presumption (that is, allowing states "to assert jurisdiction to the maximum limits allowed") (Bederman, 2001:173), in the light of U.S. law, especially the *1978 Restatement (Third) of the Foreign Relations Law of the United States*, Section 403. The paramount role of several standards emerges from the criteria listed, that is, the need to use what is "most reasonable," (only with respect to (2 above)), "comity," and the balancing of interests, before applying the doctrine of *forum non conveniens* (Bederman, 2001:179). One of the most recent and important examples of unclear and conflicted jurisdiction is apparently being addressed and is on the way to being "resolved" in the United States, in the case cited at the beginning of this section.

In the Opinion and Order (2002 U.S. Dist. Lexis 3293, Feb. 22, 2002), Judge Kimba Wood addresses the question of jurisdiction and gives the disposition of the case:

> Plaintiffs filed the first action against the corporate defendants on November 6, 2996 and filed an amended complaint on April 29, 1997. By order dated September 25, 1998 ["1998 Order"], the Court found that the corporate defendents were subject to personal jurisdiction in New York [2], but dismissed plaintiffs' amended complaint on forum non conveniens grounds. On appeal, the second Circuit Court affirmed that the corporate defendants were subject to personal jurisdiction, but reversed the Court's forum non conveniens dismissal and remanded the action for further proceedings. See Wiwa v. Royal Dutch Petroleum Company et al., 226 F.3d 88 (2d Cir. 2000). Plaintiffs filed a new action against Brian Andersonon March 5, 2001.

> Presently before the Court are: (1) defendant's motion to dismiss the actions for lack of subject matter jurisdiction; (2) defendant's motion to dismiss claims for failure to state a claim for which relief may be granted; (3) defendant's motion to abstain on the basis of act of state doctrine; and (4) defendant Anderson's motion to dismiss on the grounds of forum non conveniens. For the reasons stated below, the Court grants defendant's motion to dismiss pursuant to Fed. R. Civ. P. 12(b)(6) with respect to two claims only: Owens Wiwa's *Alien Torts Claim Act* claims, 18 U.S.C. § 1350 [ACTA], founded on an alleged violation of his right to life, liberty and security of person, and his ACTA [3] claim for arbitrary arrest and detention. Plaintiffrs are given thirty days from the date of this Order to replead those claims. Defendant's motion to dismiss is denied in all other respects.

There are both positive and negative aspects to dealing with this case under the Alien Torts Claim Act. It is indeed highly desirable to make oil corporations accountable for the havoc they wreak (Reinisch, 2001), and we will return to this point below. But it is insufficient to highlight the most obvious and serious aspect of the tragedy in Ogoniland, while ignoring the causal nexus between environmental crimes, the citizens' resistance, and the state/corporate terrorist activities that ensued. The fact that no international environmental tribunal exists today that might have brought to justice the ecocrimes that gave rise to all ensuing cascading effects, supports Judge Postiglione's pleas for the necessity of such a tribunal. (Postiglione, 2001)

In essence, Nigerian citizens in the area had no resource when their lands and waters were degraded and, with them, their only food supply. Had the ecocrimes been brought to an appropriate forum, perhaps the gross human rights violations that are now in the court, might not have occurred.

After the murder of Ken Saro-Wiwa in November 1995 (Westra, 1998:ch.5), I prepared a case study with the help of documents provided by Amnesty International, the Goldman Prize Organization and Dr. Owens Wiwa, brother of the deceased. The case is one that includes both genocide and ecocide as Saro-Wiwa himself describes it (Ibid.). After the continuing and unrelenting practice of gross abuses of human rights, ranging from the suppression of peaceful protests for the irreversible damages to the land and waters of the Ogoni people, to rapes, organized military raids and slayings, culminating with the murder of the Ogoni 9, including Ken Saro-Wiwa, no international body brought the perpetrators to justice (Ibid.; compare. "Amended Complaint," at http://www.earthrights.org/shell/complaint.html).

The main point is that "any company that profits from crimes against humanity should be brought to justice wherever they are," and the most appropriate forum for such a legal exercise should be the one best able to mount a successful prosecution (Ibid.). What is at stake is the defense of the most basic human rights, but also at the same time in this case, the defense of our common environment/habitat, and this issue is not even mentioned.

In the discussion of the case, Judge Wood clarifies the reach of ACTA and of TVPA with respect to the case:

A. ATCA and TVPA [Torture Victim Protection Act]

Plaintiffs premise jurisdiction over their international law claims on the ATCA, 28 U.S.C. §1 350, and general federal question jurisdiction, 28 U.S.C. § 1331 (1993). The ATCA provides that "the district courts shall have original jurisdiction of any civil action by any alien for a tort only, committed in violation of the laws of nations or a treaty of the United States." 28 U.S.C. § 1350. Section 1350 was enacted in 1789, but was rarely invoked until the Second Circuit's 1980 decision in Filartiga v. Pena-Irala, 630 F.2d 876 (2d Cir. 1980). In Filartiga, the Second Circuit "recognized the important principle" that ATCA "validly creates federal court jurisdiction for suits alleging torts committed anywhere in the world against aliens in violation of the law of nations." Kadic v. Karadzic, 70 F.3d 232, 236 (2d Cir.1995) ["Kadic I"].

This paragraph brings out clearly the requirement for an international crime in violation of "laws of nations," hence for violations encompassing breaches of *erga omnes* obligations. In some sense, it is insufficient to view these crimes as torts, but the presence of universal, nonderogable obligations breached in the cases ATCA considers, paves the way for further criminal prosecution, especially given the coming into force of the International Criminal Court in July 2002.

In a much simpler and lower profile case, a similar principle is upheld in the Supreme Court of Canada decision in *Ward v. Canada* ((Attorney General) (2002)

1 S.C.R. 569). This was a sealing case, where Ford Ward, was charged with using his fishing licence to kill certain seals and sell their pelts, against federal laws enacted in the common interest for the protection of these marine mammals and their habitat. Although he justly claimed he had a valid license to pursue his chosen occupation, the Supreme Court of Canada argued that Section 27 of the Marine Mammals Regulations, prohibits the sale, trade, or barter of young harp seals, and that it falls under the federal powers over fisheries, "which is not confined to conserving fish stocks, but extends more broadly to maintenance and preservation of the fishery as a whole, including its economic value" (Council Directive 83/129, 1983 O.J. (L 91) 30; Charnovitz, 1994).

Notably, the latter is clearly not the primary consideration in the case; rather, the main concern is the "management of fisheries as a public resource." It may seem strange to return to a case such as *Ward v. Canada*, where no human rights violations were at issue, in order to compare it with the murder, destruction, and torture present in the Ken Saro-Wiwa case. What they have in common is, primarily (1) the choice of jurisdiction and of law instrument based on whatever best supports the common interest; and (2) an environmental issue that is much more in evidence in the Royal Dutch Shell Case, but is not mentioned in the ATCA analysis of the case. Yet the facts show that ecological concern was indeed the starting point and foundation of the Ogoni protest, on behalf of their "basic rights" (Shue, 1996).

Ward is a case where a court upholds federal prescriptive jurisdiction, while *Royal Shell* is about interpretive adjudicative jurisdiction; in addition, the common interest institutional function within one state (Canada) is quite different from the actual scope of the ATCA. Nevertheless, it can be argued that the appeal to the common interest is the key that links the two apparently disparate cases. Even the Canadian case, ostensibly about the Canadian common interest, has several features that might bring Ward closer, in principle, to the *erga omnes* requirements of ATCA. These are: consideration of European negative assessment of seal hunting practices, the consideration, through that issue, of animal rights (a universal issue), even if it is primarily its Canadian economic aspect that emerges.

Both cases uphold universal common interests in some measure. Both cases also point to the fact that, when the environment is at issue, there is, as Judge Postiglione argues, a "juridical necessity" as well as a "social necessity" for the institution of an international environmental court, that would use the power of *erga omnes* obligations to promote the universal common good (Postiglione, 2001:68–71). The fact that such a court does not exist, and that has never been even an ad hoc international environmental court today, points to what I will term a "juridical deficit," inspired by Postiglione's words:

> The deficits of legality and justice are real and present, because, as well
> as having scientific, technical, economic and administrative instruments,

the necessary role of the judicial system in jurisprudence must be considered (Postiglione, 2001:71; author's translation).

Only an international environmental court would be the appropriate institution capable of hearing environmental cases, and of issuing decrees with *"erga omnes* efficacy," the latter a clear requirement arising from the argument of this work as well. Postiglione lists a number of reasons why an international environmental ad hoc court should be established, and the following is a translation of his main points. Postiglione says such a court is necessary, because:

(a) it is important to have jurisdiction beyond the means to resolve state conflicts, as indicated by Article 34.1 of the ICJ, statute;

(b) on environmental matters, it is imperative that NGOs should be granted access to justice;

(c) the legal principle of transboundary responsibility for damages beyond state jurisdiction has a primary and categorical character (*erga omnes*) that can best be sought by society as a whole, citizens and NGOs, but that is hard to defend through legal actions between States;

(d) in fact, many of the conflicts arising through multilateral treaties cannot be solved through voluntary cooperation of arbitral decisions, but require *erga omnes* obligations;

(e) the political basis of consensus is limited to about forty five states (out of 180), but the accelerating global ecological crisis requires immediate preventive measures;

(f) the International Court of Justice at the Hague has created no real body of jurisprudence in the last fifty years (only two arbitral cases, and no obligatory decisions);

(g) the proposed new *ad hoc* court would add a specialized, positive and interdisciplinary institution, without disrupting the unity of the present international juridical system;

(h) the obstacle of State sovereignty can be mitigated through a statute that proposes an acceptable model for international order and peace, without interfering with the primary responsibility of States to protect the environment within their jurisdiction;

(i) through the evolution and growth of a culture of human rights, it is anachronistic to view environmental matters only as State responsibility, whereas it is in the very nature of human rights and of the environment, to be substantially universal and in the common interest;

(j) there has been a rapid growth of international environmental law, so that a body of law appears ready for a global institutional organ at this time;

(k) especially the new models of multilateral conventions (climate, biodiversity, desertification, the sea, and the like), as well as the requirements of general information, participation and access, would benefit from more than proposals such as that for an ombudsman, as these fall far short of the mark;

(l) States have a legal obligation to protect the common resources of the Planet for future generations; there can be room for the violence of globalization and of the world economy, as these cannot hide the deficit of law and justice that is fostered by those activities;

(m) today there is neither a convention nor statute to reform the International Court of Justice, or to reconstruct an *ad hoc* Court, in order to establish a true and real environmental jurisdiction, despite the political interests of governments (Postiglione, 2001:68–71).

Postiglione adds that, only through an innovative instrument may it be possible to address international global damage: society and all its citizens bear the brunt of ecological harms; it is therefore fair that society should be allowed to protect itself when states fail in their duty to do so (Postiglione, 2001:78).

The Arhus Convention (June 23–25, 1998) recognizes the right of all persons to full information and to access to justice: how are these rights to be achieved in the present context? Since 1976, the European Court of Justice (Luxembourg), also recognized the right of those suffering environmental extraterritorial harms, to have access to justice beyond their borders (Bier v. Mines de Potasse d'Alsace 1976, Eur. Comm. Ct. T. Rep.1735). These rights become even clearer when one considers the relation between health and environmental damage, as argued in this work (see Chapters 2 and 7), and as supported by the WHO (Soskolne and Bertollini, 1999) as well as their 1999 London Declaration.

b. Transnational Ecological Disasters: Torts and Crimes?

The right to access to ecological justice is present in several international legal instruments, but there does not exist an ad hoc Convention to acknowledge that each person, as subject of international law . . . has a right to access to a supranational organ for all environmental matters (Postiglione, 2001:77; author's translation).

Ken Saro-Wiwa spoke of "genocide," "ecocide," and "omnicide," long before he and his fellow activists were killed. He termed the corporations "companies unholy" for what they were doing ecologically to Ogoniland, hence to his people (see Chapter 7). In essence, his own words indicted Royal Dutch Shell Oil practices as murderous, whether the killing was direct, that is through the use of conventional weapons, or through poisoning and bulldozing a habitat upon which the Ogoni had depended for centuries. The difference was one of degree, not a difference in kind, between ecological disasters on one hand, and violence against humans on the other, and the recent ATCA case does not reflect accurately the origins of the human rights violations: the environmental degradation of the region. One can understand both the activists and the lawyers, and their desire to use whatever facts are most likely to make their case, and we can also celebrate the final recognition of the gravity, and especially the public recognition, of those crimes.

There is no question that this is a positive step forward, although Terry says: "Although the idea of pursuing torturers for damages rather than jailing them may strike some as a second best solution, the tort remedy is an important complement to, and in many ways a more useful mechanism than the criminal remedy" (Terry, 2001:111).

No matter how important for the global community might be the possibility to turn to ATCA to bring (some) justice to cases involving egregious human rights violations, this approach assumes that all resulting harms are compensable. The argument of this work is—in part—that ecocrimes are forms of assaults and even crimes against humanity (see Chapters 2 and 7). But in that case monetary compensation is insufficient to compensate victims, as was argued in regard to both assaults and homicides in common law (see Chapters 4 and 5).

In the Canadian case *R. v. Ewanchuk* (see Chapter 2), Mme. L'Heureux-Dubé describes the assault of a young woman (even without the addition of rape), as "an attack on human dignity." Ewanchuck was tried and found to be guilty despite the fact that, as she was leaving the trailer where she had been confined, Ewanchuk handed $100.00 to the young woman, "for the massage." The payment did not cancel the wrong he inflicted upon her, and I do not believe that even a substantial fine established by the courts should ever be considered to replace the criminal charge of sexual assault.

Another aspect of this difficulty has been discussed in another well-known international case, the Bhopal case (see Chapter 2). The question of *forum non conveniens* was raised by the United States courts, with far less moral credibility than even the *Wiwa v. Shell* case, given that it was a U.S.-based multinational corporation, Union Carbide, that was clearly negligent and even delinquent in its practices, hence responsible for the slaughter that ensued in India. Peter Sand acknowledges the import of these procedural obstacles, and he proposes considering the "domestic alternative" (Sand, 1999:97), for transnational disputes as he shows that, at times, European domestic courts, influenced by international law may be able to deal with these cases, at least when the country where the case is tried is one of the parties to the dispute (as was the case for instance for Union Carbide in Bhopal). He cites a number of cases in support of his position, ranging from river pollution (Italy/France); to airborne pollutants for an electric power plant (Germany/France); a fishery dispute (Italy/France), and a mine vs. a garden nursery (Germany/The Netherlands) (Sand, 1999:87–97).

Yet Sands appears to think highly of the International Joint Commission (United States/Canada) and the potential role it could play, facilitated by the presence of the 1909 United States Canada Boundary Waters Treaty (Ibid.). In contrast, our earlier discussion indicated that this desirable potential has not come to fruition to date, if we judge its success from the standpoint of the conditions of the Great Lakes, rather than from the lack of serious litigation arising in the area on environmental issues (see Chapter 6). Another example Sands adduces, is that of Section 7(1)(b) of the Canadian Clean Air Act (1971):

> ... which enables the Canadian Government to prescribe national standards to control emissions 'likely to result in the violation of a term or terms of any international obligation entered into the government of Canada relating to the control or abatement of air pollution in regions adjacent to any international boundary or throughout the world (Sand, 1999:100, n.71).

Once again, the border areas between Canada and the United States, from Windsor, Ontario (Detroit, Mich.) to Toronto, Ontario (Buffalo, N.Y.) are among the most polluted areas in both countries, as they exhibit a number of "hot spots," or areas with extremely high concentrations of disease, unusual morbidity and fatality, as well as a large number of reproductive anomalies, for both human and nonhuman animals (Colborn et al., 1996; see Chapter 2). Although both Sands and others (see for instance, Falk, 1964) see an important role for domestic courts, we showed the problems arising in domestic regulations in Chapter 4, in the context of Canadian federal and provincial instruments. In both that context and the U.S. context of a Constitutional amendment (see Chapter 6), the function of environmental regulations was frustrated by corporate economic interests and their supporting governmental bureaucracies intent on consolidating their power rather than protecting the health of their citizens and the common habitat.

Beyond the procedural obstacles presented by jurisdictional questions, by far the most serious obstacle to sound ecological policies is posed by trade practices. These are supported by bureaucratic powers, and the interests and interplay of state actors in multilateral treaties, and by globally powerful regimes such as the WTO (see Chapters 3 and 6). In the next section we will consider these negotiated instruments and the related issues of implementation, compliance and effectiveness in the environmental arena.

2. STATE RESPONSIBILITY AND ENVIRONMENTAL TREATIES REVISITED

> It is probably the case that almost all nations observe almost all principles of international law and all their obligations almost all of the time (Henkin, 1968:43).

Louis Henkin's well-known words may well represent the reality of international law among states. But we have seen in the previous chapter (see Chapter 7) the grave and far-reaching effects of environmental law violations: "Violations of law attract attention and the occasional important violation is dramatic; the daily, sober loyalty of nations to the law and their obligations is hardly noted" (Ibid.).

Unfortunately, it is not an occasional violation that is dramatic in its import, but the steady ongoing results of many less dramatic violations, amount to an imminent threat to all life. The major cause of this global threat may well be the continuing reliance, at best on regimes based on dialogue, at worst, on power alliances between rich nations to the detriment of the rest. Of course, eliminating dialogue, leaves very few options, if any.

Environmental violations or wrongful acts are not isolated occurrences, nor are they easy to dismiss because they do not represent the norm for states who are mostly law-abiding. But the reality is that, typically, limited or delayed compliance with environmental treaties represents acts or omissions that lead to environmental harm to all: "While declarations and agreements proliferate, the environmental situation keeps getting worse" (Koskenniemi, 1992:123). It is for this reason, and because the environmental situation translates into violent human rights violations (described in the previous chapter and in Chapter 2), that we cannot agree fully with those who maintain that sanctions for violations are inappropriate (Chayes et al., 1995:79–80).

There are two state conditions that can be accepted as reducing, mitigating, perhaps even eliminating the culpable responsibility of states for noncompliance or breach of treaties: (1) incapacity to comply and (2) the presence of ambiguity in the norms that have been violated (Ibid.). The material, that is economic inability to comply, parallels the inability to form the required intent for the commission of a crime for reasons of mental defect, necessity, or other defenses (Roach, 2000:15–17). The states who plead inability to comply for lack of economic means or of appropriate technological or knowledge infrastructures, need and deserve the help of richer, more developed nations, not punishment. In contrast, the states who flaunt their noncompliance, and who maintain PR firms and legal teams to find ways to legitimately pursue their primary economic goals, and who are, in turn, funded and supported by those self-same economic interests, deserve the harshest condemnation of the international community.

The other cited reason for not employing coercive sanctions, that is, the vagueness and imprecision of the laws, is an unacceptable excuse for rich Northwest countries as well. Treaties are consensual instruments and, for the most part, the most powerful nations are the ones who prefer watered-down, inconclusive or vague language (couched in the terms environmental philosophers have termed "weasel words") as this language might permit them to continue to act wrongfully with some degree of impunity.

In essence, the language of treaties is one of the most significant parts of an uneven, imbalanced dialogue between states, carried on through regimes involving widely different principles, supported by polarized national interests, over time. Keohane and Nye speak of the "Club Model of Multilateral Cooperation," in a very apt metaphor (Keohane and Nye, 2000:26): it is ultimately more like a "country club" than the participants might be prepared to acknowledge. Some are admitted, largely on the basis of race, ethnic background, and socio-economic status in the global marketplace, others are not. Within such exclusive enclaves, it is to be expected that a great deal of transparency, respect, equality, and other ideals will be lost: "the opportunity for strategic manipulation of information is wide-open to decision-makers" (Ibid.).

We are facing a "democratic deficit" (Ibid. at 28), which becomes acute as the common good does not even represent a small part of what these instruments attempt to achieve, despite their rhetoric to the contrary. Perhaps a more appropriate conception of the overarching goal of most of those instruments as they apply to the environment, might be the maximum achievable common good compatible with the economic and the power interests of the richest and most powerful Western nations.

It is, therefore, unfair to blame and sanction those states actors who did not have the power to truly influence the formative dialogue in the regimes where the specifics of various conventions were decided. It is those who have a clear intent at stake, and who therefore prefer less clear and strongly worded instruments, not those whose subsistence and security (Shue, 1996) might have been protected by a stronger, hard law, but are not, in the soft language and compliance protocols that have been eventually chosen.

In the previous chapter we have argued for the radical changes proposed to eliminate this all too familiar scenario of weak ineffective, covenants, and limited effectiveness. Suggestions include (1) linking environmental violence unequivocally to reaches of international human rights law; therefore (2) insisting on the criminal nature of ecoviolence, no matter how unclear, delayed or unintended the effects of such violence; and (3) elevating environmental violence to ecocrime, and placing it under the ultimate control of international law, in order to utilize the other factors, beyond domestic practice that distinguish the latter: principles of law, *opinio juris*, and the writings of publicists (Bederman, 2001:13–17, 23–24).

Others have suggested other possible means to move forward from the existing ineffective multiplicity of treaties, to something resembling *real* environmental progress. For instance Martti Koskenniemi lists several proposals:

> . . . the creation of an international ombudsman for the environment and expansion of the notion of "threat to international peace and security," so as to allow binding action by the Security Council in environmental emergencies under Chapter VII of the UN Charter. Proposals have included giving UNEP a role in the implementation of agreements (Koskennemi, 1992:123)

Both Chapter 6 and Chapter 7 of this work supported the only conceptual move here suggested, that is, the fuller understanding (an expression preferable to the "expansion of the notion") of what a "threat to international peace and security" really means (see Chapter 6, discussion of Jutta Brunnée on "environmental security"). The other suggestions are practical rather than conceptual and these and other practical proposals will be addressed later in this chapter.

a. Koskenniemi's Analysis and the "Difficulties of Responsibility"

In his seminal article, Koskenniemi outlines some "principles" to state reponsibility, then discusses the difficulties in environmental instruments designed to define the process those responsibilities. The only clear principle listed is the *Chorzow Factory Principle:*

> The essential principle contained in the actual notion of an illegal act—
> a principle which seems to established by international practice and in
> particular by the decisions of arbitral tribunals—as far as possible, wipe
> out all the illegal act and reestablish the situation which would, in all
> probability, have existed if the act had not been committed (Chorzow
> Factory (Indemnity) Case (1928), P.C.I.J., Ser. A, No.17; Kindred et al.,
> 2000:677).

The second and third "principles" Koskenniemi lists are not really principles at all. Rather they both suggest existing customary procedures for dealing with pollution. Article 33 of the U.N. Charter indicates the most appropriate means of seeking peaceful resolution to disputes among states, as does Article 60.2 of the Vienna Convention on the Law of Treaties. Other principles we have noted in passing in the previous chapters emerge from *Trail Smelter* (see Chapters 6 and 7), and the few applicable cases and arbitrations available in international law (*Lake Lanoux, Corfu Channel,* see Chapter 7; *Gabcikovo-Nagymaros,* see Chapters 6 and 7). But the established principles apparently are insufficient to achieve the desired results.

Before proposing additional principles and strategies, later in this chapter, this section is intended to highlight the obstacles to the effective implementation not only of general principles, but also to the treaties to which responsible parties are signatories. Koskenniemi describes no less than six categories of obstacles (Koskenniemi, 1992:125–126). The first represents a recurring and basic problem: transboundary environmental pollution, despite the *Trail Smelter Arbitration,* is hard to ascribe to states, when the basis for state responsibility is the presence of an illegal "wrongful act." The latter is only occasionally the origin of the polluting activity: for the most part, transboundary pollution occurs as the result of legal and institutionalized practices, hence the reason for the present work as outlined in Chapter 1. Ecoviolence is, for the most part, the result of legal activities with both domestic and transnational effects that extend not only in space, but also in time, across both continents and generations.

Principle 21 of the Stockholm Declaration of the United Nations Conference on the Human Environment (1972), entrenches the moral principle "Do No Harm" into environmental soft law. Together with Principle 22, which prescribes the procedures to be followed in disputes, these principles establish the fact that transboundary pollution, a "wrongful act," no matter what activity generates it, thus gives rise to clear state responsibility.

Another problem, according to Koskenniemi, is the difficulty of establishing a clear line of causality that would permit the international community to isolate the responsible party. This is equally a problem in the domestic sector, because of the presence of nonpoint pollution. The only constructive approach in response to this problem is to proscribe these substances, since the reach of their synergistic and cumulative effects cannot be fully anticipated or scientifically assured (Westra, 1998). A case in point may be the proliferation of health and environmentally adverse impacts in the Great Lakes Basin. Despite the existence of the International Joint Commission, to oversee and support the binational Great Lakes Water Quality Agreement (1978, ratified 1988); see Chapter 6) the increasing presence of "hot spots" in the area demonstrates the existence of violence in the area against all forms of life including genetic mutations, (Colborn et al., 1996).

From this point of view, ascribing state or other actors' responsibility after the fact, is far less important than establishing that certain activities, products, and processes cannot be tolerated as legitimate, even less as "innocent" until proven guilty of the havoc they will eventually produce (Draper, 1991; Westra, 1998).

The third problem addresses the inability to comply on the part of developing countries, for economic reasons, and because of the lack of technological preparation, as discussed in the previous section (Chayes et al., 1995:79–80). It is easy to concede this point. Hence, it does not constitute a serious difficulty for state responsibility for the effectiveness of treaties since, for the most part, the main concern of all people ought to lie with the practices of the North, as the largest producers of pollution and polluting activities.

The fourth problem hinges on the indeterminacy and vagueness of the language of the treaties to be implemented: neither "appreciable risk," nor "significant harm" provide a clear standard for state responsibility (Koskenniemi, 1992:125). This problem parallels the one found in the language of common law environmental instruments (see Canadian example, Chapter 4). In essence, environmental violence exists in a broadly polarized world, because the North and the South play—generally speaking—in opposite camps. For the most part, the economic interests and lifestyles of the affluent North are responsible for and causative of the harms experienced more strongly and more clearly by the South (Rees, 2000; Gabadgesin, 2001).

The violence, indeed the resulting harms, are environmental, so that the whole global community of life is affected. However, those who are rich enough both as nations and as individuals can still find ways of protecting themselves at least by delaying the result of environmental violence. For instance, global warming engenders floods and great temperature imbalances, storms and various other disturbances. It is clearly easier to survive a significant sea-rise in the Netherlands than in Bangladesh; a flood in Germany or in Manitoba, Canada, than anywhere in Asia; a drought in the Canadian Prairies than in Africa; and a heatwave anywhere where individuals can afford air-conditioning.

Thus, the unclarity, with a corresponding lack of stringency in the norms and principles of environmental instruments, is not a problem for all in the same way: it plays into the hands of the rich, Western nations, as it allows them to continue their destructive practices with relative impunity, while the vagueness itself is an instrument of violence against those who are more vulnerable, and those the instruments themselves fail to protect.

The fifth point addresses the heart of the environmental problems: prevention ought to be the goal, not the ascription of responsibility after the fact. Koskenniemi says it well:

> The identification of responsibility also does little to encourage prevention. It quantifies the environment without being able to include in the quantification the value of nature as a spiritual amenity, its value to future generations and even less nature as a value in itself, regardless of its instrumental meaning for human beings (Koskenniemi, 1992:125).

This otherwise excellent passage leaves out the full impact of nonprevention: prevention is absolutely required because of the well-supported link between disintegrity and environmental degradation in the world and human health (Soskolne and Bertollini, WHO, 1999, at http://www.euro.who.int/document/gch/Globaleco/ ecorep5.pdf in Chapters 2 and 7). It is this connection that lifts environmental harms from their customary position to that of crimes against the human person and against humanity. When one understands the connection between starvation and preventable disease occurrences in children in developing countries, it is easier to acknowledge that those harms are, for the most part, incompensable. Hence, when the environment is perceived as a quantifiable entity, progress will be elusive: "Any quantification will be under inclusive, costs will be externalized and an economic incentive to pollute will remain" (Koskenniemi, 1992:125).

It is worth noting that pollution is only the most visible sign of ecological disintegrity. In addition, the expansion of the "technohuman "enterprise (Westra, 1998), leading to the encroachment in and to the utilization of too much of the Earth's surface, leads to an increasing and often irreversible loss of biodiversity and of the processes that compose the basis of nature's services (Daily, 1997).

The final critique acknowledges the dissonance between the "normative expectations" arising from soft environmental law, that despite the ongoing regimes, never seems to harden into anything more than amicable meetings aimed at consensus rather than at justice or the common good. As Koskenniemi argues, even at best, dispute settlements produce too little and much too late, as formal, punitive procedures are not in place (Koskenniemi, 1992:126).

The previous chapter proposed viewing environmental responsibility in the light of *erga omnes* obligations so that any state could plead before international tribunals. Equally important, if prevention as well as violations were to be viewed as nonderogable or *jus cogens* norms, then the failure to justly ascribe responsibility for effective change might be mitigated, as Koskenniemi argues in his sixth problem (Ibid.).

b. International Law on Responsibility and Liability

The title of our topic then means: "obligations with regard to injurious consequences of activities not prohibited by international law" (International liability for the Injurious Consequences of Acts Not Prohibited by International Law (1989)).

The question of the treatment of legal, yet harmful activities, has been a major concern in relation to state responsibility, and the topic of "International Liability for the Injurious Consequences of Acts Not Prohibited by International Law" has been on the agenda since 1978 (II-2 Y.B. I.L.C. 149 et seq. 1986), and there have been five reports, a "schematic outline" and a number of draft articles, following the first report, through 1988. The problem is that of ensuring that transboundry harm, arising primarily in the environmental field, should be considered a "liability" even if the state could be considered to be "without fault" (Boyle, 1999:1–3).

In contrast, viewing the activities under consideration as lawful, meant that "neither the payment of compensation nor the prevention of harm was seen as an absolute obligation" (Boyle, 1999:5). The emphasis is and has been on the relationship between the activities, their economic importance, and the "probability and seriousness of loss or injury": hence a balancing of interests was the main goal of any regulative effort, not ensuring that all harm would be avoided. As Boyle describes it: "In sum, what the schematic outline sought was a world in which nothing was either prohibited or made obligatory and everything was negotiable (Ibid.).

Instead of another approach based on consensus and negotiation, had the emphasis been placed on the harms themselves, the work of these Commissions ought to have sought some redefinition of risk, to indicate whether recurring but moderate pollution, or "large-scale but one-off accidents," such as Bhopal or Chernobyl might be equally harmful. Liability in all these cases ought to be strict, "in the sense that it is founded on cause, not on the lack of due diligence, or based on breach of obligation" (Boyle, 1990:7). It is disheartening that as late as 1986, Rapporteur Barboza (II—1 Y.B. I.L.C. 152, at para. 31 (1986)) stated:

> . . . within this topic there will be activities which, although they may cause significant injury, will be permitted because, on balance, the assessment of conflicting interests indicates continuation of the activity despite its risks and compensatable injury.

We have shown that ecological disasters and ongoing disintegrity will indeed cause "significant injury." In addition, most environmental injuries, as we increasingly are learning, are incompensable and, with the presence of scientific uncertainty, it is impossible to be sure which injury may be reversible or compensable at all.

Perhaps the problem should be reduced once again to that which was termed the "first obstacle," or the economic motive. The desire for "balancing interests" attempts the impossible: "balancing," or even comparing, economic interests with life and health-related interests. Hence, it will remain regressive to attempt to prohibit the harm, but not the activity that gives rise to the harm, as its consequence, as was shown for instance in the *Trail Smelter Arbitration*, where the question of making the activity unlawful was not even raised.

Here is basically one of the most serious obstacles we encounter: in the environmental realm, harm is not prohibited at source (Boyle, 1999:16); at best, "end-of-pipe" mitigation is sought instead. This happens despite the gravity of the injuries inflicted and the prohibitions and punishments these harms would easily evoke, were they inflicted by other means than through the environment. One of the Rapporteurs for the 1989 Commission attempted to include "consequences" in the meaning of obligation and in that of "responsibility":

> Rapporteur Barboza has taken "liability" to cover not only the obligation of reparation, but also the whole range of obligation, of notification, information, consultation and harm prevention with which the topic is concerned (Boyle, 1999:10; (1988) U.N. Doc. A/CN.4/413, para. 56 (1988)).

Although extending the range and meaning of "responsibility" appears to be a step forward, instead, joining "prevention" with "notification, information and consultation," once again taking the issue back to a consensus-based model, rather than indicating clearly the assaultive nature of the harm producing activities. In essence, such an approach takes, as a given, that the way business institutions presently operate, is the only way they can operate, and that is something we all, collectively, must bear, although we may attempt to mitigate the consequences of these activities, albeit in a "cost effective" manner.

This is not true, however. Business tends to operate by viewing everything through one lens only, and we jointly collaborate by allowing this to be "the way it is," instead of cutting straight to the root of the problem: the harms are indeed real, sometimes they are delayed, but they are always measurable and expected within a certain imprecise range of effects. When we divorce the activity from its immediate results and its long-range consequences, justice is not served, and human rights are not respected.

We have discussed the possibility of ascribing criminal acts to states in the previous chapter (see Chapter 7) but the nature of crime as such was not analyzed, although the arguments presented linked crime to moral principles through the appeal to *jus cogens* norms. On the topic of crime, Glanville Williams says:

> The proposition that crime is a moral wrong may have this measure of truth: that the average crime is more shocking, and has graver social consequences, that the average tort. Yet crimes of strict liability can be committed without moral wrong, while torts and breaches of trust may be, and often are, gross moral wrongs (Williams, 1955:117).

One cannot ignore the problems in this definition. The lack of a completely unitary morality in a pluralistic society, for instance, is a problem that becomes acute when it is transferred to the international community (Gilbert, 1990:348). In contrast, Lauterpacht (citing Grotius) argues that the state as a legal person, must also be viewed as subject to moral codes (Lauterpacht 1933:137), an argument we have extended to corporate legal persons as well (see Chapter 4).

Gilbert adds his voice to those who do not see the need for considering crimes of states, as he looks at international case law and some jurists; but he devotes less that a half-page to the consideration of "Massive Pollution of Land and Seas," in the ill-fated Article 19.3(d) of the 1996 I.L.C. (see Chapter 7), as he argues that the classic locus, *Trail Smelter*, cannot be authoritative enough to base criminal responsibility for transboundary harm upon it, as it is only an arbitration (Gilbert, 1990:364–365).

This is precisely the sort of opinion this work has attempted to refute: incremental scientific and medical information about the consequences of ecocrimes, makes such opinions irrelevant to the real issue, the internationally accepted protection of human rights. The bottom line is what one takes to be (1) the role of morality in the law; (2) the principled support one is prepared to accept for the basis of the connection between morality and the law. If one attempts to reduce *erga omnes* obligations, and the linked concept of *jus cogens* norms, to just another way of describing obligations that states agree to accept, on a par with treaties, then the argument for criminalization loses its starting point and much of its strength. Ecoviolence remains just one form of regulatory breach among others, not different in kind from those breaches.

I have argued that when the principles that form one of the sources on international law, are duly traced back to natural law, properly understood in its "natural" (biological) sense, then we have a solid starting point for the protection of human rights, whether the protection is required from the assaults of invading armies, or from the attacks of genocidal factions or of polluting industries (see Chapter 1).

Through this analysis of some of the difficulties besetting International environmental law instruments, we have set the stage for the major underlying problems: the economic and power differentials present in the established environmental regimes, and in the very language of the instruments that ought to protect the global commons and the global community of life, as these are inescapably connected. These differences and their effects will be our next topic.

3. THE WTO, ATCA, AND THE CONSEQUENCES OF "FREE TRADE" AND THE ECONOMIC MOTIVE

Le Monde n'est pas une merchandise—et moi non plus" (José Bové after the trial of "McDo's 10"; Barlow and Clarke, 2002:124).

In the previous section we argued that underlying each and every obstacle to the compliance and effectiveness of environmental regulatory instruments lies the overwhelming presence of North/South economic and power differences. The North (led by the United States) for the most part uses its influence to set the lowest possible standards of environmental and health protection, compatible with its interests, and often refuses to assist the South to meet even these minimum standards, while it staunchly refuses to ratify conventions that it perceives as economically damaging.

This is yet another practical reason for proposing that ecoviolence should be treated as *erga omnes* obligation, rather than one that is only assumed by signatories to specific treaties (Brunnée, 1989).

Although Brunnée prefers adopting an incrementalist, regime-development based approach today (Brunnée, private communication, Apr. 3, 2002), I have argued also for *jus cogens* norms to be used, in order to indicate the peremptory character required by ecological mandates, Dupuy characterizes them: ". . . domaine rousseauiste de la volonté génerale, a la fois la volonté de tous et déclarative du bien commun minimum irreducible a quantitatif et qualitatif coincident" (Dupuy, 1986:154).

Dupuy anticipates the words of Jose Bové at the beginning of this section. Dupuy is a well-known publicist, Bové a farmer and producer of Roquefort cheese, who issued a direct response to the "WTO ruling against the EU ban on genetically engineered crops and food products" (Barlow and Clarke, 2002:124), but their protests address similar problems.

Although we have addressed the role of ATCA applications in Section 1.a, we did not clarify under what conditions, specifically, a controversy can be brought to the attention of the court, under ATCA. Usually, this involves either biological or juridical persons rather than states, as Holwick argues in his discussion of the *Jota* case (Jota v. Texaco, Inc., 157 F.3d 153 (2d Cir. 1998); Holwick, 2000:184), where,

> Residents of regions of Ecuador brought class action against American Oil Company for environmental and personal injury, that allegedly resulted from company's exploitation of region's oil fields, and residents of Peru living downstream from that region brought class action asserting similar injuries resulting from these activities (Holwick, 2000:187, n.20).

In essence, the nature of the alleged violation is the most important point: the Jota plaintiffs "did not claim any treaty violation;" therefore they had to show that "alleged violations" were violations of universal norms, "against the law of nations." Hence, in legal terms, the plaintiffs argued that there had been a violation of *jus cogens* norms (Holwick, 2000:212).

This has been precisely the gist of the argument of this work, and the approach of ATCA supports two points. On one hand, the connection between health and disintegrity demonstrates the criminality of environmental violations that coincide with gross human rights violations (see Chapters 1 and 2). On the other hand, and following upon this argument, it is doubly important for these crimes to be prosecuted as torts as well, under ATCA: the plaintiffs' evidentiary burden, if met, hence accepted by those tribunals, may then be used to establish the criminality of the behavior that resulted in the harms for which they are being compensated, although a prior criminal conviction would prove a civil violation, *a fortiori*.

To this end, the International Criminal Court that came into force in July 2002, should be able to deal criminally with the tort cases ATCA can address in a different way. However, the only reference to the environment in the Statute of the ICC, is in Article 8, on "War Crimes" (Article 8(iv):

> . . . or widespread, long term and severe damage to the natural environment which would be clearly excessive in relation to the concrete and direct overall military advantage anticipated (Rome Statute of the International Criminal Court (1988)).

In addition, the crime of aggression (Article 5) has not yet been defined fully at this time (Kindred et al., 2000:766). Perhaps including ecoviolence in some form in that article, would be a fruitful way of ensuring that ecocrimes are found to fit within that court's mandates (see Chapter 1). At any rate, we can conclude that not only is the ATCA important on practical grounds, to ensure that egregious human rights violations are brought to the attention of the international community (Scott, 2001), but also, it can serve a vital purpose to establish the scope of these violations as real crimes, on conceptual grounds.

As more cases are brought before courts under ATCA, the current approach exemplified by the WTO tribunals, that juxtaposes human rights to economic advantage to the detriment of the former, will be under attack, even though the eventual "redress," at best, will remain monetary. These cases to date include: *Occidental Petroleum v. U'wa Indigenous People of Colombia* (http://www.earthtimes.org); *Beanal v. Freeport-McMoranty Inc.* (969 F. Supp. 362 (E.D. La. 1997)); *John Doe v. Unocal Corp.* (963 F. Supp. 880 (C.D. Cal. 1997)); *Sequihma v. Texaco, Inc.*, (157 F.3d 153 (2d Cir.1998)). All these cases list a familiar litany of "human rights abuses," "environmental torts," and even "cultural genocide" (Holwick, 2000).

They are, for the most part, cases arising from resource extraction; the accused are transnational corporations, the plaintiffs are citizens of developing countries, exploited and physically endangered together with their habitats, for the benefit of transnationals. Since governments as such, neither manufacture, process nor extract resources, they cannot be said to be directly responsible for the harms caused to health and life; we can only consider governments indirectly responsible, through the support they offer, hence their complicity in the harms caused. The interaction between governments and transnationals ranges from the straight partnership of the military regime of Sani Abbacha, with Royal Dutch Shell Oil in Ogoniland (Westra, 1998), to the immense "donations" to the Bush campaign in 2001 by a number of immoral transnationals, such as oil and tobacco companies (Borger, 2001:G2).

The difficulties of establishing ecologically sound and "secure" regimes is exacerbated by the fact that, for the most part, transnationals are not signatories or—as such—bound by the conventions their own home governments have ratified. The emergence of ATCA actions signals a ray of hope for the future, as does the coming into force of the ICC. We need to return briefly to the corporation itself, although it has been discussed in passing in most of the previous chapters.

In contrast to those who view reliance on ATCA not only as an important step forward, but also as a sufficient solution, Ratner argues that "reformulating corporate duties" to include human rights, would be the best step, because leaving those abuses entirely as torts, and relying on the presence of some "high profile tort cases" presently tried in the United States, "assumes too much about tort law and too little about human rights law" (Ratner, 2001:443, 553). Although the transformation of these cases into human rights issues is by no means a "cure-all," Ratner adds: "But reformulating the problem of business abuses as a human rights matter might well cause governments and the population to view them as a legitimate issue of public concern and not as some sort of private dispute" (Ibid.).

a. The Status and Aims of Transnational Corporations (TNCs)

Even a cursory glance through the provisions of just one UN Treaty, the International Covenant on Economic, Social and Cultural Rights (ICESCR), should bring to mind a seemingly infinite variety of possible corporate activities which could negatively affect human rights and which are at least candidates for being jurisdically sanctioned as *actual* violations of human rights (Scott, 2001:564–565; emphasis added).

Once again it will help to sum up briefly what has been argued so far. There has been a major obstacle to the criminalization of ecoviolence: the difficulty in meeting the burden of proof for some level of intent on the part of institutions, whether governments or corporations. The fault element is hard to prove when the accused is not a single biological entity. Similarly, it is not possible to adjudicate in a parallel way when the systemic accused, even if found guilty, cannot be put in jail. It is in this area that the conclusions reached in this work will need to be considered *lex ferenda*, supported by analogical reasoning and moral argument. Still, we have shown examples of attacks and callous disrespect for life, health and human rights, and traced these occurrences to the result of corporate activities in almost every chapter, as we noted:

(1) a.   the extent and particulars of the global harms (Chapters 1 and 2),
    b.   the basic conflict between the economic motive and life (Chapters 2, and 5);

(2) a.   the question of our own responsibility as citizens (Chapter 3);
    b.   the role of language, the media, and the possibility of complicity (Chapter 3),
    c.   civil disobedience and the use of force in response to ecoviolence (Chapter 3);

(2) a.   the failure of corporate self-regulations and of government deregulations (Chapter 4),
    b.   the language and practices of domestic laws in a Canadian case (Chapter 4),
    c.   the failure of "managerial standards" (Chapter 4),
    d.   the problem of corporate intent and responsibility and the CID structure (Chapter 4);

(4) a.   the nature and consequences of corporate activities (Chapter 5),
    b.   analogy between the effects of corporate activities and assaultive crimes (Chapters 2 and 5),
    c.   the problem of forms of fault;

(5) a.   the effects of corporate pressure at the international level (Chapter 6);
    b.   the language and regime processes in treaties,
    c.   the pervasive corporate pressure at the treaty level (Chapter 6),
    d.   the powerful and amoral WTO (Chapter 6).

For all these difficulties, we repeatedly encounter one basic problem: the status of corporations and institutions as legal, individual "persons" (Santa Clara County v. Southern Pacific RR Corp., (118 U.S. 394, G.S. Ct. 1132, 30 L. Ed. 118); Bowman, 1996; Kaufman et al., 1995).

This unfortunate fact of law emerges both in domestic and international law. These corporations, described by Judge Jessup as "transnational" (Kindred et al., 2000:51), are at present not subject to any clearly codified body of laws that could regulate their operations, although several instruments have made a start in that direction, for instance, the U.N. Code of Conduct on Transnational Corporations (1984), "The UN Code of Conduct never attained more than draft from and with so many matters yet to be agreed it faces an uncertain future" (Kindred et al., 2000:53).

From the point of view of this work, the most important I.C.J. decision, the one that combines the acknowledgement of the effects of corporate power, with a refusal to limit the consequences to one involved state or another only, is the Barcelona Traction, Light and Power Co. case (Belgium v. Spain, 1970 I.C.J. Rep. 3; Ragazzi, 1997). This landmark case is much cited as the basis for *erga omnes* obligations as argued especially in Chapter 7 and *passim*. In this case, the "corporate entity" is recognized in the judgment: "All it means is that international law has had to recognize the corporate entity as an institution created by States in a domain essentially within their domestic jurisdiction" (Ibid.).

But, in addition, sometimes corporate entities are "allocated to States for diplomatic protection" and in that case, "international law is based, but only to a limited extent, on an analogy with the rules governing the nationality of individuals" (*Barcelona Traction*, at 70). So that, on one hand, the transnational reach and power of corporate entities is recognized in international law as much as it is in national law, and on the other, the argument for so doing is based, as we shall see, on examples of the highest forms of criminality.

The Barcelona Traction case was not one that involved the grave violent actions described in this work, but it does present and support the foundation from which these actions and the resulting obligations can be addressed in international law:

> Such obligations derive for example in contemporary international law, from the outlawing of acts of aggression, and of genocide, as also from the principles and rules concerning *basic rights of the human person*, including protection from slavery and racial discrimination (*Barcelona Traction*, at 34, emphasis added; see Chapter 7).

In Chapters 4 and 5 the question of intentionality was discussed in detail. In sum, according to Peter French, the corporation operates as a unity. He argues that it is this aspect of its role and "nature" that warrants the ascription of a separate status to a corporate entity, beyond the legal status of each of its employees and officers (French, 1984). But unitary activities require a unitary presence and goals, hence intent. Therefore, if a corporate (separate) legal personality is accepted, then the analogical presence of intent must also be accepted, as intent of the corporation, beyond the aims and decisions of each individual within it, whose aims may only partially coincide with those of the corporate body that employs them.

Hence, recent business ethics literature may help shed light on corporate responsibility, and help clarify their intent, both in "collaborating" with and supporting national governments in order to ensure that domestic laws are not strict enough to impede their operations, and in their role in redirecting the regulatory framework of international regimes. An obvious example with both national and international implications, is the 2000 U.S. election of George W. Bush: "Big Tobacco as a whole gave $7 mill to Bush and the Republicans, 83% of the industry's total election spending" (*The Guardian*, Apr. 27, 2001).

Bush is the first U.S. president with an MBA, and as Julian Borger puts it, "corporate America bought itself a president" (Ibid.). He continues, "Business is the only voice heard in the Oval Office of the Presidency"; the AFL-CIO Union Federation has been defeated by scrapping "a raft of work safety measures"; Bush removed "rules which would have made mining companies (who donated 2.6m to his campaign) pay for clean-up costs if they contaminated the public water supply"; he also "scrapped safety limits on arsenic levels in drinking water imposed by the Clinton White House"; finally, Bush abandoned both national "legal limits on carbon dioxide emissions" and admitted that "the Kyoto Protocol on global warming" could be considered "dead and buried," thus "ending five years of transatlantic efforts" (Ibid.).

The same overwhelming influence by the United States and other Western powers is present at the WTO and in the formulation of all international environmental agreements, both in the language adopted, and in the conditions under which these documents are intended to operate (Koskenniemi, 1992).

Therefore we must conclude that the obstacles we face in the pursuit of ecologically sound policies for the protection of life, are indeed immense. They range from assuming undemocratic and unjustifiable powers nationally and internationally, by transnational corporations, to using the law for their purposes, most often contrary to the common good and to life as such. These attempts to regulate the law extend to influencing by both acts and omissions the formation of regulatory instruments, in order to maintain and support the status quo.

In the next section we will discuss the question of corporate accountability, before turning to some strategies to overcome the problems we have outlined.

b. The Foundations of the Legal Personhood of Corporations

I think that it is right that the doing of an act which one realizes may well cause grievous bodily harm should also constitute malice aforethought whether or not one realizes that one's act may endanger life (Lord Cross of Chelsea, (1974) 2 All E.R. 71).

Anthony Kenny uses this passage as an example to explain H.L.A. Hart's view on "the difference between direct and oblique intention, either being sufficient to constitute murder" (Kenny, 1977:161).

Two parallel and interwoven strands of reasoning have directed this work: the importance of principles of law, most evident in the international context; and the nature of corporate crime. The former has been easier to demonstrate than the latter, which is the subject of this section, and will be discussed under two headings (1) the legal personality of the corporation; and (2) the relevance of intent in corporate crimes.

Starting with the latter (2), we note that the research upon which the argument for criminalization of ecoviolence is based is not only readily accessible to anyone interested in the topic, but it is not protected, for the most part by trade secrets, except when corporations themselves block its access. The ecological and health/epidemiology information is not only available in learned journals and books, but also it is reprinted in newspaper articles written at the sixth-grade level. Therefore, because the effects and consequences of institutionalized business practices is so readily available globally (this is one desirable form of globalization: knowledge and information dissemination), no one can claim that they had no idea, no knowledge about the results of the activities they continue to practice. This is especially true of the TNCs whose R. and D. budgets often exceed the total budget os some developing countries.

Knowledge, as was argued in Chapter 6, is indeed part of what intent includes. It is also present in some sense in willful blindness and other lesser forms of intents.

In Canadian law, courts would "presume that criminal offences require some sort of subjective *mens rea*—intent, knowledge, recklessness or wilful blindness in relation to all aspects of the *actus reus* unless Parliament clearly indicates otherwise" (Roach, 2000:131). Roach also adds: "In English Law, however, recklessness can be an objective form of liability that only requires the accused's failure to advert to an obvious risk." (Metropolitan Police Commissioner v. Caldwell, A.C. 341 (1981), All E.R. 961, (1981) W.L.R. 509; Roach, 2000:131).

In domestic (common) law, "ignorance of the law is no excuse," so that an institution with both scientifically and otherwise well-trained individuals will not be able to claim they had no factual, scientific, or elementary legal knowledge, sufficient to enable them to understand the implications and consequences of their acts. Roach suggests that, "Because they are directed primarily at individuals, it would be helpful is Parliament addressed the issue of criminalizing omissions or failure to act in a principled and comprehensive fashion" (Roach, 2000:94).

I would add that a "principled" definition would be even more desirable and important when it is not an individual but a corporate entity that is committing the act, the omission, or failing to act.

The root of the problem is the requirement of intent (1) if an act, or an omission is to be viewed as a crime. Intent appears to be only possible for human persons, much harder to demonstrate for juridical ones. But we have argued in support of Peter French's analysis of the corporation as defined by its CID structure (see Chapter 4). The substance of French's argument for responsible personhood, can also be inferred from the Canadian acts that define corporations as persons, and ascribe to them "the capacity of natural persons" (The Interpretation Act (1985), and the Canada Business Corporations Act (1985); Welling, 1991:79, n.12).

The nature of the corporation was established as a "separate existence," and was confirmed by the House of Lords in *Salomon v. Salomon & Co.* ((1897) A.C. 22; Van Duzer, 1997:87). But this seminal case raises questions of financial responsibility for debts, not of imposition of physical harm. "Analogy" to the human person is constantly appealed to, but it is also acknowledged to be partial (Welling, 1991:76). "To clarify the corporation as a legal entity is to is thus to consign it to legal treatment by analogy to the best-known singular person present in our society, the individual human being" (Welling, 1991:77).

But analogy, although well-used in the argument of this work is—admittedly—not identity: there are indisputable differences between corporate individuals and biological ones. If the CID structure defines the corporation, then it is capable of intent, as the documents cited above imply by ascribing to it personal "capacities."

However, the limits of the analogy can also be found in the spirit behind the Charter and other documents intended to protect biological persons: corporations should not benefit from all the protections and privileges constitutionally available in civilized societies to vulnerable accused biological persons (see Chapter 5).

It seems wrong to simply subsume corporate entities under persons when in the Charter, for instance, both Sections 7 and 11(e) and especially Section 15.(1), are clearly referring to biological persons. The first two can only be understood to apply to corporations by a very stretched analogy. Section 15.(1) cannot be applied in that way: corporations have no "color," "religion," "sex," or "physical disability." Section 15.(2) is equally applicable only to biological individuals or groups, as "affirmative action" is not applicable to corporations.

As a strategy it would be highly desirable to be able to decouple corporate personhood from biological personhood, at least for noncommercial activities, that is for all cases where more is at stake than financial gains or losses, but physical health or life is at issue. This would ensure that the relevant sections of the criminal code, intended to treat accused persons in a fair and civilized manner, should not be used to harm innocents behind a legal shield inappropriate to wealthy and powerful entities, far more likely to be victimizer than victims.

c. An Aside on Corporate Crime in the Workplace: An Analogy

The problem of corporate crime has been addressed in relation the workplace, and we have already referred to this similarity (see Chapter 4). Glasbeek and Rowland found the basis for "injuring killing in the workplace," in the divided class which they define as comprising the "ruling class and the oppressed" (Glasbeek and Rowland, 1986:66). There is no doubt about their documented research that shows how hazardous the workplace truly is. It is equally indisputable that leaving "the matter of the safety at work to the bargaining of parties affected, employers and employees" (Ibid. at 70), is just as useless for the protection of health and safety as it is to do so for ecocrime at the national and the international level (see Chapters 4 and 7).

At the domestic level, business pressures governments, and lobby for "consensus" and for managerial rather than substantive standards (ISO 14000). The intent is not to preserve the environment, but to avoid prosecution by installing managerial practices to show due diligence, while continuing with business as usual, for the most part. The other tactic, employed to the same aim, is that of enacting and publishing a Code of Ethics or, of practice, applying to both workplace conditions and environmental concerns. But these documents simply entail calling meetings with the local stakeholders (read "potential victims") for the purpose of appeasing them with various public relations ploys, while continuing with their usual practices.

At the international level (see Chapter 7), as was also noted in the earlier sections of this chapter, a similar technique is applied. The Northwest developed states are involved in cooperative regimes with developing states, for the purpose of drafting joint covenants with elaborate procedural rules, intended to establish fairness. But as Pogge argues (see Section 5), the deck is stacked in favor of the affluent few from the start. The members of the G-7 group are influencing (if not dictating) the language and the terms, and even the possible penalties that will attach to the crimes they themselves commit as part of the normal functioning of their economic infrastructures and power goals. That practice seems akin to gathering a group of rapists and abusers, in order to achieve consensus on how these crimes should be defined, treated and sanctioned.

For the most part, and this is an additional obstacle worthy of mention, retributive justice is beyond the scope of international regimes, and it only comes into play for crimes against humanity, genocide, and the like. However, this is the same class of crimes, supported by *erga omnes* obligation and proscribed by *jus cogens* norms to the level of which, we have argued, ecocrimes should be raised. The importance of this move is clear when even direct harms, like those inflicted on employed workers, are often apparently beyond the reach of the law. Glasbeek and Rowland say:

"Let us make it clear at the outset that there is no expectation by us that this society will set out to control enterprise completely" (Glasbeek and Rowland, 1986:71).

This is indeed the crux of the problem. But there should remain at least a hope that justice is possible, if not guaranteed. Another example points to the immense difficulties we face. We have noted the reluctance of governments to fund a strong inspectorate and empower it to impose at least the maximum penalties presently available in the law: "Empirical studies, by sociologists point to the fact that inspectors are loath to use what they see as criminal stigmatization of employers in these kinds of circumstances" (Ibid. at 77).

At the level of general principles, the same difficulty holds true nationally as it does internationally: "We are a so-called free enterprise society, wedded to the notion that investors must be encouraged and that State interference is a disincentive to such investment" (Ibid. at 72).

The same can be said, *mutatis mutandis* at the international level, as was argued in our discussion, of the WTO (see Chapter 3). Glasbeek and Rowland are only concerned with direct harm to employees, but these are only a small fraction of the stakeholders of corporate entities, especially TNCs whose global reach cannot be underestimated. Hence, if it is or should be a crime in the context of a single business operation and its employees in one country, it clearly is and should be equally a crime now raised to the level of genocidal massacre, when the harming and killing of millions is engendered by economically motivated ecocrimes.

It is worthy of note: Glasbeek does not attempt to attribute intent to enterprises or employers generally. But he bases his argument on the failure to protect human life in the quest for profit: "It is hard to imagine that there will be many people who will publicly advocate the principle that earning a profit, even if it requires criminal conduct, is more important than the health and safety of human beings" (Ibid. at 79).

This argument seems indisputable and if it can be accepted for a single industry or corporation, surely it can be extended even more easily to the global commons and the world's peoples for whom, unlike exploited or endangered employees, it is not only unfair or undesirable to live under unsafe conditions of work, but it is absolutely impossible to "leave" the Earth for safer conditions or fairer treatment.

d. Multinationals' Accountability for Human Rights: A European Perspective

There is a global trend of shifting governance tasks from states (including their sub-entities) to non-state actors.

* * * * *

More and more private for profit and non-profit organizations step in to fill the void left by states. At the same time, there is a tendency to move governance tasks to inter- or supranational entities, like the United Nations, the World Trade Organization, or the European Union (Reinisch, 2001:270).

We have discussed the legal personality of corporations and the problem of intent for single corporate entities (see Chapter 4), and the problems of economic motivation and governance in Section 3 of this chapter. Corporations have equal protection under the law of national states, and enjoy a great deal of freedom as transnational aggregates or multinationals.

Some have argued that human rights law emerged from the struggle of property holders, and this would place a special responsibility on these entities:

Modern human rights doctrine emerged historically from the struggle of the individual property holder against the autocratic monarchic state. It is an essence of a market based theory of rights. Thus the first human right to emerge clearly is the right to private property (Muchlinski, 2001:31–33).

This appears to be incorrect: the Magna Charta was indeed intended to protect the "rights of man" against the powers of monarchs and tyrants, but it was intended as basic protection against attacks to life and freedom that were at issue, not property or markets. Of course Muchlinski is correct in his assessment, if he starts his consideration of human rights with Locke. Internationally, the progression to full human rights starts even more clearly with physical protection as most human rights instruments arise after the trials at Nuremberg, hence from humanitarian law (see Chapter 1). If we view human rights through the lens of property holders only, Muchlinski is correct as he adds: "However the traditional conception of human rights accepts only this protective approach to the relationship between corporation and human rights. It is therefore a conceptual barrier to the extension of human rights *obligations* to private corporations" (Ibid.). Muchlinski also notes that the "liberal possessive individualist origins" were at least in part viewed apart from human rights theory after Nuremberg. Although the Cold War divided world powers into easily identifiable "blocs," the antiimperialist decolonization movements in Asia and Africa, formed a "bloc" against the liberal Western powers, as it forced the latter to acknowledge the dissonance between their national observance of human rights, and their disregard of those rights in the colonies.

In addition, in many nations today, the infiltration of MNCs into the governance and power structure of states in general, and particularly those of developing states, presents a transnational conflict between pro- and anti-capitalist groups, instead of divisions based on the ideologies of specific national blocs. Against these recent developments, "traditional economic/political debates" give way to debates based on "race, gender, sexual orientation, youth culture, the 'third age' politics of the elderly, consumers and environmentalism" (Muchlinski, 2000:34).

We appear to be moving away from political power blocs, and toward corporate/economic ones, and this move to "globalization" tends to unleash powers beyond the control of states and their legal instruments. Speaking of transnational corporations, Reinisch says: ". . . their quests for profits-too often coupled with the willingness of host governments to curtail human rights for the sake of economic development, frequently escalates to a denial of human rights" (Reinisch, 2001:281). Despite the presence of (1) numerous Codes of Ethics, adopted voluntarily by corporations; (2) the OECD guidelines for Multinational Enterprises (2000); (3) the Maastricht Guidelines on Violations of Economic, Social and Cultural Rights (1997); (4) the Code of Conduct on Transnational Corporations (1988), and other legal instruments, significant violations continue to occur, as all these instruments are nonbinding. The main problem, as was noted in both the national and the international realms, is the presence of the institutional cooperation of governments, both democratic and nondemocratic, as both tend to prefer cooperating with MNCs in exchange for the economic advantages the presence of these transnationals brings to their elites, hence these governments do not hold them accountable for they harms they perpetrate (see Chapters 4 and 7) (Manzini, 2000:83).

The connection between states governance and transnational power forms the basis for what we have termed "institutionalized violence" against human rights (Westra, 2000:ch.16). The responsibility for the harms ought to be shared by governments (as facilitators) and transnationals. In fact, vigilance ought to increase sharply as "privatization of heretofore public enterprises" threatens human rights (The Realization of Economic, Social, and Cultural Rights (1991)).

However, aside from the possibility of voluntary self-imposition of standards, a doubtful enterprise at best, and aside from the presence of numerous "judicial fora" and "available legal limits," the exceptional economic power of most TNCs permits them to take advantage of their denationalization and renders them partially exempt from potentially applicable national law (Reinisch, 2001:90):

To assert that "multinationals have operated in a virtual legal and moral vacuum" may overstate the problem, but it is undeniable that TNCs are rarely held accountable for serious violations of the law, in particular, human rights (Reinich, 2001:90; Amnesty International, 1998).

In the next part of this chapter we will explore possible remedies and strategies that might include the discovery of new approaches, but also a focus—as Weeramantry proposed—on the universality already present in the law of nations (see Chapter 6). These strategies are required in order to find a more just way of dealing with ecoviolence. We will also show that the use of international law does—or at least may—offer a better way, a more justified hope to make the radical changes we need. In Chapter 6, moving from national to binational, then to international law, we argued that the latter presents elements that are absent from domestic (common) law. We now need to see how these elements, found in the principles of law and in the extensive work of publicists, may be used to fight the obstacles listed above. Another promising avenue is to learn from existing supranational regimes, such as the EU, how to live a cosmopolitanism that, in contrast with globalization, is a safer and more respectful option toward all life.

PART B: SOME NORMATIVE STRATEGIES

4. PRINCIPLED STRATEGIES TO OVERCOME THE OBSTACLES TO ECOJUSTICE: FIRST STRATEGY, COSMOPOLITANISM

A global system of a plurality of more-or-less sovereign States whose inhabitants' lives are restricted for many purposes to their own state, can injure many lives. Even if each state were more or less internally just, and they rarely are, States may injure those whom they exclude, and a system of States may systematically or gratuitously injure outsiders by wars and international conflict and by economic structures that control and limit access to the means of life (O'Neill, 1996:172).

There is a basic difference that emerges in O'Neill's passage cited above, between globalization and cosmopolitanism. While the former appears to be primarily procedural in its structures, and primarily influenced by powerful, market-oriented powers, the latter is based primarily on substantive moral principles of justice that include but also transcend the economic realm, and rely on Kantian principles, so that the difference remains a vast difference of values. States may or may not be fully just within their own borders but, even at best, (see Chapter 3) they may well injure those outside their borders by exclusionary practices, and these are direct injuries (O'Neill, 1996:175). The practices we have outlined in the previous chapters provide indirect injuries instead. This is a form of indirect injustice as "destroying parts of natural and manmade environments injure those whose lives depend on them." In addition: "Secondly, the principles of destroying natural and manmade environments, in the sense of destroying their reproductive and regenerative powers, is not universalizable (Ibid. at 176).

Ecological and biological integrity is precisely what O'Neill terms "regenerative and reproductive powers," or true sustainability: "Environmental justice is therefore a matter of transforming natural and man-made systems only in ways that do not systematically or gratuitously destroy the reproductive and regenerative powers of the natural world, so do not inflict indirect injury" (Ibid. at 177).

This is what has been argued from a scientific and a moral point of view in the work of the "Global Ecological Integrity Project" (Pimentel et al., 2000; Karr, 2000; Noss and Cooperrider, 1994; Westra, 1998), and referenced and summarized here (see Chapters 2 and 8).

In O'Neill's terms, moral principles represent the "blueprint" and the "specifications," which define the "product" to be eventually produced. In a similar sense, strategies based upon principles are not as such, the strategic tools to use in order to achieve just aims, but they define what forms such tools might take. O'Neill says: "The move from abstract and inconclusive principles of justice toward just institutions, policies and practices is analogous to moves from design specification towards finished product" (O'Neill 1996:181).

The "finished product" of this volume, or a strategy toward just and ecologically sensitive institutions, may not yet be achievable, but at least a prototype of what the finished product may look like and what it may achieve may emerge.

In this section, we are still at the blueprint and specification stage. In contrast to the procedural thrust of liberal governance, with its avoidance of moral absolutes or of any clear commitment to a specified common good, beyond the economic advantage of the most powerful groups, states and institutions, cosmopolitanism recognizes the existence of nonderogable obligations beyond borders so that its scope includes "distant strangers and future generations" (O'Neill, 1996:113). Cosmopolitanism based on Kantianism, can supply the principles and also the guidelines that are largely absent from even the best among the advocates of liberal democracy, as the roots of injustice are seldom sought out by these thinkers:

> The idea that our economic policies and the global economic institutions we impose make us causally and morally responsible for the perpetuation and even aggravation of world hunger, by contrast, is an idea rarely taken seriously by established intellectuals and politicians in the developed world (Pogge, 2001:15).

Rawls' own work distorts this basic reality: "like the existing global economic order, that of Rawls' Society of Peoples is then shaped by free bargaining" (Ibid. at 16). We will return to the strategies required to overcome "free bargaining" below. For now, the main point is that every practice that bears the prefix or qualifier "free" is, *ipso facto* not so, in the universal sense: "free" to pursue harmful practices does not render those who are harmed "free." It can be considered an obstacle to global justice, not a constructive component of it, for instance, in Rawls' liberalism in his work on justice (Rawls, 1993) and in the "Law of Peoples" (Rawls, 1999). These works emphasize and support the very lack of substantive, principled approaches that must be transcended (see Chapter 3), because they support globalization with all its inherent injustices (Pogge, 2001:22).

The alternative to globalization here proposed is a form of Kantian cosmopolitanism, an approach that embodies the respect for near and distant persons and future generations as well. In contrast, the principles that Rawls embraces and that support fairness, are said "to be internal to liberal societies" (O'Neill, 1999:47). Hence, at best, they attempt to mitigate some of the evil fostered by liberalism, but without any attempt to reach all the way to the destructive foundation on which these theories and practices rest: ". . . (a) . . . pattern of derivation shows that inclusive principles of indifference to and neglect of others also cannot be universalized" (O'Neill, 1999:193) Hence, in order to proceed from blueprints to specifics, we must ensure that our starting point is compatible with and supportive of our final aim: a Kantian form of cosmopolitanism provides such an initial blueprint.

a. Kant on Human Rights and Cosmopolitanism

The possession of fundamental, inalienable rights for all humanity finds its strongest expression in Kant's philosophy. His categorical imperative defends human dignity and the infinite value of each human life, so that the Universal Declaration of Human Rights (1948), the U.N. Charter (as signed 1945 and amended 1965, 1968, 1973) and all other international legal instruments which take a strong position in defense of human rights, originate from Kantian moral theory (Kant, 1964; Kant, 1981). But Kant also wrote on *Perpetual Peace*, and he saw a "league of nations" as "the ideal of international right" (Kant, 1957; Cavallar, 1999:113). It is not very common to find appeals to Kantian theory today either in law or even in political thought. But it is in Kant that one can find both support for absolute human rights, and the move to focus beyond the State as the ultimate source of legitimacy, to a vision of cosmopolitanism and constructive peace that comes quite close to the vision that animates the U.N. Charter.

In Kant's theory, reconciliation is achieved between individual rights and universalism, as instantiated not only through international laws but through cosmopolitanism. In 1310 the Italian poet Dante Alighieri advocated a "universal monarchy." Kant knew that a monarchy may not foster respect for individual autonomy and freedom that are foundational to human dignity and thus to his moral' theory (Cavallar, 1999:116). Kant says:

> There is only one rational way in which states coexisting with other states can emerge from the lawless condition of pure warfare. Just like individuals, they must renounce their savage and lawless freedom, adapt themselves to public coercive laws, and thus form an *international state* (Kant, 1957; Cavallar, 1999:122).

In this passage we find almost a premonition of the direction that will be taken by public international law. As we have seen in the legal instruments cited, at least three points emerge:

(1) The rule of law is the goal for individuals, states, and beyond;
(2) Public international law should be the final arbiter of what is just; it should provide the connection between individuals, single states, and the so-called "international state" or supervening regulations and laws, when required;
(3) The reason for going beyond single states, and allowing these to have the ultimate power in all matters, is to enable states to transcend warfare, as the goal of "perpetual peace" indicates in Kant.

Kant sees a "world republic," rather than a single monarchy which might give rise to a "soulless despotism," which ". . . leaves no room for rightful or lawful freedom, or public coercive laws" (Cavallar, 1999:125).

Perhaps we no longer perceive such a stark dichotomy, under the rule of democratic institutions; yet Kant's argument is well taken. What Kant aims for is that the ideal is a rule of justice that still allows individual rights and freedoms in a way that may not be always permitted when national states become the final arbiters of which (and "whose") rights to support, and which (and "whose") to ignore as we see too often in recent times, with the plight of the Rwandans, the Kurds, or the Albanians.

b. The Dual Role and the Sources of Public International Law: A Paradox

The aim of public international law, as expressed in the U.N. Charter, is, first and foremost, to support and maintain as much as possible, a state of peace and especially, to avoid armed conflicts. It is also a means to the goal of achieving civil and respectful intercourse among states. Yet, ultimately, as it is viewed in Kant's cosmopolitanism, the final aim is the defense of universal human rights, beyond the obstacles posed by the presence of harmful and disrespectful practices that might enhance certain national goals, or enrich certain groups and interests within states, while harming other individuals and peoples. The ultimate aim, within the dual role of international law and the intergovernmental organizations that support and administer the law, are addressed by legal scholars from different points of view. Brownlie says:

> The question of individuals in the scheme of things is more appropriately considered within the framework of human rights protection. In strict analytical terms, it still cannot be said that the individual per se is a subject of international law. The principal connection between the individual and the system of international law is still via the status of nationality (Brownlie, 1998:48).

But crimes against humanity or genocidal crimes against peoples cannot be carried out by a single individual, or against an individual (see Chapter 1):

> "Crimes against humanity" by virtue of their nature and scale require the use of governmental institutions, structures, resources and personnel acting in reliance upon arbitrary power uncontrolled by law. All too frequently, however, governments have managed to co-opt the legal process which produces positive law, thereby claiming "legitimacy" or "lawfulness" for which would otherwise be illegitimate or unlawful (Bassiouni, 1992:241).

This is the crux of the problem. The target of international law is, ostensibly, interstate relations; but international crimes represent institutionalized violence against individuals and peoples, not states. Conversely, the perpetrators of these crimes are states acting through persons in their organizations, bureaucracies, or command.

The argument that confers not only personhood but unitary intent upon corporations, as it explains the difference between a "mob" or a "crowd" on one hand, and a corporate body on the other, can be invoked at this level as well. All institutions act through their CID structure (French, 1984). Their intent appears in the decision they make, the orders they issue to have their decision carried out, and the effects of the decision itself. Even the domestic laws that are either tacit about these crimes, or condone them, are part of the internal decisions reached. Bassiouni says:

> It is interesting to note that throughout the twentieth century most "state action or policy" resulting in mass killings and other mass human rights violations have been committed in reliance on three interactive factors: ideology, terror and positive law. The latter being the instrument of the other two (Bassiouni, 1992:241).

In other words, we must appeal to universal basic principles, according to which we can discriminate between the positive laws that may be instruments of "ideology" and "terror," and what Bassiouni terms "general principles of law." These, he notes, are present in the definition of crimes in "the national criminal laws of the world's major legal systems" (Bassiouni, 1997:246). Although the presence of these crimes, for example murder, rape, slavery, assault, battery, kidnapping in national laws, renders them possible candidates for international crimes, it does not render them *ipso iure* international crimes unless an international connection is present: hence they are only "crimes against humanity" when they are collective crimes (Ibid.).

Hence, when we consider the sources of public, international law, a paradox emerges. These sources encompass "customary," domestic laws, and universal principles, based on the traditional moral theory of natural law (Lauterpacht, 1968; Ragazzi, 1999). The difficulty in this enterprise is clear: how to find, at least in part, the grounds to supersede national domestic laws that may not respect international human rights, within the national domestic laws themselves.

The emphasis on universal principle, on a global approach, to cosmopolitanism, and to *jus cogens* norms, in order to respond to the grave global threats to humanity that this work and many others have detailed, Kindred et al. put the reasons for this quest in a simple sentence:

> The legal doctrine of independence and equality of states must be distinguished from the political and economic reality of a finite world inhabited by globally interdependent nations . . . Fresh air and water are common resources shared by all people. Global warming and ozone depletion know no state boundaries nor are they susceptible to control by a single state. How can a system of sovereign, states take account of these global realities? (Kindred et al., 2000:19).

It is the purpose of this chapter, and of this work as a whole, to attempt to answer this fundamental question, and to clarify, where possible, the various aspects of the paradox mentioned above.

The Declaration on Principles of International Law Concerning Friendly Relations and Co-Operation Among States (1970), also manifests the dual emphasis under discussion. Although all its principles are aimed at interstate relations, it includes statements that may be viewed as self-contradictory, unless the dual purpose of international law is fully appreciated.

For instance, "(c) the duty not to intervene in matters within the domestic jurisdiction of any state in accordance with the Charter," may well conflict with "(e) the principle of equal rights and self-determination of peoples." Similarly, the "duty of states to cooperate with one another in accordance with the Charter" may need to be reconsidered if "(b) . . . universal respect for, and observance of human rights and fundamental freedoms for all" are not present and fully implemented within a state. Hence the "Principle, of sovereign equality of States" must be understood as a contingent, not an absolute principle, as the U.N. Charter provides for "investigation of disputes" (Chapter VI, Article 34); the determination of "the existence of any threat to the peace, breach of the peace, or act of aggression" (Chapter VII, Article 39); and even the decision to employ "economic," and other measures to intervene in the policies of the state whose activities provide the threats, or the presence of the unacceptable situation (Chapter VII, Article 41); finally, the "Security Council" may take such action by air, sea or land forces as may be necessary to maintain or restore international peace or security" (Chapter VII, Article 42; compare Articles 45, 47, and 51). If we understand "security" to include at least the sort of "security" Shue argued for in conjunction with "subsistence" to define basic rights (Shue, 1996), then we are a lot closer to being able to make our case that ecoviolence is-in fact-and should be considered in law, to be an international crime, and that cosmopolitan governance ought to be employed to eliminate it (see Chapter 1).

In the final analysis the paradox of the role of positive, domestic law as one of the sources of international law must be resolved from the standpoint of equity. Our main concern in this work is with equity *praeter legem* and equity, *extra legem*, where the former is used "to fill gaps in the law," and the latter "for refusing to apply unjust laws" (Kindred et al., 2000:151). In the *Diversion of Water from the Meuse* case (Netherlands v. Belgium, 1937), Judge Hudson cites the Permanent Court of International Justice (Norwegian Shipowners Claim, 1922), at 17, as, follows: "The majority of international lawyers seem to agree that these words are to be understood' to mean general principles of justice as distinguished from any particular systems of jurisprudence (Norwegian Shipowners Claims, 1922, at para. 141; 17 Am. J. Int'l. L. 362).

It is a question of substantive justice, as it is best to use moral principles to decide which of the dual roles of international laws, described at the beginning of this section, ought to be considered primary. I believe that the final aim ought to be the protection of humanity, beyond the shield of sometimes spurious legitimacy (in the moral sense) provided by the domestic laws of national states. To this end, peaceful interaction is necessary as an invaluable means, but it cannot be sufficient as such. At any rate, according to Akehurst, equity has three functions:

> . . . it can be used to adapt the law to the facts of individual cases (equity *infra legem*); it can be used to fill gaps in the law (equity *praeter legem*); and it can be used as a reason for refusing to apply unjust laws (equity *contra legem*) (Akehurst, 1976).

Unlike resolutions ex *aequo et bono*, dependent upon the agreement of the states involved in a dispute, the "three functions of equity" do not follow the same mandate. Akehurst adds: ". . . the absence of an express authorization to apply equity does not necessarily mean that an international tribunal is forbidden to apply equity" (Ibid.).

The application of equity in any of its senses, permits tribunals to apply substantive justice considerations at times, rather than "observing legal procedures and formalities" (Ibid. at 803). It is doubtful whether the application of equity in international law may succeed without the parties' agreement. Nevertheless, case law indicates that appeals to the principles of equity, rather than to entrenched procedures, may be used to achieve more just results. In the *English Channel Arbitration*, (France v. United Kingdom, 18 I.L.M. 397 (1979)), the court refers to the Geneva Convention on the Continental Shelf (1958), and to the use of Article 6 and the appeals to equity, as required by the U.N. Convention on the Law of the Sea (1982). There are special circumstances present, hence, Article 6 with its precise requirements for measurement, can only be used *prima facie*, because a delimitation to be equitable or justified, must be so in relation to both parties and in "the light of all relevant circumstances" *English Channel Arbitration* (France v. United Kingdom, 18 I.L.M. 397, at para. 197 (1979)). The close ties between the Channel Islands and the United Kingdom, the latter's obligation of defense of the former, and the economic and political importance of these islands to the UK, meant that a simple mathematical approach to the division of the continental shell "midway between two equidistant lines" (Ibid. at para. 251), would not be correct. The court stated (Ibid. at para. 202): "This second boundary must not, in the opinion of the Court, be so drawn as to allow the continental shelf of the French Republic to encroach upon the established baselines of the territorial sea of the Channel Islands."

Similarly, in the *Continental Shelf* (Tunisia v. Libya, 1982 I.C.J. Rep. 18), the majority of the court stated (Ibid. at para. 71):

Equity is a legal concept is a direct emanation of the idea of justice. The Court whose task it is by definition to administer justice is bound to apply it. In the course of the history of the legal systems the term "equity" has been used to define various legal concepts. It was often contrasted with the rigid rules of positive law, the severity of which had to be mitigated in order to do justice.

Despite the dissenting opinion of Judge Gros who said, *inter alia*, "Equity is not a sort of independent and subjective vision that takes the place of the law," our argument is that equity as the expression of principles of morality, has a substantive and defining role to play, not only in the interpretation of international law, but also in its creation (Kindred et al., 2002:153).

5. PRINCIPLED STRATEGIES TO OVERCOME OBSTACLES TO ECOJUSTICE: SECOND POINT, GLOBALIZING WORLD ORDER AND THE PRESENT "GROTIAN MOMENT"

As I look back on the post-Cold War period, the greatest surprise for me is that the affluent States have done so little toward eradicating global poverty (Pogge, 2001:6).

The problem is both systemic and legal/conceptual. As far as the systemic aspect of the issue is concerned, the basic problem is the existence of a world order that takes its legitimacy from the institutions created and supported by transnational corporations (TNCs), the veritable giants among us who dwarf all other concerns beside profits with their unforgiving power. After the Cold War period, developed countries used their economic and technological growth by cutting their military expenditures, but—at the same time—they also cut "their official development assistance (ODA) . . . by about 27 percent." Pogge adds:

"They have also reduced their allocations to multilateral development efforts, revised Part IX of the 1982 Law of the Sea to the disadvantage of developing countries" (Ibid.).

The results of these decisions and attitudes demonstrate that without a principled strategy, no morally acceptable outcome can result. When gross human rights violations are the consequence of ecological destruction and of extreme poverty, it should not be too hard to identify the policies required to ameliorate the situation, and the legal regimes needed to entrench and enforce such policies. The U.N. Charter, on occasion, permits the use of force for humanitarian interventions, and these have taken place in the past with varying results and effectiveness. In contrast, humanitarian intervention to eradicate "absolute poverty" (Shiva, 1996) and famine, would not present difficulties or be counterproductive, or cause civilian losses, as we encounter regularly in humanitarian interventions like Kosovo, no matter how well intentioned. Giving food and assistance with basic health and education would not engender violence or encounter risks of making a situation worse (Ibid. at 9).

The 1996 World Food Summit in Rome issued a pledge by the 186 participating governments that ends with the following words:

> We consider it intolerable that more than 800 million people throughout the world, and particularly in developing countries, do not have enough food to meet their basic nutritional needs. This situation is unacceptable (*Rome Declarations on World Food Security*, http://www.fao.org/wts/policy/english/96-eng.html) (Ibid. at 10).

This situation is also exacerbated and fostered by global climate change (see Chapter 2), and we have witnessed the lack of interest in signing on to the Kyoto Agreement by the countries who are the worst polluters: the United States and Canada. Yet the International Monetary Fund (IMF), the World Bank, and the World Trade Organization (WTO), led by the United States, "had unprecedented power to shape the global economic order" (Ibid. at 11). Instead of reducing global poverty, the World Bank recognizes its increase and admits "it will reach 1.9 billion by 2015" (World Bank, 1999:25).

Pogge discusses the failures of these institutions by showing "three morally significant connections between us and the global poor." In brief, these are (1) the causal/historical connections of a shared past where the presently wealthy imposed colonialism and slavery on the presently poor, so that the foundation of the formers joint powers and affluence is suspect; (2) we all depend on a single "resource basis," we share the Earth, but only in ways that benefit those better off and harm the others; (3) the present "global economic order," does not redress, but aggravates "global economic inequalities" (Pogge, 2001:14).

The second point of the "connections" is the foundation of this work's argument in our quest for, basic rights for all life. It is also the basis for the immorality of the other two connections as well (see Chapter 2 and 7). The facts adduced by Pogge, in support of his own thesis, confirm the distortion present in the priorities of the global order under the effective control of affluent liberal democracies. This power and control effectively prevent the recognition of the criminality of corporate activities.

The difficulty Pogge emphasizes through the example of global famine, supports Falk's contention that the world as a whole has arrived at a "Grotian moment" (Falk, 1998:4), but thus far we have been unable or unwilling to even attempt to reach across the "normative abyss" that is before us: "A neo-liberal world order based on the functional imperatives of the market is not likely to be a Grotian moment in the normative sense" (Falk, 1998:14).

His main point coincides with the argument here presented: while Grotius was able to "articulate a normative bridge between past and future" at a critical historical moment, the present world order is both unable and unwilling to do so.

Falk notes that the present world order "reflects mainly economistic priorities(Falk, 1998:28), and that the state system has lost much of its credibility in problem solving, in the face of "the rise of market forces" Falk adds:

> We currently confront in this era of economic and cultural globalization a more profound normative vacuum: the dominating logic of the market in a world of greatly uneven social, economics, and political conditions and without any built-in reliable means to ensure that acontinuing global economic growth does nt at some point and in certain respects cause decisive ecological damage (Falk, 1998:26).

Given his clear understanding of many of the forces we have identified as causative of our global dysfunctional condition, it is important to consider what steps Falk proposes as antidotes, if not cure.

While he does not appeal directly to Kantian cosmopolitanism, his proposals include:

(1) "An International Criminal Court with broad powers of investigatin and effective procedures to ensure implementation . . . without being subject to political controls";
(2) A "strong and effective U.N. (with) an environment program capable of protecting the global commons and . . . to ensure respect for undamental obligations to uphold human rights . . .";
(3) Because "the state appears to have lost its creativity and autonomy" as well as its ability to initiate "a new normative order," "the European Union is one exploration of another sort of agency" (Falk, 1998:27–29).

His argument makes clear that, although he thinks people should be heard and be involved in the tranformation necessary to produce a normative framework today, he conceded that we have been "lulled to ideological sleep by a mixture of consumerist allurements and a deadening market-driven ideological consensus" (Ibid. at 30), so that pulling outselves up by our own bootstraps to the demanding normativitiy required to prevent global disaster, appears to be an impossibility.

The combination of aware seenational normativity and the global rule of law Falk advocates, appear at least possible, when we consider the institutions and the juridical fremework of EU governanace.

6. EUROPEAN CITIZENSHIP: A BLUEPRINT FOR COSMOPOLITANISM? IDENTITY AND DEMOCRACY

I suggest then, that the proper grounds for a group's claim to statehood are that it is living, or could live a decent communal life which would be protected or enhanced by statehood, so long as the life of similar groups is not thereby worsened in a way that they have a right to avoid (Gilbert, 1994:123).

Paul Gilbert is here attempting to set the limits to terrorist intervention on behalf of a new or reestablished state, on the part of peoples who cannot achieve statehood simply by democratic procedures. Hence, his argument must set out the minimum acceptable conditions for the claim that taking up arms on behalf of a people might be justified. He adds: "It is not what people do desire, but what is desirable for them, that generates the right, although what is desirable for them is something that they are in a good position to judge" (Ibid.).

The appeal to the good is what has been defended in this work, often in contrast to majority preferences, but always in line with the Kantian understanding of universal laws based upon reason. And this is the first point to consider when we turn to the example of the EU as a "blueprint" for future cosmopolitanism: how do we move from democratically elected nations to a supranational entity? Weiler says: "Citizenship and nationality are more than an element in the mechanics of political organization. We live in an era—perhaps the entire century—obsessed with the question of individual and collective identity" (Weiler, 1999:326).

From the point of view of morality and the principles of international law, our obsession and our quandaries about nationality and about what can make a people, can and should be viewed from the standpoint of the common good, one that is truly universal, rather than represent the aggregate good of the most powerful individuals and institutions.

This has been and is the focus of this work as a whole: how to protect and enhance a basic, universal common good. There would be no need to seek a supranational entity if this good could be achieved and protected through the laws and the constitutions of individual states. But this in not the case; and even the presence of international law instruments, based entirely on consensus or comity represents a step forward, but it is not enough. Hence, the further question: what, if anything, is lost by seeking European citizenship, and what might be gained instead? Weiler argues that "integrationists" claim to be deeply committed to both national identity and welfare and that, "they simply argue that the European Union will enhance these goals and values rather than threaten them" (Ibid.).

The EU is intended as a union of the "peoples of Europe," thus demonstrating recognition and respect for the existence of different peoples, rather than seeking a unitary melting pot. Aside from questions of legitimacy for the EU, the basic point is that states involved may lose control of their functions, but that they have already lost much of that control of economic supranational organs of globalization, and that is what they need to regain. Minimally, they should regain control of their security, both ecological and biological, that is their own ability to protect their citizens from harm. Like laborers, the world over, have discovered, in general, unions are far more powerful than individuals.

From both the environment and the health point of view, no community, state or people, is or can be entirely independent: forming a union to repel or at least restrain unacceptable conditions of life may be the only possible way to protect the ecological integrity of a people's land and of their citizen's health. Both appear more basic and important considerations than the possible loss of national identity, as even multiculturalism in a country such as Canada, effectively masks the presence of many differences among individuals, as individuals (Ibid. at 329).

In addition, when we weigh the presence of democracy, or the effective commitment common to citizens of national states, against the possibility of a "democratic deficit" and the lack of such commitment, we should not start with a romanticized view of national governance. The reality is that, as we have argued, there are already in existence powerful supranational entities, such as the WTO, complete with their own tribunals that supersede national states in the name of trade. Susan Strange says:

> Today it seems that the heads of governments may be the last to recognize that they and their ministers have lost the authority over national societies and economies that they used to have. Their command over outcomes is not what it used to be (Strange, 1996:3).

Hence, it is disingenuous to decry the "democratic deficit" of regimes who, despite their nominal status, have already lost their claim to fully independent national democracy. We have noted the limits of power in the domestic law context (see Chapters 4 and 5), as corporate support virtually eliminates the possibility of a fair and rational choice based on one person/one informed vote, while it allows dollars, not issues, to decide not only elections, but also often, regulatory outcomes. The same occurs, albeit "writ large," in the international realm through globalization. As Strange argues, this is unfortunately not a point of debate: it is the reality of the present situation, hence the starting point of any argument for a better approach.

The proposed cosmopolitanism is intended to ameliorate the status quo by a Kantian revision designed to substitute for it a blueprint based on what Gilbert terms an "ethical revolution," to depart from the present economic hegemony. In other words, if the national state has already had its powers eroded by globalizing structures and instruments of financial power, then those democracies are already, in some sense, "on the block." Our proposal is to substitute the power of Kantian principles for the present economic control. This goal will require that global structures and instruments be accountable to all "cosmic citizens" because of universal moral norms, regardless of their ties to nationalities and ethnic or religious traditions.

The contrast between this approach and that of globalization is clearly in evidence, for instance, when one considers the effect of NAFTA on Canada's welfare state, prior to its introduction. Canada's federalist welfare policies included outright support for the poorest regions in Eastern Canada, ranging from the support of work plans to incentives to prospective corporate employers. Under NAFTA's threat of Chapter 11, such welfare measures may become illegal. If we assume that the previous welfare policies were established by the Canadian government under free democratic conditions, then NAFTA, like GATT and the WTO, runs counter to the choices of national democratic states.

Hence, the quest for a new cosmopolitan orientation based on universal moral principles is a step forward towards the respect for human rights, not a regressive move, even if it requires us to jettison some of the sacred tenets of liberal democracy. Fukuyama argues that "Western liberal democracy [has emerged] as the final form of human government" (Fukuyama, 1989:4). As we have argued, no longer are liberal democracies truly democratic in today's world, but both their economic interests, and their "warlike attitudes" to nonliberal states, have supported wars, genocide, and neocolonialism (Homer-Dixon, 1991).

Susan Marks notes that the belief that liberal democracy is the pinnacle of human achievement is questionable in the present-day context. But Marks also believes that liberal democracy corresponds to Kant's "republic" in his work on "Perpetual Peace." But this is far from the basic position of Kant's work. "Freewill" and "autonomy," the defining characteristics of human beings for Kant, are based on the self-imposition of substantive, nonderogable moral imperatives, not on the procedural emphasis that characterizes liberal democratic "choices," even leaving aside for the moment the manipulated, unfree basis for those choices at this time (Korten, 1996).

For Kant's understanding of "republic" and of the meaning of cosmopolitanism, we need to return to Stoic doctrine:

> The Stoic doctrine that those who have reason, right reason, law and justice in common, thereby belong to a single community, is therefore a reasonable and intelligible thesis (Schofield, 1999:73).

This passage lends support to the argument that Kant's cosmopolitanism is clearly influenced by the Stoic principles and tradition: it is more credible to trace Kant's historical antecedents than to view him as "anticipating" liberalism.

Although this is not the appropriate vehicle for a historical analysis of Kant's doctrine, we can look briefly at some early Stoic and later, Roman Stoic passages to support our contention starting with Chrysippus: ". . . the universe of the wise is one, citizenship in it being held by gods and men together. . . . (Chrysippus cited in Philodemus, *On Piety*, col. Vii 12–viii 4).

On the question of what constitutes a "republic," Clement adds:

The Stoics say that the universe . . . Is in the proper sense a city, but that those here on earth are not—they are called cities—but they are not really. For a city or a people (*demos*) is something morally good . . . an organization or group of men . . . administered by law (Clem. *Strom.* IV 26, SVF III 327).

Finally, turning to Cicero's argument for the cosmic city (or republic): "For the universe is as it were the common home of gods and men, or a city that belongs to both" (Cicero, *De Natura Deorum*, II 3 #154). In essence, the rationality that is viewed as "divine" in both antiquity and later Stoicism, is the foundation for the existence and the moral obligations of the cosmic citizen. Both are far removed from a liberal democracy (see Chapter 7; Weiler, 1999:343) that finds its high expression in the work of people like Rawls, who support procedural fairness, not substantive morality. In addition, there is no evidence that "democracy produces peace" (Marks, 2000:36), the ultimate aim of Kant's work on "Perpetual Peace."

As Cassese has it, the emergence of this sort of cosmopolitanism demonstrates the "coexistence of old and new patterns" (Cassese, 1986:30). Cassese refers to the old patterns of international legal institution based (1) on Hobbes, or the "realist tradition" that views states primarily as competitors; and (2) on the "Grotian, or internationalist conception," based on cooperation among states. The new international model, appears "to be largely patterned on the Kantian" tradition instead, as it seeks a "potential community of mankind" (Cassese, 1986:31). A truly Kantian model, based on moral imperatives and at the same time, embodying and developing the principles of international law, that Weeramantary believed were already implicit in it, unites the other traditions while showing continuity with them. Its main purpose may be to draw away from the wrong turn of economic globalization, in favor of seeking a true cosmopolitanism.

In sum, when we turn to a supranational entity and we appeal to the principles of Kantian cosmopolitanism, we do so to regain respect for universal human rights, not to abandon it. What remains to be considered in this regard is whether the European Union can, in practice, be viewed as capable of bearing this responsibility.

a. The Role and Function of EU Governance

Crucially, the community idea is not meant to eliminate the national state but to create a régime which seeks to tame the national interest with a new discipline. The challenge is to control at the societal level, the uncontrolled reflexes on national interest in the international sphere (Weiler, 1999:342).

In contrast with Marks' position on the commonality between liberal democracy and Kant's moral philosophy, the latter grounds both rights and obligations in the presence of human dignity, after tracing the rejection of nationalism as the ultimate expression of attachment to a group, rather than to universal principles. Weiler says:

> Supranationalism at the societal and individual rather than the state level, embodies an ideal which diminishes the importance of the statal aspects of nationality . . . as the principal reference for transnational human intercourse (Weiler, 1999:343).

Weiler recognizes that "the technology of transnational democracy" needs consideration (Ibid. at 349). Hence, it can be argued that the major perceived stumbling block to accepting an entity like the EU, may not pose as large a stumbling block as some may believe: the "democracy deficit" remains a difficulty, but the EU offers exceptional benefits through supranational governance, and democracy poses its own serious problems.

Neo-liberal democracy was discussed in some detail in Chapter 3, but it is worth adding at this point, that the often discussed democratic deficit that some see as problematic in EU governance, may not be a deficit at all, but a bonus: an indication that the form of governance under consideration may depart from a model of governance fraught with problem. C.B. Macpherson terms the Western affluent nations models of "equilibrium democracy" but, as he points out, (1) "democracy is simply a mechanism for choosing and authorizing governments, not for involving rational deliberation about political matters among citizens;" (2) this model "deliberately empties out the moral context," as democracy is not viewed as a vehicle "for the improvement of mankind"; (3) citizens are here viewed "simply as political consumers, and political society simply as a market relation between them and the suppliers of political commodities"; therefore (4) "democracy," in this model, supports "citizen consumer sovereignty" but delivers nothing better than "equilibrium in inequality" (Macpherson, 1977:77–86)

This model explains the present level of citizens' apathy: as with toothpaste brands or shampoos, for the most part, North American political parties offer no real choice. As in all market transactions, however, those with the higher socio-economic status are benefiting, whereas those who do not enjoy such status do not. Hence, this model remains unjust; in addition, it is totally unsustainable from the ecological point of view (Rees and Wackernagel, 1996: Rees and Westra, 2003). Macpherson argues that this model of democracy will continue to be considered adequate ". . . as long as we in Western Societies continue to prefer affluence to community (and to believe that the market society can provide affluence indefinitely" (Macpherson, 1977:91–92).

This understanding of democracy in Western societies clearly indicates the presence of that "normative abyss" that Falk perceives as endemic to today's political realm. It also points the way to the need for an alternative society, one that has both normativity and community as its focus. Community is emphasized instead in the EU institutions and legal instruments.

According to Article B, the Treaty on European Union (Maastricht) (1992) shall set itself the following objectives: ". . . the strengthen the protection of the rights and interests of the nationals of its member States, through the introduction of a citizenship of the Union."

Citizenship is automatically achieved by belonging to a member state. The final aim is to increase and support consensus, transparency, and political participation by "constructing a European identity" (O'Leary, 1996:39–40). The question of political participation gains prominence because of the need to judge the EU according to the "defining characteristics of a distinctively liberal-democratic legitimacy" (Beetham and Lord, 1998:5).

Beetham and Lord acknowledge that "legal or procedural legality alone" is insufficient to guarantee "political legitimacy" (Ibid. at 6). They also recognize that the purpose of government as a liberal democracy, can best be summarized in terms of Lockean rights protection (life, liberty and property)" (Ibid.).

But we have argued that it is precisely the presence of these standards: (1) the parity of Lockean rights that excludes other vital emphasis on communitarianism and, most of all, on "basic rights" (Shue 1996); and (2) that emphasis on proceduralism at the expense of normativity (we may recall Falk's expression to describe the present situation, a "normative abyss," see Chapter 7), that prompted the quest for Kant's cosmopolitanism instead.

Hence, our standard here is not the one that defines liberal democracy, as outlined above (compare Westra, 1998:ch.3). The last thing that is needed is an EU governance that is reduced to a carbon copy of the U.S. style liberal democracy, as Beetham and Lord even cite the U.S. Declaration of Independence (1776) as an example of what supports the legitimacy of a government. It is worth noting that, even aside from the Kantian/Stoic principles of cosmopolitanism, the Earth Charter (see Appendix 1) is understood to be a covenant of "interdependence" instead, hence far more suited to what we now understand to be the situation of mankind, universally.

We have argued that because of the failure of liberal democracies to recognize and respect the primacy of life and health, and the protection of their habitats as the basic rights of all humanity, there is a need to alter radically our present regulatory infrastructure and governance. The EU appears to provide a possible blueprint for a future product, or for a cosmopolitan form of governance. Of course, the main consideration will remain what the strengths of the EU are, and what might be its powers for remediation in the present global context.

Simon Hix's analysis of the "re-regulative policies" of the EU offers positive support for future strategies. Speaking of the "values" implemented by the EU, Hix says: "As a result EU environmental and social policies may not redistribute resources, but they do produce a reallocation of values in European society" (Hix, 1999:224).

After listing all the EU environmental regulations since 1970, Hix adds that the EU "addresses single market failures," as it "sets standards at both the national and the European levels," adapting the "high standards" of Denmark, Germany, and the Netherlands, rather than the "low standards of Britain, Ireland, and Southern Europe" (Hix, 1999:225–226). Therefore, environmentally speaking, the EU has been able to raise the standards of environmental regulations to a higher level than those prevalent in member states. This remains a desirable result for the protection of everyone's basic rights, even if it is not, as such, the majoritarian choice of all Europeans.

b. EU Governance and the Protection of Life and Public Health

Treaty Establishing the European Community [1957] Article 30 (ex Article 36)

The provisions of Articles 28 and 29 shall not preclude prohibitions or restrictions on imports, exports or goods in transit justified on grounds of public morality, public policy or public security; the protection of health and life of humans, animals or plants; the protection of national treasures possessing artistic, historic or archaeological value; or the protection of industrial or commercial property. Such prohibitions or restrictions shall not, however, constitute a means of arbitrary discrimination or a disguised restriction on trade between Member States.

There are a fair number of EC cases that involve public health issues, and these involve Article 30 (EC Treaty, Part Three, Title 1, Chapter 2), where grounds are sought to validate measures that might otherwise be considered discriminatory (De Burca and Craig, 2002:634). For example in the *Sandoz* case (174/82, Officier van Justitie v. Sandoz, BV (1983) ECR 2445), the Dutch authorities "refused to allow the sale of muesli bars that contained added vitamins, on the grounds that the vitamins were dangerous to health. Article 30 was also fundamental in *Preussen-Elektra* (Case c-379/98, Preussen-Elektra AG v. Schleswag AG, (2001) ECR 1-2099), and doubts were even cast on whether the list of "grounds" in Article 30 was truly exhaustive in *Preussen-Elektra*

. . . Advocate General Jacobs re-examined the issue. He argued that the approach in the Walloon Waste case was flawed, in the sense that, whether a measure was discriminatory was logically distinct from whether it could be justified. He suggested however, that there could be good reasons for allowing environmental protection to be pleaded as a justification, even in cases where there was direct discrimination (De Burca and Craig, 2002:633–634).

In the *Cassis de Dijon* case (Case 120/78, Rewe-Zentrale AG v. Bundes-monopolverwaltung fur Brantwein), the ECJ, in contrast, deemed that the protection of public health was not (in this case) a "decisive consideration" (Ibid. at para. ll) to establish that the rejected import's alcohol content, although it was lower than that prevalent in Germany, was necessarily conducive to addiction or other harmful health effects. But the *Simmenthal* case (Simmenthal SpA v. Commission (Case 92/78) (1979) ECR 777, (1980) 1 CMLR) demonstrates that extraordinary health measures (e.g., a second veterinary opinion) may be necessary to protect the public in the case of transboundary movement of beef and beef products. Yet the case is viewed in the literature as an example of the affirmation of the supremacy of community law over national law, with some overtones of market protectionism for Italy's own beef producers.

At any rate, the combination of a forward-looking "teleological" law, as exemplifies for instance by Article 308 (ex Article 235), often used to introduce and justify measures for environmental protection or other normatively desirable outcomes, on one hand, and the presence of "judicial activism" on the other (Lord Howe of Aberavon, (1996) European Law Rev. 187, at 190–193; compare Tridimas, (1999) European Law Rev.), together appear to distance EU Law from all other trade agreements as we noted in Chapter 6. Lord Howe cites Sir Thomas Bingham in *Customs and Excise v. Samex:*

> The interpretation of Community Instruments invokes very often . . . the creative process of supplying flesh to a spare and loosely constructed skeleton, and the taking of a broader view of what the orderly development of the Community requires (1983, 1 All E.R. 1042, 1056).

This approach, present in ECJ judgments is similar to the position of Mme. L'Heureux-Dubé's judgments, discussed in Chapter 2, and it also supports the view of Prof. V. Dicey pro "judge made law," also present in the words of Article 4 from the Code Napoleon: "Le juge qui se refuse de juger, sous prétexte du silence, de l'obscurité ou de l'insuffisance de la loi, pourra etre poursuivi comme coupable de déni de justice" (cited in Dicey, 1926).

This forward-looking approach to law, coupled with a supranational form of governance that is inherently (though not exclusively) normative, manifests a deep contrast with the approach of trade organizations such as the GATT or the WTO (see Chapter 3).The conflict between the two approaches comes to a head in *the Hormones* case (EC Measures concerning Meat and Meat Products (Hormones), Appellate Body Report, Adopted Feb. 13, 1998, WTO Doc. WT/DS26/AR/R and WT/DS48/AD/U). In this case, the United States tried without success to remove the EC import ban "on meat raised with growth hormones" (Fidler, 2000: 233),which according to Fidler's report are at least five hormones. The case hinged upon several issues: (1) the use of the Precautionary Principle; (2) public health protection; (3) the nature and import of risk assessment on the part of the European Community. All these issues were brought into question in the case the United States brought to the WTO.

The Panel Report, issued Aug. 18, 1997 (WTO Doc. WT/DS26/R/USA), is a lengthy and complex document, hence we will limit our discussion to the three areas listed above. The first difference between the EC and the WTO centers on the nature and the role of the Precautionary Principle. The EC viewed it as a "general, customary rule of international law," or least, as "a general principle of law." Further, the EC believed that it was "not necessary for *all* scientists around the world to agree on the possibility and the magnitude" of the risk, nor for all of the WTO members to perceive and evaluate the risk in the same way (Ibid. at para. 121). In the following paragraph the United States, position is outlined: "The United States does not consider that the 'precautionary principle' represents customary international law and suggests it is more 'an approach' than a 'principle.'"

The implication here, of course, is that if it is not a principle of law, then its use does not have the legitimacy it might otherwise have; and, if the U.S. position is accepted, the use of the principle might be termed "arbitrary."

The second problem concerns the nature of public health, based on international standards and the debate between the possible interpretations of Article 3.1 of the SPS Agreement, which states:

> To harmonize sanitary and phytosanitary measures on as wide a basis as possible, Members shall base their sanitary or phytosanitary measures on international standards, guidelines or recommendations, where they exist, except as otherwise provided for in this Agreement, and in particular in paragraph 3.

The question is whether it is possible to equate measures "based on international standards," with "measures which *conform to* such standard," therefore, whether one or the other interpretation is the basis of the EC's understanding of "public health" (Scott, 2000:144–158). It is clear that "based on" certain standards is not the same as being in conformity or compliance with these standards. Hence, the scientific justification required by the EC may well be understood to exceed international standards, rather than simply to conform to them.

Finally, on the question of risk assessment, Paragraph 4 of Annex A of the SPS Agreement defines risk assessment: ". . . the evaluation of the *potential* for adverse effects on human or animal health arising from the presence of additives, contaminants, toxins, or disease—causing organisms in food, beverages or feed-stuffs (emphasis added; Fidler, 2001:240). The problem is that, although the Panel refers to "potential" as an alternative to "probability," "potential" is a concept much closer to "possible" than to "probable" and the European Community's understanding of risk assessment sees risk as present when the mere *possibility* of harm to human health is present. Five levels of protection of human health are required by the EC:

(1) the level of protection in respect of natural hormones when used for growth promotion;
(2) the level of protection in respect of natural hormones occurring endogenously in meat or other food;
(3) the level of protection in respect of natural hormones when used for therapeutic or zoo technical purposes;
(4) the level of protection in respect of synthetic hormones (zeranol and trenbolone) when used for growth promotion; and
(5) the level of protection in respect to carbadox and olaquindox.

Aside from details pertaining to point (5), which are both technical and complex (Fidler, 2001:245–247), all other listed levels of protection indicate a perfectly understandable and scientifically supportable stance, which eliminated the possibility of an arbitrary position on the part of the EC. Even if the EC has economic interests in addition to the health concerns, that is, if it had an interest in protecting its own beef sources, the fact remains that there is a solid position in defense of public health, in the face of the cancer epidemic that exists (Epstein, 1989). Nor is this case unique. In the later case of *Portugal v. Council* (Case C-149/96, (1999) ECR I-8395), the ECJ judgment stated (Ibid. at para. 47): "It follows for all those considerations, that having regard to their nature and structure, the WTO agreements are not in principle among the rules in the light of which the Court is to review the legality of measures adopted by the Community institutions." Aside from cases which place the main goals of the community laws ahead of the economic goals of trade agreements, there are also some ECJ cases that reaffirm the primacy of life and health of individuals explicitly, and the direct effect of Community law over national law, in cases where these are at issue (Guerra v. Italy, (1998) 26 EHRR 357) and Lopez-Ostra v. Spain, (1995) 20 EHRR 277, (1994) ECHR 16798/90)). Both cases were brought to the ECJ after the plaintiffs failed to receive satisfaction from their respective countries. For the *Guerra* case, although at first the Italian government expressed a preliminary objection based on "non-exhaustion of domestic remedies," the court did not accept their argument: had they pursued such remedies, at best they might have caused a temporary closure of the plant, perhaps even a criminal conviction of the factory's managers. However, such a course of action would not have provided them with the information they sought, or any redress.

The court judged, in the merits of the complaint that the state had failed to act:

> Direct effect of basic emissions on applicant's right to respect for private and family life meant that Article 8 was applicable. Applicants complained not of an act of State, but of its failure to act—object of Article 8 was essentially that of protecting individuals against arbitrary interferences by public authority—it did not merely compel State to abstain from such interference: in addition to that primarily negative undertaking, there might be positive obligations inherent in effective respect for private or family life.

This case concerns a group of citizens of Manfredonia, located one kilometer away from Erichem Agricoltura, a chemical factory involving the release of large quantities of inflammable gas. Often the operation caused chemical explosions that spewed highly toxic substances into the air. In 1988 the factory was classified as "high risk" according to Council Directive (EEC) 82/501m, that is, the major accident hazard of industrial activities, "dangerous to the environment and the well being of local populations" (Guerra v. Italy, "Head note").

Forty citizens complained to the European Commission of Human Rights that the action and especially the omissions of the Italian authorities had violated Article 10, as well as Articles 8 ("Respect for Family and Home,") and 2 ("Right to Life") of the EU Convention. Article 10, Freedom of Expression, emphasizes something on which this work has focused: the exercise of freedom is and must be limited by responsibilities and duties:

Article .10(2)—Freedom of Expression

> The exercise of these freedoms, since it carries with it duties and responsibilities, may be subject to such formalities, conditions, restrictions and penalties as are prescribed by law and are necessary in a democratic society, in the interest of national security, territorial integrity or public safety, for the prevention of disorder or crime, for the protection of health or morals, for the protection of the reputation or rights of others, for preventing the disclosure of information received in confidence, or for maintaining the authority and impartiality of the judiciary.

This article is outstanding among other international human rights instruments because of the thorough and painstaking way it outlines the "duties and responsibilities" that balance and limit all "freedoms" not only freedom of expression, but also "freedom of thought, conscience and religion" (Article 9): "public safety," "the protection of health and morals" and, in Article 9 (a), in addition, "the protection of the public order." Hence, the freedom of the corporate enterprise is by no means absolute, and it does not appear to extend as far as it does in North American instruments, as it is clearly limited even in the realm of legally sanctioned activities.

In turn, the freedom of citizens to be safe in their homes, and to retain their health is openly considered to have been under attack. The right to protection extends, according to Article 8, to the right of respect for the "well-being" of persons, and the "respect for their private and family life." The failure of the Italian authorities to protect the "right to life" extends to the protection of "physical integrity," as guaranteed by Article 2 of the European Covenant (1950). Although this extension is not explicitly spelled out in the language of the covenant, it represents a juridical extension by analogy (Judge Amedeo Postiglione, Oct. 2, 2002, private communication). The logic of this extension has also been argued as the necessity for microintegrity given its clear connection to ecological (macro) integrity, in my earlier work (Westra, 1998).

Returning to *Guerra* ((1998) 26 EHRR, 357), eventually several steps were taken to impose government restraints on the corporation, because of the status of the latter under Council Directive (EEC) 82/501 (under the *Seveso* directive). In 1993, the Ministry of the Environment issued an order, jointly with the Ministry of Health prescribing measures to be taken (Ibid. at para. 17), and in 1994 the factory permanently stopped the production of fertilizer (Ibid. at para. 18).

But already in 1985, 420 residents of Manfredonia complained of the health effect of the air pollution, and criminal proceedings had been brought to bear against seven directors of the company (Ibid. at para. 19). The court declared that "a complaint is characterized by the facts alleged in it and not merely by the legal grounds or arguments relied on" (Ibid. at para. 44), hence, despite objections on various legal points, it concluded: "46. Having regard to the foregoing and to the Commission's decision on admissibility, the Court holds that it has jurisdiction to consider the case under Articles 8 and 2 as well as under art.10." Aside from the disposition of the case ordered by the court in favor of Guerra and the other citizens, it is instructive to read a paragraph in the "Concurring Opinion of Judge Jambrek" as he, as well as Judge Walsh, hold that this case clearly represents a violation under Article 2:

> *Article 2* states that "Everyone's right to life shall be protected by law. No one shall be deprived of his life intentionally save . . ." The protection of health and physical integrity is, in my view as closely associated with the right to life as with "respect for private and family life." An analogy may be made with the court's case law on art 3 concerning the existence of "foreseeable consequences" where *mutatis mutandis*-substantial grounds can be shown for believing that the person(s) concerned face a real risk of being subjected to circumstances which

endanger their health and physical integrity, and thereby put at serious risk their right to life, protected by law. If information is withheld by a government about circumstances which foreseeable, and on substantial grounds, present a real risk of danger to health and physical integrity, then such a situation may also be protected by art 2 of the convention: "No one shall be deprived of his life intentionally."

This case, I believe, demonstrates, without a doubt, the strength of the EU Covenant and the position of the European Court of Human Rights, in contrast with other venues discussed above, both domestic and international, but also in the United States, based on the example of the Constitution of Pennsylvania (see Chapters 4 and 6). What is striking is the lack of any effort to "balance interests," and the lack of any argument citing the "economic and social interests" of the legal persons involved in maintaining a noxious operation, despite its effects on the health of citizens.

This is a major consideration in our quest for a blueprint for an improved regime, based on a supranational regulatory framework. Another case offers further evidence of the judicial superiority of the EU Court of Human Rights: the case of *Lopez-Ostra v. Spain* ((1995) 20 EHRR 277, (1994) ECHR 16798/90). Mrs. Lopez-Ostra lived in Lorca (Murcia), a town with a high concentration of leather industries, all of which belonged to SACURSA, a company that also had a plant for the treatment of liquid and solid waste, built with a state subsidy on municipal land, 12 miles away from Lopez-Ostra's home, in July 1998 (Ibid. at para. 8).

The gas fumes and other contamination, arising from the tanneries and the waste treatment operation, caused health problems to many in Lorca, and in September 1988 health authorities, and the Environmental and Nature Agency (Agencia para el Medio Ambiente y la Naturaleza), forced the company to cease some of its activities, and relocated elsewhere a number of residents. However, some of the practices of the operation were allowed to continue, such as the treatment of waste water contaminated with chromium (Ibid. at para. 9). Mrs. Lopez-Ostra sought protection of her fundamental rights, and the language of her complaint in worthy of note (Ibid. at para. 10):

> She complained, inter alia, of an unlawful interference with her home and her peaceful enjoyment of it, a violation of her right to choose freely her place of residence; attacks on her physical and psychological integrity, and infringements of her liberty and her safety (Articles 15, 17(1), 18(2) and 19 of the (Spanish] Constitution.

Despite the strong evidence available, both the Municipal and the Supreme Court of her country dismissed both her case and her appeal, respectively. Evidence was eventually accumulated by the National Toxicology Institute, the

Ministry of Justice Institute of Forensic Medicine (Cartagena) and even by three police offices called to the home. The health effects were listed as "a clinical picture of nausea, vomiting, allergic reactions, and anorexia," in addition to acute symptoms of "bronchopulmonary infections" (Ibid. at para. 19), all in clear conflict with Article 15 of the Spanish Constitution: "Article 15: Everyone shall have the right to life and to physical and psychological integrity."

Hence, once again, we see the protection of fundamental human rights and environmental protection provisions, coupled explicitly in a way that justifies the imposition of severe penalties, including imprisonment and hefty fines, and allows the temporary or permanent closure of the establishment in question. Under the EU Covenant, the Court found that there had been a breach of Article 8 and awarded 4 million pesetas for damages, and 1.5 million for costs and expenses to Mrs. Lopez-Ostra.

In sum, not only are the relevant article of the EU Convention on Human Rights progressively and analogically applied and understood, but there is little or no effort to view as comparable economic (corporate) rights on one hand, and health/life rights (individual or group based), on the other. Therefore, the EU appears to be far ahead of other similar courts. In the next section we will see a similar case, argued in a similar way by Greek Authorities, around 400 B.C. in a tannery edict, that is thought to be the first environmental regulation and decree known (see Section 6.c).

Both cases show first of all, that the right to life can be extended analogically to the right to health and to biological integrity, hence that the connection between the latter and the environment, possibly even environmental rights themselves gain support, at least in principle. Second, those omissions to protect and to give information to citizens, on the part of a state, are perceived as culpable. Like direct interference, negligent omissions that support or enable operations that impose risks, constitute a punishable harm, even if specific intent to harm is not present. Article 10(2) of the Convention may be viewed as prohibiting a government from preventing citizens from receiving information (Lender v. Sweden, A/116 (1987) 9 E.HR.R. 433).

The Council Directive of June 7, 1990 on the Freedom of Access to Information on the Environment states: "Article 1—The object of this directive is to ensure the freedom of access to and dissemination of information on the environment held by public authorities and to set out the basic terms and conditions on which such information should be made available."

In addition, Article 4 enables whoever considers that the request for information has been unreasonably refused or ignored, or has been inadequately answered by a public authority has the right to seek "judicial or administrative review." This position of the Court represents, in part, one of the bases for the successfully conclusion of both cases cited.

Third, in the *Lopez-Ostra* case, the Court stated (Ibid. at para. 52):

Admittedly, the Spanish authorities, and in particular the Lorca municipality were theoretically not directly responsible for the emissions in question. However, as the Commission pointed out, the town allowed the plant to be built on its land, and the State subsidized the plant's construction.

This is a significant point, and a version of this argument was advanced in Chapter 4 in relation to the *Walkerton* case (Chapter 4). Although the Ontario conservative government had not provided funding for factory farms, nevertheless it had directly or indirectly allowed those practices and limited the regulation and inspection regimes that were used to protect public health. Under these conditions, a government ought to be seen at least as complicit, if not directly responsible for harmful industrial practices it has permitted.

Although there are no specific environmental rights in the European Convention of Human Rights, these cases come close to deriving such rights not only from Article 8, but also from Article 3. Kiss and Shelton (1997:84), cite Article 45, para. 11 of the 1978 Spanish Constitution, which ". . . speaks of the right to enjoy an environment suitable for the development of the person."

Principle 1 of the Stockholm Declaration says:

Man has the fundamental right to freedom, equality and adequate conditions of life, in an environment of a quality that permits a life of dignity and well-being, and he bears a solemn responsibility to protect and improve the environment for present and future generations.

The link between the right to life and that to a "suitable" environment is in the fact that both life and health depend upon environmental conditions (Kiss and Shelton, 1997:85; compare Soskolne and Bertollini, 1999).

Fourth, Article 3, Prohibition of Torture, states:" No one shall be subjected to torture or to inhuman or degrading treatment or punishment." In *Lopez-Ostra*, the Court did not view the severe health effects suffered by the applicant and her family as sufficiently grave to be termed "inhuman or degrading treatment" (Ibid. at paras. 59 and 60), although Mrs. Lopez-Ostra had so characterized her ordeal (Ibid. at para. 30) (see also Birnie and Boyle, 2002:252–254, 287, n.10). The Court's response appears to be less a rejection in principle of the possibility of viewing environmental harm in that light, than a matter of the gravity of a specific instance of harm. The Court's decision would allow the harm to be viewed as a difference of degree of "inhumanity" or "degradation," rather than a difference in kind between environmental harms and torture. This interpretation supports the understanding of ecocrime in this work.

Finally, moving from substantive to procedural matters, both cases support the choice of a supranational regulatory entity, as better able than either internal or international tribunals to restrain, and, if necessary, redress environmental harms.

The Supremacy of the European Convention on Human Rights over (European) state law is shown to be absolute, as is its ability to redress environmental human rights violations, rather than being hampered by economic agreements that might prescribe, and, in fact, demand a different course.

c. EU Governance and the Protection of Nature

. . . and let the king provide. The present decree should be transcribed on blocks of stone and placed on both sides. It is forbidden to throw out leather to rot in the Ilissus river near the Temple of Hercules, also the practice of tanning, and disposing of the wastes in the Ilyssus river (author's translation) (440–430 B.C., Karousos, "Apo to Heraklion touKounosargos" Archaiologicon Deltion 8 (1923) 96–98).

The one here cited is the first ecologically based decree in the Western world, to my knowledge. Livio Rossetti argues that it is not a "sacred edict," or only a "local norm." Probably spurred by the presence of a pestilence erupting in Athens around that time, the citizens intended to protect human life, health, and the environment, particularly the watercourses, as other documents speak of noxious odors, or of water that is no longer limpid. Moreover, they connected these environmental conditions to human health, an insight that apparently has taken humankind a long time to recover. In addition, unlike modern humans, these ancient Greeks were prepared to prohibit one of the most lucrative business operations in their country, leather tanning for sandals and other paraphernalia for their soldiers, despite the ensuing damage to their economy (Rossetti, 2002).

Perhaps this early decree was a portent of things to come, and Europe, even today, may show its superiority through the presence of a great number of environmental decrees, although, not all the countries of the present EU are equally enthusiastic in their promotion of environmental protection. At any rate, most European countries have adopted general laws on environmental protection, the earliest Sweden (1969), the latest to date Slovenia and the Netherlands (1993), and the most recent, France (1994) (Kiss and Shelton, 1997:17).

In addition, there is a global trend present in Europe, but especially in the Eastern European countries, to entrench constitutional protection of environmental rights, such as Article 72 of the Republic of Slovenia:" . . . each person shall have the right in accordance with the statute to a health environment in which to live (1991)" (Kiss and Shelton, 1997:15)

Another important trend can be found in Section 5.1. of the Netherlands Environmental Protection Act of May 1993, regarding orders in council for environmental quality. No. 4 states: "the options for restricting as far as reasonably possible *the risks to the environment* caused by environmentally damaging factors occurring as the result of the requirements" (Kiss and Shelton, 1997:15) (emphasis added). The important point is that the risk to be avoided is to the environment: this trend is one of the many EC Directives for the protection and conservation of natural habitats, based on the mandates of the UNESCO Convention of the Protection of the World's Cultural and Natural Heritage (1972), which obliges each state ". . . to identify and delineate the different natural areas situated in its territory that are of outstanding interest and need to be preserved as part of the world heritage of mankind" (Kiss and Shelton, 1997:196).

We have referred to the need to conserve wild areas in order to support all life by retaining nature's services (Daly, 1997). In this regard, we have cited the Wildlands Project and the work of Reed Noss in North America (Noss, 1992; Noss and Cooperrider, 1994). The Wildlands Project recommends the formation of a connected ecological network of natural habitats, and this is the main focus of Natura 2000, a similar enterprise supported by the EU. But the North American project is not part of a regulatory regime: it is simply funded by private charitable institutions like the Pew Foundation. In contrast, the World Heritage Convention (1972) and the Ramsar Convention on Wetlands (1971) establish general guidelines, and they leave the required task to prescribe more specific plans to each party state, as part of their regulative framework.

From the standpoint of the protection of ecological integrity, one of the goals of the original Wildlands Project, many of the European countries (such as Spain or Germany), not only establish nature reserves and parks, but also they have laws that provide special control for the buffer zones around protected areas. Sweden, for instance, under the Swedish Water Act ". . . calls for denying permits for proposed activities upstream of a natural park or nature reserves when the activity will result in damage to the protected area" (Kiss and Shelton, 1997:199). The creation of buffer zones, in general, is an integral part of what I have termed "living in integrity" (Westra, 1998), that is, ensuring that our activities are compatible with and respectful of fully protected wild areas of sizes equal to the task of providing life support through the systemic processes present in these areas. The size and number of protected, wild lands in Europe vary greatly from country to country; for instance, France only has 10 percent, while Norway's figure is 5.6 percent. According to Danish law, all activities incompatible with conservation, including agriculture, are restricted around these areas, which are to remain "uninhabited and, as much as possible, undisturbed" (Kiss and Shelton, 1997:200).

These areas may be termed (1) nature reserves; (2) national parks; (3) game preserves or sanctuaries; (4) national monuments; and (5) wilderness reserves. The latter comprises 4.4 percent of the country in Finland, and in Italy "mountains above 1,600 metres line are protected from quarrying, building and road construction" (Kiss and Shelton, 1997:201). In addition, as indicated above, EU protection appears to be both comprehensive and fully integrated into the regulatory framework of the Union. Best of all, the difficult and debated question of intrinsic value, so problematic in North America and in general, even in the environmental ethics literature, is confronted head on:

The *Convention on the Conservation of European Wildlife and Natural Habitats* (Berne, September 19, 1979) reflects many modern concepts of nature conservation. It refers to wild flora and fauna as a natural heritage of intrinsic value that must be preserved and handed on to future generations and emphasizes the importance of conserving natural habitats as one of the essential elements of conservation (Kiss and Shelton, 1997:203).

The protection of ecological complexity in natural systems also extends to coastal and marine ecosystems, to specially protected areas of Mediterranean importance (SPAMI List), and to a Special Convention for the Protection of the Alps (1991), which involved the EC, Austria, France, Germany, Italy, Lichtenstein, Switzerland, and Yugoslavia (Kiss and Shelton, 1997:205). It is also well-known (see Chapter 6) that the EU has far more stringent regulations than the United States in place to control the handling of genetically modified organisms (GMOs) at the laboratory level, but also for their possible release into ecosystems, whether for the purpose of conducting tests or for commercial exploitation (Kiss and Shelton, 1997:207). In fact, the Council of Europe Convention on Civil Responsibility for Damage Resulting from the Exercise of Activities Dangerous for the Environment, includes measures for damage caused by GMOs (EC Directive on the Containment of GMOs, 90/219/EEC,OJ No. L 117, May 8, 1990 at 209–210).

In addition the U.K., Environmental Protection Act (1990) prohibits the release of "substances" into the environment, that might cause harm, under Sections 7(2)(i), (ii), and (3)(b), in a way that may apply not only to polluting substances, but perhaps also to GMOs, and that is highly reminiscent of the classic *Rylands v. Fletcher* (1866) case (see Chapter 5).

A particularly interesting case in point is that of the Netherlands. Both the Meuse and the Rhine Rivers are extremely polluted, and the country as a whole is highly industrialized so that urbanization and intensive agriculture have been taking a heavy toll on the environment. By the 1980s the Dutch government was well aware of the sad state of its natural systems. In 1988 Queen Beatrix addressed a speech to these problems, as she spoke of "the special responsibility of the present generation" as she proposed "that attention be paid to the 'rights of nature'" (van der Zande and Wolters, 1997:219).

The Netherlands represents a special, extreme case, as most of its land is utilized, leading to that "fragmentation of nature" their government termed "a form of pollution" in their Outlook document (Punter, Olieman and Partners, 1992).

Hence the Dutch faced the necessity of "withdrawing" presently used land to enlarge and even create nature reserves (Ibid. at 221).

This brief, cursory overview of some of the proposed regulatory regimes and environmental goals in Europe, reveals a more advanced stance, for the most part, than what can be found in North America and emphasizes certain interesting features of these regulations. First, there seems to be a strong common interest in both protection and respect for wild/natural areas, due perhaps to the much smaller quantities of available land in each state than one finds in North America's states and provinces. Second, there appears to be less difficulty in accepting not only the instrumental, but also the intrinsic value of natural ecosystems and habitats across nations, than one might find in the American continent. As an example, the Netherlands no longer limits its regulations to prescribing some sort of "wise use" of natural resources, including flora and fauna, but they now favor "the intrinsic value of the animal" as the guideline, which means that habitats will be protected even outside national ecological networks (Ibid. at 225). Of course, the Netherlands is a particularly interesting state as only the future will tell whether it is even possible to recreate natural, wild areas, when these have been lost to ecologically unsound practices a long time ago.

Another point worthy of note is that both the science and the language of these environmental documents shows clearly the acceptance of European nations of both complexity of natural systems, and the value of the ecosystem approach, something that has been (and still is) fought in both scientific and policy-making fora in North America (Shrader-Frechette and McCoy, 1993; Simberloff, 1982), where many powerful players, including government granting agencies, supported the failed "populations" approach to ecology, or preferred to avoid ecology and even conservation biology altogether (Pimm, 1991), when proposing public policy objectives.

One may be encouraged by the fact that, roughly at the same time that Western philosophy and moral reasoning was initiated in Greece, one can also find the birth of ecological concern, at least in the decree cited above. One can also point to the Stoic concept of "cosmic citizenship" for a positive approach to principled national governance, of which the EU appears to provide an example worthy of study.

7. THE EUROPEAN UNION COMMUNITY: A MODEL FOR WORLD GOVERNMENT

> The Community vision is . . . premised on limiting or sharing sovereignty in a select albeit growing number of fields, on recognizing, and even celebrating the reality of interdependence, and on counterposing to the exclusivist ethos of statal autonomy a notion of a community of states and peoples sharing values and aspirations (Weiler, 1991:2479).

To propose the EU as a template of expanding human rights protection is to transcend the view of the EU as a "federation" (Lenaerts, 1994: 846), like the

United States or Canada, but to view it instead as a community, whose most important aspect is the vision upon which it is based. To do so is not to be able to trace a clear, linear path from the way ecocrimes are approached (or denied) in national and international law, to the model of a legal system where the acceptance and treatment of ecocrimes as such is a legal given. It is not to acknowledge and research the presence of *lex lata*, but to advocate strongly a *lex ferenda* that recognizes and celebrates human interdependence with all natural systems. Just as my earlier work was presented as a "proposal for ethics" (Westra, 1994) suggesting that a radically different understanding of morality is now necessary, as earlier doctrines had not (and could not have) understood the interdependence between natural systems and human biological ones, so too I now can only propose that this interdependence must be incorporated in legal regimes, globally, if the protection and the defense of human rights is to become complete and a reality.

In order to achieve this goal in human ethics, individual self-interest must be transcended, and this is the accepted starting point of morality: our self-concern must be limited by respect for others and by the recognition that their fulfillment and their happiness must be of equal concern to us, for justice to be present. In international law, in order to achieve global justice, a similar argument must be accepted: each state must be prepared and willing to give up sovereignty in certain areas (that is, to abandon the primacy of self-concern), in order to achieve a higher level of joint justice. This is not to abandon democracy, but to expand social policy into "major substantive areas," of which "environmental protection" is one (Weiler, 1991:2452).

Although in many areas jurisdictional limits remain within the ambit of state law, when conflicts of competence arise, the doctrine of absorption entails that "community competence must prevail" (Weiler, 1991:2441). Absorption is only one of the categories of mutation present in EU law; extension is another: "Extension is mutation in the area of autonomous Community jurisdiction. The most striking example of this change is the well-known evolution of a higher law of human rights in the Community" (Weiler, 1991:2437).

Although there is not, at this time, an EU "Bill of Rights," the present legislative framework represents a step towards a review of present instruments, in view of creating such a document in the future.

The main point to note then, is that the blueprint referred to earlier in O'Neill's work is present here, unlike governance under treaties and agreements which give primacy to trade and economic issues, hence to state interests analogous to prudential self-interest in individuals. The EU form of governance instead represents a competing vision, so that the strategies it proposes and implements do not simply move from positive to strategic analysis, bypassing altogether the normative aspects of their decisions, but that normatively is clearly incorporated into the pillars of the EU (Laffan, 2001:709), as is the "centrality of law" in their supranational legal order: "The compulsory/obligatory part of the EU's patrimony has produced its own Euro-term—the *acquis communautaire*. In the absence of other glue, the *acquis* (the body of law/policies that currently runs to over 80,000 pages) is sacrosanct" (Laffan, 2001:712). Laffan traces the core characteristics of the EU, thus also tracing "the consolidation of a supranational polity" (Puchala, 1999:329). This supranational polity is in evidence also through our brief examination of case law in regard to human health (see Section 6.b), as the ECJ clearly supports the focus on "values and norms as guideline to social and political behavior" that prevail in the EU as a "community of values" (Laffan, 2001:714). To be sure, many of these norms are procedural rather than substantive. Nevertheless, the supremacy of the community's norms in the law renders the EU ongoing "transformation" a valid model on which to rest future human rights. Equally significant, the increasing power of the EU augurs well for the possibility of an increasing global influence and power against the presence of other purely economic power alliances.

This argument's conclusion does not represent the laying out of an adopted practical legal system, but it indicates more than a vague direction to which the EU might be moving. It shows that the European Community's "transformation" (to use Weiler's felicitous expression once again), already contains within it the embryonic form of what it can become, and more than likely, what it will become in time. Support for this argument may be found in the existence of the *acquis communautaire* on which EU policy depends. The *acquis* represents the nonderogable aspect of EU governance; its presence and that of the normative pillar of which it is a part, render the EU form of governance close to embodying, at least in the areas where community supremacy prevails, *erga omnes* obligations. These are equally nonderogable, nonnegotiable and based upon principles, hence unlike treaties or even politically negotiated internal laws. In fact the presence of the *acquis* and of the "normative vision" to which Weiler refers, render the EU regulatory framework opposite to the rules of trade organizations such as the GATT or the WTO (see Chapter 3). For instance, we noted that the Preamble of Article XX of the WTO privileges trade/economic issues over the protection of health and the environment. In contrast, the ECJ in its judgments gives primacy to health even over trade fairness, as we saw in Section 6.b.

It could be objected that all strategies proposed in this chapter remain largely in the realm of theory. That is true, to some extent: if ecocrimes were already accepted in international or domestic laws and their true impact recognized, there would have been no need to write this work in the effort to make the case that they should be so viewed, in the name of science, morality, and justice, as has been argued. But theory like natural law (see Chapter 1) is implicit in the principles of international law, and is explicit in the normative aspect of the EU *acquis* and in the teleological transformation of the European Community. The theory therefore is like an acorn, eventually to become a full-grown, majestic oak tree, representing a legislative framework for the complete protection of human rights, beyond the protection of procedural rights or simple human preferences. The respect and protection that is the goal of this unfolding, is, in essence, the respect and protection of the biological and functional integrity that defines the most basic right of humanity.

In sum, although we must acknowledge the number and the magnitude of the obstacles we face to protect human rights and life on Earth, the few strategies we can propose, on balance, have a strength of their own. The biological understanding of natural law; the tradition of deontological moral principles, as superior to economic preferences, the re-birth of aspirations to respect for natural entities and processes (witness the mounting protests to globalization in that regard); and the historical permanence of law, from Ancient Greece to today's aspirations to a functioning International Criminal Court, or an International Environmental Court, all offer a promise on which we can build a morally sound cosmopolitanism, based on national governance and law.

a.   A Recent Canadian Development: Former Bill C-45 on Corporate Criminality

The focus of this work has been for the most part on the need to transcend domestic law and its limitations in order to emphasize supranational regulatory regimes. Nevertheless a new domestic law development is worthy of note: on November 7, 2003, the final draft of An Act to Amend the Criminal Code S.C. 2003, C.21 [formerly Bill C-45] was completed and received Royal Assent (and thus became law). This bill addressed some of the lacunae and limitations of the Canadian Criminal Code, amending the language of several sections with that aim in mind.

Corporations were originally formed and given a juridical personality separate from that of the aggregate of their officers, shareholders, employees, and agents for one reason only: to ensure their economic protection, thus to encourage investment in their activities. It was never the intention of the legislators and the courts to declare that corporations would be granted a new form of immunity from criminal prosecution, similar to the immunity enjoyed by the representatives of States, and those involved in activities on behalf of various nations. Thus criminal prosecution should equally be available when the accused is an organization, that is a group joined in a common purpose as well as a corporation. The example given in Bill C-45 is that of a municipality. The substitution of "organization" for "corporation" in several Sections of the Criminal Code is one of the objectives of Bill C-45.

Another main objective of Bill C-45 is to address the question of *mens rea*, which posed a serious difficulty for any court attempting to impose criminal liability to an organization, as was discussed in Chapters 4 and 5. The inability to ascribe the requisite form of criminal intent on the part of corporations and associations, ensured that a wide array of regulatory breaches for workplace safety and public health or environmental offences, would be viewed as "quasi-crimes," rather than "true crimes."

This work has argued for both of these points (see Chapter 8-A, Section 3.a for a summary of the arguments), and it is gratifying to realize that, although there is no case law at this time based on Bill C-45, many of the changes proposed earlier as possible *lex ferenda* have now acquired the status of *lex lata* instead

Therefore, it might be useful:

(1) to review briefly the actual changes Bill C-45 introduces in the Criminal Code; and

(2) to show precisely where the Bill does not go far enough to provide grounds to redress the wrong it clearly acknowledges by the changes it implements; and

(3) to propose a possible international effect resulting from the implementation of the Bill.

i. Bill C-45 and the Canadian Criminal Code

The main changes effected to the Criminal Code are as follows:

S 1. (1) extends the definition of "every one," "person," and "owner" to include "an organization." In turn, "organization" means"

(2) (a) a public body, body corporate, society, company, firm, partnership, trade union or municipality, or

(b) an association of persons that

(i) is created for a common purpose,

(ii) has an operational structure, and

(iii) holds itself out to the public as an association of persons.

Here, and in the amendments to Section 22.1, Bill C-45 ensures that a wide array of actors within an organization may be viewed as responsible for an offence, "whether by act or omission" (Section 22.1 (ii)); it also ensures that if the prosecution is required "to prove fault other than negligence" (Section 22.2), then senior officers or representatives may manifest the requisite "mental state" also by "(c) knowing that a representative of the organization is or is about to be a party to the offence, or does not take all reasonable measures to stop them from being a party to the offence." The Bill also adds a Section (217.1) to define "the legal duty to take reasonable steps to prevent bodily harm," on the part of anyone who is in the position to direct and order how work is to be done.

In addition, several sections deal with making or causing to be made false statements with respect to the financial conditions of the organization (Section 362 (1) (c)), or in general, committing fraud or causing it to be committed. For the sake of the present purposes, the discussion here will be limited to the aspects of Bill C-45 that are directly relevant to this work, thus to ecocrime rather than white collar crime in general.

ii. Bill C-45 and Ecocrime

The expanded definition of organizations is of cardinal importance in cases where the authority other responsible senior party, or those directed by the senior individuals, "depart-markedly from the standard of care" (5.22.1) that could reasonably be expected, could be found to be Provincial or Federal officials. There is no case law yet to determine whether this interpretation might eventually be part of the positive developments arising out of Bill C-45, and of course "depart markedly" from the standard of care does not define the "standard of care" itself or what, precisely, a "marked" departure from a non-specified form of behaviour might be: in fact it may be the case that the standard of "due diligence" (also largely undefined) that has been the expected test, is not different from the standard included or implied by the changed wording of Bill C-45.

Nevertheless, in the *Walkerton case* (see Chapter 4),this approach would have made a great difference to the outcome of the case, by recognizing and penalizing the organizational (i.e. governmental) officials complicit in the crimes, and guilty of engendering precisely that "culture" of negligence and attention to the bottom line at the expense of human rights that eventually gave rise to the multiple homicides and other crimes in that case. With the coming into force of the Bill, this might still be possible in the future.

Another important point worthy of attention is that after Section 718.2, the Act now provides in Section 718.21 on "Organizations" the "factors regarding the offence" that must be taken in consideration in sentencing. Some of the most interesting of these factors, in relation to our main concern, are:

(a) any advantage realized by the organization as a result of the offence;
(b) the degree of planning involved in carrying out the offence, and the duration and complexity of the offence;

. . .

(g) whether the organization or any of its representatives were convicted of a similar offence or sanctioned by a regulatory body for similar conduct;

. . .

(j) any measures that the organization has taken to reduce the likelihood of it committing a subsequent offence.

Briefly, the first factor cited shows that economic advantage renders the offence graver; the second parallels the premeditation aspect as it renders a homicide committed by an individual, a murder instead; planning may also include "conspiring," something that has become a crime in itself according to the Nuremberg Charter (see Chapter 3). Previous crimes are now admissible at sentencing: (g) recognizes that an organization does not require the same Constitutional (Charter) protections as does the individual offender, at least implicitly. The commitment not to repeat the crime (j) also allows a degree of official intervention that is not possible with individual persons.

The Problem of Mens Rea in Organizational Crime

We can now consider the major difficulties present in the Criminal Code of Canada that Bill C-45 is intended to correct. In Chapters 4 and 5, the major problem was identified as the view that corporate (or, as it is now viewed) "organizational" crime, was considered a "quasi-crime," a regulatory breach, rather than a true crime, even when environmental crime was the reason for the infliction of grave harm even death. The main reason for the discrepancy between the consequences of organizational crime and the way it was treated in law, is the "fact" that intent is hard to prove when the crime is not the discrete, wrongful conduct of individuals (Legislative Summary, p.3), whereas the "identification theory" model of the corporation appeared to be insufficient to explain the responsibility of directors and officers for serious crimes.

In Chapter 4, the Corporate Internal Decision Making Structure (CID Structure) was discussed in detail (French, 1984; French, 1979), and some far-reaching implications of the theory were proposed, eventually showing that through the CID Structure, a corporate body represented an example of pure intent, as none of the human, personal failings and emotions that are appropriate for natural persons apply to a juridical person instead. In the Netherlands, Article 51 of the Criminal Code, states that "offences can be committed by human beings and corporations" (Field and Jorg, 1991:157), and these offences include "battery and involuntary manslaughter" as, for instance, in the Dutch Hospital case (Dutch Hospital Case, Rechtbank Leeuwarden, Dec.23, 1987, partially reported at N.J. 1988, 981).

The root of the problem is that criminal liability requires both *acts reus* and *mens rea*, thus

> [U]sing the rule of vicarious liability, corporations were sued in torts for acts of their agents and servants. However, when there were civil wrongs, in which malice or motive were involved, the view of the court was that "no action could lie"—i.e., there is no cause for action because it is impossible for a corporation to have malice or motive. (Frenkel and Lurie, 2002:466).

The work of Peter French on CID Structure (French 1979; French, 1984), however, shows the contrary to be true, as was argued in Chapter 4. In brief, because corporations are viewed as making rational decisions through their decision-making structure, and because they are only juridical, not natural persons corporations (now organizations) cannot lay claim to any human failing, that is, neither psychological nor emotional nor yet any actual extenuating circumstances could possibly make a difference to their implemented rational choices.

In the case of these legal persons, rationality therefore excludes both emotions and willfull blindness, as components of the reasonably expected consequences of their behavior, 'thus the corporate institutional "limited liability," should not protect individuals within the organizational milieu from criminal and moral liability (Frenkel and Lurie, 2002:467). Thus criminal liability may be ascribed to an organization, but without eliminating individual liability. An individual who is convicted of a *mala per se* crime may be sentenced to imprisonment, (Frenkel and Lurie, 2002:486); therefore the new additional requirement introduced by Bill C-45,that is the consideration of organizational criminality as well as the individual one, will be basic to the sentencing of corporate organization crime.

iii. Some Consequences of Bill C-45

The best result of this Bill is that it encourages an integrated approach to organizational crime: both the general, intended activities will be stigmatized by

(1) heavy economic penalties;
(2) disclosure (and sentencing considerations)of prior offences;
(3) continued monitoring of corporate/organizational activities (comparable to the monitoring of parolees); and
(4) full criminal prosecution and jailing of all those responsible not only for the decisions and execution of the crime itself, but also for the imposition and fostering of the corporate culture that permits, and in fact encourages such activities.

Victor Ramraj argues that:

[W]e can consistently affirm the significance of the corporate criminal liability while denying both that corporations ought to be subject to the same principles of liability as individuals, and that constitutional rights ought to apply with equal vigour to corporations (Ramraj, 2001:30).

The argument developed in this book derives from the work of Peter French also contends that individuals and organizations cannot and should not claim the same rights, while their duties remain, to say the least, similar although the far-reaching presence of corporate power demonstrates why the corporate duties ought to be correspondingly far-reaching. That is why the constitutional protection of an individual's liberty cannot be simply transferred to the criminal organization, as Ramraj also argues:

Moreover, the scope of the constitutional protection depends not, as L'Heureux-Dubé J. suggested in *Thomson Newspapers*, on whether the rights claimant is a corporation or a natural person, but rather on the nature of the regulated activity (Ramraj, 2001:43–44).

We noted above the changes introduced to Section 22.1 and 22.2 of the Canadian Criminal Code. Understood in the light of these changes, even Section 21.(1) and (2),describing the "parties to offence" as those who aid and abet, or have a "common intention" in regard to the criminal activity, comes quite close, as I suggested above, to pointing to "complicity" as a crime in itself (see Chapter 3).

After considering all useful changes introduced by Bill C-45, two important questions remain to be answered: first, are the amendments that have been legislated sufficient to eliminate the grave concerns expressed and defended in the rest of this work in regard to the basic understanding of ecocrime and its treatment in domestic (common) law; second, are these emendations significant enough to withstand the globalized presence of transnational organizations (Held and McGrew, 2002:128–129),and the problems we have discussed in connection with the formulation and applications of international law (Chapters 6, 7 and 8A).

The first question is the easier to answer: the attempts to fully capture all the consequences of organizational crime, do not explicitly address the problem of governmental complicity (although eventually the case law may do so), thus they are not far-reaching enough to ensure that human biological rights to life/health and normal function, hence public health itself, be fully protected. The second question evokes a double-edged response: it is seemingly irrelevant to the formulation of international legal instruments, but it may be extremely useful in the case of crimes committed by Canadian transnational organizations, such as mining operations for instance.

In addition, in order to extradite and try those who might be nationals of other countries, but either employed by or directors of Canadian enterprises, the crime they are accused of needs to be present in the Canadian Criminal Code, especially because the formerly used "list of offences" are no longer in force after the 1999. Extradition Treaty came in force (Extradition Act, S.C. 1999, c.18). All that is now required is that the crime be known as such in Canada, even if a different expression might be used to define it in another country. Extradition Treaties are used to prevent persons escaping justice, and "It involves a common fight against crime" (Williams, 2004:94). Thus Bill C-45 may be used to attack some of the most intractable consequences of globalization: the largely unchecked spread of transnational harm through ecocrime (see Chapter 7).

Admittedly, Bill C-45 neither states nor defends any great moral or legal principle it promotes no immediate supranational or normative response to ecocrime. Yet we cannot discount it as "useless" as some characterize all efforts to criminalize wrongful corporate activites (Khanna, 1996). The new law does propose some substantive differences in our approach to ecocrime, and it supports some significant procedural improvements in Canadian law and—perhaps—indirectly, in international law as well.

8. A POSTSCRIPT ON INTRINSIC VALUE AND ECOLOGICAL INTEGRITY IN LAW

... it is not difficult to conceive of humanity as being morally responsible to protect the integrity of the whole ecosystem, and for that responsibility to be translated into such mechanisms as standard-setting in a manner which is cognizant of ecological thresholds (Taylor, 1998:382–383).

Thus far I have concentrated almost entirely on human life and health, in order to better support my argument that breaches of environmental regulations should not be met with economic penalties but with criminal ones, because of their effects on basic human rights.

The basis for this argument is the fact that, for the most part, ecocrimes are perpetrated by corporate/industrial enterprises, with the domestic support of national governments and with the international support of trade organizations and negotiated legal instruments. Hence, economic advantage and power represent the foundations and the goals of ecocrimes.

Nevertheless there is, increasingly, a parallel movement to recognize the intrinsic value of both the components and the processes of natural systems, not only in philosophy (Devall and Sessions, 2000; Callicott, 2000; Leopold, 1949; Stone, 2000; Westra, 1998), but also in the law (Brooks et al., 2002). A number of international legal instruments also reflect the emerging ecological concerns that are present globally; hence, they include in their language, respect for the intrinsic value of both natural things and processes. Prudence Taylor says: ". . . the debate in international law has focused on the development of environmental rights . . . (and) the debate on the creation of a new environmental human right is well advanced" (Taylor, 1998:310–311). Her point is confirmed by the UNEP funded project involving the Supreme Court Justices of the world, as outlined in its goal by Judge Arthur Chaksalson of South Africa (see Chapter 7), as one of the most important results of the Johannesburg meeting (Rio+ 10), and by the 2000 Draft International Covenant on Environment and Development.

The latter is involved at this time in incorporating the mandates and the letter of the Earth Charter in its language, which therefore includes articles on ecological integrity and on the intrinsic value of nature (see Chapter 6).

Taylor traces the history of the development of human rights instruments from civil and political rights, to economic, social, and cultural rights, through to the "third generation of human rights," that she terms "solidarity rights" (Taylor, 1998:318; Birnie and Boyle, 2002:253).

But the rights set out in Articles 2-21 of the Universal Declaration (1948), include the "right to life, liberty and security of the person; freedom from slavery or involuntary servitude; freedom from torture," and Taylor suggests that the core concept here is that of liberty from state abuses (Taylor, 1998:318).

In contrast, I have argued that these "freedom from" rights are implicitly based on the rights Shue terms basic rights, because without physical security and subsistence, that is, without the protection of life and health as required for survival, all other rights are meaningless. Falk argues that human rights must include "the rights of individuals and groups (including those of unborn generations) to be reasonably secure about their prospects of minimal physical well-being and survival (and) the duty of governments and peoples to uphold this right by working to achieve sustainable forms of national and ecological sustainability" (Falk, 1981:558).

Although the position advanced here is present in the law, as many legal instruments accept the ecosystem approach or speak about respect for natural entities, as we have argued, economic power blocs in society manage to paper over the vast differences between these basic rights of persons and peoples, and the property rights of legal entities and institutions, with the result that various courts weigh these incommensurable values as though they were level: the right to life and the survival of peoples is not comparable to economic benefits or even the survival of corporate and industrial enterprises.

Hence, we have the need to seek the principled approach to *jus cogens* norms, of cosmopolitanism in general. The latter is exemplified in the supranational governance of the EC, as we noted in this part of Chapter 8. This normative approach in its various instances is complementary to Taylor's quest for ecological limits to property rights, and can be viewed as a mandatory first step to curtail and contain "emergent risks" (Hiskes, 1998) and to mitigate perhaps the assaultive attacks on life and health that are part of the present status quo.

The implicit presence of basic rights I propose, bind together all rights. Taylor says: "Some states have for example argued that despite the differences in wording, all types of rights are *indivisible*, creating an interdependent 'mutually self-supporting whole'" (Taylor, 1998:319).

The EC recognizes the importance of environmental rights, as for the OECD "fundamental human rights should include a right to a decent environment" (OECD, 1984).

The United Nations Economic Commission for Europe (UNECE) also ". . . affirmed the universal right to an environment adequate for general health and well-being, as well as the responsibility to protect and conserve the environment for present and future generations" (Taylor, 1998: 348)

An additional connection arises from a consideration of ecological integrity, a complex concept that, after several years of funded work, the Global Ecological Integrity Project eventually defined in 2000 (Westra et al., 2000). The protection of basic human rights through the recognition of our need for ecological integrity as Rolston acknowledges (Rolston, 1993), is a step in the emerging awareness of humanity as an integral part of the biosphere (Westra, 1998; Taylor, 1998).

In that case, there is a false dichotomy in any attempt to separate human rights and ecological rights. Ultimately, the latter are equally necessary for all natural entities, human and nonhuman. Limits to property rights would perhaps preserve the integrity of some wild areas; for the reasons cited by Gretchen Daily (1997), all life need some areas of the global environment to be wild, others to be "buffers" or "corridors" in the protection of the former, in order to support the natural evolutionary processes needed to maintain all life, including humanity.

Hence, the defense of any ecological right, ultimately can be understood as all mandating respect for parts of the biosphere, as does any right directly or indirectly applicable to nonhuman entities, be they trees (Stone, 2000), large carnivores (Noss, 1992) or earth worms (Loucks, 2000). In other words, the conclusion is unavoidable: if we protect and respect trees and large carnivores or earthworms, essentially we are not only protecting aggregates of natural entities, but we also thereby protect the ecosystem where they exist and their natural processes, thus ecosystem "services" at the same time. It is impossible to separate the former from the latter. Earthworms, for instance, are not charismatic megafauna, or WWF "poster boys," but by ensuring their survival, ultimately we also ensure ours. That is the reality.

But that reality can be presented honestly under any of its interconnected aspects, as long as these interconnections are not denied, without losing its legitimacy. It would be more than difficult, in fact, probably impossible, to ask for jail terms for those whose negligence killed the proverbial canary in the mine, but, I argue, that sentence can and should be demanded for the death of the miner instead. Without abandoning our understanding of the biocentric reasons for our stance, we need to move toward the twin goals of strong deterrence and restraint, as is done in the case of assaults, rapes, and other violent crimes. Laws that restrain unbridled property rights represent a first target; but we cannot stop with property issues, that is, we ought not to limit our efforts to action within the realm of tort law. The reason is obvious: economic harms are transferable, thus acceptable to the harm imposers, although the real harms produced are often incompensable. As Brooks et al. (2002) indicate, speaking of U.S. law, science is now available to support appeals to interdependence:

The Culmination of Ecosystem Regimes—In the 1990s we have witnessed the culmination of the relations between ecology and environmental law. Not only has conservation biology as a discipline and biodiversity as a concept become an important part of national forest and endangered species management, but major court cases reviewing biodiversity determinations have been decided (Brooks et al., 2002:373).

Law and ecology are, increasingly, joined in both domestic common law and international law. In addition, Earth System Science (ESS) has been increasingly providing "multidisciplinary and interdisciplinary science framework for understanding global scale problems," including the relations and the functioning of "global systems that include the land, oceans and the atmosphere" (Ibid. at 345). In essence, the ecosystem approach, and systemic science have contributed to support what A.A. Cancado Trindade terms "the globalization of human rights protection and of environmental protection" (Cancado Trindade, 1992:247).

Additional support can be found in the Third Report on International Liability for Injurious Consequences Arising out of Acts Not Prohibited by International Law (1982; 4th Report, 1983), so that some hazardous products and activities are blacklisted, so that: ". . . when pollution is caused by substances that are highly dangerous to human life and health, there is no need to prove a significant impact or injury." (Vicuna, 1992:135). Hence, the awareness of what specific environmentally hazardous activities cause harm to natural systems, is foundational to the defense of public health in the law, without the need for immediate evidence of harm. But present approaches, with these significant (and growing exceptions), are insufficient for the protection of public health and the emphasis on state sovereignty is actually often counterproductive (Vicuna, 1992; Fidler, 2001).

The problem remains the one emphasized in this work: the effort to harmonize competing interests that is prevalent in international law instruments, is in direct conflict with the reality of the violent harms to all life that result from such a conciliatory attitude. This is our earlier analogy with sexual attacks (see Chapter 5), and other criminal cases where no "harmonization of interests" is possible or allowed. The right to health, proceeding from the right to life, or the "right to living" as Cancado Trindade (1992) defines it, is clearly the focus of *erga omnes* obligations. These proscribe all attacks against the human person or groups and are rendered particularly desirable because of their preventive character (Cancado Trindade, 1992:261).

Some of these documents now propose the extension of genocide to cultural genocide or ethnocide, but also to ecocide (in the case of irreparable alteration to the environment threatening the existence of entire populations). Some have proposed instead that ecocide constitutes a crime against humanity rather than only genocide (Cancado Trindade, 1992:261; Falk, 1998).

The cosmopolitan conception of law proposed in this chapter, and the universal protection of human rights it embraces fit well the ideal and the practice of a life-centred ethic. A biocentric global ethic reaches across borders and ideologies (Westra, 1994), and it no longer represents only a trivialized view seen as too radical even by environmental ethicists. It has moved beyond the limits imposed by local dialogues all equally embedded in the neo-liberal status quo. Such an ethic seeks to reaffirm the indissoluble synthesis of humans and their habitat (Westra, 1998).

We noted that these ideals are present in the language and the principles of the Earth Charter (see Chapter 6), and the latter was recently adopted by a UNESCO Resolution (Oct. 16, 2003; see Appendix 3). The global reach of these ethics and charters, to be effective, must be supported by a supranational juridical entity such as the EC. As the case for environmental or, better yet, ecological rights, becomes stronger and more accepted in the international law, we might seek the best solution as Birnie and Boyle suggest (citing Hurrell and Kingsbury, 1992) in empowering the U.N. It might be desirable ". . . to invest the UN Security Council, or some other UN organ with the power to act in the interests of "ecological security," taking universally binding decisions in the interests of all mankind and the environment" (Birnie and Boyle, 2002:754). The abundant evidence linking ecology and human rights makes such a development a highly desirable one, for a new global environmental/human order.

THE EARTH CHARTER

March 2000

PREAMBLE

We stand at a critical moment in Earth's history, a time when humanity must choose its future. As the world becomes increasingly interdependent and fragile, the future at once holds great peril and great promise. To move forward we must recognize that in the midst of a magnificent diversity of cultures and life forms we are one human family and one Earth community with a common destiny. We must join together to bring forth a sustainable global society founded on respect for nature, universal human rights, economic justice, and a culture of peace. Towards this end, it is imperative that we, the peoples of Earth, declare our responsibility to one another, to the greater community of life, and to future generations.

Earth, Our Home

Humanity is part of a vast evolving universe. Earth, our home, is alive with a unique community of life. The forces of nature make existence a demanding and uncertain adventure, but Earth has provided the conditions essential to life's evolution. The resilience of the community of life and the well-being of humanity depend upon preserving a healthy biosphere with all its ecological systems, a rich variety of plants and animals, fertile soils, pure waters, and clean air. The global environment with its finite resources is a common concern of all peoples. The protection of Earth's vitality, diversity, and beauty is a sacred trust.

The Global Situation

The dominant patterns of production and consumption are causing environmental devastation, the depletion of resources, and a massive extinction of species. Communities are being undermined. The benefits of development are not shared equitably and the gap between rich and poor is widening. Injustice, poverty, ignorance, and violent conflict are widespread and the cause of great suffering. An unprecedented rise in human population has overburdened ecological and social systems. The foundations of global security are threatened. These trends are perilous—but not inevitable.

The Challenges Ahead

The choice is ours: form a global partnership to care for Earth and one another or risk the destruction of ourselves and the diversity of life. Fundamental changes are needed in our values, institutions, and ways of living. We must realize that when basic needs have been met, human development is primarily about being more, not having more. We have the knowledge and technology to provide for all and to reduce our impacts on the environment. The emergence of a global civil society is creating new opportunities to build a democratic and humane world. Our environmental, economic, political, social, and spiritual challenges are interconnected, and together we can forge inclusive solutions.

Universal Responsibility

To realize these aspirations, we must decide to live with a sense of universal responsibility, identifying ourselves with the whole Earth community as well as our local communities. We are at once citizens of different nations and of one world in which the local and global are linked. Everyone shares responsibility for the present and future well-being of the human family and the larger living world. The spirit of human solidarity and kinship with all life is strengthened when we live with reverence for the mystery of being, gratitude for the gift of life, and humility regarding the human place in nature.

We urgently need a shared vision of basic values to provide an ethical foundation for the emerging world community. Therefore, together in hope we affirm the following interdependent principles for a sustainable way of life as a common standard by which the conduct of all individuals, organizations, businesses, governments, and transnational institutions is to be guided and assessed.

PRINCIPLES

1. Respect And Care For The Community Of Life

1. *Respect Earth and life in all its diversity.*

   a. Recognize that all beings are interdependent and every form of life has value regardless of its worth to human beings.
   b. Affirm faith in the inherent dignity of all human beings and in the intellectual, artistic, ethical, and spiritual potential of humanity.

2. *Care for the community of life with understanding, compassion, and love.*

   a. Accept that with the right to own, manage, and use natural resources comes the duty to prevent environmental harm and to protect the rights of people.
   b. Affirm that with increased freedom, knowledge, and power comes increased responsibility to promote the common good.

3. *Build democratic societies that are just, participatory, sustainable, and peaceful.*

   a. Ensure that communities at all levels guarantee human rights and fundamental freedoms and provide everyone an opportunity to realize his or her full potential.

b. Promote social and economic justice, enabling all to achieve a secure and meaningful livelihood that is ecologically responsible.

4. *Secure Earth's bounty and beauty for present and future generations.*

   a. Recognize that the freedom of action of each generation is qualified by the needs of future generations.
   b. Transmit to future generations values, traditions, and institutions that support the long-term flourishing of Earth's human and ecological communities.

In order to fulfill these four broad commitments, it is necessary to:

II. ECOLOGICAL INTEGRITY

5. *Protect and restore the integrity of Earth's ecological systems, with special concern for biological diversity and the natural processes that sustain life.*

   a. Adopt at all levels sustainable development plans and regulations that make environmental conservation and rehabilitation integral to all development initiatives.
   b. Establish and safeguard viable nature and biosphere reserves, including wild lands and marine areas, to protect Earth's life support systems, maintain biodiversity, and preserve our natural heritage.
   c. Promote the recovery of endangered species and ecosystems.
   d. Control and eradicate non-native or genetically modified organisms harmful to native species and the environment, and prevent introduction of such harmful organisms.
   e. Manage the use of renewable resources such as water, soil, forest products, and marine life in ways that do not exceed rates of regeneration and that protect the health of ecosystems.
   f. Manage the extraction and use of non-renewable resources such as minerals and fossil fuels in ways that minimize depletion and cause no serious environmental damage.

6. *Prevent harm as the best method of environmental protection and, when knowledge is limited, apply a precautionary approach.*

   a. Take action to avoid the possibility of serious or irreversible environmental harm even when scientific knowledge is incomplete or inconclusive.
   b. Place the burden of proof on those who argue that a proposed activity will not cause significant harm, and make the responsible parties liable for environmental harm.
   c. Ensure that decision making addresses the cumulative, long-term, indirect, long distance, and global consequences of human activities.

    d.   Prevent pollution of any part of the environment and allow no build-up of radioactive, toxic, or other hazardous substances.

    e.   Avoid military activities damaging to the environment.

7.   *Adopt patterns of production, consumption, and reproduction that safeguard Earth's regenerative capacities, human rights, and community well being.*

    a.   Reduce, reuse, and recycle the materials used in production and consumption systems, and ensure that residual waste can be assimilated by ecological systems.

    b.   Act with restraint and efficiency when using energy, and rely increasingly on renewable energy sources such as solar and wind.

    c.   Promote the development, adoption, and equitable transfer of environmentally sound technologies.

    d.   Internalize the full environmental and social costs of goods and services in the selling price, and enable consumers to identify products that meet the highest social and environmental standards.

    e.   Ensure universal access to health care that fosters reproductive health and responsible reproduction.

    f.   Adopt lifestyles that emphasize the quality of life and material sufficiency in a finite world.

8.   *Advance the study of ecological sustainability and promote the open exchange and wide application of the knowledge acquired.*

    a.   Support international scientific and technical cooperation on sustainability, with special attention to the needs of developing nations.

    b.   Recognize and preserve the traditional knowledge and spiritual wisdom in all cultures that contribute to environmental protection and human well-being.

    c.   Ensure that information of vital importance to human health and environmental protection, including genetic information, remains available in the public domain.

III. Social And Economic Justice

9.   *Eradicate poverty as an ethical, social, and environmental imperative.*

    a.   Guarantee the right to potable water, clean air, food security, uncontaminated soil, shelter, and safe sanitation, allocating the national and international resources required.

    b.   Empower every human being with the education and resources to secure a sustainable livelihood, and provide social security and safety nets for those who are unable to support themselves.

    c.   Recognize the ignored, protect the vulnerable, serve those who suffer, and enable them to develop their capacities and to pursue their aspirations.

10. *Ensure that economic activities and institutions at all levels promote human development in an equitable and sustainable manner.*

   a. Promote the equitable distribution of wealth within nations and among nations.

   b. Enhance the intellectual, financial, technical, and social resources of developing nations, and relieve them of onerous international debt.

   c. Ensure that all trade supports sustainable resource use, environmental protection, and progressive labor standards.

   d. Require multinational corporations and international financial organizations to act transparently in the public good, and hold them accountable for the consequences of their activities.

11. *Affirm gender equality and equity as prerequisites to sustainable development and ensure universal access to education, health care, and economic opportunity.*

   a. Secure the human rights of women and girls and end all violence against them.

   b. Promote the active participation of women in all aspects of economic, political, civil, social, and cultural life as full and equal partners, decision makers, leaders, and beneficiaries.

   c. Strengthen families and ensure the safety and loving nurture of all family members.

12. *Uphold the right of all, without discrimination, to a natural and social environment supportive of human dignity, bodily health, and spiritual well-being, with special attention to the rights of indigenous peoples and minorities.*

   a. Eliminate discrimination in all its forms, such as that based on race, color, sex, sexual orientation, religion, language, and national, ethnic or social origin.

   b. Affirm the right of indigenous peoples to their spirituality, knowledge, lands and resources and to their related practice of sustainable livelihoods.

   c. Honor and support the young people of our communities, enabling them to fulfill their essential role in creating sustainable societies.

   d. Protect and restore outstanding places of cultural and spiritual significance.

IV. Democracy, Nonviolence, And Peace

13. *Strengthen democratic institutions at all levels, and provide transparency and accountability in governance, inclusive participation in decision making, and access to justice.*

   a. Uphold the right of everyone to receive clear and timely information on environmental matters and all development plans and activities which are likely to affect them or in which they have an interest.

   b. Support local, regional and global civil society, and promote the meaningful participation of all interested individuals and organizations in decision making.
   c. Protect the rights to freedom of opinion, expression, peaceful assembly, association, and dissent.
   d. Institute effective and efficient access to administrative and independent judicial procedures, including remedies and redress for environmental harm and the threat of such harm.
   e. Eliminate corruption in all public and private institutions.
   f. Strengthen local communities, enabling them to care for their environments, and assign environmental responsibilities to the levels of government where they can be carried out most effectively.

14. *Integrate into formal education and life-long learning the knowledge, values, and skills needed for a sustainable way of life.*

   a. Provide all, especially children and youth, with educational opportunities that empower them to contribute actively to sustainable development.
   b. Promote the contribution of the arts and humanities as well as the sciences in sustainability education.
   c. Enhance the role of the mass media in raising awareness of ecological and social challenges.
   d. Recognize the importance of moral and spiritual education for sustainable living.

15. *Treat all living beings with respect and consideration.*

   a. Prevent cruelty to animals kept in human societies and protect them from suffering.
   b. Protect wild animals from methods of hunting, trapping, and fishing that cause extreme, prolonged, or avoidable suffering.
   c. Avoid or eliminate to the full extent possible the taking or destruction of non-targeted species.

16. *Promote a culture of tolerance, nonviolence, and peace.*

   a. Encourage and support mutual understanding, solidarity, and cooperation among all peoples and within and among nations.
   b. Implement comprehensive strategies to prevent violent conflict and use collaborative problem solving to manage and resolve environmental conflicts and other disputes.
   c. Demilitarize national security systems to the level of a non-provocative defense posture, and convert military resources to peaceful purposes, including ecological restoration.
   d. Eliminate nuclear, biological, and toxic weapons and other weapons of mass destruction.

e. Ensure that the use of orbital and outer space supports environmental protection and peace.

f. Recognize that peace is the wholeness created by right relationships with oneself, other persons, other cultures, other life, Earth, and the larger whole of which all are a part.

THE WAY FORWARD

As never before in history, common destiny beckons us to seek a new beginning. Such renewal is the promise of these Earth Charter principles. To fulfill this promise, we must commit ourselves to adopt and promote the values and objectives of the Charter.

This requires a change of mind and heart. It requires a new sense of global interdependence and universal responsibility. We must imaginatively develop and apply the vision of a sustainable way of life locally, nationally, regionally, and globally. Our cultural diversity is a precious heritage and different cultures will find their own distinctive ways to realize the vision. We must deepen and expand the global dialogue that generated the Earth Charter, for we have much to learn from the ongoing collaborative search for truth and wisdom.

Life often involves tensions between important values. This can mean difficult choices. However, we must find ways to harmonize diversity with unity, the exercise of freedom with the common good, short-term objectives with long-term goals. Every individual, family, organization, and community has a vital role to play. The arts, sciences, religions, educational institutions, media, businesses, nongovernmental organizations, and governments are all called to offer creative leadership. The partnership of government, civil society, and business is essential for effective governance.

In order to build a sustainable global community, the nations of the world must renew their commitment to the United Nations, fulfill their obligations under existing international agreements, and support the implementation of Earth Charter principles with an international legally binding instrument on environment and development.

Let ours be a time remembered for the awakening of a new reverence for life, the firm resolve to achieve sustainability, the quickening of the struggle for justice and peace, and the joyful celebration of life.

The Earth Charter Initiative, International Secretariat The Earth Council
P.O. Box 319-6100
San Jose, Costa Rica
Tel: +506-205-1600
Fax: +506-249-3500
Email: info@earthcharter.org

APPENDIX 2

THE INTERNATIONAL LAW COMMISSION ON STATE RESPONSIBILITY

What is the responsibility of States for attacks on human rights in International Law? *The International Law Commission* (1996) characterizes an "Internationally Wrongful Act of a State" in Article 3:

There is an internationally wrongful act of a State when:

(a) conduct consisting of an action or omission is attributable to the State, under International Law; and

(b) that conduct constitutes a breach of an international obligation of the State.

Article 4 adds the conditions that render the act not only "wrongful," but specifically so on international grounds:

An act of a State may only be characterized as internationally wrong by international law. Such characterization cannot be affected by the characterization of the same act as lawful by internal law.

From our point of view, Article 19, "International Crimes and International Delicts" is the most important among the Draft articles on State Responsibility, although it is admittedly controversial:

A.19

1. An act of a State which constitutes a breach of an international obligation is an internationally wrongful act, regardless of the subject matter of the obligation breached.

2. An internationally wrongful act which results from the breach by a State of an international obligation so essential for the protection of fundamental interests of the international community that its breach is recognized as a crime by that community as a whole, constitutes an international crime.

3. Subject to paragraph 2, and on the basis of the rules of international law in force, an international crime may result, *inter alia*, from:

    (a) a serious breach of an international obligation of essential importance for maintenance of international peace and security, such as that prohibiting aggression;

    (b) a serious breach of an international obligation of essential importance for safeguarding the right of self-determination of peoples, such as that prohibiting the establishment or maintenance by force of colonial domination;

    (c) a serious breach on a widespread scale of an international obligation of essential importance for safe guarding the human being, such as those prohibiting slavery, genocide, *apartheid*;

    (d) a serious breach of an international obligation of essential importance for the safeguarding and preservation of the human environment, such as those prohibiting massive pollution of the atmosphere or of the seas.

4.   Any internationally wrongful act which is not an international crime in accordance with paragraph 2, constitutes an international delict.

UNESCO RESOLUTION ON THE EARTH CHARTER

16 October 2003

Item 5.23—UNESCO's support for the Earth Charter

31. The Commission III recommends to the General Conference that it adopt, for the records of the General Conference, the draft resolution 32 C/COM.III.DR.1 (submitted by Jordon, supported by Costa Rica) as amended orally by Jordon. The resolution reads as follows:

The General Conference, Considering that:

— Over the decade of the 1990's, there has been a worldwide, multi-cultural, multisectoral consultation process for the creation of an instrument that contains the shared values, principles and ethics that can guide our efforts towards a sustainable future,
— Today, the international community has the Earth Charter as an instrument, which contains fundamental principles for building a just, sustainable and peaceful global society,
— The Earth Charter sets forth an integrated approach to addressing our interrelated problems the world community faces. This ethical framework involves respect and responsibility for the community of life, ecological integrity, social and economic justice and equity, democracy, alleviation of poverty, non-violence and peace,
— The Earth Charter is a part of a continuing process generated by the United Nations Brundtland Commission's (1987) call for a new code of ethics for sustainable development, and the unfinished issue of the Rio Earth Summit, which attempted adoption of an ethical framework for sustainability, and
— UNESCO is a Task Manager in the United Nations system of Chapters 15 (Science) and 36 (Education) of Agenda 21, 32 C/73—page 16

Resolves to:

1. Recognize the Earth Charter as an important ethical framework for sustainable development, and acknowledge its ethical principles, its objectives and its contents, as an expression that coincides with the

vision that UNESCO has with regard to their new Medium-Term Strategy for 2002–2007;

2. Affirm our intention, as Member States, to utilize the Earth Charter as an educational instrument, particularly in the framework of the United Nations Decade for Education for Sustainable Development;

3. Invite the UNESCO General Conference to analyse with the UNESCO Director-General how to reinforce, in a practical way, the vision and principles of the Earth Charter in UNESCO programmes.

BIBLIOGRAPHY

Adams, Hussein M. "Somalia: Environmental Degradation and Environmental Racism," *in* L. Westra and P. Wenz, eds., *Faces of Environmental Racism* at 181 (1995).

Ago, R. "The Concept of "International Community as a Whole," *in* J. Weiler, A. Cassese & M. Spimedi eds., *International Crime of State—A Critical Analysis of the ILC Draft Article 19 on State Responsibility* at 252 (Walter de Gruyter: Berlin, 1989).

Akehurst, Michael. "Equity and General Principals of Law," 25 *Intl. & Comp. Law Q.* 801 (1976).

Al-Saleh. "Lead Exposure in Saudi Arabia and Its Relationship to Smoking," 8 (3) *Biometals* 243–45 (July 1995).

Anderson, H.R. et al. "Air Pollution and Daily Admissions for Chronic Obstructive Pulmonary Disease in 6 European Cities; Results from the APHEA Project," 10 (5) *Eur. Respiratory J.* 1064–1071 (1997).

Aquinas, Thomas. *On Law, Morality, and Politics* (W. Baumgarrten & R.S.J. Regan eds., Hackett Publishing Co.: Indianapolis, IN, 1988).

Arendt, H., Eichmann. *Jerusalem: A Report on the Banality of Evil* (Viking Press: NY, 1964).

Ashford, Nicholas. "A Conceptual Framework for the Use of the Precautionary Principle in Law," *in Protecting Public Health and the Environment* at189–206 (Island Press, Washington, DC, 1999).

Atik, J. "Two Hopeful Readings of *Shrimp-Turtle*," 9 *Y.B. Int'l Envtl. L.* 6–12 (1998).

Aunan, K. "Exposure-Response Functions for Health Effects of Air Pollutants Based on Epidemiological Findings," 16 (5) *Risk Analysis* 693–709 (1996).

Baier, Annette, "Violent Demonstrations," *Symposium on Terrorism* (Bowling Green State University, OH, 1988).

Baird, R.M. & Rosenbaum, S.E., 1995, *Punishment and the Death Penalty* (Prometherus Books: Amherst, NY, 1995).

Barash, David, D. "International Law," *in Approaches to Peace* at 106 (D. Baresh ed., Oxford University Press, 2000).

Baratte, Alessandro, "Ecologia, Economia, Democrazia eil Patto Sociale della Modernita," 1–2 *Dei Delitti e delle Pene* 9–23 (2000).

Barile, Giuseppe. "Obligationes Erga Omnes e individui nel diritt internazionale umanitario," 68 *Rivista di Diritto Internazionale* 5,17–27 (1985).

Barker, Ernest, *The Politics of Aristotle* (Oxford University Press: London, UK, 1973).

Barlow, Maude & Clarke, Tony. *Global Showdown* (Stoddard Publishing House: Don Mills, Ontario, 2002).

Barlow, Maude. *Blue Gold* (A Special Report Issued by the International Forum of Globalization (IFG),1999).

Barry, Brian. *The Liberal Theory of Justice* (Clarendon Press: Oxford University Press, 1973).

Bassiouni, M. Cherif. "International Crimes: *Jus Cogens* and *Obligatio Erga Omnes*," 59 (4) *Law & Contemp. Probs.* 64, 67 (1996).

Bassiouni, M. Cherif. "Searching for Peace and Achieving Justice: The Need for Accountability," 59 (4) *Law & Contemp. Probs.* 9 (1996).

Bassiouni, M. Cherif. *Crimes Against Humanity in International Criminal Law* (Martinus Nijhoff Publishers: Dordrecht, The Netherlands,1992).

Battin, Margaret P. "The Way We Do It, the Way They Do It," in Thomas Mappes and David De Grazia, *Biomedical Ethics* at 393–400 (McGraw Hill: NY, 4th ed. 1996).

Baxi, Upendra. "Voices of Suffering and the Future of Human Rights," 8 *Transnat'l L. & Contemp. Probs.* 125 (1999).

Baxi, Upendra & Paul, Thomas. *Mass Disasters and Multinational Liability: The Bhopal Case* (Indian Law Institute: Delhi, 1986).

Bay, Christian. "Civil Disobedience: Prerequisite for Democracy in Mass Society," *in Civil Disobedience and Violence* at 73–92 (Wadsworth, 1971).

BCSD (Business Council for Sustainable Development) *Getting Eco Efficient*, Report of the BSCD First Report of the Eco efficiency Workshop (Geneva: Nov. 1993).

Beard et al. "Exposure to Pesticides in Ambient Air," 19 (4) *Aust. J. Pub. Health* 357–62.

Beckwith, Francis. "Argument from Bodily Rights: A Critical Analysis" *in* Jones and Bartlett, *The Abortion Controversy* at 155–173 (Boston, 1994).

Bederman, David J. *International Law Frameworks* (Foundation Press: New York, 2001).

Beetham David, & Lord, Christopher. *Legitimacy and the European Union* (Longman: London, UK, 1998).

Bell, E.A. "Mankind and Plants: The Need to Conserve Biodiversity," 106 *Parasitology* S47–S53 (1993 supp.).

Biddle, Francis. "The Nuremberg Trials," 33 *Va. L. Rev.* 679–696 (1974).

Birnie, Patricia W. and Boyle, Adam. *International Law and the Environment* (Oxford University Press: UK, 2d ed. 2002).

Birnie, Patricia W. and Boyle, Alan E. *International Law and the Environment* (Clarendon Press: New York, 1992).

Black's Law Dictionary (5th ed.1979).

Bodin, Jean. *Six Books of a Commonwealth (London)* (trans. R. Knolles, ed. Kenneith D. McRea) (Harvard University Press: Cambridge, MA, 1962).

Bok, Sissela. "Nuclear Deterrence, Ethics and Strategy," in *Distrust, Secrecy and the Arms Race* at 339–354 (University of Chicago Press: Chicago, 1985).

Bonaventura. "Commentary on the Sentences," in *Opera Omnia* (Paris: Berton ed., 1856).

Borger, Julian. "All The President's Business Men," in *The Guardian* (UK: April 27, 2001).

Boss, Judith. "Treading on Harrowed Ground: The Violence of Agriculture," *in* D. Curtin & R. Lietke, eds., *Institutional Violence* at 263–277 (Value Inquiry Books, Rodopi, BV: Amsterdam, 1999).

Bourette, S., "Ontario Ignored Water Alert," *The Globe and Mail*, Toronto, Ont., June 6, 2000, p. A1.

Bowman, M.E. "Is International Law Ready for the Information Age?," 19 *Fordham Int'l L.J.* 935–946 (1996).

Boyd, David R. *Unnatural Law (Rethinking Canadian Environmental Law and Policy)* (UBC Press: Vancouver, 2003).

Boyle, Adam, "Problems of Compulsory Jurisdiction and the Settlement of Disputes Relating to Straddling Fish Stocks" 14 (1) *J. Marine & Coastal L.* 1–25 (March 1999).

Brenkert, G. "Marketing, The Ethics of Consumption, and Less Developed Countries," *in* L. Westra and P. Werhane, eds., *The Business of Consumptions* (Rowman Littlefield: Lanham MD, 1998).

Brewer, Scott. "Exemplary Reasoning: Semantics, Pragmatics and the Rational Force of Legal Argument by Analogy," 109 *Harv. L. Rev.* 925, 938–939 (1996).

Bridgeford, Tawny Aine. "Imputing Human Rights Obligations on Multi National Corporations:The Ninth Circuit Strikes Again in Judicial Activism," 18 *Am. U. Int'l L. Rev.* 1009 (2003).

Brooks, Richard, Jones, Ross & Virginia, Ross. *Law and Ecology* (Ashgate: Aldershot, Hants, UK, 2002).

Brown Don. "The State of the Planet at the Five Year Review of Rio and the Prospects for Protecting Worldwide Ecological Integrity," *in Ecological Integrity: Integrating Environment, Conservation and Health* at 369, 382 (Island Press: Washington, DC, 2000).

Brown, D. A. "The Role of Law in Sustainable Development and Environmental Protection Decisionmaking," *in Sustainable Development: Science, Ethics and Public Policy* at 64–76 (Kluwer Academic Press: Dordrecht, The Netherlands, 1995).

Brown, D., Manno, J., Westra, L. Pimentel, D., & Crabbe, P., eds., "Implementing Global Ecological Integrity: A Synthesis," *in Ecological Integrity: Integrating Environment, Conservation and Health* at 385–405 (2000).

Brown, Donald, *American Heat* (Rowman Littlefield: Lanham, MD, 2002).

Brown, Lester. "Challenges of the New Century," *in State of the World 2000* 3–21 (The Worldwatch Institute, W.W. Norton: NY, 2000).

Brownlie, Ian. *The Rule of Law in International Affairs* (Martinus Nijhoff, Kluwer Law International: The Hague, Netherlands, 1998).

Brownlie, Ian. *Principles of Public International Law* (Clarendon Press: Oxford, 3d ed. 1979).

Brownlie, Ian. *The Rule of Law in International Affairs* (Maartinus Nijhoff: The Hague, The Netherlands, 1990).

Brown-Weiss, Edith, "Our Rights and Obligations to Future Generations for the Environment," 84 *Am. J. Int'l L.* 198 (1990).

Brown-Weiss, Edith, ed. *Environmental Change and International Law* (United Nations University Press: Tokyo, 1992).

Bruckmann, E. "Rural Ontario: Industrial Hog Barns, Industrial Waste," 25 (1) *Intervenor* (Jan.–Mar. 2000).

Brunnée, Jutta. "The Responsibility of States for Environmental Harm in a Multinational Context—Problems and Trends," 34 *Les Cahiers de Droit* 827 (1993).

Brunnée, Jutta. "Environmental Security in the Twenty-First Century: New Momentum for the Development of International Environmental Law?," 18 *Fordham Int'l L.J.* 1742 (1995).

Brunnée, Jutta. *Acid Rain and Ozone Layer Depletion, International Law and Regulation* (Transnational: New York, 1988).

Brunnée, Jutta. "A Fine Balance: Facilitation and Enforcement in the Design of a Compliance Regime for the Kyoto Protocol," 13 (2) *Tulane Envtl. L. Rev.* 223–270 (2000).

Brunnée, Jutta, & Toope, Stephen. "Environmental Security and Freshwater Resources: Ecosystem Regime Building," 91 *Am. J. Int'l L.* 26–59 (1997).

Bullard, R. *Dumping in Dixie (Race Class and Environmental Quality)* (Westview Press: Boulder, CO, 1994).

Bullard, Robert. "Decision Making" in L. Westra and B. Lawson, eds., *Faces of Environmental Raci* at 3–28 (Rowman Littlefield, 2001).

Burkitt, Denis M.D. "Are Our Commonest Diseases Preventable?," 54 (1) *The Pharos of Alpha Omega Alpha Winter* 19–21 (1991).

Caldwell, Lynton. "The Ecosystem as a Criterion," *in* L. Caldwell & K. Shrader-Frechett, eds., *Policy for Land and Ethics* at 183–208 (1993).

Callicott, J. Baird. *In Defense of the Land Ethic* (SUNY Press: NY, 1989).

Callicott, J. Baird. "Animal Liberation: A Triangular Affair" *in* L. Pojman, ed., *Environmental Ethics* at 51–61 (Wadsworth: Belmont, CA, 2000).

Callicott, J. Baird. *The Land Ethic Revisited* (SUNY Press, Albany, NY, 1999).

Campbell, Colin. *The Myth of Social Action* (Cambridge University Press: Cambridge, UK, 1998).

Canadian Bar Association Report, *Principles of Criminal Liability* (Canadian Bar Association: Ottawa, Ont., 1992).

Cancado Trindade, A.A. "The Contribution Of International Human Rights Law To Environmental Protection, With Special Reference To Global Environmental Change," *in* E. Brown-Weiss, ed., *Environmental Change and International. Law* at 244–312 (1992).

Carson, Rachel. *Silent Spring* (Houghton Mifflin: Boston, 1962).

Carswell, Swanson, John. "Dow-Corning and the Breast Silicone Implants," paper presented at the Business Ethics Society Meeting, Aug. 10, 1996, Québec City, Canada.

Cassese, Antonio, *International Law in a Divided World* (Clarendon Press, Oxford: NY, 1986).

Cassese, Antonio, "International Crimes of State: A Critical Analysis of the ILC Draft Article 19 on State Responsibility," *in* J.H. Weiler, A. Cassese & M. Spinedi, eds., *International Crimes of State* at 376 (Walter de Gruyter: Berlin, 1989).

Cavallar, George, *Kant and the Theory and Practice of International Right* (University of Wales Press, Cardiff, 1999).

Charnovitz, Steve, "Free Trade, Fair Trade, Green Trade: Defogging the Debate," 27 *Cornell Int'l L.J.* 459–525 (1994).

Chayes, A. Handler, Abram Chayes & R.B. Mitchell. "Active Complaince Committed Abroad," *in* C. Scott, ed., *Torture as Tort: Comparative* (1995).

Chayes, A. Handler, Chayes, Abram & Mitchell, R.B. "Active Compliance Management in Environmental Treaties" *in* W. Land, ed., *Sustainable Development and International Law* at 75–89 (Kluwer Law: London, 1995).

Chen, Lung-Chu, *An Introduction to Contemporary International Law: A Policy Oriented Perspective* (Yale University Press: New Haven, CT, 1989).

Cheng, Bin, "The Legal Regime of Airspace and Outer Space in the Boundary Problem, Functionalism versus Spatialism: The Major Premises," 5 *Annals of Air and Space Law* 323, 337 (1980).

Cheyne, Ilona. "Africa and International Trade in Hazardous Wastes," 6 RADIC 493 (1994).

Chick, Timothy, *Corporations and the Canadian Charter of Rights and Freedoms* (Dalhousie University: Halifax, 1993).

Christensen, Randy L., "Canada's Drinking Problem, Walkerton, Water Contamination and Public Policy," *in* S.C. Boyd, D.E. Chunn & R. Menzies, eds., *Toxic Criminology* at 97–111 (Fernwood Publishing: Halifax, 2002).

Christopher, Paul. *The Ethics of War & Peace: An Introduction to Legal and Moral Issues* (Prentice Hall, NJ, 1994).

Cicero, *De Re Publica* and De Legibus (tr. Clinton W. Keyes; G.P. Putnam Sons: NY, 1928).

Clark, K. & Yacoumidis, A. *CELA 5 Year Report on the "Common Sense Revolution"* (2001).

Cohen, J. "Tobacco Money Lights Up a Debate," 272 (5261) *Science* 488–94 (Apr. 26, 1996).

Cohen, Robert. *Milk, The Deadly Poison* (Argus Publishing, NJ, 1998).

Colborn, Theo, Dumanoski, Dianne, Myers & John Peterson. *Our Stolen Future* (Dutton, Penguin Books: NY, 1996).

Coleman, Jules. *Risks and Wrongs* (Cambridge University Press, Cambridge, U.K., 1995).

Colvin, Eric. *Principles of Criminal Law*, (Thomson Professional Publishing, Carswell Publications, Canada, 1991).

Colwell, Rita. "Global Climate and Infectious Disease: The Cholera Paradigm," President's Lecture, Feb. 10,1996, American Association for the Advancement of Science, 274 *Science* 2025–2031 (Dec. 20, 1996).

Cooney, John F., Starr, Judson W., Block, Joseph G., Kelly, Thomas J. Jr., Herrup, Andrew R., Mann, Valerie K., & Baker, Gregory. *Environmental Crimes*

Desk Book (Environmental Law Institute: Washington, 1996).

Craig, Paul & De Burca, Grainne, *EU Law—Text, Cases and Materials* (Oxford University Press: Oxford, UK, 3d ed. 2002).

Cranor, Carl F. *Regulating Toxic Substances (Philosophy of Science and the Law)* (Oxford University Press: NY, 1993).

Crawford, James. *The International Law Commission's Articles on State Responsibility* (Cambridge University Press: UK, 2002).

Crowe, Michael, B. "St. Thomas and Ulpian's Natural Law" *in St. Thomas Aquinas 1274–1974 Commemorative Studies* at 261–282 (Pontifical Institute for Medieval Studies: Toronto, Canada, 1974).

Curtin, D. & Litke, R., eds. *Institutional Violence* (Value Inquiry Book Series, No. 88: Rodopi, Amsterdam, 1999).

D'Amato, Anthony. "Agora: What Obligation Do Our Generation Owe to The Next? An Approach to Global Environmental Responsibility," 84 *Am. J. Int'l L.* 190 (1990).

Daily, Gretchen. "Introduction," *in Nature's Services* at 3–4 (Island Press: Washington, DC, 1997).

Daly Herman & Cobb, John B, Jr. *For the Common Good* (Beacon Press Books: Boston, MA. 1989).

Daly, Herman. "From Empty World Economics to Full World Economics: Recognizing an Historical Turning Point in Economic Development," *in* R. Goodland, H. Daly, S. El Serafy, & B. Von Droste, eds., *Environmentally Sustainable Economic Development: Building on Bruntland* (UNESCO: Paris, 1991).

Daly, Herman. *Beyond Growth* (Beacon Press: Boston, MA, 1996).

Daly, Herman, "Consumption: The Economics of Value Added and the Ethics of Value Distributed," *in* L. Westra & P. Werhane, eds., *The Business of Consumption* at 17–30 (Rowman Littlefield: Lanham, MD, 1998).

Daniels, Norman, "Reflective Equilibrium and Justice as Political" *in* V. Davion & C. Wolf, eds., *The Idea of a Political Liberalism* at 127–145 (Rowman Littlefield: Lanham, MD, 2000).

Dartois, A.M. & Casamitjana, F. "Drinking Water," 46 (10) *Pediatrie* 663–667 (1991).

Davis, Karen. *Prisoned Chickens, Poisoned Eggs: An Inside Look at the Poultry Industry* (The Book Publishing Co: TN, 1996).

De Fiumel, H. "Critical Observations on Crimes of State and the Notion of International Community as a Whole," *in* J.H. Weiler, A. Cassese & M. Spimedi, eds., *International Crime of State—A Critical Analysis of the ILC Draft Article 19 on State Responsibility* at 251 (Walter de Gruyter: Berlin, 1989).

De George, R. "The Environment, Rights and Future Generations," *in* E. Partridge, ed., *Responsibilities to Future Generations* (Prometheus Books, Buffalo, NY, 1981).

De Laat, J.M.T. & De Gruijl, F.R. "The Role of UVA in the Aetiology of Non-Melonoma Skin Cancer," 26 *Cancer Surveys* 173–192.

De Sousa Santos, Boaventura. *Towards a New Legal Common Sense: Law, Globalization and Emancipation* (Butterworth, Lexis/Nexis, UK, 2002).

De Sousa Santos, Boaventura. "Global Bovernance," paper presented at Sheffield University Law School for the International Global Governance and Democracy Conference (April 30, 2003).

De Sousa Santos, Boaventura. "Towards a Multicultural Conception of Human Rights," 18:1–15 1999 *Zeitschung fur Recgtsoziologie* z42 (1997).

Deets, Stephen. "Solving the Gabcikovo-Nagymaros Dam Conflict," 1988 East European Studies Meeting Reports,Woodrow Wilson Centre.

DeGrazia, David. *Taking Animals Seriously* (Cambridge University Press: NY, 1996)

Dernbach, John. "Taking the Pennsylvania Constitution Seriously When It Protects the Environment: Part I—An Interpretative Framework for Article I, Section 27" 103:4 *Dick. L. Rev.* 693–734 (1999).

Dernbach, John. "Taking the Pennsylvania Constitution Seriously When It Protects the Environment: Part II—Environmental Rights and Public Trust," 104:1 *Dick. L. Rev.* 97–164 (1999).

Dillon, J.C. "Risks Associated with Pesticide Residue Contamination of Foods in Developing Countries," 30 (5) *Cahiers de Nutrition et de Dietetique* 294–299 (1995).

Domitius, Ulpianus, *Commentary on the Sentences* (Quaracchi: Milano, 1889).

Downs, G. et al. "Is the Good News About Compliance Good News About Cooperation?" 50 *Int'l Org.* (1996).

Draper, E. *Risky Business* (Cambridge University Press: Cambridge, 1991).

Duff, A., *Philosophy and the Criminal Law* (Cambridge University Press: Cambridge, 1990)

Dupuy, Pierre-Marie. "The Institutionalization of International Crimes of State," in J.H. Weiler, A. Cassese & M. Spinedi, eds., *International Crime of State* at 170–188 (Walter de Gruyter: Berlin, 1989).

Dupuy, R.-J. A9-86 (11) *La Communauté Internationale entre le Mythe et l'Histoire, Anuario Argentino de Derecho International* at 291–294 (1984).

Dupuy, René Jean, "Humanity and the Environment," 2 Colo. *J. Int'l L. & Pol'y* 201–204 (1991).

Dworkin, Ronald *Taking Rights Seriously* (Harvard University Press: Cambridge, MA, 1978).

Eckhout, Piet, "The EU Charter of Fundamental Rights and the Federal Question," 39 *Common Mkt. L. Rev.* 945–994 (2002)

Edgerton, H.W. "Negligence, Inadvertence and Indifference" 39 *Harv. L. Rev.* 849 (1927).

Ehrenfeld, D. "The Management of Diversity: A Conservation Paradox," *in* F.H. Bormann & S.R. Kellert, eds., *Ecology, Economics and Ethics* at 26–39 (Yale University Press: New Haven, CT).

Ehrlich, Paul and Ehrlich, Anne. *The Population Explosion* (Simon and Schuster: NY, 1990).

Eickmann, T. "Waste Sites, Former Waste Sites, Contaminated Sites and Health Effects—A Survey," *Wissenshaft and Umwelt,* Issue 2 at 75–79 (1994).

Eisler, R., *The Chalice and the Blade* (Viking Press, NY, 1988).

Eisnitz, Gail. *Slaughterhouse: The Shocking Story of Greed, Neglect, and Inhumane Treatment Inside the U.S. Meat Industry* (Prometheus Books, NY, 1997).

English, Jane. "Abortion and the Concept of a Person," 5 (2) *Can. J. Phil.* (October 1975), *reprinted in* Mappes and Zembaty, *Biomedical Ethics* at 447–453 (McGraw-Hill: NY, 1991).

Epstein, Samuel S. *The Politics of Cancer* (Sierra Club Books, CA, 1978).

Estrich, Susan. "Rape," 95 *Yale Law Journal* 1087 (1986).

Esty, Daniel C. "Unpacking the Trade and Environment Conflict." 25 *Law & Pol'y Int'l Bus.* 1259 (1994).

Faber, Daniel, ed. *The Struggle for Ecological Democracy* (The Guilford Press: NY, 1998).

Faber, Daniel. "The Political Ecology of American Capitalism: New Challenges for the Environmental Justice Movement," *in* D. Faber, ed., *The Struggle for Ecological Democracy*, The Guilford Press: NY, 1998).

Falk, Richard A. *The Role of Domestic Courts in the International Legal Order*, (Syracuse University Press: NY, 1964).

Falk, Richard A. *The Status of Law in International Society* (Princeton University Press: NJ, 1970).

Falk, Richard. *Law in an Emerging Global Village* (Transnational Publishers: Ardsley, NY, 1998).

Feyerband, *Science in a Free Society* (NLB: London, UK, 1978).

Fidler, David P. *International Law and Public Health* (Transnational Publishers: Ardsley, NY, 2001).

Field, Stewart and Jorg, Nico, "Corporate Liability and Manslaughter: Should We Be Going Dutch?," *Criminal Law Quarterly* 156–171 (1991).

Finnis, John, *Natural Law and Natural Rights* (Clarendon Press: Oxford, 1980).

Fitzmaurice, G.G. "The Law and Procedure of the International Court of Justice: General Principles and Substantive Law," *B.Y.I.L.* 1–70 (1950).

Fletcher, G. P., "The Theory of Criminal Negligence: A Comparative Analysis," U. 119 (3) *Penn. L. Rev.* 401–437 (Jan. 1971).

Forbes, Valery & Calow, Peter. "Costs of Living with Contaminants: Implications for Assessing Low-Level Exposures," 4 (3) *Belle Newsletter* 1–8 (1996).

Forman, Dave. "EarthFirst!" *in* Peter C. List, ed., *Radical Environmentalism* at 187–191 (1993).

Fox, Michael. "Ecofeminism and the Dismantling of Institutional Violence" in D. Curtin & R. Lietke eds., 88 *Institutional Violence* 263–272 (Value Inquiry Books: Rodopi BV Amsterdam, 1999).

Frederick Hernandez-Garduno, E., Perez-Neria, J., Paccagnella, A.M., Pina-Garcia, M.A., Manguia-Castro, M., Catalan-Vazquez, M., Rojas-Ramos, M. "Air Pollution and Respiratory Health in Mexico City," 39 (4) *J. Occupational & Envtl. Med.* 299–307 (1997).

French, Hilary & Mastney, Lisa, "Controlling International Environmental Crime," *State of the World 2001* 166–188 (The Worldwatch Institute, W. W. Norton and Co.: NY, 2001).

French, Peter A. *Collective and Corporate Responsibility* (Columbia University Press: NY, 1984).

French, Peter A. *Responsibility Matters* (University Press of Kansas: Lawrence, KS, 1992).

French, Peter, A. "Corporate Moral Agency," *in* Tom L. Beauchamp and Norman E. Bowie, eds, *Ethical Theory and Business* 58–69 (Prentice Hall: Englewood Cliffs, N.J.,1979).

Frenkel, David A. and Lurie, Yotam, "Culpability of Corporations–Legal and Ethical Perspectives", 45 *Criminal Law Quarterly* 465–487 (2002).

Froman, Dave. "More on Earth First! And the Monkey Wrench Gang," *in* Peter C. List, ed., *Radical Environmentalism* at 253–254 (1993).

Fukuyama, F. "The End of History?," 16 *National Interest* 3–18 (1989).

Gaylord, C. & Bell, E. "Enviornmental Justice: A National Priority," *in* L. Westra & P. Wenz, eds., *Faces of Environmental Racism* at 29–40 (Rowman Littlefield: Lanham, MD, 1995).

Gbadegesin, Segun. "Multinational Corporations, Developed Nations and Environmental Racism: Toxic Waste, Oil Explorations and Ecocatastrophes," *in* L. Westra and B. Lawson, eds, *Faces of Environmental Racism* at 187–202 (Rowman Littlefield: Lanham, MD, 2d ed. 2001).

Gerhring, Thomas and Jactenfuchs. "International Environmental Regimes: Dynamic Sectoral Legal Changes," 1 *Y.B. Int'l Env. L.* 35–56 (1990).

Gertner, Eric, "Are Corporations Entitled to Equality?," 19 *Canadian Rts. Rep.* 288–301 (1986).

Gewirth, A. *Human Rights: Essays on Justification and Applications*, (University of Chicago Press: IL, 1982).

Gilbert, Geoff. "The Criminal Responsibility of States," 39 *I.C.L.Q.* 345 (1990).

Gilbert, Paul. *Terrorism, Security and Nationality (An Introductory Study in Applied Political Philosophy)* (Routledge: London, UK, 1994).

Glasbeek, H. and Tucker, E. "Death by Consensus: The Westray Mine Story," 3 (4) *New Solutions* 14–41 (1993).

Glasbeek, Harry and Rowland, Susan, "Are Injuring and Killing in the Workplace Crimes?," *in* Neil Boyd, ed., *The Social Dimensions of Law* (Prentice Hall: Scarborough, Ont., 1986).

Glennon, Michael J. "American Hegemoney in an Unplanned World Order, 5 (1) *J. Conflict & Security L.* 3–25 (2000).

Goedhuis, "Some Recent Trends in the Interpretation and the Implementation of International Space Law" 19 *Colum. J. Transnat'l L.* 213, 218–219 (1981).

Goerner, Sally, J., *Chaos and The Evolving Ecological Universe* (Gordon and Breach Science Publishers, S.A. (Overseas Publishers Association): Amsterdam, The Netherlands, 1994).

Goetz, David, "Bill C-45: An Act to Amend the Criminal Code (Criminal Liability of Organizations), Legislative Summary, 2003.

Goldie, L.F.E. "Concepts of Strict and Absolute Liability and the Ranking of Liability in Terms of Relative Exposure to Risk," XVI *Netherlands Y.B. Int'l L.*175 (1985).

Goodland, Robert and Pimentel, David, "Environmental Sustainability and Integrity in the Agriculture Section", in D. Pimentel, L. Westra and R. Noss eds. *Ecological Integrity: Integrating Environment, Conservation and Health* 121–138 (Island Press: Washington, D.C., 2000).

Goodland, R. "The Case that the World Has Reached Limits" *in* R. Goodland, H. Daly, S. El Serafy & B. van Droste, eds., *Environmentally Sustainable Economic Development: Building on Bruntland* (Paris, UNESCO, 1991).

Goodwin, Robert E. "No Moral Nukes," 90 (3) *Ethics* 417–449 (April, 1980).

Graefrath, B. "On the Reaction of the 'International Community as a Whole': A Perspective of Survival," *in* J.H. Weiler, A. Cassese & M. Spimedi, eds., *International Crime of State—A Critical Analysis of the ILC Draft Article 19 on State Responsibility* at 253 (Walter de Gruyter, Berlin, 1989).

Grantstein, R.D. "Photoimmunology" 9 (1) *Seminars in Dermatology* 16–24 (1990).

Green, Leslie. *The Authority of the State* (Clarendon Press, Oxford, UK, 1990).

Grotius, Hugo. *The Law of War and Peace* (Francis W. Kelsey, trans., Bobbs-Merrill: Indianapolis, IN, 1962).

Grotius, Hugo. *De jure belli ac paces libri tres*, (1625), II, XXV, sec. vi, at 582.

Guidotti, T.L. "Ambient Air Quality and Human Health; Current Concepts (Part 2)," 3 (1) *Canadian Respiratory J.* 29–39 (1996).

Guidotti, Tee L. & Gosselin, Pierre, eds. *The Canadian Guide to Health and the Environment* (University of Alberta Press: Edmonton, AL, 1999).

Gutto, Shadrack, B.O. "The Synergy of Sociology of Law and Human and People's Rights: A Critical African and Third World Perpective," *in Human and Peoples' Rights for the Oppressed* at 38–51 (Lund Studies in Law and Society, Lund University Press: Sweden, 1993).

Habermas, Jurgen, "Three Normative Models of Democracy," *in The Inclusion of the Other Studies in Political Theory* at 239–252 (MIT Press, 1998).

Hacker, P.M.S. and Raz, J., *Law, Morality and Society* (Clarendon Press: Oxford, UK, 1977).

Halász, Zoltan, "Sull'applicazione per analogia delle disposizioni penali," XLIV *La Giustizia Penale* 358–368 (1938).

Handl, Gregory. "Compliance Control Mechanisms and International Environmental Obligations," *Tul. J. Int'l & Comp. L.* 29 (1997).

Hannikainen, L. *Peremptory Norms (Jus Cogens) in International Law—Historical Development, Criteria, Present Status* (Helsinki, 1988).

Hardin, G. "The Tragedy of the Commons", 162 *Science* 1243–48. 365 (1968).

Harrington, Courtney. "*Doe v. Unocal Corp.* (2002 WL 31063976 (9th Cir.2002))," 16 *Tul. Envtl. L.J.* 247–249 (2002).

Harris, C.E. "The Ethics of Natural Law," *in* Mark Timmons, ed., *Conduct and Character* at 100–113 (Wadsworth Publishing, 1990).

Hart, H.L.A. *The Concept of Law* (Oxford University Press: London, UK, 1961).

Hart, H.L.A. and Honoré, T. *Causation in the Law* (Clarendon Press, Oxford, UK, 2d ed. 1985).

Hart, Henry M. Jr. & Sacks, Albert M., "The Legal Process: Basic Problems in the Making and Application of Law," in N. Eskridge, Jr., and Philip P. Frickey eds., *Cases and Material on Legislation: Statutes and the Creation of Public Policy* (West Publishing Co.: St. Paul, MN, 1995).

Harte, J. Torn, M. and Jensen, D. "The Nature and Consequences of Indirect Linkages Between Climate Change and Biological Diversity," R.L. Peters and T. Lovejoy, eds, *Global Warming and Biological Diversity* (Yale University Press: New Haven, CT, 1992).

Healy, Patrick. "The Creighton Quartet: Enigma Variations in a Lower Key," 23 C.R. (4th) 265 (1993).

Henkin, L. *How Nations Behave: Land and Foreign Policy* (Frederick A. Praeger: NY, 1968).

Henkin, Louis et al. *Rights and Might: International Law and the Use of Force* (New York Council on Foreign Relations Press: NY, 1989).

Herman, Edward S. and Chomsky, Noam. *Manufacturing Consent* (Pantheon Books, Random House: NY, 2002).

Hervey, Tamara K. "Up in Smoke? Community (Anti)-Tobacco Law and Policy," 26 *E.L. Rev.* Apr.101–125 (Apr. 2001).

Hey, Ellen. *Reflections on an Environmental Court* (Kluwer Law International: Dordrecht, The Netherlands, 2000).

Higgins, Rosalynn. *Problems and Process: International Law and How We Use It* (Clarendon Press: Oxford, UK, 1994).

Hill, Julia Butterfly. *The Legacy of Luna* (Harper Collins Publishers: San Francisco, CA, 2000).

Hiskes, Richard P. *Democracy, Risk and Community* (Oxford University Press: NY, 1998).

Hix, Simon. *The Political System of the European Union* (Palgrave Publishers: NY, 1999).

Hobbes, Thomas. *Leviathan* (Bobbs-Merrill: NY, 1958).

Hogg, Peter. "Gun Control and the Criminal Law Power," *Constitutional Cases* (Osgood Hall Law School Professional Program 2000).

Hohfeld, W.N. *Fundamental Legal Conceptions* (Yale University Press: New Haven, CT, 1923).

Holwick, Scott, "Transnational Corporate Behaviour and Its Disparate and Unjust Effects on the Indigenous Cultures and the Environment of Developing Nations: *Jota v. Texaco*, A Case Study," *Colo. J. Int'l Envtl. L. & Pol'y* 183–221 (2000).

Homer Dixon, Thomas. "Environmental Scarcity and Violent Conflict: Evidence from Cases," 19 (1) *Int'l Security* 5–40 (Summer 1994).

Homer-Dixon, Thomas. "On The Threshold: Environmental Changes as Causes of Acute Conflict," 16 (2) *Int'l Security* 76–116 (Fall 1991).

Homer-Dixon, Thomas F., *Environment Scarcity and Violence* (Princeton University Press: NJ, 1999).

Homer-Dixon, Thomas F. & Gizewski, Peter. *Environmental Scarcity and Violent Conflict: The Case of Pakistan* (Project on Environment, Population and

Security University of Toronto, University College and the American Assoc. for the Advancement of Science (1996).

Honoré, Tony. *Responsibility and Fault* (Hart Publishing: Oxford, UK, 1999).

Howe of Aberavon, The Rt. Hon. Lord. "Euro-Justice:Yes or No?" 21 *E.L. Rev.* 187–198 (June 1996).

Howse, Robert. "Democracy, Science, and Free Trade: Risk Regulation on Trial at the World Trade Organization," 98 *Mich. L. Rev.* 2329–2357 (2000).

Hummel, Monte. *Endangered Spaces—The Future for Canada's Wilderness* (Key Porter Books: Toronto, 1989).

Hurrell and Kingsbury. *The International Politics of the Environment* (Oxford University Press: Oxford, UK, 1992).

Hutchinson, A. and Peter, A. "Private Rights, Public Wrongs," The Liberal Lie of the Charter 38 *Ut. L.J.* 278 (1988).

International Council on Human Rights Policy (Geneva). *Beyond Voluntarism: Human Rights and the Developing International Legal Obligations of Companies* (2002).

Janis, Mark W. "The Nature of *Jus Cogens*," 3 *Conn. J. Int'l L.* 359 (1998).

Jenks, C. Wilfred. *Law, Freedom and Welfare* (Stevens and Sons: London, UK, 1963).

Jennings, Sir R.Y. "Universal International Law in a Multicultural World," *in* M. Bos & I. Brownlie, eds., *Liber Amicorum for the Rt. Hon. Lord Wilberforce* at 187–197(Oxford University Press: UK, 1987).

Jonas, Hans. *The Imperative of Responsibility* (University of Chicago Press: Chicago, IL, 1984).

Jutro. "Biological Diversity, Ecology, and Global Climate Change," 96 *Envtl. Health Perspective* 167–70 (Dec. 1991).

Kant, Immanuel. *Methaphsics of Morals* (trans. James Ellington, Bobbs Merrill, Indianapolis, IN, 1981).

Kant, Immanuel. "Duties to Oneself," in *Lectures on Ethics* at 116–126 (trans. Louis Infield, Hackett Publishing Company: Indianapolis, IN, 1979).

Kant, Immanuel. *Groundwork of the Metaphysics of Morals* (trans. H.J. Paton, Harper Torchbooks: NY, 1964).

Kant, Immanuel. *Perpetual Peace* 23 (Lewis White Beck ed., Bobbs-Merrill: Indianapolis, IN, 1957).

Karr, James & Chu, Ellen. "Ecological Integrity: Reclaiming Lost Connections," *in* L. Westra & J. Lemons eds., *Perspectives on Ecological Integrity* at 34–48 (Kluwer Academic Publishers: Dordrecht, The Netherlands, 1995).

Karr, James R. "Health, Integrity and Biological Assessment: The Importance of Measuring Whole Things," *in* D. Pimentel, L. Westra & R.F. Noss, *Ecological Integrity: Integrating Environment, Conservation and Health* at 209–226 (Island Press: Washington, DC, 2000).

Karr, James, R., & Chu, Ellen, W. *Restoring Life in Running Waters* (Island Press: Washington, DC, 1999).

Kaufman, Robert S. and Haggard, S. *The Politcal Economy of Democracy*, (Princeton University Press: Princeton, N.J., 1995).

Kay, James J. & Regier, Henry A. "Uncertainty, Complexity, and Ecological Integrity: Insights from an Ecosystem Approach," *in* P. Crabbé, A. Holland, L Ryszkowski & L. Westra, eds., *Implementing Ecological Integrity* at 121–156 (NATO Science Series, Vol. 1, Kluwer Academic Publishers: Dordrecht, The Netherlands, 2000).

Kay, James J., and Schneider, E. "The Challenge of the Ecosystem Approach," 20 (3) *Alternatives* 1–6 (1994), *reprinted in* L. Westra & J. Lemons, eds., *Perspectives on Integrity* at 49–59 (Kluwer Academic Publishers: Dordrecht, The Netherlands, 1994).

Kekes, John. *Against Liberalism* (Cornell University Press: Ithaca, NY, 1997).

Kelman, Herbert C. & Hamilton V. Lee, *Crimes of Obedience* (Yale University Press: New Haven, CT, 1989).

Kenny, Anthony John Patrick. *The Aristolian Ethics: A Study of the Relationship between the Eudemian and Nicomachan Ethics of Aristotle* (Clarendon Press: Oxford, UK, 1978).

Kendall, H.W. and D. Pimentel. "Constraints on the Expansion of the Global Food Supply," 23 (3) *AMBIO*,198–205 (1994).

Keohane, R.O. and Nye J.S., "Globalization: What's New, What's Not and So What," 118 *Foreign Policy* 104–19 (2000).

Khanna, V.S., "Corporate Criminal Liability: What Purpose Does It Serve?," 109 (7) *Harvard Law Review* 1477–1534 (1996).

Kindred, H., Mickelson, K., Provost, R., Reif, L.C., McDorman, T.L., DeMestral, Williams, S.A. *International Law* (Edmond Montgomery: Toronto, 6th ed. 2000).

King, Martin Luther, Jr. "Letter from a Birmingham Jail" *in* R. Holmes, ed., *Non-Violence in Theory and Practice* 69 (Wadsworth, 1990).

Kiss, Alexandre & Shelton, Dinah. *Manual of European Environmental Law* (Cambridge University Press: Cambridge, UK, 2d ed. 1997).

Kiss, Alexandre. *Droit International de l'environment*, (A. Pedone ed., Paris, 1989).

Kiss, Alexandre. "The Implications of Global Change for the International Legal System," *in* E. Brown-Weiss, ed., *Environmental Change and International Law* at315–339 (United Nations University Press: Tokyo, 1992).

Kissell, Judith Lee. "Causation—The Challenge for Complicity" (Paper presented at the Eastern Meeting American Philosophical Association, 1999).

Klein, Naomi, "Reclaiming the Commons," 9 *New Left Review* 81–89 (May/June 2001).

Kohlberg, L. *The Psychology of Moral Development: The Nature and the Validity of Moral Stages* (Harper and Row: San Franscisco, CA, 1984).

Kokole, Omari H. "The Political Economy of the African Environment," *in Faces of Environmental Racism* at 163, 177 (Rowman Littlefield: Lanham, MD, 1995).

Korsgaard, Christine, M. *Creating the Kingdom of Ends* (Cambridge University Press: UK, 1996).

Korten, David C. "Do Corporations Rule the World? And Does It Matter?," 11 (1) *Org. & Env.* 389–396 (December 1998).

Korten, David. *When Corporations Rule the World* (Kumarian Press, Berret Koehler Publishers: West Hartford, CT, 1995).

Koskenniemi, M. "Breach of Treaty or Noncompliance? Reflections on the Enforcement of the Montreal Protocol," 3 *YB Int'l Envtl. Law* 123–128 (1992).

Koskenniemi, Martti. *From Apology to Utopia* (Finnish Lawyers' Publishing Company: Helsinki, 1989).

Kumate, J. "Infectious Diseases of the 21st Century," 28(2) *Archives of Medical Research* 155–161 (1997).

Kummer, K. "The International Regulation of Transboundary Traffic in Hazardous Wastes: The 1989 Basel Convention," 41 *ICLQ* 530 (1992).

Kuper, Adam. *Culture: The Anthropologists Account* (Harvard University Press: Cambridge, MA, 1999).

Kwame-Appiah, Anthony. "Racism" *in* Larry May et al., ed., *Applied Ethics: A Multicultural Approach* at 417 (Prentice Hall: Edgewood Cliffs, NJ, 1998).

Kymlicka, Will. *Multicultural Citizenship* (Clarendon Press: Oxford, UK, 1997).

L'Heureux-Dubé, Claire, "By Reason of Authority or By Authority of Reason," 27 *U.B.C. L. Rev.* 1 (1993).

L'Heureux-Dubé, Claire, "Making Equality Work in Family Law," 14 *Can. J. Fam. L.* 103 (1997).

L'Heureux-Dubé, Claire, "Conversations on Equality," 26 *Man. L.J.* 273–298 (1999).

Lacey, N. & Wells, C. *Reconstructing Criminal Law* (Butterworths: London, UK, 1998).

Laffan, Brigid. "The European Union Polity: A Union of Regulative, Normative and Cognitive Pillars," *J. Eur. Pub. Pol'y* 709–727 (2001).

LaFollette, H. & May, Larry. "Suffer the Little Children," *in World Hunger and Morality* at 70 (Prentice Hall: NJ, 2d ed. 1996).

Lagrega, M. D., Buckingham, P. L., & Evans J. C. *Hazardous Waste Management* (McGraw-Hill: NY, 1994).

Larschan, Bradley and Brennan, Bonnie C. "The Common Heritage of Mankind Principle in International Law," 21 *Colum. J. Transnat'l L.* 305–337 (1983).

Lauterpacht, Hersch. *International Law and Human Rights* (Archon Books: NY, 1968).

Lauterpacht, Hersch. *International Law and Human Rights* (Stevens Publishers: London, UK, 1950).

Lauterpacht, Hersch. *The Function of Law in the International Community* (Clarendon Press: Oxford, UK, 1933).

Law Reform Commission of Canada. *Our Criminal Law* (1976).

Law Reform Commission of Canada. "Protection of Life, Crimes against the Environment," (Working Paper # 44, 1985).

Laxer, James. *Inventing Europe: The Rise of a New World Power* (Lester Publications: Toronto, ON, 1991).

Lazarus, Richard J. "Thirty Years of Environmental Protection Law in Supreme Court" 19 *Pace Envtl. L. Rev.* 619–666 (2002).

Lazarus, Richard, "A New Fault Line—*Mes Rea,*" *Envtl. F.* 9 (May/June 1995).

Lebowitz, M.D. "Epidemiological Studies of the Respiratory Effects of Air Pollution," 9 (5) *Eur. Respiratory Jv.* 1029–1054 (1996).

Lechat et al. "Accident and Disaster Epidemiology," 21 (3–4) *Pub. Health Rev.* 243–253 (Catholic University of Louvain: Brussels, Belgium, 1993–94).

Lemons, John, Heredia, R., Jamieson, D., & Spash, C. "Climate Change and Sustainable Development," *in* J. Lemons & D. Brown, eds., *Sustainable Development: Science, Ethics and Public Policy* (Kluwer Academic Publishers: Dordrecht, The Netherlands, 1995).

Lenaerts, Ken. "The Principle of Subsidiary and the Environment in the European Union: Keeping the Balance of Federalism," 17 *Fordham International Law Journal* 846–895 (1994).

Leopold, A. *A Sand County Almanac and Sketches Here and There* (Oxford University Press: NY, 1949).

Levinstein, C & Wooding, J., "Dying for a Living: Workers, Production and the Environment," in D. Faber, ed., *The Struggle for Ecological Democracy* at 60–80 (The Guilford Press: NY, 1998).

Linden, Allen M. *Canadian Tort Law* (Butterworth's: Toronto, 6th ed. 1997).

Lindgren, Richard et al. "Tragedy on Tap," (CELA: Toronto, Ont., 2001).

Lindgren, Richard, McShane, Lisa, Patterson, Grace & Wordsworth, Anne. "Tragedy on Tap: Why Ontario Needs a Safe Drinking Water Act," (Submission of the Concerned Walkerton Citizens and the Canadian Environmental Law Association to Part II of the Walkerton Inquiry, 2001).

List, Martin & Rittberger, Volker. "Regime Theory and International Environmental Management," *in* A. Hurrell & B. Kingsbury, eds., *The International Politics of the Environment* at 85–109 (Clarendon Press: Oxford, 1992).

Liu, Mimi. *A Prophet with Honour: An Examination of the Gender Equality Jurisprudence of Madam Justice Claire L'Heureux-Dubé of the Supreme Court of Canada* (2000).

Longino, Helen. *Science as Social Knowledge* (Princeton University Press: NJ, 1990).

Longstretch, Janice D. & Frank R. de Grujil et al. "Effects of Increased Solar Ultraviolet Radiation on Human Health," 24 (3) *Ambio* 153–165 (May 1995).

Loretti, A. and Tegegn, Y. "Disasters in Africa: Old and New Hazards and Growing Vulnerability" 49 (3–4) *World Health Stat. Q.* 179–184 (1996).

Loucks, O.L. "Pattern of Forest Integrity in the Eastern United States and Canada: Measuring Loss and Recovery," *in* D. Pimentel, L. Westra & R.F. Noss, eds., *Ecological Integrity: Integrating Environment, Conservation and Health* at 177–190 (Island Press, Washington, 2000).

Lucas, J.R. *Principles of Politics* (Clarendon Press: Oxford, UK, 1966).

MacIntyre, A. *Whose Justice? Whose Rationality?* University of Notre Dame Press:Notre Dame, IN, 1988).

Macpherson, Crawford Brough, *The Life and Times of Liberal Democracy* (Oxford University Press: UK, 1977).

Malanczuk, Peter, *Akehurst's Modern Introduction to International Law* (Routledge: London, UK, 7th rev. ed., 1997).

Malla, U.M "Conservation of Environment and Protection of Health of the People: A Task for Policy Makers," 3 (4) *Int'l Med. J.* 277–287 (1996).

Manzini, Pietro, *Diritto Internazionale dell Ambiente* (Giuffré ed., Milano, Italy, 1998).

Marks, Stephan P. "Emerging Human Rights: A Generation for the 1980's," 33 *Rutgers L. Rev.* 435–452 (1981).

Marks, Susan. *The Riddle of All Constitutions* (Oxford University Press: UK, 2000).

Marquis, Don. "Why Abortion Is Immoral" *in J. Phil.* 183–202 (1989).

Mazrui, Al. *The Africans: A Triple Heritage* 11–21 (1986).

McBride, S. & Shields, J., "Embracing Free Trade: Embedding Neo-Liberalism," *in Dismantling a Nation: Canada and the New World Order* at 161–187 (Fernwood, 1993).

McCaffrey, S. "The Objectives of a New Regime and the Means for Accomplishment," *in* J.H. Weiler, A. Cassese & M. Spimedi, eds., *International Crime of State—A Critical Analysis of the ILC Draft Article 19 on State Responsibility* (Walter de Gruyter: Berlin, 1989).

McCaffrey, S.C. "Assessment of Environmental Impact: Some Reflections on the American Experience," *in Environmental Law International and Comparative Aspects* at 159–169 (Oceana Publications, 1976).

McCalman, Iain et al. *Mad Cows and Modernity* (Humanities Research Centre, The Australian National University, National Academies Forum, 1998: Canberra, Australia).

McDermott, J., "Technology: The Opiate of the Intellectuals," *in* L. Westra & K. Shrader Frechette, eds., *Technology and Values* (Rowman Littlefield: Lanham, MA, 1997).

McGinn, R.E. "Technology, Demography, and the Anachronism of Traditional Rights," *in* K. Shrader-Frechette and L. Westra, eds., *Technology and Values* at 167–186 (Rowman Littlefield: Lanham, MD, 1997).

McKibben, Bill, "Indifferent to the Pain," NY Times, Sept. 4, 1999, op-ed.

McMahan, Jeff. "Deterrence and Deontology," *in* R. Hardin, J. Mearsheimer, G. Dworkin & R. Goodin, eds., *Nuclear Deterrence Ethics and Strategy* at 141–160 (Chicago University Press: IL, 1985).

McMichael, A.J. "Global Environmental Change in the Coming Century: How Sustainable Are Recent Health Gains?" *in* D. Pimentel, L. Westra & R. Noss, *Ecological Integrity: Integrating Environment, Conservation and Health* 245 (Island Press: Washington, DC, 2000).

McMichael, A.J. Haines, A., Slooff, R. & Kovats, S., eds. *Climate Change and Human Health* (WHO Publication: Geneva, 1996).

McMichael, A.J. "Global Environmental Change and Human Health: New Challenges to Scientist and Policy-Maker," 15 (4) *J. Pub. Health Pol'y* 407–419 (1994).

McMichael, A.J. *A Planetary Overload* (Cambridge University Press: U.K. (1995a).

McMichael, A.J. "The Health of Persons, Populations, and Planets: Epidemiology Comes Full Circle" in *Epidemiology and Society* (Epidemiology Resources, Inc., 1995b).

McMichael, A.J. "Global Environmental Change in the Coming Century: How Sustainable Are Recent Health Gains?" *in* D. Pimentel, L. Westra & R. Noss, eds., *Ecological Integrity: Integrating Environment, Conservation and Health* at 245 (Island Press, Washington, DC, 2000).

Mellon, M. and Fondriest, D. "Pearls Before Pigs," 23 (1) *Nucleus* 1 (Spring 2001).

Meron, Theodor. *Human Rights Law-Making in the United Nations* (Clarendon Press: Oxford, UK, 1986).

Meron, Theodor. *Human Rights and Humanitarian Norms as Customary Law* (Clarendon Press: Oxford, UK, 1989).

Meron, Theodor, "On the Inadequate Reach of Humanitarian and Human Rights Law and the Need for a New Instrument," 77 *Am. J. Int'l L.* 589 (1983).

Mickelson, Karin, "Rereading *Trail Smelter*," *Canadian Y.B. Int'l L.* 219 (1993).

Middleton, J. and Saunders, P. "Paying for Water," 19 (1) *J. Public Health Medicine* 106–115 (1997).

Midlarsky, Manus I. "Raison d'état, raison d'église: Realpolitik and the Onset of Genocide" (Paper presented to the 2001 Annual Meeting of the American Political Science Association, Aug. 30–Sept. 1, 2001).

Mill, J.S. *On Liberty* (George Routledge and Sons: London, UK, 1910).

Miller, Peter and Westra, Laura. *Just Integrity* (Rowman Littlefield: Lanham, MD, 2002).

Minow, Martha, *Making All the Difference: Inclusion, Exclusion and American Law* (Cornell University Press, Ithaca, NY, 1990).

Morris, Madeline H. "International Guidelines Against Impunity: Facilitating Accountability," 59 (4) *L. & Contemporary Problems* 29 (1996).

Muchlinski, Peter. "Human Rights and Multinationals—Is There a Problem?," 77 *Int'l Aff.* 31 (2001).

Muldoon, Paul. "Feds Fail to Protect Public Health: CEPA Passes," 24 (2) *The Intervenor* (April–June 1999).

Murphy, Jeffrie G. "The Vietnam War and the Right to Resistance," *in Civil Disobedience and Violence* at 73–92 (Wadsworth, 1971).

Murray, C.J.L. and Lopez, A.D. "Global Mortality, Disability, and the Contribution of Risk Factors: Global Burden of Disease Study," 349 *Lancet* 1436–1442 (1997).

Nagel, Thomas. "War and Massacre" *in* M. Cohen, T. Nagel, T. Scanlon, eds., *War and Moral Responsibility* (Princeton University Press: NJ, 1974).

Nash, Roderick. *Wilderness and the American Mind* (Yale University Press: New Haven, CT, 1967).

Nathanson. "Capital Punishment" *in* D. Curtin and R. Lietke, eds., *Institutional Violence* at 53–59 (Value Inquiry Books: Rodopi, BV Amsterdam, 1999).

Newark, F.H. "Non-Natural User and Rylands v. Fletcher." 24 *Modern Law Review* 557 (1961).

Noonan, John. "An Almost Absolute Value in History," *in* Mappes and Zembaty, eds., *Biomedical Ethics* 434–438 (McGraw Hill, NY).

Noss, Reed F. "The Wildlands Project: Land Conservation Strategy," *Wild Earth* 10–25 (Special Issue, 1992).

Noss, Reed F. & Cooperrider, A.Y. *Saving Nature's Legacy* (Washington, DC, 1994).

Noss, Reed. "Maintaining the Ecological Integrity of Landscapes and Ecoregions," in D. Pimentel, L. Westra & R. Noss eds. *Ecological Integrity: Integrating Environment, Conservation and Health* 191–208 (Island Press, Washington, DC, 2000).

Noss, Reed. "At What Scale Should We Manage Biodiversity?" F.L. Bunnell J.F. Johnson, eds., *The Living Dance* 96–116 (University of British Columbia Press: Vancouver, 1998).

Nye, Joseph S. and Donahue, John D., eds., *Governance in a Globalizing World* (Brookings Institution Press, Washington, DC, 2000).

OECD, "Responsibility and Liability of States in Relation to Trans frontier Pollution," 13 *Envtl. Policy and L.* 122 (1984)

O'Leary, Siofra. *European Union Citizenship Institute for Public Policy Research* (London, UK, 1996).

O'Neil, Onora. *Towards Justice and Virtue* (Cambridge University Press: Cambridge, MA, 1996).

O'Neil, Onora. "Agents of Justice," *in* T. Pogge, ed., *Global Justice* at 188–203 (Blackwell Publishers: Oxford, UK, 2001).

Oppenheim, 1 *International Law and Treaties* (Longman's London, 8th ed. 1995).

Olsen, Frances. "Socrates on Legal Obligation: Legitimate Theory and Civil Disobedience," 18 *Ga. L. Rev.* 929. (1984).

Orenstein, R. & Ehrlich, Paul. *New World, New Mind* (Doubleday: NY, 1989).

Owens, Joseph, *A History of Ancient Western Philosophy* (Applecroft Century Crofts, Inc.: N.Y., 1959).

Parfit, Derek. *Reasons and Persons* (Oxford University Press, Oxford, UK. 1984).

Parsons, J. "Banality on Our Dinner Plates: A Comparative Analysis on the Moral and Ethical Shortcomings of the Meat and Dairy Industries," (Conference paper produced for "Environmental Ethics" course, at Sarah Lawrence College, May 2000).

Partridge, E. "On the Rights of Future Generations," *in* D. Scherer, ed., *Upstream/Downstream* 40–66 (Temple University Press, Philadelphia, PA).

Pauly, Daniel. "Global Change, Fisheries, and the Integrity of Marine Ecosystems: The Future has Already Begun," *in* D. Pimentel, L. Westra & R. Noss, eds., *Ecological Integrity: Integrating Environment Conservation and Health* at 227–239 (Island Press, Washington, DC, 2000).

Peel, Jacqueline. "New State Responsibility Rules and Compliance with Multilateral Environmental Obligations: Some Case Studies of How the New

Rules Might Apply in the International Environmental Context" 10 (1) *RECIEL* 82–97 (Blackwell Publishers; Oxford, UK, 2001).

Pegis, Anton C., ed. *Basic Writings of Thomas Aquinas* (Random House: NY, 1945).

Pellet, Alain. "Vive le Crime! Remarques sur les Degrées de l'Illicite en Droit International," *in International Law on the Eve of the Twenty-First Century* 287 (United Nations, NY, 1997).

Pennybacker, M. 104 (4) *Envtl. Health Prospect* 362–369 (National Cancer Institute, Bethesda, MD, 1996).

Perry, Michael, J. *Morality, Politics and the Law* (Oxford University Press: NY, 1988).

Pimentel, D. et. al. "Environmental and Economic Effects of Reducing Pesticide Use," 41 (6) *Bioscience* (1991).

Pimentel, D. et. al., "Conserving Biological Diversity in Agricultural / Forestry Systems" 42 (5) *BioScience* (1992).

Pimentel, D., Kirby, C. et al. "The Relationship Between Cosmetic Standards for Food and Pesticide Use," *in* D. Pimentel, ed., *The Pesticide Question: Environment, Economics and Ethics* (Chapman and Hall: NY, 1993).

Pimentel, D., Westra, L. & Noss, R. *Ecological Integrity: Integrating Environment, Conservation and Health* (Island Press, Washington, DC, 2000).

Pimentel, David. *Ecological Effects of Pesticides on Non-Target Species* (Office of Science and Technology: Washington, DC, 1971).

Pimentel, David, Maria Tor, Linda D'Anna, Anne Krawic et al. "Ecology of Increasing Disease" 48 (10) *BioScience* 817–826 (Oct. 1998).

Pimm, S. L. *The Balance of Nature? Ecological Issues in the Conservation of Species and Communities*, (University of Chicago Press: IL, 1991).

Pogge, Thomas W. ed., *Global Justice* (Blackwell Publishers: Oxford, 2001).

Pogge, Thomas W. "Priorities of Global Justice," *in* T. Pogge, ed., *Global Justice* at 6–23 (Blackwell Publishers: Oxford, UK, 2001).

Pojman, Louis & Reiman, Jeffrey. *The Death Penalty: For and Against* (Rowman Littlefield, Lanham, MD, 1997).

Pojman, Louis, "A Critique of Ethical Relativism" in *Ethical Theory* at 24–32 (Wadsworth: Belmont, CA, 1989).

Posner, Richard. "Strict Liability: "A Comment," 1 *J. Leg. Stud.* 2 (January 1973).

Postiglione, Amedeo. *Giustizia e Ambiente Globale* 95–102 (Giuffré Editore: Milano, 2001).

Provost, René. *International Human Rights and Humanitarian Law* (Cambridge University Press: Cambridge, UK, 2002).

Puchala, Donald J. "Institutionalism, Intergovernmentalism and European Integration," 2 *J. Common Mkt. Stud.* 317–337 (1999).

Punter, Olieman and Partners, *National Environmental Outlook 2 (1990–2010)*, National Institute of Public Health and Environmental Protection, Leiden University and Groningen University, RIVM, Bilthoven, the Netherlands. 1992.

Rachels, James. "Vegetarianism and "the Other Weight Problem" *in* L. Pojman ed., *Environmental Ethics* 367–373 (Wadsworth: Belmont, CA, 1997).

Radelet, M., Bedeau, H.& Putnam, C.E. "Punishment of the Innocent" *in* Baird & Rosenbaum eds., *Punishment and the Death Penalty* (Prometheus Books: Amherst, NY, 1995).

Raffenserger, Carolyn & Tickner, Joel. *Protecting Public Health and the Environment (Implementing the Precautionary Principle)* (Island Press, Washington, DC, 1999).

Ragazzi, Maurizio. *The Concept of International Obligatins Erga Omnes* (Clarendon Press: Oxford, UK, 1997).

Rall, D.P. "Toxic Agent and Radiation Control: Progress Toward Objectives for the Nation for the Year 1990" 104 (4) *Public Health Rep.* 342–347 (July–Aug. 1988).

Ramraj, Victor V. "Disentangling Corporate Criminal Liability and Individual Rights," 45 *Criminal L.Q.* 29–45 (2001).

Rapport, David J. "Ecosystem Health: More than a Metaphor?," 4 *Environmental Values* 287–309 (1995).

Ratner, S. "Corporations and Human Rights: A Theory of Legal Responsibility," 111 *Yale Law Journal* 443 (2001).

Rawls, John. *A Theory of Justice* (Harvard University Press: Cambridge, MA, 1971).

Raz, Joseph. *The Authority of Law* (Clarendon Press: Oxford, UK, 1979).

Reed, D. "Three Realms of Corporate Responsibility: Distinguishing Legitimacy, Morality and Ethics," 21 *J. Bus. Ethics* 23–35 (1999).

Rees, W.E. & M. Wackernagel. "Urban Ecological Footprints: Why Cities Cannot Be Sustainable and Why They Are a Key to Sustainability," Rev. 16 *Environmental Impact Assess.* 223–248 (1996).

Rees, W.E. & M. Wackernagel. *Our Ecological Footprint* (New Society Publishers: Gabriola Island, BC, 1996).

Rees, William. "Reducing the Ecological Footprint of Consumption" *in* L. Westra & P. Werhane, eds., *The Business of Consumption* 113–130 (Rowman Littlefield: Lanham, MD, 1998).

Rees, William. "Patch Disturbance, Ecofootprints, and Biological Integrity: Revisiting the Limits to Growth (or Why Industrial Society Is Inherently Unsustainable)," *in* D. Pimentel, L. Westra & R. Noss, eds., *Ecological Integrity: Integrating Environment, Conservation and Health* at 139–156 (Island Press, Washington, DC, 2000).

Rees, William & Westra, Laura. "When Consumption Does Violence: Can There Be Sustainability and Environmental Justice in a Resource Limited World?," *in* J. Agyeman, R. Bullard & B. Evans, eds., *Just Sustainabilities* at 99–124 (Earthscan Ltd: London, UK, 2003).

Regan, T. *The Case for Animal Rights* (University of California Press: Berkeley, CA, 1983).

Reiff, F.M., Roses, M., Venczel, L., Quick, R. & Witt, V.M. "Low-Cost, Safe Water for the World: A Practical Interim Solution," 17 (4) *J. Public Health Pol'y* 389–408 (1996).

Reinisch, August. "Governance Without Accountability," *German Y.B. Int'l L.* 270–306 (2001).

Richards, David A.J. "Conscience, Human Rights and the Anarchist Challenge to the Obligation to Obey the Law," 18 *Ga. L. Rev.* 771 (1984).

Richardson, Geneva. "Strict Liability for Regulatory Crime: The Empirical Research," *Crim. L. Rev.* 295 (1987).

Ridenour, Andrew. *"Doe v. Unocal Corporation*, Apples and Oranges: Why Courts Should Use International Standards to Determine Liability for Violations of the Law of Nations Under the Alien Tort Claims Act," 9 *Tul. J. Int'l & Comp. L.* 581 (2001).

Rifkin, Jeremy. *Beyond Beef: The Rise and Fall of the Cattle Culture* (Plume Books: NY, 1992).

Rifkin, Jeremy. "The Cattle Culture" *in* C. Pierce & D. Van de Veer, eds., *People, Penguins and Plastic Trees* at 445–451.

Ripstein, Arthur. *Equality, Responsibility, and the Law* (Cambridge University Press: NY, 1999).

Rissler, Jane and Mellon, Margaret. "Perils Amidst the Promise," *Ecological Risks of Transgenic Crops in a Global Market* (Cambridge, MA), Union of Concerned Bcientists. 1993.

RIVM. *National Environmental Outlook, 1990–2010* (Rijksinstituut voor Volksgezondheid en Milieuhygiene: Bilthoven, The Netherlands, 1986).

Roach, Kent, *Criminal Law* (Irwin Law: Toronto, 2d ed. 2000).

Rockefeller, Steven C. "Earth Charter," *Principles of Environmental Conservation Summary and Survey* (April 1996).

Rockefeller, Steven. "Foreword," *Just Ecological Integrity* x–xiv (Rowman Littlefield: Lanham, MD, 2002).

Rogers, R.G. and Wofford, S. "Life Expectancy in Less Developed Countries Socioeconomic Development or Public Health?," 21 (2) *J. Biosocial Science* 245–252 (1989).

Rolston, Holmes, III. "Rights and responsibilities on the Home Planet," 18 *Yale J. Int'l L.* 59–262 (1993).

Romano, Roberta. "Metapolitics and Corporate Law Reform," 36 *Stanford Law Rev.* 923 (1984).

Rosas, Allan. "Case Law—A Court of Justice Case C-149/96, *Portugal v. Council*. Judgment of the Full Court of 23 Nov.1999," 37 Common Mkt. L. Rev. 797–816 (2000).

Ruhl, J. B. "The Metrics of Constitutional Amendments and Why Proposed Environmental Quality Amendments Don't Measure Up," 74 (2) Notre Dame L. Rev. 245–281 (1999).

Sachs, Jeffrey. "Globalization and the Rule of Law," (Paper presented at the Yale Law School, Oct. 16, 1998).

Sagoff, M. *The Economy of the Earth: Philosophy, Law and the Environment* (Cambridge University Press: UK, 1988).

Sagoff, Mark. At the Monument to General Meade, or the Difference Between Beliefs and Benefits," 42 (2) *Ariz. L. Rev.* 433–462 (2000).

Sagoff, Mark. "At the Shrine of Our Lady of Fatima, or Why Political Questions Are Not All Economic," *in* L. Pojman, ed., *Environmental Ethics* at 467–473 (Wadsworth/Thomson Learning: Belmont, CA, 2001).

Salmond, Sir John. "Torts," *in* R.F.V. Henson, ed., *Salmond on the Law of Torts* (Sweet and Maxwell: UK, 14th ed. 1965).

Sampat, Payal. "Uncovering Groundwater Pollution," *State of the World 2001* 21–42. (Worldwatch Institute, W. W. Norton and Co.: NY, 2001).

Sand, Peter H. *Transnational Environmental Law* (Kluwer Law International: London, UK, 1999).

Sandel, Michael J. *Liberalism and the Limits of Justice* (Cambridge University Press, Cambridge, MA. 1982).

Saxe, Dianne. *Environmental Justice, The Corporation and the Corporate Executive* (D. Jur. Thesis, York University Law Library, 1991).

Schabas, William, *On Genocide* (Kluwer Law Publishers: Dordrecht, The Netherlands, 2000).

Scherer, D. and Attig, T. *Upstream/Downstream* (Temple University Press: Philadelphia, PA, 1990).

Schmitz et al. "Long-Wave Ultraviolet Radiation (UVA) and Skin Cancer," 45 (8) *Hautarzt* 517–25 (Aug. 1994).

Schofield, Malcolm, *The Stoic Idea of the City* (University of Chicago Press, Chicago, Ill. 1999).

Schwarts, J. & Katsouianni, K., "Air Pollution and Daily Admissions for Chronic Obstructive Pulmonary Disease in 6 European Cities: Results from the APHEA Project," 10 (5) *Eur. Respiratory J.* 1064–1071 (1997).

Scott, Craig. "Translating Torture into Transnational Tort: Conceptual Divides in the Debate on Corporate Accountability for Human Rights Harms," *in* C. Scott ed., *Torture as Tort* at 45–63 (2001).

Scott, Craig, "Multinational Enterprises and Emergent Jurisprudence on Violations of Economic, Social and Cultural Rights," *in* A. Eide et al., eds., *Economic, Social and Cultural Rights* 563–595 (2d ed. 2001).

Scott, Joanne, "On Kith and Kine (and Crustaceans): Trade and Environment in the EU and the WTO," *in* J.H. Weiler, ed., *The EU, the WTO, and the NAFTA* at 129–168 (Oxford University Press: UK, 2000).

Sebba, Leslie, 71 *J. Crim. L. & Criminology* 127–135 (1980).

Seck, Sara, "Environmental Harm in Developing Countries Caused by Subsidiaries of Canadian Mining Corporations: The Interface of Public and Private International Law," 37 *Canadian Y.B. Int'l L.* 139–221 (1999).

Sessions, George and Devall, Bill, "Deep Ecology" *in* Louis Pojam ed., *Environmental Ethics* 157–161 (Wadsworth Publishing House: Belmont, CA, 2000).

Sheehy, Elizabeth A., "Regulatory Crimes and the Charter: *R. v. Wholesale Travel, Inc.*, 3 (2) *J. Human Justice* 111–124 (Spring 1982).

Sherwin, Emily "A Defense of Analogical Reasoning in Law," 66 *U. Chi. L. Rev.* 1179 (1999).

Shields, Natalie S. & Gamble, John King, "International Legal Scholarship: a Perspective on Teaching and Publishing," 39 *J. Legal Edu.* 40 (1989).

Shiva, Vandana, *Staying Alive* (Zed Books: London, UK, 1989).

Shrader-Frechette, K. *Nuclear Power and Public Policy* (Kluwer Academic: Dordrecht, The Netherands, 1982).

Shrader-Frechette, K. *Risk and Rationality* (University of California Press: Berkeley, CA, 1991).

Shrader-Frechette, K. & E.D. McCoy, *Method in Ecology* (Cambridge University Press: NY, 1993).

Shrader-Frechette, K. "Ecological Risk Assessment and Ecosystem Health: Fallacies and Solutions," 3 (2) *Ecosystem Health* 73–81 (June 1997).

Shrader-Frechette, K. *Burying Uncertainty* (University of California Press: Berkeley, CA, 1993).

Shrivastava, P. *Greening Business: Profiting Corporations and the Environment* (Thompson Executive Press: Cincinnati, OH, 1995).

Shue, Henry, *Basic Rights: Subsistence, Affluence and American Foreign Policy* (Princeton University Press, NJ, 1996).

Simberloff, D. "A Succession of Paradigms in Ecology: Essentialism to Materialism and Probabilism," *in* E. Sarinen ed., *Conceptual Issues in Ecology* 61–100 (Reidel: Boston, 1982).

Simmons, A. John, *Moral Principles and Political Obligations* (Princeton University Press, Englewood Cliffs, NJ, 1979).

Simmons, John A., 1984, "Consent, Free Choice and Democratic Government," *Georgia Law Reivew*, Vol. 18: 791.

Singer, P. *Practical Ethics* (Cambridge University Press: NY, 2d ed. 1993).

Singer, P. *Animal Rights and Human Obligations* (Prentice Hall: Englewood Cliffs, NJ, 1976).

Smith, J.A.C. & J. Kerby. *Private Law in Canada—A Comparative Study* (University of Ottawa Press: Ottawa, 1975).

Sophocles, *Antigone,* (E.F Watling, trans. 1947).

Sopinka, J. "The Charter of Rights and the Corporations," *in The Cambridge Lectures: 1989* at 129 (1989).

Soskolne Colin and Bertollini, Roberto, *Ecological Integrity and Sustainable Development: Cornerstones of Public Health* (1999) *available at* (http://www.euro.who.int/document/ghc/Globaleco/ecorep5/pdf).

Soskolne, Colin. "International Transport of Hazardous Waste: Legal and Illegal Trade in the Context of Professional Ethics," 1 *Global Bioethics* 3–9 (Mar. 2001).

Soskolne, Colin, Sieswerda, Lee, & Scott, Morgan. "Epidemiologic Methods for Assessing the Health Impacts of Diminishing Ecological Integrity," in D. Pimentel, L. Westra & Noss, R., eds, *Ecological Integrity: Integrating Environment, Conservation and Health* in 261–278 (Island Press, Washington, DC, 2000).

Spinedi, Marina. "Convergences and Divergencies on the Legal Consequences of International Crimes of State: With Whom Should Lie the Right of Response?" *in* J.H. Weiler, A. Cassese, M. Spinedi, eds., *International Crime of*

State—A Critical Analysis of the ILC Draft Article 19 on State Responsibility at 244 (Walter de Gruyter: Berlin, 1989).

Stace, Walter. "Ethical Relativism" *in* J. Feinberg ed., *Reason and Responsibility* (Wadsworth Publishing: Belmont, CA, 1985).

Stein, Peter. *Legal Institutions*—The Development of Dispute Settlements (Butterworth: London, UK, 1984).

Steiner, Henry J. and Alston, Philip, *International Human Rights in Context* (Oxford University Press: UK, 2d ed. 2000).

Sterba, James. *Justice Here and Now* (Cambridge University Press: Cambridge, MA, 1998).

Sterba, James. "A Biocentric Defense of Environmental Integrity," *in* D. Pimentel, L. Westra & R. Noss, eds., *Ecological Integrity: Integrating Environment, Conservation and Health* at 335–350 (Island Press: Washington, DC, 2000).

Stone, Christopher. "Should Trees Have Standing? Toward Legal Rights for Natural Objects," *in* L. Pojman ed., *Environmental Ethics* at 240–248 (Wadsworth Publishing: Belmont, CA, 2000).

Stone, Christopher. "Moral Pluralism and the Course of Environmental Ethics," 10 *Environmental Ethics* 139–154 (1988).

Strange, Susan. *The Retreat of the State: The Diffusion of Power in the World Economy* (Cambridge University Press: Cambridge, MA, 1996).

Stribopoulos, James. "The Constitutionalization of "Fault" in Canada A Normative Critique," 42 *Crim. L.Q.* 227–285 (1999).

Strong, Maurice. *Where on Earth Are We Going* (Knopf Publishing: Toronto, 2000).

Stuart, Don. *Criminal Law* (Carswell, Thomson Canada Ltd., 1995).

Sunstein, Cass R. "On Analogical Reasoning," 106 *Harv. L. Rev.* 741 (1993).

Sutherland, Harry. *Company Law of Canada* (Carswell: Toronto, 6th ed. 1993).

Swanson, John. "Dow-Corning and the Breast Silicone Implants" (Paper presented at the Business Ethics Society Meeting, Aug. 10, 1996, Québec City, Canada).

Tanzi, Attila, "Diritto di veto ed esecuzione della sentenza della Corte Internazionale di Guistiza fra Nicaragua e Stati Uniti," *Rivista di Diritto Internazionale* r405–70 at 293–305 (1987).

Taylor, C., "Can Canada Survive the Charter?," 30 *Alta. Law. Rev.* 427 (1992).

Taylor, P. *Respect for Nature: A Theory of Environmental Ethics* (Princeton University Press: NJ, 1986).

Taylor, Prudence E., "From Environmental to Ecological Human Rights: A New Dynamic in International Law?," 10 *Geo. Int'l Envtl. L. Rev.* 309 (1998).

Teichman, J. *Pacifism and the Just War* (Oxford University Press, Blackwell; Oxford, UK, 1986).

Terry, John. "Taking *Filartiga* on the Road: Why Courts Outside the United States Should Accept Jurisdictions Over Actions Involving Torture Committed Abroad," in C. Scott, ed., *Torture as Tort: Comparative Perspectives on the Development of Transnational Human Rights Litigation* 109–129 (Hart Publishing: Oxford, 2001).

Téson, Fernando. "The Kantian Theory of International Law," 92 *Colum. L. Rev.* 53 (1992).

Tesón, Fernando R. "Two Mistakes About Democracy," *Proceedings of the Ninety-Second Annual Meeting of the American Society of International Law* (1998).

Thomson, J.J. *The Realm of Rights* (Harvard University Press, 1990).

Thoreau, Henry David. "Civil Disobedience," *in Walden and Other Writings* (Modern Library, NY, 1950).

Tickner, Joel. "A Map Toward Precautionary Decision Making," *in Protecting Public Health and the Environment* at 162–186 (Island Press: Washington, DC, 1999).

Timmons, Mark. *Conduct and Character*, Wadsworth Publishing: Belmont, CA, 1990).

Tomuschat, Christian, "International Liability for Injurious Consequences Arising Out of Acts Not Prohibited by International Law: The Work of the International Law Commission," *in* F. Francioni & T. Scovazzi, eds., *International Responsibility for Environmental Harm* at 37–72 (Graham & Trottman: UK, 1991).

Toope, Stephen & Brunnee, Jutta, "Freshwater Regimes: The Mandate the International Joint Commission," 15 (1) *Ariz. J. Int'l & Comp. L.* 273–287 (1998).

Tourmaa, "The Adverse Effects of Tobacco Smoking on Reproduction and Health; A Review from the Literature," 10 (2) *Nutritional Health* 105–201 (1995).

Toyokawa, H. & Nishikawa, H. "A New Estimation of the Intake of Contaminants, based on Daily Consumption Data," 49 (2) *Japanese J. Hygiene* 606–615 (1994).

Tridimas, Takis. "The Court of Justice and Judicial Activism," 21 *E.L. Rev.* 199–210 (June 1996).

Trimble, Phillip R. "International Law, World Order and Critical Studies," 42 *Stan. L. Rev.* 811 (1990).

Tunkin, Grigorli Ivanovich. *Theory of International Law* (Harvard University Press: Cambridge, MA, 1974).

Turpel, M.E., et al. "Peremptory International Law and Sovereignty: Some Questions," 3 *Conn. J. Int'l L.* 364–369 (Spring 1998).

Ulanowicz, R. *Ecology, The Ascendent Perspective* (Columbia University Press: NY, 1997).

Ulanowicz, Robert, "Toward the Measurement of Ecological Integrity," *in* D. Pimentel, L. Westra & R. Noss, *Ecological Integrity: Integrating Environment Conservation and Health* at 99–113 (Island Press: Washington, DC, 2000).

Ulanowicz, Robert. "Ecosystem Integrity: A Causal Necessity," *in* L. Westra & J. Lemons, eds., *Perspectives on Ecological Integrity* at 77–87 (Kluwer Academic: Dordrecht, The Netherlands, 1995).

Ulanowicz, Robert E., "Towards the Measurement of Ecological Integrity," *in* D. Pimentel, L. Westra and R. Noss, eds. *Ecological Integrity: Integrating Environment, Conservation and Health* (Island Press: Washington, D.C., 2000).

Ullman, Richard, H. "Denuclearizing International Politics," *in* R. Hardin, J. Mearsheimer, G. Dworkin & R.E. Goodin, eds., *Nuclear Deterrence, Ethics and Strategy* 191–212 (The University of Chicago Press: Chicago, 1985).

Vallette, J. *The International Trade in Waste: A Greenpeace Inventory* (Greenpeace: Washington, DC, 1989).

Van den Bosch, C.A. *The Pesticide Conspiracy* (Doubleday: NY, 1978).

VanDuzer, Anthony, J. *The Law of Partnerships and Corporations* (Irwin Law: Concord, Ont., 1997).

Velasquez, Manuel. *Business Ethics Concepts and Cases* (Prentice Hall: Englewood Cliffs, NJ, 1991).

Velasquez, Manuel. *Business Ethics Concepts and Cases* (Prentice Hall: Edgewood Cliffs, NJ, 1993).

Velasquez, Manuel. *Business Ethics: Concepts and Cases* (Prentice Hall, Belmont, CA, 1998).

Vicuna, Francisco Orrego. "State Reponsibility,Liability,and Remedial Measures Under International Law: New Criteria for Environmental Protection" *in* E. Brown Weiss, ed., *Environmental Change and International Law* at 124–158 (1992 United Nations University Press: Tokyo, 1992).

Von Schirnding, Y.E.R. & Ehrlich, R.I. "Environmental Health Risks of Toxic Waste Site Exposure—An Epidemiological Perspective," 81 (11) *S. Afr. Med. J.* 546–549 (1992).

Wagner, Hartmut. "Problemi degli effetti 'del diritto dell 'ambiente," 1–2/2000 *Dei Delitti e delle Pene* 28–31.

Wallach, L. and Sforza, Michelle. *Whose Trade Organization? Corporate Globalization and the Erosion of Democracy* (1999).

Walsh, J.F., Moyneux, D.H. & Birley, M.H. "Deforestation: Effects on Vector Borne Disease," 106 *Parasitology* S55–S75 (Suppl. 1993).

Warren, Mary Anne. "On the Moral and Legal Status of Abortion," 57 (1) *The Monist, reprinted in* T. Mappes & J. Zembaty, *Biomedical Ethics* 438–444 (McGraw-Hill, NY, 1991).

Warrick, R.A. et al., "Integrated Model Systems for National Assessments of the Effects of Climate Change: Applications in New Zealand and Bangladesh," 92 (1–2) *Water, Air and Soil Pollution* 215–227 (1996).

Wasserstrom, R. "The Relevance of Nuremberg," *in* M. Cohen, T. Nagel & T. Scanlon, eds., *War and Moral Responsibility* (Princeton University Press, NJ, 1974).

Wasserstrom, Richard, "War,Nuclear War and Nuclear Deterrence: Some Conceptual and Moral Issues" in R. Hardin, J. Mersheimer, G. Dworkin & R. Goodin, eds., *Nuclear Deterrence, Ethics and Strategy* at 15–36 (University of Chicago Press: Chicago, 1985).

Watson, Paul, *Sea Shepherd, My Flight for Whales and Seals* 26 (W.W. Norton & Co., 1982).

Weiler, J.H., Cassese, Antonio, Spimedi, Marina eds., *International Crime of State—A Critical Analysis of the ILC Draft Article 19 on State Responsibility* (Walter de Gruyter, Berlin, 1989).

Weiler, J.H. "Does Europe Need a Constitution? Demos,Telos and the German Maastricht Decision," 1 (3) *ELJ* 219–258 (1995).

Weiler, J.H. "The Transformation of Europe" *Yale L.J.* 2403–2483 (1991).

Weiler, J.H. & Lockhart, N.J.S. "Taking Rights Seriously" Seriously: The European Court and Its Fundamental Rights Jurisprudence," 32 *Common Mkt. L. Rev.* 579–627 (Part II) (1995).

Weiler, J.H. *The Constitution of Europe* (Cambridge University Press: UK, 1999).

Weinreb, Lloyd. *Natural Law and Justice* (Cambridge University Press: Cambridge, MA, 1987).

Welling, Bruce. *Corporate Law in Canada*, Butterworth: Toronto, 1991).

Wells, Celia, "Corporate Criminal Liability in Europe and Beyond," *New S. Wales L. Society J.* 62–66 (2001).

Wesseling, C. McConnell, R. Powtanen, T. & Hogstedt, C. "Agricultural Pesticides Use in Developing Countries: Health Effects and Research Needs" 27(2) *Int'l J. Health Services* 273–308 (1997).

Westra, L. "A Transgenic Dinner? Ethical and Social Issues in Biotechnology and Agriculture," 24 (3) *J. Social Phil.* 215–232 (Winter 1993).

Westra, L. *An Environmental Proposal for Ethics: The Principle of Integrity*, (Rowman, Littlefield, Lanham, MD, 1994).

Westra, L. "Institutionalized Violence and Human Rights" *in* D. Pimentel, L. Westra & R. Noss, eds., *Ecological Integrity in the World's Environment and Health*, (Island Press: Washington, DC, 2000).

Westra, L. "Terrorism, Self-Defence and Whistleblowing," 20 (3) *J. Social Phil.* 46–58 (Winter 1989).

Westra, L. "Ecosystem Integrity and Sustainability: The Foundational Value of the Wild," *in* L. Westra & J. Lemons, eds., *Perspectives on Ecological Integrity* (Kluwer Academic: Dordrecht, The Netherlands, 1995).

Westra, L. "Environmental Racism and the First Nation People of Canada: Terrorism at Oka," *in* W. Cragg and A. Wellington, eds., *Canadian Studies in Applied Ethics* at 274–291 (Broadview Press: Toronto, Canada, 1997).

Westra, L. & Lawson, B., *Faces of Environmental Racism* (Rowan Littlefield: Lanham, MD, 2d ed., 2001).

Westra, Laura. "On War and Innocence," XV (4) *Dialogue* 735–740 (Winter 1986).

Westra, Laura & Werhane, Patricia. *The Business of Consumption Environmental Ethics and the Global Economy* (Rowman & Littlefield, Lanham, MD, 1998).

Westra, Laura. "The Disvalue of Contingent Valuation and the Accounting *Expectation* Gap," 9 *Environmental Values* 153–171 (White Horse Press: Lancaster, UK, 2000a).

Westra, Laura. *Living in Integrity: A Global Ethic to Restore a Fragmented Earth* (Rowman Littlefield, Lanham, MD, 1998).

Westra, Laura. "From Aldo Leopold to the Wildlands Project: The Ethics of Integrity," 1 *(23) Envtl. Ethics* 261–274 (Fall 2001).

Westra, Laura, "The Faces of Environmental Racism: Titusville, Alabama, and

BFI," *in* L. Westra & W. Lawson, eds., *Faces of Environmental Racism* 113–140 (2d ed. 2001).

Westra, Laura, Miller, Peter, Karr, James R., Rees, William E. & Ulanowicz, Robert E. "Ecological Integrity and the Aims of the Global Ecological Integrity Project," *in Ecological Integrity: Integrating Environment, Conservation and Health* at 19–41 (Island Press, Washington, DC, 2000).

Williams, Glanville Llewelyn, *The Proof of Guilt: A Study of the English Criminal Trial* (Stevens Publishing: London, UK, 1955).

Williams, John Fischer. *Aspects of Modern International Law: An Essay* (Oxford University Press: London, UK, 1939).

Williams, Paul R. "International Environmental Dispute Resolution: The Dispute Between Slovakia and Hungary Concerning Construction of the Gabvikovo and Nagymaros Dams," 19 (1) *Colum. J. Envtl. L.* 1. (1994).

Williams, Sharon A. "Public International Law and Water Quantity Management in a Common Drainage Basin: The Great Lakes," 18 *Case Western Res. Int'l L.* 155–201 (1986).

Williams, Sharon A. "Light Out of Darkness: The New International Criminal Court," *Proceedings of the Annual Conference of the Canadian Council on International Law* 23 (1998).

Williams, Sharon, "The Rome Statute of the International Criminal Court: From 1947–2000 and Beyond," 38 (2) *Osgoode Hall L.J.* (Summer 2000).

Wilson, E.O. "Biodiversity, Prosperity and Value," *in* F.H. Bormann & S.R. Kellert, eds., *Ecology, Economics and Ethics, The Broken Circle* at 3–10 (Yale University Press: New Haven, CT, 1991).

Wilson, Edward O. "Biophilia and the Conservation Ethic," *in* S.R. Kellert & E. Wilson, eds., *The Biophilia Hypothesis* 31–41 (Island Press, Washington, DC, 1993).

Wilson, Edward O. *The Diversity of Life* (Harvard University Press: Cambridge, MA, 1992).

Wise, Edward M. "International Crimes and Domestic Criminal Law," XVI *DePaul L. Rev.* 175 (1989).

Wood, Ellen Meiskins, "The Origin of Capitalism," *The Monthly Review Press* 67–94 (1999).

Wordsworth, Anne, *Tragedy on Tap, Volume I, An Overview* (CELA 2001).

Zinn, Howard, "A Fallacy on Law and Order: That Civil Disobedience Must Be Absolutely Nonviolent," in *Civil Disobedience and Violence* at 103–111 (Wadsworth Publishing, 1971).

TABLE OF CASES

RJR-MacDonald Inc. v. Canada (Attorney General) [1995] 3S.C.R. 199
Snell v. Farrell (1990) 72 D.L.R. (4th) 289 SCC
Thomson Newspapers Co. v. Canada (A.G.) (1998) 1 S.C.R. 877
Trinity Western 1996) 27 OR (3d) 132 DLR 4th
Vriend v. Alberta (1994) 6 WWC 414 (Alta QB), B2 DLR (4th) 595 (Alta)
Waite v. The Queen (1989) 48 C.C.C. 3d 1

International

Advisory Opinion (WHO) (1996) I.C.J. Rep. 66
Barcelona Traction, Light and Power Co. Ltd. (Belgium v. Spain) 1970 I.C.J.
    50, 54
Chorzow Factory Indemnity Case (1928), P.C.I.J., Ser. A, No. 17 (Merits)
Continental Shelf Tunisia v. Libya Case 1982), ICJ Rep. 18
Corfu Channel Case (U.K.) v. Albania (1949) I.C.J. Rep. 4, 17
Diversion of Water from the Meuse Case (1937) P.C.I.J. Ser. A/B No. 70
East Timor Case (1995) I.C.J. Rep. 90
English Channel Arbitration, France v. U.K. (1979) 18 ILM 397
Gabcikovo—Nagymaros Case (1997) I.C.J. Rep. 7
ICCPR Case Timari Lausman et al. v. Finland, Comm. No. 511/1992; Finland
    08/11/94
ICTFY (1995) Tadic Case No. IT-94-L-AR72, 2 Oct. 1995
Lake Lanoux Arbitration (1957) 12 R.I.A.A. 281, 241. L.R. 101
Nicaragua v. United States of American (1986) I.C.J. Ref. 14
Norwegian Shipowners Claims (1922) 17 *Am.J. Int. L.* 362
Nuclear Tests Case—Australia v. France; New Zealand v. France (1974) I.C.J.
    Rep. 253United States v. Ian (1980) I.C.J. Rep. 369

United Kingdom

Beaver v. the Queen (1957) 116 C.C.C. 129
Commissioner of Police of Metropolis v. Caldwell (1982) A.C. 3341 (1981) 2
    W.L.R. 509, 73 Cr. Ap.R.13 (1981) 1 All E.R. 961 at 966
Continental Tyre and Rubber co. Ltd. Vs. Daimler Co. Ltd. (1915), K.B. 89
Custom and Excise v. Samex (1983) 1 A 11 E.R. 1042
Dherras v. De Rutzen [1985] 1 Q.B. 918
Donooghue v. Stevenson (1932) A.C. 562 A 11 E.R. Rep. 1 101
Fletcher v. Rylands (1866) LR 1 Exch. 265, Exch. Rev. (1865) 3 H & C 774
Harding v. Price (1948)
Le Louis, 2 Dodson Rep. 238
McGhee v. National Coal Board (1973) 1 W.L.R. 1
R. v. Miller, House of Lords (19983) AC 161 (1983) All ER 978 2 WLR
Rylands v. Fletcher (1868) LR 3 HR 330; 37 LJ 161

European

Cassis de Dijon Case (Case 120/78, Rewe Zentrale AG v.
  Bundesmonopolverwaltung fur Brantwein
Freussen Elektra (Case c-379/98) Freussen-Elektra AG v Schleswag, AG (2001)
  ECR 1-2099
Guerra and others v. Italy (116/1996/735/932), 19 February 1998
Lender v. Sweden, Aa/116 (1987) 9 E. HR.R. 433
Lopez Ostra v. Spain (1995) 20 EHRR 277, (1994) ECHR 16798/90
Sandoz Case 1974/82 Officer van Justitie v. Sandoz, BV (1983) ECR 2445
Simmethal Case (Simmenthal SPA v. Commission (Case 92/78) (1979) ECR
  777 (1980) 1 CMLR

WTO

Hormones Decision (EC Measures Concerning Meat and Meat Products
  (Hormones) AB-1997-4 WT/DS 26/AB/R,WT/DS 48/AB/R
Shrimp/Turtle Case (United States Prohibition of Shrimps and Certain Shrimp
  Products, WTO Doc.WT/DS58/R(15 May 1998)
Tuna/Dolphin Case (United States Restrictions on Imports of Tuna, 39 GATT
  BISD 155 (1993)

United States

Beaanel v. Freeport-McMoranty Inc., 969 F. Supp.362 (ED La. 1997)
Canterbury v. Spence US County of Appeals (D.C. Cir. May 19, 1972)
Commonwealth v. National Gettysburg Battlefield Tower, Inc. (302) A.2d 886,
  PA Commonwealth Ct.; 311 A.2d 588,598 n.3PA 1973
Commonwealth v. Welansky 316 Mass. 383, 55 N.E.2d 902 (1944)
Filartiga v. Pena-Irala, 630 F.2d 876 (2d Cir. 1980)
Frre v. Spock, 424 U.S. 828 (1976)
John Doe v. Unocal Corp. 963 F. Supp. 880 (C.D.Cal. 1977)
Jota v. Texaco, Inc. 157 F.3d 153 (2d Cir 1998)
Kkadic v. Karadzic, 70 F.3d 232 (2d Cir. 1995)
Lehman v. City of Shaker Heights, 418 U.S. 298 (1974)
Occidental Petroleum v. U'wa Indigenous People of Colombia
Pagraf v. Long Island R.R. Co. (1928) 248 NY 339
Payne v. Kassab (312) A.2d 86, PA Commonwealth Ct. 1973
R.A.V. v. City of St. Paul, 1125 S.Ct. 2538 (1992)
Santa Clara County v. Southern Pacific R.R. Corp. (1886)
Sequinhar v. Texaco, Inc. 157 F3d 153 (2d Cir. 1998)
Trail Smelter Arbitration (US v. Canada 1931–1941 3 R.I.A.A. 1905
United States v. Britain 731 F. 2d 1413,21 ELR 21092 (10thCir. 1991)
Wiwa v. Royal Shell Petroleum et al., 226 F.3d 88 (2d Cir. 2000)

TABLE OF DOCUMENTS

Alien Torts Claim Act 18 U.S.C §1350

Alien Torts Statute 28 U.S.C.§1350

Alien Torts Claim Act (1789) 28 U.S.C. §1350

American Convention on Human Rights (1969) OAS Tr. Ser./. No.36; 1144 U.N.T.S. 123

An Act to Amend the Criminal Code S.C. 2003, C.21 [formerly Bill C-45].

Canada Business Corporations Act (1985), R.S.C 1985,c. C-44, s.15(1)

Canadian Clear Air Act (1971), 19–20 Eliz.2, Statutes of Canada 1970-71-72 Can. 1971, chapter 47.

Canadian Criminal Code (1985), R.S., Chapter C-46

Canadian Environmental Protection Act (1985) R.S.C. 1985, Chapter 16 (4th Supp.); as Amended by 1999 Chapter 31, s. 39, in force June 17, 1999.

Canadian Red Mountain Residents and Property Owner's Association v. B.C. (Ministry of Forests) (2000), 35 C.E.L.R. (N.S) 127 (B.C.S.C.).

Code of Conduct on Transnational Corporations (1988) UNESCOR, UNDoc.E/19/1988/39, Add.1 (1988).

Commission of Human Rights, Sub-Commission on Prevention of Discrimination, Protection of Minorities, 43rd Sess., Agenda item 8, UNDoc.E/CN.4/Sub2/ 1991/17 (1991) para.85 (Second Progress Report submitted by Mr. Danilo Turk, Special Rapporteur, UN ESCOR)

Convention for the Prevention and Punishment of the Crime of Genocide (1951), 78 U.N.T.S. 277; 1949 Can.T.S. No. 27

Convention of the Law of Treaties (1969) (Vienna), 8 ILM (1969), 689. In force 27 January 1980.

Convention on Wetlands of International Importance (Ramsar) (1971) 996 UNTS 245

Conventions on the Prevention and Suppression of the Crime of Genocide (1951), 78 U.N.T.S. 277

Council Directive on the Freedom of Access to Information on the Environment (90/313/EEC, O.J. No.L158, June 23, 1990).

Council of Europe Convention on Civil Responsibility for Damage Resulting from the Exercise of Activities Dangerous for the Environment; (EC Directive on the Containment of GMOs, 90/219/EEC,OJ No.L 117, May 8, 1990, at 201–210).

Declaration of the United Nations Conference on the Human Environment (Stockholm), U.N. Doc. A/CONF/$'/#$/REV.1;

Declaration on Principles of International Law Friendly Relations and Co-Operation Among States in Accordance with the Charter of the United Nations (1883rd Pinary Meeting, 24 October, 1970)

Declaration on the Right toDevelopment (1986) U.N. 41st Session, Rep. A/RES/ 41/128

Declaration on the Rights of the Child, G.A.Res.1386(XIV), UN Doc.A/4354 (1959)

Definition of Aggression, U.N. GA Res. 3314 (XXIX), U.N. GAOR, 29th Sess. Supp. No. 31, 142; U.N. Doc. A/9631 (1974), 13 Int. Leg. Mat. 710 REVA (1999) "Rexognizing and Encouraging Voluntary Actions," Ministry of the Environment published *Policy Framework*.

Ontario Safe Drinking Water Act (2002), S.O. 2002, Chapter 32

Ontario Water Resources Act (1990) R.S.O 1990, Chapter 0.40

Proceedings, (1985) London Tribunal on Nuclear Warfare

Protocol to the Framework Convention on Climate Change (Kyoto), 37 ILM (1998), 22. Not in force.

Refuse Act of 1899 33 U.S.C §§407, 411 (section 13 and 16 if the Rivers and Harbors Appropriation Act of 1899).

Special Convention for the Protection of the Alps, (1992) 31 ILM 767

Statute of the International Court of Justice (as signed in 1945)

Statute of the International Criminal Court (Rome) U.N. Doc. A/CONF./83/19; 37 ILM (1998), 999

Technical Standards and Safety Act (2000), S.O. 2000, Chapter 16, in force June 27, 2001.

The Charter and Judgment of the Nurnberg Tribunal: History and Analysis, U.N. Doc. A/C/N. 4/5 (1949)

The Convention Against Torture and Other Cruel, Inhuman or Degrading Treatment or Punishment (1984), 23 Int. Leg. Mat. 1027 and (1985) 24 Int. Leg. Mat. 535

The International Covenant on Civil and Political Rights (ICCPR) (1966) 999 U.N.T.S. 171

The International Covenant on Econbomic, Social and Cultural Rights (ICESCR) (1966) U.N.T.S. 3

The Nuremberg Charter, 1945—Charter of the International Military Tribunal, 82 U.N.T.S.279

The Universal Declaration of Human Rights (1948) Res. 217A(III) U.N. Doc. A/810

Torture Victims Protection Act (1988) H.R. 1662,s.1629

Treaty Banning Nuclear Weapons Tests in the Atmosphere, in Outer Space and Under Water (Moscow), 480 UNTS 3 (1964) In Force October 10 1963

Treaty of Rome (1957), establishing the European Community (EEC Treaty)

Treaty on European Union 1992 (TEU/Maastricht)

U.N. Code of Conduct on Transnational Corporations (1984), 23 Int. Leg. Mat., 626

UNESCO Convention Concerning the Protection of the World Cultural and Natural Heritage UKTS 2(1985); 11 ILM (1972) 1358.

United Kingdom Salomon v. Salomon and Co. C.A. [1985] 2 Ch.323; H.L.(E.) [1896] W.N. 160(5), [1897] A.C.22

Vienna Convention on the Law of Treaties (1969), 1155 U.N.T.S. 331, in force 1980., 8 ILM (1969), 689.

World Charter for Nature, UNGA Res. 37/7, 37 UNGAOR Suppl. (no.51) at 17 U.N. Doc. A/37/51 (1982).

World Medical Association Declaration of Helsinki, "Recommendations Guiding Physicians in Biomedical Research Involving Human Subjects" (1964) As Amended by the 52nd General Assembly, Edinburgh, Scotland, October 2000

World Trade Organization, 1994 Marrakesh Agreement Establishing the World Trade Organization, WTO Legal Texts, 3

INDEX

- FUTURE GENERATS / PRECAUTIONARY PRINC
- DEMOC THEORY
- CRITIQUE F CORPS 133